FEDERAL TAX PROCEDURES FOR ATTORNEYS

To Professor Ricketts ⸺

I hope you find this useful.

Regards,

Pat Cantrell

Class of '67

FEDERAL TAX PROCEDURES

FOR ATTORNEYS

W. PATRICK CANTRELL

Cover design by Tamara Kowalski/ABA Publishing.

The materials contained herein represent the views of each chapter author in his or her individual capacity and should not be construed as the views of the author's firms, employers, or clients, or of the editors or other chapter authors, or of the American Bar Association or the Solo, Small Firm and General Practice Division, unless adopted pursuant to the bylaws of the Association. Nothing contained in this book is to be considered as the rendering of legal advice for specific cases, and readers are responsible for obtaining such advice from their own legal counsel. This book is intended for educational and informational purposes only.

Printed in the United States of America

19 18 17 16 15 5 4 3 2 1

Library of Congress Cataloging-in-Publication Data

Cantrell, W. Patrick, author.
   Federal tax procedures for attorneys / By W. Patrick Cantrell. — Second edition.
     pages cm
Includes bibliographical references and index.
   ISBN 978-1-63425-259-1 (print : alk. paper)
   1. Tax administration and procedure—United States. I. Title.
   KF6320.C36 2015
   343.7304—dc23

                        2015027472

Discounts are available for books ordered in bulk. Special consideration is given to state bars, CLE programs, and other bar-related organizations. Inquire at ABA Publishing, American Bar Association, 321 North Clark Street, Chicago, Illinois 60654-7598.

www.ShopABA.org

CONTENTS

ACKNOWLEDGMENTS

The author acknowledges the generous support of a number of individuals who contributed their talent and insight for no compensation. Foremost of these is the late Professor Samuel W. Chisholm of the Texas Tech University College of Business Administration. Professor Chisholm opened my eyes to the world of tax law more than four decades ago and propelled my career into a direction that I have never regretted.

Heartfelt thanks go to my family: my wife, Carol, and daughters Emily and Rebecca. Their support and encouragement kept me going through many tedious hours of research.

To the many dedicated tax professionals I had the privilege to know inside the government: you know who you are and there are too many to name. You all had an impact on my career and my life.

A special debt of gratitude is owed to my colleague and friend Melanie D. Bragg. An accomplished author and attorney in her own right, she first suggested ABA Book Publishing as the way to get this work published.

And finally, to the editors at ABA Book Publishing, many thanks for your helpful suggested modifications to the manuscript. They were greatly appreciated.

ABOUT THE AUTHOR

W. Patrick Cantrell received his bachelor's degree in accounting from Texas Tech University in Lubbock, Texas, and followed up with a law degree from the University of Houston Law Center. He is licensed as a certified public accountant and a Texas attorney. He is also certified as a tax attorney by the Texas Board of Legal Specialization. He began his career by working for the Internal Revenue Service for seven years (revenue agent and appeals officer). After 33 years practicing as a CPA, Patrick opened a tax law practice, Cantrell & Cantrell, PLLC, in Houston, Texas. For more information, access http://www.cctaxlaw.com.

INTRODUCTION

My reason for writing this book has to do with perceived necessity. I was unaware of a practical reference book delineating rules for dealing with real-life problems faced by a typical practitioner whose clients have confronted otherwise unsolvable IRS problems. The IRS is a huge bureaucracy with approximately one hundred thousand employees across the United States and in foreign countries. The powers of these employees rival those of the most despotic governments in history. The disparity of power between IRS employees and the typical taxpayer is my raison d'être.

This book is intended as a reference manual to be used by the casual practitioner of tax procedure as well as by serious scholars. Unlike casebooks used in the curricula of most law schools, this publication is much more of a nuts-and-bolts approach to solving specific problems that arise in everyday tax practice. One of the unique features I have employed is the injection of tricks and techniques that go well beyond the boundaries of rigid procedural rules. Unfortunately, this requires the injection of my own personal biases and sometimes irreverent opinions, which may differ from those of mainstream practitioners of this often frustrating art.

The incredible complexity of the Internal Revenue Code, which has evolved over the past hundred years, has spawned an industry comprising tax lawyers and accountants who deal primarily with the labyrinthine substantive tax rules. Simplicity is a concept foreign to the drafters of federal tax law. In any event, the focus of practitioners on substantive tax rules, while well understood, is often misplaced. What you will not find in this book are any substantive tax law rules. Instead, I deal primarily with Internal Revenue Code sections 6000 to 9000. It is my steadfast belief that without a thorough knowledge of these procedures, the most learned tax practitioner will encounter nothing but frustration.

If there is a moral higher ground for the tax professional, it is undoubtedly the desire to change the tax structure systemically. Those of us who lack the courage or inclination to do that are relegated to the mundane world of dealing with the tax system as we find it—and not as it ought to be. I am frequently asked, "Wouldn't it be a much fairer tax system if only . . . ?" My answer is always the same: "Yes, of course, but the chances of that happening, given the current political landscape, are equivalent to your winning the lottery within the next thirty days."

Similar to tax law generally, procedural tax law changes daily. To employ an old platitude, attempting to set forth definitive procedural tax rules is a bit like shooting a moving target. Any such attempt is obsolete the day it is published.

I have chosen the outline format for the presentation of these materials to make the information more reader-friendly.

In the second edition of this book I have included appendices consisting of lists of (1) acronyms and abbreviations, (2) IRS forms and notices, (3) form letters commonly sent to taxpayers by the IRS, and (4) tax procedure publications. I hope you find them useful.

W.P.C.

CHAPTER I

Examination

IRS Audit Procedures

I. Introduction and Background

A. *Background*

Anyone who does any significant tax practice inevitably will be required to deal with the examination personnel of the Internal Revenue Service (IRS). In the event of an audit, a client justifiably expects his or her representative to be able to defend positions taken on tax returns. Thus a certified public accountant (CPA) or lawyer should be reasonably conversant with the intricacies and pitfalls of handling a tax audit.

B. *Organizational Structure*

There are four operating divisions within the IRS that are responsible for the Examination function. These are as follows:

1. *Small Business/Self-Employed (SB/SE)*

This division handles the examination of 1040s with Schedules C, E, and F as well as other business returns with assets of less than $10 million.

2. *Large Business and International (LB&I)*

This division handles the audits of business returns (1065, 1120, and 1120S) having assets of more than $10 million. LB&I is organized into five industry groups:

a. communications, technology, & media,

b. financial services,

c. heavy manufacturing and transportation,

d. natural resources and construction, and

e. retailers, food, pharmaceuticals, and health care.

1

3. *Tax-Exempt and Governmental Entities (TEGE)*
4. *Wage and Investment (W&I)*
    This division handles all other taxpayers; that is, individuals who have only wage and investment income. W&I does not conduct field audits. If it is necessary to do a field examination of a W&I taxpayer, it is done by SB/SE.

C. *Initial Screening*
    In the initial processing of a return at regional service centers (now called "campuses"), returns are manually edited and computer scanned for math errors, defects in form or execution, and potentially unallowable items.[1] Returns may be classified as to audit potential according to various criteria predetermined through National Research Program (NRP) audits. The NRP is a program designed to provide information used in designing the discriminant function (DIF) formulas.[2] DIF is a mathematical technique used to score income tax returns as to examination potential based on NRP-developed data. A DIF formula is applied to each return, and each is assigned a three-digit DIF score. The hypothesis is that the higher the score, the greater the potential for audit deficiency. Corporate returns with balance sheets or assets over $10 million are not DIF scored.[3] The highly sophisticated formulas developed by the IRS to score tax returns are secret and thus unavailable to taxpayers.[4]

    As a subset of the DIF procedures, the IRS has developed a tool for identifying returns with a high probability of unreported income. They call it the Unreported Income Discriminant Index Formula, known by its acronym UI DIF.[5] All filed returns now receive a UI DIF score in addition to the traditional DIF score.

D. *Selection of Type of Audit*
    If a DIF score indicates the need for an audit, the IRS first considers the types of potential issues. If the matter can be satisfactorily resolved by correspondence, then that will be the method. If not, and only a few documents need to be inspected, the taxpayer will be asked to bring them to the office ("office examination"). If several complex issues or many books are involved, a "field examination" will be made. Typically, only individuals will be scheduled for office exams. Business returns (corporations, partnerships, etc.) are always subject to field exams by revenue agents. The IRS determines whether an examination should be a field exam or an office exam based on the complexity of the return.[6]

II. Rules Governing Powers of Attorney

A. During any kind of examination, the taxpayer under audit is entitled to be represented by a lawyer, CPA, enrolled agent, or other representative allowed by Circular 230.[7] Because of the anti-disclosure laws, the IRS scrupulously observes the rules regarding who is authorized to receive confidential tax information. Without a properly executed written authorization, the IRS will not disclose information to a representative.

B. A power of attorney (POA) need not follow any prescribed form;[8] however, the IRS has provided Form 2848 for this purpose.[9] It should be prepared with great care; otherwise, it will be rejected. At a minimum, it must contain the following:[10]

1. The taxpayer's complete name;
2. The taxpayer's identifying number (employee identification number [EIN] or Social Security number [SSN]);
3. The representative's
   a. name,
   b. address,
   c. telephone number,
   d. fax number, and
   e. Central Authorization File (CAF) number (optional according to the regulations);[11]
4. The exact years or periods;[12] e.g.,
   a. 0903 (i.e., for quarter ended 3-31-2009),
   b. 2010, or
   c. year ended 12-31-13;
5. The type of tax (e.g., income, estate, or employment) or civil penalty;
6. The form number (e.g., 1040, 1120, 5500, 941, or SS-8); and
7. The declaration of authority (on the back of Form 2848).
   Be careful that the client signs the POA *after* the representative does so; otherwise, it may be rejected for having an invalid date.

C. *Bypassing the Representative*
   Examination personnel are forbidden from contacting the taxpayer directly where there is a valid POA on file, unless the representative has been dilatory or has unreasonably hindered the examination, in which case the revenue agent must request permission from the appropriate supervisory personnel.[13]

D. *Multiple Cases*
   A 2848 (POA) may cover more than one matter; for example, a 1040 and a 941 (for employment tax issues).[14] For business clients, it is generally advisable to cover "civil penalties" in addition to other types of taxes.

E. *Signature of Representative*
   Form 2848 does *not* permit a representative to sign tax returns on behalf of the client. Nor does it permit the endorsing of checks.[15] However, a taxpayer may modify a POA to authorize his or her representative to perform these functions.[16]

In addition to a signature, a representative must provide his license number and PTIN.

A representative may represent both a husband and wife, regardless of whether a joint return was filed. However, in all cases, separate POAs must be obtained for each spouse.

Practice Tip

If the husband and wife are currently divorced, separated, or otherwise having marital difficulties, it is advisable for them to have separate representatives.

F. *Photocopies*
    A photocopy of a POA will suffice for the IRS. It need not be an original, despite the occasional protestations of some revenue personnel.[17] A POA received by fax will also be accepted.[18]

G. *Arrangements for Audits*
    Whenever there is a valid POA, all arrangements for the audit of a taxpayer are conducted through the authorized representative.

H. *CAF Numbers*
    The IRS maintains a Central Authorization File for all representatives who have submitted a POA to represent their clients. Each authorized representative is assigned a unique CAF number and is asked to use that number when submitting a POA to the IRS.[19] However, it should be noted that a POA will *not* be rejected solely because it does not contain a CAF number.[20]

III. Correspondence and Office Audit

A. *Initiation of Audits*
    Correspondence audits are usually initiated by computer-generated letters from the IRS service center. Office examinations are initiated by form letters from the office audit appointment clerk in the local IRS office. The initial letter will have a list of possible items the IRS wants to look at. This letter will also either set a specific appointment date or give a telephone number to call to set up the appointment.

B. *Correspondence Audits*
    Each service center has an audit branch that conducts correspondence audits. Taxpayers are required to mail in certain documents and information. If an issue is raised, taxpayers are given an opportunity to appeal using regular appeals procedures.[21]

Another variation of the correspondence audit is the so-called cross-match audit. Because of statutory "information return" requirements, the IRS receives many millions of documents (W-2s, 1099s, K-1s, etc.) that contain information that should be reported on income-recipient tax returns. If, after matching the information returns with the corresponding income tax returns, there appears to be some discrepancy, a "proposed change" notice is mailed to the taxpayer. This frequently takes the form of a CP-2000 or CP-2501 computer-generated notice.[22] If there is no response to a CP-2000 or -2501 notice, the IRS will issue a statutory notice of deficiency as prescribed by Internal Revenue Code (I.R.C.) § 6212.[23]

C. *Office Audit*

In an office examination case,[24] the taxpayers are required to bring their records to the IRS office. The office auditors (now known as tax compliance officers, or TCOs) will not have screened the return before the audit. They will go through a routine questionnaire, asking if the taxpayer has ever been audited, among other questions (see list below). They will also have an Information Return Program (IRP) (1099, cross-match, etc.) report in front of them. If the auditor tries to go beyond questions indicated on the initial appointment letter, it is within the representative's rights to tell the auditor that he or she is not prepared to discuss these other areas since they were beyond the scope of the original request.

Preliminary questions typically asked by auditors before the actual auditing begins may include some or all of the following:

1. Where does the taxpayer do his or her banking?
2. Is the taxpayer current on all of his or her tax return filing?
3. Have any amended returns been filed?
4. Are there any other tax return filing requirements?
5. Have there been any other prior-year IRS audits?
6. Is the taxpayer a member of any barter club?
7. Does the taxpayer have any foreign bank accounts?
8. What is the taxpayer's age?

   Taxpayers always have the right to raise new, favorable issues during the office interview process.[25]

D. *Repetitive Audits*

If a taxpayer was audited and "no-changed" for the same issue in one of the two years preceding the one under examination, the auditor has the discretion to discontinue the audit for the current year.[26]

E. *Conclusion of Office Audit*

Generally, at the conclusion of an office audit, which lasts usually two to four hours, the auditor will request additional information. If the information is not provided within a few days, a machine-prepared report will be issued, disallowing all questioned items. If additional information is subsequently received, a "corrected" report will be issued. If no additional information is needed by the auditor, the report can be generated by computer and printed at the auditor's desk.

IV. Field Audit Procedures

A. *Initiation of Field Audits*

Field examinations are normally initiated by a telephone call or letter from a revenue agent. Unannounced visits from revenue agents are rare. Accompanying the audit notice will also usually be a request for documents. This is called an Information Document Request, Form 4564.

B. *Pre-Audit Procedures*

Before the first field visit by a revenue agent, the agent will have done a significant amount of analysis and other work. The first thing the agent must do is a "risk analysis." He or she must weigh the benefits of auditing a return against the resources required to complete the job. If the benefits do not outweigh the cost, the return will not be opened for examination.[27]

By the time the revenue agent shows up at your office, he or she already knows a great deal about the taxpayer. Using online capability with services such as ChoicePoint or Accurint, the agent will have checked all public record sources for auto titles, real estate transactions, and court records. He or she may bring printouts of this information to the audit. The agent also has computer access to prior- and subsequent-year tax return information. This information contains line-by-line details, even for Schedules C, E, and F. He or she will also have IRP information based on information reporting.

IRS personnel often pick up leads and other relevant information from media sources such as newspapers. They can also access "public record" information such as lawsuits either by going to the courthouse or by Internet access. A practitioner should assume that the revenue agent already knows, before the start of the audit, everything about the taxpayer that the general public has access to (vehicle titles, real estate ownership, etc.).

Agents also have the capability of downloading tax return information without ever having seen a copy of the tax return. However, this computer information will not have detailed schedules that are attached to the tax return. Agents can even begin the audit with this computer information without a copy of the return in their file.

The agent may also have done a preliminary "cash T" analysis for sources and application of funds. This is done for purposes of a "rough and dirty" indication of unreported income.[28]

A representative should remember that he is entitled to have a copy of all this preliminary and third-party information. Unfortunately, the typical revenue agent will not provide it voluntarily. The required course of action is to file a Freedom of Information Act (FOIA) request as soon as the case is closed out of the examination group. Of course this FOIA request should be prepared only if things have not gone well during the audit.

C. *General Authority of Revenue Agents*
Revenue agents have extremely broad authority in the auditing of tax returns. By statute, for the purpose of ascertaining the correctness of any return (or making a return where none has been made) and determining the tax liability of any person, an IRS agent is authorized to examine (1) books, (2) papers, (3) records, or (4) other data that may be relevant or material to the inquiry.[29]

D. *Revenue Agent Qualifications*
Revenue agents typically have a degree in accounting (or equivalent accounting hours) and are much more technically competent than office auditors. Revenue agents are field personnel who, unlike office auditors, do not conduct their audits in the IRS office.

E. *Time and Place of the Audit*
Normally, the time and place of examination shall be such as may be determined by the revenue agent and as are reasonable under the circumstances.[30]

Practice Tip

It is a good idea not to let the revenue agent work at the taxpayer's place of business, where he or she has free and unfettered access to all of the taxpayer's confidential data, much of which may be irrelevant to the agent's inquiry. The best approach is to convince the agent to work in the representative's office. *See* IRM 4.10.2.7.6 (5-14-99).

There may be circumstances under which a taxpayer may request a transfer of the place of examination from one place to another. For example, if a taxpayer has moved to a different area or can demonstrate that books and records are located elsewhere, the IRS will consider a transfer to another IRS office.[31]

F. *Use of Summons*
An IRS agent has the right to interview a taxpayer or his or her employee, but where there is a POA, that right is enforceable only by

the use of an administrative summons. In the absence of a summons, it is generally not advisable to have the taxpayer who is represented submit to an interview.[32] Similarly, an agent can summons any third party having custody of a taxpayer's books of account.[33] If the agent insists on issuing a summons to the taxpayer or to third parties, there is an increased likelihood of a criminal investigation referral. See the separate subchapter in this chapter dealing with administrative summonses.

G. *Recording of Interviews*
Taxpayers and their authorized representatives are permitted to make audit recordings of in-person interviews relating to the determination or collection of any tax. However, videotaping is not permitted. Nor may a taxpayer record telephone conversations with IRS personnel. Ten days' advance written notice is usually required to record an interview.[34]

H. *Claim-Auditing Procedures*
When claims (1040Xs, 1120Xs, and 843s) are audited, the same procedures are followed by the IRS as when the original returns are audited. Also, the taxpayer has the same appeal rights.[35]

I. *Oral Opinions of IRS Personnel*
Oral statements and opinions are not binding on the IRS upon subsequent audit, even though the taxpayer or his or her representative may have relied on them to their detriment.[36]

Practice Tip

Never rely on verbal statements made by a revenue agent. Get an agent to commit his or her positions in writing whenever possible.

J. *Access to Accountant's Working Papers*
In 1984, the IRS won a great victory in the U.S. Supreme Court, which decided, in *Arthur Young*,[37] that the IRS could have full access to an auditing firm's tax accrual working papers. Nevertheless, the IRS has self-imposed restraints.[38] Such requests are generally limited to those cases where unusual circumstances make it necessary to have access to complete an audit.[39]

K. *Tour of Business Premises*
Field agents are told to conduct a tour of the business site early in the examination process. The purpose of this procedure is for the agent to attain a familiarity with the business operations and internal control.

Theoretically, it also allows agents to identify potential sources of unreported income and confirm the existence of assets. That is, such a tour may reveal areas of audit concern not evident on the tax return.[40]

Practice Tip

Nothing in the rules says that the business owner has to conduct the tour of the business site. To prevent the agent from having a free shot at harassing the business owner with intrusive questions, it is a better plan to have the tour conducted by another employee.

L. *Requests for Technical Advice*

Occasionally a revenue agent will raise an issue requiring the national office of the IRS to make a ruling. A request for technical advice may be made by a taxpayer or his or her representative during an audit if there is

1. a lack of uniformity among authorities or
2. unusual or complex issues.[41]

Requests for technical advice are helpful to maintain consistent holdings throughout the IRS. If a taxpayer or his or her representative makes the request, it is submitted to the examining agent or appeals officer and must contain a full statement of facts and a discussion of relevant law.[42]

M. *Providing Photocopies of Documents*

Contrary to prevailing opinion, the IRS cannot require a taxpayer to provide photocopies of requested documents during an audit. It is frequently recommended to provide such copies, however, particularly where they support a taxpayer's position.

N. *Analytical Procedures*

There is some question as to whether agents can require representatives to do analytical work. Generally, CPAs should not be required to do the agent's auditing work. Agents are trying to come up with the maximum deficiency with a minimum amount of thought and effort. Consequently, they will try to get the CPA to do as much of the work as possible. But there is nothing in the code or regulations that requires a representative to do anything more than furnish records and answer questions.

O. *Extension of the Statute of Limitations*

To avoid interruption of an audit, the regulations suggest (if the case is old) that taxpayers execute Form 872 or 872-A to extend the statute of limitations.[43] However, in the author's opinion, this should not be done routinely. The reason that consent forms 872 and 872-A should not be executed is that they simply can give the IRS agent an unlimited amount of time to do what he or she was going to do anyway. And it is far easier to defend a poorly developed case than a well-developed case, even if a U.S. Tax Court petition has to be prepared.

P.   *Issues Favorable to the Taxpayer*
During an audit, representatives should be on the alert for any adjustments in the taxpayer's favor. Then raise those issues at the *conclusion* of the audit. Be assured that the agent is not *looking* for issues in the taxpayer's favor, but he or she is permitted to make such adjustments in his or her report.

Q.   *Sworn Statements*
IRS agents are authorized to take sworn statements from taxpayers.[44] This power is not frequently used, however. If a revenue agent wants to do it, the representative is within his or her rights to ask the reason for this extraordinary procedure.

R.   *Specialty Groups*
There are several specialty groups within the IRS Examination Division, including the following:
- Estate and gift
- Economists
- Engineers
- Wage and excise
- Employee plan/exempt organizations
- Computer specialists
  A more detailed discussion of these specialty audits is reserved for a later chapter.

S.   *Litigation Hazards*
An agent may not consider hazards of litigation or take a position contrary to that announced by the IRS. Do not expect subtlety to work on a revenue agent. Even if a tax court case is unfavorable to the IRS, a revenue agent will not follow it unless the national office has issued an acquiescence.

T.   *"Package" Audits*
During a field examination of an income tax return of a business taxpayer, the agent will typically inspect returns for other types of taxes to ensure voluntary compliance. Be prepared, therefore, to submit copies of employment tax returns (941, 942, and 940) and excise tax forms (e.g., 720 and 2290) to the agent for inspection.[45] If the agent selects an employment tax return for audit, the representative should consult the Internal

Revenue Manual (IRM), chapter 4.23. The agent will also ask to inspect copies of the taxpayer's prior- and subsequent-year tax returns. This is for the purpose of spotting inconsistencies between years. If the representative is also the preparer, he or she is required by law to allow the agent to inspect such returns.[46] Otherwise, he or she is under no obligation to allow such inspection unless the years are under audit. Before the commencement of the audit, the practitioner should always make sure that all required 1099s have been issued with correct Social Security numbers on them. This will prevent imposition of backup withholding.

U. *Income Probe*

Typically, field agents will request copies of personal bank statements. Their purpose in doing this is to see whether there are bank deposits representing unreported income. If the taxpayer has maintained personal bank statements and if he or she chooses to turn them over to the agent, then the taxpayer should make sure he or she has first inspected each deposit and determined the source of each one to establish its taxable or nontaxable nature. In nonbusiness audits, examiners are advised not to routinely ask for bank statements, canceled checks, or deposit slips.[47]

V. *Corporate Audits*

It is particularly important in audits of corporations for practitioners to be alert for the possibility of the agent raising certain issues. Before the agent arrives, the practitioner should ensure that the corporate minutes book is available and up to date. The minutes book should cover such things as (1) officer/director compensation, (2) formula bonus arrangements, (3) reimbursement policy for business expenses incurred by executives, (4) use of company vehicles by employees, (5) the necessity for retaining earnings rather than declaring dividends, and (6) authorization for loans to executives.

V. Estate Tax Examinations

A. *In General*

Estate tax returns (Form 706) are examined in much the same way that income tax returns are. Estate tax examinations are under the jurisdiction of the SB/SE operating division of the IRS. Since estate tax examiners are always lawyers, the cases tend to be better developed than is the case with income tax audits. Estate tax examiners have no "settlement" authority. That is, they may not base their decisions on "hazards of litigation."

B. *Internal Revenue Manual Provisions*

Guidance for estate tax examiners is contained in the IRM at 4.25.1. Included in this provision are guidelines for scope, surveying, and other processes.

These provisions specify examination methods and techniques for issues, including the following:

- Valuation of real property
- Valuation of stocks and bonds
- Mortgages, notes, and cash
- Life insurance
- Jointly owned property
- Miscellaneous property interests
- Transfers
- Powers of appointment
- Survivorship annuities
- Deductions—marital, charitable, and administrative expenses
  Practitioners should review these provisions in preparing for an estate tax examination.

C. *Statute of Limitations*

It is IRS policy to complete an examination of a 706 within eighteen months of the filing of the return.[48] The reason for this eighteen-month rule is that the federal estate tax return is the only return in which an extension of the statute of limitations for assessment cannot be secured.[49]

D. *Related Returns*

As a part of his or her examination, an estate tax lawyer will always inspect related returns. These may include the following: (1) the decedent's 1040s for the last several years, (2) fiduciary returns (testamentary or inter vivos) filed on Form 1041, (3) gift tax returns (Form 709), or (4) entity returns (1065s, 1120s, etc.).

E. *Closing Letter*

If the estate tax audit is agreed to by the executor, a "closing" letter is issued. If the case is unagreed, no letter is issued until after the case is settled in appeals. If the case is litigated, no closing letter is issued. Note that the closing letter is *not* the same thing as a closing *agreement*.[50]

Practice Tip

If you are facing a large estate tax deficiency on a controversial issue, agree with the examining lawyer, sign an agreement form (waiver of assessment restrictions), then file an amended 706 with a slightly lower value, claiming a refund. Then, after disallowance of this claim, file suit in district court so that you can have a jury hear your case. This procedure is a cheap ticket to the federal district court.

VI. Concluding the Audit

A. *Closing Conference*

At the conclusion of an audit, a revenue agent is required to give the taxpayer or his or her representative an opportunity to agree or disagree with any proposed adjustments.[51] During this "exit" conference, the representative has an opportunity to obtain information from the agent's files that may assist in the defense of the taxpayer's case. The representative should always ask for copies of *all* working papers that support the agent's position on each item for which an adverse adjustment is being proposed. If the agent allows an inspection of his or her file, the representative should also be on the alert for documents that will support a later claim for administrative or litigation costs. In the event that the agent refuses to allow photocopying, he or she should be advised that such documents can be obtained anyway through a FOIA request.

B. *Agreement and Payment*

If the taxpayer agrees with the agent, the agent is required to solicit immediate payment of the tax. Failing that, the taxpayer (or representative) will be asked to sign agreement Form 870 (or the equivalent). This form effectively waives any restrictions on assessment of the deficiency; therefore, one should be careful before signing it.[52] At the conclusion of the audit, the agent will often solicit immediate payment of the agreed deficiency. If the taxpayer does not have the available funds for payment, the agent has the authority to enter into an installment payment agreement with the taxpayer.

C. *Options Available at the Conclusion of an Audit*

The options available at the conclusion of the audit are as follows:
1. Accept the proposal and sign Form 870 or Form 4549, following which the tax will be assessed and collection procedures will commence.
2. Do nothing and wait for the thirty-day or ninety-day letter.
3. Pay the tax, then
   a. forget it, or
   b. file a claim for a refund, wait six months, then file suit in federal district court.
4. Ask for a conference with a group manager.
5. Ask for an appeals conference.

   In the author's opinion, conferences with a group manager are almost always an exercise in futility, as group managers will typically support the positions taken by their auditors or agents.

D. *Issuance of Deficiency Notice*

If the statute of limitations is about to expire, either an office audit or field audit may be abruptly concluded when a deficiency notice (ninety-day letter) is issued. The only appropriate response when a deficiency notice is received (assuming you do not want to pay the tax in full and initiate refund litigation in federal district court) is to file a petition with the U.S. Tax Court within ninety days of the date of the deficiency notice. A petition can be filed either by the taxpayer or by a representative (usually a lawyer) who is admitted to practice before the U.S. Tax Court.[53]

E. *Protests*

In the event of disagreement, the representative may have to draft a protest. However, protests are *not* required after a correspondence or office audit, or after a field audit where the deficiency is less than $2,500. In those cases, a simple request for an appeals conference is sufficient.[54] No fee is required for the filing of a protest. They need not be filed under oath, but they must be certified as true under the penalty of perjury.

F. *Time Limits for Protests*

Written audit reports in unagreed cases are accompanied by "thirty-day letters." This means that the representative has thirty days within which to prepare and submit a written protest to the Examination function. The regulations do not provide for an extension of time to reply to a thirty-day letter by preparing a protest. However, as a matter of practice, extensions may be granted under reasonable circumstances enumerated in the IRM.[55]

G. *Contents of Protest*

The contents of a protest are not fixed by law, but IRS instructions require the following:
1. A statement that the taxpayer seeks to appeal the examiner's findings to the nearest appeals office.
2. The taxpayer's name, address, and daytime telephone number.
3. The date and symbols shown on the thirty-day letter (or a copy of the letter showing proposed changes).
4. The tax period(s) or year(s) involved.
5. An itemized schedule of the disputed adjustments.
6. A statement of facts supporting the taxpayer's position in any contested factual issue.
7. A statement outlining the law or other authority upon which the taxpayer relies.
8. A paragraph, signed by the taxpayer under oath, that the statement of facts is true and correct.
9. If prepared by a representative, this person is required to state that he or she prepared the protest and whether or not he or she knows the facts to be true.[56]

H. *Full versus Skeleton Protest*

There are two schools of thought on preparing a protest:

1. *Skeleton* (the author's favorite—save back a few cards to play at the conference)—but be sure to identify all the issues, including those in your favor.
2. *Full*—but putting too much in the protest may "freeze" a taxpayer's position.

I. *New Issues Raised by the IRS*

A major disadvantage of the appeals process is in providing the IRS the opportunity to strengthen its case against the taxpayer or to raise new issues during the administrative appellate review. Of course appeals officers are prohibited from raising new issues except upon a showing of fraud or malfeasance, or misrepresentation of a material fact.[57]

Practice Tip

A possible ploy if your case has some soft spots not initially recognized by the agent is to go ahead and get the case docketed in tax court, where it is more difficult for the government to raise new issues.

J. *Ex Parte Prohibition*

When an unagreed case gets to appeals, the revenue agent and appeals officer are generally precluded from having ex parte conversations without the taxpayer or his representative being a party to those conversations.[58]

VII. Second Audits

A. *Successive Audits after "No Change"*

IRS has an internal policy whereby once an item is questioned and accepted, the following years will not be questioned as to that item, assuming the facts are substantially identical. For a general discussion of the prohibition on "repetitive audits," see IRM 4.10.2.

B. *General Rule*

Taxpayers are not to be subjected to unnecessary audits, and only *one* inspection of a taxpayer's books of account shall be made for each taxable year unless the taxpayer requests otherwise or unless the IRS notifies the taxpayer, in writing, that an additional inspection is necessary.[59]

C. *Circumstances for Reopening*

A tax case may be reopened, after the first audit is concluded, only if there has been

1. fraud, concealment, or the like;
2. a serious administrative omission; or
3. a clearly defined substantial error.[60]

A case is considered closed when the taxpayer is notified in writing of adjustments to tax liability or acceptance of the return without change.[61]

D. *Doctrine of Estoppel*

Taxpayers who are aware of a second inspection of books and records and do not object to it are estopped from raising the issue in a tax court petition.[62]

E. *Pass-through Entities*

Under prevailing case law, after the first audit is concluded, a second audit may be made as the result of a flow-through adjustment of a partnership or S-Corp without violating § 7605(b).[63]

F. *Closing Agreement*

If there is legitimate concern regarding a subsequent audit, the representative should consider entering into a statutory closing agreement.[64] One would want to use this procedure when there appears to be an advantage in having a case permanently and conclusively closed.

G. *Audit Reconsideration*

When an audit deficiency was assessed and the practitioner convinces the collection employee that the taxpayer did not get sufficient opportunity to present documentation substantiating the disallowed items during the audit process, according to the Internal Revenue Manual that employee may recommend that an audit reconsideration be granted.[65] Audit reconsiderations are discretionary. The following three conditions must be present for an audit reconsideration:

1. The taxpayer's address has changed since the original return was filed, and the deficiency notice was not sent to the taxpayer's new address.
2. The taxpayer has not received any notification from the IRS on any assessment or as to how the assessment was determined before receipt of the bill.
3. The taxpayer has not had an opportunity to submit any required substantiation to support his side of the story.

It is up to the practitioner to convince the collection employee that, had the taxpayer been allowed to present the documentation that is now being offered, the result of the audit would have been different.

H. *Service Center Inquiries and Math Correction Notices*

A taxpayer contacted by the IRS service center under a limited-contact program not involving the examination of records will not subject the

IRS to the prohibition of a "second inspection." The most important of these programs are math correction notices and the Information Returns Program.

Practice Tip

Note that the way to circumvent the "math correction" rule is to require the IRS to issue a deficiency notice, petition the Tax Court, then agree to the deficiency. The case will thereafter be closed under the doctrine of *res judicata*.

VIII. Conclusions and Recommendations

A. *Preparation*

Be thoroughly prepared. Nothing wins cases like being better prepared than the revenue agent. During an audit, documentation is king. The representative should ensure that there is enough evidence to support the taxpayer's position, and all data should be reviewed with the client before the audit.

B. *Cooperation and Attitude*

Always cooperate fully and do not be the cause of any delay. On the other hand, do not do the agent's work for him or her or furnish information not required by law. Remember, you are working for the client, not the government. Nevertheless, a representative should not do or say anything that will cause a revenue agent to become irritated. Should the revenue agent develop an "attitude" toward you or your client, he or she can and usually will make life miserable for you.

C. *Procedural Rules*

In dealing with revenue agents, it is far more important to know procedural rules than substantive tax law. You can always look up the tax law, but you may have to make a snap decision on procedural issues that will significantly affect the result of the audit.

D. *Intimidation*

Many times agents try to win by intimidation. So do not be afraid to challenge their authority. Remember that, as a rule, you are more intelligent and more experienced than the revenue agent. In practice, agents routinely go beyond the announced scope of the audit. Their most common transgression is asking for information about tax years other than the one under examination. The representative should not permit this to happen. If the agent wants to look at records pertaining to other years, then he or she needs to officially open those years for audit.

E. *Volunteering Information*
Do not volunteer information that is not asked for, no matter how innocuous it may seem. Do not give revenue personnel one scrap of information that you do not have to. Also, do not tip your hand as to what you intend to do procedurally or substantively.

F. *Early Commitment*
A representative should get the agent committed to a position in writing as early as possible during the examination process. You can always disagree, but the agent will not likely come back with higher deficiency numbers. Lock the agent into a position before you commit to an agreement.

G. *Time Is Always on the Side of the Taxpayer*
If, during the pendency of an audit, the agent (for whatever reason) is not actively pursuing the case, this is not necessarily a bad sign. He or she may be preoccupied with other matters or in training classes, for example. The representative should let as much time pass as possible so that the agent will be ultimately pressured by management to close the case out without incurring any additional time.
Another ploy, if too much time goes by, is to ask for an interest abatement.[66] This is appropriate where there has been a ministerial or managerial delay that is not the fault of the taxpayer.

H. *Personal Living Expenses*
Occasionally a revenue agent will ask a taxpayer to fill out Form 4822, Statement of Annual Estimated Personal and Family Expenses. This is part of a recent emphasis on "economic reality" or "financial status" audits. The better part of wisdom, however, is not to fill out this form. Nothing good can come of its completion. And it is not required by law to be filled out. In all "financial status" audits, taxpayers should refuse to answer such questions on the grounds that they are not relevant to any item being examined.

I. *Representative-IRS Relationship*
Never forget that while your relationship with the IRS agent should be professionally cordial, it is inherently adversarial. Do not be lulled into a false sense of security. Remember whom you represent. You never know what examination has elements of civil or criminal fraud.

IX. Notes

1. Treas. Reg. § 601.105(a).
2. *See* IRM 4.1.3.2 *et seq.* for an overview of the DIF system and its application.
3. IRM 4.1.3.2.3(1).
4. IRM 4.1.3.2(3).

5. IRM 1.4.40.7.3(3).
6. Treas. Reg. § 301.7605-1(c).
7. 31 C.F.R. pt. 10.
8. Treas. Reg. § 601.503(b)(2).
9. *See* Treas. Reg. § 601.503 for POA requirements generally.
10. Treas. Reg. § 601.503(a).
11. Treas. Reg. § 601.506(d)(2).
12. POAs may cover up to three years beyond the year in which the POA is received by the IRS. Treas. Reg. § 601.506(d)(3)(ii).
13. Treas. Reg. § 601.506(b); IRM 4.10.1.6.1 (5-14-1999).
14. Treas. Reg. § 601.503(a)(5).
15. Treas. Reg. § 601.504(a)(5).
16. Treas. Reg. § 601.504(a)(5),(6).
17. Treas. Reg. § 601.504(c)(4).
18. *Id.*
19. *See* IRM 21.3.7.5.1 (10-1-05) regarding the assignment of CAF numbers to representatives.
20. Treas. Reg. § 601.506(d)(2).
21. Treas. Reg. § 601.105(b)(2)(i).
22. A CP-2501 may precede the CP-2000. The CP-2501 does not calculate a proposed tax change; it is merely an inquiry that requires a response. A CP-2000, on the other hand, calculates a proposed tax deficiency, statutory interest, and any applicable penalties. This is part of the IRS automated underreporter program (AUP), a discussion of which can be found in IRM 4.19.2.1 (9-1-03).
23. All references here to the I.R.C. or to section numbers refer to Title 26 U.S.C., the Internal Revenue Code of 1986, as amended, unless specifically otherwise designated.
24. *See* Treas. Reg. § 601.105(b)(2)(ii) for a discussion of office examinations at local IRS offices.
25. *Id.*
26. IRM 4.10.2.4.2.
27. IRM 4.10.2.4.1.2.1.
28. *See* IRM §§ 4.10.2.4, 4.10.4.3.3.1.
29. I.R.C. § 7602(a)(1).
30. Treas. Reg. § 601.105(b)(3) provides that field examinations are to be conducted on the taxpayer's premises. However, for the convenience of all concerned, audits are frequently conducted at the offices of the representative. *See also* Treas. Reg. § 301.7605-1(e) regarding requests by taxpayers to change the place of examination.
31. Treas. Reg. § 601.105(k).
32. Indeed, the statute provides that a revenue agent may not require the taxpayer to attend such an interview in the absence of a summons where the representative holds a valid power of attorney. *See* I.R.C. § 7521(c).
33. I.R.C. § 7602(a)(2).
34. I.R.C. § 7521(a); Notice 89-51, 1989-1 CB 691.
35. Treas. Reg. § 601.105(e)(2).
36. Treas. Reg. § 601.201(k)(2); United States v. Guy, 92-2 USTC ¶ 50,581 (6th Cir. 1992); Williams v. United States, 92-1 USTC ¶ 50,160 (N.D. Ala. 1992); First Ala. Bank NA v. United States, 93-1 USTC ¶ 50,138 (11th Cir. 1993).

37. United States v. Arthur Young & Co., 84-1 USTC ¶ 9305 (S. Ct. 1984).

38. IRM 4.10.20; I.R.S. Ann. 2002-63, 2002-27 I.R.B. 72.

39. *Arthur Young*, 84-1 USTC at ¶ 83,677.

40. IRM 4.10.4.3.3.3; IRM 4.10.4.3.3(1)C.

41. Treas. Reg. § 601.105(b)(5).

42. Rev. Proc. 98-2, 1998-1 I.R.B. 74.

43. *See generally* Treas. Reg. § 601.105(f).

44. I.R.C. § 7602(a)(3); I.R.C. § 7622.

45. IRM 4.10.52.6.1.

46. I.R.C. § 6107(b)(2). Failure to comply with this provision can subject the preparer to a civil penalty under I.R.C. § 6695(d) and to a possible lifetime injunction from preparing returns for clients. *See* United States v. Nordbrock, 90-1 USTC ¶ 50,089 (D. Ariz. 1990), *aff'd*, 94-1 USTC ¶ 50,532 (9th Cir. 1994).

47. IRM 4.10.4.3.2.1(1).

48. IRM 4.25.1.5.1(1).

49. I.R.C. § 6501(c)(4)(A).

50. *See* I.R.C. § 7121.

51. Treas. Reg. § 601.105(b)(4).

52. *Id.*

53. *See* I.R.C. §§ 6212–6213.

54. Treas. Reg. § 601.105(c)(1).

55. Treas. Reg. § 601.105(d); IRM 4.71.4.4.7 (1-1-06).

56. I.R.S. Publ'n No. 5 (revised Jan. 1999).

57. IRM 8.6.1.6(1).

58. IRS Restructuring and Reform Act of 1998, Act § 1001(a)(4).

59. I.R.C. § 7605(b); IRS procedures for reopening cases are contained in Rev. Proc. 85-13, 85-1 CB 514.

60. Treas. Reg. § 601.105(j).

61. Rev. Proc. 85-13.

62. Harrington v. Comm'r, 48 T.C. 939, at 953 (1967).

63. Williams v. United States, 80-1 USTC ¶ 9740 (W.D. Tex. 1980).

64. I.R.C. § 7121.

65. *See generally* IRM 4.13.1.

66. I.R.C. § 6404(e).

Alternative Audit Techniques

I. History and Background

A. Traditional audit techniques involve verification of items that appear on tax returns or financial statements. What is eminently more difficult, however, is determining what does not appear on a tax return or what is not obvious from looking at books and records. As a result of this difficulty, the IRS has developed nontraditional or alternative procedures designed to reveal previously undisclosed, but reportable, income.

   There is statutory authority for using alternative audit techniques. If no method of accounting has been regularly used by the taxpayer, or if the method used does not clearly reflect income, then the IRS is authorized to reconstruct taxable income under whatever method, in the opinion of the IRS, *does* clearly reflect income.[1] Agents often make liberal use of this authority.

B. *History of Financial Status Audits*
   During the 1990s the IRS began a formalized program to ferret out, or probe for, the existence of taxpayers' unreported income. The IRS instituted what are known as "financial status" audits (or FS audits), formerly known as "economic reality" audits. The idea was for agents to come up with circumstantial or indirect evidence that the taxpayer's lifestyle belies, or is inconsistent with, his or her reported income. The two primary means of doing this were through the use of "lifestyle" questions propounded to the taxpayer and through development information through third-party sources.

C. *Traditional Audit Focus versus FS Audit Focus*
   There are two distinct types of methods of proof in tax cases: the direct ("specific-item") method and the indirect method. The IRS does not use specific items to support an inference of unreported income from unidentified sources.[2]

   Traditional audits focus principally on books and records that have a direct bearing on the accuracy of a tax return. In an FS audit, on the other hand, the focus is on detecting unreported income at the outset of the proceeding.

D. *"Cash T" Method*
  1. When a revenue agent determines that income cannot be determined from books and records, he or she will sometimes use the cash transaction (cash T) method to compute unreported income.[3]
  2. All accounting students are familiar with "T" accounts, with the left-hand side of the T containing debits and the right-hand side containing credits. All of the T accounts must balance within the theoretical general ledger. The cash T method is a variation of that technique.
  3. The cash T is an alternative method for determining gross receipts.
  4. Generally the IRS is looking for uses or application of funds that is greater than the reported sources of funds. Generally a cash T analysis is done at the individual level rather than at the entity level.
  5. Pre-contact analysis requires an agent to prepare a preliminary cash T based on tax return information and other information in the case file. If the cash T is materially out of balance, the examiner is guided to use subsequent interviews and information gathered during the audit to resolve those discrepancies. Note that in the audit of a business taxpayer, a review of a taxpayer's bank statements is considered to be a "minimum probe" for unreported income.[4]

II. FS Audit Techniques

A. *Rationale*
The goal of using FS techniques is to determine whether a taxpayer's lifestyle belies his or her reported income.

B. *Primary Techniques*
The IRS uses various techniques in FS audits. The most common are the following:
  1. In-depth interview of the taxpayer and his or her spouse;
  2. Obtaining asset and income information from third-party sources, including public records sources; and
  3. Coercing the taxpayer to complete a Form 4822, "Estimated Personal and Family Expenses."
Financial status audit techniques are not defined in the I.R.C. But the General Accounting Office reports requested by Congress before the enactment of I.R.C. § 7602(e) describe financial status or economic reality audit techniques as consisting of IRS indirect methods of examination, such as the bank deposits method, the cash transaction method, the net worth method, the percentage of markup method, and the unit and volume method. When the IRS is using such indirect

methods, a taxpayer's finances are reconstructed through circumstantial evidence. Indirect methods are then used to support an inference of unreported income.

C. *Timing*

IRS agents prefer to employ these FS techniques at the beginning of the audit before the taxpayer has a chance to consult with a competent adviser, who, most likely, would advise the client not to submit to such an intrusive invasion of his or her privacy.

III. Form 4822

A. Form 4822, a one-page form, asks for extremely detailed information about a taxpayer's spending patterns and habits. It is also sometimes referred to as a Personal Living Expenses (PLE) form. This form has not been revised since 1983.

B. No specific authority exists to require a taxpayer to fill out a PLE form. If a taxpayer refuses, the examiner's options include filling out the form himself based on known expenditures or the use of Bureau of Labor statistics.

C. Form 4822 is often used during an audit where books and records are judged by the IRS auditor to be inadequate. Most frequently the taxpayer is asked to fill out the form and submit it to the auditor.[5] The auditor then uses this information to reconstruct the taxpayer's income indirectly, often in conjunction with a cash T analysis.

D. Because of I.R.C. § 7602(e), the IRS has become more cautious in its recommended use of Form 4822. In fact, their manual states that it is "inappropriate" for an auditor to ask the taxpayer to complete this form.[6] Instead, examiners are asked to estimate personal living expenses.

Practice Tip

Practitioners should *never* allow their clients to fill out Form 4822. The reason is that, if they do, the IRS will surely use this information to develop a justification for determining unreported income, resulting in civil penalties or criminal sanctions. In the author's opinion, submission of this form is tantamount to committing malpractice.

IV. Specific-Item versus Indirect Methods

A. *Specific-Item Method*

The specific-item method of auditing involves the use of direct evidence to determine omitted income, overstated expenses, or both. Direct evidence is evidence from which only one logical conclusion can be reached. This method is appropriate when the taxpayer maintains adequate books and records. The specific-item method is not useful if the taxpayer's gross receipts are generated from numerous sources or in small amounts such as in a grocery store.[7]

B. *Indirect Method*

The indirect method involves the use of circumstantial evidence to prove omitted income, overstated expenses, or both. Conclusions drawn from such evidence must be reasonable. Financial status analysis and bank account analysis are not prohibited by I.R.C. § 7602(e). Note (as mentioned above) that a minimum income probe for a business return will always include a bank account analysis.[8]

C. *Formal Indirect Methods*[9]

The formal indirect methods are audit techniques used to determine the amount of unreported income. They include the
1. bank deposit and cash expenditures method,[10]
2. source and application of funds method,[11]
3. percentage of markup method,[12]
4. unit and volume method,[13] and
5. net worth method.[14]

V. Criminal Investigation Possibilities

A. The obvious danger inherent in an FS audit is that an agent may become, with or without justification, suspicious at some point and refer the case to the IRS Criminal Investigation function for possible prosecution.
B. The primary criticism of FS audits is that they blur the distinction between civil audits and criminal investigations.

VI. Interview Process

A. *Sample Questions*

Typical questions asked in an FS audit interview might include the following:
1. What is your educational background?
2. Where did you go on vacation? How much did you spend?
3. Where do your children attend school?
4. How many automobiles do you own? What kind are they? What are the amounts of your car payments?
5. Do you own any large assets (> $10,000) besides automobiles and your home? What are they? Where are they located?
6. What currency did you have on hand at the beginning and at the end of the year under audit?
7. Do you have a safe deposit box? What information and/or assets are kept in it?

Practice Tip

An alert practitioner will not allow an agent to ask these kinds of questions of a taxpayer or the representative. The response should be something like "This question relates to a 'lifestyle' or 'financial status' inquiry, forbidden by I.R.C. § 7602(e)."

B. *Statutory Rights*

IRS agents are pressured to force the taxpayer to submit to a face-to-face interview. However, the practitioner should be alert to this technique and be prepared to invoke the statute that states that agents have *no right* to insist that a taxpayer be present during any interview.[15]

C. *Recommendation*

While each situation is unique and professional judgment must always be exercised, in most if not all cases, practitioners should advise their clients *not* to submit to a personal interview or fill out Form 4822.

VII. Role and Benefit of Counsel

A. If a taxpayer is interviewed by the IRS without the benefit of counsel being present, he or she may unwittingly make statements that (especially in the context of FS audit techniques) may be misinterpreted or create unnecessary problems or concerns.

B. Note that the right to representation is statutory. In the opinion of this author, if a client appears for an interview pursuant to the issuance of a summons, the representative *must* appear with him or her, or run the risk of committing malpractice.[16]

C. A practitioner's pre-audit activity should include an evaluation of whether the client would generate significant interest to an agent performing an audit using FS techniques.

D. There is no duty imposed on a practitioner by the I.R.C., Treasury Circular 230, or the AICPA Code of Professional Conduct to request personal living expense and lifestyle information from his or her client.

VIII. Miscellaneous

A. *Bank Statements*

Revenue agents, in virtually all cases where an individual taxpayer is being audited, will ask for bank statements. This procedure occurs in traditional as well as FS audits. Agents define bank statements as including all savings, money market, CD, and brokerage accounts. If the taxpayer does not produce them, agents are more than willing to serve an administrative summons on the financial institutions. Taxpayers will thereafter be asked to explain every deposit and how it relates to his or her tax return.

B. *Summons*

Any time an agent issues a summons, the practitioner should be on high alert. Issuance of a summons pursuing financial status information is seen as an indication that unreported income is a significant audit issue.

C. *Right to Information in IRS Files*

On August 8, 1995, the assistant commissioner of examination issued a memorandum to the regional chief compliance officers, providing that "[e]xaminers are reminded that, except for informant information, taxpayers and representatives should be provided with available third-party information on request. If an examiner has indications of unreported income, there should be no hesitation to discuss this issue with the taxpayer or practitioner as soon as possible."

IX. Notes

1. I.R.C. § 446(b).
2. I.R.S. Priv. Ltr. Rul. 2002-06-055.
3. Hawkins v. Comm'r (T.C. Summary Opinion 2003-154).
4. CCA 200311032.
5. *See, e.g.*, Wenz v. Comm'r, 69 T.C.M. (CCH) 2961 (1995); Cherry v. Comm'r, 76 T.C.M. (CCH) 626 (1998).
6. IRM 4.10.4.5.2.
7. IRM 4.10.4.2.7.
8. IRM 4.10.4.2.8.
9. Also known as financial status audit techniques.
10. IRM 4.10.4.6.4.
11. IRM 4.10.4.6.3; also known as the "cash T" method discussed above.
12. IRM 4.10.4.6.5.
13. IRM 4.10.4.6.6.
14. IRM 4.10.4.6.7.
15. In the absence of a summons, of course. *See* I.R.C. § 7521(c).
16. *See* I.R.C. § 7521(c).

Taxpayer Interviews

I. Background

A. Audit Technique

The IRS's authority to interview taxpayers and others in connection with the determination of tax liability is contained in I.R.C. § 7602. This includes the ability to take testimony under oath, if necessary. These interviews are used to obtain leads, develop information, and establish evidence.[1]

Prior to the enactment of various Taxpayer Bills of Rights,[2] the IRS greatly emphasized the taxpayer interview as a wonderful audit technique. Particularly where an IRS agent could catch the taxpayer by surprise, before he or she had an opportunity to contact tax counsel, the agent could obtain all sorts of information that was otherwise unavailable. Typically an agent will have a computer-prepared list of questions at the initial interview. The representative is well advised to be thoroughly prepared to answer questions regarding the taxpayer's history and his or her business.

B. 1987 Policy re Whom to Interview

In 1987 IRS Commissioner Lawrence Gibbs announced a policy shift that provided that the IRS would not insist on a taxpayer being present during an interview as long as a knowledgeable representative could answer all of the examiner's questions. (Note: This policy presented obvious problems since the representative could not possibly have as much knowledge about the facts as would the taxpayer.) Nevertheless, this policy was obviated by subsequent legislation. Despite the statutory change, however, agents are encouraged to request a taxpayer's "voluntary" presence at the interview.[3]

C. The Taxpayer Bill of Rights

The Technical and Miscellaneous Revenue Act of 1988[4] enacted the first Taxpayer Bill of Rights (TBR) to promote taxpayer rights and to protect taxpayers when dealing with the IRS. One of the provisions of the TBR was the enactment of new Code § 7521 dealing with taxpayer interviews.

27

D. *Effective Dates*
   Code § 7521 was signed into law on November 10, 1988. The provisions of the TBR dealing with taxpayer interviews were effective with respect to interviews conducted thirty days after the enactment date, or December 10, 1988.

E. Prior to the enactment of the TBR, IRS agents had the annoying habit of not always honoring powers of attorney and would often "audit around the representative." They would typically insist that a taxpayer personally be interviewed, whether or not the representative was present.

F. According to the TBR conference report, the IRS may continue to request that taxpayers "voluntarily" attend interviews.

II. Recordings of Interviews

A. *Recordings by the Taxpayer*
   Any IRS employee who wishes to conduct an in-person interview with a taxpayer, for any reason, must allow the taxpayer to make an audio recording of the interview. But the taxpayer must provide his or her own recording equipment.[5] In a 2003 U.S. Tax Court case, the word "interview" was extended to include an appeals conference conducted pursuant to I.R.C. § 6330. The court decided that the term "interview" was broad enough to include a collection due process "hearing."[6]

B. *Recordings by the IRS*
   IRS employees may also record interviews with taxpayers, but only if the taxpayer is informed of the recording prior to the interview. And, upon request by the taxpayer, the IRS must furnish the taxpayer a copy of the recording or a transcript of the recording. If a copy or transcript of the recording is requested, the taxpayer must pay the cost of transcription or reproduction.[7]

C. *Place of the Recording*
   The IRS has a policy that all recordings should take place in their office, where recording equipment is available. However, as a practical matter, the IRS will do the recording in the representative's office.[8]

D. *Identification*
   All participants in the recording session must identify themselves and their role at the beginning of the recording.[9]

E. *Payment for Reproduction Costs*
   Where the IRS does the recording and the taxpayer wants a copy, a taxpayer must submit payment therefor with his or her request for a copy or a transcription.[10]

F. *Prior Notification*

Taxpayer requests for recordings must be received by the IRS at least ten days prior to the interview. The IRS must also give taxpayers ten days' advance notice.[11] If the IRS is not given ten days' advance notice, they may continue with the interview or reschedule for a later date at their discretion.

III. Right to Representation

A. *Suspension of Interview*

If, during an interview conducted by an IRS agent, a taxpayer states that he or she wishes to consult with a representative (attorney, CPA, etc.), the IRS employee must immediately suspend the interview even if the taxpayer has not answered a single question. Note, however, that an IRS employee is not required to suspend the interview if the taxpayer has appeared for the interview in response to an administrative summons.[12]

B. *Mandatory Representative Presence*

An attorney or CPA holding a written power of attorney must be allowed by the IRS to represent the taxpayer during any interview. It is important to note that the IRS cannot compel a taxpayer to accompany his or her representative to an interview unless the taxpayer has been issued an administrative summons.[13] But even with a summons, a taxpayer can always invoke his or her Fifth Amendment privilege.

C. *Who May Act as a Representative*

Circular 230 describes the type of persons who may represent a client before the IRS during an interview.[14] Generally this includes attorneys, CPAs, enrolled agents, and enrolled actuaries—as long as they are not under suspension or disbarment from practice.[15]

D. *Unreasonable Delay*

If a representative has unreasonably delayed or hindered an audit, an agent, with proper supervisory approval, may contact the taxpayer directly for an interview.[16] Unfortunately, illegal direct contacts with taxpayers by the IRS occur all too frequently.

E. *Reason for Having a Representative*

In the opinion of the author it is absolutely essential that a taxpayer be represented during confrontation with a revenue agent or officer. The reason is that a knowledgeable representative can frame replies to questions in a manner that better supports the taxpayer's position than most taxpayers could on their own.

F. *Non-taxpayer Witness*

A non-taxpayer witness has a right to have his or her own counsel present during an interview by an IRS agent even if that attorney also represents the taxpayer.[17] Note, however, that the taxpayer's attorney does not have an automatic right to attend such an interview unless, of course, he or she also represents the non-taxpayer witness.[18]

IV. Criminal Investigation Interviews[19]

A. *General Rule*

The statutory provisions regarding taxpayer interviews do not apply to cases being investigated by the IRS Criminal Investigation function (CI) or to cases being investigated by the Treasury Inspector General for Tax Administration (TIGTA).[20] Your client will know when he or she is being interviewed by CI for two reasons: (1) The client will be read his or her rights (the so-called Miranda warning), and (2) the agents, who carry gold badges, always work in teams.

B. As a general rule, it is best not to let your client (the taxpayer) be interviewed by the IRS. This is particularly true in CI cases. In most cases, in an effort to be "cooperative," a taxpayer will say far more than is necessary and possibly cause irreparable damage to his or her case.

C. *Prior Notification*

If the case has been referred to CI, the taxpayer must be notified that he or she is a target of an investigation before the beginning of an initial interview.

D. *Witnesses*

Occasionally the CI will issue a summons to a third-party witness. If so, the witness may want to hire his or her own attorney, particularly if the witness has had any financial transactions with the taxpayer-target. If there is a realistic possibility of the witness becoming a subject of an investigation, the witness has the right to invoke his or her Fifth Amendment right to remain silent.

V. Place for the Interview

A. *General Rule*

In recent years, the IRS has conceded that the taxpayer's representative can dictate where the interview will take place. Of course, in an "office audit"[21] context, the interview takes place in the IRS office, since office auditors do not have authorization to make field visits. In a "field" audit context representatives should insist that the interview *not* take place in the taxpayer's place of business. The best place is in the representative's office.

B. According to the committee reports on the Technical and Miscellaneous Revenue Act of 1988, the regulations will take into account the physical danger to an IRS agent when determining the place for an interview.

C. A representative should always insist that the interview be conducted in the representative's office.

VI. Explanations

A. *General Rule*

Before beginning an in-person interview with a taxpayer, a revenue agent is required to give the taxpayer an explanation of the audit process and an explanation of the taxpayer's appeal rights. If the interview is to be conducted by a revenue officer or employee of the Collection function, the collection process must be explained to the taxpayer.[22]

B. *Written Explanations*

An explanation of rights can be accomplished by handing the taxpayer a written statement.[23] This is most often what happens since most IRS personnel are incapable of speaking extemporaneously on the subject of taxpayer rights. The material most often used is the IRS's Publication 1, "Your Rights as a Taxpayer." Routine telephone calls are not considered interviews for purposes of the explanation of rights.

VII. Interviews Pursuant to the Administrative Summons

A. A taxpayer must appear personally in response to a summons, even if he or she is represented by counsel.[24]

VIII. Planning Suggestions

A. *General Rule*

Practitioners should make extensive use of I.R.C. § 7521 to shield their clients as much as possible from the IRS's intimidation tactics.

B. *"Fishing Expeditions"*

Usually, agents are on a "fishing expedition" when interviewing a taxpayer. That is, they will ask open-ended questions, hoping that they will be led into productive areas they would not otherwise have discovered. Astute practitioners will force agents to ask specific, relevant questions.

C. When asked to submit interview questions in advance, in writing, agents will always refuse. Why? Because they don't want the answers carefully thought out.

IX. Notes

1. IRM 4.10.4.3.2.
2. There have actually been three Taxpayer Bills of Rights: one in 1988, one in 1996, and then in 1998 there was the IRS Restructuring and Reform Act, which contained many pro-taxpayer provisions.
3. IRM 4.10.3.2.1.
4. Pub. L. No. 100-647.
5. Notice 89-51, 1989-1 CB 691.
6. Keene v. Comm'r, 121 T.C. 8 (2003).
7. I.R.C. § 7521(a)(2).
8. Notice 89-51, 1989-1 CB 691.
9. *Id.*
10. *Id.*
11. *Id.*
12. *See* I.R.C. § 7602(a)(2) for the statutory authority regarding summonses; I.R.C. § 7521(b)(2).
13. I.R.C. § 7521(c).
14. *See* CCH Standard Federal Tax Reports, ¶¶ 43,499 *et seq.*, for a reproduced copy of Circular 230, issued as part of Title 31 regulations.
15. *Id.* § 10.3.
16. I.R.C. § 7521(c).
17. Backer v. United States, 275 F.2d 141, 5 AFTR2d 824 (5th Cir. 1960). In this case a taxpayer's CPA was allowed to have the taxpayer's attorney attend his "third-party" interview.
18. United States v. Taylor, 79-1 USTC ¶ 9231 (E.D. Va. 1979); *Backer*, 275 F.2d 141.
19. *See generally* IRM 9.4.5 regarding interviews conducted by special agents of CI.
20. *See* I.R.C. § 7521(d); TIGTA is charged with maintaining and monitoring integrity of IRS employees and tax practitioners.
21. Sometimes referred to as a "desk audit."
22. I.R.C. § 7521(b)(1).
23. Committee Reports on Pub. L. No. 100-647.
24. United States v. Leach, 90-1 USTC ¶ 50,291 (D. Kan. 1990).

Use of Administrative Summonses by Federal Agents

I. **Introduction**

A. The purpose of this subchapter is to discuss the various methods by which taxpayers and third parties can be legally compelled to produce books, records, and testimony pursuant to a civil or criminal tax investigation. Also discussed are ways to protect such evidence from compelled production through the exercise of privileges and defenses.

B. To determine whether taxpayers are voluntarily complying with internal revenue laws, the IRS has been given broad investigatory powers to issue summonses for records and testimony.[1] And this power has survived a variety of constitutional challenges. Although existing records and testimony may be compelled with a summons, a summons authorizes neither a search of the taxpayer's premises nor a seizure of his or her property.[2]

C. A summons is generally used in the case of recalcitrant taxpayers in civil examinations or in criminal cases. This document used by IRS personnel is referred to as an "administrative summons" and is similar in many respects to a subpoena. If a summons requires a witness to produce books, papers, records, and the like, it is the equivalent of a subpoena duces tecum.[3]

D. A summons may be issued by the Collection function of the IRS as well as the Examination and Criminal Investigation functions.[4] Issuance of a summons is the exception rather than the rule. Investigators are required to explore all other means of securing the required information before issuing a summons in view of the action required to enforce compliance.[5]

E. *Types of Summonses*
Different summonses are used for different purposes within the IRS. Typical are the following:
1. Taxpayer summons[6]
2. Third-party summons[7]
3. Third-party record keeper summons[8]
4. John Doe summons[9]

5. Designated summons[10]
6. Church summons[11]

F. *Authority to Issue Summonses*
Only certain types of government employees can issue summonses:
- Internal revenue agents (including special agents)
- Estate tax attorneys
- Estate tax examiners
- Revenue service representatives
- Tax auditors
- Revenue officers (GS-9 and above)
- Tax law specialists
- Compliance officers
- Tax resolution representatives
- Property appraisal and liquidation specialists (GS-12 and above)[12]

II. Technical Requirements of a Summons

A. *Date, Time, and Place for Appearance*
The summons is required to name a specific time and place for the person summoned to appear.[13] The time and place must be reasonable. The date fixed for appearance before the IRS official cannot be less than ten calendar days from the issuance date of the summons.[14]

The person issuing the summons can, and often will, agree to change the time and place of appearance to suit the convenience of the person summoned. The investigator can also waive appearance, but if he or she does so, the IRS may be precluded from resorting to judicial process to enforce the summons.[15]

B. *Persons Who Can Be Summoned*
The IRS is authorized by statute to "examine" books, papers, and so on.[16] However, in the event that cooperation is not obtained by the examining auditor or agent, the IRS is further authorized to issue (administrative) summonses to any of the following persons:
1. The taxpayer under examination or investigation,[17]
2. The taxpayer's employee or agent,
3. A person having custody of a taxpayer's books or records, or
4. Any other person.[18]

C. *Records to Be Produced*
1. *Description*
When the summons requires the production of records, they must be described with "reasonable certainty."[19] The IRM describes this standard as "reasonable particularity," a factual matter depending on the circumstances of each case.[20]

2. *Electronic/Internet*

Questions have arisen regarding whether the IRS can compel the production of a taxpayer's restricted website and whether such website constitutes "records." In answering affirmatively and interpreting § 7602 broadly, the IRS has issued a ruling that states that a taxpayer's restricted website constitutes "records, or other data" within the meaning of section 7602(a)(2).[21]

For purposes of § 7602, the term "records" includes electronic storage media, not just visible and legible records. Moreover, where part of a company's accounting records are maintained on computer tapes, the IRS is entitled to the originals, not just copies, of such tapes.[22]

Other electronic records that must be produced include tax preparation software being used under a license.[23]

D. *Methods of Service*

A summons may be served on a taxpayer by an IRS employee in only one of two ways:

1. By hand delivery in person, or
2. By leaving it at a last and usual place of abode.[24] There is at least one authority holding that merely leaving a summons on the front door of a dwelling, without more, is insufficient. What is required is to leave the summons at the residence with someone of "suitable age and discretion." That would not include young children. Other authorities have reached a contrary result, however.[25]

Leaving the summons at a taxpayer's office, without personally handing it to the taxpayer, is apparently insufficient, although there is no case law on point.

E. *Signatures*

The summons must also be signed by the person serving it.[26] This is done by completing a "certificate of service" that is printed on the summons form. Summonses issued to third-party witnesses must contain the signature of an approving supervisory official.[27] Form 2039 has a signature line for "signature of approving officer (if applicable)." Absence of such an approval may be a valid reason for alleging a defective summons.

F. *Attestation*

If a copy of the summons served on taxpayers or third-party record keepers does not include a signed written notation that the copy is a correct copy of the original, it will not be considered to be an "attested copy." And since the service of an "attested" copy is a statutory requirement of I.R.C. § 7603, this administrative step will not have been complied with, resulting in a possible non-enforcement of the summons by a federal district court, depending on whether the IRS has acted in "good faith."[28]

G. *Oath*

An IRS agent who has summoned a taxpayer may put the taxpayer or a third party under oath before questioning begins.[29] Note that the IRS is not authorized to take a *written* sworn statement from the taxpayer. Compelled testimony can only be *oral.*

H. *Documents Not in Existence*

A summons should not require the witness to do anything other than to appear on a given date to give testimony and to bring existing books, papers, and records. A summons cannot require a witness to prepare or create documents, including tax returns, that are not currently in existence.[30] For example, often a revenue officer will issue a summons requiring a taxpayer to complete a financial statement (Form 433) and bring it with him or her on the summons appearance date. Such a summons is invalid and could justifiably be ignored.

I. *Right to Photocopy*

It is clear under the statute that a taxpayer must appear and "produce" records for "examination" upon demand by the revenue service. What is not clear is whether the IRS can force a taxpayer to make photocopies of such records for the IRS's files. According to the Internal Revenue Manual, the person serving a summons for records has the right to photocopy the summonsed records, although there appears to be no statutory or regulatory authority for such photocopying.[31]

III. The Third-Party Summons

A. *General Rule*

The IRS has the right not only to issue a summons to the taxpayer under examination or investigation but also to issue summonses to third parties.[32] Third parties fall into one of two categories: (1) third-party record keepers, and (2) other.

B. *Duties of a Third-Party Record Keeper*

On receipt of a summons, a third-party record keeper must proceed to assemble the records requested and produce them on the day specified in the summons.[33]

C. *Who Are "Third-Party Record Keepers"?*

Third-party record keepers can be just about anybody (other than the taxpayer), but by statute they include only the following:[34]
1. Banks and other financial institutions,
2. Securities brokers,
3. Barter exchanges,

4. Attorneys,[35]
5. Enrolled agents,[36]
6. Computer software code developers,[37]
7. Accountants,[38]
8. Consumer reporting agencies,
9. Credit card issuers,[39] and
10. Regulated investment companies.

D. *Method of Service*

Unlike summonses served on taxpayers, a summons served on a third-party record keeper may be served via certified or registered mail sent to the third party's last known address.[40] It does not have to be hand-delivered. Note, however, that this rule does not apply in the case of a third party who is merely a witness instead of being a record keeper. Witnesses who are not record keepers must be served in the manner discussed in II.D., *supra*.

E. *Notice (to Taxpayer) Requirement*

If a summons is served on a third-party record keeper, then notice of the summons must be given to the identified taxpayer within three days after the service date (by certified mail) but not later than the twenty-third day before the appearance date.[41] Such notice must also attach a copy of the summons and must explain a taxpayer's right to file a motion to quash. A person (i.e., the taxpayer) who is entitled to notice of a third-party summons has the right to intervene in any U.S. district court enforcement action.[42] Note that if a summons is served on a third-party witness who is not a record keeper, then there is no notice requirement.[43] In such cases, the IRS is under no duty to reveal even the existence of such a witness.

F. *Motions to Quash*

A taxpayer cannot bring a proceeding to quash a summons served on him or her personally.[44] These procedures are available only in the event of a third-party summons. Any person who is entitled to notice of a third-party summons is entitled to file a motion to quash such summons within twenty days after the notice is given. In such proceeding the IRS may seek to compel compliance with the summons.[45] The act of mailing the notice triggers the twenty-day period, not the receipt of the notice by the noticee taxpayer.[46]

Federal district courts have exclusive jurisdiction to hear motions to quash. The district court's order denying a petition to quash a third-party summons or a John Doe summons is considered to be a final order that may be appealed.[47] Note that some judges will rule on the motion to quash based solely on the pleadings without giving the parties the benefit of a hearing.

If a motion to quash is filed, the running of the three-year assessment statute of limitations is suspended for the period that the enforcement proceeding is pending. In the absence of a resolution of the matter, the period of suspension begins six months after the summons service date and ends with the final resolution of the matter.[48]

G. Liability for Disclosure by Third Parties

A third-party record keeper who discloses information pursuant to an IRS summons cannot be held liable to any person for such disclosure.[49]

H. Authority to Issue

Revenue officers may generally issue summonses to taxpayers as authorized by Delegation Order 25-1.[50] All revenue agents, special agents, tax auditors, and estate tax examiners have authority to issue summonses.

I. Third-Party Rights

1. Right to Counsel

A third-party witness has just as much right to have counsel present during an interview mandated by a summons as does the taxpayer.[51] However, the third party must have his or her own attorney; the taxpayer's attorney has no right to be present during the third party's interview unless he or she also represents the interviewee.[52]

2. Rights of Interviewees Interrogated by CI

Any person summoned by a criminal investigator to appear and give testimony is entitled to be represented by an attorney and obtain a transcript of the testimony.[53] Special agents, however, typically take the position that release of such transcript may be delayed until such time as it will not interfere with the development or successful prosecution of an investigation.

J. Taxpayer Right to Privacy

Normally a taxpayer may be able to enjoin a disclosure by a third-party custodian of records under the Right to Financial Privacy Act (RFPA).[54] However, it is noteworthy that the third-party summons procedures of § 7609 are exempted from the procedures of the RFPA.[55]

IV. Requirement for Summons Legality

A. Relevancy

According to the Internal Revenue Code, the information and testimony sought in a summons must be "relevant" to the inquiry or "material" to the inquiry.[56] Courts have held that a summons is enforceable if it seeks relevant information and is not designed to harass a taxpayer.[57] Once the IRS has made a minimal showing of relevancy, the burden shifts to the taxpayer to show why the summons might represent "an abuse of the court's process" that should not be enforced.[58] "Relevancy" is liberally construed. An IRS summons can even reach copyrighted material.[59]

Note that an IRS summons is not to be judged by the relevance standards used in deciding whether to admit evidence at trial, because the IRS cannot be expected to know whether the summoned information will in fact be relevant until it is procured and scrutinized.

B. *"Powell" Requirements*
An individual's right to privacy will not defeat an IRS summons if:
1. The summons is issued for a legitimate (which may be civil or criminal) purpose;
2. The IRS does not already possess the information sought;
3. The inquiry is relevant to tax liability, i.e.,
   a. The summons should not be overly broad, and
   b. The information sought should shed some light on the "correctness" of a taxpayer's liability;
4. The requisite administrative steps are followed; and
5. The summons is not issued as a harassment tactic.[60]

C. *Other Constitutional Objections*
1. A summons issued pursuant to § 7602 will generally survive a constitutional challenge.[61]
2. *Fifth Amendment (Self-Incrimination)*
   To raise a Fifth Amendment objection to producing records or testimony, a taxpayer must overcome the "fear of prosecution" test. That is, a summoned taxpayer must be faced with a real and substantial hazard of self-incrimination.[62]

   A partnership or other collective entity cannot challenge a third-party summons on Fifth Amendment grounds unless it is a "small family partnership."[63]

   A handwriting exemplar is not testimony, and a taxpayer cannot refuse to provide it based on the Fifth Amendment.[64]

D. *Successful Defenses*
Successful defenses to the production of records or testimony pursuant to summonses include the following:
1. Where the IRS has decided to pursue criminal prosecution,
2. Where the IRS is attempting to harass the taxpayer or apply pressure to settle a collateral dispute,

3. Where the IRS is acting as an information-gathering agency for any other federal agency,
4. Where the summoned material is already in the possession of the IRS,
5. Where the material sought is not relevant to the purpose for which the summons was issued,
6. Where a privilege (e.g., attorney-client) is applicable,[65]
7. Where the IRS failed to follow the required administrative procedures (such as getting managerial approval for third-party summonses), and
8. Where the information sought is, through no fault of the recipient of the summons, not in the possession of and cannot be obtained by the person upon whom the summons was served.
9. Where the summons request for documents is overly broad or vague.[66]

V. Enforcement for Noncompliance

A. Summons Enforcement—Generally[67]

When a taxpayer refuses to comply with an administrative summons, the IRS has several options from which to choose:

-   It can decline to pursue summons enforcement and proceed with its case based on incomplete information.
-   It can seek civil enforcement through
    1. judicial enforcement to compel attendance[68] or
    2. judicial enforcement through contempt proceedings.[69]
-   It can seek a misdemeanor indictment for a taxpayer who neglects to appear and produce summoned documents.[70]

Summons enforcement proceedings are intended to be summary in nature so that an investigation can advance to an ultimate determination as to whether and to what extent tax liability exists.[71]

B. Rules for Civil Enforcement

An administrative summons is not self-enforcing; it requires judicial intervention to enforce compliance. A taxpayer may not be punished for failing to comply with an IRS summons, but instead, a taxpayer may be punished only for failing to comply with a subsequent order of the court. If there is noncompliance with a summons issued by the Examination function, IRS can seek approval of counsel to forward the case to the Department of Justice for civil enforcement.[72] Federal district courts have jurisdiction to compel (through their contempt power) compliance with a summons in what amounts to an adversary proceeding.[73]

The required showing necessary to obtain enforcement is generally made by the affidavit of the agent or officer who issued the summons and who is seeking enforcement. The IRS's burden is a slight one, and it may be satisfied by a declaration of the summons issuer that the *Powell* requirements have been met.[74]

C. *Criminal Enforcement: Statutory Criminal Sanctions*

A failure to appear and produce records as required by a summons can result in a fine of $1,000 and a one-year jail sentence.[75] Prosecutions under this statute are relatively rare because the IRS typically seeks civil enforcement of a summons rather than conviction of a misdemeanor for failure to comply.[76]

D. *Contempt Procedures*

1. *Statutory Rule*

   When a person ignores or refuses to obey a summons, the IRS may apply to the appropriate federal district court for an attachment against him or her as for contempt. If the application is satisfactory, the judge may issue the attachment (after an appropriate hearing), directed to an officer, for the arrest of the person summoned.[77]

2. *Court "Order" Required Prior to Contempt Finding*

   If the party whose attendance is "required" fails to attend, the IRS may ask the district court by appropriate process to compel such attendance, testimony, or production of books, papers, or other data.

   A subpoena is such an appropriate process. If it is disregarded, then contempt proceedings may ensue. A person served with a summons cannot be punished summarily by the court for contempt of court for his or her failure to obey the summons of the IRS. Thus, there can be no contempt prior to a court's order of enforcement.[78]

3. *Timing for Asserting Defenses*

   It is inappropriate for a taxpayer to assert for the first time at a contempt proceeding his or her inability to comply with a summons because he or she does not possess the records. Such a defense must be raised at the summons enforcement proceeding and not a contempt proceeding.[79]

4. *Civil Rules to Apply*

   Contempt proceedings resulting from noncompliance with an IRS summons are civil in nature, and the rules governing civil appeals therefore apply.[80]

5. *Habeas Corpus*

   Once a taxpayer is in jail for failure to produce records in compliance with an IRS summons, he or she cannot get out on a writ of habeas corpus.[81]

VI. Witness Fees and Costs

A. *General Rules*

Persons asked to give information to the IRS, including those persons who have been issued a summons, may receive payment from the IRS for costs incurred in complying with the summons. Witnesses generally will not be reimbursed for actual expenses incurred but instead will be paid in accordance with the payment rates established by regulations.[82] Directly incurred costs are those incurred solely, immediately, and necessarily as a consequence of searching for, reproducing, or transporting records to comply with a summons. No overhead allocation is allowed. No payment will be made until after the summoned party appears and has submitted any necessary receipts or other evidence of cost to the IRS employee before whom the person was summoned.[83]

B. *Schedule of Reimbursement Rates*
Persons summoned to appear before the IRS may be reimbursed for a variety of costs, including the following:

Transportation (auto)	$0.20 per mile*
Travel (common carrier)	Actual **
Subsistence (if overnight)	$35.00 per day
Search costs (for locating records)	$8.50 per hour***
Reproduction costs	$0.10 per page***
Attendance fees	$30.00 per day[84]

* Adjustable, depending on current rate payable to government employees.
** Must use most economical means available.
*** Available to third-party record keepers only, not the taxpayer or his or her agent.[85]

C. *Form for Reimbursement*
When payment of a witness fee is requested, Form 1157 is prepared by the examiner, signed by the payee, and processed for payment. Third parties who receive summonses should fill out Form 6863, Invoice and Authorization for Payment of Administrative Summons Expenses.[86]

D. *Prepayment of Fees*
Prepayment of witness fees and travel expenses is not a prerequisite to the enforcement of an IRS summons.[87] Unless a taxpayer is financially unable, he or she must comply with the summons and await reimbursement.

E. *Exceptions to Payment of Expenses*[88]
Payment of fees and expenses may *not* be made to any of the following individuals:
1. A summoned person who has a proprietary interest in the records being sought; or
2. The taxpayer's
    - Agent,
    - Employee,
    - Officer,

- Accountant, or
- Attorney.

F. *Banks*

Banks and other financial institutions are frequently served with summonses from the IRS. Pursuant to statute, they are entitled to be reimbursed by the government for costs that are reasonably necessary and that have been directly incurred in searching for and reproducing the records sought by the summons.[89] Depending on the volume of transactions sought, this can be extremely expensive for the government.

VII. Other Procedural Matters

A. *John Doe Summons*
   1. *Statutory Provisions*

   A summons issued that does not identify the person with respect to whose liability the summons is issued (a so-called John Doe summons) may be served only after a court proceeding in which the IRS must establish the following:
      a. The summons relates to the investigation of a particular person or ascertainable group of persons;
      b. There is a reasonable belief that such person(s) may have failed to comply with tax law; and
      c. The information sought is not readily available from other sources.[90]
   2. *Jurisdiction*

   Jurisdiction for John Doe summons proceedings lies with the federal district court for the district within which the summoned person(s) resides or can be found.[91] A John Doe summons proceeding in federal district court can be made ex parte and solely on the basis of the petition and supporting affidavits.[92]
   3. *Offshore Credit Card Abuse*

   Starting in 2000, the IRS began to use John Doe summonses to access records of credit card companies such as Visa, MasterCard, and American Express for the purpose of ferreting out people who may have evaded U.S. taxes through the use of offshore credit cards.[93] A typical scheme might involve, for example, the diversion of funds overseas by claiming false deductions for payments to a foreign entity that, in turn, would establish a foreign account accessible by nontraceable credit or debit card transactions. Additionally, John Doe summonses were recently issued to airlines, hotels, and rental car companies who have accepted the use of offshore cards. As a result of these summonses, IRS suspicions were confirmed that the use of offshore credit cards has "gone retail."[94]

B. *"Designated" Summons*[95]

In general, the issuance of a summons does not toll the assessment statute of limitations. However, in the case of a corporation (or any person to whom a corporation has transferred records), the IRS may issue a "designated" summons in situations where a corporation is being examined under the "coordinated issue case" program. This means a large corporate case referred to in the Internal Revenue Manual as a coordinated industry case.[96] When such a summons is issued the assessment statute of limitations[97] is suspended for the period of judicial enforcement and for 120 days after final resolution of the summoned person's response.

For the IRS to issue a designated summons, it must first take the following steps:

*   It must be reviewed by counsel's office.
*   The summons must be issued at least sixty days before the assessment period of the tax under examination expires.
*   The summons must clearly state that it is a designated summons.

It is not necessary, in issuing a designated summons, for the government to demonstrate a lack of cooperation on the part of a taxpayer to justify such issuance.[98]

C. *Criminal Matters*

While the IRS has the authority under § 7602(b) to use the summons power to investigate tax crimes, § 7602(d) provides a "bright line" preclusion rule. Under this statute no summons may be issued if, in a criminal tax case, there has been a referral of the case to the Department of Justice for prosecution. A Justice Department referral is in effect whenever the IRS has recommended a grand jury investigation or the criminal prosecution of a person for an offense connected with internal revenue laws.[99] Even where the summons is issued prior to such referral, the summons must still be issued in good faith (i.e., it meets the *Powell* requirements) if it is "likely" to lead to criminal prosecution.[100] For purposes of § 7602(d), each tax year and each tax imposed by a separate chapter of the I.R.C. are treated as separate investigations.[101]

D. *"Original" Records*

The IRS cannot deny a taxpayer access to his or her own original records once they have been removed from the taxpayer's possession.[102] Once a taxpayer has withdrawn his or her voluntary permission to inspect books and records, the IRS must return the documents and any copies made after permission is withdrawn.[103]

E. *Accountant-Client Privilege in Audit Context*

No accountant-client privilege can be invoked if the IRS issues a summons for a CPA's audit working papers, particularly where a corporation's reserve account for contingent tax liability is relevant to the IRS in determining the correctness of the corporation's tax returns.[104]

F. *Damages and/or Injunctive Relief*
Neither damages nor injunctive relief may be obtained by the taxpayer against the IRS for summons enforcement actions taken within the scope of their authority.[105]

G. *Violation of Procedure by the IRS*
The fact that the IRS may have violated its own regulations is not a defense to production of material sought by an IRS summons.[106]

H. *Partnership Audits*
Issuance of a Final Partnership Administrative Adjustment (FPAA) does not preclude further issuance of an administrative summons.[107]

I. *Cases Docketed in U.S. Tax Court*
Once a case has become docketed in the U.S. Tax Court, IRS personnel, including trial attorneys, may not use administrative summonses to circumvent the discovery rules promulgated by the tax court.[108] The reasoning behind this rule is that there would be unfair advantage to the respondent, as the petitioner does not have the ability to issue summonses to witnesses in tax court. Cases have consistently held that the IRS, during the pendency of U.S. Tax Court cases, cannot exploit summonses or summoned information.

J. *Computer Software Code*
1. The general rule is that a summons may not be issued by the IRS to obtain tax-related computer software source code.[109]
2. There is an exception to this rule, however, where the IRS is unable to reasonably ascertain the correctness of a return item from the taxpayer's books and records.[110]

VIII. Production of Foreign Records

A. *Possession and Control Issues*
To compel production of foreign-based records pursuant to a summons, a court must have personal jurisdiction over the custodian of records. Records outside the United States are subject to production if they are in the U.S. entity's control and a court has jurisdiction over the entity.[111]

A domestic entity is presumed to be in control of its books and records, and clear proof of lack of possession and control is necessary to rebut that presumption.[112] "Control" is defined as whether a party has the legal power to produce the records.[113]

"Possession and control" issues are important also for individuals. For example, if a foreign bank refuses to honor a voluntarily executed consent directive, a district court must make a determination as to whether the individual taxpayer actually possesses or controls the subject records. If a taxpayer prevails in his or her burden of proving that he or she does not have possession of the records, then enforcement will be denied.[114]

B. *Domestic Corporate Parent*
A domestic corporation may be ordered to produce books and records under the custody and control of a foreign subsidiary.[115]

C. *Domestic Partner*
A partner in a foreign partnership may be ordered to produce books and records of the partnership if he or she can exercise control over the partnership's affairs.[116]

D. *Foreign Parent Corporation*
Ordinarily, a domestic subsidiary corporation will not have control over a foreign parent or sister corporation. Despite the general rule, some courts have allowed the IRS to summons records from foreign parents.[117]

E. *Formal Document Requests*
Enacted by the Tax Equity and Fiscal Responsibility Act (TEFRA), I.R.C. § 982 precludes a taxpayer from introducing into evidence in any civil proceeding any foreign-based documentation that has been previously requested by the IRS through a Formal Document Request (FDR) and that the taxpayer has not furnished by a certain date. The FDR form number is 4546. This rule is effective for FDRs made after September 3, 1982. There must be "substantial compliance" with the FDR; otherwise, the only way to avoid the exclusionary rule is to invoke the "reasonable cause" exception.[118]

F. *Consent Directives*
In view of the difficulty of obtaining records in foreign countries, particularly bank records, the IRS has begun to use what is known as a "consent directive."[119] A consent decree essentially authorizes a financial institution in a foreign country to release records regarding its taxpayer-customer to the IRS.
    In this author's view, a government's ability to force a taxpayer to sign a document over his or her strenuous objection raises serious constitutional issues. Nonetheless, the U.S. Supreme Court has ruled that, since a consent directive is not "testimonial" in nature, a recalcitrant taxpayer may not raise a Fifth Amendment objection.[120]

Despite a federal district court's broad authority to force a signature on a consent directive under § 7402(a), the IRS may be further frustrated. If the foreign jurisdiction has a bank secrecy law, it may very well rule that a consent decree was obtained under "compulsion" and is, therefore, invalid.[121]

IX. Conclusions

A. It is important to note the seriousness of failing to comply with a summons, while at the same time to recognize certain limitations on the IRS's power to enforce it. Noncompliance with a summons does not mean "automatic arrest." A taxpayer will always have an opportunity to contest the validity of a summons in a court proceeding.

B. On the date for appearance, a taxpayer's representative has a right to be present, note any objections to improper questions, and instruct his or her client not to answer improper questions. A taxpayer also has the right to make an audio recording of any testimony given pursuant to a summons. While a representative may appear along with his or her taxpayer-client, the representative may not appear *in lieu of* the taxpayer.[122] Without a summons, however, a taxpayer's appearance for an interview is purely voluntary.[123]

C. When it appears imminent that a revenue agent is going to summons a bank to get copies of deposit slips, the representative should offer to do it for him or her to avoid the agent's gaining access to nonrelevant material (such as financial statements).

X. Notes

1. In certain criminal investigations, where the special agents are cooperating with a grand jury, subpoenas are sometimes used in lieu of administrative summonses.
2. United States v. Morgan, 85-1 USTC ¶ 9397 (4th Cir. 1985).
3. *Duces tecum* is the name of a species of writs, of which the subpoena duces tecum is the most common, requiring a party who is summoned to appear in court to bring with him some document, piece of evidence, or other thing to be used or inspected by the court.
4. Treas. Reg. § 301.7602-1(b).
5. IRM 5.17.6.1; IRM 25.5.1.4. Before issuing a summons, the investigator should consider the possibility that judicial enforcement will be required and the adverse effect on future voluntary compliance if enforcement is abandoned.
6. I.R.C. § 7602(a)(2).
7. I.R.C. § 7609.
8. *See* I.R.C. § 7603(b)(2) for a list of who are considered to be third-party record keepers.
9. I.R.C. § 7609(f).
10. I.R.C. § 6503(j)(2).
11. I.R.C. § 7611(e).

12. IRM 25.5.1.3.3.
13. I.R.C. § 7602(a)(2).
14. I.R.C. § 7605(a).
15. United States v. Malnik, 33 AFTR2d 74-692 (5th Cir. 1974).
16. I.R.C. § 7602(a)(1).
17. A summons for books and records of the taxpayer can be issued by a revenue officer as well as by a revenue agent. United States v. Davila, 90 AFTR2d 2002-7416 (N.D. Tex. 2002).
18. I.R.C. § 7602(a)(2); Treas. Reg. § 301.7602-1(b).
19. I.R.C. § 7603(a). "Reasonable certainty" has been broadly construed by district courts. For example, in *United States v. Moseley*, 93-2 USTC ¶ 50,440 (W.D.N.Y. 1993), a summons for "general correspondence and administrative files" was held to be reasonably certain. Similarly, "all statements of account (detailing account numbers)" (*see* Nelson v. United States, 95-1 USTC ¶ 50,003 (N.D. Cal. 1994)) also satisfied the statutory standard. However, in *United States v. Lewis*, 87-2 USTC ¶ 9374 (D. La. 1985), a request for "all relevant documents" was deemed to be overly broad.
20. IRM 5.17.6.5.
21. I.R.S. Priv. Ltr. Rul. 200233002 (Aug. 6, 2002).
22. United States v. Davey, 76-2 USTC ¶ 9724 (2d Cir. 1976).
23. United States v. Norwest, 97-2 USTC ¶ 50,510 (8th Cir. 1997).
24. I.R.C. § 7603(a).
25. *See, e.g.*, the discussion in United States v. Giertz, 8702 USTC ¶ 9505 (S.D. Fla. 1987); *but see* United States v. Bichara, 87-2 USTC ¶ 9540 (11th Cir. 1987) for a contrary result.
26. I.R.C. § 7603(a).
27. IRM 25.5.1.3.3.
28. Mimick v. United States, 92-1 USTC ¶ 50,022 (8th Cir. 1991), *rev'g* 91-1 USTC ¶ 50,070 (D. Neb. 1991).
29. I.R.C. §§ 7602(a)(3), 7622; IRM 25.5.4.2.
30. IRM 5.17.6.3 (9-20-00); 25.5.4.2.1.
31. IRM 5.17.6.2.1.
32. I.R.C. §§ 7602(a)(2), 7602(c), 7603(b), 7609.
33. I.R.C. § 7609(i)(1).
34. I.R.C. § 7603(b)(2). Note that the Code does *not* use the phrase "but not limited to." One could possibly conclude, therefore, that if a summoned person or entity is not on that list, and is not an agent or employee of the taxpayer, the summons could be successfully resisted by the summoned party. *See also* IRM 25.5.6.3.2.
35. Note that although the statute specifically includes attorneys as a "third-party record keeper," it does not address the issue of attorney-client privilege, which should always be asserted in appropriate cases.
36. That is, enrolled agents who are authorized to practice before the Service under Circular 230.
37. *But see* I.R.C. § 7612 for restrictions and circumstances under which computer source code can be provided.
38. Note that for attorneys and accountants to be considered "third-party record keepers," they must have some kind of state license. *See* Treas. Reg. § 301.7603-2(a)(1),(2).

39. Credit card issuers do not include a seller of goods or services who honors credit cards issued by other parties. *See* Treas. Reg. § 301.7603-2(a)(3). For this purpose, a debit card is not considered a credit card.
40. I.R.C. § 7603(b)(1).
41. I.R.C. § 7609(a)(1),(2).
42. I.R.C. § 7609(b)(1).
43. Boyd v. United States, 2004-1 USTC ¶ 50,199 (6th Cir. 2003).
44. I.R.C. § 7609(c)(2)(A); Muratore v. Dep't of Treasury, 2004-1 USTC ¶ 50,265 (W.D.N.Y. 2004).
45. I.R.C. § 7609(b)(2)(A).
46. Camaro Trading Co. v. United States, 91-1 USTC ¶ 50,275 (N.D. Ga. 1991).
47. I.R.C. § 7609(h)(1).
48. I.R.C. § 7609(e)(1).
49. I.R.C. § 7609(i)(3).
50. IRM 5.17.6.4.
51. Backer v. United States, 275 F.2d 141, 5 AFTR2d 824 (5th Cir. 1960).
52. United States v. Jones, 99-2 USTC ¶ 50,748 (D. S.C. 1999).
53. 26 C.F.R. § 601.107(b)(1) (criminal investigation function); 5 U.S.C. § 555(c).
54. 12 U.S.C. § 3410.
55. 12 U.S.C. § 3413(c).
56. I.R.C. § 7602(a)(2); Treas. Reg. § 301.7602-1(b).
57. *See* United States v. Bisceglia, 35 AFTR2d 75-702; 420 U.S. 141 (S. Ct. 1975), which held that the IRS could serve a John Doe summons to ascertain the depositor of several old hundred-dollar bills.
58. United States v. Davey, 76-2 USTC ¶ 9724 (2d Cir. 1976).
59. United States v. Norwest Corp., 97-2 USTC ¶ 50,510 (8th Cir. 1997).
60. United States v. Powell, 14 AFTR2d 5942; 85 S. Ct. 248 (1964). The *Powell* test for relevance is generous, reflecting Congress's express intention to allow the IRS to obtain items of even *potential* relevance to an ongoing investigation *See, e.g.,* Boyd v. United States, 2004-1 USTC ¶ 50,199 (6th Cir. 2003).
61. United States v. Morgan, 85-1 USTC ¶ 9397 (4th Cir. 1985), holding that a summons does not require a warrant based on probable cause.
62. United States v. Troescher, 75 AFTR2d 95-2118 (C.D. Cal. 1995).
63. Bellis v. United States, 417 U.S. 85 (S. Ct. 1974).
64. United States v. Tanoue, 95-1 USTC ¶ 50,120 (D. Haw. 1994).
65. Similarly, where a tax memorandum, prepared at the request of an attorney in anticipation of a contemplated transaction resulting in a large tax loss, was sought by means of a summons, the "work-product" will prevent the production thereof. United States v. Adlman, 98-1 USTC ¶ 50,230 (2d Cir. 1998).
66. United States v. Klir, 81-1 USTC ¶ 9422 (E.D. Tex. 1979) (request for "all relevant information" not enforceable).
67. For a summary discussion of summons enforcement, see Philip N. Jones, *Has the Second Circuit Weakened Summons Enforcement Powers?*, 103 J. Taxation 101 (Aug. 2005).
68. I.R.C. § 7604(a).
69. I.R.C. § 7604(b).
70. I.R.C. § 7210. However, one should note that at least one circuit has opined that indictments under 26 U.S.C. § 7210 shall not lie and contempt sanctions under 26 U.S.C. § 7604(b) shall not be levied based on disobedience of an IRS

summons unless and until the summoned party, after having been given a reasonable opportunity to comply with the court's order, has refused. Schulz v. Internal Revenue Serv., 95 AFTR2d 2005-3007 (2d Cir. 2005) (*Schulz II*).

71. Muratore v. Dep't of Treasury, 2004-1 USTC ¶ 50,265 (W.D. N.Y. 2004).
72. *See* IRM 25.5.10.3 for general summons enforcement procedures.
73. I.R.C. §§ 7604(a), 7402(b).
74. United States v. Abrahams, 90-1 USTC ¶ 50,310 (9th Cir. 1990).
75. I.R.C. § 7210.
76. *But see* United States v. Becker, 1 AFTR2d 1437 (S.D.N.Y. 1958).
77. I.R.C. § 7604(b).
78. United States v. Bookstaff, 80-2 USTC ¶ 9557 (E.D. Wis. 1980).
79. United States v. Rylander, 83-1 USTC ¶ 9300 (Sup. Ct. 1983).
80. McCrone v. United States, 307 U.S. 61, 22 AFTR 324 (S. Ct. 1939).
81. Zimmerman v. Spears, 78-1 USTC ¶ 9223 (5th Cir. 1977).
82. For example, a third-party witness may not recover compliance costs in excess of the regulatory amounts when it uses an independent storage facility to search, reproduce, and transport summonsed records. CCA 200417032 (Mar. 25, 2004).
83. Treas. Reg. § 301.7610-1(c).
84. Or, if higher, the rate payable pursuant to 28 U.S.C. § 1821(b) to witnesses in attendance at courts of the United States at the time of the summoned person's appearance.
85. I.R.C. § 7610(b).
86. For a description of general rules regarding payment to third parties, see IRM 25.5.9.
87. United States v. Money, 84-2 USTC ¶ 9876 (11th Cir. 1984).
88. I.R.C. § 7610(b).
89. United States v. Fain, 78-2 USTC ¶ 9540 (M.D. S.C. 1978).
90. I.R.C. § 7609(f).
91. I.R.C. § 7609(h)(1).
92. I.R.C. § 7609(h)(2). Similarly, the IRS can petition the court on an ex parte basis if there is a reasonable belief that giving of notice may result in intimidation of witnesses, fleeing to avoid prosecution, etc. I.R.C. § 7609(g).
93. *See, e.g., In re* Tax Liabilities of John Does, 92 AFTR2d 2003-7188 (W.D. Tenn. 2003).
94. Charles P. Rettig & Steven Toscher, *Deadline Looms to Come Clean on Offshore Credit Card Schemes*, 26 L.A. LAW. 12 (2003).
95. *See generally* I.R.C. § 6503(j).
96. IRM 25.5.3.3.
97. I.R.C. § 6501.
98. United States v. Derr, 92-2 USTC ¶ 50,369 (9th Cir. 1992).
99. I.R.C. § 7602(d).
100. Donaldson v. United States, 27 AFTR2d 71-482 (Sup. Ct. 1971).
101. I.R.C. § 7602(d)(3).
102. United States v. Miller, 33 AFTR2d 74-1076 (5th Cir. 1974).
103. Mason v. Pulliam, 77-2 USTC ¶ 9579 (5th Cir. 1977).
104. United States v. Arthur Young & Co., 84-1 USTC ¶ 9305 (Sup. Ct. 1984).
105. Shupak v. Groh, 34 AFTR2d 74-5671 (5th Cir. 1974).
106. United States v. Caceres, 79-1 USTC ¶ 9294 (Sup. Ct. 1979).

107. PAA Mgmt., Ltd. v. United States, 92-1 USTC ¶ 50,261 (2d Cir. 1992).

108. IRM 25.5.4.4.8 (2).

109. I.R.C. § 7612(a).

110. I.R.C. § 7612(b).

111. *In re* Marc Rich & Co., A.G. v. United States, 707 F.2d 663 (2d Cir. 1983).

112. First Nat'l City Bank of N.Y. v. Internal Revenue Serv., 271 F.2d 616 (2d Cir. 1959).

113. *Id.* at 618.

114. United States v. Gippetti, 96 AFTR2d 2005-6978 (3d Cir. 2005), *cert. denied.*

115. United States v. First City Nat'l Bank of N.Y., 396 F.2d 897 (2d Cir. 1968); Application of Chase Manhattan Bank, 297 F.2d 611 (2d Cir. 1962); United States v. First Nat'l Bank, 699 F.2d 341 (7th Cir. 1983); United States v. Field, 532 F.2d 404 5th Cir. 1976); United States v. Germann, 370 F.2d 1019 (2d Cir. 1967), *vacated*, 389 U.S. 329 (1967); United States v. Vetco, Inc., 644 F.2d 1324 (9th Cir. 1981); United States v. Chase Manhattan Bank, N.A., 584 F. Supp. 1080 (S.D.N.Y. 1984); United States v. Bank of Nova Scotia, 691 F.2d 1384 (11th Cir. 1982); United States v. Ghidoni, 732 F.2d 814 (11th Cir. 1984); Doe v. United States, 487 U.S. 201 (1988).

116. United States v. Hayes, 722 F.2d 723 (11th Cir. 1984).

117. United States v. Toyota Motor Corp., 83-2 USTC ¶ 9468 (C.D. Cal. 1983); United States v. Ross, 196 F. Supp. 243 (S.D.N.Y. 1961), *aff'd*, 302 F.2d 831 (2d Cir. 1962).

118. I.R.C. § 982(b)(1).

119. IRM 25.5.4.4.9; IRM 34.6.3.7.

120. Doe v. United States, 88-2 USTC ¶ 9545 (S. Ct. 1988); *See also* United States v. Ghidoni, 84-1 USTC ¶ 9498 (11th Cir. 1984). *But see* United States v. Kao, 96-1 USTC ¶ 50,203 (9th Cir. 1996) (to the contrary).

121. For example, the Cayman Islands.

122. United States v. Leach, 90-1 USTC ¶ 50,291 (D. Kan. 1990).

123. *See generally* I.R.C. § 7521(c).

Audits of Partnership Entities

I. Background

   A. *Problems with Pre-TEFRA Procedures*
   Prior to the enactment of the Tax Equity and Fiscal Responsibility Act (TEFRA), there were significant administrative problems in auditing partnerships. For example, locating all of the partners was a significant burden on the IRS. Further, tracing through multiple tiers of pass-through entities was difficult and time-consuming. In some cases, the IRS found it impossible to locate the actual taxpayer prior to the expiration of the statute of limitations—which was measured from the filing of the partners' individual tax returns.

   B. *General Rule of TEFRA*
   TEFRA added sections 6221 through 6232 to the I.R.C. This new Subchapter C revolutionized the procedures used for auditing partnership returns. These provisions provide for a unified way to resolve disputes involving "partnership items" even though the ultimate tax liability resulting from such disputes is imposed on the partners separately.

   Subchapter C will be referred to as "TEFRA procedures." They are to be contrasted with Subchapter B procedures, which contain the "normal" deficiency procedures in I.R.C. § 6211 *et seq.*

   C. *Years to Which TEFRA Procedures Apply*
   The new partnership audit rules, enacted as a part of TEFRA, are applicable to partnership taxable years "beginning after" September 3, 1982.[1] For purposes of determining when a partnership year begins, it is neither the formation date nor the date appearing at the top of the Form 1065 that controls. Instead, it is the date at which more than 50 percent of the capital and profits interests were sold that controls.[2]

   D. *Entities Excluded from TEFRA Rules*
   Partnerships electing out of Subchapter K are not subject to the TEFRA rules since they are not required to file partnership returns.[3] Although

originally treated as partnerships for audit purposes, effective in 1997, S corporations are not subject to TEFRA audit rules.[4] Estates and trusts have never been subject to such rules.

II. Duty of Consistency

A. *General Consistency Rules*

The tax treatment of "partnership items" is determined at the partnership level, not the partner level.[5] A partner is required to treat a "partnership item" consistent with the way it was treated at the partner level.[6] Similarly, a partner must be consistent from one year to the next. He or she cannot claim status as a partner in one year and then claim that he or she was a mere employee in a subsequent year.[7]

B. *Inconsistency*

The consistency rule need not be followed if the taxpayer notifies the IRS by means of a statement identifying the inconsistency.[8] In the case of a failure of a partner to notify the IRS of an inconsistency, the consequences are that the statute of limitations continues to run with respect to the partnership item in question. Thus, the IRS can issue a Final Partnership Administrative Adjustment (FPAA) even after the three-year period of § 6229 has expired.[9] There are three purposes of a Form 8082:[10]

1. To notify the IRS of an inconsistent treatment of an item appearing on the K-1 of a 1065;
2. To notify the IRS of a failure to receive a K-1; or
3. For a Tax Matters Partner (TMP) to file a request for an administrative adjustment.

C. *Reliance on K-1*

The consistency rule is satisfied if a 1040 is prepared in accordance with the numbers reflected on the K-1.[11]

D. *Cross-Match Audits*

In previous years, the IRS did not match K-1 information against the 1040 information reported by partners or S corporation shareholders. This is no longer the case. The IRS has now implemented a matching program that has resulted in the issuance of a significant number of "mismatch" notices.

E. *Sanctions for Failure to Be Consistent*

If a taxpayer does not comply with the consistency-reporting rules, the consequences are that he or she will be subject to the accuracy-related penalty on underpayments.[12]

III. Settlement of Partnership Appeals

A. *General Rule*

The IRS can enter into a settlement agreement with a partner that binds all parties to the agreement (which may or may not be all the partners) plus "indirect" partners where "pass-through" partners are parties to the agreement.[13]

B. *Nonnotice Partners*

A partner who is not a "notice" partner is bound by any settlement agreements entered into by a TMP. However, if such a partner files a required statement with the IRS, he will not be bound.[14] A statement by a "nonnotice" partner not to be bound by the TMP agreement must
1. be filed with the IRS thirty days before the TMP agreement is entered into; and
2. do the following:
   - clearly identify denial under § 6224(c)(3),
   - clearly identify the partnership and partner,
   - specify the tax year, and
   - contain a partner's signature.[15]

C. *Fairness by the IRS*

Upon timely demand, any partner may insist on settlement terms identical to those offered to any other partner.[16]

IV. Litigation of Partnership Disputes

A. *Choice of Forum*

An FPAA is usually sent to all "notice" partners by certified mail. After receiving an FPAA, a TMP has a choice of three different courts in which to file a petition for readjustment:
1. The U.S. Tax Court,
2. The U.S. Federal District Court, or
3. The U.S. Claims Court.
   This readjustment petition must be filed by the TMP within ninety days of receiving the FPAA.[17]

B. *TMP Default*

If the TMP chooses not to file a readjustment petition with one of the three designated courts, any "notice" partner may, within sixty days of the close of the ninety-day period, file such a petition.[18] Note that if the partnership statute of limitations has previously been extended, then there is no reason for the IRS to issue an FPAA. Instead, they will issue a letter inviting agreement or the preparation of a protest to the IRS Appeals Office. Any partner is given the right to prepare such a protest.

C. *Successive Litigation*

If a partner has a judicial determination made on a non-TEFRA matter, his or her tax liability can be further affected by a TEFRA adjustment.[19]

D. *Non–Tax Court Litigation*

When a petition for readjustment is filed in either the U.S. district court or the claims court, the partner filing the petition must deposit with the IRS the amount of tax that would be due on his or her individual return if the FPAA adjustments were allowed to stand.[20]

E. *General Jurisdiction*

The court in which a petition is filed has jurisdiction to determine all partnership items to which the FPAA relates.[21]

F. *Appeal of Trial Court Determination*

A trial court's determination is reviewable by circuit courts of appeal just as any tax court's determination would be. But only a TMP or 5 percent "notice" group[22] may appeal the trial court's decision.[23]

G. *Tax Court Rules*

In 1988 the tax court found it necessary to substantially amend its initial set of rules relating to partnership actions (see Tax Court Rules 240 to 251), which were issued in 1984.

V. Statute of Limitations (S/L) Issues

A. *General Three-Year Rule*

Tax attributable to a "partnership item" may not be assessed after three years after the partnership Form 1065 was filed.[24] This three-year period may be extended by an agreement entered into by the IRS and the TMP. This agreement binds all partners. Any other authorized person may also enter into this binding extension agreement.[25] The extension, Form 872-P, must be executed by a partner or by someone else who is authorized in writing.[26]

B. *Effect of the FPAA on the Statute of Limitations*

A tax assessment attributable to a partnership item cannot be made prior to 150 days (90 + 60) after the FPAA is mailed out.[27] If an FPAA is issued, the three-year S/L period is suspended. In this sense, the FPAA is the equivalent of a deficiency notice.[28] The running of the S/L is tolled by timely mailing of the FPAA (which is usually sent by certified mail) and does not expire for one year after either the period for filing a readjustment petition expires, or a court decision with respect to such a petition becomes final.

C. *Injunction*
If an assessment is made in violation of the I.R.C. § 6225(a)(1) rule, such action may be enjoined, § 7421 notwithstanding.[29]

D. *Unidentified Partners*
The assessment S/L is suspended with respect to unidentified partners until one year after such identification is furnished to the IRS.[30]

E. *Mathematical or Clerical Errors*
Math or clerical errors can be corrected by the IRS without regard to the assessment S/L rules of § 6225.[31]

F. *Pass-Through Entity S/L versus Individual S/L*
If the statute of limitations on assessment expires for adjustments to a pass-through entity, the IRS can adjust pass-through items on a shareholder or partner's individual return for the same years even though the S/L for such pass-through return has otherwise expired.[32]

VI. "Partnership Items"

A. *Definition*
A partnership item is one that is more appropriately taken into account at the partnership level than at the partner level.[33] (Note: This distinction is important because non-partnership items are not covered by TEFRA procedures.)

B. *Examples*
There are several categories of "partnership items":
1. "Return items" (including all K-1 items),
2. Nondeductible items (e.g., charitable contributions),
3. Tax preference items,
4. Tax-exempt items,
5. Partnership liabilities,
6. Items necessary to determine various credits and amounts at risk,
7. Guaranteed payments,
8. Basis adjustments (including § 754 basis adjustments), and
9. Determinations of transactions necessary for the partnership's books and records.[34]
Additionally, matters such as accounting practices and legal matters affecting the timing, amount, and characterization of items of income, deductions, and so on, are considered to be "partnership items."[35]

C. *Conversion from Partnership to Non-partnership Item*
The I.R.C. delineates various circumstances in which partnership items can be transformed into non-partnership items.[36] If a partnership item

becomes a non-partnership item (e.g., because of a bankruptcy filing), then the IRS must issue a regular (i.e., non-TEFRA) deficiency notice within one year of the triggering event.[37]

D. *Bankruptcy*

If a partner files a bankruptcy petition, all pre-bankruptcy partnership items are converted to non-partnership items. Therefore, TEFRA procedures will not apply as to that partner.[38]

E. *"Computational Adjustments"*

If there is merely a computational adjustment, then TEFRA procedures apply as if it were a partnership item.[39] Penalties and additions to tax are generally considered computational adjustments and are, therefore, subject to TEFRA procedures. Accordingly, a separate deficiency notice will generally not be sent out for penalties. However, see the discussion below of "affected items."[40]

VII. The Tax Matters Partner

A. *General Rules*

The TMP is the central figure in partnership proceedings. During both administrative and litigation proceedings, the TMP serves as the focal point for service of all notices, documents, and orders on the partnership. The TMP's initiative during proceedings and the execution of his or her statutory duties have a substantial effect upon the rights of all the partners in the partnership. The TMP is usually a general partner designated as such by the partnership itself. If there is no TMP designated, the general partner with the largest profits will be the TMP by default. In the event of a tie, the IRS will go alphabetically. If it is impractical for the IRS to designate a general partner, then the IRS can designate *any* partner (including a limited partner) to act as the TMP.[41]

B. *Selection of TMP by the IRS*

The IRS has issued a revenue procedure describing circumstances and criteria under which it will select a TMP pursuant to I.R.C. § 6231(a)(7).[42] Note that the IRS is not required to appoint a TMP for a deficiency notice to be valid, as long as partners receive adequate notice and opportunity to protect their interests.[43]

C. *Duty to Notify*

The TMP must keep all other partners informed at all times as to what is going on administratively and judicially.[44]

D. *TMP Outside of the United States*

If a TMP resides outside of the United States or the partnership books and records are maintained outside the United States, then no loss or credit is allowed to any partner until all partnership-filing require-ments of I.R.C. § 6031 are complied with for the year in question.[45]

VIII. "Affected Items"

A. *General Rules*

"Affected items" are not controlled by TEFRA procedures.[46] Instead, regular deficiency procedures (i.e., Subchapter B) apply. An affected item is one that is affected by a partnership item.[47]

Affected items play a unique role in partnership audit procedures because they are not considered in the partnership-level audit, yet they are controlled by the partnership-level statute of limitations. Thus, it is possible that the partner-level statute of limitations may have run for non-partnership items, but that a partner could still be sent a notice of deficiency with regard to affected items. Indeed, a partner could receive multiple subsequent deficiency notices with regard to affected items.[48]

Section 6230(a) allows the IRS to issue a second deficiency notice for any tax year to determine deficiencies attributable to affected items and to assess (without a deficiency notice) for computational adjust-ments.[49] Of course, this rule does not apply to assessments resulting from the disallowance of unrelated, non-partnership items.

B. *Examples of "Affected Items"*
1. Medical expense percentage limitations
2. Basis in a partnership interest
3. Application of at-risk rules to partnership loss
4. Penalties attributable to a partnership loss[50]
5. Carryback of a disallowed partnership item (e.g., an investment tax credit)[51]

IX. Small Partnerships

A. *General Rule*

The TEFRA partnership audit rules do not apply to partnerships with ten or fewer partners, each of whom is a natural person.[52] The deter-mination regarding whether a "small" partnership qualifies as such is made each year.[53]

B. *Election by Small Partnerships to Have TEFRA Apply*

A small partnership (ten or fewer partners) may elect to have TEFRA procedures apply anyway.[54] The election to have TEFRA procedures apply to a small partnership is effective for the current and all subse-quent years, unless revoked with the consent of the IRS. The election is made by attaching a written statement (signed by all partners) to a timely filed partnership return for the first taxable year for which the election is effective. Merely checking the "S" block on page 1 of the 1065 form will not suffice.[55]

C. *Husbands and Wives*

For purposes of determining whether there are ten or fewer partners, husbands and wives (and their estates) are treated as one partner.[56]

X. Miscellaneous Topics

A. *Notice of Beginning of Administrative Proceeding (NBAP)*

The IRS is required, at the beginning of a partnership audit, to mail to each affected partner a "notice of the beginning of an administrative proceeding."[57] However, this notice is not required for partners who own less than a 1 percent interest in the partnership profits and are members of partnerships with greater than one hundred partners.[58] The NBAP notice must precede the FPAA notice by at least 120 days.[59]

B. *Final Partnership of Administrative Adjustment (FPAA)*

The IRS cannot issue a series of FPAAs; only one is permitted. In this sense, an FPAA is similar to a deficiency notice (see I.R.C. § 6212(c)).[60]

C. *Types of Partners*

There are four general types of partners to keep in mind when handling partnership audits under TEFRA. They are as follows:

- Tax matters partner (I.R.C. § 6231(a)(7)1)
- Indirect partner (I.R.C. § 6231(a)(10)1)
- Pass-through partner (I.R.C. § 6231(a)(9)1)
- Notice partner (I.R.C. § 6231(a)(8)1)

Notice partners are all those to whom the IRS is required to send an NBAP notice. Basically, this includes all partners. An indirect partner is one who holds his or her profits interest through a "pass-through" partner. Pass-through entities are defined elsewhere in the I.R.C. as partnerships and S corporations.[61] If pass-through partners receive notices from the IRS, they are required to forward copies of such notices to the indirect partners within thirty days of receipt.[62]

D. *Notices*

The IRS maintains an information base for TEFRA notices. For notices and other TEFRA purposes, the IRS is entitled to rely on partnership name, address, and profits interest information reflected on the Form 1065 and its K-1s unless otherwise notified.[63]

E. *Right of Participation*

Any partner has the right to participate in the partnership audit or appeal thereof.[64] However, a partner may waive his or her right to participate in any administrative proceeding.[65] Furthermore, a partner has the right to participate as a party to any court action.[66]

F.   *Requests for Administrative Adjustments (RAA)*
If there is an error in a partnership return, any partner may file a request for administrative adjustment. This request must be filed within three years of the filing date of the Form 1065.[67] If the TMP files an RAA, the IRS can treat the change as the correction of a math error, resulting in a "substituted return." If any part of an RAA is disallowed by the IRS, the TMP can seek a review of that determination in any one of the three trial courts.[68] An RAA is filed by filling out a Form 8082 and attaching a pro forma 1065 to accomplish what amounts to an amended 1065. In other words, one does not just file an "amended partnership return." There is no partnership equivalent of the Form 1040-X.

G.   *Cross-Matching K-1s*
In the past, the IRS has not been effectively cross-matching pass-through items shown on K-1s. However, they now possess the technology to do this, and practitioners can expect "cross-match" notices in the future where there are discrepancies.

H.   *Agreement at Conclusion of Audit*
If a TEFRA partnership audit is concluded by an agreed settlement, the TMP will be asked to sign a Form 870-P. Once executed, this form becomes an agreement, binding on both parties in the absence of fraud, malfeasance, or misrepresentation of a material fact. In a sense, then, this form is similar in effect to a closing agreement, as it is in the nature of a contract.[69]

XI. Notes

1. I.R.C. § 6221 fn.
2. *See generally* I.R.C. § 706(b)(1) re partnership taxable years; Estate of Somashekar v. Comm'r, 53 T.C.M. (CCH) 315 (1987).
3. *See* Treas. Reg. § 1.6031(a)-1(c)(1)(ii) regarding the filing of returns by partnerships excluded from Subchapter K.
4. *See* former I.R.C. § 6241.
5. I.R.C. § 6221.
6. I.R.C. § 6222(a).
7. Blonien v. Comm'r, 118 T.C. 541 (2002) (re "duty of consistency").
8. *See* Form 8082; I.R.C. § 6222(b)(1)(B).
9. I.R.C. § 6222(c).
10. Form 8082 instructions.
11. I.R.C. § 6222(b)(2).
12. I.R.C. § 6222(d).

13. I.R.C. § 6224(c)(1).
14. I.R.C. § 6224(c)(3).
15. Treas. Reg. § 301.6224(c)-1.
16. I.R.C. § 6224(c)(2).
17. I.R.C. § 6226(a).
18. I.R.C. § 6226(b)(1).
19. I.R.C. § 6231(e)(1)(A).
20. I.R.C. § 6226(e).
21. I.R.C. § 6226(f).
22. *See* I.R.C. § 6223 for categories of partners who are entitled to "notice."
23. I.R.C. § 6226(g).
24. I.R.C. § 6229(a).
25. I.R.C. § 6229(b)(1).
26. I.R.C. § 6229(b)(1)(B).
27. I.R.C. § 6225(a)(1).
28. I.R.C. § 6229(d).
29. I.R.C. § 6225(b).
30. I.R.C. § 6229(e).
31. I.R.C. § 6230(b).
32. Bufferd v. Comm'r, 93-1 U.S.T.C. 1 ¶ 50,038 (S. Ct. 1993), which overruled the *Kelley* line of cases; *see also* Fendell v. Comm'r, 92 T.C. 708 (1989), allowing IRS to adjust pass-through items on a beneficiary's open returns.
33. I.R.C. § 6231(a)(3).
34. Treas. Reg. § 301.6231(a)(3)-1.
35. Treas. Reg. § 301.6231(a)(3)-1(b).
36. I.R.C. § 6231(b).
37. I.R.C. § 6229(f).
38. Treas. Reg. § 301.6231(c)-7(a).
39. I.R.C. § 6230(a)(1).
40. Treas. Reg. § 301.6231(a)(6)-1(a)(2).
41. I.R.C. § 6231(a)(7).
42. Rev. Proc. 88-16, 1988-1 CB 691.
43. Seneca, Ltd. v. Comm'r, 92 T.C. 363 (1989).
44. I.R.C. § 6223(g).
45. I.R.C. § 6231(f).
46. I.R.C. § 6230(a)(2)(A).
47. I.R.C. § 6231(a)(5).
48. I.R.C. § 6231(e)(1).
49. *See* N.C.F. Energy Partners v. Comm'r, 89 T.C.741 (1987).
50. Treas. Reg. § 301.6231(a)(5)-1.
51. Cf. Maxwell v. Comm'r, 87 T.C. 783 (1986).
52. I.R.C. § 6231(a)(1)(B).
53. Treas. Reg. § 301.6231(a)(1)-1(a)(3).
54. I.R.C. § 6231(a)(1)(B)(ii).
55. Treas. Reg. § 301.6231(a)(1)-1(b).
56. I.R.C. § 6231(a)(1)(B).
57. I.R.C. § 6223(a)(1).
58. I.R.C. § 6223(b)(1).
59. I.R.C. § 6223(d)(1).

60. I.R.C. § 6223(f).
61. I.R.C. § 267(e)(2).
62. I.R.C. § 6223(h).
63. I.R.C. § 6223(c).
64. I.R.C. § 6224.
65. I.R.C. § 6224(b).
66. I.R.C. § 6226(c).
67. I.R.C. § 6227(a).
68. I.R.C. § 6228(a)(1)
69. *See* I.R.C. § 7121; Alexander v. United States, 95-1 USTC ¶ 50,105 (5th Cir. 1995).

Audits by IRS Specialists

I. Background

A. Specialty Groups

The IRS has an official Examination Specialization program. This allows agents to specialize their knowledge in a concentrated area.[1]

There are several specialty groups within the IRS's Examination section. Currently these include the following:

- Estate and gift[2]
- Engineers
- Employment
- Excise[3]
- Employee plans
- Exempt organizations
- Economists
- Computer specialists
- Large case (coordinated industry cases)

B. Package Audits

Revenue agents typically ask to inspect retained copies of returns other than the one they have under audit. For example, an agent auditing a corporate Form 1120 is required to inspect the controlling shareholder's return and the various employment and excise tax returns required to be filed. This is called a "package audit." If the agent feels that the inspected returns need to be audited, the agent can either do it him- or herself or, in some cases, refer it out to a specialist.

C. Engineering

"Engineering" is actually a misnomer. The agents who work in these groups are not necessarily degreed engineers. The Engineering Branch of the Examination function is frequently called in to address questions concerning the valuation, depreciation, obsolescence, or depletion of particular assets. Engineering teams are located across the

United States. They assist and support all IRS organizations on engineering and valuation issues.[4]

D. *Computer Specialists*

The IRS has specially trained agents in the computer field. These are called computer audit specialist (CAS) agents.[5] Typically CAS agents provide analysis of complex computer accounting systems employed by large corporate taxpayers.[6]

E. *Employee Plan Audits*

Another audit specialty program within the IRS is the Employee Plan (EP) examination process. EP examiners are primarily concerned with the auditing of 5500 forms to determine the adequacy of compliance. Cases may be referred to EP groups by W&I, SB/SE, or LB&I.[7]

F. *Exempt Organizations*

Exempt organization examinations are done within specialty groups throughout the United States. Agents assigned to these groups are generally responsible for auditing returns filed by organizations exempt from taxation under Subchapter F of the I.R.C.[8]

G. *Economists*

Requests for an economist are mandatory in all coordinated industry cases.[9] They are also appropriate in cases involving § 482 issues. Economists may also be utilized by examiners for issues such as "reasonable compensation."

II. Industry Specialization

A. The IRM contains handbooks provided to field agents who examine particular industries such as insurance, auto dealers, textiles, timber, brokerage firms, railroads, construction, oil and gas, banking, public utilities, and barter exchanges.

B. The IRS has an active Industry Specialization Program. Periodically coordinators of this program promulgate lists of issues peculiar to an industry for the guidance of field agents. For example, agents who audit banks are required to look into issues raised by "other real estate owned" (OREO).

C. The specialization program has devolved into what is known as the Market Segment Specialization Program (MSSP).

D. The IRS has published audit guidelines for the following industries as part of their MSSP:

- Artists and art galleries,
- Attorneys,

- Auto body and repair,
- Architects,
- Banking and commercial,
- Bars and restaurants,
- Beauty and barber shops,
- Bed and breakfasts,
- Bus—tour,
- Computers and electronics,
- Entertainment,
- Farmers,
- Furniture manufacturers,
- Garment manufacturers,
- Gas retailers,
- Liquor retailers,
- Ministers,
- Mortuaries,
- Restaurants—pizza,
- Passive activity losses,
- Taxicabs,
- Timber industry, and
- Trucking companies.

The IRS has published handbooks for its agents who operate in various industry specialties. These are contained in the IRM as follows:

- Financial products and transactions   IRM 4.37
- Oil and gas   IRM 4.41
- Insurance   IRM 4.42
- Retail   IRM 4.43
- Farmers' cooperatives   IRM 4.44

III. Employment Tax Audits[10]

A. One of the specialties in the Examination Division is employment tax. These agents are concerned with the adequacy and accuracy of compensation reported in 941 forms. For example, these agents may look at 1120s and 1120Ss to determine if officer-owners are paying themselves adequate compensation. If they are not, the IRS will prepare an adjustment to the 941 liability.

B. The IRS has published—for the benefit of all examiners, not just employment tax specialists—an Employment Tax Examination Handbook.[11] An everyday reference guide, it is the single official compilation of policies, procedures, instructions, and guidelines relating to employment taxes.

C. *Employment Tax Examination Objectives*

The primary objective of these types of audits is to ensure that all employers and workers are "in the system," that is, they are filing timely, accurate, and fully paid returns. The IRS also wants to make sure that workers are properly classified as employees or independent contractors. It goes without saying that the implied objective is to encourage voluntary compliance. The IRS also seeks to achieve consistency from year to year and from taxpayer to taxpayer. There must also be consistency between the I.R.C. and the Social Security Act.

D. *Compliance Checks Distinguished*

Potential examination involvement will initially be determined to warrant a full audit or merely a "compliance check." A compliance check is clearly different from an examination in that it does not seek to make a determination of tax liability. Its purpose is to educate the taxpayer and encourage compliance. The scope of a compliance check is to look only at documents already on file with the IRS.

E. *Section 3402(d) Procedures*

Many employment tax audits involve a reclassification of alleged subcontracted workers to the status of common law employees. Section 3402(d) states that the IRS cannot collect the tax from an employer if the employee has already reported the income. However, the employer has the burden of proving that the employee has reported the tax. For this purpose, a Form 4669 is submitted to the examiner.

F. *Section 3509 Procedures*

An alternative to the 3402(d) procedures is section 3509. This a less draconian penalty imposed to bring the taxpayer into compliance. When this procedure is used by an examiner, however, the 3402(d) relief provisions do not apply.

IV. Large Case Audits

A. As U.S. companies and individuals have increasingly been involved in global commerce, the IRS has likewise increased its emphasis on international tax compliance and enforcement. International examiners have been hired and trained for this work.[12]

Large corporations present special audit problems for the IRS. Audits of large companies are difficult and complex because they are often highly diversified and have many locations, some of which are often overseas. Clearly all publicly owned corporations as well as privately owned corporations with assets and revenues exceeding a certain amount fall into this category. The determination of whether the taxpayer will be considered a large corporation for this purpose is based on a formula with points assigned to various factors such as assets, revenues, number of subsidiaries, and so on. *Very* large corporations are audited on a permanent basis each and every year.

B. All large case audits fall into the jurisdiction of the LB&I function. The manual contains procedures for both coordinated industry cases as well as industry cases.[13]

C. Due to this diversity and organizational complexity, the IRS has adopted a team audit approach.

D. The recent trend toward mergers and acquisitions continues to create multilayered structures with divisions, branches, and subsidiaries.

E. One of the IRS's objectives in large case audits is to identify the best litigating vehicles (issues) and settle everything else.

V. International Tax Audits

A. The IRM provides guidance and instruction on the classification and assignment of returns with international tax issues.[14] The IRS has a classification process to identify which returns with international implications have the most audit potential. During the international classification process, returns are identified as having "tax haven" or "boycott" characteristics. Most international audits involve U.S. corporations operating abroad through various subsidiaries or branches. However, the IRS may also focus on U.S. corporations that are foreign owned.

B. The first determination for a representative to make is whether his or her client's transactions are with companies in countries with which the United States has an income tax treaty. If the proposed adjustment would result in double taxation, the IRS may be required to take up the particular issue with the "competent authority" in the foreign country to try and resolve any differences.

C. Every foreign-chartered corporation that is subject to U.S. taxation must file a Form 1120F regardless of whether it has taxable income or gross income.[15] International examiners will also review Forms 5471 and 5472 to determine if there are any transfer pricing issues or whether certain income realized by a foreign subsidiary should be treated as Subpart F income.

D. Among the special powers the IRS has in the area of international tax audits is the authority to require the production of foreign documents. If a taxpayer fails to produce such documents, he or she cannot introduce them as evidence at trial.

VI. Miscellaneous

A. *Bank Secrecy Act*
The IRS also employs specialists to audit issues under the Bank Secrecy Act (BSA). This includes money laundering and I.R.C. § 6050I (currency-reporting) issues.[16]

B. *Bankruptcy*

The IRS has an Insolvency Support section to assist examiners whose taxpayers have filed for bankruptcy protection under 11 U.S.C.[17]

VII. Notes

1. IRM 4.28.1.1.
2. Estate tax (Form 706) audits are always done by attorneys employed by the government. IRM 4.25.1.1. These specialists also examine gift tax and generation-skipping tax issues.
3. IRS employs excise tax specialists to assist in auditing returns filed under I.R.C. §§ 4000–4999 (Subtitle D of the Code). Excise tax examiners are concerned with examining the following forms: 11C, 637, 720, 730, and 2290. IRM 4.24.
4. IRM 4.48.1.1.
5. IRM 4.47.1.1.1.
6. IRM 4.47.1.1.2.
7. IRM 4.71.1.2.
8. *See generally* IRM 4.75, 4.76.
9. IRM 4.49.1.2.
10. *See* IRM 4.23 *et seq.*
11. *See generally* IRM 4.23.
12. IRM 4.61.1.
13. IRM 4.46.1.1.
14. IRM 4.1.8.1.
15. IRM 4.1.8.2.5.
16. IRM 4.26.1.1.
17. IRM 4.27.2.2.

CHAPTER 2

Administrative Appeals

The IRS Appeals Office[1]

I. General Information

A. *History*

Prior to October 1, 1978, there were two administrative levels of appeal within the IRS:

1. District conference
2. Appellate conference

This effectively gave taxpayers two bites at the apple prior to any court action. Now, under the present system, assuming you cannot reach agreement with the examiner, you have only one shot at appealing administratively within the IRS. The Appeals Office was formerly known as the Appellate Division, and appeals officers were formerly known as appellate conferees.

It is generally much more cost-effective to resolve a tax controversy at the "function" (revenue agent or office auditor) level than at the appeals level. However, sometimes you have no choice because examination personnel are often inflexible, poorly trained, or simply unqualified to make a quality decision in a tax case. Most importantly, though, examiners are unable to base decisions on "hazards of litigation."

There are two types of appeals officials: appeals officers (AOs) and settlement officers (SOs). SOs are officers who originally came from IRS Collections. AOs, on the other hand, came up through the ranks from IRS Examination. SOs typically handle cases such as offers in compromise, trust fund recovery penalties (TFRPs), and collection due process (CDP) hearings. AOs are generally less partial to the IRS's case than are revenue agents. However, sometimes you draw a new AO who was formerly a revenue agent and who has not quite made the attitude adjustment.

B. *Qualifications of Appeals Officers (AOs)*
1. Generally AOs are former revenue agents.
2. They need not be attorneys or CPAs, but they frequently are.
3. They are generally much more experienced and qualified than revenue agents.
C. The Appeals Office is not under the jurisdiction of the management structure in charge of IRS Collections or Examination and is, therefore, theoretically considered to be independent of and not prejudiced by the field personnel.

II. Protests

A. In a nondocketed case (i.e. a pre-ninety-day-letter case, or pre-90 case), one can generally obtain an appeals conference only by preparing a "protest."
B. A protest is required only when there has been a field audit (i.e., conducted by a revenue agent, and not an office audit) *and*
1. The deficiency (or overassessment) is greater than $2,500.
2. If the deficiency is between $2,500 and $10,000, a brief written statement of disputed issues is all that is needed in lieu of a formal protest.
3. For purposes of the dollar limits discussed in 1 and 2, one counts the amount of penalties and interest as well as tax.[2]
4. In the event of an office audit, all that is required is a simple written statement that you wish to appeal.
C. As to the contents of a protest, there are two schools of thought:
1. Full disclosure (playing all your cards), *or*
2. Skeleton approach.

D. *Minimum Requirements of a Protest*
1. Statement that you disagree with the findings proposed in the thirty-day letter and accompanying audit report (sometimes referred to as an RAR) and a statement that you wish to appeal.
2. Date and symbols on the thirty-day letter.
3. The taxable periods covered by the examination.
4. A schedule detailing the specific items to which the taxpayer takes exception.
5. A statement of facts relied on by the taxpayer.
6. A section containing all of the law and argument supporting the taxpayer's position, citing all pertinent authorities.
7. A statement that you are requesting a conference with an AO.
8. A declaration of truth and a signature.
9. Name and address of the taxpayer.
E. When the thirty-day[3] letter arrives, it is very important that it be promptly responded to. It states that you have only thirty days within which to prepare your protest and submit it to the office that issued the letter.

Extensions of time within which to file the thirty-day letter are entirely discretionary with examination management. The examination office, assuming the protest is in order, sends the case (the "administrative file") forward to the appropriate Appeals Office for consideration. Before sending it to appeals, however, the revenue agent has an opportunity to review the protest and prepare a written rebuttal. After the records section of the Appeals Office receives the case, the assigned AO generally sends out an acknowledgment letter and thereafter schedules a mutually convenient time for a settlement conference. All conferences are held at the Appeals Office location. AOs are generally not permitted to travel to other locations to hold conferences.

F.   A protest can be signed by a representative qualified to practice before the IRS (see Circular 230) if the power of attorney (generally, a Form 2848) is attached or has previously been filed with the IRS. Protests and briefs should be submitted at least five days before the scheduled conference date.

Practice Tip

A practitioner should protest all issues even if some are weak. This gives you some bargaining chips to be conceded as a part of the overall settlement.

G.   *Disadvantages of Filing a Protest*
   1.   Additional cost.
   2.   Further delay in closing the case.
   3.   Possibility that new issues will be raised at the appeals level.
   4.   Interest and time-sensitive penalties will continue to accrue.
       There is a school of thought that theorizes that protests should rarely, if ever, be prepared. The rationale is that forcing the IRS to issue a deficiency notice minimizes the involvement of the revenue agent in the settlement process, thereby enhancing the prospects for a favorable settlement. A petitioner is still entitled to an appeals conference followed by settlement opportunities with counsel.

Practice Tip

Consider filing two separate protests. File the first one within the thirty-day period allowed and make sure that it contains the minimum requirements to confer jurisdiction on the Appeals Office. This protest will be read and analyzed by the revenue agent. Then, just a few days before the scheduled appeals conference, submit a supplemental protest containing the substance (including law, argument, and documentary evidence) of your defense. This prevents the examiner from shoring up his or her case and having an undue influence on the AO.

III. Appeals Conference Procedures

A. *Jurisdictional Matters*

If a representative and his or her client reside in different parts of the country, the Appeals Office with the jurisdiction will be the one nearest the residence of the taxpayer. However, in docketed cases, the representative can select whatever city he or she wants with a trial designation.[4]

B. An appeals conference is very informal. No rules of evidence are followed. It is not considered a "hearing." There is generally no tape recording equipment, and no court reporter or stenographer present.[5] The purpose of this informality is to encourage all parties to be more frank and candid about the relative strengths and weaknesses of their respective cases. Typically the only people present are the AO and the taxpayer and/or his or her representative. Of course, the representative may appear with or without his or her client and may bring other witnesses, both factual and expert.

C. As a tactical matter, it is usually not a good idea for a representative to bring his or her client to the appeals conference. The reason is that the taxpayer is more likely to blurt out statements that could later prove to be damaging. There appears to be no provision for an AO to require that a taxpayer appear and give testimony during an appeals conference. If a representative appears alone, the AO will verify that he or she is indeed admitted to practice before the IRS. If the taxpayer appears with his or her representative, then the representative need not possess a power of attorney.

D. *Functions of an Appeals Officer (AO)*
   1. Identify the issue(s).
   2. Evaluate the facts.
   3. Evaluate the relevant tax law.
   4. Consider the case on a fair and impartial basis.
   5. Close as large a percentage of his or her cases as possible on an "agreed" basis.

E. Statements of fact should be submitted to the AO in affidavit form, signed under penalty of perjury. Do not depend on verbal arguments to persuade the AO; put all arguments in writing.

F. Practitioners should always be thoroughly prepared.

G. AOs are supposed to make a careful analysis of all legal authorities, including statutory, administrative, and judicial authorities.

H. *New Issues*
   1. New issues will be raised by the AO only if the tax is material and the grounds (probability of winning) are substantial. However, according to the Internal Revenue Manual, an issue on which the

taxpayer and IRS Compliance are in agreement should not be reopened by the Appeals Office.[6]

2. But taxpayers may raise a new issue at any time without restriction while the case is under consideration of the Appeals Office.

3. Even the IRS raises a new issue in docketed cases, it is called an "affirmative" issue and the IRS has the burden of proof with respect to it and must amend their pleadings accordingly.

I. Form 872-As (assessment statute extensions) will be solicited by the AO if there are less than 120 days left in the statute of limitations period.

Practice Tip

Do not submit a large amount of new evidence (documents) to the AO. If the field agent or officer has not seen it, the AO may send the entire case file back to the original revenue agent for consideration of the new evidence. This can be very dangerous; the revenue agent will have yet another opportunity to develop new issues. The AO will not play the role of an auditor. Sometimes the AO receives a case from the field that, in his or her opinion, is "poorly developed." In such a case, he or she will often send back the case for further development or comment by the original examining agent.

J. *Prohibited Ex Parte Communications*

The 1998 IRS Restructuring Act prohibits AOs from having *ex parte* communications or conversations with IRS Examination or Collections personnel about issues in a case under consideration by the Appeals Office. Taxpayers or their representatives must be allowed to participate in such conversations or conferences.[7] The purpose of not allowing one-sided conversations between the AO and other IRS personnel is to avoid compromising the independence of the Appeals Office. During the conference it is a good idea always to ask the AO if he or she has had any communication with the revenue agent or officer about your case.

K. Statements and representations made by either party during an appeals conference are always inadmissible as evidence. If the AO insists on having a revenue agent participate in the appeals conference, the representative should normally consider objecting to the agent's presence. Agents are usually called as fact witnesses at trial. Statements made in settlement conferences are not admissible at trial.[8] If the agent hears something in the appeals conference, such as an admission of weakness by a taxpayer, it may unfairly influence and alter the agent's trial testimony. This would effectively emasculate Rule 408.

L. After the AO has made a decision, he or she will draft what is called an "appeals conference memorandum." This document is similar to a written opinion in a court case and attempts to justify the AO's opinions to the AO's superior, an "associate chief" or "team leader." This is an internal document and is not available to the taxpayer or his or her representative. The decision of the AO is not final and must be approved by his or her superior.

M. *Third-Party Information*
    If there is third-party information in the appeals officer's files, he or she is required to give it to the taxpayer or the taxpayer's representative without the necessity of filing a Freedom of Information Act request.[9]

N. *Conference Memorandum*
    It is always a good idea to prepare a conference memorandum at the conclusion of each meeting with an AO. If a copy of this memo is furnished to the AO, any misunderstandings of how particular issues are to be handled can be cleared up. Further, all deadlines should be reduced to writing.

O. *Docketed Cases*
    A practitioner should be particularly careful in docketed cases that too much time does not slip by during Appeals Office consideration. Once a case appears on a tax court trial calendar, discovery deadlines start coming up very quickly. The recommended procedure is to issue a *Branerton* letter (informal discovery) as soon as you are notified of a trial date. This tends to push the case along faster. However, if the AO has already committed to a settlement in writing, this should not be necessary.

IV. Types of Cases Considered by Appeals

A. For income, estate, and gift tax cases, there are three different categories:
    1. *Docketed:* This is following the issuance of a ninety-day letter (a statutory notice of deficiency under I.R.C. § 6212).[10]
    2. *Nondocketed* (pre-90): These cases are heard pursuant to the issuance of a statutory notice of deficiency.
    3. *Claims:* This is where the taxpayer has already paid the tax and has filed a claim for refund that has been rejected by the IRS (by means of a statutory notice of claim disallowance). The taxpayer has just as much right to an administrative appeal of a claim disallowance as in a regular deficiency case.[11]

A claimant desiring an administrative settlement conference must file a request for Appeals Office consideration within the time period for bringing suit.[12] However, the receiving Appeals Office may decline to take jurisdiction of the request for a disallowed claim hearing if less than 120 days remain in the two-year period for filing suit.[13]

If no agreement is reached in the Appeals Office in this type of case, the taxpayer cannot proceed to U.S. Tax Court (because there is no "deficiency"). Instead, he or she must proceed to either the U.S. district court or the federal claims court.

B. *Non–income tax cases heard by appeals:*
    1. Penalty appeals
    2. Trust fund recovery penalty cases (§ 6672)
    3. Excise tax cases
    4. Employment tax cases
    5. Offers in compromise
    6. Estate and/or gift tax cases
    7. Collection due process (CDP) cases

C. *Docketed cases:*
    1. After issuance of the deficiency notice (ninety-day letter) and the filing of a petition by the taxpayer or his or her representative, the case is considered to be "docketed."
    2. AOs usually handle docketed cases where the deficiency notice (sometimes referred to as a "stat notice") was issued by the Examination function.
    3. If the Appeals Office issues the deficiency notice, it usually means that an AO has already considered the case and has held an appeals conference while the case was in pre-90 status.
    4. If the AO and the taxpayer cannot reach agreement in a docketed case, the AO then forwards the file to the chief counsel trial attorney for trial preparation.
    5. Of course, you can always attempt to settle the case with the trial attorney before, during, or after the trial.
    6. If a docketed case is settled, a "decision document" is prepared for the signature of both counsel. This document is also ultimately signed by the tax court judge and thereafter becomes the final decision of the court.
    7. There are two types of docketed cases:
        a. Regular
        b. "S" cases (see I.R.C. § 7463)
    8. If it becomes obvious that an AO is procrastinating or is having difficulty making a decision, the counsel for the petitioner should send out a *Branerton* letter to speed up the process. Ordinarily, the

Appeals Office should be able to come to a decision within ninety days of receiving the case file initially from counsel. Calendars should be marked for follow-up by this date.

D. *Pre-90 Cases (Income, Estate, or Gift Tax Cases)*
    1. Where the Appeals Division considers a case prior to the issuance of a deficiency notice, it is called a pre-90 case. Usually, this is where a thirty-day letter has been issued.
    2. If, during Appeals Office consideration of a case, the three-year assessment statute of limitations is about to expire and the taxpayer wants to avoid the issuance of a deficiency notice, the AO will ask the taxpayer to sign an 872-A, extending the statute indefinitely, unless terminated by an 872-T.
    3. If a pre-90 case is settled, the AO will usually request the execution of one of the following forms:
        a. 870 or
        b. 870-AD: This is where future years are affected, there are mutual concessions, and substantial tax is involved. This form is signed by both the taxpayer and the AO. Note that there is a conflict among the circuits regarding whether it bars a later refund claim.[14]
        c. Collateral agreement.
        d. Closing agreement: Where absolute finality is desired.

E. *Trust Fund Liability Cases*
    1. AOs have authority to consider cases arising under § 6672 of the I.R.C.
    2. Sometimes delay is important, even if you have a weak case, because interest does not start accruing on this liability until it is assessed. And, generally, assessment has not occurred at the time of appeals consideration of these cases.
    3. These cases usually involve multiple parties.
    4. The IRS posture in these cases is very tough; do not expect much leniency.

V. Settlement Practices

A. *Settlement Policy*
    1. The taxpayer is expected to make the initial proposal of settlement of the case.
    2. If the AO rejects the taxpayer's proposal of settlement, he or she is expected to make a counterproposal. The AO will generally not back off from his or her counterproposal once it is made.
    3. The AO is under pressure to close a large number of his or her cases on an agreed basis.

4. Usually, the best way to settle is issue by issue.
5. "Flat-sum" settlements are permitted but discouraged.
6. Settlements usually involve mutual concessions.

B. *"Split-Issue" Settlements*
The AO will use "split-issue" (or "flat-sum") settlements only as a last resort and when there is no continuing problem. The distinguishing feature of a split-issue settlement is that it is a result that would not be reached by a court. Split-issue settlements should be expressed in terms of changes to taxable income rather than a percentage of the tax.

C. *Nuisance Value Settlements*
These settlements (those reflecting the respective litigating costs) are to be avoided by AOs.

D. *Equitable Considerations*
An AO will not consider settlements based on equity, justice, individual hardship, inability to pay, and so on. However, in CDP hearings these issues are considered.

E. *Hazards of Litigation*
1. Unlike revenue agents and other compliance personnel, an AO can take into consideration the so-called hazards of litigation. Hazards of litigation are those uncertainties about a tax case regarding the outcome in the event of a trial. For example, if a key witness for the IRS is deceased, this would be considered a hazard for the IRS and might cause a more favorable settlement for the taxpayer.
2. Typical litigating hazards for the IRS are the following:
   a. Doubt as to the court's view of the law
   b. Doubt as to conclusions of fact
   c. Credibility of witnesses
   d. Probative value of evidence
   e. Death or unavailability of a witness
   f. Inability to meet burden of proof
   g. Inability to go forward with evidence once the taxpayer has presented his or her evidence
   h. Doubt as to legal conclusions[15]

F. Once you have reached agreement with the AO, immediately reduce your understanding of that agreement to writing so that there will be no misunderstanding. Also, the AO will be less likely to renege on the agreement once it is reduced to writing.

G. Always know the bottom-line tax effect (including penalty and interest) of any proposal of settlement before you make the proposal. Sometimes you can work out a settlement that, at first, seems very favorable to the IRS but that, after the tax is calculated, is favorable to the taxpayer. That is, do not make proposals blindly.

VI. Early Settlement

A. *Early Referrals*
Effective in 1998 Congress enacted a statutory provision mandating that the IRS establish procedures by which a taxpayer can request an "early referral" of one or more unresolved issues from the Examination or Collections function.[16]

B. *Fast-Track Settlement (FTS)*
IRS Announcement 2006-61[17] establishes the SB/SE FTS program to expedite case resolution and expand the range of dispute resolution options to SB/SE taxpayers.[18] These procedures are available to a taxpayer before his or her case is closed out of the Examination group. In the event that the FTS procedure is unsuccessful, the standard appeals process remains available. Thus, in this case the taxpayer still has two bites at the appeals apple.

C. *Mediation*
Additionally, procedures are required to be established under which either the taxpayer or an AO can request nonbinding mediation on any unresolved issue at the conclusion of the appeals process.[19]
Mediation is an extension of the appeals process to enhance voluntary compliance. It is a nonbinding procedure that uses the services of a mediator, a neutral third party, to help the taxpayer and the Appeals Office reach their own negotiated settlement.[20]

D. *Fast-Track Mediation*
Procedures for prompt resolution of tax issues are described in IRS Publication 3605 (Rev. 12-2001).

E. *Arbitration*
The IRS is also required to establish a pilot program under which the IRS can jointly request binding arbitration at the conclusion of the appeals process.[21] See the full text of Rev. Proc. 2006-44 for IRS implementation of arbitration procedures.[22]

VII. Notes

1. For further information, go to the IRS home page: http://www.irs.gov. Then, from the bottom margin menu, select "Appealing a Tax Dispute."
2. *See* Treas. Reg. § 601.105(c)(2)(ii).
3. In the case of a proposed liability under § 6672 (trust fund recovery penalty), the response period is sixty days.

4. *See generally* IRM chapter 8.4 for materials related to docketed and ninety-day cases.

5. IRM 8.6.1.2.5; *but see* Mesa Oil, Inc. v. United States, 2001-1 USTC ¶ 50,130 (D. Colo. 2000), *non-acq.*, re the requirements for a "record" in collection due process (CDP) hearings to allow for a proper appeal. Moreover, the Tax Court has held that in a CDP hearing a taxpayer may audio-record his section 6330 hearing under the authority of I.R.C. § 7521(c). Keene v. Comm'r, 121 T.C. 8 (2003).

6. IRM 8.6.1.6, citing Policy Statement P-8-49; *see also* Interim Guidance (AP-08-0713) effective July 18, 2013, Appeals Judicial Approach and Culture (AJAC).

7. 1998 "Act" § 1001(a)(4), not amending any Code section; Notice 99-50; Rev. Proc. 2000-43; Rev. Proc. 2012-18, 2012-10 I.R.B. 455; IRM 8.1.10.

8. *See* Fed. R. Evid. 408.

9. See 1995 and 1996 memoranda from the assistant commissioner of examination. This document is an "internal use only" document and is not generally available to the public. As a practical matter one may have to wait until the case becomes docketed in Tax Court. As part of *Branerton* discovery, IRS counsel will generally allow petitioner's counsel to review the entire administrative file.

10. *See* Rev. Proc. 87-24, 1987-1 CB 720, re settlement authority of appeals officers in docketed cases.

11. *See* Procedural Treas. Reg. § 601.105(e)(2).

12. IRM 8.7.7; *see also* I.R.C. § 6532(a), which requires that a refund suit be brought within two years of receiving a statutory notice of claim disallowance.

13. IRM 8.7.7.

14. *See* Whitney v. United States, 87-2 USTC ¶ 9503 (9th Cir. 1987) (holding that an 870-AD, which purports to prevent a taxpayer from reopening a tax case, is in fact invalid since it does not comply with the closing agreement procedures of I.R.C. § 7121).

15. *See* IRM 8.6.3 re the requirement for appeals officers to follow rulings, etc.

16. I.R.C. § 7123(a); Pub. L. No. 105-206.

17. 2006-36 I.R.B. 390.

18. *See also* IRM 8.26.2.1. for a discussion of fast-track settlement for SB/SE taxpayers.

19. I.R.C. § 7123(b)(1).

20. Rev. Proc. 2002-44, 2002-26 I.R.B. 10.

21. I.R.C. § 7123(b)(2).

22. 2006-44 I.R.B. 800.

Freedom of Information Act Requests

I. History and General Rules

A. There are several ways to access government information and documents, but the most effective and widely used method is via the so-called Freedom of Information Act (FOIA).[1] This statute was enacted in 1966 as an amendment to the public disclosure section of the Administrative Procedure Act. In addition to an agency's organization, function, and policies, the federal government is required to disclose "agency records," which may be disclosed to any person who reasonably describes such records in a request prepared in accordance with published rules.[2] As one might expect, the IRS is one of the agencies that must comply with the FOIA rules.[3]

B. *Materials the IRS Must Disclose*
FOIA suits have triggered the disclosure of private letter rulings (PLRs), large portions of the Internal Revenue Manual (IRM), and numerous other types of internal IRS memoranda. Materials disclosed by the IRS provide a tax practitioner with valuable insights into IRS positions and policies. For example, inconsistent rulings by the IRS can show an abuse of discretion, or the good faith of a taxpayer's position in a penalty or criminal context.

II. Minimum Requirements of an FOIA Request

A. *Specific Items Required*
A formal FOIA request must contain the following items at a minimum:
1. The request must be in writing and signed by the person making the request.
2. The request must state that it is made pursuant to the FOIA, 5 U.S.C. § 552.
3. The request must be addressed to the IRS official (disclosure officer) who is responsible for the control of the records.
4. The request must reasonably describe the records sought.

5. The request must establish the identity of the person making the request and his or her right to the disclosure.
6. The request must state the address where the copies are to be sent.
7. The request must state an agreement to pay for copying costs.
8. The request must identify the "category" of the requester.[4]

B. *Reasonable Description*
While no specific formula for a "reasonable description" of a record can be established, the requirement will generally be satisfied if the requester gives the name, subject matter, location, and years at issue of the requested records.[5]

C. *Power of Attorney*
A representative seeking disclosure of his or her client's tax files from the IRS will be required to submit a copy of his or her properly executed power of attorney along with the FOIA request.[6]

D. *Category Requirement*
An FOIA requester must state in the request which of the following categories he or she falls in:
1. Commercial use requester,
2. Media requester,
3. Educational institution requester,
4. Noncommercial scientific institution requester, or
5. "Other" requester.[7]
   Tax practitioners typically fall into the "other" category.

III. Exemptions

A. Several matters are exempt from FOIA disclosure. Some of the more important of these are the following:
1. Information related to national defense or foreign policy
2. Instructions related to enforcement tolerances or criteria
3. Enforcement investigative techniques, etc.
4. Trade secrets
5. IRS personnel files[8]

B. If a document has exempt and nonexempt material in it, the exempt portion may be deleted if, after deletion, the remaining material still conveys meaningful information that is not misleading.[9]

C. *FOIA Litigation*
1. Litigation under the FOIA has generally centered on the interpretation of the nine disclosure exemptions.
2. Exemptions to the disclosure statute are specifically made exclusive and must be narrowly construed.[10]

3. Discriminant function (DIF) formulas developed as a result of Taxpayer Compliance Measurement Program (TCMP)[11] audits are not discoverable through the use of FOIA requests.[12]
4. Documents relevant to an ongoing criminal investigation are not discoverable through the FOIA. The IRS can sustain its "exemption" burden through the use of affidavits.[13]
5. Courts have also held that statements prepared by IRS appeals officers[14] and criminal referral letters are exempt from disclosure on the grounds that the government's strategy might be revealed.[15]

D. *Informants*
Production of documents under the FOIA may not include disclosure of the identity of a confidential source, otherwise known as an informant.[16] This generally means that the IRS need not disclose to a requester any informant's communication in the taxpayer's administrative file.[17]

IV. When and Where to File

A. The timing of filing an FOIA request is important. One should file it after the investigative work of the agency is complete; otherwise, you may miss obtaining evidence obtained by the agency after the request is filled. But the request should be made before an administrative appeals hearing or conference in order to prepare the best case possible. For IRS matters, all FOIA requests are filed with the local Disclosure Office in each IRS office.
B. Addresses of all IRS Disclosure Offices throughout the United States are published in the regulations.[18]

C. *Assessment Records*
Requests for copies of assessment records (Form 23-C) have to be made to the director of the IRS Service Center, not the local office.[19]

V. Response Date

A. After the IRS Disclosure Office receives the FOIA request, a letter is sent to the requester advising him or her of the date within which a response may be expected.[20] Where the FOIA request cannot be filled within ten days of receipt, the requester is so notified and given an opportunity for an administrative appeal. As a practical matter, FOIA requests are seldom filled with the ten-day period.[21] In the author's experience, it is not unusual to have to wait for four to six months to receive the requested documents.

VI. Fees

A. After the copies are made, a statement of fees due is mailed to the requester. And only after the fees are paid will the copied materials be released.[22] Payment may be made with a personal or company check.

B. In some specific instances, the regulations provide for situations where the copying fee may be waived.[23]

C. To avoid incurring unexpected fees, a requester should state the maximum dollar amount he or she is willing to pay without specific authorization from the requester.[24]

VII. Miscellaneous Topics

A. *The FOIA versus Litigation Discovery*

Access to information in IRS files pursuant to disclosure statutes may be sought at any time, without regard to active litigation. It is usually advantageous for a taxpayer to obtain information through the use of disclosure statutes prior to initiating court proceedings against the IRS for the reason that FOIA discovery is usually broader than civil litigation discovery. For example, under the FOIA, one does not have to demonstrate relevance or materiality as would be the case with civil discovery. Moreover, one need not specify a reason or offer any justification whatsoever for making an FOIA request.[25]

B. *Agency Burden*

After having received an FOIA request, the agency must make a search reasonably calculated to uncover all relevant documents.[26] However, the responding agency is *not* required to tabulate or compile information for purposes of creating a record.[27] Nor is the IRS required to make a nationwide search for records when a taxpayer makes a request to one field office.

C. *District Court Opinions*

The U.S. Supreme Court has held that under the FOIA, the Department of Justice's Tax Division must make available to the public copies of district court opinions that it receives in the course of litigation.[28]

D. *Revenue Agent Report "Transmittal" Letters*

Normally an FOIA request would not ask for a copy of a revenue agent's report because that document would have already been sent to the taxpayer as a matter of policy. However, there is a document called a transmittal letter that accompanies such a report. It contains information that the agent does not want the taxpayer to see. Obviously, this is a critical document and one that can be obtained through an FOIA request.[29]

E. *Jurisdiction for Suits to Compel Disclosure*
   Lawsuits brought by taxpayers to compel the IRS to disclose information sought by an FOIA request must be filed in federal district courts. The tax court has no statutory authority over those issues.

VIII. Notes

1. 5 U.S.C. §§ 552 *et seq.*
2. 5 U.S.C. § 552(a)(3).
3. *See* Treas. Reg. § 601.702(a).
4. Treas. Reg. § 601.702(c)(4).
5. *Id.*
6. Treas. Reg. § 601.702(c)(5)(iii)(C).
7. Treas. Reg. § 601.702(c)(4)(i)(H).
8. *See* Treas. Reg. § 601.702(c)(9).
9. *Id.*
10. E.P.A. v. Mink, 410 U.S. 73 (S. Ct. 1973).
11. Now known as NRP (national research program) audits.
12. Long v. Internal Revenue Serv., 87-2 USTC ¶ 9484 (9th Cir. 1987).
13. Lewis v. Internal Revenue Serv., 87-2 USTC ¶ 9548 (9th Cir. 1987).
14. Presumably this would include what are known as appeals conference memoranda.
15. *See, e.g.,* Casa Investors, Ltd v. Gibbs, 90-2 USTC ¶ 50,553 (D. D.C. 1990).
16. 5 U.S.C. § 552(b)(7)(D).
17. Luzaich v. United States, 77-1 USTC ¶ 9250 (D. Minn. 1977), *aff'd in unpubl. opinion* (8th Cir. 1977).
18. Treas. Reg. § 601.702(h).
19. *See* Parenti v. Internal Revenue Serv., 91 AFTR2d 2003-1136 (D. Wash. 2003).
20. Treas. Reg. § 601.702.
21. *Id.*
22. *Id.*
23. *Id.*
24. *Id.*
25. N.L.R.B. v. Sears, Roebuck & Co., 421 U.S. 132 (1975).
26. Treas. Reg. § 601.702(c).
27. *Id.*
28. U.S. Dep't of Justice v. Tax Analysts, 492 U.S. 136, 89-1 USTC ¶ 9386 (S. Ct. 1989).
29. Branerton Corp. v. Comm'r, 64 T.C. 191 (1975).

Closing Agreements

I. Introduction and Background

A. IRS's Statutory Authority

1. The IRS is authorized to enter into a written agreement with any person relating to the tax liability of such person for any tax period.[1]

B. IRS's Discretion

Whether or not a closing agreement will be entered into is a matter within the IRS's discretion and, therefore, within the discretion of those to whom the commissioner has delegated his or her authority.[2]

C. Requests by Taxpayers

In practice, if the taxpayer shows good reasons for requesting the agreement and furnishes necessary facts and documentation, and the IRS will suffer no disadvantage therefrom, a closing agreement will ordinarily be entered into provided that the content of the agreement can be satisfactorily agreed upon. No request to enter into a closing agreement will be denied solely because granting the request would result in no apparent advantage to the IRS.[3]

D. Examples of Acceptable Reasons

1. A taxpayer wishes to definitely establish its tax liability so that a transaction may be facilitated, such as the sale of its stock.
2. The fiduciary of an estate desires a closing agreement so he or she can be discharged by a probate court.
3. A corporation is in the process of liquidating and desires a final determination before a distribution is made or its affairs wound up.
4. A taxpayer wishes to fulfill creditors' demands for authentic evidence of the status of its tax liability.
5. A taxpayer wishes to assure itself that a controversy between it and the IRS is conclusively disposed of.[4]

E. *Purpose of Closing Agreements*

The purpose of I.R.C. § 7121 is to protect the taxpayer against the government reopening the case at a later date and to prevent the taxpayer from later filing a claim or instituting a lawsuit for refund of taxes paid.[5]

F. *"Whipsaw" Situations*

To "whipsaw" is to gain the advantage over an opponent in two ways at once. The IRS uses closing agreements to prevent whipsaw situations such as those that could result in a related taxpayer conceding an issue (with the result that the other related party obtains a benefit) and then, after the statute of limitations period has expired against the other related party, contesting the issue by filing a claim.[6]

II.   What Does *Not* Constitute a Closing Agreement?

A. *Collateral Agreements*

There is a distinction between a collateral agreement and a closing agreement. The former does not purport to bind the IRS. That is, collateral agreements are unilateral commitments on the part of the taxpayer. The IRS does not enter into and sign collateral agreements as a party.[7]

B. *Assessment Waivers*

A taxpayer's execution of restrictions on assessment (via Forms 870, 870-AD, and 4549) does not constitute entering into a closing agreement under I.R.C. § 7121.[8]

C. *Offer in Compromise*

A closing agreement is not the same thing as a "compromise." See the offer in compromise provisions of I.R.C. § 7122.

III. Grounds for Rescission

A. *General Rule: No Reopening*

Once a closing agreement has been entered into, the case cannot normally be reopened by the IRS or the taxpayer as to the matters agreed on.[9]

B. *Mistakes of Fact and Law*

Mere mistakes of fact as well as of law are insufficient grounds for rescission of a closing agreement.[10]

C. *Mistakes by the Taxpayer*

A taxpayer's unintentional mistake in taking an unallowable deduction on a return will not constitute "misrepresentation of material fact," particularly where the facts are before the IRS in an audit setting.[11]

D. *Mistakes by the IRS*

A revenue agent's unintentional oversight in failing to include certain deductions in arriving at the result upon which the closing agreement was based does not constitute misrepresentation of a material fact relied upon by the taxpayer.[12]

E. *Misrepresentation*

To set aside a closing agreement, proof of misrepresentation in the original return is, alone, insufficient; there must be such proof as to the closing agreement itself.[13] Congress intended that innocent mistakes be buried in closing agreements.

F. *Tax Court Review*

The tax court has the power to review the determination of the IRS in setting aside a closing agreement. The burden of proof is on the IRS in such a controversy.[14]

IV. Finality of Closing Agreements

A. *Statutory Finality*

By statute, all closing agreements approved and signed by an authorized IRS official are considered to be final and conclusive except upon a showing of
1. fraud,
2. malfeasance, or
3. misrepresentation of a material fact.[15]

B. *Binding Effect*

Unlike a private ruling by the IRS, a closing agreement is legally binding on both parties to the agreement (the taxpayer and the IRS) regardless of mistakes of fact or law by either side.

C. *Related Parties*

A closing agreement with a corporation does not bind its stockholders.[16]

D. *Depreciation Example*

Where a closing agreement involved gain from the sale of property on which no adjustment was made for depreciation, taxpayers are estopped from claiming a deduction for depreciation.[17]

V. Execution of Closing Agreements

A. *Authority by Delegation*

By delegation order, only certain officials of the IRS are empowered to execute closing agreements. The commissioner of internal revenue is the primary official who has such authority. This authority has been redelegated to certain field officials. The practical result is that most closing agreements are entered into by such field officials.[18]

B. *Execution by Taxpayer's Representative*
A taxpayer's representative or, in the case of a case being litigated, the counsel of record can execute a closing agreement for his or her client only if he or she has previously furnished to the IRS a power of attorney (Form 2848) authorizing him or her to execute such an agreement. If, however, a closing agreement covers, for example, "all future years," the representative cannot sign on behalf of his or her client because there is no way the power of attorney can cover all future years.[19]

C. *Authority of Field Personnel*
Revenue officers (the IRS Collections function) have no authority to enter into closing agreements.[20] Presumably this rule applies also to revenue agents and other field personnel of the IRS.

D. *Order of Execution*
Closing agreements must always be signed by the taxpayer before they are signed by the IRS. The taxpayer's signature constitutes an offer to agree, and the IRS's signature constitutes an acceptance and approval of the offer.[21]

E. *Corporate Execution*
Corporate resolutions authorizing execution of closing agreements are no longer required to be submitted with the agreement. All that is required is a name and title of the authorized corporate officer.[22]

VI. Forms to Be Used

A. *General Rule*
All closing agreements are to be executed on forms prescribed by the IRS.[23]

B. *Prescribed Forms*
Forms to be used for closing agreements are as follows:
1. Form 866: Closing Agreement (Final Determination) and
2. Form 906: Closing Agreement (As to Specific Matters).

C. *Plain Paper*
Plain bond paper may be used where the agreement covers both specific matters and ultimate tax liability.[24]

VII. Applicability of Legal Principles

A. *Drafting the Contract*
The Internal Revenue Manual (IRM) does not specify which party must draft the agreement, although in virtually all cases it is done by

the IRS. However, there is no legal prohibition against a taxpayer's preparation of the agreement.[25]

B. *Executory Provisions*
   The agreement should not depend on executory provisions, that is, where the taxpayer agrees to do something in the future. This avoids the difficulties that may ensue if the taxpayer does not do what he or she promises.[26]

C. *Consideration*
   Absence of consideration does not alter the conclusive and binding effect of a closing agreement. Thus, closing agreements, while exhibiting some of the attributes of a contract, are not governed by the law of contracts.[27]

VIII. Prior and Subsequent Years

A. *General Rule*
   The regulations provide that closing agreements may relate to future taxable periods.[28]

B. *Subsequent Tax Legislation*
   A closing agreement regarding future years is subject to changes or modifications to the tax law as may be subsequently enacted, and each closing agreement must recite this fact.[29] But a valid closing agreement is not affected by retroactive legislation applicable to the taxable period to which the agreement relates where the legislation is silent as to its effect on closing agreements.[30]

C. *Subsequent Court Decisions*
   A closing agreement bars a suit for refund even though a later Supreme Court decision holds that the tax involved is unconstitutional.[31]

D. *Subsequent IRS Action*
   An agreement as to only one year does not preclude the IRS from challenging the agreed-upon matter in a subsequent year. Each tax year stands on its own. Further, the IRS has the right to examine a taxpayer's books and records even after a closing agreement has been entered into to determine whether there has been any fraud, malfeasance, or misrepresentation of a material fact.[32]

E. *Prior Years*
   Sometimes a closing agreement will adjust prior and otherwise barred years, not for the purpose of assessing a deficiency, but for raising a new issue in the event of a carryback.

IX. Miscellaneous Provisions

A. *No Requirement for Liability*

A closing agreement may be executed even though under the agreement the taxpayer is not liable for any tax for the period to which the agreement relates. Also, there may be a series of closing agreements relating to the tax liability for a single period.[33]

B. *General versus Specific Agreements*

Closing agreements with respect to taxable periods ended prior to the date of the agreement may relate to the total liability of the taxpayer or to one or more separate items affecting the tax liability of the taxpayer, as, for example, the amount of gross income, deductions for losses, depreciation, depletion, the year in which an item of income is to be included in gross income, the year in which an item of loss is to be deducted, or the value of property on a specific date.[34]

C. *Deficiency Dividends*

A closing agreement may also be entered into for the purpose of allowing a deficiency dividend under I.R.C. § 547.[35]

D. *Mitigation Applicability*

A closing agreement constitutes a "determination" for mitigation purposes under I.R.C. § 1313(a)(2).[36]

E. *Establishing Basis*

If a taxpayer is uncertain about basis in an asset, he or she can enter into a closing agreement with the IRS establishing such basis for all purposes.[37]

F. *Cases Docketed in U.S. Tax Court*

Once a case has become docketed in tax court, requests for closing agreements will not be granted where they relate to years before the court. However, agreement *can* be reached relating to future years not before the court.[38]

G. *Internal Revenue Manual*

The Internal Revenue Manual contains a section detailing information and instructions pertaining to the procedures and technical aspects involved in the drafting, processing, reviewing, and signing of closing agreements under I.R.C. § 7121. This section is a subset of the appeals (chapter 8) section of the IRM and is found at 8.13 *et seq.*

H. *Transferee Liability*

Closing agreements can determine transferee liability under I.R.C. § 6901. A transferee closing agreement should not be combined with the liability of the transferor.[39]

X. Conclusions and Recommendations

A. If, during the administrative appeals process, the IRS requests a closing agreement as a condition of settling a disputed tax controversy, you can be assured that the agreement will not contain provisions favorable to your client. These types of agreements typically tie your client's hands regarding what he or she can or cannot do in future years. Nevertheless, you may not have a choice if that is the only way a settlement can be reached.

B. In a tax case, if there are some buried skeletons you would not like for the IRS to dig up, you should consider a closing agreement to prevent a reopening of the case. Thus a practitioner should always consider requesting a closing agreement where there is a danger that subsequent reopening of the case would raise substantial civil or criminal issues. However, in a case being litigated, this should not be necessary since the court's decision makes the case res judicata (meaning the case cannot be reopened for any reason).

C. Because of their finality, the IRS is reluctant to enter into closing agreements at the request of taxpayers. Therefore, it may take some creative persuasion to convince the IRS that you have a valid reason for wanting the agreement.

D. To avoid the result in the *Himmelwright*[40] case, counsel for taxpayers should insert a provision in a closing agreement that any subsequent, and at present unknown, net operating loss or similar event giving rise to a carryback may be carried back for purposes of claiming a refund of all or part of any tax agreed to in the closing agreement for the taxable year.

XI. Notes

1. I.R.C. § 7121(a).
2. Rev. Proc. 68-16, 1968-1 CB 770.
3. *Id.*
4. *Id.*
5. Rev. Rul. 73-459, 1973-2 CB 415.
6. *See generally* IRM 8.13.
7. IRM 8.13.1.1.3.
8. Maloney v. Comm'r, 51 T.C.M. (CCH) 572 (1986).
9. I.R.C. § 7121(b)(2).
10. Wolverine Petrol. Corp. v. Comm'r, 75 F.2d 593, 15 AFTR 254 (8th Cir. 1935).
11. Phx. Ins. Co. v. Comm'r, 29 B.T.A. 291 (1933).
12. Rev. Rul. 73-459, 1973-2 CB 415.
13. Comm'r v. Ingram, 87 F.2d 915, 18 AFTR 839 (3d Cir. 1937).
14. Holmes & Jaynes, Inc., 30 B.T.A. 74 (1934).
15. I.R.C. § 7121(b).
16. Phillips v. Comm'r, 38 AFTR 1038 (3d Cir. 1949).
17. Wheelock v. Comm'r, 28 B.T.A. 611 (1933).

18. IRM 8.13.1.1.4; *see* Delegation Order No. 97 (Rev. 9), 1971-1 CB 656.
19. Treas. Reg. § 601.502(c)(1); IRM 8.13.1.2.5.2.
20. Dorl v. Comm'r, 34 AFTR2d 74-6230 (2d Cir. 1974).
21. IRM 8.13.1.2.5.
22. IRM 8.13.1.2.5.
23. Treas. Reg. § 301.7121-1(d)(1); IRM 8.13.1.2.
24. IRM 8.13.1.2.3.
25. *See* IRM 8.13.1.1.1.
26. IRM 8.13.1.3.1.
27. IRM 8.13.1.1.1.
28. Treas. Reg. § 301.7121-1(b)(3).
29. Treas. Reg. § 301.7121-1(c).
30. Rev. Rul. 56-322, 1956-2 CB 963.
31. Great S. Life Ins. Co. v. United States, 70 Ct. Cl. 439, 8 AFTR 11,139 (Cl. Ct. 1930).
32. Harrah's Club v. United States, 81-2 USTC ¶ 9677 (Cl. Ct. 1981); Rev. Rul. 72-487, 1972-2 CB 645.
33. Treas. Reg. § 301.7121-1(b)(1).
34. Treas. Reg. § 301.7121-1(b)(2).
35. *Id.*
36. *Id.* § 301.7121-1(b)(2).
37. *Id.* § 301.7121-1(b)(4).
38. *Id.* § 301.7121-1(d)(1).
39. IRM 8.13.1.2.19(2) (5-3-2001).
40. Himmelwright v. Comm'r, 55 T.C.M. (CCH) 403 (1988). Note, however, that *Himmelwright* involved a "settlement" agreement in a case pending before the Tax Court, not a "closing" agreement. Regardless, the same advice should apply.

Collection Due Process (CDP) Hearings

I. Introduction

A. History

Availability of CDP hearings was brought about by the IRS Restructuring and Reform Act of 1998.[1] When President Clinton signed this act into law, a major policy shift occurred, primarily as a result of prior congressional testimony unfavorable to the IRS's "collection tactics." Before this enactment, taxpayers were not entitled to an administrative or judicial review of actual and threatened enforcement actions of the IRS. But as a result of this new law, the playing field has now been leveled somewhat.

B. Effective Date

Section 6320, enacted as part of the new act, is effective as of January 19, 1999. Accordingly, relief in the form of CDP hearings is unavailable for liens filed before that date.[2] Note that new section 6330 (regarding levies) has the same effective date for levies issued after January 19, 1999. If a lien is filed before the effective date of Public Law No. 105-206, but a levy action is commenced after the effective date, does the tax court acquire jurisdiction? The answer is yes, since § 6320 and § 6330 create separate causes of action.[3]

C. Coordination of Due Process Provisions

There are two separate provisions in the Internal Revenue Code dealing with due process. One has to do with liens,[4] and the other deals with levies.[5] For the sake of efficiency, hearings conducted pursuant to I.R.C. § 6320 are, if possible, coordinated with those held under § 6330.[6] Sections 6320 and 6330 are companion sections, with the former dealing with liens and the latter dealing with levies, but essentially the two different provisions are procedurally identical.

II. Notice of Lien Filings

A. *General Notice Requirements*

The IRS is required to notify a taxpayer in writing each time a notice of federal tax lien (NFTL) is filed in the public records (typically in the courthouse of the county in which the taxpayer resides).[7] There are various online services available to determine whether such a lien has been filed in a particular county.

B. *Delivery of Notice*

There are specific statutory requirements that the IRS must meet to satisfy the "notice" requirement. The lien notice must be delivered in one of three ways:

1. Hand delivery,
2. Leaving the notice at the taxpayer's home or office, or
3. Sending the notice by certified or registered mail to the taxpayer's "last known address."

Importantly, the notice must also be delivered within five days of the filing of the lien notice.[8]

Since the delivery date starts a critical thirty-day period running, one should carefully determine when this occurs. Notice properly sent to the taxpayer by certified mail is sufficient to start the running of this thirty-day period. Actual receipt is not a prerequisite for the validity of the CDP notice.[9]

C. *Information to Be Included*

The lien-filing notice must include an explanation of four items, in simple and nontechnical terms:

1. The amount of the unpaid tax,
2. The right of the taxpayer to request a hearing during the thirty-day period beginning five days after the filing of the lien,
3. The administrative appeals available to the taxpayer with respect to the lien and the procedures relating to such appeals, and
4. The procedures related to obtaining a release of the lien.[10]

D. *Appeals Hearing Request*

If the taxpayer feels that the lien filing is defective, illegal, or otherwise inappropriate, he or she may request that a hearing be held in the nearest IRS Appeals Office.[11]

E. *Multiple NFTLs*

A taxpayer is entitled to only one CDP hearing under § 6320 for the type of tax and the tax periods with respect to the *first* filing of an NFTL. Thereafter, if a taxpayer does not request a CDP hearing with respect to that first NFTL in a timely manner, he or she forgoes the right to a CDP hearing with respect to any subsequent NFTL regarding the same period(s).[12]

III. Notice before Levy

A. *General Notice Rules*

Unlike a notice of tax lien filing, a notice of levy must be given in writing *before* the fact.[13] This notice must advise the taxpayer that he or she has the right to a CDP hearing. The IRS must send this notice only once per tax period. Unfortunately, this means that years can go by before the taxpayer actually experiences a levy. In the intervening time period, a taxpayer may become complacent and may not realize that a levy could come at any time. For this reason, notices of intent to levy must be dealt with seriously and quickly. In any event, the IRS must wait at least thirty days after the notice of intent to levy before the first levy is actually attempted.[14]

B. *Methods of Levy Notice*

There are only three specified methods of giving a notice of intent to levy. These are as follows:
1. Personal hand delivery,
2. Left at the taxpayer's home or office, or
3. Sent by certified mail (return receipt requested) to the taxpayer's last known address.[15]

If a levy is attempted without proof of delivery of this notice, the IRS is required to release the levy.

C. *Information to Be Included*

The levy notice provisions contain a companion statute to § 6320, with the difference being that the notice of intent to levy is somewhat more detailed. All of the following "simple and nontechnical" terms must be included:
1. The amount of the unpaid tax;
2. The right of the taxpayer to request a CDP hearing within the thirty-day period specified in § 6330(a)(2); and
3. A statement that sets forth
   a. An explanation of levy and sales procedures,
   b. The administrative appeals available regarding levies,
   c. Alternatives available that could prevent a levy (such as installment agreements), and
   d. Provisions relating to redemption of property and release of liens.[16]

Note that the notice of intent to levy is not required to itemize the property the IRS seeks to levy on.[17]

D. *Time Limit for Submitting Request*

The thirty-day time limit for § 6320 requests are slightly different from those of § 6330 requests. For "lien" hearings, the thirty days begin to run after the five-business-day period following the filing of the NFTL. For "levy" hearings, the thirty-day period commences the day after the date of the CDP notice letter.[18]

IV. Appeals Hearings

A. *Matters Considered*

Generally, the matters to be considered at CDP hearings are the same at both "lien" hearings as well as "levy" hearings. Similarly, the suspension of the "collection" statute of limitations applies to both types of hearings.[19] It is anticipated that the IRS will combine "levy" and "lien" hearings whenever possible. If multiple hearings are held, to the extent practicable the same officer will handle all issues. If there is a single hearing covering lien as well as levy issues, the taxpayer is obligated to raise all relevant issues at such hearing.[20]

A taxpayer may raise any relevant issue at a CDP hearing, including any of the following:

1.   Any innocent spouse defenses;
2.   Challenges to the appropriateness of collection actions;
3.   Offers of collection alternatives, which may include the following:
     a.   Posting of a bond,
     b.   Substitution of other assets,
     c.   Withdrawal of an NFTL in circumstances that will facilitate collection of the tax,[21]
     d.   An installment agreement, or
     e.   An offer in compromise; and
4.   A challenge to the validity of the underlying tax liability if, for example, a taxpayer did not receive a deficiency notice or have an opportunity to dispute the liability, even if it is a liability reported on a duly filed return.[22]

     The ultimate decision of the appeals or settlement officer handling the hearing must take into consideration the following items:
     •   Verification obtained from collection personnel;
     •   All issues raised by the taxpayer; and (most importantly)
     •   Whether any proposed collection action balances the need for efficient collection of taxes with the legitimate concern of the person that any collection action be no more intrusive than necessary.[23]

B. *Precluded Issues*

A taxpayer may not raise an issue at a CDP hearing if such issue was raised and considered at any previous hearing, administrative proceeding, or judicial proceeding. This assumes that the taxpayer participated meaningfully in such hearing or proceeding. Of course, if there has been a change of circumstances, the previously considered issue may be revisited.[24]

If a taxpayer has chosen previously not to contest the validity of a proposed assessment, the officer may not include a discussion of that issue in his or her final determination. For example, if a taxpayer was sent a deficiency notice and chose not to petition the tax court, he or she is precluded from challenging the existence or amount of the tax liability in a subsequent CDP hearing.[25] Similarly, if a "responsible person" has received a sixty-day letter inviting him or her to challenge a trust fund recovery penalty (TFRP) under § 6672, this person must avail him- or herself of the opportunity to appeal administratively. If the person does not do so, he or she forfeits the right to challenge the TFRP assessment in a CDP hearing.[26]

C. *One Hearing per Period, and Impartiality*

A taxpayer is entitled to only one hearing per taxable period to which the lien filing relates.[27] Note that there appears to be no prohibition, though, against having a single hearing for purposes of discussing multiple periods.

CDP hearings conducted pursuant to § 6320 or § 6330 must be presided over by an IRS employee who has had no prior involvement with the particular case under consideration.[28] This means that typically a hearing will be conducted by an appeals or settlement officer instead of a revenue officer or his or her group manager. A taxpayer may also waive this requirement, although this author cannot think of a good reason to do so.

The ex parte communications prohibition[29] applies to the Appeals Office's consideration of CDP cases and other cases arising in the IRS Collection function. IRS Appeals may not engage in discussions of the strengths and weaknesses of the issues and positions in the case, which appear to compromise IRS Appeals' independence.[30]

D. *Investigation*

At a CDP hearing the AO is required first to obtain verification from IRS Collection personnel that all requirements of any applicable law or administrative procedure have been met.[31]

IRS verifications are required to include (but are not limited to) showings that

1. the revenue officer recommending the collection action has verified the taxpayer's liability;
2. the estimated expenses of levy and sale will not exceed the value of the property seized;

3. the revenue officer has determined that there is sufficient equity in the property to be seized to yield net proceeds from sale to apply to the unpaid tax liabilities; and

4. with respect to the seizure of the assets of a going business, the revenue officer recommending the collection action has thoroughly considered the facts of the case, including the availability of alternative collection methods, before recommending the collection action.[32]

E. *Suspension of Enforcement and Collection Statute of Limitations*

If a "levy" CDP hearing request is filed, all levy actions and the running of the § 6502 statute of limitations are automatically suspended. The suspension period starts on the day of the filing of the hearing request and ends ninety days after the AO issues his or her final "determination" letter. Notwithstanding § 7421(a), the anti-injunction statute, IRS may be enjoined from taking levy action during the CDP hearing process, including any court appeal.[33] As a precautionary measure, a practitioner who requests a CDP hearing would be well advised to reemphasize this enforcement prohibition in his or her cover letter accompanying the Form 12153.

Note that once a § 6330 CDP notice is issued, only *levy* action is required to be suspended. Revenue officers may file liens, even nominee liens, while a CDP hearing and appeal thereof are pending.[34]

A taxpayer is entitled to only one CDP hearing for the periods specified in the CDP notice. Accordingly, any subsequent consideration by IRS Appeals pursuant to its retained jurisdiction is not a continuation of the original CDP hearing and does not suspend the periods of limitation.[35]

F. *Hearings Procedures*

Unfortunately, the statutory provisions do not define the nature of a CDP hearing. The formal hearing procedures required under the Administrative Procedure Act, 5 U.S.C. §§ 551 *et seq.*, do not apply to CDP hearings. CDP hearings are informal in nature and do not necessarily require face-to-face meetings. A transcript or recording of the proceeding is not required. The taxpayer does not have the right to subpoena and examine witnesses at these proceedings.[36] Taxpayers are given the option of having the hearings conducted by correspondence or by telephone.[37] Taxpayers are expected to provide all relevant information requested by IRS Appeals, including financial statements, for its consideration of the facts and issues involved in the hearing.[38]

At least one district court has held that CDP hearings are required to be somehow preserved through audiotape, videotape, or stenographic recording. Otherwise, the administrative record is inadequate for judicial review.[39] Following the promulgation of this decision, the

IRS issued a nonacquiescence, stating, "We do not believe that § 6320 and 6330 require a CDP hearing to be recorded verbatim. Congress did not intend [for] CDP hearings to be conducted in a manner different from proceedings in Appeals instituted prior to the 1998 Act."[40]

Subsequent to the nonacquiescence to the *Mesa Oil* case, the IRS's chief counsel's office issued a notice approving audio recordings by taxpayers in face-to-face conferences with IRS Appeals. This notice also emphasized that if a taxpayer's arguments consist solely of frivolous or groundless positions, a face-to-face conference will not be allowed.[41]

The current position of the tax court seems to be that an audio recording will be permitted in CDP hearings held at the IRS Appeals Office. However, if an audio recording is not made at the original hearing, the court will not remand the case back to IRS Appeals so that such a recording can be made.[42] In the author's opinion, the better practice is always to make an audio recording of a CDP hearing if you plan to appeal an adverse determination.

G. *Innocent Spouse Defenses*

A taxpayer may not raise an innocent spouse defense at a CDP hearing if the IRS has already made a final determination on that issue in a statutory deficiency notice. If such a defense is permitted, all the rules and regulations under § 66 and § 6015 must be followed.[43]

H. *Assessment Validity*

During a CDP hearing a taxpayer may question the validity of a tax assessment. However, it is not an abuse of an AO's discretion to rely on a Form 4340 to verify that a valid assessment existed.[44]

I. *Final Determination*

At the conclusion of the CDP hearing process, the appeals or settlement officer is required to send to the taxpayer a "notice of determination" by certified mail. This letter must address all issues considered and all taxpayer defenses and allegations. Unless a taxpayer withdraws, in writing, his or her request for a CDP hearing, an AO is required to issue the official notice of determination.[45] This determination is not required to be verified under penalties of perjury.[46]

From a jurisdictional standpoint, the AO's "determination" letter is the equivalent of a notice of deficiency. An absence of such a determination will be grounds for a tax court's dismissal for lack of jurisdiction.[47]

J. *Retained Jurisdiction*

Once the IRS Appeals Office has concluded a CDP hearing and issued a determination letter, it will thereafter retain jurisdiction with respect to that taxpayer in all subsequent hearings. Those subsequent hearings can involve collection actions (taken or proposed) or changes in the taxpayer's circumstances.[48]

V. Late-Filed Requests

A. *Equivalent Hearings*

If a taxpayer fails to make a timely request for a CDP hearing, he or she is not entitled to a CDP hearing. Nevertheless, in such circumstances, he or she may request an "equivalent" hearing at which the same issues may be raised and considered by the AO. The difference between an "equivalent" hearing and a regular CDP hearing is that with the former,

1. there is no suspension of the collection statute of limitations,
2. collection enforcement is not stayed,[49] and
3. there is no judicial review available.[50]

B. *Timeliness Rules*

The timeliness of a CDP hearing request is determined under the rules of I.R.C. § 7502 (timely mailing treated as timely filing and paying) and I.R.C. § 7503 (time for performance of acts where the last day for performance falls on a weekend or holiday).[51]

VI. Judicial Review

A. *General Rules, and Choice of Forum*

At some point after the CDP hearing is held, the AO is required to issue an official determination letter. Within thirty days of the issuance of this determination letter, the taxpayer, if he or she does not agree with the determination, may appeal to a court. The appeal is normally to the U.S. Tax Court. Appeal to the tax court is mandatory if the tax court would have jurisdiction over the type of tax in the CDP notice (for example, income or estate tax).[52] Effective October 2006, the U.S. Tax Court now has jurisdiction to hear all types of CDP litigation, regardless of whether it would have had original jurisdiction of the underlying type of tax liability.[53]

B. *Appeal Period Rules*

If an appeal of the AO's determination is based solely on his or her denial of an innocent spouse defense under § 6015, then, in lieu of the thirty-day appeal period, the taxpayer has ninety days to petition the tax court for review.[54]

If a taxpayer misses the appeal deadline of § 6330(d)(1) following receipt of the AO's determination letter, he or she may not thereafter file a petition with a different court. For example, if he or she petitions the district court late, the tax court cannot thereafter acquire jurisdiction.[55]

C. *De Novo versus Abuse of Discretion Standard*

If the validity of the liability is an issue following an AO's determination, then the court will consider that issue on a de novo basis. On all other issues the appellant taxpayer may challenge the AO's determination on the basis of abuse of discretion.[56]

A claim that the statute of limitations has expired constitutes a challenge to the underlying liability. Accordingly, a court will consider that matter on a de novo basis.[57]

On the other hand, whether a tax has been properly assessed is not considered an issue involving the validity of the underlying tax liability. Accordingly, a court will review such an issue on an abuse of discretion basis. For example, an unsigned Form 4340 is a presumptively valid assessment.[58] Similarly, whether to reinstate a defaulted offer in compromise is an issue to be considered only on an abuse of discretion basis.[59]

D. *Precluded Liability and/or Jurisdiction Issues*

Even if the AO erroneously allows the taxpayer to offer information at the CDP hearing regarding underlying liability, the taxpayer will not be allowed to present such arguments in an appeal to the tax court. This follows the rule that it is only where a taxpayer failed to receive a deficiency notice, or otherwise lacked an earlier opportunity for disputing the liability, that the tax court will consider the underlying liability.[60]

During a CDP hearing an AO is not required to look behind a deficiency notice to determine whether it was properly issued.

As long as the deficiency notice was, in fact, received by the taxpayer, consideration of the underlying liability by the AO is precluded.[61]

Following an examination of his tax or her return by the IRS, if a taxpayer signs a consent to the assessment (Form 870, Form 4549, etc.), he or she is thereafter precluded from raising an underlying liability issue in an appeal of the AO's determination.[62]

The tax court may not expand its jurisdiction in CDP matters to issues it could not otherwise hear. For example, it will dismiss for want of jurisdiction any case brought with respect to a frivolous return penalty.[63]

E. *New and/or Affirmative Issues*

In seeking a tax court or district court review of an AO's determination, the taxpayer can request that the court consider only those issues raised in the CDP hearing. That is to say, the taxpayer may not raise a new or affirmative issue for the first time in the judicial proceeding.[64]

F. *Interest Abatement*

The tax court has jurisdiction to review an AO's determination with regard to interest that is the subject of IRS collection activities. For example, whether IRS delays, justifying abatement under § 6404, are "ministerial acts" may be considered.[65]

G. *Lack of Notice*

If a taxpayer deliberately refuses delivery of a deficiency notice, this will not defeat actual notice. Therefore, if this occurs, he or she will be presumed to have had the opportunity to contest the underlying liability, and the tax court will not entertain an argument of an invalid liability.[66]

H. *Postpetition Motion to Dismiss*

After filing a tax court petition to review an adverse Appeals Office decision, a taxpayer-petitioner will be permitted to file a motion to dismiss his or her own case. In these cases, I.R.C. § 7459(d), regarding dismissal of "deficiency" cases, does not apply.[67]

VII. Miscellaneous Topics

A. *Jeopardy Determinations*

Pre-levy CDP hearings do not normally apply if the IRS has made a determination that the collection of the tax is in jeopardy.[68] However, such hearings are allowed within a reasonable period of time *after* the levy.[69] Expedited administrative and judicial review procedures are also available under I.R.C. § 7429.

A jeopardy or termination assessment must be approved by the IRS District Counsel responsible for the case. Failure to obtain such approval would render the jeopardy or termination assessment void.[70]

B. *Nominee Liens*

A nominee[71] of, or a person holding property of, the taxpayer is not entitled to a CDP hearing. Such a person is not described in I.R.C. § 6321.[72]

C. *Forms Used, Mailing Address*

A request for a CDP hearing cannot be done orally. Such a request can take any written form, but must include the taxpayer's name, address, and daytime telephone number. It must also be signed by the taxpayer or his or her authorized representative. It is recommended that an IRS Form 12153 be completed for this purpose. A Form 12153 can be used for either a lien notice or a threatened levy.[73]

Generally the CDP hearing notice will contain an address to which hearings requests are to be mailed. According to the Form 12153 instructions, if you are working with a particular revenue officer, then the request should be mailed directly to that person for forwarding to the local Appeals Office. Otherwise, use the address indicated.[74]

D. *Time Limit for IRS Appeals to Act on a Request*
There is no period of time within which IRS Appeals must conduct a CDP hearing or issue a notice of determination. However, they will attempt to resolve these matters "as expeditiously as possible under the circumstances."[75]

VIII. Final Observations

Practice Tip

Requests for CDP hearings should be sent via certified mail. Additionally, and particularly where requests are being filed on short notice, a right to supplement should be reserved.[76]

A. It is noteworthy that, with respect to the filing of lien notices, an opportunity for a hearing is not afforded until after the fact, when the damage is already done. Lien-filing notices are frequently noted by business competitors, lenders, and credit-reporting agencies. Subsequent release of an erroneously filed lien may not remove the taint created by the lien.[77]
B. It is expected that a rather large volume of CDP cases will be filed, both administratively and judicially, in the future. It is also anticipated that the mix of cases considered by IRS Appeals and the tax court will be increasingly skewed toward collection issues and away from the more traditional and substantive tax issues.[78]
C. It has been suggested that a practitioner's failure to file a request for a CDP hearing may be tantamount to committing professional malpractice in giving up a substantial procedural right for his or her taxpayer-client.[79]

IX. Notes

1. Pub. L. No. 105-206.
2. Inman v. Comm'r, 81 T.C.M. (CCH) 1583 (2001).
3. Parker v. Comm'r, 117 T.C. 63 (2001).
4. Subch. C, pt. I.
5. Subch. D, pt. I.
6. I.R.C. § 6320(b)(4).
7. I.R.C. § 6320(a)(1).
8. I.R.C. § 6320(a)(2).
9. Temp. Treas. Reg. § 301.6320-1(a)(2), Q-A 11.
10. I.R.C. § 6320(a)(3).
11. I.R.C. § 6320(b)(1).
12. Treas. Reg. § 301.6320-1(b)(3), Q-A B 1.
13. I.R.C. § 6330(a)(1).
14. I.R.C. § 6330(a)(2).

15. Note that these methods are identical to the delivery methods for lien notices.
16. I.R.C. § 6330(a)(3).
17. H.R. Conf. Rep. No. 105-599.
18. Treas. Reg. § 301.6320-1(c) (2), Q-A C 3.
19. I.R.C. § 6320(c).
20. H.R. Conf. Rep. No. 105-599.
21. Treas. Reg. § 301.6320-1(e)(3), Q-A E6.
22. I.R.C. § 6330(c)(2); Montgomery v. Comm'r, 122 T.C. 1 (2004).
23. I.R.C. § 6330(c)(3).
24. I.R.C. § 6330(c)(4).
25. Treas. Reg. § 301.6320-1(e)(4), ex. 1.
26. Dami v. Internal Revenue Serv., 2002-1 USTC ¶ 50,433 (W.D. Pa. 2002).
27. I.R.C. § 6320(b)(2).
28. I.R.C. § 6320(b)(3).
29. *See* Pub. L. No. 105-206, Act § 1001(a)(4).
30. Rev. Proc. 2000-43, 2000-43 I.R.B. 404.
31. I.R.C. § 6330(c)(1). Note that a proposed collection action should not be approved solely because the IRS shows that it has followed appropriate procedures. S. Conf. Rep. No. 105-174.
32. S. Conf. Rep. No. 105-174.
33. I.R.C. § 6330(e)(1); Treas. Reg. § 301.6320-1(g)(2), Q-A G3.
34. CCA 199934019.
35. Treas. Reg. § 301.6320-1(h)(2), Q-A H1.
36. Treas. Reg. § 301.6320-1(d)(2), Q-A, D6; *see also* Davis v. Comm'r, 115 T.C. 35 (2000).
37. Treas. Reg. § 301.6320-1(d)(2), Q-A, D7.
38. Treas. Reg. § 301.6320-1(e)(1).
39. Mesa Oil, Inc. v. United States, 2001-1 USTC ¶ 50,130 (D. Colo. 2001). For a discussion of the *Mesa Oil* case, see Paul W. Raymond, *Collection Due Process: What's New, What's Changed, and Lingering Issues*, 3(1) J. Tax Prac. & Procedure 19 (2001).
40. CBS 200140081.
41. Chief Counsel Notice CC-2003-031.
42. Keene v. Comm'r, 121. T.C. 8 (2003); Frey v. Comm'r, 87 T.C.M. (CCH) at 1181 (2004).
43. Treas. Reg. § 301.6320-1(e)(1).
44. Lunsford v. Comm'r, 117 T.C. 159 (2001).
45. Treas. Reg. § 6320-1(e)(3), Q-A E8.
46. Davis v. Comm'r, 115 T.C. 35 (2000).
47. Offiler v. Comm'r, 114 T.C. 492 (2000).
48. I.R.C. § 6330(d)(2).
49. H.R. Conf. Rep. No. 105-599.
50. Treas. Reg. § 301.6320-1(i).
51. Treas. Reg. § 301.6320-1(c), Q-A C4.
52. Treas. Reg. § 301.6330-1(f), Q/A F3; Cortes v. United States, 2002- 2 USTC ¶ 50,601 (D. Nev. 2002).
53. I.R.C. § 6330(d)(1), amended effective for determinations made after the date which is 60 days after August 17, 2006.
54. Treas. Reg. § 301.6320-1(f)(2), Q-A F2.

55. McCune v. Comm'r, 115 T.C. 114 (2000).
56. H.R. Conf. Rep. No. 105-599; Lunsford v. Comm'r, 117 T.C. 159 (2001).
57. Boyd v. Comm'r, 117 T.C. 127 (2001).
58. Nicklaus v. Comm'r, 117 T.C. 117 (2001).
59. Robinette v. Comm'r, 2006-1 USTC ¶ 50,213 (8th Cir. 2006).
60. Behling v. Comm'r, 118 T.C. 572 (2002).
61. Nestor v. Comm'r, 118 T.C. No. 10 (2002).
62. Aguirre v. Comm'r, 117 T.C. 324 (2001).
63. Johnson v. Comm'r, 117 T.C. 18 (2001).
64. Treas. Reg. § 301.6320-1(f)(2), Q-A F3.
65. Katz v. Comm'r, 115 T.C. 329 (2000).
66. Sego v. Comm'r, 114 T.C. 604 (2000) (citing Goza v. Comm'r 114 T.C. 176 (2000)).
67. Wagner v. Comm'r, 118 T.C. 330 (2002).
68. *See* I.R.C. §§ 6861 *et seq.*
69. I.R.C. § 6330(f).
70. H.R. Conf. Rep. No. 105-599.
71. *See* Andrews v. United States, 99-1 USTC ¶ 50,359 (N.D. Ohio) for a discussion of nominee liens.
72. Treas. Reg. § 6320-1(b)(2), Q-A B5.
73. Treas. Reg. § 301.6320-1(c)(2), Q-A C1.
74. Treas. Reg. § 301.6320-1(c)(2), Q-A C6.
75. Treas. Reg. § 301.6320-1(e)(3), Q-A E9.
76. Paul W. Raymond, *Collection Due Process: New Rules, Procedures, and Traps for the Unwary*, 1 J. Tax Prac. & Procedure 25 (1999).
77. Elliott H. Kajan, *A Kinder, Gentler IRS*, 21 L.A. Law. 29 (1998), *reprinted in* 49 Monthly Digest of Tax Articles 10 (1999).
78. Carol M. Luttati, *Knowing and Invoking Your Clients' Collection Due Process Rights*, 1 J. Tax Prac. & Procedure 8 (1999).
79. William A. Roberts, *Collection Due Process Hearing: An Underutilized Tool*, 3(1) J. Tax Prac. & Procedure 30 (2001).

CHAPTER 3

Civil Tax Litigation

Choice of Forum

I. Introduction

A. *General Considerations*

Taxpayers and the Internal Revenue Service have a mutual interest in settling disputed tax cases without the necessity of litigation. Litigation necessarily involves the consumption of enormous amounts of resources. But there are those occasions when litigation of a tax case becomes necessary. Fortunately, tax litigators get to forum-shop. They typically make the decision as to choice of forum based on the tax lawyer's assessment of where the case law is better and whether or not the client can pay the tax before litigation.

B. *Courts of Original Jurisdiction*

There are three[1] possible courts in which to litigate federal tax cases, all of which have concurrent jurisdiction:[2]
1. U.S. Court of Federal Claims,
2. U.S. district courts, and
3. U.S. Tax Court.[3]

C. *Consideration of Precedents*

Avoiding unfavorable precedents may be the primary consideration in selecting a trial forum. One must consider decisions, both favorable and unfavorable, of the following courts: (1) U.S. Tax Court, (2) federal district courts, (3) U.S. Court of Federal Claims, and (4) the circuit court to which appeal would lie.

D. *Orientation of the Judges*

The experience and orientation of the judges of the three courts of original jurisdiction are significantly different. Therefore, this is an important factor in the selection process.

E. *Recovery of Litigation Costs*

If the government's position is not substantially justified, a successful taxpayer can file a motion for recovery of litigation costs regardless of the forum in which suit was brought.[4]

II. U.S. Court of Federal Claims

A. *Jurisdiction*

The U.S. Court of Federal Claims (also known as the claims court) is located in Washington, D.C., and its jurisdiction is limited to claims against the federal government. Therefore, a potential litigant must first pay the tax and then sue for a refund to get into this court. The defendant in these cases is always the United States. Unlike the tax court, the court of federal claims has jurisdiction over any type of federal tax, not just income, estate, or gift taxes.

B. *Location of Trial*

The court of federal claims' hearings and trials are normally heard in Washington, D.C., although the court does have the authority to travel. The cost of litigating in Washington, D.C., can be prohibitively expensive. Therefore, the court of federal claims is best avoided by novices and nonspecialists.

C. *Expertise of Judges*

Judges in the court of federal claims hear all types of claims litigation, not just tax cases. Their expertise is in hearing claims against the government. Accordingly, their tax law expertise may be somewhat limited. This makes it difficult to argue logical but novel positions.

D. *Opposing Counsel*

The government is represented in the court of federal claims by the Department of Justice—Tax Division.

E. *Rules of Practice*

The operative rules for the court of federal claims are the federal rules of the U.S. Court of Federal Claims.

F. *Appeal*

The court of federal claims accepts as binding precedent the published decisions of its own cases, unless modified by the federal circuit or the U.S. Supreme Court. The federal circuit is the only court to which an appeal from the court of federal claims will lie.[5]

III. Federal District Court

A. *Claims for Refund*

Litigation in federal district court is also known as "refund litigation" for the reason that one must pay the tax in full and file a claim for refund (generally by a Form 843 or by an amended return) to get into this court.

B. *Variance Doctrine*

Another factor that must be considered is the "variance doctrine." This doctrine requires that one sue only on claims that are part of the claim for refund. One cannot add additional claims. This means that a claim must be prepared very carefully to include all possible available claims. If a claim omits an essential element, the refund litigation may be impossible for the claimant to win.

C. *Full Payment Rule*

To commence a refund suit in federal district court, the entire amount of income tax must be prepaid to establish the proper jurisdictional prerequisite.[6]

D. *Statutory Periods*

To initiate refund litigation, there are some statutory waiting periods. First, the litigant-taxpayer must file a claim for a refund and then wait until the expiration of the earlier of (1) claim disallowance notification, or (2) six months from the date of claim filing. Moreover, refund litigation may *not* be filed after the expiration of two years from the date of claim disallowance notification. This two-year period may be extended by written agreement.[7]

E. *Orientation of Judges*

In federal district courts the dockets are heavily criminal, and very few tax cases ever get heard there. For the most part the judges have little or no background in tax law. They are generalists, presiding over a wide variety of both criminal and civil litigation.

F. *Jury Trials*

The unique distinction of federal district courts is the availability of juries to try fact issues. That is to say, a taxpayer who wants a trial by jury must bring suit in a federal district court. Jury trials are considered to be appropriate in cases involving the following:
1. Trust fund liability (§ 6672) cases,
2. Valuation issues,
3. Reasonable compensation issues, and
4. Other assessable penalties.

G. *Opposing Counsel*

Opposing counsel in tax cases tried in federal district courts is the Department of Justice—Tax Division. Because the responsibility for defense of a refund suit lies not with the IRS but with the Department of Justice, the Tax Division lawyer is more likely to tax a position that is different from the initial IRS position. Justice Department lawyers have none of the institutional loyalty that is often felt by chief counsel lawyers. Therefore, the possibility for a more reasonable settlement is greater outside the tax court.

H. *Appeal*

Appeal of a federal district court case is made to the court of appeals for the local circuit.

I. *Exclusive Jurisdiction in Specialized Cases*
   1. Preparer penalty litigation can only be brought in federal district court. The tax court and court of federal claims have no jurisdiction to hear these cases.[8]
   2. All actions involving injunctions and summons enforcement are brought only in federal district court.[9]
   3. Suits for wrongful levy are brought only in federal district court.[10]

J. *Summary of District Court Advantages*

If your client can possibly pay the price of admission to the district court, the practitioner should consider not only the saving of interest but also the following advantages:
   1. Having the Justice Department for an opponent,
   2. More and better discovery,
   3. Increased and different settlement pressures,
   4. Flexibility in choosing the finder of fact,
   5. More pressure from the judge to settle,
   6. Availability of "equity" considerations,
   7. A better stage on which to present the case, and
   8. A happier client, regardless of the outcome.[11]

IV. U.S. Tax Court[12]

A. *Organization and Operation*

Details of the organization and operation of the tax court are reserved for another subchapter.

B. *Time for Making a Decision*

Whatever forum is chosen, the decision must be made before the deadline for filing a tax court petition. Once a tax court petition has been filed, § 6512(a) precludes litigation in any other court with respect to the year to which the deficiency notice relates. Therefore, the taxpayer has ninety days from the date of a deficiency notice to make up his or her mind as to which court to litigate his or her case in. In some cases (i.e., in cases other than those involving income, estate, or gift tax), a taxpayer will not have received a deficiency notice. In those cases, the only two choices are the district court and the court of federal claims.

C. *Tax Court Advantages*

The U.S. Tax Court is the forum of choice for many reasons. Most importantly, one does not have to pay the tax before filing suit. Additionally, tax court judges hear nothing but tax cases, and they are very good at it. Tax court judges generally come from a background of tax law practice, either in or out of government service. Therefore, they have significant technical expertise not usually found on the district court and court of federal claims benches.

The tax court is the least expensive of the three available tribunals. This is because of the restricted "discovery" process, an emphasis on the stipulation process, and the shortness of the trials.

D. *Tax Court Disadvantages*

In addition to the unavailability of a jury, a tax court judge is far less likely to yield to equitable arguments than is the case with a district court or claims court judge. Additionally, settling a case with IRS counsel following an adverse appeals officer decision often becomes problematic. This is because of the symbiotic relationship that exists between appeals officers and counsel. On the other hand, Department of Justice lawyers are more removed from the people who set up the deficiency in the first place.

E. *Institutional Bias*

If a practitioner is considering which court to litigate in, it is probably because things have not gone well within the administrative machinery of the IRS. If the Appeals Office adopts the examiner's position, there is an institutional bias toward staying with that position into the litigation arena. This is a danger when litigating in tax court because your opponent is the IRS's lawyer, as opposed to some other agency's lawyer. In district court or the court of federal claims, the Justice Department lawyers tend to be less prosecutorial than the chief counsel lawyers in tax court.[13] There are those practitioners who cynically observe that, despite its relatively new "constitutional" status, the tax court is and always will be an arm of the executive branch of the government.

F. *Discovery*

As a general proposition, discovery usually benefits only the IRS. This is because the taxpayer is in full command of all of the facts giving rise to the dispute. District court discovery procedures are much more liberal than in tax court. The discovery restrictions in tax court are contained in its Rules of Practice and Procedure.[14] Also, the tax court rules require the parties to stipulate all relevant, nonprivileged matters to the fullest extent possible.[15] This is the reason that tax court practitioners rely so heavily on Freedom of Information Act requests, *Branerton* exchanges, and the stipulation process.

G. *Appeal*

Appeal of a tax court decision is heard by a circuit court for the circuit in which the petitioner's legal residence is located.[16] Note that the tax court will normally follow decisions in the circuit to which an appeal of its decisions would lie.[17] A taxpayer's "residence" has been defined to mean his or her "domicile."[18] In the case of an estate, there is some question as to whether it is the residence of the executor(s) or the residence of the decedent at the time of his or her death is controlling on the appeals venue question.[19] The Eleventh Circuit treats as binding precedent decisions of the Fifth Circuit issued before the creation of the Eleventh Circuit in 1981.

The tax court is the only forum where the taxpayer gets to select the geographical area where his or her case is tried. At the time he or she files a petition, the taxpayer may select any city he or she wishes as long as it is a city where the tax court customarily hears cases. This selection is, however, not controlling on the question of appeals venue. Thus, while a taxpayer gets to forum-shop and venue-shop (in tax court), he or she does not get to "circuit-shop."

H. *Financial Considerations*

More often than not, a taxpayer's financial circumstances determine where suit is filed. Often the U.S. Tax Court is the forum of choice because only there can the merits of the case be litigated prior to the payment of the tax. For this reason the tax court presides over the vast majority of tax litigation. Indeed, the I.R.C. itself is structured to channel tax litigation to the tax court.[20]

Interest is also a factor in deciding where to litigate. If the taxpayer is an astute investor, he or she may choose the tax court on the theory that, even if he or she loses, he or she can earn more than the underpayment interest rate charged by the IRS under § 6621(a). If not, he or she can either litigate in district court (where prepayment of the tax is mandated) or litigate in the court of federal claims. If prepayment of the tax is desired in tax court to stop the running of interest, there are two ways to do it. A taxpayer can make a remittance before the issuance of a deficiency notice by following the procedures of Rev. Proc. 84-58,[21] or by making a remittance after filing a tax court petition. Otherwise a taxpayer would run the risk of depriving the tax court of jurisdiction, which depends on the existence of a "deficiency."[22]

I. *Equitable Considerations*

The tax court is far less likely than either the district court or the court of federal claims to hear equitable arguments.

J. *Jurisdictional Limitations*

While the current trend has been toward expansion of tax court jurisdiction, there are certain types of cases that it simply has no jurisdiction to hear. For example, litigation involving "trust fund" liability
must be brought in either the federal district court or the court of federal claims.[23]

V. Notes

1. Note that if a taxpayer is also a debtor in a bankruptcy case, the federal bank-
    ruptcy court hearing the Title 11 case has plenary jurisdiction also to determine
    federal tax liabilities by conducting a full trial on the merits.
2. Subject to some unique jurisdictional requirements of each court.
3. See the separate subchapter dealing in greater detail with the jurisdiction and
    operation of the U.S. Tax Court. Greater emphasis is given to the Tax Court than
    to other courts because of its popularity and its handling of the vast majority of
    litigated federal tax cases.
4. I.R.C. § 7430(c)(6).
5. 28 U.S.C. § 1295(a)(3).
6. Flora v. United States, 5 AFTR2d 1046 (S. Ct. 1960).
7. I.R.C. § 6532(a).
8. *See* I.R.C. § 6694(c)(2).
9. I.R.C. § 7402.
10. I.R.C. § 7426.
11. For an excellent discussion on this topic, see Roberts, *Bringing Tax Cases in District
    Court: The Other Considerations*, Taxes—Tax Mag., Mar. 1991, at 167. Also see Jones,
    Challenging the IRS in Court, J. Tax Prac. & Procedure, June–July 2001, at 27.
12. The predecessor of the U.S. Tax Court was known as the Board of Tax Appeals,
    which functioned between the years 1924 and 1942. The name was changed to
    the United States Tax Court by the Revenue Act of 1942. The Tax Reform Act of
    1969 established the Tax Court as a constitutional court and removed it from
    the Executive Branch of the government.
13. *Supra* note 11.
14. T.C. Rules 75, 90(a).
15. T.C. Rule 91.
16. I.R.C. § 7482(b)(1); T.C. Rule 190.
17. Golsen v. Comm'r, 54 T.C. 742 (1970). Note also that appeals venue can lie in any
    circuit if both parties so stipulate in writing. I.R.C. § 7482(b)(2).
18. Brewin v. Comm'r, 72 T.C. 1055 (1979). Domicile is the place where a person has
    his true, fixed, and permanent home, and to which whenever he is absent he
    has the intention of returning.
19. See the discussion in Judge Gerber's concurring opinion in *Estate of Clack v.
    Comm'r*, 106 T.C. 131 (1996), a case reviewed by the entire court.
20. Estate of Mueller v. Comm'r, 101 T.C. 551 at 564 (1993).
21. 1984-2 CB 501.
22. Paccon, Inc. v. Comm'r, 45 T.C. 392 (1966).
23. *See, e.g.*, Gordon v. Comm'r, 39 T.C.M. (CCH) 769 (1979).

Deficiency Procedures

I. Definitions

A. *Definition of a Deficiency*

Since the U.S. Tax Court has jurisdiction only if there is a "deficiency," it is important to know what a deficiency is and is not. Its definition is the amount by which the "correct" tax (including self-employment tax) exceeds the tax shown by a taxpayer upon his or her return ("tax per return"; see definition below):

+ any previous assessments,
– any "rebates" (defined as previous refunds resulting from a change to reported liability).

The "correct" tax is the tax as determined by the IRS whether or not the taxpayer ultimately agrees with it.[1]

B. *Tax per Return*

The tax per return is determined without regard to withholding credits under § 31.[2] If a taxpayer has not filed a return, the tax per return is considered to be zero.[3]

C. *Estimated Tax Payments*

Payments of estimated tax are also disregarded in the determination of a deficiency.[4]

D. *Amended Returns*

Any amount shown as additional tax on an amended return (1040-X, 1120-X, etc.) is treated as an amount shown by the taxpayer "upon his [or her] return" for purposes of computing a deficiency.[5]

E. *Disallowed Earned Income Credit*

Effective in 1988 the definition of a deficiency was expanded to permit taxpayers to contest the disallowance of refundable credits[6] in tax court, notwithstanding that these credits reduce the net tax liability to less than zero.[7]

II. "Notices" of Deficiency

A. Mailing Requirements

If the IRS determines, as a result of an audit of a tax return, that there is a "deficiency," they are authorized to send a "notice" of that deficiency to the taxpayer by certified or registered mail. Unknown to many practitioners is the fact that this notice is actually the beginning of litigation with the government.[8]

B. Nonreceipt by the Taxpayer

It is the IRS's burden to prove that it sent the deficiency notice to the taxpayer by certified mail. If the IRS can show that its Form 3877 (a listing of all deficiency notices mailed on a particular day) had the taxpayer's name and a certified mail number, it will have met its burden. Even if the taxpayer never ultimately receives the deficiency notice, the IRS will prevail in subsequent litigation concerning whether the tax court has jurisdiction over an untimely filed petition.[9]

C. Last Known Address

Notices of deficiency are required to be sent by the IRS to taxpayers at their last "known address." This rule applies even if a taxpayer is deceased or a corporate taxpayer has gone out of existence. An exception applies, however, if a deceased's fiduciary files the proper notice with the IRS. If the IRS fails to use proper diligence in determining a taxpayer's address, the deficiency notice can be set aside in court.[10]

D. Joint versus Separate Returns

If a joint return is filed, a single deficiency notice is sent to both husband and wife. However, if the IRS has been notified of a separation, they are required to send a duplicate original to each spouse.[11]

E. Estate Tax

In the case of an estate tax deficiency, the "notice" is required to be sent to the estate's executor or other personal representative of the estate.[12] Issuance of an estate tax "closing letter" does not preclude the IRS from reopening an examination of a decedent's estate tax return in determining a deficiency.[13]

F. Additional Notices and Issues

If the IRS issues a deficiency notice, it cannot thereafter issue additional notices for the same year as long as the taxpayer files a proper petition with the U.S. Tax Court.[14] If no petition is filed, however, this rule would seem not to preclude the issuance by the IRS of multiple deficiency notices.

However, one should note that the IRS lawyer can still raise additional issues in court and the tax court can determine additional tax beyond what is in the deficiency notice.[15]

The IRS can amend its answer and include an issue not raised in the deficiency notice as long as the taxpayer's efforts to prepare for trial are not hindered.[16]

G. *Time within Which to File a Petition*

Following the issuance of a deficiency notice, the taxpayer has only ninety days within which to file a "petition" with the U.S. Tax Court. This ninety-day period is strictly observed and cannot in any way be extended.[17]

Pursuant to the 1998 IRS Restructuring and Reform Act, in an uncodified provision, the IRS is required on each notice of deficiency to include the date that is the last date on which the taxpayer may file a petition to the U.S. Tax Court.[18] The question of what happens when this date is omitted has been litigated. In a reviewed opinion (10–6), the tax court has held that a deficiency notice without such a date is valid and that a taxpayer's untimely petition will be dismissed.[19]

H. *Untimely Notices*

Once a taxpayer establishes a prima facie case that a deficiency notice was not timely, the burden of proof shifts to the government, which must then produce an extension agreement executed by the taxpayer.[20] If the IRS cannot do this, the deficiency will be barred by the statute of limitations.

Practice Tip

An astute practitioner should always raise the statute of limitations as an issue any time that an untimely petition is received by his or her client.

I. *IRS Errors*

An inconsequential transposition error on the cover page of the deficiency notice will not cause such notice to be invalid, as long as the taxpayer is not misled by the error.[21]

III. Assessment of a Deficiency

A. A deficiency cannot be assessed if a taxpayer has filed a tax court petition. If no petition is filed, the deficiency is assessed by default after the ninety days have expired. If a petition is filed, there is no assessment until the tax court decision becomes final.[22]

B. Whatever amount of deficiency is finally determined by the U.S. Tax Court is thereafter assessed and can be collected by the IRS in the normal enforcement manner. If the tax court reduces the amount of the original deficiency, the amount of that reduction cannot be assessed or collected.[23]

IV. Rescission of a Deficiency Notice

A. *General Rule*
Starting in 1987 the IRS has authority to rescind a deficiency notice after its issuance, but only with the consent of the taxpayer.[24] Once the notice is properly rescinded, it is treated as if it never existed. In the experience of the author, this rescission procedure has never been utilized.

B. *Grounds*
Grounds for rescission of a deficiency notice:
1. The notice was issued due to an administrative error.
2. A taxpayer submits information showing a lesser amount of tax due.
3. A taxpayer wants a conference with the IRS Appeals Office and the case is susceptible of settlement.[25]

V. "Math" Errors

A. A notice from the IRS of a mathematical or clerical error (appearing on the return) is not normally considered a "deficiency notice." However, within sixty days of such a notice a taxpayer may file an abatement request. The IRS must then abate the tax, and any subsequent reassessment is subject to deficiency procedures.[26]

VI. Penalties

A. *Underpayment Penalty*
The "failure to pay" penalty (0.5 percent per month up to 25 percent) can be imposed on a "deficiency" as well as on a tax per return that has not been paid.[27] In the case of a deficiency, the underpayment penalty can be imposed only after the IRS mails out a demand notice.[28]

B. *"Additions" to Tax*
The type of penalties known as additions to tax are contained in part I of chapter 68 of the I.R.C.[29] They may be imposed and collected without the requirement of a deficiency notice and assessment.[30]

C. *Preparer and Other Penalties*

Normal deficiency procedures do not apply to the following penalties:

1. Promoting abusive tax shelters (I.R.C. § 6700),
2. Aiding and abetting understatement of tax liability (I.R.C. § 6701), and
3. Frivolous tax return (I.R.C. § 6702).

Instead, these cases must be litigated in federal district court, where the burden of proof is on the IRS.[31]

VII. Prepayments

A. If all or part of the tax is paid *after* the mailing of a deficiency notice, the tax court still will not be deprived of jurisdiction.[32]

B. A portion of any proposed deficiency can be prepaid to stop the running of interest. A taxpayer can also specify the amount of his or her payment allocated to interest.[33]

VIII. Miscellaneous

A. *Tax Shelter Promotion Penalties*

Normal deficiency procedures do not apply to tax shelter promotion penalties imposed pursuant to I.R.C. § 6700, 6701, and 6702.[34]

B. *Estate Tax Payouts*

If an estate tax deficiency has been assessed at a time when the estate has elected a long-term payout under I.R.C. § 6166, the amount of the deficiency is prorated over the remaining unpaid installments.[35]

C. *Deficiency Payment Extensions*

The IRS may extend the time for the payment of any amount determined as a deficiency for a period not to exceed eighteen months plus another twelve months in exceptional circumstances.[36]

D. *Thirty-Day Letters*

If a taxpayer is sent a thirty-day letter instead of a deficiency notice, then follow the procedures for preparing protests if you do not agree with the proposed deficiency.[37]

Practice Tip

Note that there are some practitioners who always prefer the receipt of a deficiency notice under the theory that it is far less likely that the government will discover or raise a new issue when a case is in docketed status.

E. *Tax Court Jurisdiction*

It is the existence of a deficiency at the time of issuing a deficiency notice that confers jurisdiction upon the tax court. If there is a net overassessment at that time, the case will be dismissed for want of jurisdiction.[38]

There is a substantive requirement that the IRS "determine" a deficiency prior to issuing a notice. Where the "notice" is patently defective on its face, it will not confer jurisdiction on the tax court. For example, the IRS's failure to review a taxpayer's 1040 is a fatal defect.[39]

F. *Nonfilers*

A valid determination of a deficiency can be determined against a taxpayer even though he or she has not filed any tax return.[40]

G. *Partnership Items*

"Partnership items" are not included in computing a deficiency notice of non-partnership items.

IX. Notes

1. I.R.C. § 6211(a).
2. I.R.C. § 6211(b).
3. Treas. Reg. § 301.6211-1(a).
4. *Id.*
5. *Id.*
6. Primarily the refundable child credit (I.R.C. § 24(d)), the earned income credit (I.R.C. § 32), and nonresident alien withholding credits (I.R.C. § 33).
7. I.R.C. § 6211(b)(4); Wilson v. Comm'r, 81 T.C.M. (CCH) 1745 (2001).
8. I.R.C. § 6211(a).
9. Barrash v. Comm'r, 54 T.C.M. (CCH) 1230 (1987).
10. I.R.C. § 6212(b)(1).
11. I.R.C. § 6212(b)(2).
12. I.R.C. § 6212(b)(3).
13. Bommer Estate v. Comm'r, 69 T.C.M. (CCH) 2541 (1995).
14. I.R.C. § 6212(c).
15. I.R.C. § 6214(a).
16. Braude v. Comm'r, 87-1 1 USTC ¶ 9140 (4th Cir. 1986).
17. I.R.C. § 6213(a).
18. Pub. L. No. 105-206, Act § 6463(a).
19. Rochelle v. Comm'r, 116 T.C. 356 (2001), *aff'd*, 2001 USTC ¶ 50,447 (5th Cir. 2002) (per curiam).
20. Persson v. Comm'r, 58 T.C.M. (CCH) 409 (1989).
21. Stussy v. Comm'r, 84 T.C.M. (CCH) 439 (2002).
22. I.R.C. § 6215.
23. I.R.C. § 6215(a).
24. I.R.C. § 6212(d).

25. Rev. Proc. 88-17, 1988-2 CB 692.
26. I.R.C. § 6213(b).
27. I.R.C. § 6651(a)(3).
28. Treas. Reg. § 301.6651-1(a)(3).
29. Generally I.R.C. §§ 6651–6658.
30. *See, e.g.,* Bob Hamrick Chevrolet, Inc. v. United States, 94-1 USTC ¶ 50,178 (W.D. Tex. 1994).
31. I.R.C. § 6703.
32. I.R.C. § 6213(b)(4).
33. Rev. Proc. 84-58, 84-2 CB 501; Perkins v. Comm'r, 92 T.C. 749 (1989).
34. I.R.C. § 6703.
35. I.R.C. § 6166(e).
36. I.R.C. § 6161(b)(1).
37. Treas. Reg. § 601.105(c)(1).
38. Paccon, Inc. v. Comm'r, 45 T.C. 392 (1966); *See also* Huene v. United States, 81-1 USTC ¶ 9133 (E.D. Cal. 1980).
39. Scar v. Comm'r, 87-1 USTC ¶ 9277 (9th Cir. 1987).
40. Hartman v. Comm'r, 65 T.C. 542 (1975).

Last Known Address Problems

I. General and Statutory Rules

A. The purpose of imposing a last known address standard was to relieve the Internal Revenue Service (IRS) of the obviously impossible task of keeping an up-to-date record of taxpayers' addresses.[1] There has been much litigation over the years whenever the IRS sends out a statutory deficiency notice[2] and the taxpayer never receives it. As a consequence of not receiving the required notice, typically the taxpayer never responds by filing a tax court petition, and the tax deficiency is thereafter assessed by default.

B. Unless the IRS is notified of a fiduciary relationship (see requirements under I.R.C. § 6903), a notice of deficiency (ND) is sufficient if it is mailed to a taxpayer at his or her "last known address," even if the taxpayer is deceased and even if a corporation has gone out of existence.[3] There is a similar rule in the assessable penalty section of the I.R.C. Before the IRS can make an assessment of trust fund liability, it must notify the taxpayer in writing by mail at his or her last known address before the penalty can be assessed.[4]

C. Generally, it is not necessary that the ND be sent to the "correct" address—merely that it is sent to the *last known* address.

D. The last known address of a taxpayer has reference to the last known permanent address or legal residence of the taxpayer, or the last known temporary address of a definite duration or period to which all communications during such period were to be sent.[5]

II. The IRS's Burden: General Rules

A. When a notice of deficiency is to be sent, the IRS is required to exercise ordinary care to ascertain the correct address of a taxpayer and mail the ND to that address.[6]

B. The last known address is that address that the IRS reasonably believed the taxpayer wished it to use.[7] Reasonable diligence does not require the IRS to send duplicate notices to every address of which it has knowledge or to look to outside sources for other addresses.[8]

C. The appropriate address is the address to which, in light of all the surrounding facts and circumstances, the IRS reasonably believes the taxpayer wishes for the ND to be sent.[9]

D. The IRS cannot merely rely on an address on the last tax return where prior correspondence to that address had been returned as undeliverable. It must demonstrate what steps were taken to ascertain the correct address.[10]

III. Filing a Tax Return as Notification of Address

A. The last known address of a taxpayer is the address appearing on the tax return in question filed in the investigating district, and in the absence of a definitive notice of a change of address, the IRS is entitled to use that address for official communications.[11]

B. The rule, as enunciated in *Marcus*, was modified slightly in 1988 when the tax court decided the *Abeles* case.[12] Until that case, the tax court treated the address of the taxpayer appearing on the return under examination as the taxpayer's last known address unless the taxpayer proved a "clear and concise notification" of an address change. Acknowledging the technological advancements made in the IRS's computer system and the ready access to the address used on the taxpayer's most recently filed return, the majority of the tax court decided to establish a new rule, in which a taxpayer's last known address would, in most cases, be the address shown on the most recently filed return, absent clear and concise notice of a change of address.[13]

C. *2001 Regulations*
Regulations adopted in 2001 for the most part adopt the rules enunciated in the *Abeles* case. The regulations now state that a taxpayer's last known address is the address that appears on the taxpayer's most recently filed and properly processed federal tax return, unless the IRS is given clear and concise notification of a different address.[14]

D. Note, however, that a Form W-2 or 1099 listing a new address is *not* clear and concise notification of an address change.[15]

IV. Other Address Change Notices

A. It is clear that the burden is on the taxpayer (although the IRS has certain responsibilities as well) to provide the IRS with a clear and concise notification of the new address.[16]

B. After written notification to the IRS of a change of address, the mere filing of a return indicating a subsequent different address is not sufficient to change a last known address.[17]

C. A notice of change of address filed by the taxpayer must be unequivocal. The recommended way to notify the IRS of an address change is by filling out and filing a Form 8822.

D. *Address Obtained from Third Party*

A change of address that a taxpayer provides to a third party, such as a payor or another government agency, is not clear and concise notification of a different address for purposes of determining a last known address.[18]

E. Starting in 2001 the IRS began to use the U.S. Postal Service's (USPS) National Change of Address database to update taxpayers' last known address.[19] This is an exception to the rule that the tax return address always controls. Examples of how the USPS change of address system affects the IRS are listed in the regulations.

V. Problems of Actual Notice

A. Where the IRS mails an ND to a clearly wrong address and the taxpayer never receives it, the ND has no legal efficacy.[20]

B. If the mailing results in actual notice without prejudicial delay, it meets the conditions of § 6212(b)(1) no matter to what address the notice was successfully sent.[21] In other words, mailing a deficiency notice to a wrong address does not automatically invalidate the notice as long as the taxpayer actually receives it in a timely manner.[22] Several courts have held that a technically defective notice (as to address) may still be valid if it is actually received by the taxpayer without undue prejudice to the taxpayer's rights.[23]

VI. Jurisdictional Matters

It has been held that an injunction preventing distraint against the taxpayer's property will be granted by a district court where the ND was *not* mailed to the last known address.[24] For a federal district court to grant an injunction, the taxpayer must show irreparable harm and lack of adequate remedy at law.[25] The tax court has jurisdiction to hear a case even though the petition was not timely for purposes of determining whether the ND was improperly addressed.[26]

VII. Fact-Specific Cases

A. The IRS could not reasonably believe that the taxpayer wished to be reached at her mother's address since the taxpayer did not authorize her mother to accept her mail.[27]

B. The IRS is not required to treat the address of a temporary sojourn as the last known address (e.g., where the taxpayer is in jail).[28]

C. An ND sent to a taxpayer's accountant has been held to be reasonable.[29] Similarly, notices sent to a taxpayer's lawyers (designated in a filed power of attorney) have been held to be valid.[30]

D. Reasonable diligence was not exercised when, through negligent mishandling of a power of attorney, an ND was not sent the last known address.[31]

E.   An ND mailed to the address of one of the executors of the decedent taxpayer, pursuant to instructions by the other executor to a revenue agent, was properly addressed.[32]

F.   Where the Department of Justice (DOJ), as assisted by the IRS, prosecuted a taxpayer for criminal tax evasion, the DOJ's knowledge of the whereabouts of the taxpayer is imputed to the IRS. Therefore, the IRS must exercise due diligence in determining the last known address of the taxpayer by inquiring of its sister agency. Moreover, a *copy* of a deficiency notice (as opposed to an original) sent to the taxpayer's lawyer will not suffice as adequate notice.[33]

G.   In the *Taylor* case,[34] the IRS sent an ND to an old address of the taxpayer used by her prior to her marriage. By the time the ND was sent, the taxpayer had filed two joint tax returns with her new husband showing a different address. The ND was returned from the old address as undeliverable. The court concluded that the IRS did not properly discharge its obligation to exercise reasonable diligence to ascertain Taylor's correct address through a computer search.

VIII. Conclusions

A practitioner should never assume that the IRS knows where his or her client lives. Particularly where you have a "high-audit-risk" client, the better part of wisdom mandates that whenever that client changes his or her address, you ask him or her to fill out and send in a Form 8822. This will ensure that the client will get all required notices. In the cases of death, the decedent's personal representative should always submit a Form 56 (Notice of Fiduciary Relationship) to the IRS indicating the address to which all notices should be sent.

IX. Notes

1. *See generally* Rev. Proc. 90-18, 1990-1 CB 491, for rules demonstrating how a taxpayer is to inform the IRS of a change of address.
2. Internal Revenue Code (I.R.C.) § 6212(a).
3. I.R.C. § 6212(b)(1).
4. I.R.C. § 6672(b), enacted as part of the Taxpayer Bill of Rights 2. Other references in the Code to last known addresses include the following: § 414(p)(2)(A) (qualified domestic relations orders); § 982(c)(1) (admissibility of documents maintained in foreign countries); § 6110(f) (resolution of disputes relating to disclosure); § 6303(a) (notice and demand for tax); § 6325(f) (release of lien); § 6331(d) (notice before levy); § 6332(b) (levy on life insurance policy); § 6335(a) (sale of seized property); § 6901(g) (transferee liability); and § 7609(a) (third-party summonses).
5. Gregory v. United States, 57 F. Supp. 962, 33 AFTR 232 (Cl. Ct. 1944).
6. United States v. Lehigh, 9 AFTR2d 616 (W.D. Ark. 1961); *see also* Sicari v. United States, 136 F.3d 925, 98-1 USTC ¶ 50,237 (2d Cir. 1998).

7. Kennedy v. United States, 403 F. Supp. 619, 76-1 USTC ¶ 9229 (W.D. Mich. 1975); where the IRS had sent multiple notices to the correct address, it was on notice as to where to send the deficiency notice.

8. Armstrong v. Comm'r, 94-1 USTC ¶ 50,083 (10th Cir. 1994).

9. Delman v. Comm'r, 20 AFTR2d 5543 (3d Cir. 1967).

10. Crawford v. Comm'r, 72 T.C.M. (CCH) 999 (1996).

11. Marcus v. Comm'r, 12 T.C. 1071 (1949).

12. Abeles v. Comm'r, 91 T.C. 1019 (1988). Acq.

13. *See* Richards, *When Will Notice of Change of Address Bind the IRS?*, 74 J. TAXATION 226 (1990).

14. Treas. Reg. § 301.6212-2(a).

15. White v. Comm'r, 60 T.C.M. (CCH) 958 (1990).

16. Alta Sierra Vista, Inc. v. Comm'r, 62 T.C. 367 (1974).

17. Budlong v. Comm'r, 58 T.C. 850 (1972). Note that this case is now of questionable validity in view of the 1988 decision in *Abeles*.

18. Treas. Reg. § 301.6212-2(b)(1).

19. T.D. 8939; Treas. Reg. § 301.6212-2(b)(2).

20. *See* United States v. Lehigh, 9 AFTR2d 616 (W.D. Ark. 1961).

21. Clodfelter v. Comm'r, 527 F.2d 754 (9th Cir. 1975). Presumably this same rule would follow if the ND were sent by regular mail as opposed to the required certified mail. I.R.C. § 6212(a).

22. Frieling, Jr. v. Comm'r, 81 T.C. 42 (1983); *see also* Mulvania v. Comm'r, 769 F.2d 1376, 85-2 USTC ¶ 9634 (9th Cir. 1985).

23. Boren v. Ridell, 241 F.2d 670 (9th Cir. 1957).

24. Slaven v. United States, 45 AFTR 1168 (S.D. Cal. 1953).

25. Gruber v. Comm'r, 81-2 USTC ¶ 9763 (D. N.J. 1981).

26. Shelton v. Comm'r, 63 T.C. 193 (1974).

27. Austin v. Voskuil, 80-2 USTC (E.D. Mo. 1980).

28. Cohen v. United States, 297 F.2d 760, 9 AFTR2d at 728 (9th Cir. 1962).

29. *See* Delman v. Comm'r, 20 AFTR2d 5543 (3d Cir. 1967).

30. Expanding Envelope & Folder Corp. v. Shotz, 385 F.2d 402, 20 AFTR2d 5758 (3d Cir. 1967).

31. Johnson v. Comm'r, 611 F.2d 1015, 80-1 USTC ¶ 9219 (5th Cir. 1980).

32. United States v. Lyman, 36 F. Supp. 53 (D. Mass. 1940); Irwin v. Larson, 94 F.2d 187.

33. Keeton v. Comm'r, 74 T.C. 877 (1980); *see also* Rev. Proc. 61-18, 1961-2 CB 550.

34. Taylor v. Comm'r, 55 T.C.M. 596 (1988) (citing McPartlin v. Comm'r, 81-2 USTC ¶ 9569 (7th Cir. 1981)).

Tax Claim and Refund Procedures

I. Introduction

A. Claim Definition
When an amended return is filed reflecting an overpayment of tax and requesting a refund, it is considered by the IRS to be a "claim." And claim procedures are specifically delineated in the I.R.C.

B. Statutory Authority
There is no statutory authority that entitles taxpayers to file amended tax returns.[1] Nevertheless, it has been the long-standing policy of the IRS to recognize them as long as they are for the purpose of correcting errors or mistakes on the original return.

C. IRS Explanations
An explanation of tax claims can be found in IRS Publication Number 556.

D. General Requirements
The most important requirement of a claim is that it state the grounds and supporting facts of the taxpayer's claim. However, this requirement should be liberally interpreted. As long as the claim apprises the IRS of the essential nature of the claim, it should be seen as satisfying this requirement.[2]

II. Audit Procedures for Claims

A. Audit Risk
Taxpayers are frequently concerned that filing an amended tax return will trigger an audit by the IRS. But that is not necessarily true; it all depends on the nature of the claim. It has been reported that claims (amended returns) are subject to "special review" by IRS personnel. It is true that an amended return is usually subject to closer scrutiny than an originally filed return. The IRS reviews the reasons for the amendment as well as the type and size of the changes. Returns with

large or unusual items are referred to examiners for further review and possible audit. As a result of this extra analysis, practitioners should consider whether the benefits of filing an amended return may not be outweighed by the higher risk that other items on the original return may also be examined.

B. *Administrative Review of Claim*
    The I.R.C. provides that the IRS's decision in disallowing all or part of any claim is not administratively reviewable.[3] However, the IRS's own procedural regulations are contrary to this statutory rule and provide that when claims are audited by the Examination Division, substantially the same procedure is followed (including appeal rights afforded to taxpayers) as when returns are originally examined.[4] Occasionally, a taxpayer will file an amended return on Form 1040-X, which has the effect of reducing an assessment but does not claim a refund because the original assessment was never paid. When this happens, the IRS will treat the 1040-X as an "informal" claim. If the examining agent does not agree with the issues raised in the 1040-X, he or she will inform the taxpayer that his or her decision is not reviewable.[5]

C. *IRS Choices*
    The IRS is required to act on a claim; it cannot just ignore it. The IRS has three choices:
    1. Allow the claim in full and issue a refund check;
    2. Allow the claim in part; or
    3. Disallow the claim in full.

D. *Required Comment*
    If a revenue agent is in the process of auditing an original return and a claim is filed for the same year before the audit is completed, the agent is required to comment on the disposition of the claim in his or her report.

E. *Offsetting Adjustments*
    When the IRS audits a claim, offsetting adjustments may be proposed. That is, the IRS can raise nonclaim issues to offset and disallow the claim even though a deficiency may be barred in the carryback year.[6]

F. *Audit Conclusions—Forms Required*
    An explanation of income tax changes is made on Form 4549. This form can be used on claim cases. The consent at the bottom is the equivalent of "waiver" Form 870. If a taxpayer accepts an IRS disallowance of a claim, he or she usually signs a Form 3363. To obviate the IRS having

to issue a statutory notice of claim disallowance, a taxpayer must also sign a Form 2297.

G. *Tentative Carryback Applications*[7]
In the case of a tentative carryback adjustment, the IRS can audit the carryback year and can determine a deficiency, but only to the extent of the amount previously refunded.[8]

III. Statute of Limitations Rules

A. *General Rules*
Claims for refund must be filed within certain statutory time periods. The general rule is that they must be filed within three years from the time the return was originally filed or two years from the time the tax was paid, whichever of such periods expires later.[9] For purposes of claim filing, tax paid before the due date of the original return is considered to be paid on the due date.[10] If, on the other hand, no return was filed, the period expires two years from the time any tax was paid.[11] If the refund claim is not filed within the prescribed periods, the IRS will not issue a refund check.[12]

Claims for refund of tax filed after the statute of limitations has expired are void, and any refund thereon is considered erroneous.[13]

B. *Withheld Tax*
For purposes of the two-year rule, withheld tax is deemed to be paid on April 15 of the year following the year of withholding.[14]

C. *Delinquent Original Returns*
Section 6511 must be read to refer to a "timely" filed original return. If the return is delinquent (even by one day), the three-year rule is unavailable, and the two-year statute of limitations rule must be used.[15] Another trap that taxpayers frequently fall into is the thought that an overpaid original return can be filed at any time and that the refund check will be duly issued. This is not the case. Where original returns are delinquent by more than three years, plus an extension period, any refund claim will not be allowed.[16]

D. *Extensions of the Statute*
If the taxpayer and the IRS agree to an extension of the deficiency assessment statute,[17] such agreement also extends the time for filing a refund claim plus an additional six months.[18]

E. *Special Rule regarding Bad Debts or Worthless Securities*
If a claim relates to bad debts[19] or worthless securities,[20] in lieu of the normal three-year period, a seven-year period is substituted.[21]

F. *Special Rule for Carrybacks*
In the case of a net operating loss (NOL) carryback[22] or a corporate capital loss carryback,[23] the three-year period does not expire for the carryback year until three years after the filing date of the NOL or capital loss year (including an extension period).[24]

G. *Effect on "Assessment" Statute*
The filing of an amended return does not extend the "assessment" statute.[25] It is the filing of the original return, not the amended return, which starts the running of the assessment statutory period.[26]

H. *Equitable Tolling*
Largely in response to the *Brockamp* case,[27] Congress enacted I.R.C. § 6511(h). This provision, effective in 1998, specifies an equitable tolling rule that the statute of limitations is suspended during any period of an individual's life that he or she is "financially disabled." Financial disability is defined to mean physical or mental impairment of significant duration. There is an exception to this rule, however, when the impaired taxpayer has a guardian or a spouse.[28]

I. *Informal Claim Doctrine*
Courts occasionally recognize an informal claim doctrine for limitations period purposes even though not all of the regulation's requirements are satisfied. This doctrine generally prevents technical defects in refund claims, such as no signature, from preventing an otherwise justifiable refund from being issued. However, mere discussions with revenue service personnel, or mention of the possibility of a claim being filed in a revenue agent's report, will not be sufficient to constitute such an informal claim. Cases allowing the informal claim doctrine to overcome the limitations period require that the taxpayer at least have some communication with the IRS indicating an intention to file a refund claim.[29]

IV. Refund Litigation

A. *Authority to Sue the Government*
In the case of tax refund litigation, there is a waiver of governmental sovereign immunity from suit. By statute, federal courts have authority to adjudicate any civil action against the United States for the recovery of any tax erroneously or illegally assessed or collected.[30]

There is also Supreme Court authority for the proposition that even non-taxpayers, under certain circumstances, have standing to bring a refund action against the IRS.[31]

B. *General Rule of Forum*
While to some extent there is overlapping jurisdiction where "claim" issues are involved, suffice it to say that lawsuits for refunds of federal

tax can only be brought in the U.S. district courts or the U.S. Courts of Federal Claims. The district court offers the flexibility of jury availability, while the claims court, like the U.S. Tax Court, does not.

C. U.S. Tax Court Involvement

Of course tax refund litigation may not be instituted in the U.S. Tax Court because its jurisdiction depends on a preexisting "deficiency," which would not be the case where there is an alleged overpayment.[32] After a deficiency case has become docketed before the tax court, the IRS will not allow a claim for refund.[33] This is the apparent reason that the income tax refund claim forms (1040-X and 1120-X) ask the question whether the original return was, or will be, audited.

However, if, in a deficiency case, the tax court finds that a taxpayer has in fact overpaid his or her tax, it does have jurisdiction to determine the amount of that overpayment as long as the issues are properly pleaded and argued.[34]

Once a petition has been filed in U.S. Tax Court, the court has exclusive jurisdiction to hear the case, to the exclusion of the federal district court. That is, after such filing with the tax court, no claim for refund can be filed, nor can a refund suit be instituted.[35]

Where a taxpayer has not filed a return (reflecting an overpayment) by the time a statutory notice of deficiency is mailed to him or her by the IRS, and the notice is mailed more than two years after the date on which the taxes are deemed paid, a two-year "look-back" period applies under § 6512(b)(3)(B), and the tax court lacks jurisdiction to award a refund.[36]

Once a case is docketed with the tax court, an NOL carryback issue can apparently be raised even though the year giving rise to the NOL is otherwise barred as long as a carryback claim *could* have been filed at the time the deficiency notice was issued.

D. Subsequent Deficiency Notice

If a refund suit is brought in federal district court or the claims court and thereafter a deficiency notice (§ 6212) is sent to the taxpayer, the action in federal district court is temporarily suspended. If the taxpayer files a petition with the tax court within ninety days, the district court relinquishes jurisdiction. If, on the other hand, the taxpayer does not file such a petition, the district court resumes its jurisdiction of the case.[37]

E. District Court Jurisdictional Requirements

Refund litigation in federal district court cannot be initiated until a claim for refund is first filed. That is, the filing of such a claim is a jurisdictional prerequisite.[38]

Further, a federal district court refund suit cannot begin until after six months have elapsed from the date of filing the claim. Nor can such a suit be commenced after two years have elapsed from the date of an official IRS claim disallowance. But this two-year period can be extended by agreement between the taxpayer and the IRS.[39]

If the taxpayer signs a written waiver of notice of claim disallowance (Form 2297), then the two-year period for filing suit starts to run when the waiver is "filed."[40] Note that courts are not unanimous as to what the "filing" date is: the date that the taxpayer signs the form, or the date it is received by the IRS.

F. *Full Payment Rule*

To commence a refund suit in federal district court, the entire amount of income tax sought to be refunded (plus any statutory accruals of interest and penalties) must have been fully paid to establish a jurisdictional prerequisite.[41] This is known as the "full payment" rule and prevents most taxpayers from being able to litigate "deficiency" cases in this relatively friendly forum.

G. *Administrative Appeals Consideration*

The IRS Office of Administrative Appeals has jurisdiction to consider a disallowed claim case, but the taxpayer must file a request for a settlement conference (protest) within the period for filing suit.[42] Appeals may refuse to consider a case if less than 120 days remain in the two-year period.[43] If a taxpayer is within the 120-day period, the Appeals Office will accept jurisdiction only if the taxpayer agrees to extend the two-year period by executing a Form 907.[44]

V. Tentative Refund Applications

A. *General Rule*

Although these refund applications are sometimes referred to as "quickie claims," it is clear, by statute, that an application for tentative carryback adjustment does *not* constitute a "claim" for refund.[45]

If, for any reason, the application is rejected, the applicant taxpayer has no recourse but to go through the normal claim (amended return) procedures. If the IRS finds that an application contains material omissions or errors, it may disallow the application in whole or in part without further action.[46] The usual application involves a carryback of a net operating loss or an unused credit of some sort.

B. *Time Limitations*

The attractiveness of a tentative refund application is that the IRS is required to act on the application within ninety days of filing by either rejection or issuance of the refund check.[47] This is much preferable to going through the normal claim procedures with their inordinate delays. However, one must be careful to file within certain prescribed deadlines. For example, the application must be filed, for a particular year, within twelve months after the end of the year giving rise to the NOL.[48]

C. *Other Provisions*

The forms to use for tentative refund applications are Form 1045 for individuals and Form 1139 for corporations. An important distinction between tentative application forms and amended return forms is that the former can cover all of the carryback years in the same form. If, on the other hand, an 1120-X or 1040-X is used, a separate form must be prepared for each carryback year being amended.

VI. Interest on Refunds

A. *General Rule*

The IRS is required to pay statutory interest on a refund of any over-payment of federal income tax.[49]

B. *Interest Rate*

The interest rate paid on overpayments fluctuates on a quarterly basis, just like the rate charged on underpayments. But note that the rate *paid* by the IRS on overpayments is 1 percent point less than what is *charged* by them on underpayments in the case of corporations.[50] For individuals the rate is the same for both underpayments and overpayments. Several computer software packages are available that calculate this interest for practitioners.

C. *Restrictions on Interest Payable by the IRS*

1. *Delinquent returns:* In the case of a delinquent return (filed after the last extension deadline), no interest will be paid for the period preceding the filing date.[51]

2. *Carryback claims:* In the case of a carryback claim, interest is not calculated from the carryback year to the date of refund payment. Instead, interest is payable only from the due date of the return giving rise to the carryback to the date of payment.[52] This is known as "restricted" interest.

3. *Forty-five-day rule:* No interest accrues on a refund within the first forty-five days after a return is filed.[53] The rationale for this rule is that the IRS should not have to pay interest for the period of time that it takes for normal return processing.

D. *Erroneous Refunds*

If the IRS refunds an amount to a taxpayer in error under circumstances where they could sue to get it back, interest will be charged against the taxpayer at the rate specified in § 6621.[54]

VII. Employment or Excise Tax Claims

A. *Section 6672 (Trust Fund Liability) Cases*
If a trust fund liability has been proposed and assessed, the IRS cannot enforce collection of that amount if a minimum payment (tax for one quarter on one employee) is made, a claim for refund for that tax is filed, and a bond is furnished. Additionally, within thirty days of the denial of such a claim, suit must be brought in either the claims court or federal district court.[55]

B. *Request for Immediate Rejection*
One can file a claim with a request that it be immediately rejected. Usually this is done in anticipation of litigation—for example, in a section 6672 case, which is headed for federal district court.

C. *Forms Used*
Refund claims can also be made for overpaid employment taxes. For these purposes, use Form 941c or an 843 form. An 843 may also be used to request abatement of employment or excise tax.[56] The regulations contain other rules relating to adjustment of overpayments of employment tax.[57] Where refunds are claimed on Forms 720, 730, and 2290 (relating to various forms of excise tax), taxpayers are asked to file a claim Form 8849.

D. *Fuel Tax Penalty*
Penalties are imposed on taxpayers who file a claim for overpaid fuel tax for an amount that is excessive.[58]

VIII. Filing Requirements

A. *General Rule*
The general rule is that claims and amended returns are to be filed in the IRS service center where the original return was filed. However, if the taxpayer has moved in the interim, he or she should file the claim in the new jurisdiction if it is served by a different service center.

B. *Proof of Filing*
Particularly where a claim is being filed to protect a taxpayer's rights or a position, it is important to be able to prevent the IRS from subsequently denying that the claim was ever filed. For this reason, it is recommended that claims containing possibly controversial positions be hand-carried to the local IRS office. The IRS will, upon request, stamp a copy of the return with a "received" stamp.

To illustrate the problem in one particular case, the claims court refused to accept jurisdiction of a case because the taxpayer could not prove that his or her claim was mailed. A preparer's affidavit that the claim was mailed by regular mail was insufficient.[59]

C. *Tentative Carryback Applications*
   Tentative carryback applications (so-called quickie claims) are filed by sending them to the following address:
       IRS [city, state, depending where you filed your original return]

IX. Miscellaneous Topics

A. *Estimated Tax (Corporate)*
   A corporation (but not an individual) may file a claim for refund of over-paid estimated tax, even before the return for the year in question is filed.[60] This is accomplished by filing a Form 4466. If a corporation files an original return showing an estimated tax penalty, it cannot thereafter have that penalty abated by filing an amended return. The determination of estimated penalty is based on the tax shown on the original return.[61]

B. *Tax Preparer Claims*
   Tax return preparers who are assessed preparer penalties can file a claim for not less than 15 percent thereof and get a hearing in federal district court to determine their liability.[62] An income tax preparer files such a claim on Form 6118.

C. *Erroneous Refunds*
   Occasionally the IRS makes a refund to the taxpayer in error. If the taxpayer keeps the money, the IRS can recover that money by suing the taxpayer to get it back.[63] Such suits must be brought within two years of the making of the erroneous refund.[64]

D. *Overpayment Offsets*
   1. *Against underpayments:* The IRS can offset any overpayment against any underpayment owed by the same taxpayer.[65]
   2. *Against estimated tax:* A prior-year overpayment can be credited against current year estimated tax.[66]
   3. *Child support obligations:* The IRS can offset any refund against past-due family support obligations.[67]
   4. *Federal agency debt:* The IRS can also offset any refund against debts owed to other federal agencies.[68]

E. *Joint Committee Cases*
   A filed refund claim of greater than $2 million must ultimately be reviewed by the Joint Committee on Taxation of the U.S. Congress before it can be allowed.[69] One hundred percent of these claims are audited.

F. *Abatement*
   "Abatement" relates to tax that has been assessed but not paid. One cannot "abate" certain types of tax (i.e., income, estate, and gift tax). Only employment and excise tax may legally be abated. For this

purpose, Form 843 is used. One can also use an 843 form for the abatement of interest under § 6404(e).[70] The IRS has taken a more liberal view, however, and has allowed abatement of income tax in some limited circumstances.[71]

G. *New Issues—Untimely*

A taxpayer cannot raise a new issue in an untimely claim despite the fact that a previous timely claim was filed on other grounds.[72] This is the reason that it is recommended that a claim contain language to the effect that the taxpayer is additionally claiming such sums "that may be legally due and owing to the taxpayer."

H. *Claim Forms*

The general claim form is an 843. But it is important to note that this form cannot be used to claim a refund of income tax. Instead, a 1040-X is used where the original return was a 1040, 1040-A, or 1040-EZ. For corporations, an 1120-X is used where the original return was an 1120, 1120-S, 1120-DISC, or 1120-L.[73] A claim for refund due a decedent is accomplished with a form 1310.

I. *Elections*

A taxpayer cannot make an election in an amended return that was required to be made in the original return.

J. *Deficiency Dividends*

If the IRS proposes a "personal holding company" tax, such a tax can be avoided by payment of "deficiency dividends." A deduction for such deficiency dividends is allowed as of the date a "claim" is filed. This claim must be filed within 120 days of the IRS's determination.[74]

K. *Filing a Claim after Agreeing to a Deficiency*

Execution of an 870 (by the taxpayer) or an 870-AD by the taxpayer and the IRS generally does *not* preclude a taxpayer's later filing of a refund claim. That is, an 870-AD does not constitute a "closing agreement."[75] The IRS language on the form is contradictory and is, therefore, mostly ignored.[76] Note that there may be a conflict among the circuit courts on this point.[77]

L. *Consolidated Returns*

A parent corporation may not file a carryback claim for a net operating loss and apply against its income earned in an earlier year the loss sustained by one of its subsidiaries during a later year when a consolidated return was filed.[78]

M. *Ex-Spouses*

Where net operating loss refund claims relate to ex-spouses, the IRS provides a procedure whereby a separate refund can be determined so that the refund check can be issued in a separate name.[79]

N. *Refund Check Endorsement*

A power of attorney will not allow a return preparer to endorse a refund check of a client without imposition of a penalty under § 6695(f), which calls for a $500 fine per occurrence.[80]

O. *Deposit versus Payment*

Under I.R.C. § 6401(c), an amount paid as a tax may still be a tax overpayment even though it was remitted to satisfy a nonexistent tax liability. Nevertheless, the IRS permits taxpayers to designate payments either as tax payments or as deposits. When the taxpayer designates a remittance as a deposit, the funds will be held by the government without any obligation to pay interest if the taxpayer prevails in tax litigation and is entitled to its return. Moreover, since a deposit is not a payment of tax, formal refund procedures do not apply to its retrieval.[81]

X. Summary and Recommendations

A. *Ethical Considerations*

If a tax practitioner becomes aware of a mistake or omission on a client's tax return or any document previously submitted to the IRS, he or she is required to advise the client promptly of the fact and consequences of the error or omission.[82] However, the practitioner is not required to ensure that an amended tax return is filed to correct the error.

B. *Protective Claims*[83]

The IRS also permits the use of so-called protective claims. These are claims that are used to protect a taxpayer's position on a given issue where the statute of limitations is about to expire. For example, if there is a controversy over which year is the proper one in which to take a deduction, the taxpayer may want to file an amended return for the earlier year to claim such deduction before the statute expires. This procedure assumes, of course, that one would not otherwise be protected by the mitigation[84] statutes. It is highly recommended that protective claims be used in appropriate circumstances. Not doing so may constitute malpractice on the part of a practitioner.[85]

C. *Increasing Use of Claims*

Filing a claim while taking an aggressive position is far less dangerous than filing an original tax return with the same position. Why? Because numerous penalties attach to a potential deficiency, whereas with a claim, the worst that can happen is that the claim is disallowed. That is, the IRS simply says, "No," in which case you are no worse off than you were before.

XI. Notes

1. Miscovsky v. United States, 24 AFTR2d 69-6074 (3d Cir. 1969).
2. Treas. Reg. § 301.6402-2(b)(1).
3. I.R.C. § 6406.
4. Proc. Reg. § 601.105(e)(2).
5. *See generally* IRM 4.4.4 regarding the processing and examination of claims filed by taxpayers.
6. *See* Lewis v. Reynolds, 284 U.S. 281 (S. Ct. 1932).
7. I.R.C. § 6411.
8. I.R.C. § 6501(k).
9. I.R.C. § 6511(a).
10. I.R.C. § 6513(a).
11. I.R.C. § 6511(a).
12. I.R.C. § 6511(b).
13. I.R.C. § 6514(a).
14. Arnzen v. Internal Revenue Serv., 91-1 USTC ¶ 50,020 (W.D. Wash. 1990); *see also* Anastasoff v. United States, 223 F.3d 898,2000-2 USTC ¶ 50,705 (8th Cir. 2000), which indicated that the "mailbox rule" of I.R.C. § 7502 (timely mailing is timely filing) does not apply where a claim is mailed before the three-year period expires but is received by the IRS after the three-year period expires. *But see* Anderson v. United States, 92-1 USTC ¶ 50,308 (9th Cir. 1992), to the contrary, where extrinsic evidence (a taxpayer's own sworn testimony) was admitted to prove up timely mailing of a refund claim.
15. *Id.*
16. I.R.C. § 6511(b)(2)(A). Note that the statute refers to late-filed "claims." In practice, IRS applies this rule to all late-filed original returns, which are not technically "claims."
17. *See* I.R.C. § 6501(c)(4) re extension by agreement, usually accomplished by execution of Form 872 or 872-A.
18. I.R.C. § 6511(c)(1).
19. I.R.C. § 166.
20. I.R.C. § 165(g).
21. I.R.C. § 6511(d)(1).
22. I.R.C. § 172(b)(1)(A).
23. I.R.C. § 1212(a)(1)(A).
24. I.R.C. § 6511(d)(2)(A).
25. *See* I.R.C. § 6501(a) for the general assessment statute rule.
26. Kaltreider Constr., Inc. v. United States, 9 AFTR2d 1577 (3d Cir. 1962). This assumes, of course, that there is nothing tentative or defective in the taxpayer's original tax return.
27. United States v. Brockcamp, 97-1 USTC ¶ 50,216 (S. Ct. 1997).
28. I.R.C. § 6511(h)(2)(B).
29. BCS Fin. Corp. v. United States, 97-2 USTC ¶ 50,514 (7th Cir. 1997).
30. 28 U.S.C. § 1346(a)(1).
31. *See* United States v. Williams, 95-1 USTC ¶ 50,218 (S. Ct. 1995). In that case, a former spouse paid tax under protest to remove a federal tax lien on property she had received in a divorce settlement. She was found to have standing to sue, despite that she was not the taxpayer. *See* Minton, *Waiver of Sovereign*

Immunity: A Nontaxpayer Has Standing to Bring a Tax Refund Action, DIGEST OF TAX ARTICLES, Mar. 1997.

32. *See* Huene v. United States, 81-1 USTC ¶ 9133 (E.D. Cal. 1980).
33. I.R.C. § 6512(a).
34. I.R.C. § 6512(b).
35. I.R.C. § 6512(a).
36. Comm'r v. Lundy, 96-1 USTC ¶ 50,035 (S. Ct. 1996), *rev'g* 95-1 USTC ¶ 50,085 (4th Cir. 1995). *See* Gould, *Supreme Court Puts Two-Year Limit on Tax Court Refunds*, 56 TAXATION FOR ACCT. 260 (May 1996).
37. I.R.C. § 7422(e).
38. I.R.C. § 7422(a). *But see* Tobin v. Troutman, 2002-1 USTC ¶ 50,392 (W.D. Ky. 2002), where a premature refund suit was allowed to stand after the plaintiff "cured" the defective suit by filing an amended complaint.
39. I.R.C. § 6532(a).
40. I.R.C. § 6532(a)(3).
41. Flora v. United States, 5 AFTR2d 1046 (S. Ct. 1960). 28 U.S.C. § 1346(a)(1). Note that the full payment rule also applies in the case of excise and employment tax cases (including trust fund cases arising under I.R.C. § 6672). However, it is sufficient if the employer or responsible person pays the tax with respect to the wages of one employee for one quarter. *See* Peyser, *Is Full Payment Always Required before Filing a Refund Suit?*, 74 J. TAXATION 162 (Mar. 1991).
42. IRM 8.7.7.2.
43. *Id.*
44. IRM 8.7.7.2.5.
45. I.R.C. § 6411(a).
46. Treas. Reg. § 1.6411-3(c).
47. I.R.C. § 6411(b).
48. I.R.C. § 6411(a).
49. I.R.C. § 6611(a).
50. I.R.C. § 6621(a).
51. I.R.C. § 6611(b)(3).
52. I.R.C. § 6611(f).
53. I.R.C. § 6611(e).
54. I.R.C. § 6602.
55. I.R.C. § 6672(c)(2).
56. I.R.C. § 6413(a)(1).
57. Treas. Reg. § 31.6413.
58. I.R.C. § 6675.
59. Buttke v. United States, 87-2 USTC ¶ 9502 (Cl. Ct. 1987).
60. I.R.C. § 6425(a).
61. Evans-Cooperage, Inc. v. United States, 83-2 USTC ¶ 9544 (5th Cir. 1983).
62. I.R.C. § 6694(c).
63. I.R.C. § 7405(a). The IRS has a choice of remedies when this occurs. If a taxpayer's remittance did not extinguish an existing deficiency (i.e., was a deposit rather than a payment), the IRS can still collect the tax administratively. On the other hand, an extinguished deficiency is not revived by a subsequent erroneous refund, and the IRS would be limited to a suit to recover the erroneous refund under § 7405 or by asserting a new deficiency. *See* Bishop, *IRS' Choice of*

Remedy for Recovering an Erroneous Refund Determines Taxpayer's Response, 82 J. TAXATION 296 (May 1995).

64. I.R.C. § 6532(b).

65. I.R.C. § 6402(a); however, it should be noted that the IRS's National Office has ruled that the IRS has no authority to credit prior years' overpayments against a subsequent year's *potential* deficiency for the reason that a potential deficiency is not an outstanding liability. I.R.S. Priv. Ltr. Rul. (TAM) 9739003.

66. I.R.C. § 6402(b).

67. I.R.C. § 6402(c).

68. I.R.C. § 6402(d).

69. I.R.C. § 6405.

70. Treas. Reg. § 301.6404-1(b). For abatement of "math error" tax due, see I.R.C. § 6213(b). IRS has the authority to abate an assessment of interest where a deficiency is attributable in whole or in part to the delay of an IRS employee. *See* I.R.C. § 6404(e).

71. *See, e.g.*, FSA 2751 (1996).

72. United States v. Andrews, 19 AFTR 1243 (S. Ct. 1938).

73. Proc. Reg. § 601.105(e)(1).

74. I.R.C. § 547.

75. *See* I.R.C. § 7121 for statutory provisions regarding closing agreements.

76. *See* Whitney v. United States, 826 F.2d 896; 87-2 USTC ¶ 9503 (9th Cir. 1987).

77. See an excellent discussion of these issues in Spence, *Taxpayers' Rights to Refund Claims after Administrative Settlements with IRS*, 72 J. TAXATION 290 (May 1990). *See also* Stair v. United States, 35 AFTR2d 75-1515 (2d Cir. 1975) (holding that the taxpayers were estopped from bringing a refund action where they had signed a Form 870-AD representing that they wouldn't seek a refund); McGraw-Hill, Inc. v. United States, 90-1 USTC ¶ 50,053 (S.D.N.Y. 1990).

78. Trinco Indus., Inc. v. Comm'r, 22 T.C. 959 (1954).

79. Rev. Rul. 86-57, 1986-1 CB 362.

80. I.R.S. Priv. Ltr. Rul. 8720021. Circular 230, § 10.31.

81. Rev. Proc. 84-58, 1894-2 CB 501. *See also* Aquilio, *Make Sure Tax Deposits Are Not Payments*, 54 TAXATION FOR ACCT. 89 (Feb. 1995).

82. Circular 230, § 10.21.

83. *See also* SCA 199941039 re "incomplete" claims filed just before the statute of limitations expires.

84. I.R.C. §§ 1311 *et seq.*

85. *See* Treas. Reg. § 301.6402-2 for detailed requirements for filing claims generally. *See also* Benway, *Protective Claims Preserve Taxpayer's Right to Refund of Credit*, 41(6) TAXATION FOR ACCT. (Dec. 1988).

The U.S. Tax Court: Organization, Jurisdiction, and Operation

I. History and Organization of the U.S. Tax Court

  A. History

   The U.S. Tax Court has its roots in the Board of Tax Appeal (BTA), an independent agency originally set up within the executive branch of the government.

   The BTA was formed by the Revenue Act of 1924. Its name, but not its status, was later changed by the Revenue Act of 1942 from the Board of Tax Appeals to the U.S. Tax Court. The court's status was subsequently changed from that of an "independent agency" to that of an Article I "constitutional court" in 1969.[1]

  B. Court of Equity versus Court of Law

   Traditionally the tax court has been thought of as a court of law, not a court of equity. But nothing is further from the truth. While the tax court may not expand its jurisdiction beyond statutory limits, it most certainly can apply equitable principles in the disposition of cases that come within its statutory jurisdiction. For example, reformation of a document containing a drafting mistake to reflect the parties' true intent is an equitable power that the tax court may exercise.[2]

   Similarly, a taxpayer may raise the equitable doctrine of equitable recoupment as a defense to a government claim of statute of limitations to reduce an asserted deficiency.[3] Thus within its specialized and limited jurisdiction, the tax court operates virtually indistinguishably from a federal district court.

  C. Tax Court Judges

   The tax court is composed of nineteen members, all of whom are appointed for a fifteen-year term by the president of the United States. There is a chief judge and eighteen other "regular" members. They receive the same salary as do federal district court judges.[4] The mandatory retirement age for a tax court judge is seventy years of age.[5]

D. Tax Court Hearings and Trials

The principal office of the tax court is in Washington, D.C., but any of its judges may hear cases at any place within the United States.[6] A single judge will come and hear each case on his or her assigned docket.

The tax court judges hear cases in sixty-three principal cities throughout the country to minimize the inconvenience and expense to taxpayers.[7] For example, in Texas the tax court sits in Dallas, El Paso, Houston, Lubbock, and San Antonio.

II. Tax Court Rules

A. Admission to Practice

One does not have to be a lawyer to practice (i.e., represent taxpayers) in tax court.[8] However, to be admitted to practice in tax court, a nonlawyer must take and pass a rigorous examination given once every two years in Washington, D.C. But experience shows that only a small portion of those candidates who take this examination ever pass.

The tax court is authorized to impose an annual registration fee on practitioners admitted to practice before the court. This fee is limited to $30 per year. However, to date, the registration fee has never been imposed.[9]

Each practitioner admitted to practice before the tax court is assigned a unique bar number, which must be placed on each pleading filed with the court. For example, CW0531 is the author's tax court bar number.

B. General Rule

The U.S. Tax Court prescribes its own rules of practice and procedure in accordance with the rules of evidence applicable in trials without a jury in the U.S. District Court of the District of Columbia.[10]

C. TEFRA Rules

In 1982, the Tax Equity and Fiscal Responsibility Act (TEFRA) gave the tax court[11] jurisdiction to hear disputes at the entity level (i.e., for partnerships).[12] In 1984 the tax court added Rules 240 through 247 to its Rules of Practice and Procedure to provide special rules for entity-level partnership actions under I.R.C. §§ 6226 and 6228.

Thereafter, in May 1988, the tax court adopted extensive amendments to its rules relating to partnership actions. Three problems developed under these rules, which are addressed in the 1988 rule changes:

1. A missing or uncooperative tax matters partner (TMP);
2. Settlement of partnership actions; and

   3.   Elections to intervene or participate.[13]

However, two problem areas still exist:

   1.   The tax court rules still fail to set forth the manner in which trials with multiple participating partners are to be conducted; and

   2.   The tax court rules also fail to deal with the situation where more than one partner files a petition in response to the same Final Partnership Administrative Adjustment (FPAA).[14]

  D. *Recent Rule Changes*

Effective in 1990, the tax court promulgated new rules providing for several changes, including the following:

   1.   Rule 76 permitting depositions of opposing expert witnesses without the consent of the opposing party;

   2.   Rule 124 permitting parties to agree to resolve a factual issue by what is essentially voluntary binding arbitration; and

   3.   Rule 24(f) setting out areas of lawyer conflict of interest where

      a.   he or she was involved in the promotion of a tax shelter,

      b.   he or she is a potential witness, or

      c.   he or she represents more than one person with differing interest in the case.

III. Small Case Procedures

  A. *Statutory Authority*

The I.R.C. provides for special, simplified procedures applicable, at the option of the taxpayer, to "small" cases, defined as those involving disputes of less than $50,000 per tax year.[15] These cases are also known as "S" cases.[16]

     For purposes of calculating the $50,000 maximum amount in controversy in S cases, one considers penalties ("additions to tax") but not statutory interest.[17]

  B. *Disadvantages*

The primary disadvantage to an S case is that it is not appealable (reviewable) by any other court, and it cannot be cited as precedent by any future case.[18] Nevertheless, S case opinions are now available on the tax court website.[19] S case opinions are referred to as summary opinions and are available on this website if issued after January 1, 2001.

     Additionally, the filing fee for an S petition is the same $60.00 as for a regular tax court petition.[20] This fee may be waived upon submission of an affidavit of hardship.

  C. *Special Trial Judges*

All S cases are heard by "special" trial judges. Special trial judges are appointed from time to time by the chief judge of the tax court to hear not only S cases but also the following matters:

1. Declaratory judgment proceedings;
2. Appeals of collection due process (CDP) determinations; and
3. Other matters designated by the chief tax court judge.

These special judges receive a salary equal to 90 percent of that received by regular tax court judges.[21]

IV. Jurisdictional Matters

A. *Rushed Deficiency Notices*
Many times tax court litigation results from the fact that the time between the opening of a case in the field and the date of the expiration of the assessment statute of limitations[22] is often short. Revenue agents frequently, due to the lack of time, make ill-conceived and arbitrary adjustments to close their case in time to issue a deficiency notice.

B. *Threshold Jurisdictional Prerequisite*
It is the existence of a deficiency at the date of sending the notice of deficiency that confers jurisdiction upon the tax court. If there is a net overassessment at that time, the case will be dismissed for lack of jurisdiction.[23]

C. *Jurisdiction over Substantive I.R.C. Chapters*
The I.R.C. confers specific jurisdiction on the U.S. Tax Court for controversy resolution of the following areas:
1. Subtitle A (Income Taxes): I.R.C. § 1-1564.
2. Subtitle B (Estate and Gift Taxes): I.R.C. §§ 2001–2704.
3. Chapter 41 (Public Charities): I.R.C. §§ 4911–4912.
4. Chapter 42 (Tax-Exempt Organizations): I.R.C. §§ 4940–4963.
5. Chapter 43 (Qualified Pension, etc., Plans): I.R.C. §§ 4940–4963.
6. Chapter 44 (Qualified Investment Entities): I.R.C. §§ 4981–4982.

Note that the tax court does *not* have jurisdiction to hear employment tax cases, including employee FICA tax[24] and trust fund liability cases.[25] However, the Tax Relief Act of 1997[26] created § 7436, which provides for tax court review of certain employment tax determinations. Also see Notice 98-43, which explains how taxpayers may petition the tax court for review of worker status.

Nor does the tax court have jurisdiction to hear the following types of cases:
1. Retail excise tax,
2. Manufacturer's excise tax,
3. Wagering tax,
4. Environmental tax, or
5. Alcohol, tobacco, and miscellaneous taxes.[27]

The cases over which the tax court has no jurisdiction must be litigated in either the federal district court or claims court.

D. Penalty Issues

The tax court has jurisdiction to hear issues involving penalties imposed as additions to the tax deficiency, including, for example, the I.R.C. § 6654 underestimate penalty.[28] All penalties are reviewable by the court as long as they are proper subjects of a deficiency notice.[29]

However, the tax court has no jurisdiction to hear issues regarding a penalty imposition for submission of a false W-4 form.[30] The tax court also has the power to impose its own penalty on a taxpayer. If it appears to the tax court that (1) proceedings before it have been instituted primarily for delay, (2) the taxpayer's position is frivolous or groundless, or (3) the taxpayer unreasonably failed to pursue available administrative remedies, then the court can assess a penalty of up to $25,000 on the taxpayer. The tax court can also impose similar sanctions on lawyers who have acted "unreasonably and vexatiously."[31]

E. Interest Issues

The general rule is that the tax court has no jurisdiction to abate or reduce interest on deficiencies.[32]

However, there is one exception. The tax court has very limited jurisdiction over statutory interest but only after the deficiency has been assessed following a tax court decision and the tax (plus interest) has been paid. In those circumstances, if the taxpayer feels that he or she has overpaid the interest, then the tax court may reopen the case solely to determine the proper amount of the interest.[33]

F. Declaratory Judgments

1. Definition

A declaratory judgment is one that simply declares the rights of the parties or expresses the opinion of the court on a question of law, without ordering that anything be done. But it must deal with a real dispute of real fact.

2. Rule

Congress has given the tax court jurisdiction to issue declaratory judgments only in very limited circumstances. For example, the tax court has jurisdiction to issue a declaratory judgment regarding the qualification of a retirement plan under I.R.C. Subchapter D.[34]

G. Late Petitions

After a deficiency notice has been issued, a taxpayer may file a petition with the tax court within ninety days after the deficiency notice is mailed (usually the same day it is dated). If the petition is late by only a day, the tax court will not acquire jurisdiction over the case and the case will be dismissed. There is no grace period.[35] In counting the ninety days, the date of the deficiency notice is considered to be day zero.[36]

If a taxpayer does not file a tax court petition within ninety days of the deficiency notice, the tax will simply be assessed by default.[37] This ninety-day period is suspended if the taxpayer files a bankruptcy action.[38]

If a petition is late because of a "last known address" problem, then the tax court has limited jurisdiction to determine the validity of the deficiency notice, following which the court will grant either the petitioner's or the respondent's motion to dismiss based on lack of jurisdiction.[39]

If a petition filed by a taxpayer is dismissed by the tax court (for lateness or whatever reason), the effect of such dismissal is that the deficiency determined by the IRS is in all respects approved.[40]

H. *Statute of Limitations Expiration*

If the tax court determines that the statute of limitations has run on assessment, then the effect of that is that there is no deficiency.[41]

I. *Exclusivity*

Once a tax court petition has been filed, the tax court acquires exclusive jurisdiction with regard to all federal tax matters for that year. Accordingly, a taxpayer may not file a separate refund claim or institute refund litigation in district court for the year before the tax court. All "claim" issues should be raised in the tax court case.[42]

J. *Jeopardy Assessment Jurisdiction*

If the IRS makes a jeopardy assessment under I.R.C. § 6861, then the IRS is required to issue a deficiency notice within sixty days after making such an assessment.[43] The IRS may abate all or part of a jeopardy assessment at any time prior to a tax court decision, to the extent the IRS believes the amount to be excessive.

K. *TEFRA Jurisdiction*

Prior to TEFRA (1982), the tax court had no jurisdiction over entity-level partnership issues. But effective with respect to partnership years beginning after September 3, 1982, the tax court has jurisdiction over TEFRA partnership issues. The way this is done is by a partner filing a request for administrative adjustment (RAA) with the tax court. This is very similar to a petition, and it always follows the issuance by the IRS of an FPAA. Taxpayers also have the option of filing requests for administrative adjustment in either the federal district court or the court of federal claims.[44]

L. *New Issues*

The tax court has jurisdiction to redetermine the correct amount of the deficiency even if the amount so redetermined is greater than the amount reflected in the deficiency notice.[45]

M. *Other Years*

Although the tax court can consider facts in years not before it, it has no jurisdiction to determine tax liability for years not before it.[46]

N. *Jurisdiction to Determine Collection Issues*

I.R.C. § 6330(d) confers upon the tax court jurisdiction to determine the propriety of certain collection actions of the IRS. This jurisdiction is exercisable only after the issuance of a "determination letter" by an appeals officer and a timely filed petition for review. However, if the appeals officer does not offer an opportunity for a hearing prior to the determination letter, such letter will be considered invalid.[47] But note that the *Meyer* case was overruled in *Lunsford*,[48] which held that the tax court should not look behind the determination letter to determine whether a proper hearing opportunity was given to the taxpayer.

V. Pretrial Procedures

A. *Commencement of Case*

The initiation of tax court litigation is accomplished by filing a petition, which must clearly and concisely set out the IRS's errors and the facts regarding each contested issue. The filing fee for filing a petition in the U.S. Tax Court is $60.00, usually with a check payable to "Clerk, U.S. Tax Court," sent along with the petition.[49] At this time the petitioner is also required to designate a city for a place of trial.

B. *Service of Process*

According to the IRS, service of process (e.g., pleadings, decisions, orders, or notices) is accomplished by means of certified mail.[50] The initial pleading (i.e. the petition) can be sent to the court by any means, including a commercial service like FedEx. Certified mailing is recommended, however. After the petition is filed, all future pleadings are generally served via electronic procedures prescribed by the court.[51]

C. *Pleadings*

All pleadings filed with the tax court must be in an original with one conformed copy.[52] However, there is an exception for petitions,[53] which require only an original copy.

After the petition has been filed and a docket number assigned to it, the IRS has only sixty days within which to file an "answer."[54] Once a number has been assigned, the case is said to be "docketed." After the answer is filed, the case is said to be "joined."

After the answer is filed by the government's lawyer, a further pleading called a "reply" may be filed, but usually this is only in cases where the commissioner has the burden of proof.[55]

Generally, the tax court cannot render a decision on an issue not raised in the pleadings.[56] However, the tax court may receive evidence at trial even though the issue is not raised in the pleadings and allow the pleadings to be conformed to the proof.[57]

If a party in a tax court proceeding fails to plead properly, the other party may move for dismissal by default.[58]

D. *Informal Discovery*

The tax court expects the parties to obtain discovery through informal means before using formal discovery procedures, such as depositions and interrogatories.[59] The tax court is unique in mandating attempts by the IRS and taxpayers to informally agree, through the stipulation process. By contrast, other courts cannot compel parties to stipulate undisputed facts.[60]

In summary, the bias of the tax court toward informal agreement and informal disposition of tax controversies is pervasive in the tax court rules. This bias is particularly noticeable in two areas:

1. The prohibition on formal discovery until informal means of obtaining information are exhausted[61] and
2. The mandatory stipulation requirement.[62]

E. *Formal Discovery*

Available formal discovery procedures in the tax court include the following:

- Interrogatories[63]
- Production of documents and things[64]
- Examination by transferees[65]
- Depositions[66]
- Requests for admission[67]

F. *Settlement*

Once a case becomes docketed in the tax court, the petitioner-taxpayer is afforded an opportunity to attend a settlement conference. Accordingly, after the district counsel lawyer answers the petition, he or she will immediately forward the case to the IRS's Appeals Office for consideration of settlement opportunities. Of course, if the Appeals Office has issued the deficiency notice, this means that they have already held a settlement conference with the taxpayer that was unsuccessful. In the latter case, the chief counsel lawyer retains the case for trial preparation.[68]

However, even after the Appeals Office has rejected a taxpayer's settlement offer, counsel has the authority to settle the case at any time prior to trial.

The settlement policy in tax court cases is very different than it is in private litigation. Chief counsel's office has a strict policy of not considering litigation costs and, therefore, will not consider "nuisance settlements."[69]

General contract principles govern tax court settlements. An agreement between the parties is enforceable even though formal settlement documents have not been signed.[70]

G. *Motions for Continuance*[71]

The standing pretrial orders will usually state that motions for continuance will not be looked upon favorably even where there is no opposition from opposing counsel. They are to be granted only in exceptional circumstances. Regardless, the movant is required to state the position of the opposing party. Motions filed within 30 days of calendar call will generally be deemed to be dilatory. As a practical matter, however, if a party has good cause, first-time motions are generally granted.

VI. Trial Procedures

A. *Jury Availability*

There are no juries available in tax court trials.[72] The tax court judge is the final arbiter of the facts and the law, as he or she conducts a "bench trial."

B. *IRS Representation*

In tax court trials the IRS is represented by chief counsel, a lawyer appointed by the president and headquartered in Washington, D.C.[73] In practice, tax court cases are tried on behalf of the IRS by lawyers in local offices throughout the country, where they are known as "area counsel" (formerly "regional counsel" or "district counsel").

C. *Burden of Proof*

In tax court trials the general rule is that the burden of proof is on the taxpayer-petitioner. However, the burden of proof is on the IRS-respondent in respect to (1) fraud issues, (2) new matters not raised in the deficiency notice, (3) increases in deficiency (i.e., beyond what is in the notice), and (4) affirmative defenses.[74]

In some limited circumstances, where the taxpayer introduces credible evidence, the burden of proof shifts to the government with respect to the issue involved. For this to occur, the taxpayer must have satisfied all requirements as to substantiation and cooperation.[75]

D. *Witnesses*

If witnesses appear for trials or depositions, they are entitled to witness fees and automobile mileage reimbursement. Payments for these fees are to be made to the witness by the party at whose instance the witness appears.[76]

E. *Contempt Powers*

For misbehavior or disobedience to the tax court's orders, a tax court judge has powers of punishment via contempt.[77]

F. *Stenographic Recording of Trial Proceedings*

The testimony at a tax court trial is stenographically reported by tape recording.[78] Transcripts of the stenographic reports of tax court trials and hearings are considered to be public record, open to inspection by anybody.[79]

VII. Posttrial Procedures

A. *Decision of the Court*

A decision by a single judge is considered a decision by the entire tax court.[80]

B. *Written Opinion*

It is the duty of a tax court judge, following a trial, to issue a written opinion on its findings of facts and law.[81] Cases that advance a new issue of law or contribute to the body of existing law are published as regular decisions. All others are issued as memorandum decisions. The court issues about fifty to seventy-five "regular" decisions in an average year.

C. *Rendering Date*

A decision of the tax court is said to be "rendered" upon the date that an order specifying the amount of the deficiency is entered into the records of the tax court.[82]

D. *Publishing of Opinions*

Tax court regular decisions are printed and published by the U.S. Government Printing Office.[83] However, it is up to private publishers, such as Commerce Clearing House and Prentice Hall, to publish "memorandum" decisions. Recent tax court opinions, including regular, memorandum, and S case opinions, are also found on the tax court's website.[84]

E. *Finality of Tax Court Decisions*

A decision of the tax court becomes final only after the expiration of the time allowed (ninety days) for filing a notice of appeal.[85] After expiration of this ninety-day period, the tax court has no authority to vacate its original decision.[86] In S cases, the tax court decision becomes "final" ninety days after the decision is entered.[87]

F. *Appeal of Tax Court Decisions*

Except for S cases, all tax court decisions are appealable to one of the eleven U.S. Circuit Courts of Appeal, but not the federal circuit.[88] Venue for a particular circuit court of appeals is the circuit in which is located the legal residence of the petitioner at the time the petition is filed.[89] In the case of a corporation or a partnership, venue for appeal of a tax court decision is based on the principal place of business.[90]

After a tax court decision has been rendered, a notice of appeal must be filed within ninety days after the date the decision is rendered.[91] Following an adverse tax court decision, if an appeal is desired by the taxpayer, the assessment (and collection) of the tax may be stayed only if the taxpayer files an appeals bond not exceeding double the amount of the deficiency.[92]

G. *Lawyer Fees and Litigation Costs*

In any federal court proceeding, including the tax court, a taxpayer can be awarded lawyer fees or other litigating costs incurred in connection with such court proceeding. Of course, all administrative remedies must have first been exhausted, the taxpayer must have substantially prevailed, and the IRS position must not have been substantially justified.[93]

Taxpayers who have been unreasonably forced to resort to a judicial remedy as a result of their IRS audit have the right to seek recovery of "reasonable litigation costs" under I.R.C. § 7430, including lawyer fees, witness and trial preparation expenses, and court costs.[94]

The procedure for filing a motion for litigation costs under I.R.C. § 7430 in the tax court is found in the U.S. Tax Court Rules of Practice and Procedure. In general, the motion must be filed within thirty days after the court issues its opinion in a case that has gone to trial. If the taxpayer "substantially prevails" in a settlement without trial, the § 7430 motion will typically be filed at the same time as the stipulated decision.[95] A detailed discussion of litigation and administrative cost recovery is reserved for a separate subchapter.

H. *Mistake of Fact*

Occasionally a mistake will be made in calculating the final stipulated deficiency or there will be a mutual mistake of fact in reaching a tax court settlement. When that happens, obviously the parties will seek to correct it. The availability of mechanisms for correcting or otherwise modifying a final tax court decision appears to depend on the reason for the error, such as a mutual mistake in stipulation or on which the judgment is based, or a fraud committed on the court.

The best way to correct a mistake is to convince the IRS to abate the tax.[96] The IRS can always agree to abate the tax if it so chooses by correcting the error without the parties applying to the tax court for a correction of its decision. However, if the IRS refuses to make the correction, the taxpayer's ability to modify a tax court decision is extremely limited. The tax court will probably not grant any motion to reopen its decision after the ninety-day period[97] has expired unless a fraud on the court has been committed.[98]

I.   *Assessment of Final Decision*

Subject to appeal availability, the entire amount of a deficiency as determined by the tax court is assessed and collected by the IRS in the usual manner.[99] Of course, if any part of the deficiency was reduced by the court, that reduction may not be assessed and collected by the IRS.[100] The exact amount to be assessed depends on the petitioner and respondent agreement on the deficiency redetermination under a (tax court) Rule 155 calculation. If the parties cannot agree on the calculation, the matter must be taken up with the court.

VIII. Notes

1. Tax Reform Act of 1969, Pub. L. No. 91-172, '951, 83 Stat. 730; *see also* amendment notes to I.R.C. § 7441.
2. Woods v. Comm'r, 92 T.C. 776 (1989).
3. Estate of Branson v. Comm'r, 2001-2 USTC ¶ 50,622 (9th Cir. 2001), *aff'g* 113 T.C. 6.
4. I.R.C. § 7443.
5. Note that, unlike Tax Court judges, federal district judges are appointed for life and can only be removed by impeachment.
6. I.R.C. § 7445.
7. I.R.C. § 7446.
8. I.R.C. § 7452.
9. I.R.C. § 7475(a).
10. I.R.C. § 7453.
11. Note that concurrent, but mutually exclusive, jurisdiction is also given to federal district courts as well as the Court of Federal Claims.
12. *See* I.R.C. § 6226. Note that S Corporations are no longer subject to TEFRA procedures.
13. *Id.*
14. *Id.*
15. I.R.C. § 7463(a).
16. The "small tax court" proceedings were added to the Code by the Tax Reform Act of 1969.
17. I.R.C. § 7463(e).
18. I.R.C. § 7463(b).
19. www.ustaxcourt.gov.
20. T.C. Rule 173(a)(2).
21. I.R.C. § 7443A(d).
22. *See* I.R.C. § 6501.
23. Paccon, Inc. v. Comm'r, 45 T.C. 392 (1966).
24. Anderson v. Comm'r, 80 T.C.M. (CCH) 461 (2000).
25. *See* I.R.C. § 6672.
26. Pub. L. No. 105-34.
27. *See* I.R.C. Subtitles D, E.
28. Conovitz v. Comm'r, 39 T.C.M. (CCH) 929 (1980).

29. I.R.C. § 6214(a).
30. I.R.C. § 6682(c); Castillo v. Comm'r, 84 T.C. 405 (1985).
31. I.R.C. § 6673.
32. Costanza v. Comm'r, 50 T.C.M. (CCH) 280 (1985); *but see* I.R.C. § 6404(e) and Rev. Proc. 87-42 for authority to abate interest where a delay was caused by the IRS. The Tax Court has limited jurisdiction, under an abuse of discretion standard, to review IRS's determination not to abate under § 6404(e). *See* I.R.C. § 6404(h).
33. I.R.C. § 7481(c).
34. I.R.C. § 7476(a).
35. I.R.C. § 6213(a).
36. T.C. Rule 25(a)(1).
37. I.R.C. § 6213(c).
38. I.R.C. § 6213(f).
39. *See, e.g.*, Shelton v. Comm'r, 63 T.C. 193 (1974).
40. I.R.C. § 7459(d).
41. I.R.C. § 7459(e).
42. I.R.C. § 6512(a).
43. *See* I.R.C. § 6861(b).
44. I.R.C. §§ 6226, 6227.
45. I.R.C. § 6214(a).
46. I.R.C. § 6214(b).
47. Meyer v. Comm'r, 115 T.C. 417 (2000).
48. Lunsford v. Comm'r, 117 T.C. No. 16 (2001). Note, however, that the *Lunsford* decision was reviewed by the entire court and contained several dissenting opinions.
49. I.R.C. § 7451.
50. I.R.C. § 7455.
51. T.C. Rule 21(b).
52. T.C. Rule 23(b).
53. *See* T.C. Rule 34(e).
54. With leave of the court and a showing of no prejudice to the petitioner, the respondent may obtain an extension of this sixty-day period.
55. T.C. Rule 37.
56. Lepson v. Comm'r, 44 T.C.M. (CCH) 19 (1982).
57. T.C. Rule 41(b).
58. T.C. Rule 123(a).
59. T.C. Rule 70(a)(1).
60. *Id.*
61. T.C. Rule 70.
62. T.C. Rule 91(a).
63. T.C. Rule 71.
64. T.C. Rule 72.
65. T.C. Rule 73.
66. T.C. Rules 74–85.
67. T.C. Rule 90.
68. Rev. Proc. 87-24, 1987-1 CB 720.
69. See position of Chief Counsel expressed in CCA 200013032.
70. Treaty Pines Invs. P'ship v. Comm'r, 1992-2 USTC ¶ 50,418 (5th Cir. 1992).
71. T.C. Rule 133.

72. I.R.C. § 7453.
73. I.R.C. § 7452.
74. T.C. Rule 142; *see also* I.R.C. § 7454 re the burden of proof in fraud cases.
75. I.R.C. § 7491.
76. I.R.C. § 7457. *See also* T.C. Rule 148.
77. I.R.C. § 7456(c).
78. I.R.C. § 7458.
79. I.R.C. § 7461(a).
80. I.R.C. § 7459(a).
81. I.R.C. § 7459.
82. I.R.C. § 7459(c).
83. I.R.C. § 7462.
84. http://www.ustaxcourt.gov.
85. I.R.C. § 7481(a)(1).
86. Lasky v. Comm'r, 49 AFTR 1696 (9th Cir. 1956) 1027; Abatti v. Comm'r, 88-2 USTC ¶ 9548 (9th Cir. 1988).
87. I.R.C. § 7481(b).
88. I.R.C. § 7482(a)(1).
89. I.R.C. § 7482(b).
90. *Id.*
91. I.R.C. § 7483.
92. I.R.C. § 7485(a)(1).
93. I.R.C. § 7430.
94. I.R.C. § 7430 was enacted as part of TEFRA. Previously, litigation costs had been recoverable in tax cases under the Equal Access to Justice (EAJA), which was limited to costs incurred in refund suits.
95. T.C. Rule 231.
96. I.R.C. § 6404.
97. *See* I.R.C. § 7483.
98. Abatti v. Comm'r, 88-2 USTC ¶ 9548 (9th Cir. 1988).
99. I.R.C. § 6215(a).
100. *Id.*

Burden of Proof

I. Introduction

What is a "burden of proof"? The textbook definition in the law of evidence is the necessity or duty of affirmatively proving a fact on an issue in dispute between two litigants in a court case. In federal tax cases the litigants are, by and large, the IRS and the taxpayer. Burden of proof has a double meaning. It may mean the burden of persuading the trier of the fact, whether judge or jury, or the burden of introducing evidence. Since triers of tax cases conduct no independent investigation, courts must apportion between the parties the burden of persuasion.

In civil tax cases the burden of proof is typically on the taxpayer. This means that the taxpayer must prove his case in justifying the accuracy of his tax return. It requires generally that the taxpayer document his case at the examination or appeals level within the IRS, or in whatever court he decides to litigate in if settlement cannot be reached. If the taxpayer cannot substantiate his case (i.e., "carry his burden"), then he loses.

In court cases the party having the burden must go first in presenting evidence. If the party having the burden does not present any evidence, whether it be oral (sworn testimony in court), documentary, or demonstrative, then the party without the burden wins without having to do anything.

There are different levels of proof in tax cases. In increasing order of difficulty, they are (1) preponderance of the evidence, (2) clear preponderance of the evidence, (3) clear and convincing evidence, and (4) evidence beyond a reasonable doubt. In most cases that tax practitioners will handle, the standard of proof required is simply a preponderance of the evidence. This means merely that the quantity and competency of the evidence must be greater than that of your opponent. On the other hand, in a criminal prosecution the government must present its case against the defendant with evidence that establishes evidence of guilt beyond a reasonable doubt—a very difficult

154

task in many instances. In civil tax cases, with some limited exceptions noted here, there is no such thing as "innocent until proven guilty."

II. Taxpayer Burden: General Rules

A. *Presumption of Correctness*

Whenever the IRS makes a deficiency determination, it is entitled to a presumption of correctness. This presumption imposes upon the taxpayer the burden of proving that the assessment is erroneous. The presumption is not, however, irrefutable. When an assessment is shown to be without rational foundation or is arbitrary and erroneous, the presumption is not recognized.[1]

B. *Refund Actions and Bankruptcy Cases*

In tax refund suits in federal district court, the IRS may always raise counterclaim issues. If it does so, the taxpayer bears the burden of proof with respect to those issues as well as the issues in the original refund claim. Thus the same burden applies whether in a tax court deficiency redetermination hearing or in district where a refund claim or a government counterclaim is being heard.[2] If the counterclaim relates to fraud, however, the IRS bears the burden. In bankruptcy cases a claimant, typically a creditor, bears the burden of persuasion.[3]

C. *Corporate Reorganizations*

In corporate reorganizations and tax-free incorporations, assumption of a liability is not treated as the receipt of money (i.e., "boot") unless the purpose with respect to such receipt had a tax avoidance motive. The taxpayer has the burden of proving a bona fide business purpose by a *"clear* preponderance" of the evidence.[4]

D. *Expatriation*

Generally U.S. citizens may not give up their U.S. citizenship to escape U.S. taxation. The burden of proving that loss of citizenship did *not* have a tax avoidance motive is on the taxpayer.[5]

E. *Accounting Methods*

I.R.C. §§ 446 and 471 vest the IRS with broad discretion in determining matters involving accounting methods. Thus, taxpayers have a heavy burden of proof in challenging the IRS's determinations.[6] If a taxpayer's books and records do not accurately reflect income, the IRS's determinations, even if based on indirect methods, are entitled to a presumption of correctness.[7]

F.   *Estate Tax Value Issues*
In estate tax cases, the burden is on the estate to establish values lower than those determined by the IRS.[8]

III. Taxpayer Burden: Business and Other Deductions

A.   *General Rule, and Inadequate Records*
It is the taxpayer's burden to prove that the IRS's determination is incorrect by a preponderance of the evidence. However, a lack of records does not give the IRS carte blanche authority to impose draconian absolutes.[9]

B.   *Ordinary and Necessary*
Regarding business expenses, it is always the taxpayer's burden of proof to show that such expenses were not only paid or incurred, but also "ordinary and necessary" in the conduct of business.[10]

C.   *Incomplete Records*
Where records are incomplete or documentary evidence is unavailable, it may be possible to establish the amount of business expenses by approximations based on reliable secondary sources of information and collateral evidence.[11]

D.   *Reasonableness Required*
Regarding business expenses, due consideration will be given to the reasonableness of the stated expenditures for the claimed purpose in relation to the taxpayer's circumstances (such as his or her income and the nature of his or her occupation).[12]

E.   *Absence of Canceled Checks*
Taxpayers who are unable to provide the IRS with canceled checks as proof of expense payment to substantiate deductions may submit account statements prepared by financial institutions. The IRS will accept the following:
1.   Account statements of check clearance,
2.   Electronic funds transfer statements, and
3.   Credit card statements.[13]

F.   *Cohan Rule*
Where an individual has evidently incurred some deductible expenses but does not possess documentary proof thereof, he or she is allowed a reasonable approximation of such items by resorting to reliable secondary sources of information and collateral evidence. The burden of proof in all such cases necessarily falls upon

the taxpayer, and doubts resulting from vague and unsatisfactory evidence may properly be resolved "against him whose inexactitude is of his own making."[14]

IV. IRS Burden

A. *Deductibility of Illegal or Unethical Payments*

If the IRS denies a business deduction on the ground of illegality, the government bears the burden of proving that a payment constitutes an illegal bribe, kickback, or other illegal payment. The IRS's burden in this regard is one of "clear and convincing evidence."[15]

B. *Penalties*

Starting with examinations commencing after July 22, 1998, the IRS, in any court proceeding, has the burden of production (coming forward with the appropriate evidence) with respect to all types of penalties.[16] The burden of production is to be distinguished from the burden of proof. The burden of production is less strenuous than the burden of proof. The former requires only that the government come forward with sufficient evidence indicating that it is appropriate for the IRS to have imposed a penalty.[17]

The IRS has the burden of proof with respect to penalties proposed in the following "abusive" circumstances:
1. Promotion of abusive tax shelters,
2. Aiding and abetting understatement of tax liability, and
3. Filing a frivolous tax return.[18]

The IRS also has the burden of proof in attempting to assert a preparer penalty where the preparer acted willfully.[19] Where the preparer penalty has been asserted under the negligence subsection, however, apparently the taxpayer retains the burden of proof, although the statute is silent on the burden question except for subsection (b).[20]

C. *Criminal and Civil Fraud*

In any proceeding involving the issue of whether the taxpayer has been guilty of fraud with intent to evade tax, the burden of proof is always on the IRS.[21] In criminal tax evasion cases, the IRS bears the burden of providing evidence of guilt beyond a reasonable doubt.[22] Where the IRS has the burden to establish *civil* fraud, the standard is clear and convincing evidence.[23]

D. *"Information" Returns*

If a taxpayer has a reasonable quarrel with the IRS regarding the accuracy of a 1099, or other similar "information" return, assuming the taxpayer has cooperated with the IRS during the audit, the IRS has the burden of producing "reasonable and probative information" in addition to the numbers reflected on the 1099.[24]

E. *Section 83 Property Value Issues*
Where an employer transfers property subject to a restriction that, by its terms, will never lapse and is subject to a formula valuation, the burden of proof is on the IRS to establish a contrary value.[25]

F. *Golden Parachute Issues*
Under I.R.C. § 280G, no deduction is allowed for an "excess" golden parachute payment. A parachute payment includes one that violates securities laws. The IRS has the burden of proof of such a violation.[26]

G. *Accumulated Earnings Tax*
The IRS has the power to impose an accumulated earnings tax (AET) on a corporation whose earnings have accumulated beyond the reasonable needs of the business.[27] If the IRS does not notify the taxpayer by certified mail that a proposed deficiency notice will include an AET amount, then the burden of proof with respect to an unreasonable accumulation shifts to the IRS.[28]

H. *Compelled Disclosure*
The IRS must generally disclose to the public and allow inspections of all written determinations (rulings, etc.). If the IRS refuses such disclosure and the person seeking disclosure has to file suit to compel disclosure, the burden of proof with respect to disclosure is on the IRS.[29]

I. *Transferee Liability*
In a tax court proceeding, the burden of proof is on the IRS to show that a petitioner is liable as a transferee of property of a taxpayer, but *not* to show that the taxpayer-transferor was liable for the tax.[30]

J. *Termination or Jeopardy Assessments*
In the case of termination or jeopardy assessments, the burden of proof regarding reasonableness of the assessment is always on the IRS.[31] However, where the *amount* of the assessment is the issue, the burden remains with the taxpayer.[32]

K. *Six-Year Statute of Limitations*
If the taxpayer has omitted more than 25 percent of his or her gross income, then in lieu of the normal three-year assessment statute, the I.R.C. provides for a six-year rule.[33] When the IRS invokes this extended statutory period, it bears the burden of proving the omission of more than 25 percent of gross income.[34] The IRS must meet this burden only

by affirmative evidence. It may not rely only on the normal presumption of correctness.[35]

V. Burden Shifting

A. *General Rule*
Once the taxpayer overcomes the government's presumption of correctness by presenting "competent and relevant credible evidence" establishing that the IRS's position is erroneous, the burden of going forward shifts to the IRS.[36] The reason behind the burden-shifting principle in unreported income cases is that the taxpayer bears the difficult burden of proving a negative, that is, that he or she did not receive the income in question.

B. *Statutory Shifting*
1. *Credible Evidence Required*
   In any court proceeding, if a taxpayer introduces "credible" evidence with respect to any relevant fact issue, the burden of proof then shifts to the IRS.[37] Although this rule was a new statutory enactment effective in 1998, it is not radically different from the rules as they existed before 1998. The taxpayer still has the burden of going forward with the production of evidence before the burden can shift.

   A taxpayer's self-serving testimony that is not considered credible by the trier of fact will not serve as a basis for shifting the burden.[38]
2. *Limitations on Statutory Rule*
   The courtroom burden does not shift to the government for any issue where it is established that the taxpayer has failed (presumably at the examination level) to substantiate any item.[39] Moreover, the taxpayer must have maintained all records required by law and must have been responsive with regard to all IRS requests for information and interviews.[40]

VI. Income Issues

A. *Necessity for Substantive Evidence*
On an income issue, before the government can rely on a presumption of correctness, it must offer some substantive evidence showing that the taxpayer received income from the charged activity.[41]

B. *Taxpayer Testimony*
In unreported income cases the ultimate burden of proof shifts to the IRS. A trial court must give proper weight to a taxpayer's testimony where the taxpayer rebuts the IRS's assertion of understated income.[42]

C. *Necessity for Predicate Evidence of Income*

Where there is an income issue, the IRS must provide some predicate evidence of understated income before issuing a deficiency notice. Otherwise the taxpayer is relieved of the burden of going forward with the evidence.[43]

D. *Use of Statistics by the Government*

The IRS is not accorded the presumption of correctness where income is concerned. Therefore, the IRS cannot simply assume that a taxpayer's income is the same as the year before, increased by an inflationary factor.[44] Similarly, the IRS cannot use statistics to recalculate someone's income where the taxpayer has contemporaneous records of his or her income.[45]

In the case of an individual taxpayer, the IRS has the burden of proof in any court proceeding with respect to income items where the adjustment was developed through the use of statistical data obtained from unrelated taxpayers.[46]

E. *Net Worth Method*

The IRS is generally permitted to determine income based on indirect means. One of their favorite indirect techniques is the net worth method. The burden of establishing opening net worth, however, is on the IRS.[47]

VII. U.S. Tax Court

A. *Tax Court Rules*

In U.S. Tax Court, the IRS bears the burden of proof in regard to the following:
1. New matters raised subsequent to the issuance of the deficiency notice,
2. Increases in deficiency, and
3. Affirmative defenses pleaded in the answer.

Otherwise, the burden of proof is on the petitioner, except as otherwise provided by statute.[48]

B. *New Matters*

A new position taken by the IRS in tax court is not necessarily a "new matter," especially when it merely clarifies or develops the original determination without being inconsistent or increasing the amount of the deficiency.[49]

C. *Closing Agreements*

The tax court has the power to review the determination of the IRS in setting aside a closing agreement, and the IRS has the burden of proof in such cases.[50]

VIII. Miscellaneous Rules

A. *Bankruptcy Court*
In bankruptcy court, if the IRS submits a proof of claim for taxes, it is presumptively valid unless a party in interest (typically the taxpayer) submits an objection.[51]

B. *Motions for Summary Judgment*
On motions for summary judgment, the moving party bears the initial burden of proof to establish that no genuine factual issue exists. Where the moving party satisfies its burden, the burden of going forward shifts to the nonmoving party to demonstrate that a genuine issue of material fact indeed exists.[52]

C. *Litigation Costs*
In some cases, the I.R.C. allows taxpayers to recover litigation costs where they substantially prevail and the government's position is not substantially justified.[53] The Taxpayer Bill of Rights 2 (1996) provides that the burden of proof is on the IRS to establish that it was substantially justified in maintaining its position.[54]

D. *Extensions of the Statute of Limitations*
Once a taxpayer establishes a prima facie case that a deficiency notice was not timely, the burden of proof shifts to the IRS, which then must produce a valid extension agreement executed by the taxpayer. If it cannot do this, the court will hold that the statute of limitations has expired and invalidate the deficiency.[55]

IX. Conclusion

A tax controversy practitioner should not automatically assume that his or her client bears the burden of proof in a federal tax case. While the taxpayer burden is the general rule, there are numerous statutory and judicial exceptions.

X. Notes

1. Pittman v. Comm'r, 96-2 USTC ¶ 50,658 (7th Cir. 1996); Price v. United States, 14 AFTR2d 5519 (5th Cir. 1964).
2. Carson v. United States, 78-1 USTC ¶ 16,280 (5th Cir. 1977).
3. *In re* Paul E. Abel, 96-2 USTC ¶ 50,498 (E.D. Pa. 1996).
4. I.R.C. § 357(b)(2).
5. I.R.C. § 877(f); *See also* § 2107(d) regarding a similar rule regarding expatriation to avoid estate tax.
6. I.R.S. Priv. Ltr. Rul. 8811001.
7. Mallette Bros. Constr. Co. v. United States, 83-1 USTC ¶ 9144 (5th Cir. 1988).
8. Rev. Rul. 76-112, 1976-1 CB 276; Rev. Rul. 67-276, 1967-2 CB 321.

9. Carson v. United States, 78-1 USTC ¶ 16,280 (5th Cir. 1977).
10. Treas. Reg. § 1.162-17(d)(2).
11. Treas. Reg. § 1.162-17(d)(3).
12. *Id.*
13. Rev. Proc. 92-71, 1992-2 CB 61.
14. Rev. Rul. 54-195, 1954-1 CB 1; Cohan v. Comm'r, 39 F.2d 540, 8 AFTR 10,552 (2d Cir. 1930).
15. I.R.C. § 162(c)(2); Treas. Reg. § 1.162-18(a)(5).
16. I.R.C. § 7491(c).
17. *Id.*; Spurlock v. Comm'r, 85 T.C.M. (CCH) 1236 (2003).
18. I.R.C. § 6703(a).
19. Treas. Reg. § 1.6694-3(h).
20. I.R.C. § 7427).
21. I.R.C. § 7454(a); T.C. Rule 142(b).
22. McGirl v. Comm'r, 72 T.C.M. (CCH) 66 (1996), fn.14.
23. Rev. Rul. 80-334, 1980-2 CB 61.
24. I.R.C. § 6201(d). Note that this is a codification of the rule first enunciated in *Portillo v. Comm'r*, 91-2 USTC ¶ 50,304 (5th Cir. 1991).
25. I.R.C. § 83(d)(1).
26. I.R.C. § 280G(b)(2)(B).
27. *See* I.R.C. §§ 531 *et seq.*
28. I.R.C. § 534(a)(1).
29. I.R.C. § 6110(f)(4)(A).
30. I.R.C. § 6902(a).
31. I.R.C. § 7429(g)(1).
32. I.R.C. § 7429(g)(2).
33. *See* I.R.C. § 6501(e)(1)(A).
34. Reis v. Comm'r, 1 T.C. 9 (1942).
35. Kavoosi v. Comm'r, 51 T.C.M. (CCH) 993 (1986).
36. Demkowicz v. Comm'r, 77-1 USTC ¶ 9318 (3d Cir. 1977).
37. I.R.C. § 7491(a)(1).
38. Blodgett v. Comm'r, 86 T.C.M. (CCH) 90 (2003).
39. I.R.C. § 7491(a)(2)(A).
40. I.R.C. § 7491(a)(2)(B).
41. Weimerskirch v. Comm'r, 79-1 USTC ¶ 9359 (9th Cir. 1979).
42. Anatasato v. Comm'r, 86-2 USTC ¶ 9529 (3d Cir. 1986).
43. Sealy Power, Ltd. v. Comm'r, 95-1 USTC ¶ 50,103 (5th Cir. 1995).
44. Senter v. Comm'r, 70 T.C.M. (CCH) 54 (1995).
45. Krause v. Comm'r, 63 T.C.M. (CCH) 2968 (1992), a case involving bartender tips.
46. I.R.C. § 7491(b).
47. Yoon v. Comm'r, 98-1 USTC ¶ 50,245 (5th Cir. 1998).
48. T.C. Rule 142.
49. Estate of Jayne v. Comm'r, 61 T.C. 744 (1974).
50. Holmes & James, Inc. v. Comm'r, 30 BTA 74 (1934).
51. *In re* Vines, 96-2 USTC ¶ 50,603 (M.D. Fla. 1996).
52. Kenny v. United States, 79 AFTR2d 97-2189 (Bankr. N.D. Ga. 1997).
53. *See* I.R.C. § 7430.
54. I.R.C. § 7430(c)(4)(B).
55. Mantzel v. Comm'r, 41 T.C.M. (CCH) 1237 (1981).

Recovery of Costs under I.R.C. § 7430

I. Background and Legislative History

A. Pre-TEFRA

Prior to the enactment of TEFRA in 1982, taxpayers were limited in their pursuit of lawyer fees against the government to the Equal Access to Justice Act.[1] Under that law a prevailing taxpayer in an Article I court (federal district courts, but not the tax court) could be awarded reasonable lawyer fees where the government's position (e.g., refusal to grant a refund, issue a favorable ruling, etc.) was not "substantially justified."[2] Congress decided that additional legislation was needed to provide a greater measure of relief in circumstances where taxpayers are compelled to engage in litigation with the government to assert their rights regarding tax matters whether as petitioner or as defendant. There appeared to be no rational reason for excluding from the coverage of such rules litigation in the tax court solely because its powers are constitutionally limited.

B. Congressional Purpose: Economic Circumstances

The congressional purpose behind awarding litigation and administrative costs to taxpayers is to enable individual taxpayers to vindicate their rights regardless of their economic circumstances and to deter abusive actions and overreaching by the IRS.[3] Obviously the desire was to create a level playing field for tax controversy opponents with disparate economic resources.

C. TEFRA

The current rule authorizing an award of lawyer fees in tax cases was a result of TEFRA in 1982.[4] TEFRA added new I.R.C. section 7430, Awarding of Costs and Certain Fees.

As the statute is presently crafted, it reads,

> In any administrative or court proceeding which is brought by or against the United States in connection with the determination,

collection, or refund of any tax, interest, or penalty under this title, the prevailing party may be awarded a judgment or a settlement for—(1) reasonable administrative costs incurred in connection with such administrative proceeding within the Internal Revenue Service, and (2) reasonable litigation costs incurred in connection with such court proceeding.

In tax cases brought in forums other than the U.S. Tax Court, both the Title 26 (TEFRA) provisions and Title 28 (EAJA) provisions are available as alternative remedies. Thus, if the plaintiff in a refund suit prevails but the court denies a claim for litigation costs under § 7430, court costs are still recoverable under 28 U.S. Code (U.S.C.) 2412, which provides for the awarding of such costs as may be allowed under common law or any statute. Of course, in tax court, the prevailing taxpayer is limited to using Title 26 as a remedy for recovery of costs.

D. *Hourly Rate Caps*
The Tax Reform Act of 1986 (TRA) eliminated the old $25,000 cap on the award of lawyer fees and substituted a $75 per hour limitation unless the court determined that a higher rate was justified.[5] This act also changed the "unreasonable" standard to "not substantially justified," the standard applicable to the EAJA. The Taxpayers Bill of Rights 2 (TBOR 2; 1996) raised the $75 per hour limit on lawyer fees to $110, indexed for inflation beginning after 1996. The IRS Restructuring and Reform Act of 1998 (RRA) increased the base rate to $125 per hour, adjusted for inflation starting in 1997. Of course, a higher rate can be approved but only upon a showing of special factors such as the difficulty of the case or the limited availability of qualified lawyers.

II. Litigation Costs

A. *"Position" Issues*
Where litigation costs are involved, the IRS's position is the government's position taken by counsel in the litigation proceeding to which § 7430(a) applies.[6] Nevertheless, prelitigation conduct can be considered by the court because the IRS's position at the highest administrative level is what engenders the court action.[7]

B. *Definition of Court Proceeding*
A "court proceeding" means any civil tax action brought in any of the following courts of original jurisdiction: (1) federal district court, (2) bankruptcy court, (3) tax court, or (4) court of federal claims.[8] Although the bankruptcy court is not mentioned by name in § 7430, an action, for

example, to hold the IRS in civil contempt for collection in violation of a bankruptcy discharge concerns tax, and it is, therefore, a court proceeding for litigation expense purposes.

C. *Types of Litigation Costs That May Be Awarded*
"Reasonable litigation costs" include the following:
1. Reasonable expenses of expert witness(es);
2. Costs of any study, analysis,[9] engineering report, test, or project that is found by the court to be necessary for the preparation of the case;[10]
3. Fees of an individual authorized to practice before the court or the IRS (whether or not a lawyer),[11] generally not in excess of $125 per hour (indexed to inflation, with increase multiples rounded to $10); and
4. Reasonable court costs.[12]
   a. Note that reasonable court costs include filing fees.[13]

D. *Expert Witness Fees*
Expert witnesses cannot be compensated at a rate higher than that paid by the U.S. government for similar fees.[14]

E. *Reasonableness of Fees*
Reasonable litigation costs must be based upon prevailing market rates for the kind and quality of services furnished.[15] It is advisable to submit contemporaneous billing records as one of the exhibits in support of the litigation costs motion.[16] Vague testimony that does not establish the total number of hours or the hourly rate of the billing lawyer will not suffice. Fees of a "consulting" lawyer will not be allowed to the extent that his or her services are duplicative of those of the primary lawyer.[17]

F. *Pro Bono Services*
The court may award reasonable lawyer fees in excess of those actually incurred if such fees are intentionally low (or even zero) because the lawyer was working on a "pro bono" basis for his or her client.[18]

G. *Recent Litigation*
In a blistering attack on the way the IRS conducted its audit, the tax court awarded the following to the taxpayer:
1. Five hours for accounting services at $75 per hour;
2. Forty-three hours for law clerks and paralegals at a rate of $30 per hour; and
3. Over $29,000 in lawyer fees, representing 242 hours of lawyer time, which the tax court found to be reasonable.[19]

H. *Contingency Fee Cases*

Where actual costs incurred by a taxpayer who had contracted with a lawyer for services under a contingency fee arrangement are less than they would have been under an hourly arrangement, the statutory award is limited to the lower of the two. That is, nothing in excess of the amount due under the contingency arrangement was "incurred" by the taxpayer.[20]

III. Administrative Costs

A. *Definition*

"Administrative proceeding" means any procedure or other action before the IRS, as opposed to court proceedings. This means generally that the costs of the administrative appeals process may be recovered.[21] Note, however, that certain administrative proceedings are *not* covered by § 7430. For example, *no costs* can be recovered for the following:

1. Proceedings involving hearings on regulations, forms, revenue rulings, etc.;
2. Proceedings involving private letter rulings;
3. Proceedings involving technical advice memoranda; and
4. Collection actions. "Collection actions" are defined as follows:
   a. Anything generally done by the IRS's Collection function,
   b. Failure to release a lien, or
   c. Unauthorized collection actions.
   d. Note, however, that procedures relating to claims for refund after payment of tax are not considered collection actions.[22]

B. *Date of "Position"*

Administrative costs may not be recovered if they were incurred prior to the date the IRS takes an official position in a case. This is also known as the "administrative proceeding date."[23] In the case of administrative costs, the IRS's position is the position taken as of the earliest of the following:

1. The date the taxpayer received a decision notice from the IRS Office of Appeals (usually a letter from an appeals officer or associate chief);[24]
2. The date of the deficiency notice (ninety-day letter); or
3. The date on which the first letter of proposed deficiency allows the taxpayer an opportunity for administrative review in the Appeals Office (thirty-day letter).[25]

C. *Procedures under the Regulations*

The IRS has issued proposed regulations under which taxpayers prevailing in administrative proceedings before the IRS may recover costs. This is done by filing an application with the IRS to recover costs in connection with the determination, collection, or refund of any tax.

The following conditions must be satisfied:

1. The issues must never have been before a court;
2. There must have been an "administrative proceeding";
3. The costs must have been incurred after the "administrative proceeding date";
4. The costs must qualify as "reasonable administrative costs" as defined in the regulations;
5. The taxpayer must have prevailed;
6. The taxpayer must not have unreasonably prolonged the proceeding; and
7. The taxpayer must follow the application procedures for filing a "request" as outlined in the regulations.[26]

D. *Procedures for Filing an Administrative Costs "Request"*[27]

No administrative costs will be allowed unless a written request is filed that meets the following requirements:

1. File the request with the office having jurisdiction over the tax matter in question.
2. Contents:
   a. Statement that the issues have never been before any court;
   b. Statement of reasons that the IRS's position is not substantially justified;
   c. Statement that the taxpayer has substantially prevailed;
   d. Statement that the taxpayer has not unreasonably protracted the proceedings;
   e. Statement supported by a detailed affidavit specifying each item of costs sought to be recovered;
   f. Affidavit regarding net worth;
   g. Billing records of the representative for the requested fees; and
   h. An address to which the determination should be mailed.
3. No specific form is required.
4. The request (application) must be filed before the ninety-first day after the date the IRS's final decision is mailed to the taxpayer.[28] If the IRS does not respond to the request within six months, a denial may be presumed.
5. A denial of a request for administrative costs may be appealed to the U.S. Tax Court by filing an appropriate petition.[29] Such a petition must be filed before the ninety-first day after the certified or registered mailing of a decision denying (in whole or in part) an award for reasonable administrative costs.[30]

E. *Types of Recoverable Costs*

The types of costs recoverable in an administrative cost request are similar to those recoverable in a litigation context. They include, for example, the following:

1. Any administrative fees or similar charges imposed by the IRS; and
2. Expenses, costs, and fees described in II.C., *supra*, except that all "reasonableness" issues are determined by the IRS instead of a court.[31]

IV. Reasons for Denial of Award of Costs

A. *Exhaustion of Administrative Remedies*

No costs will be awarded where the prevailing party failed to exhaust all of the administrative remedies available within the IRS.[32] The requirement that administrative remedies be exhausted is designed to permit the IRS to pass upon the merits of a person's claim before litigation commences. This generally means that the taxpayer or his or her representative must participate in the conference procedures of the IRS's Appeals Office where such procedures are available. "Participation" means disclosure of all relevant information that the taxpayer knew or should have known about. That is, the taxpayer may not hold back any of his or her cards to play later. The regulations contain eleven examples of the application of these rules.[33]

The regulations formerly specified that a party has not exhausted his or her administrative remedies unless he or she has participated in an appeals conference (if available) prior to filing a tax court petition and, furthermore, has extended the three-year assessment statute of limitations, if necessary.[34] Now the regulations specify that failure to extend the assessment statute will not be fatal to a claim for costs.

In a 1987 tax court case, the taxpayers had refused to extend the statute of limitations by executing a requested Form 872 or 872-A. The taxpayers subsequently filed a motion for litigation costs under I.R.C. § 7430. The tax court held that the regulations were invalid insofar as they provide that a refusal to extend the statute of limitations will be considered a failure to exhaust administrative remedies.[35] The regulations have now been redrafted to reflect the *Minahan* rule.[36]

In cases where no appeals conference was offered prior to the issuance of a deficiency notice, the taxpayer cannot refuse to participate in an Appeals Office conference while the case is in tax court docketed status.[37]

B. *Delay*

Costs will be denied for any portion of the proceeding where the prevailing party caused unreasonable delay.[38]

C. *Receipt of Thirty-Day Letter*

If a taxpayer receives a thirty-day letter, he or she must respond by filing a protest; otherwise, the taxpayer will forfeit his or her right to litigation costs due to not having exhausted his or her administrative remedies.[39] If, on the other hand, the IRS issues a deficiency notice (ninety-day letter) in lieu of a thirty-day letter, the taxpayer has been effectively denied the opportunity to have a prelitigation appeals conference. In such a case, refusal to participate in an appeals conference at the administrative level will be an ineffective argument by the government, as no appeals conference would have been offered.[40]

V. "Reasonableness" Issues

A. *General Policy*

Congress did not authorize payment in every case where the taxpayer prevails.[41] The fact that the government loses the case is not determinative.[42] The rules are designed to limit recoveries to situations where the pursuit of a case was unreasonable because the IRS knew or should have known that it had little or no chance of winning. The position of the IRS is not substantially justified where action is taken without factual or legal support, or without adequate investigation and analysis of its position. Most circuits have interpreted "substantial justification" to be virtually synonymous with "reasonable."[43]

B. *Examples of "Unreasonable" Conduct*

The IRS's steadfastly clinging to an inflexible position despite a petitioner's efforts to conduct meaningful negotiations can result in a court's finding of unreasonableness.[44] In the same case, the tax court took into consideration "whether the government used the costs and expenses of litigation against its position to extract concessions from the taxpayer that were not justified under the circumstances of the case."

Where the government never explained why it required the taxpayer to litigate over previously allowed deductions or where it issued further deficiency notices in the face of a prior court's order can serve as the basis for an award of costs.[45]

The IRS's presumption of correctness is not a basis in both fact and law for the IRS's position where the IRS had no information and made no attempt to obtain information about the case before adopting the position.[46]

The IRS's failure to accept a *limited* consent to extend the statute of limitations may result in that refusal being per se unreasonable, resulting in an award of costs to the taxpayer. Also, this case reinforced the rule that substantial justification must exist on the day the deficiency notice is issued, not just in the period following its issuance.[47]

In a case where the taxpayer had requested a change of place of audit and had executed one extension of the statute of limitations, the IRS sat on the file for over ten months without action until only 2.5 months were left. When the taxpayer refused to extend the statute further, the revenue agent arbitrarily disallowed 75 percent of the claimed deductions. After a tax court petition was filed, 97 percent of the disallowed deductions were conceded by the government. The court held that the government's "frittering away" ten months was unreasonable and the basis for an award of costs.[48]

The IRS's ignoring of the appraisal (in the amount of $500,000) of an artwork for forty-four months and insisting on a value of $1,500 even into litigation was an abuse of discretion justifying an award of costs under § 7430.[49]

Inordinate and unexplained delay by the IRS and/or its counsel can, in and of itself, support a determination of unreasonableness.[50]

"Unreasonable" conduct does not necessarily have to be "outrageous." Where, for example, the IRS imposed a delinquency penalty when, in fact, the taxpayers mailed a Form 4868 automatic extension request in a timely manner, an award of costs was made. The taxpayer's uncontroverted, credible testimony prevailed where the government could not produce a postmarked envelope to refute that evidence.[51]

In a 1987 case, the government argued that a letter sent to the taxpayer following a deficiency notice that the government admitted was sent to the wrong address was sufficient to put the taxpayer on notice that the ninety-day period started to run. The court held this to be patently "unreasonable" and awarded the petitioner his costs.[52]

Unreasonableness does not require a showing of bad faith on the part of the government. In a trust fund recovery[53] case recently, a district court stated that the "government's inability to keep its personnel on the same page" forced the taxpayer to file suit and prosecute his lawsuit. During the pendency of the lawsuit, the IRS had levied on his pension checks while his meritorious challenge was pending and even after the assessment had been paid![54]

C. *Timing of Determination of Reasonableness*

In determining the reasonableness of the IRS's position, reference should be made to the IRS's prelitigation position at the time the court action (petition) is initiated, as well as during the litigation process itself, but not during the entire administrative proceedings.[55]

D. *Substantiation Cases*

Taxpayers cannot withhold information from the IRS until the very last minute and then hope to recoup their administrative or litigation costs. Indeed, whenever there is a factual determination, the IRS need not concede the case until it receives the necessary documentation to prove the taxpayer's contentions.[56] Nevertheless, where taxpayers cooperate extensively with the IRS's auditor and agents and provide substantiation when requested, the IRS cannot use the "withholding of evidence" argument.[57]

VI. Prevailing Party

A. *Who Makes the Determination?*
The determination as to who is a prevailing party is made by the IRS at the administrative level or by the court in a litigation context.[58] The determination may also be made by agreement of the parties. A "prevailing party" cannot be the United States or a creditor of the taxpayer.[59]

B. *General Rule*
A taxpayer is held to have "substantially prevailed" in a particular case if he or she has substantially prevailed with respect to the amount in controversy or with respect to the most significant issue or set of issues presented.[60] But note that there is no per se rule that litigation costs are recoverable whenever the IRS concedes the case, no matter how prompt the concession. That is, the fact that the government ultimately loses the case is not determinative as to whether the taxpayer is entitled to an award of reasonable litigation costs.[61]

C. *Recent Litigation*
In a 1994 case the taxpayer lost an attempt to claim costs because the IRS won 80 percent of its claimed deficiency and five of the seven issues in the case.[62]

D. *Qualified Offers*[63]
   1. *Federal Rules of Civil Procedure (FRCP)*
   Rule 68 of the FRCP provides for a procedure under which a party may recover costs if the party's offer for settlement was rejected and the subsequent court judgment was less favorable to the opposing party than the offer. The FRCP generally apply to tax litigation in the district courts and the U.S. Court of Federal Claims. They do not apply to tax court litigation.
   2. *General Rules*
   An award of fees and costs may be available if, after a taxpayer has a right to administrative review in the IRS Office of Appeals, the taxpayer makes a "qualified" offer that the IRS rejects and the IRS obtains a judgment against the taxpayer in an amount that is equal to or less than the taxpayer's offer (without regard to interest).[64] In this situation, the taxpayer should be treated as the prevailing party. (Note: The "qualified offer" rule does not apply to judgments issued pursuant to a *settlement*[65] or in a proceeding in which the amount of tax liability is not at issue, such as a declaratory judgment proceeding or a summons enforcement proceeding.[66])
   Qualified offers may be submitted in any type of federal tax controversy. They are not limited to income tax cases. For example,

if an offer is made to the Department of Justice in a trust fund liability case and a jury subsequently finds that a corporate officer was not responsible or did not act willfully, then he or she will be treated as the prevailing party.[67]

3. *Other Rules*
   - "Qualified offer" means the last offer made with reference to the particular tax liability, and costs include only those incurred after the date of such offer.[68]
   - If the taxpayer is a "prevailing party" under any other definition, then the "qualified offer" provisions will not apply.[69]
   - Whenever a taxpayer makes a qualified offer to fully resolve all adjustments at issue, he or she may not thereafter attempt to reduce his or her offer by attempting to renegotiate it. For example, an after-the-fact attempt to apply net operating losses against the previously negotiated settlement number will not work.[70]
   - Even if the government wins at trial, but the taxpayer is found to be liable for an amount less than what the taxpayer conceded in a qualified offer, the IRS will be treated as having lacked substantial justification in rejecting the settlement offer and going to trial.[71]

4. *Technical Requirements for "Qualified Offers"*
   - Offers must be made by a taxpayer during a "qualified offer period" defined as the period beginning on the date on which the first letter of proposed deficiency allows the taxpayer an opportunity for an appeals conference and ending thirty days before the date the case is first set for trial.[72] In the case of a qualified offer, the taxpayer is entitled to costs incurred from the date of the offer forward even if the government's position before the date of the offer was substantially justified.[73]
   - An offer must specify the offered amount of the taxpayer's liability.
   - An offer must be designated specifically as a "qualified offer."
   - An offer must remain open during the period beginning on the date it is made and ending on the earliest of the three following dates: the date the offer is rejected, the date the trial begins, or the ninetieth day after the date the offer is made.[74]

E. *Adverse Decisions in Other Circuits*

In determining whether the position of the IRS is substantially justified, the court will take into account whether the IRS has lost in appeals courts of other circuits on substantially similar issues.[75]

VII. Net Worth Limits

A. *General Rule*
An award of costs may be made only if the taxpayer meets certain net worth limitations. The net worth limit is $2 million, set by another federal statute.[76] The $2 million rule applies to individual[77] taxpayers, trusts, and estates.

B. *Definition*
Although the term "net worth" is not statutorily defined, the legislative history indicates that in determining the value of assets, the cost of acquisition rather than fair market value should be used.[78]

C. *Recent Cases*
A movant must present proof in his or her motion for costs that his or her net worth is less than $2 million. Otherwise, a court will not even reach the other § 7430 tests.[79] For example, in a 1994 case the taxpayer lost because he failed to submit an affidavit that his net worth was less than $2 million.[80] Representations of counsel regarding net worth are insufficient; there must be an affidavit signed by the taxpayer.

D. *Corporations and Business Taxpayers*
Corporations, partnerships, and sole proprietorships meet the net worth test if their net worth does not exceed $7 million *and* they do not have more than 500 employees.[81]

E. *Proof of Net Worth*
Mere submission of an affidavit regarding net worth may be inadequate. In close cases, it is always advisable to submit a cost-basis balance sheet with a claim for § 7430 costs.[82]

VIII. Tax Court Rules

A. The Rules of Practice and Procedure for the U.S. Tax Court contain a section regarding claims for litigation and administrative costs.[83]
B. Additionally, the tax court rules contain a section dealing strictly with actions for administrative costs.[84]
C. Tax court cases do not have to be tried for there to be an award of costs. In agreed cases, the award is included in the stipulated decision submitted by the parties for entry by the court.[85] However, the government's failure to stipulate recovery of litigation costs under this rule, standing alone, does not entitle a taxpayer to such costs.[86]
D. If there is no agreement as to a party's entitlement to costs, a claim is made by the petitioner's filing of a motion:
   1. Within thirty days after a written opinion has been issued by the court;

2. Within thirty days of service of the transcript pages following a Rule 152 bench (oral) ruling; or

3. After the parties have settled all issues other than litigation costs.[87]

E. A written motion for costs must contain at least the following:

1. A statement that the moving party is a party to an appropriate action;

2. If it is a claim for administrative costs, a statement that the administrative proceeding was commenced after November 10, 1988;

3. A statement that the moving party has substantially prevailed;

4. Reasons why the position(s) of the IRS were not substantially justified (including a statement of facts);

5. A statement that the moving party's net worth does not exceed $2 million;[88]

6. A statement that the movant has exhausted all administrative remedies;

7. A statement that the movant has not unreasonably protracted the court or administrative process;

8. A statement (supported by an affidavit) of specific costs claimed;

9. If a hearing is requested, a statement of reasons why the motion cannot be disposed of without a hearing; and

10. A prayer for relief.[89]

F. *Petition*

A claim for litigation or administrative costs is *not* included in a tax court petition.[90]

G. *Hearing*

Ordinarily the § 7430 issues will be disposed of by the tax court without an evidentiary hearing unless it is clear from the motion and the response that there is a bona fide factual dispute that cannot be resolved without a hearing.[91]

IX. Appeal

A. An order granting or denying an award for litigation costs becomes part of the decision or judgment in the case and is subject to appeal in the same manner as the decision or judgment.[92]

B. A decision by the IRS granting or denying (in whole or in part) an award for reasonable administrative costs can be appealed to the U.S. Tax Court under rules similar to those for S cases[93] without regard to the amount in dispute.[94]

X. Miscellaneous Provisions

A. *Appropriation of Funds*

Funds are appropriated for administrative costs under Title 31, § 1304 of the U.S.C. Awards payable under § 7430 are payable in the case of the tax court in the same manner as such an award by a district court.[95]

B. *Multiple Actions*

For purposes of litigation costs, multiple actions that could have been consolidated or joined are treated as one court proceeding.[96]

C. *Pro Se Litigants*

The tax court held in a case of first impression in 1986 that a pro se litigant, even though he was a lawyer, was not entitled to the value of his own services under § 7430 even though he proved that the IRS's position was unreasonable.[97] However, in 1987 a federal district court in North Carolina held that a pro se litigant, a lawyer, was entitled to an award of lawyer fees at $90 per hour for 97.8 hours of his own time. The district court found the tax court's reasoning in *Frisch* (the 1986 case) "unpersuasive." Clearly, the defendant "paid" for his services by forgoing other opportunities.[98] Unfortunately the district court was reversed on appeal by the government.[99]

D. *Dismissal for Lack of Jurisdiction*

Section 7430 permits an award of litigation costs following a determination that a case should be dismissed for lack of jurisdiction.[100] The reasoning for this rule is that an order of dismissal for lack of jurisdiction is a final order, appealable as such, and surely is either a "judgment" or a "decision" within the meaning of § 7430(f)(1).

E. *Burden of Proof*

Prior to 1996, taxpayers bore the burden of proof in § 7430 cases. However, pursuant to TBOR 2, the statute was amended to require the IRS to prove that its position was substantially justified.[101] The effect of this provision was to bring § 7430 into line with the EAJA, which had always placed the burden on the government. This new rule shifts the burden only with respect to "substantial justification." The taxpayer retains the burden of proof as to the other elements of a lawyer's fee action, including (1) net worth limitation, (2) whether the taxpayer has substantially prevailed, and (3) whether the taxpayer has exhausted his or her administrative remedies.

F. *Statutory Presumption of "No Justification"*

For purposes of the burden of proof being on the IRS to establish justification, the position of the IRS is presumed *not* to have justification if the IRS field personnel did not follow their "applicable published guidance" in the administrative proceeding. This presumption is rebuttable. For this purpose, applicable published guidance means the following: (1) regulations, (2) revenue rulings, (3) revenue procedures, (4) information releases, (5) notices, (6) announcements, (7) private letter rulings, (8) technical advice memoranda, and (9) determination letters. Note that items 7 through 9 are applicable only if they were issued to the taxpayer being investigated.[102]

G. *Employment Tax Cases*

Litigation and administrative costs may also be sought in actions brought in the tax court for the determination of the employment status of workers.[103] Appropriate actions for costs may be brought where field personnel make determinations contrary to the manifest weight of the common law factors relevant to independent contractor status.

H. *Tax Protesters*

A litigant's status as an IRS-branded "tax protester" will not deprive him or her of the right to protection afforded by § 7430.[104]

I. *Criminal and Civil Fraud Cases*

Will § 7430 or the EAJA provide any relief to criminal tax defendants who have substantially prevailed after having been investigated and indicted? Probably not.[105] But there is hope. In the Hyde Amendment, a new statute provides for the award of lawyer fees for criminal defendants who can prove that the government's position is not substantially justified.[106] This statute incorporates many provisions of the EAJA.[107]

Acquittal of criminal fraud will not necessarily result in the government not having "substantial justification." Even where the government cannot prove a civil fraud case, it may yet prevail as having substantial justification. Where the government could "reasonably believe" that a court would find evidence of civil fraud, no litigation costs will be awarded.[108]

J. *Costs of Arguing the Motion for Costs*

Obviously counsel for the movant-taxpayer must spend sometimes a considerable amount of time in preparing and litigating the issue of costs under § 7430. In the cases that have considered whether such costs are covered by the statute, recovery has generally been allowed.[109]

K. *Setoff Issue*

If an award of costs is made when the taxpayer owes money to the government in an unrelated matter, the government will often refuse to pay, arguing its statutory right of setoff. Taxpayers will likely prevail in this argument, however, under the theory that the government is precluded from exercising its right of setoff due to a lack of "mutuality of debt." That is, while such an award is nominally made to the prevailing party (taxpayer), the *real* party in interest is the lawyer, not his or her client.[110]

L. *Unauthorized Disclosure*

There is a split of authority among the circuits as to whether a § 7431 (civil damages for unauthorized disclosure) action automatically qualifies for an award of costs under § 7430.[111]

M. *Partnerships*

Partnerships governed by the TEFRA audit rules[112] can be awarded § 7430 costs just as individuals and corporations can. First-tier partners who meet the net worth tests are eligible to receive the award, but only to the extent of their allocable share.[113]

XI. Notes

1. 28 U.S.C. § 2412 provides that a judgment for costs and reasonable lawyer fees may be awarded to prevailing parties in civil actions brought by or against the United States or any agency thereof or any official acting in an official capacity. But the provisions of 28 U.S.C. § 2412 do not apply to costs and expenses awarded under 26 U.S.C. § 7430.
2. Pub. L. No. 94-48, 28 U.S.C. § 2412(d)(1)(A).
3. H.R. Rep. No. 97-404, at 11 (1982).
4. Tax Equity and Fiscal Responsibility Act of 1982, § 292(a).
5. Committee Report on Pub. L. No. 99-514, Tax Reform Act of 1986.
6. I.R.C. § 7430(c)(7)(A).
7. Powell v. Comm'r, 86-2 USTC ¶ 9486 (5th Cir. 1986).
8. I.R.C. § 7430(c)(6).
9. In reversing the tax court, the Fifth Circuit has held that reasonable litigation costs include the fees of an accounting firm not working under the direction or employ of an individual authorized to practice before the court. The fees of one who prepares an analysis or report necessary for a party's case are recoverable as reasonable litigation costs, irrespective of whether the person is admitted to practice before the tax court, or employed by someone who is. Ragan v. Comm'r, 98-1 USTC ¶ 50,209 (5th Cir. 1998).
10. Based on prevailing market rates. I.R.C. § 7430(c)(1)(B).
11. I.R.C. § 7430(c)(3)(A).
12. I.R.C. § 7430(c)(1)(A).
13. Frisch v. Comm'r, 87 T.C. 838 (1986).
14. I.R.C. § 7430(c)(1)(B)(i).
15. I.R.C. § 7430(c)(1)(B).
16. Heasley v. Comm'r, 92-2 USTC ¶ 50,412 (5th Cir. 1992).
17. Human v. Comm'r, 75 T.C.M. (CCH) 1814 (1998).
18. I.R.C. § 7430(c)(3)(B) enacted as a part of the IRS Restructuring and Reform Act of 1998.

19. Han v. Comm'r, 66 T.C.M. (CCH) 499 (1993). In the *Han* case the court relied on the Committee Reports behind § 7430 and cited the "abusive tactics and over-reaching" language. But the court went on to say that the facts support the petitioners' contention that the facts present a textbook example of how respondent should not conduct an examination. The petitioners had cited numerous examples of being bullied and verbally assaulted.
20. Marre v. United States, 94-2 USTC ¶ 50,615 (5th Cir. 1994).
21. I.R.C. § 7430(c)(5).
22. Treas. Reg. § 301.7430-3(a),(b). "Tax matters" for purposes of § 7430 include collection issues, but "administrative proceedings" do not. Note that "collection" actions and issues in a litigation context apparently would not be subject to this prohibition. *See, e.g.,* Treas. Reg. § 301.7430-1(b)(3). *See also In re* Thibodaux, 96-2 USTC ¶ 50,534 (Bankr. N.D. Ala. 1996). In that case a debtor was allowed to recover lawyer fees where the IRS had attempted to collect pre-petition, discharged payroll taxes in a Chapter 13 plan. The IRS had failed to file a claim for the payroll taxes in the Chapter 13 proceeding. Taxpayers can also be awarded costs where the IRS Collection Division has issued a wrongful levy. Wilkerson v. United States, 95-2 USTC ¶ 50,569 (5th Cir. 1995). Costs have also been awarded when the IRS Collection Division persisted in enforcement action even though it knew that the taxpayers had prevailed in an appellate court decision. Wittstadt, Jr. v. Comm'r, 74 T.C.M. (CCH) 396 (1997).
23. Treas. Reg. § 301.7430-3(c).
24. This must be a written document signed by someone to whom settlement authority has been delegated. *See* Treas. Reg. § 301.7430-3(c)(2).
25. I.R.C. § 7430(c)(2), as amended by the IRS Restructuring and Reform Act of 1998. Prior to January 1999, taxpayers could not recover costs incurred *prior to* the earlier of a deficiency notice or an appeals decision. Previously no costs were recoverable between the dates of the thirty-day letter and the issuance of the ninety-day letter.
26. Treas. Reg. 301.7430-2.
27. Note that these requirements are virtually identical to those involving motions for costs in a litigation context.
28. *See also* I.R.C. § 7430(b)(4).
29. Treas. Reg. § 301.7430-2(c).
30. I.R.C. § 7430(f)(2).
31. I.R.C. § 7430(c)(2).
32. I.R.C. § 7430(b)(1); Treas. Reg. § 301.7430-1.
33. Treas. Reg. § 301.7430-1(f).
34. Treas. Reg. § 301.7430-1(b).
35. *Minahan,* 88 T.C. 492 (1987); note that the "*Minahan*" rule has now been codified in I.R.C. § 7430(b)(1).
36. *See* Treas. Reg. § 301.7430-1(b)(4).
37. Treas. Reg. § 301.7430-1(f)(2).
38. I.R.C. § 7430(b)(3).
39. Munley v. United States, 95-1 USTC ¶ 50,169 (D.C. Nev. 1995); Burke v. Comm'r, 73 T.C.M. (CCH) 2291 (1997).
40. Swanson v. Comm'r, 106 T.C. at 76 (1996).
41. Williford v. Comm'r, 67 T.C.M. (CCH) 2542 (1994).
42. Baker v. Comm'r, 83 T.C. 822 (1984).
43. *See, e.g.,* the discussion in R.C. Lindsey Plumbing, Inc. v. Comm'r, 55 T.C.M. (CCH) 196 (1988).

44. Frisch v. Comm'r, 87 T.C. 838 (1986).
45. Pohl Corp. v. United States, 93-2 USTC ¶ 50,474 (Fed. Cl. 1989).
46. Powers v. Comm'r, 100 T.C. 457 (1993).
47. Lennox v. Comm'r, 93-2 USTC ¶ 50,444 (5th Cir. 1993).
48. Maddox v. Comm'r, 76 T.C.M. (CCH) 1040 (1998).
49. Williford v. Comm'r, 67 T.C.M. (CCH) 2542 (1994).
50. Hall v. Comm'r, 57 T.C.M. (CCH) 232 (1989).
51. Lewis v. United States, 98-1 USTC ¶ 50,441 (9th Cir. 1998), reversing the district court holding.
52. Hubbard v. Comm'r, 89 T.C. 792 (1987).
53. I.R.C. § 6672, the so-called 100 percent penalty.
54. Nixon v. United States, 83 AFTR2d 99-610 (W.D. Pa. 1999).
55. Powell v. Comm'r, 86-2 USTC ¶ 9486 (5th Cir. 1986).
56. Brice v. Comm'r, 60 T.C.M. (CCH) 118 (1990); Pan Pac. Trading Corp. v. Comm'r, 67 T.C.M. (CCH) 2374 (1994); Caparaso v. Comm'r, 65 T.C.M. (CCH) 2930 (1993); Salopek v. Comm'r, 76 T.C.M. (CCH) 741 (1998); Uddo v. Comm'r, 76 T.C.M. (CCH) 200 (1998); Simpson v. Comm'r, 69 T.C.M. (CCH) 2517 (1995); Evans v. Comm'r, 77 T.C.M. (CCH) 1339 (1999).
57. Tinsley v. Comm'r, 63 T.C.M. (CCH) 2629 (1992); *See also* Powers v. Comm'r, 100 T.C. 457 (1993), where the IRS had decided not to contact the petitioner to obtain information from him.
58. I.R.C. § 7430(c)(4)(C).
59. I.R.C. § 7430(c)(4)(A).
60. I.R.C. § 7430(c)(4)(A)(i).
61. Sokol v. Comm'r, 92 T.C. 760 (1989).
62. Bragg v. Comm'r, 102 T.C. 715 (1994).
63. Temporary and proposed regulations were issued on qualified offers on January 3, 2001.
64. Even though an offer amount is determined without interest, presumably it would include applicable penalties. Treas. Reg. § 301.7430-7(a).
65. A tax settlement is a contract that should be interpreted according to ordinary principles of contract law.
66. I.R.C. § 7430(c)(4)(E), as amended by the 1998 act.
67. United States v. Scheingold, 2004-1 USTC ¶ 50,116 (D.C. N.J. 2003).
68. I.R.C. § 7430(c)(4)(E)(iii).
69. I.R.C. § 7430(c)(4)(E)(iv).
70. Johnston v. Comm'r, 2006-02 USTC ¶ 50,538 (9th Cir. 2006).
71. Urban v. United States, 2006-1 USTC ¶ 50,211 (N.D. Ill. 2006).
72. I.R.C. § 7430(g)(2).
73. Trucks, Inc. v. United States, 2002-2 USTC ¶ 50,723 (N.D. Ga. 2002).
74. I.R.C. § 7430(g)(1).
75. I.R.C. § 7430(c)(4)(B)(iii).
76. I.R.C. § 7430(c)(4)(A)(ii); I.R.C. § 7430(c)(4)(D); 28 U.S.C. § 2412(d).
77. I.R.C. § 7430(c)(4)(D). For this purpose individual taxpayers filing a joint return are treated as one taxpayer, except in the case of a taxpayer who is relieved of liability as an innocent spouse. *See* Treas. Reg. § 301.7430-5(f)(1). *But see Hong v. Comm'r,* 100 T.C. 88 (1993). The *Hong* case was a case of first impression which, essentially, overruled what at that time was a proposed regulation. In the *Hong* case the combined net worth of husband and wife was in excess of $2 million, but individually their respective net worths were less than the statutory amount.

78. Swanson v. Comm'r, 106 T.C. 76 (1996).

79. Doyle v. Comm'r, 56 T.C.M. (CCH) 260 (1988).

80. Bragg v. Comm'r, 102 T.C. 715 (1994).

81. Treas. Reg. § 301.7430-5(f)(2).

82. *See* King v. United States, 93-2 USTC ¶ 50,442 (D. Md. 1993).

83. *See* Title XXIII of the Tax Court Rules, Rules 230 through 233.

84. *Id.*, Rules 270 through 274.

85. T.C. Rule 231(a).

86. Sokol v. Comm'r, 92 T.C. 760 (1989).

87. T.C. Rule 231(a)(2).

88. *See* 28 U.S.C. § 2412(d)(2)(B).

89. T.C. Rule 231(b).

90. T.C. Rules 34(b), 233.

91. T.C. Rule 232(a)(2).

92. I.R.C. § 7430(f).

93. *See* I.R.C. § 7463.

94. I.R.C. § 7430(f)(2).

95. I.R.C. § 7430(d).

96. I.R.C. § 7430(e)(2).

97. Frisch v. Comm'r, 87 T.C. 838 (1986).

98. United States v. McPherson, 87-2 USTC ¶ 9512 (M.D. N.C. 1987); *but see* Overton v. United States, 83 AFTR2d 99-349 (10th Cir. 1999), for a contrary result.

99. 88-1 USTC ¶ 9194 (4th Cir. 1988).

100. Weiss v. Comm'r, 88 T.C. 1036 (1987); Sponza v. Comm'r, 88-1 USTC ¶ 9294 (9th Cir. 1988).

101. *See* § 7430(c)(4)(B) for the change in the burden of proof with respect to actions commenced after July 30, 1996. Note that the tax court has consistently held that the petition filing date is to be used when applying the effective date of amendments to I.R.C. § 7430. Maggie Mgmt. Co. v. Comm'r, 108 T.C. 430 (1997).

102. I.R.C. § 7430(c)(4)(B)(ii), (iv).

103. I.R.C. § 7436(d)(2). Apollo Drywall, Inc. v. Comm'r, 96-1 USTC ¶ 50,196 (W.D. Mich. 1993); JJR, Inc. v. United States, 99-1 USTC ¶ 50,313 (W.D. Wash. 1999); Beck v. United States, 83 AFTR2d 99-621 (D. S.C. 1999) (regarding exotic dancers).

104. Hanson v. Comm'r, 92-2 USTC ¶ 50,554 (5th Cir. 1992).

105. Indeed, I.R.C. § 7430(c)(6) defines "court proceedings" to include only *civil* actions.

106. Pub. L. No. 105-119, § 617, 111 Stat. 2440, 2519 (1997).

107. For an excellent discussion of the history of this statute and its application to a criminal tax defendant (here, a "tax preparer"), see *United States v. Gardner*, 82 AFTR2d 198-5393 (N.D. Okla. 1998).

108. Terrell Equip. Co. v. Comm'r, 84 T.C.M. (CCH) 259 (2002), *aff'd*, CA-5, 203-2 USTC ¶ 50,625 (2003).

109. *See, e.g.*, Cassuto v. Comm'r, 93 T.C. 256 (1989).

110. United States v. Smith, 98-1 USTC ¶ 50,338 (N.D. Ind. 1998).

111. *See* the discussion in *Scrimgeour v. Internal Revenue Serv.*, 82 AFTR2d 1 98-5100 (4th Cir. 1998).

112. I.R.C. §§ 6221 *et seq.*

113. Foothills Ranch Co. P'ship v. Comm'r, 110 T.C. 94 (1998).

CHAPTER 4

Statutes of Limitations in Tax Cases

Statutes of Limitations: General Rules

I. History and Background

A. *Definition*

A statute of limitations (S/L) is a legislative enactment prescribing the period of time within which an action may be brought upon certain claims or within which certain rights may be enforced.

B. *Types of S/L*

The I.R.C. has a variety of different statutes of limitations. There are, in fact, five major types of statutes of limitations affecting federal tax matters:
1. Assessment,
2. Collection,
3. Transferee liability,
4. Penalties, and
5. Criminal tax prosecutions.

II. Tax S/L Definitions

A. *Assessment*

Assessment is the act of recording a tax liability on the books of the IRS service center or other appropriate government office. There can be no collection action (liens, demands, levies, etc.) without "assessment" having first occurred.[1] A taxpayer may determine the exact date of assessment by inspecting a record (transcript) of account. The IRS is required to furnish this information to a taxpayer or his or her representative free of charge. An assessment may occur summarily, as, for example, with a mathematical correction, or through the deficiency notice procedure.

B. *Deficiency*

A deficiency is the excess of the true tax liability over the tax as reflected on a filed tax return. Generally, a deficiency is determined by examination (audit) of a tax return. A service center math correction for this purpose does not constitute a deficiency determination. A deficiency *proposed* by the Examination Division is not an assessment. As long as a deficiency is being contested in either the IRS Appeals Office or the tax court, there is no assessment and thus no collection can occur.[2]

C. *Tax Collection*

This is either a voluntary payment of the tax by a taxpayer or an involuntary payment through IRS enforcement action (levy).

D. *Levy*

A levy means seizure or distraint of a taxpayer's money (bank account) or property by any means whatsoever.[3]

III. General Assessment Rules

A. *General Rule*

As a general rule, all income taxes (including reported taxes and tax deficiencies) must be assessed within three years after an income tax return is filed.[4]

B. *Early Filed Returns*

Normally the return filing date initiates the S/L period for assessment. But if a return is filed before its due date, the three-year period starts running on such due date.[5]

C. *Incomplete or Invalid Returns*

To start the running of the S/L for assessment purposes, a filed return must disclose income and deductions in a uniform and complete manner so that the handling and verifying of the return can be easily accomplished. Moreover, modification of printed forms, such as striking out the language that the form is signed under penalty of perjury, invalidates an otherwise valid return, thereby preventing the S/L from beginning to run.[6]

The test to determine whether a document is sufficient for S/L purposes has several elements:

- There must be sufficient data to calculate tax liability.
- The document must purport to be a tax return.
- There must be an honest and reasonable attempt to satisfy the requirements of the tax law.
- The taxpayer must execute the return under penalties of perjury.[7]

D. *Returns Completed by the IRS*

If the IRS is forced to prepare and execute a return for the taxpayer under the procedures prescribed by I.R.C. § 6020(b), the assessment S/L will not start to run.[8]

E. *Employment Tax Returns*

For employment tax returns (941s), the three-year S/L period begins running on April 15 of the *succeeding* calendar year.[9]

F. *Joint Return after Separate Returns*

In the case of filing a joint return after separate returns have been filed by spouses, the S/L begins to run on the new joint return on the date the *latest* separate return was filed.[10]

G. *Amended Tax Returns*

1. *Effect Of*

   When the return as required by law has been filed and thereafter an amended return is filed, the S/L period begins to run from the date the *original* return was filed.

2. *Amended Return with Tax Due*

   Where an amended return is filed showing additional tax due (within sixty days of the S/L expiration), the IRS has sixty days after receiving the return to assess the tax.[11]

H. *25 Percent Omission Rule*

If the taxpayer omits from gross income an amount in excess of 25 percent of the amount of gross income stated in the return, a six-year assessment limitation period applies in lieu of the normal three-year period.[12]

1. *Calculation of the 25 Percent Omission*

   For purposes of the 25 percent omission rule, gross income means gross receipts without reduction for cost of sales.[13]

2. *Disclosure of Omission*

   An item will not be considered as omitted from gross income if information, sufficient to apprise the IRS of the nature and amount of such item, is disclosed on the return.[14]

3. *Burden of Proof*

   The burden of proof of omission of more than 25 percent of gross income for purposes of the six-year S/L period is on the IRS.[15] The IRS must possess evidence of the 25 percent omission *before* a deficiency notice is issued.[16]

4. *Overstated Deductions*

   The IRS cannot invoke the six-year S/L based on overstated deductions; it can do so only based on omitted gross income.[17]

5. *Basis Overstatements*
   A basis overstatement is not an "omission from gross income" and will not, therefore, trigger the six-year S/L.[18]

I. *Assessment of Interest*
   The assessment and collection S/L rule applicable to statutory interest follows the same rule as that applicable to the underlying tax.[19]

IV. The Collection Statute of Limitations

A. *General Collection Statute*
   Once a tax has been assessed, the IRS has ten years within which to *collect* the tax by levy (see definition in II.D, above) or otherwise. The ten-year collection S/L starts to run on the date of assessment.[20]

B. *Extension of Collection Statute*
   As a part of the IRS Restructuring and Reform Act of 1998, the IRS is no longer permitted to solicit an extension of the collection statute of limitations. The prior extension authorization[21] is repealed effective for extension requests made after December 31, 1999.

C. *Suit for Judgment*
   If the ten-year S/L period for collection is about to expire, the IRS's remedy is to sue in federal district court and secure a judgment against the taxpayer, and therefore collection may be had only by enforcing the judgment by execution. This judgment is renewable every ten years. (Note: As a practical matter, the IRS is reluctant to bring these kinds of lawsuits except in unusual cases.)[22]

D. *Offer in Compromise*
   If a taxpayer files an offer in compromise (OIC; Form 656) with the IRS, he or she must waive the collection S/L for the entire period during which the offer is being considered (including administrative appeals) by the IRS and for 30 days thereafter.[23]

E. *Suit to Set Aside Fraudulent Conveyance*
   Although state law determines what constitutes a fraudulent conveyance, federal (I.R.C. § 6502) law controls the timeliness of the action where the United States is a party. Thus, a state fraudulent conveyance statute with a statute of limitations shorter than ten years will not be controlling on the government.

V. Extensions of the Assessment Statute

A. *General Rule*
   The three-year assessment period can be extended by a written agreement between the taxpayer and the IRS. The agreement must be signed

by both the taxpayer and a representative of the IRS.[24] Each time an S/L extension is requested, the IRS must, by law, advise the taxpayer of his or her right to refuse to extend the statute.[25] Failure by the IRS to advise a taxpayer of this right may result in an invalid extension.[26] Note, however, that extension of the S/L relative to the estate tax is not permitted.[27]

B. *Burden of Proof*

When the IRS relies on a written extension of the assessment S/L, the IRS bears the burden of proving that a written agreement was entered into. For example, if a Form 872 is signed and dated by the taxpayer and signed, but not dated, by the IRS, the IRS will fail in its burden of proof.[28]

Whether a Form 872 extension was properly signed by a taxpayer is always a fact issue for the judge or jury. An individual's signature on a document creates a mere rebuttable presumption that the signature is genuine. If a taxpayer denies that he or she signed an 872, and if his or her testimony is credible, the court may find that the statute of limitations was not properly extended.[29]

C. *Restricted Consents*

There are provisions in the Internal Revenue Manual for restricting a consent to extend the assessment S/L to one or more specific issues. Generally, restricted consents cannot be used where there are more than two issues to be held open. And no restricted consents will be accepted by the IRS until the examination of the tax return in question has been completed and approved. While the taxpayer has a right to *request* a restricted consent, IRS is not compelled to grant that request.[30]

D. *Termination of Extension Agreements*

Previously executed extension agreements (872-A forms only) may be terminated by filing a Form 872-T. The IRS then has ninety days within which to issue a deficiency notice. A detailed discussion of this termination process is reserved for another subchapter.

E. *Effect of Extensions on Claim Filing*

If the assessment (three-year) S/L period is extended by agreement, this automatically extends the period for filing a claim for the extended period plus six months.[31]

F. *Examination Cutoff Dates*

The IRS's examination agents generally ask a taxpayer to execute an S/L waiver when a return under audit becomes "old." Whether it is old depends on the number of months left in the assessment S/L period. The cutoff dates for closing cases without extensions are as follows:

1.	Agreed cases (general)	5 months
2.	Agreed Personal Holding Company cases	8 months
3.	Joint committee cases	15 months
4.	Unagreed cases (general)	9 months
5.	Unagreed § 531 cases	10 months
6.	Cases going to suspense (audit cannot be completed; e.g., partnership under audit in another district)	12 months[32]

G. *Appeals*

As a rule, field personnel will not transfer a case to IRS Appeals with less than 180 days remaining before the assessment statute expiration date (ASED). If such a case is received in IRS Appeals, the appeals team manager has the option of accepting it or returning it.[33]

H. *Forms Used*

The following forms are customarily used to extend voluntarily the assessment S/L:

Form No.	Explanation
1. 872	Extends the S/L to a future date certain. It cannot be terminated.
2. 872-A	Extends the S/L indefinitely. It can be terminated with an 872-T.
3. 2750	Extends the assessment S/L in regard to trust fund liability (100 percent penalty) to a future date certain.
4. 872-P	Extends the S/L attributable to partnership items to a date certain.
5. SS-10	Extends the assessment S/L for FUTA, FICA, and WHT to a future date certain. Note that Form SS-10 does not extend the statute for purposes of a trust fund liability assessment under § 6672.

VI. Claims and Carrybacks

A. *Claim-Filing Limitations*

Many times it is to the taxpayer's advantage to file an amended return to claim a refund of an overpayment or otherwise correct return errors. Generally the filing of an 1120-X or 1040-X showing a refund due will constitute a claim for this purpose. A claim for refund of an overpayment of tax must be filed within whichever of the following periods expires the later:

1. Three years from the time the return was filed or
2. Two years from the date the tax was paid.[34]

B. *Carrybacks—General Rule*

Whenever a carryback claim of any sort, including tentative carryback allowances (net operating loss [NOL], etc.), is filed, the S/L period remains open in such carryback year to the same extent as the year giving rise to the NOL.[35]

C. *Carrybacks—Deficiencies*

Deficiencies attributable to a carryback of an NOL or capital loss may be assessed within the S/L period that applies to the loss or credit year.[36]

D. *Overpayments on Original Returns*

The IRS will not refund an overpayment if a tax return is delinquent by more than three years (plus an extension period).[37] This rule surprises many taxpayers, who believe that they can always receive a refund of an overpaid tax return. This is yet another reason for careful practitioners to advise clients to file their returns timely.

E. *Tentative Applications for Refunds (1045 and 1139 Forms)*

1. Must be filed before the end of the year following the NOL, investment tax credit, and so on.[38]
2. The IRS has ninety days after receipt of the application to make a preliminary review and issue the refund check.[39]
3. A deficiency can be assessed in the carryback year, but only to the extent of the amount tentatively refunded.[40]

F. *Mailbox Rule*

Under the "mailbox rule," a return (or other document) is considered to be mailed in a timely manner even though it is received by the IRS after its due date as long as the postmark on the envelope is dated on or before the due date of the document.[41] In such cases the date of receipt by the IRS is considered to be the filing date. Nevertheless, if a return constitutes a claim for refund, the postmark date will be considered the filing date even if it is received after the due date as long as the postmark date is within three years (plus an extension period) from the time the tax was paid or considered paid.[42]

VII. Fraud and Delinquency

A. *General Rule*

There are no limitations on assessment or court proceeding to collect the tax if a return is fraudulent or filed with the intent to evade tax.[43] Note that this rule pertains to civil assessment of tax; it does not apply to the criminal prosecution of a taxpayer.

B. *Subsequent Nonfraudulent Filing*

An assessment of a tax deficiency for a year in which the taxpayer filed a false or fraudulent return may be made at any time, notwithstanding any later filing of a nonfraudulent amended return. The I.R.C. provision allowing unlimited time for assessment where fraudulent returns are filed applies to original, not amended, returns.[44] Under the *Badaracco* ruling, the one exception to this rule is where an amended nonfraudulent return is filed on or before the due date. In such a case the amended return will be treated as the original.[45]

C. *Criminal Prosecutions*

A criminal indictment for a federal tax crime must be brought within six years after the commission of the offense where the offense involves defrauding the government or any type of tax evasion. This is the reason that, in the case of nonfiling, delinquent tax returns are generally prepared only for the last six years.[46] Note, however, that when a taxpayer commits a series of evasive acts over several years after incurring a tax liability, the six-year S/L begins to run on the date of the last affirmative act of evasion. For example, continuing to deny the existence of a foreign bank account is such an act that will keep the prosecution statute from starting to run.[47]

D. *Nonfiling*

If no return has been filed, the S/L period does not start running until the return is filed.[48] This is one of the reasons that a return should be filed, even if it may be based on incomplete information.

E. *IRS-Executed Returns*

If the taxpayer declines to file a return that is due, the IRS has the power to examine the facts and sign a return for him or her. The execution of such returns by the IRS will not, however, start the S/L period running.[49]

F. *Expatriates*

Note also that the prosecution S/L is tolled during the period that a taxpayer is physically out of the country.[50]

G. *Preparer Fraud*

What if the taxpayer did not have a fraudulent intent, but his or her preparer did? The tax court has ruled that the statute of limitations does not protect a taxpayer from a deficiency assessment on a fraudulent return when the fraud was committed by a preparer. An argument that the unlimited statute applies only when a taxpayer has fraudulent intent will fail.[51]

VIII. Court Proceedings

A. *General Rule*

If there is no assessment within the three-year period, the IRS must commence a proceeding in court within the same period.[52]

B. *Notices of Deficiency (ND)*

When an ND (ninety-day letter) is mailed to the taxpayer, the running of the period of limitations on assessments is suspended for ninety days, plus an additional sixty days.[53] The date on which the ND is *mailed*, not the date of receipt by the taxpayer, determines whether the ND is timely.[54]

C. *Effect of a Tax Court Petition*

If the taxpayer files a tax court petition in response to the ND, the S/L period is further suspended until a settlement has been reached or a decision has been rendered by the court, and for an additional sixty days thereafter.[55]

D. *Tax Court Decision*

If the assessment S/L has expired at the time the deficiency notice is issued, the decision of the tax court will be that there is no deficiency in respect of such tax.[56]

E. *Pleadings*

In a court action, a taxpayer must affirmatively plead the S/L as a bar to the deficiency determined by the commissioner. If it is so pleaded, the burden is placed on the IRS to allege affirmatively the exception it is relying on.[57]

F. *Claim Filing*

As long as a tax court proceeding is pending, no claim for refund may be filed with respect to that year.[58] Instead, the proper procedure is to raise and plead an affirmative issue.

G. *Erroneous Refunds*

Whenever the IRS has made an erroneous refund, it may sue the taxpayer to get it back within two years after the refund was paid, or within five years if the refund was induced by fraud or misrepresentation.[59]

H. *Disclosure Damage Suits*

Lawsuits against the IRS for civil damages resulting from unauthorized disclosure of tax return information to third parties must be brought within two years after the plaintiff's discovery of the disclosure.[60]

IX. Special Exceptions and Rules

A. *Bad Debts or Worthless Securities*

Where an overpayment relates to a bad debt or a worthless security, there is a seven-year S/L for filing a claim in lieu of the normal three-year period.[61]

B. *Partnership Rules*

In the case of a partnership, the period for assessing any tax attributable to any partnership item does not expire until three years after the partnership return is filed. There are also special rules for extension of the S/L where the name, ID number, and address of a partner are not furnished on a partnership return.[62]

C. *Flow-Through Entities*

After a great deal of inconsistency among the various circuits, the U.S. Supreme Court finally ruled that the limitations period for a deficiency assessment against an S corporation shareholder was properly measured with reference to the date on which the shareholder filed his individual return, not the date on which the S corporation filed its information return. In affirming the Second Circuit Court, the Supreme Court rejected the Ninth Circuit's conclusion in *Kelley*.[63]

D. *Mitigation*

If it were not for the mitigation rule, the S/L could have a disastrous effect on the IRS. Under this rule, if the IRS makes a "determination" (e.g., disposes of a claim), and correction of the effect of an error in a prior year is otherwise barred by operation of the S/L, then the correction of the error, assessment of the error, and assessment of the tax may be made anyway.[64] A detailed discussion of the mitigation provisions is reserved for another subchapter.

E. *Equitable Recoupment*

Equitable recoupment may also be raised as a defense to the S/L. It is designed to protect a party from paying twice on a single obligation. Equitable recoupment arises when a single transaction, item, or taxable event is subject to two inconsistent taxes. The doctrine permits a party to a tax dispute to raise a time-barred claim to reduce or eliminate the money owed on the timely claim. Equitable recoupment cannot be used offensively to seek a money payment, only defensively to offset an adjudicated deficiency.[65]

F. *Request for Prompt Assessment*

An administrator of an estate of a decedent or a corporation in liquidation may request a prompt assessment of tax. This request must be made within three years after a return has been filed. The IRS must then make the assessment within eighteen months after the request has been received.[66]

G. *Items Triggering S/L Suspensions*
Certain actions or events suspend or extend the statute of limitations. These "extenders" may include the following.
1. *Assessment S/L*
    - The issuance of a deficiency notice,[67] including a deficiency notice mailed to a transferee of property.[68]
    - Where a taxpayer has filed for bankruptcy protection under Title 11 of the U.S.C.[69]
    - Where a proceeding to quash a third-party summons has been brought.[70]
    - The IRS's issuance of a designated summons.[71]
2. *Collection S/L*
    - The filing of an application for taxpayer assistance order (Form 911).[72]
    - Where the taxpayer's assets come under the control of a court.[73]
    - Where the taxpayer is outside the United States for a continuous period of at least six months.[74]
    - Where a taxpayer has filed for bankruptcy protection under Title 11 of the U.S.C.[75]
    - The filing of an offer in compromise (Form 656).[76]
    - The failure to appoint a fiduciary representative following a taxpayer's death.[77]
    - A taxpayer's request for a CDP hearing.[78]
    - A taxpayer's request for an installment agreement under I.R.C. § 6159.[79]

H. *Payments Made after the S/L Period Has Expired*
If a tax is assessed or collected after the applicable S/L period has expired, it is treated as an "overpayment" and can be refunded.[80]

I. *Redemption of Corporate Stock by Family Members*
Where a distributee-shareholder redeems his or her corporate stock in a transaction that qualifies for capital gain treatment, he or she may not reacquire an interest in the corporation within the ensuing ten years. If he or she does so, the § 6501 and the § 6502 limitations periods will not start to run until the distribute-shareholder notifies the IRS.[81]

J. *Gift Tax Returns*
If a gift is not adequately disclosed, the limitations period on the assessment of a gift tax for that gift will not begin to run.[82]

X. Conclusions and Recommendations

There are many things the IRS is not good at, but it is *very* good at maintaining control of the statute of limitations in a pending tax case. Examining revenue agents are responsible for protecting the S/L on tax returns within their control. Inadvertently letting a statute expire is extremely embarrassing for the IRS. If this happens, the taxpayer is relieved of all liability for potential tax deficiencies. The number of cases where the IRS has inadvertently let an S/L lapse is a statistic that the IRS chooses not to publish.

The S/L has record-keeping implications for taxpayers. Normally, records of income and deductions need be kept for only three years (the assessment S/L period). However, for basis purpose, records need to be preserved for as long as the asset is owned.

The S/L is a two-edged sword. It operates against the IRS (for deficiency assessment purposes) and taxpayers (in claim-filing cases).

It is a good idea not to be intimidated by revenue personnel requesting clients' signatures on S/L "waivers." Revenue agents have no power to assess tax; all they can do is *propose* a deficiency and cause a notice of deficiency to be issued.

XI. Notes

1. I.R.C. § 6203.
2. I.R.C. § 6211.
3. I.R.C. § 6331(b); I.R.C. § 7701(a)(21).
4. I.R.C. § 6501(a).
5. I.R.C. § 6501(b)(1).
6. Nat'l Contracting Co. v. Comm'r, 37 B.T.A. 689 (1938); Schroeder v. Comm'r, 52 T.C.M. (CCH) 620 (1986).
7. Beard v. Comm'r, 82 T.C. 766, 777 (1984) *aff'd*, 86-2 USTC ¶ 9496 (6th Cir. 1986).
8. I.R.C. § 6501(b)(3).
9. I.R.C. § 6501(b)(2).
10. I.R.C. § 6013(b)(3)(A).
11. I.R.C. § 6501(c)(7).
12. I.R.C. § 6501(e)(1).
13. *Id.*
14. Treas. Reg. § 301.6501(e)-1(a)(1)(ii).
15. Reis v. Comm'r, 1 T.C. 9 (1942).
16. United States v. Crisp, 99-2 USTC ¶ 50,719 (E.D. Cal. 1999).
17. Shaheen, Jr. v. Comm'r, 54 T.C.M. (CCH) 661 (1987); Courtney v. Comm'r, 28 T.C. 658 (1957).
18. United States v. Home Concrete & Supply, LLC, 12-1 USTC ¶ 50,315 (S. Ct. 2012), following the *Colony* case.
19. I.R.C. § 6601(g).
20. I.R.C. § 6502(a)(1).
21. *See prior law*, I.R.C. § 6502(a)(2).
22. Treas. Reg. § 301.6502-1(a)(1).

23. Treas. Reg. § 301.7122-1(g),(i).
24. I.R.C. § 6501(c)(4).
25. I.R.C. § 6501(c)(4)(B).
26. F.S.A. 200106010.
27. I.R.C. § 6501(c)(4)(A).
28. Mantzel v. Comm'r, 41 T.C.M. (CCH) 1237 (1981).
29. Steingold v. Comm'r, 80 T.C.M. (CCH) 95 (2000).
30. IRM 25.6.22.8.2.
31. I.R.C. § 6511(c)(1).
32. Note that policies may vary among different IRS offices.
33. IRM 8.2.1.3.
34. I.R.C. § 6511(a).
35. I.R.C. § 6501(h)(1).
36. I.R.C. § 6511(d)(2)(A).
37. I.R.C. § 6511(b)(2)(A).
38. I.R.C. § 6411(a).
39. I.R.C. § 6411(b).
40. I.R.C. § 6501(k).
41. Emmons v. Comm'r, 92 T.C. 342 (1989), *aff'd*, 90-1 USTC ¶ 50,217 (1990).
42. Treas. Reg. § 301.7502-1(f)(1).
43. I.R.C. § 6501(c)(1).
44. Badaracco v. Comm'r, 84-1 USTC ¶ 9150 (S. Ct. 1984).
45. *Id.*
46. I.R.C. § 6531(1), (2).
47. United States v. Anderson, 2003-1 USTC ¶ 50,237 (10th Cir. 2003).
48. I.R.C. § 6501(c)(3).
49. I.R.C. § 6020(b); 6501(b)(3).
50. I.R.C. § 6531; United States v. Yip, 248 F. Supp. 2d 970 (D. Haw. 2003).
51. Allen v. Comm'r, 128 T.C. No. 4 (2007).
52. I.R.C. § 6501(a).
53. I.R.C. § 6503(a)(1).
54. Frieling, Jr. v. Comm'r., 81 T.C. 42 (1983).
55. I.R.C. § 6503(a)(1).
56. I.R.C. § 7459(e).
57. T.C. Rule 39.
58. I.R.C. § 6512(a).
59. I.R.C. § 6532(b).
60. I.R.C. § 7431(d).
61. I.R.C. § 6511(d)(1).
62. I.R.C. § 6229(a).
63. Bufferd v. Comm'r, 93-1 USTC ¶ 50.038 (S. Ct. 1993) (rejecting *Kelley*, 89-1 USTC ¶ 9360).
64. I.R.C. §§ 1311, 6521.
65. Estate of Branson v. Comm'r, 2001-2 USTC ¶ 50,622 (9th Cir. 2001).
66. I.R.C. § 6501(d).
67. I.R.C. § 6503(a).
68. I.R.C. § 6901(f).
69. I.R.C. § 6503(h), 6872.
70. I.R.C. § 7609(e).

71. I.R.C. § 6503(j)(1).
72. I.R.C. § 7811(d).
73. I.R.C. § 6503(b).
74. I.R.C. § 6503(c).
75. I.R.C. § 6503(h).
76. Treas. Reg. § 301.7122-1(g),(i).
77. United States v. Besase, 26 AFTR2d 70-5158 (N.D. Ohio 1970). Note that the mere act of dying does not appear to toll any statutory period.
78. I.R.C. §§ 6320(c), 6330(e).
79. Treas. Reg. § 301.6331-4(c)(1), effective Dec. 18, 2002; Seagrave v. United States, 99 AFTR2d 2007-1989 (7th Cir. 2007). Note that while the S/L is suspended during the pendency of a request for installment agreement (IA), once an IA is entered into, the S/L clock continues to run.
80. I.R.C. § 6401(a).
81. I.R.C. § 302(c)(2)(A).
82. I.R.C. § 6501(c)(9); Rev. Proc. 2000-34, 2000-34 IRB 186.

Termination of Form 872-A

I. Introduction

A. Over the years there have been a number of tax cases involving attempts by taxpayers to terminate previously executed consents to extend the statute of limitation pursuant to I.R.C. § 6501(c)(4). This statute expressly provides that

> where, before the expiration of time prescribed . . . for assessment of any tax . . . both the [IRS] and the taxpayer have consented in writing to its assessment after such time, the tax may be assessed at any time prior to the expiration of the period agreed upon.

B. There are several possible reasons that a taxpayer may want to terminate a previously agreed-upon extension, including the following:
1. The IRS is unreasonably delaying closure of an examination, resulting in unnecessary accrual of interest;
2. The taxpayer wishes to cause the immediate issuance of a statutory deficiency notice, thereby depriving the examiner of the opportunity to fully develop his or her case; or
3. It is apparent that further attempts at settlement at the examination level will be fruitless.

C. *Extension Forms*
The IRS has printed three different forms relating to extension of the statute of limitations that are relevant to this discussion. Instead of being printed on white paper, these forms are printed in colors (green for the 872 and 872-A and pink for the 872-T). The author's opinion is that this color scheme was concocted to alert IRS personnel as to their importance. However, in at least one case,[1] a photocopy of Form 872-T was submitted and received without objection on the ground that an original form was not used.

The forms are as follows:

1. *Form 872*

   This form extends the three-year assessment statute of limitations from the normal expiration date to a "date certain" in the future. That is, the extension of time is for a fixed, predetermined period ending on the date agreed to by the parties. Typically, the "extension" period is for at least six months and for not more than two years. But the important point to remember is that 872 forms, once executed by the taxpayer, *may not be unilaterally terminated*. The forms automatically terminate on their own by lapse of time.

2. *Form 872-P*

   This form relates to assessments attributable to "partnership items" involved with examinations conducted under the TEFRA procedures applicable to pass-through entities. The form is titled Consent to Extend the Time to Assess Tax Attributable to Partnership Items.[2] Similar to Form 872, the 872-P is not "open ended," and permits extension of the statute of limitations only to a date certain. This extension may not be terminated with a Form 872-T.

3. *Form 872-A*

   This form extends the § 6501 three-year assessment statute of limitations for an indefinite period of time. Notice that, like the 872, it is required to be executed by both the IRS as well as the taxpayer(s). Unless it is signed by both parties, it does not constitute an "agreement" and is therefore ineffective to extend the statute. The 872-A is also known as an "open-ended waiver."

   A consent to extend the period for assessment of an income tax is essentially a unilateral waiver of a defense by a taxpayer and is not a contract. Contract principles are significant, however, because § 6501(c)(4) requires that the parties reach a written "agreement" as to the extension.[3]

   If a taxpayer refuses to execute a Form 872-A, preferring instead to execute an 872, the 872 will be accepted by the IRS. Of course, this presents problems to the IRS of having to maintain "statute control" over the case to prevent the expiration of the assessment statute during administrative consideration of the case. In Rev. Rul. 71-11,[4] the IRS stated that the reason Form 872-A was adopted was to relieve taxpayers and the IRS from the irritations and difficulties of obtaining renewal consent forms during the minimum time required for IRS Appeals consideration.

   The important distinction between the 872 and the 872-A is that the latter may be unilaterally terminated by either the IRS or the taxpayer. The original printed agreement on the 872-A required only a ninety-day "notification" by either party to the other to effectively terminate the agreement.

Form 872-A was revised effective March 1979 to comply with Rev. Proc. 79-22 in respect of the termination procedures. The critical language on the revised 872-A is that the tax may be assessed at any time "before the 90th (ninetieth) day after: (a) the Internal Revenue Service office considering the case receives Form 872-T." Of course, the IRS can also terminate the 872-A by issuing an 872-T. And if the IRS issues a deficiency notice (see I.R.C. § 6212) prior to termination of the 872-A, then the termination thereof is rendered moot.

4. *Form 872-T*

The apparent reason for the promulgation of this form was to eliminate all confusion as to what constituted "notice." The form is titled Notice of Termination of Special Consent to Extend the Time to Assess Tax, and it is to be signed unilaterally by either the taxpayer or his or her representative.

If the 872-T form relates to a joint Form 1040, both husband and wife must sign (unless their representative signs for them). If a representative signs, he or she must hold a valid power of attorney (Form 2848) from the taxpayers.

To effectively terminate an 872-A, the 872-T must be submitted to the IRS office from which the 872-A originated unless the IRS has issued a Form 872-U, notifying the taxpayer of a different address to be used.[5]

It is interesting that the 872-A form requires "receipt" of an 872-T, and that the 872-T form requires "mailing" of such form. The case law, however, resolves this issue to a certain extent. It is clear that, in the case of mailing, it is the date of "receipt," not the date of "mailing," that starts the ninety days running.[6]

II. Case Law Analysis

A. *Tapper v. Commissioner*[7]

This case makes it clear that merely sending a certified letter purporting to rescind an 872-A will be ineffective. In denying the taxpayer's motion for summary judgment, the Ninth Circuit sustained the tax court's determination that an 872-T was required.

B. *Grunwald v. Commissioner*[8]

In this case the IRS appeals officer, during IRS Appeals consideration of an unagreed examination, wrote a letter to the taxpayer's lawyer. This letter requested that additional information be furnished, failing receipt of which, he would issue a deficiency notice. One hundred and thirty-two days later, the IRS issued its deficiency notice. The taxpayer argued that the appeals officer's letter effectively terminated the previously filed 872-A and that the letter from the appeals officer to the taxpayer's lawyer did not conform to the terms of the consents signed by the taxpayer and, therefore, cannot constitute termination thereof.

C. *Brown v. Commissioner*[9]

This case involved an attempted termination of Form 872-A. Here, the taxpayer's accountant mailed Form 872-T to the IRS service center in Austin, Texas, "Attention: Chief, Examination Division." The district office handling the case at that time was located in El Paso, Texas. The deficiency notice was issued to the taxpayer more than ninety days after the 872-T had been mailed but fewer than ninety days after the 872-T had been received in Austin.

The tax court held for the IRS on the termination issued for two reasons:

> First, the form was not mailed to the office considering the case; and Second, it is the date of receipt of the Form 872-T, and not the date of mailing, that controls.

D. *Freedman v. Commissioner*[10]

In this case the taxpayer successfully terminated a Form 872-A resulting in an untimely deficiency notice. The 872-T was delivered to one of the IRS's suboffices in Manhattan. Actually, the case was being handled out of another building in Manhattan.

This case is important in two respects. First, the IRS conceded that it is not necessary that the 872-T be mailed and that hand delivery is sufficient. Second, it is not necessary that the hand delivery be to the actual building where the file is located. It is sufficient if it is delivered to one of the IRS buildings in the district. The court noted that the instructions on Form 872-A do not require delivery to a specific address.

E. *Roberson v. Commissioner*[11]

Relying on the *Grunwald* decision, the court held that a letter from an accountant to the IRS district director requesting a "ninety-day" letter was insufficient to terminate a previously executed 872-A.

F. *Burke v. Commissioner*[12]

This case involves facts somewhat analogous to those in the *Freedman* case, discussed, *supra*. Unfortunately, the tax court chose to distinguish the facts and hold for the IRS.

The facts were that, following execution of an 872-A, the taxpayers and their representative executed a photocopy of Form 872-T and hand-delivered it to the Collection Division Teller Unit, where they received a stamped copy. Subsequently, the 872-T was routed to the proper office (the Examination—Quality Review Staff of the district office) after first having traveled from the Collection Division Teller Unit to the service center and then to the Appeals Office. Only then did the form end up in the Examination Division, which was considering the case.

The IRS subsequently issued a deficiency notice more than ninety days after the 872-T had been received by the Collection Division Teller Unit but fewer than ninety days after it had been received (ultimately) by the Examination Division, which was considering the case. The taxpayers, thereafter, contended that the deficiency notice was untimely.

In holding for the IRS, the court noted the following:

1. The hand delivery was without directions that the 872-T be routed to the Examination Division.
2. The purpose of the specific instructions on the 872-A form is to in-sure that those persons within the IRS considering the taxpayer's return have sufficient time (ninety days) to complete their consideration of it after receiving actual notice that the time for assessment is coming to an end.
3. The *Freedman* case is distinguishable because, in *Freedman*, the taxpayer marked the 872-T for the proper division.

III. Conclusions

For obvious reasons, the IRS is very careful to maintain strict controls over statute of limitations expiration. Because of hypersensitivity to cases involving "blowing the statute," procedures have been established to ensure that it almost never happens.

It is clear that nothing short of a Form 872-T will terminate an 872-A. Since the promulgation of Rev. Proc. 79-22, virtually all attempts at other methods of termination have failed in court.

It is not necessary for a taxpayer to use an original Form 872-T; a photocopy will suffice. Nor is it necessary that an 872-T be *mailed* to the IRS. Hand delivery is perfectly acceptable, and, in the author's view, is preferable. But one must be careful in how the hand delivery is accomplished. The recommended way is to type (in bold letters) prominently on the 872-T the words "ATTENTION, CHIEF EXAMINATION [OR APPEALS] DIVISION."[13] The 872-T form should then be delivered to the IRS office considering the case under examination (or appeal). The taxpayer should then have the IRS employee receiving the 872-T form stamp a copy of the 872-T to prove that it had in fact been received.

Certified mail is another way to submit an 872-T form. However, it should be noted that the certified mail receipt proves only that an envelope was received. The envelope could be empty—or the IRS could assert that the contents of the envelope were never received. For this reason, the author recommends hand delivery.

Issuance of Form 872-T is a very powerful tool in the hands of an astute practitioner for the following reasons:

1. It can force revenue agents to complete their audit within the statutorily mandated three years of filing date. It can catch revenue agents unprepared ("asleep at the wheel") where they have a previously executed 872-A in their possession.

2. Faced with only ninety days within which to issue a statutory deficiency notice, examination personnel have insufficient time within which to properly develop their case, thereby making it much easier for the taxpayer to defend his case.

IV. Notes

1. Burke v. Comm'r, discussed *infra* at note 12.
2. Pursuant to I.R.C. § 6229(b), if executed by the tax matters partner, all partners are bound by this extension.
3. Piarulle v. Comm'r, 80 T.C. 1035, 1042; *see also* Kovens v. Comm'r, 91 T.C. 74 (1988).
4. 1971 CB 679.
5. Per Form 872-T instructions.
6. *See Kovens*, 91 T.C. 74.
7. 85-2 USTC ¶ 9569 (9th Cir. 1985).
8. Grunwald v. Comm'r, 86 T.C. 85 (1986).
9. 51 T.C.M. (CCH) 1171 (1986), *aff'd*, 817 F.2d 754 (5th Cir. 1987).
10. 51 T.C.M. (CCH) 1264 (1986).
11. 52 T.C.M. (CCH) 851 (1986).
12. 53 T.C.M. (CCH) 1279 (1987); *Burke* was also followed in *O'Harren v. Comm'r*, 60 T.C.M. (CCH) 20 (1990).
13. *See generally* IRM § 25.6.22.

Mitigation of the Statute of Limitations

I. Introduction

There are a number of common law doctrines and statutory provisions intended to prevent the inequitable results arising from the exploitation of the statute of limitations. While the primary focus of this subchapter is mitigation, we also explore estoppel, equitable recoupment, equitable tolling (suspension), and claim of right. Note, however, that statutory mitigation preempts all other equitable doctrines. That is, these other doctrines can only be applied to situations not covered by mitigation.

The concept of mitigation is symptomatic of the classic struggle between simplicity and fairness. The statute of limitations provides a simple, workable rule. On the other hand, mitigation, albeit murky and arcane, exists to achieve fairness and balance. At first blush it would seem that the concept of viewing fairness over a span of several years flies in the very face of the regime of an annual accounting period.

The U.S. Treasury recognized the need for legislative amendment to the statute of limitations as early as 1933. It endorsed proposals ensuring that income and deductions should be reported or taken into account once and only once. The mitigation provisions of the I.R.C. were originally enacted in 1938 during the Great Depression. The ensuing six decades of experience with these provisions have proven to be a frustrating exercise in dealing with complexity.

As to the overriding goal of consistency, Congress has observed the following:

> To preserve unimpaired the essential function of the statute of limitations, corrective adjustments should (a) never modify the application of the statute except when the party or parties in whose favor it applies shall have justified such modification by active inconsistency, and (b) under no circumstances affect the tax save with respect to the influence of particular items involved in the adjustment.[1]

The overriding purpose of the mitigation statute is to permit an equitable adjustment by treating an error as if it had never existed, the statute of limitations notwithstanding. The obvious reason for a statute of limitations—staleness of evidence—is generally absent in mitigation cases.[2] Literally, the definition of "mitigation" is something that makes something else less severe or intense. It has also been defined as alleviation or abatement of a penalty or punishment imposed by law.[3]

I.R.C. §§ 1311 to 1314 (the "mitigation" provisions) provide relief from the often draconian results of the statute of limitations (S/L). While the S/L prevents the litigation of stale claims, the mitigation provisions were enacted to eliminate any benefit from changing positions after a tax year has closed. The purpose of the mitigation statute is to prevent either the IRS or the taxpayer from assuming an inconsistent position and then finding cover behind the statute of limitations. The theory behind mitigation is that the protection afforded by the S/L is not needed by a party who changes position, because that party currently has facts to correct the prior tax treatment of an item. Accordingly, under § 1311(b)(2) the party seeking to avoid the bar of the statute of limitations has the burden of proving that the mitigation provisions apply.[4]

While mitigation is a creature of statute, it is really a remedial rule of equity, seeking to fix what otherwise could not be fixed. Query: Does the mitigation statute supplement or preempt equitable remedies that judges could have dispensed as a matter of discretion? See the discussion below regarding distinctions drawn between mitigation and doctrines of equitable tolling, equitable recoupment, and the statutory rule of claim of right.

II. General Rules

A. *Statutory Provision*
   Mitigation involves the "correction of errors" that otherwise could not be corrected due to the effect of rules of law such as the S/L. That is, if mitigation applies, an adjustment can be made in a year otherwise barred by the S/L.[5] Note that mitigation applies to Title 26 taxes *other than* employment taxes.[6]

B. *Four Threshold Requirements*
   To invoke mitigation, the party seeking relief must meet four threshold requirements:
   First, there must be a substantive error on a tax return filed for a year that is time-barred.
   Second, there must be a "determination" (statutorily defined).
   Third, the error must be of a particular type covered by statutorily defined "circumstances of adjustment."

Fourth, in most cases, there must be an interyear inconsistency maintained by a party against whom mitigation is invoked.

C. *Inconsistency between Years*

Mitigation normally applies only if either the taxpayer or the IRS has maintained an inconsistent position. If an error correction would result in a refund to the taxpayer, then the inconsistency must have been maintained by the IRS; conversely, if an adjustment would result in a deficiency, then the inconsistency must have been maintained by the taxpayer.[7]

1. *Example of Government Inconsistency*

   If the taxpayer erroneously included an item of income on his return for year #1, which is now closed, and the IRS successfully requires it to be included in year #4, then the correction of the effect of the erroneous inclusion of that item in the closed year may be made since the IRS has maintained a position inconsistent with the treatment of such item in year #1.

2. *Example of Taxpayer Inconsistency*

   If the taxpayer deducted an item in year #1, which is now closed, and she successfully contends that the item should be deducted in year #4, then the correction may be made since the taxpayer has taken an interyear inconsistent position that would result in an additional tax assessment in the closed year.

D. *Exceptions to the Inconsistency Rule*

Assume that an income item has not been reported at all and the IRS raises the inclusion issue in a court proceeding. If the court determines that the item is not reportable for the year before the court, but in fact for another year that is not before the court, then the IRS can invoke mitigation to include the item in the proper year *as long as* the proper year was not closed at the time the IRS first took its position in a deficiency notice.[8]

Now assume, conversely, that a taxpayer claims a refund based on an expense not previously deducted. If it is ultimately determined that the deduction properly belongs in another year, then mitigation may be invoked to put the deduction in the proper year *as long as* the proper year was not closed at the time the taxpayer first claimed the deduction.[9]

Note that in both of the two previous examples, neither the taxpayer nor the government had maintained inconsistent positions. These situations typically arise in cases involving the timing, for example, of deductions for bad debts or worthless securities.

E.   *Law Applicable in the Determination of Error*
     In the event that there is a change in the law (administrative or judicial
     only) between the barred year of the error and the later year of the
     determination, a special rule applies. The interpretation of the law at
     the time the error occurred is not controlling; it is the law as ultimately
     later interpreted that controls.[10]

III. Determination

A.   For mitigation to apply, there must exist a determination. A deter-
     mination can be only one of four things. If it is not one of these four,
     then you can forget about mitigation. These four are the following:
     1.   A court decision (whether pursuant to a trial or settlement) that
          has become final;[11]
     2.   A § 7121 closing agreement;[12]
     3.   A final disposition by the IRS of a claim for refund;[13] or
     4.   An agreement (bilateral) signed by both the IRS and the taxpayer
          whose tax liability is in question.[14]
          a.   Agreements made pursuant to I.R.C. § 1313(a)(4) must meet
               strict content and execution requirements specified in the
               regulations. Merely signing a standard agreement form such
               as an 870-AD will not suffice.[15]
          b.   Additionally, an agreement under § 1313(a)(4) will not achieve
               finality, as would a closing agreement. The taxpayer or the IRS
               can, therefore, subsequently adopt a position at variance with
               this agreement.

IV. Circumstances of Adjustment

A.   I.R.C. § 1312 delineates seven circumstances under which mitigation
     adjustments can be made. Mitigation avoids the limitations statute
     only in precisely defined instances. Thus, if a situation does not fit any
     of these, then there can be no adjustment. The party seeking to use the
     mitigation provisions must show that the determination comes within
     one of the following categories:
     1.   *Double Inclusion of an Item of Gross Income*
          •   *Example:* W-2 form in year #1 reports a paycheck that was not
              actually received until year #2. By the time the IRS makes a
              determination that the amount is taxable in year #2, it is too
              late for the taxpayer to file a refund claim for year #1. Mitiga-
              tion will apply to correct the error in year #1 and allow the
              refund.
     2.   *Double Allowance of a Deduction or Credit*
          •   *Example:* Taxpayer claims a bad debt in year #1, then he decides
              that the year of worthlessness is really year #4 and claims the
              deduction in that year as well. If there is a determination that

year #4 is correct, mitigation will allow the IRS to issue a deficiency notice in otherwise barred year #1.

3. *Double Exclusion of an Item of Gross Income*
   - *Example:* Father and son have a 50–50 partnership. In year #1 the father reports 100 percent of the income and the son reports none. Just before the statute expires in year #3, the father corrects his return to report his correct 50 percent share of the income. If the father's claim is allowed, the IRS would be allowed to open up the son's return for year #1 and issue a deficiency notice.

4. *Double Disallowance of a Deduction or Credit*
   - *Example:* Taxpayer deducts a bad debt in year #2. The IRS denies the deduction on the basis that it properly belongs in year #1. The taxpayer will be permitted to file a refund claim even after the I.R.C. § 6511 period has expired.

5. *Correlative[16] Deductions or Inclusions for Fiduciaries and Beneficiaries*
   - *Example:* A trust takes a deduction for a distribution of income to its beneficiary under I.R.C. § 651. The beneficiary reports the distribution as income under I.R.C. § 652. If the IRS makes a determination that the income either should not have been distributed or did not carry out distributable net income (DNI), then the beneficiary will be permitted to file a refund claim to adjust the income.

6. *Correlative Deductions or Credits for Related Corporations*
   - *Example:* Subsidiary corporation S pays an amount to its parent, P, and deducts the amount as interest expense. P reports the interest income. If there is a subsequent determination that the amount is actually a dividend and it is disallowed to S, then P will be allowed to amend and claim a dividend received deduction.

7. *Basis of Property after Erroneous Treatment of a Prior Transaction* (Note: An example of a prior erroneous treatment would be where a taxpayer erroneously capitalized a deductible item.)[17]
   - If a determination results in the establishing of proper basis of property, then there must have been one of the following errors in a prior year:
     a. Erroneous inclusion or exclusion from gross income;
     b. Erroneous recognition or nonrecognition of gain or loss; or
     c. Erroneous deduction of an item properly chargeable to capital account, or vice versa.[18]
   - For 1312(7) "basis" adjustments to apply, the persons involved in the transaction must have been
     a. The same taxpayer;
     b. The taxpayer and the person he or she acquired title from if there was a carryover basis; or

      c.   The taxpayer and a donor where "gift" basis was determined under § 1015.[19]
- *Examples:*
  a. In year #1, individual taxpayer A transfers depreciable property to a corporation in exchange for stock and excludes gain under § 351.

    In year 4 the transferor, taxpayer A, sells his corporate stock and maintains that gain should have been recognized in year #1; therefore, a larger basis should have been used for gain calculation purposes. His position is confirmed in a closing agreement. *Held:* Mitigation applies because (1) it is the same taxpayer, and (2) there was an erroneous nonrecognition of income in year #1.

  b. In year #1 taxpayer A receives a preferred stock dividend (excludable under § 305). In year #2 taxpayer A makes a gift of the preferred stock to unrelated taxpayer B. In year #3 taxpayer B sells the preferred stock, claiming that the basis should be the full basis at the time A received it. The higher basis was confirmed in a closing agreement. *Held:* Year #1 is open for purposes of recalculating A's gain. *Reason:* erroneous omission of income and basis carryover under § 1015.

  c. In year #1 taxpayer receives a corporate distribution and reports it as an ordinary dividend. In year #4 the corporation liquidates and a determination is made that the year #1 distribution should have reduced stock basis instead of being treated as a dividend. *Held:* Year #1 is opened up through mitigation because (1) it is the same taxpayer, and (2) there was an erroneous inclusion in income in the barred year.[20]

B. In the case of an income exclusion, adjustment can be made only if the issue was raised by the IRS in a timely deficiency notice.[21]

C. In the case of the disallowance of a deduction or a credit, adjustment can be made only if any refund would not have been time-barred at the time the taxpayer first maintained before the IRS in writing that he or she was entitled to the deduction or credit.[22]

D. Filing a return is an example of "maintaining a position in writing before the IRS."[23]

V. Related Taxpayers

A. *General Rule*
Mitigation adjustments can be made with respect to different taxpayers as long as they are "related" and the relationship existed at the time the taxpayers first maintained an inconsistent position on a return or

a tax court petition.[24] Related taxpayers are those that are not involved in the proceeding giving rise to the determination.

The relationship to "the taxpayer with respect to whom a determination is made" must have existed at some time in the taxable year in which the erroneous tax treatment occurred. Further, if it is the IRS that seeks an adjustment against a related taxpayer, the relationship with the taxpayer with respect to whom the determination is made must, with one exception,[25] exist at the time the taxpayer first maintains the position upheld in the determination or at the time of the determination.

B. *Types of Relationships*
Mitigation adjustments can be made with respect to "related taxpayers," which are defined as the following:
1.   Husband and wife,
2.   Grantor and fiduciary,
3.   Grantor and beneficiary,
4.   Fiduciary and beneficiary,
5.   Decedent and his or her estate,
6.   Partners, and
7.   An affiliated group of corporations (see § 1504).[26]
C. If a relationship exists, it is not essential that the error involve a transaction made possible *only* by reason of the existence of the relationship.
   •   *Example:* Partner A erroneously assigned rent to Partner B. If there is a determination with respect to Partner A, an "adjustment" may be made with respect to Partner B despite the fact that the assignment had nothing to do with the business of their partnership.[27]

VI. Making the Adjustment

A. In ascertaining the amount of the adjustment to be made in the otherwise time-barred year, the IRS simply reconstructs taxable income as it should have been done originally to reflect consistent treatment, then recalculates the tax liability. This reconstructed liability is then compared with the original liability, and any difference is the amount of the "adjustment."[28]
B. Once the adjustment amount has been determined, the tax is then either refunded or assessed and collected as if the year involved were not time-barred.[29]
C. If the adjustment results in a deficiency in the otherwise barred year, the IRS is required to issue a deficiency notice, unless the taxpayer waives his or her right to go to tax court. The taxpayer against whom the adjustment is sought may contest the deficiency in the tax court or may pay the deficiency, file a claim for refund, and then file a refund

suit in district court or in the court of federal claims. In the case of an overpayment, the taxpayer is required to file a refund claim.[30] If the IRS denies the refund claim, the taxpayer must file suit for the refund.

The manner in which the statute functions sometimes requires two adjudications of the same anomaly: one to establish an inconsistency, and a second to establish that the inconsistency is the sort that warrants relief from the statute of limitations.

D. If the determination permits an adjustment, the adjustment must occur within one year of the determination.[31]

E. Query: If a barred year is opened up by mitigation, does one who has successfully invoked mitigation receive statutory interest going all the way back to the barred year?

VII. Similar Doctrines Distinguished

A. *Claim of Right*

"Claim of right" comes into play whenever an income item is thought to be taxable in year #1 and in fact is reported in year #1.[32] Then it is later determined that the reporting taxpayer did not have a right to that income and has to pay it back in a subsequent year. It is further assumed that the taxpayer is entitled to a deduction for the item paid back.[33] For illustration purposes, we will refer to the subsequent year as "year #2."

Unlike mitigation, the claim of right doctrine allows the taxpayer a choice of methods to correct the error:

> *Method #1:* Calculate the tax in year #2 with the deduction of the amount paid back.[34]
> *Method #2:* (1) Calculate the tax in year #2 *without* the "payback" deduction, then (2) subtract the decrease of tax in year #1 that would have resulted *without inclusion* of the income item.[35]

The taxpayer then pays the lesser of either method #1's tax or method #2's tax.

Does it matter that the statute of limitations may have expired on year #1 at the time the claim of right calculation is made? Apparently not.

B. *Equitable Recoupment*

This doctrine is usually raised as an affirmative defense by taxpayers who have been subjected to double taxation based on inconsistent legal theories. Typically a taxpayer-litigant wants to offset a deficiency with a refund claimed for a year otherwise barred by the statute of limitations. To invoke this doctrine, four things must occur:

- There must be a single transaction or taxable event involved in the controversy;
- This transaction must be subjected to double taxation based on an inconsistent theory;
- The offset claimed in the recoupment must have been barred by the statute of limitations, while the litigated amount must be timely; and
- There is an "identity of interest" between the party who paid the erroneous tax and the party seeking recoupment.[36]

Example: Decedent dies in year #1. In year #2, Form 706 is filed, reflecting a stock valued at $500 per share. Also in year #2 the estate sold the stock for $900 per share and distributed the proceeds to the beneficiary, who reported gain on the difference between $500 and $900 per share on the year #2 income tax return. In year #5, the IRS examines the 706 and determines an estate tax deficiency based on an increased stock value. In year #7 the tax court sustains the commissioner's determination. The beneficiary did not file a timely refund claim to recoup her overpaid year #2 income tax but, instead, raised equitable recoupment to offset the estate tax deficiency.

Held: All four criteria (see above) have been satisfied and, therefore, equitable recoupment applies.[37]

Query: Why couldn't mitigation be invoked in the above example?

Note that an equitable recoupment claim cannot be raised as a separate, stand-alone basis for jurisdiction in a refund action. Equitable recoupment can only be raised as a defensive offset in a different and independent case.[38] This is an example of progressively stronger restrictions on the use of equitable recoupment.

C. *Equitable Tolling*

  1. *Pre-1998 Reform Act Rules*

     Prior to the 1998 IRS Restructuring and Reform Act,[39] one had to look to the common law for relief in situations where taxpayers sought equity when there were circumstances beyond their control.

     Judicial relief was sometimes available to remedy the harsh result of the expiration of the statute of limitations when extraordinary circumstances beyond a taxpayer's control made it impossible to act within the applicable limitations period.

     For example, three district court cases have held that mental incompetency constituted a sufficient condition to toll the statute until an executor could be appointed.

  2. *1998 Act*

     In July 1998, Congress passed the IRS Restructuring and Reform Act.[40] Included in its provisions was Act § 3202(a), which added new I.R.C. § 6511(h). Prior to this act, the requirement of I.R.C. § 6511(a) prescribing three years within which to file a claim for a refund was strictly construed, equitable considerations notwithstanding.[41] The *Brockcamp* decision made it clear that the principles of equity did not apply to override the statutory requirement.

Effective with respect to periods of liability after July 22, 1998, the act permits the tolling of the statute of limitations on refund claims during any period that an individual is "financially disabled." An individual is financially disabled if he or she is under a medically determinable medical or physical impairment that

a. can be expected to result in death or that has lasted or can be expected to last for a continuous period of not less than one year, and

b. renders the person unable to manage his or her financial affairs.[42]

D. *Equitable Estoppel*

Prior to the enactment of the mitigation statute in 1938, the equitable remedy of estoppel was considered inadequate because of its inflexibility, conceptual limitations, and one-sidedness. It is now available to the taxpayer only under limited circumstances.

The common law doctrine of equitable estoppel is also sometimes referred to as "detrimental reliance." While this doctrine can be imposed judicially to mitigate the effect of the statute of limitations, it is applied against the government only with the utmost caution and restraint.[43]

The elements that must be shown before the doctrine will be applied include the following:

- A false representation or a wrongful misleading silence has been made;
- The error must be in a statement of fact and not in an opinion or a statement of law;
- The person claiming the benefits of estoppel must be ignorant of the true facts; and
- He or she must be adversely affected by the acts or statements of the person against whom an estoppel is claimed.[44]

Similarly, the doctrine of judicial estoppel prevents a litigant or his or her counsel from asserting a position in a legal proceeding that is contrary to a position successfully taken in the same or some earlier proceeding. This doctrine, which protects the integrity of the judicial process, is properly applied against the IRS to estop it from taking inconsistent positions in the same or related litigation.[45]

VIII. Judicial Authorities Discussing Mitigation

A. As the following cases will demonstrate, judicial interpretation of mitigation has been, at best, inconsistent.

B. *Brigham v. United States*[46]

In this case, the plaintiff-taxpayers sought to obtain refunds of tax in closed years based on a change in judicial posture on a particular issue. The IRS, in fact, had allowed such refunds to other taxpayers similarly situated when those taxpayers had filed timely claims. The claims court declined to extend the mitigation relief to these circumstances.

C. *Chertkof v. United States*[47]

In this case the decedent's estate used a lower securities valuation than determination; however, a sale of some of these securities occurred in which the lower estate tax return values were used as basis. After the statute of limitations had tolled, the executor filed refund claims using the higher basis as determined by the court. The IRS denied the claims on the basis that the genesis of the claims was grounded in estate tax law, not income tax law. The Fourth Circuit disagreed, however, and allowed the claims pursuant to the mitigation provisions.[48]

D. *Cocchiara v. United States*[49]

The taxpayer in this case was audited by the IRS in reference to the disallowance of installment sale treatment of mineral lease proceeds. After paying the tax in the initial year of sale, the taxpayer sought to recover the tax paid in subsequent years, after the expiration of the statute of limitations, under the mitigation provisions. The court rejected the IRS's superficial reading of the statute and allowed the taxpayer to recover her claimed refund.

E. *Esterbrook Pen Company*[50]

In this case the taxpayer took a deduction in 1952 that properly belonged in 1953. The IRS audited the 1952 return and disallowed the deduction. The taxpayer paid the resulting 1952 deficiency. Subsequently the taxpayer filed a claim for 1953, claiming the same amount that was disallowed in 1952. However, this claim was not filed within the statutory time period for filing claims and the claim was, therefore, disallowed on this basis.

The court held that the taxpayer was entitled to relief under § 1311 since the disallowance of the claim was a determination and since correction of the error in 1953 was otherwise time-barred.

F. *Gant v. United States*[51]

In years #1 through #4, the taxpayer reported partnership earnings based on withdrawals rather than the distributed share of partnership earnings. In year #6 the taxpayer discovered his error and filed claims for refund for years #1 through #4. The IRS allowed all claims except for year #1, which it said was untimely. In year #7 the taxpayer filed a second claim for year #1, claiming that year #1 was open under mitigation.

Held: The "mitigation" claim was improperly denied.

G. *Heineman v. United States*[52]

In this case the claims court drew a distinction between the "passive" and the "active" maintenance of a position to deny the taxpayer relief under mitigation.

The case involved the years 1944 through 1954. The taxpayer, in all of those years, claimed that certain corporate distributions were nontaxable distributions in liquidation. The IRS, on audit, disagreed and taxed them as ordinary dividends. The resulting deficiencies were paid for each year. Later, in an unrelated case, a court ruled that such distributions were, indeed, nontaxable.

The taxpayer thereafter filed a timely refund claim for the year 1954 only, claiming that the distributions were nontaxable. This claim was subsequently allowed in full by the IRS. But after the period of limitations for claim filing for the years 1944 through 1953 had expired, the taxpayer also filed claims for those years, urging that mitigation applied. The court disagreed, however, and said that the IRS's allowance of the 1954 claim was the maintenance of a position of the *taxpayers*, not the IRS.

H. *Hindes v. United States*[53]

During year #1 the taxpayer wanted to sell his ranch for $300,000. Instead, in year #1, the taxpayer and his lawyer transferred the ranch to a newly formed corporation for $265,000 on the installment basis over a ten-year period. The corporation then sold the ranch for $300,000 to the ultimate buyer for cash. The corporation paid tax in year #1 on the difference between $265,000 and $300,000.

In year #3 the IRS examined the taxpayer's return, held that the corporation was a sham, and set up tax against the taxpayer for gain on the full $300,000. This was also the position that was ultimately determined by the court.

Held: Since the corporation was not "related" to the taxpayers under I.R.C. § 1313(c), there is no mitigation relief.

I. *United States v. Rachal*[54]

In this case the taxpayer was a large Texas cattle rancher required to use the inventory method of accounting for calculating gross profit from cattle sales. He was audited twice by the IRS. The first time, the agent adjusted the unit price of the cattle, which affected the ending inventory (as well as gross profit) in two successive years. Mr. Rachal paid substantial deficiencies as a result of these adjustments. Later Mr. Rachal filed claims for refunds for these two years, alleging that the IRS had erred. The IRS then reexamined the years in question and made a downward adjustment in costs and inventories.

The IRS issued refund checks for most, but not all, of the amounts claimed. Checks were issued only for the portion of the tax paid within the two preceding years under the theory that the balance was barred by the statute of limitations. The taxpayer appealed, arguing that mitigation opened up the closed years to allow the full refund.

The district court, affirmed by the Fifth Circuit, held that in allowing most of the amounts claimed, there was a concurrent determination on the portion of the claims disallowed. Moreover, a change to inventory constitutes a change in income; therefore, there was effectively a double inclusion of income. Therefore, mitigation applied and the barred years were opened.

J.   *Rasmussen v. United States*[55]
In this case the taxpayer was unable to use the mitigation provisions because his situation did not fit the definition of a determination. The signing of a Form 870 setting forth his liability did not qualify under a § 1313 determination.

IX. Notes

1. S. Rep. No. 75-1567 (1938).
2. *Id.*
3. Black's Law Dictionary (8th ed. 2007).
4. John D. Rice, *When and How Will the Courts Apply the Mitigation Provisions?*, 69 J. Taxation 106 (1988).
5. I.R.C. § 1311(a).
6. I.R.C. § 1314(e).
7. Treas. Reg. § 1.1311(a)-1(b).
8. This is an example of the § 1312(3)(B) exception.
9. This an example of the § 1312(4) exception.
10. Treas. Reg. § 1.1312-8.
11. Generally the decision of a court becomes final upon the expiration of time allowed for filing an appeal. *See, e.g.*, I.R.C. § 7481(a)(1). In the case of the tax court, a notice of appeal must be filed within ninety days of the tax court's entry of decision. I.R.C. § 7483. *See also* Treas. Reg. § 1.1313(a)-1.
12. Treas. Reg. 1.1313(a)-2 specifies that a closing agreement may relate to the total tax liability of the taxpayer for a particular tax year or to one or more separate items affecting such liability. A closing agreement becomes final for the purposes of mitigation on the date of its approval by the commissioner.
13. A final disposition of a claim includes two things: (1) items claimed by the taxpayer and (2) IRS offsets to claimed items. A disposition becomes final upon the expiration of the period for filing suit for refund. Treas. Reg. § 1.1313(a)-3(c).

14. I.R.C. § 1313(a)(4).
15. Treas. Reg. § 1.1313(a)-4.
16. Defined as reciprocally related.
17. I.R.C. § 1312(7)(C)(iii).
18. I.R.C. § 1312(7)(C); Treas. Reg. § 1.312-7(a).
19. I.R.C. § 1312(7)(B).
20. Treas. Reg. § 1.1312-7(c) examples.
21. I.R.C. § 1311(b)(2)(A).
22. I.R.C. § 1311(b)(2)(B).
23. Treas. Reg. § 1.1311(b)-2(b).
24. I.R.C. § 1311(b)(3).
25. *Id.*
26. I.R.C. § 1313(c).
27. Treas. Reg. § 1313(c)-1.
28. I.R.C. § 1314(a).
29. I.R.C. § 1314(b).
30. Treas. Reg. § 1.1314(b)-1(a).
31. I.R.C. § 1314(b).
32. I.R.C. § 1341(a)(1).
33. I.R.C. § 1341(a)(2).
34. I.R.C. § 1341(a)(4).
35. I.R.C. § 1341(a)(5).
36. Estate of Branson v. Comm'r, 2001-2 USTC ¶ 50,622 n.7 (9th Cir. 2001), *aff'g* 78 T.C.M. (CCH) 78 (1999). The Ninth Circuit held, further, that the tax court has jurisdiction to hear equitable recoupment arguments.
37. *Id.*
38. United States v. Dalm, 494 U.S. 696, 90-1 USTC ¶ 50,154 (1990) *rev'g* 89-1 USTC ¶ 50,154 (6th Cir. 1989).
39. Pub. L. No. 105-206, § 3202(a), applicable to periods of disability before, on, or after July 22, 1998, but does not apply to any claim for refund or credit that (without regard to such amendment) is barred by the operation of any law or rule of law (including res judicata) as of July 22, 1998.
40. Pub. L. No. 105-206.
41. *See, e.g.,* United States v. Brockamp, 97-1 USTC ¶ 50,216 (S. Ct. 1997).
42. I.R.C. § 6511(h)(2).
43. Dillard v. Comm'r, 63 T.C.M. (CCH) 2255 (1992).
44. *Id.*
45. Marre v. United States, 98-1 USTC ¶ 50,321 (S.D. Tex. 1998).
46. 31 AFTR2d 73-534 (Cl. Ct. 1972).
47. 82-1 USTC ¶ 9282 (4th Cir. 1982).
48. *But see* O'Brien v. United States, 85-2 USTC ¶ 9492 (7th Cir. 1985) for a contrary result, focusing on "in respect of" language of I.R.C. § 1312(7)(A).
49. 86-1 USTC ¶ 9152 (5th Cir. 1986).
50. 6 AFTR2d 5123 (D.N.J. 1960).
51. 26 AFTR2d 70-5046 (M.D. Fla. 1970), *aff'd,* 26 AFTR2d 71-596 (5th Cir. 1971).
52. 21 AFTR2d 931 (Ct. Cl. 1968).
53. 19 AFTR2d 408 (5th Cir. 1967).
54. 312 F.2d 376, 11 AFTR2d 353 (5th Cir. 1962).
55. 87-1 USTC ¶ 9206 (5th Cir. 1987).

CHAPTER 5

Penalties and Interest

Federal Penalty Structure

I. Introduction

A. Scope of Presentation

The intent of this presentation is to provide the reader with a bird's-eye view of the civil penalty structure of the Internal Revenue Code to see how it all fits together. The process of securing a reduction or abatement of any asserted penalty is discussed later in this chapter under "Penalty Abatement." Additionally, the following specific penalties, because of their relative importance, are discussed elsewhere in some depth:
1. Underestimate penalties (later in this chapter),
2. Civil fraud (chapter 8),
3. Trust fund liability (later in this chapter), and
4. Preparer penalty (chapter 9).

B. Background

There are over 150 penalties in the Internal Revenue Code. As it is presently configured, the existing system is a patchwork maze of inconsistent, overlapping, and often draconian levies. This subchapter will attempt to explain and make some sense of this system and highlight some of the more common penalties that the average practitioner is likely to encounter.

C. IRS Policy and Procedure

The IRS's stated policy is that a penalty is to be imposed only to ensure voluntary compliance with the tax law.[1] However, the result of penalty imposition is also to raise revenue, punish the taxpayer, and reimburse the IRS for the cost of enforcement. According to existing policy, IRS agents may not use penalties as a bargaining ploy to extract an agreement on other issues.[2] In any "notice" that gives a taxpayer a right of appeal, the IRS is required to provide an explanation for any proposed penalty. However, failure to do so will not invalidate such a notice.[3]

D. *Civil and Criminal Penalties Distinguished*
Penalties couched in terms of a percentage of the tax owed are called "ad valorem" civil penalties and are designed to encourage or coerce compliance with the law. Nearly all civil penalties are ad valorem, whereas criminal penalties, imposed only after conviction in court, do not depend on the amount of the tax involved. Thus, there are two principal penalty classifications: (1) *specific* penalties, consisting principally of fines with maximum limits and imprisonment; and (2) *ad valorem* penalties, measured by a percentage of the tax liability. Note that acquittal on a criminal charge does not prevent the later imposition of a civil fraud penalty.[4] The ad valorem provisions of the I.R.C. are often referred to in the statute as "additions" to tax, but the generic term is "penalty." Ad valorem penalties may be determined and assessed by the IRS, but specific criminal penalties cannot be so assessed and are enforceable only by a suit and prosecution.

E. *Assessable versus Nonassessable*
Chapter 68 of the I.R.C. refers to "assessable penalties" and "additions to the tax," as if there were some important distinction between the two categories. "Additions to the tax" are found in I.R.C. §§ 6651 through 6665. "Assessable penalties" are found in I.R.C. §§ 6671 through 6751. But, as a practical matter, there are no distinctions between the two categories.

F. *Constitutional Objections*
Civil tax penalties have survived a number of constitutional challenges, most notably the double jeopardy clause, which forbids a second "punishment" for the same offense.[5]

G. *Penalty "Stacking"*
There are some judicially imposed limits on the IRS's attempts to impose multiple penalties on the same deficiency. For example, the IRS cannot stack penalty on top of penalty just because of an understatement of tax attributable to investment in a tax shelter, particularly where the taxpayer is inexperienced and uneducated.[6]

II. Failure to File or Pay

A. *Failure to File*
   1. *General rule:* In the case of a failure to file a return, or late filing of a return, the I.R.C. imposes a penalty equal to 5 percent of the tax

due, per month of delinquency or fraction thereof, up to 25 percent in the aggregate. As can be seen, this is a significant deterrent to filing late. This penalty can be avoided or abated upon a showing of reasonable cause.[7] This penalty is also commonly referred to as the "delinquency" penalty.

2. *Extended returns:* Merely paying the tax within an approved extension period will not avoid the § 6651(a)(1) penalty if the return is filed after the extension period expired, absent a showing of reasonable cause. Thus, in the event of late filing, the penalty is based on the total correct tax, unreduced by the payment made after the due date.[8]

3. *Accrual starting point:* For purposes of the "per month" calculation, the date of accrual is the first day after the final extension period has expired.[9]

4. *De minimis rule:* The failure-to-file penalty will never be lower than the *lesser* of (1) $135 or (2) 100 percent of the tax liability. Thus, if the late-filed return reflects a refund or zero liability, the delinquency penalty will likewise be zero.[10]

5. *Mailbox rule:* When there is a dispute as to when (or whether) an extension was filed, a taxpayer's own sworn statement when coupled with other circumstantial evidence will be sufficient to establish timely filing under the "mailbox" rule.[11]

6. *Fraud:* If a failure to file is fraudulent, the penalty rate is tripled. Five percent per month becomes 15 percent per month, and the 25 percent maximum becomes 75 percent.[12]

7. *Exempt organization returns:* In the case of failure to file an exempt organization return (see Form 990), the penalty is $20 for each day during which the failure continues. The maximum penalty is the lesser of $10,000 or 5 percent of the gross receipts of the tax-exempt organization.[13] This penalty can also be abated upon a showing of reasonable cause.[14]

8. *Pension or profit-sharing returns:* In the case of failure to file a return (Form 5500 series) for a deferred compensation plan, the penalty is $25 per day, not to exceed $15,000.[15]

B. *Failure to Pay*

1. *General rule:* Regardless of whether a return is filed in a timely manner, or within an approved extension period, a failure-to-pay penalty is imposed if 100 percent of the tax due is not paid on or before the original due date of the return. This penalty is calculated at a rate of 0.5 percent (of the unpaid tax), per month (or fraction thereof), up to 25 percent in the aggregate. This penalty may also be avoided by a showing of reasonable cause.[16]

2. *Deficiency cases:* The failure-to-pay penalty can also be imposed with respect to a tax deficiency, but only after twenty-one days

(ten days in the case of a deficiency of more than $100,000) after "notice and demand" for payment. That is, it cannot be imposed retroactively to the original due date of the return.[17]

3. *Increased rate:* If the failure to pay continues for ten days following a "Notice of Intent to Levy,"[18] then the penalty rate is doubled from 0.5 percent per month to 1 percent per month.[19] Note that a notice of intent to levy is *not* the same thing as a notice and demand.

4. *Failure to file cases:* Generally the IRS may not impose a failure-to-pay penalty where a taxpayer has not filed his or her return. However, this prohibition may be overcome by the government if it can prove that it prepared returns under "substitute" procedures.[20]

C. *"Balance Due" Rule*

The delinquency penalty is based only on the net amount due. Payments made before the return due date are offset against the total liability before the penalty is calculated.[21] This "balance due" rule also applies to failure to pay an amount per the tax return as well as to a deficiency.[22]

D. *Mutual Exclusivity*

When both the delinquency and failure-to-pay penalties apply to a particular period, the delinquency penalty is reduced by the failure-to-pay penalty during such period. That is, they are not "stacked."[23]

E. *Substitute for Returns (SFR)*

Where returns are prepared for a taxpayer under § 6020(b) (SFR procedures), then the delinquency penalty cannot be imposed; however, the failure-to-pay penalty *can* be imposed in such circumstances.[24]

F. *Installment Agreements*

The failure-to-pay penalty is cut in half during the period that an installment agreement is in effect.[25]

III. Accuracy-Related Penalty

A. *General Rule*

If there is an "underpayment"[26] of tax, the I.R.C. imposes a penalty equal to 20 percent of the portion of the underpayment to which § 6662 applies.[27] In the event of a tax return audit, the IRS will routinely add this penalty to any proposed deficiency unless the deficiency is nominal in amount. It is up to the practitioner, then, to come up with a defense to this penalty based on one of the statutory exceptions.

B. *Components of the Accuracy-Related Penalty*
Section 6662 can apply to any one, or more, of the following violations:[28]
1. Negligence or disregard of rules or regulations,
2. Substantial understatement of income tax,
3. Substantial valuation misstatement,
4. Substantial overstatement of pension liabilities,
5. Estate or gift tax valuation understatement,
6. Disallowance of a transaction due to lack of economic substance, or
7. Any undisclosed foreign financial asset understatement.

C. *No Civil Fraud Overlap*
The accuracy-related penalty cannot be imposed in a case where the civil fraud penalty[29] has been imposed.[30]

D. *Negligence*
"Negligence" includes any failure to make a reasonable attempt to comply with tax law. "Disregard" includes any careless, reckless, or intentional disregard.[31]

E. *Substantial Understatement*
1. *General rule:* There is a "substantial understatement" if the understatement of tax exceeds the greater of the following:
   a. 10 percent of the correct tax or
   b. $5,000 ($10,000 in the case of a C corporation).[32]
2. *Two methods of avoidance:* The "substantial understatement" portion of the accuracy-related penalty can be avoided by one of two methods:
   a. A showing that there is "substantial authority" for the treatment of any return item or
   b. Adequate disclosure of relevant facts, coupled with a "reasonable basis" for an item's tax treatment.[33]
3. *Substantial authority:* Note that the "substantial authority" (one-in-three) standard is *less* stringent than the "more likely than not" (>50 percent) standard.[34]
4. *Adequate disclosure:* To "adequately disclose" a departure from substantial authority, a taxpayer must attach a Form 8275 to his or her return.[35] In the author's opinion, attaching a Form 8275 to a return is the equivalent of attaching a request to be audited by the IRS. The better practice is to not take a position if there is no substantial authority and then consider filing a protective claim shortly before the statute of limitations expires, depending on the dollar amount at stake.
5. *Reasonable cause:* The 20 percent accuracy-related penalty can be avoided if the taxpayer can show reasonable cause, coupled with "good faith."[36] An honest misunderstanding of facts or

law (given the experience and education of the taxpayer), or reliance on professional advice, constitutes "reasonable cause" for the purposes of § 6664(c)(1).[37] An isolated computational or transcription error can also be evidence of reasonable cause and good faith.[38]

6. *Illustration of various standards:*
   Percentage of Chance of Success
   - 51 percent: More likely than not
   - 34–50 percent: Substantial authority
   - 33 percent: Realistic possibility of success
   - 15–32 percent: Reasonable basis
   - 0–14 percent: Frivolous

IV. Miscellaneous Penalties

A. *Failure to Deposit Taxes*
   Primarily in the case of payroll (employment) or excise taxes, the I.R.C. has penalties for failure to deposit those taxes in a timely manner. Unless there is reasonable cause, the penalty is equal to the "applicable percentage" of the amount not deposited. The applicable percentage means the following:
   1. 2 percent if five or fewer days late;
   2. 5 percent if six to fifteen days late; and
   3. 10 percent if more than fifteen days late.[39]

   This penalty will not be imposed if the taxpayer is a "first time" depositor.[40]

B. *Hot Check Penalty*
   If any check issued to the government is not duly paid, there is a penalty of 2 percent of the amount of the check. If the amount of the check is less than $750, the penalty is the lesser of $15 or the amount of the check.[41]

C. *Tax Court Delay*
   If a taxpayer starts or continues a tax court case for improper reasons, the court can impose a penalty of up to $25,000. Any one of the following reasons can trigger this penalty:
   1. The case was brought primarily for the purpose of delay.
   2. The taxpayer's position is frivolous or groundless.
   3. The taxpayer unreasonably failed to pursue available administrative remedies (i.e., go to the Appeals Division first for a settlement conference prior to the issuance of the deficiency notice).[42]

D. *Failure to Furnish a W-2 Form*
   If an employer fails to furnish a W-2 form or furnishes a false W-2 form to an employee, the I.R.C. imposes a $50 per W-2 penalty.[43]

E. *Foreign Trusts*

If a taxpayer fails to file an information return required when creating a foreign trust, the I.R.C. imposes a penalty equal to 35 percent of the value of the trust's assets.[44]

F. *False W-4 Form*

If an employee submits a false (i.e., no reasonable basis) W-4 form to an employer, he or she can be assessed a penalty equal to $500 for each such statement.[45]

G. *Partnership Delinquency*

1. *General rule:* If a partnership fails to file a Form 1065 (or files it late), the partnership is liable for a penalty equal to $195 times the number of partners during any part of the taxable year, up to a maximum of 12 months.[46] There is an equivalent penalty for failing to file an S corporation return.[47]

2. *Partner liability:* The partnership delinquency penalty can be assessed directly against the partners personally despite the language of I.R.C. § 6698(c).[48] This is based on the common law and statutory rule that general partners are jointly and severally liable for all partnership debts. Also, the penalty is not divisible and must be paid in full under the *Flora* rule to be contested in federal district court.[49]

3. *Exception:* The § 6698 penalty can be avoided if there are ten or fewer partners, all of which have reported their share of the partnership income.[50]

H. *Tax Shelter Promotion*

Any person who promotes an abusive tax shelter can be assessed a penalty equal to the lesser of $1,000 or 100 percent of the income derived by the promoter from the tax shelter activity.[51] For purposes of this penalty, a "gross valuation overstatement" means greater than 200 percent of the correct valuation.[52]

I. *Aiding and Abetting*

A person who assists in, or advises with respect to, a tax return, resulting in an understatement of tax liability, can be assessed a penalty equal to $1,000.[53] Note that this is in addition to a possible felony criminal violation for "aiding or assisting" in connection with a false return or document.[54]

J. *Frivolous Tax Return*

If a taxpayer files an incomplete or patently incorrect return and the IRS determines that it is frivolous, the IRS can assess a penalty of $500.[55]

K. *Burden of Proof and Choice of Forum*

For penalties under §§ 6700–6702, the burden of proof is always on the IRS.[56] Also, for these types of penalties, the "deficiency" procedures do not apply and, therefore, one must litigate them in district court or the claims court.[57]

L. *Failure to File Information Returns*

1. *General rule:* In the case of failure to file (or omission of any required information regarding) 1099 or other information returns, the IRS can assess $50 per return. However, if the return is filed within thirty days of the required due date, the penalty drops from $50 to $15 per return. If, on the other hand, the failure to file is due to intentional disregard, the penalty is the greater of $100 per return or 10 percent of the amount required to be reported.[58] Fortunately, however, a taxpayer must engage in "flagrant and egregious" conduct to be assessed a 10 percent "intentional disregard" penalty.[59]

2. *Failure to furnish copy to payee:* In addition to the penalty for failing to file an information return with the IRS, the I.R.C. also imposes a penalty for failing to give a copy to the payee. The amount of this penalty is $50 for each failure, not to exceed $1,500,000.[60]

V. Federal Penalty Matrix

Just in case you cannot remember the rules outlined above, or are too lazy to look them up, I have prepared a quick-reference cheat sheet.

Federal Penalty Matrix

Code Section	Name	Amount	Reasonable Cause Exception?	Remarks
6651(a)(1)	Failure to File Return	5% of the balance due, per month, or fraction thereof, up to 25% in total	Y	If fraudulent, 15% per month up to 75%. (a)(1) and (a)(2) are mutually exclusive. $100 minimum. No penalty if taxpayer (TP) is in bankruptcy.

Federal Penalty Matrix *(continued)*

Code Section	Name	Amount	Reasonable Cause Exception?	Remarks
6651(a)(2)	Failure to Pay Amount Due on Return	0.5% of amount due, per month, up to 25%	Y	(a)(1) and (a)(2) are mutually exclusive. $100 minimum. Becomes 1% per month 10 days after notice and demand. No penalty if TP is in bankruptcy.
6651(a)(3)	Failure to Pay Deficiency	0.5% of amount due, per month, up to 25%	Y	$100 minimum. No penalty if TP is in bankruptcy.
6652(c)	Failure to File Exempt Organization Return (990)	$20 per day, up to lesser of $10,000 or 5% of gross receipts	Y	Higher penalty limits if the gross receipts of the organization are > $1 million.
6652(e)	Failure to File Pension Plan (5500 Forms)	$25 per day, up to $15,000	Y	
6654	Failure to Pay Individual (including estate/trust) Estimated Tax (Form 2210)	Underpayment rate of § 6621 for "period of underpayment"	Y	No daily compounding of rate. No penalty if < $1,000. See separate subchapter for further discussion. No penalty if TP is in bankruptcy.
6655	Failure to Pay Corporate Estimated Tax (Form 2220)	§ 6621 rate × underpayment × period of underpayment	N	No "safe" estimate for "large" corporations. No penalty if TP is in bankruptcy.
6656	Failure to Deposit Payroll, etc. Taxes	2% if < 6 days late 5% > 5, but < 15 days late 10% if > 15 days late	Y	Exception for "first-time" depositors.
6657	Bad ("Hot") Check	2% of amount of check	Y	$15 penalty if dishonored check < $750.

Code Section	Name	Amount	Reasonable Cause Exception?	Remarks
6662	Accuracy-Related Penalty (includes: negligence, substantial understatements, valuation misstatements, and understatements of pension liability)	20% of portion of underpayment that applies	N*	* There are various exceptions, involving (1) de minimis dollar amounts, (2) adequate disclosure, (3) substantial authority, and (4) good faith. Underpayment means, generally, a tax deficiency.
6663	Civil Fraud	75% of underpayment attributable to fraud	N	Spouse exempted unless he or she was fraudulent. Government has burden of proof.
6672	Trust Fund Liability (100% penalty) [Failure to Collect & Pay Over Payroll Taxes]	100% of the tax not collected and paid over to the IRS (not the employer portion)	N*	*Requires "willfulness." Must bring suit in federal district court if administrative appeal is unsuccessful.
6673	Frivolous Tax Court Action	Not > $25,000	NA	Cannot unreasonably fail to pursue administrative remedies.
6674	Failure to Furnish or Furnishing of False W-2	$50 per W-2	N	See § 6051 for filing requirement. See § 7204 for criminal penalty.
6677	Failure to File Information re Foreign Trusts	35% of gross reportable amount	Y	
6682	False W-4 Information	$500 per W-4	N*	*"Reasonable basis" exception.
6694	Return Preparer Liability	$1,000 per return or claim	N*	*"More likely than not" standard. Administrative appeal can result in abatement. Must litigate (if necessary) in federal district court.

(continued)

Federal Penalty Matrix *(continued)*

Code Section	Name	Amount	Reasonable Cause Exception?	Remarks
6695(a),(d)	Failure to Furnish Return Copy to Client	$50 for each failure, up to $25,000 in any one year	Y	Same penalty for failure to retain a copy of the return (or list).
6695(f)	Refund Check Negotiation	$500 per check	N	Cannot use an agent to avoid penalty.
6698	Failure to File Partnership Form 1065	$195 × number of partners, per month, up to 12 months	N	Exception per Rev. Proc. 81-11.
6699	Failure to File S Corp Form 1120S	$195 × number of shareholders per month, up to 12 months	N	Same as partnership penalty.
6700	Promotion of Abusive Tax Shelter	Lesser of $1,000 per activity or 100% of gross income derived from the activity	Y	Includes "gross valuation overstatements" (> 200% of correct valuation).
6701	Aiding and Abetting Understatement of Tax Liability	$1,000 ($10,000 if corporate liability)	N	
6702	Frivolous Tax Return	$500 per return	N	Where correctness of the return cannot be determined.
6721(a)	Failure (negligent) to File Information Returns	$50 per return, up to $250,000 per year	Y	Includes failure to include all (unless de minimis) required information.
6721(e)	Failure (intentional) to File Information Returns	Greater of $100 or 10% of $ amount to be reported	Y	Per case law, there must be "flagrant and egregious" conduct for penalty to apply.
6722	Failure to Furnish Statements to Payees	$50 per statement, not to exceed $100,000 per year	Y	Higher penalty limits in case of intentional disregard.

VI. Notes

1. IRM 20.1.1.13.
2. IRM 4.10.6.4(1). Arguably, this tactic by the IRS could conceivably also violate the criminal statute, I.R.C. § 7214(a)(1), dealing with extortion under color of law.
3. I.R.C. § 7522(a).
4. Helvering v. Mitchell, 303 U.S. 391 (1938).
5. *Id.*
6. Heasley v. Comm'r, 90-1 USTC ¶ 50,314 (5th Cir. 1990).
7. I.R.C. § 6651(a)(1).
8. Rev. Rul. 81-237, 1981-2 CB 245.
9. Fergen v. Comm'r, 47 T.C.M. (CCH) at 911 (1984).
10. I.R.C. § 6651(a).
11. Lewis v. United States, 98-1 USTC ¶ 50,441 (9th Cir. 1998).
12. I.R.C. § 6651(f)(1),(2).
13. I.R.C. § 6652(c)(1)(A).
14. I.R.C. § 6652(c)(4).
15. I.R.C. § 6652(e).
16. I.R.C. § 6651(a)(2).
17. I.R.C. § 6651(a)(3).
18. *See* I.R.C. § 6331(d).
19. I.R.C. § 6651(d)(1).
20. I.R.C. § 6020(b); Spurlock v. Comm'r, 85 T.C.M. (CCH) at 1243 (2003).
21. I.R.C. § 6651(b)(1).
22. I.R.C. § 6651(b)(2),(3).
23. I.R.C. § 6651(c)(1).
24. I.R.C. § 6651(g).
25. I.R.C. §§ 6651(h), 6159.
26. Defined generally to be a "deficiency." See I.R.C. § 6664 for the precise definition.
27. I.R.C. § 6662(a).
28. I.R.C. § 6662(b).
29. I.R.C. § 6663.
30. I.R.C. § 6662(b).
31. I.R.C. § 6662(c).
32. I.R.C. § 6662(d)(1)(A).
33. I.R.C. § 6662(d)(2)(B).
34. Treas. Reg. § 1.6662-4(d)(2); Collins v. Comm'r, 64 T.C.M. (CCH) at 570 (1992).
35. I.R.S. Notice 90-20, 1990-1 CB 328.
36. I.R.C. § 6664(c)(1).
37. Zurcher v. Comm'r, 73 T.C.M. (CCH) 2532 (1997); Allied Marine Sys., Inc. v. Comm'r, 73 T.C.M. (CCH) 2124 (1997).
38. Treas. Reg. § 1.6664-4(b)(1).
39. I.R.C. § 6656(b)(1)(A).
40. I.R.C. § 6656(c).
41. I.R.C. § 6657.
42. I.R.C. § 6673(a).
43. I.R.C. § 6674.
44. I.R.C. § 6677.
45. I.R.C. § 6682(a).

46. I.R.C. § 6698(a),(b).

47. I.R.C. § 6699.

48. Simons v. United States, 89-1 USTC ¶ 9238 (S.D. Fla. 1989).

49. Flora v. United States, 5 AFTR2D 1046 (S. Ct. 1960); Christian Laymen P'ship, Ltd. v. United States, 90-1 USTC ¶ 50,042 (W.D. Okla. 1989).

50. Rev. Proc. 81-11, 1981-1 C.B. 651.

51. I.R.C. § 6700(a).

52. I.R.C. § 6700(b).

53. I.R.C. § 6701(b)(1).

54. *See* I.R.C. § 7206(2).

55. I.R.C. § 6702.

56. I.R.C. § 6703(a).

57. I.R.C. § 6703(b).

58. I.R.C. § 6721.

59. *In re* Quality Med. Consultants, Inc. v. United States, 96-1 USTC ¶ 50,115 (Bankr. M.D. Fla. 1995).

60. I.R.C. § 6722.

Penalty Abatement

I. Introduction and General Rules

A. There are over 150 civil penalties in I.R.C. §§ 6651 through 6724. Most of these penalties can be avoided or abated for reasonable cause, although additional requirements may also have to be met. Tax professionals should be familiar not only with the statutory civil penalty provisions, but also with the proper use of reasonable cause as a defense. Reasonable cause and good faith can serve as exceptions to the various civil penalties. Because of the subjective nature of the penalty area, a precise definition of "reasonable cause" remains elusive.

Reasonable cause cases are necessarily fact specific. One must look at the unique facts and circumstances of each case separately. The Internal Revenue Manual (IRM) also requires that, in the interest of equitable treatment of the taxpayer and effective tax administration, the penalty abatement determination must be made in a consistent manner.[1]

B. *Failure to File or Pay*
A reasonable cause exception clause is primarily invoked in the case of a failure to file a tax return (also known as "delinquency") and in the case of failure to pay a balance due. These two penalties contain exactly the same waiver language. Neither penalty will be imposed if the failure is due to "reasonable cause and not willful neglect."[2]

C. *Other "Reasonable Cause" Sections*
1. The accuracy-related (§ 6662) and the civil fraud (§ 6663) penalties can also be abated if reasonable cause can be shown.[3]
2. The failure to deposit (generally, payroll taxes) penalty can be avoided if reasonable cause can be shown.[4]
3. Penalties for failure to file information returns (1099s, 990s, 5500s, etc.) may also be avoided by the reasonable cause exception.[5] Similarly, failure to file correct information returns or to make

timely corrections may result in an avoidable penalty if such failure results from reasonable cause and not from willful neglect.[6]

4. Penalties for understatements for "reportable transactions" can be abated if it is shown that there was reasonable cause and that the taxpayer acted in good faith with respect to the portion of the understatement attributable to such transactions.[7]

D. *Internal Revenue Manual (IRM)*
Reasonable cause penalty exceptions are discussed generally in the IRM at § 20.1.1.3.1. Its provisions should be carefully reviewed before preparing a request for abatement to be filed with the IRS.

E. *Burden of Proof*
In federal tax controversy cases, the burden of proof is, in some limited circumstances, shifted to the government.[8] In the case of penalties or additions to tax, the I.R.C. specifically requires that the government bear the burden of *production* in any court proceeding.[9] In case of penalties involving promoting abusive tax shelters, aiding and abetting understatement of tax, and filing frivolous tax returns, the burden of *proof* is on the government.[10]

F. For an excellent analysis of reasonable cause issues in the failure-to-file arena in cases recently litigated, see a recent article in *Taxes* magazine.[11]

II. Reliance on a Tax Adviser

A. Failure to file a tax return in a timely manner is not excused by a taxpayer's reliance on an agent, such as a lawyer. Reliance on the advice of a professional tax adviser or an appraiser does not necessarily demonstrate reasonable cause and good faith.[12] Such reliance is not reasonable cause under § 6651(a).[13] The rationale for this rule is that it requires no special training or effort on the taxpayer's part to ascertain a deadline and ensure that it is met.

B. However, cases have frequently held that reasonable cause is established when a taxpayer shows that he or she reasonably relied on the advice of an accountant or lawyer that it was unnecessary to file a return even when such advice turned out to be mistaken.[14]

C. There are legitimate arguments that *Boyle* should be limited to its narrow set of facts and that reliance on advice of counsel remains a viable defense in many cases.[15]

D. According to the IRM, reliance on a tax adviser generally relates to the reasonable cause exception in I.R.C. § 6664(c) for the accuracy-related penalty under I.R.C. § 6662. However, in very limited circumstances, reliance on the advice of a tax adviser may apply to other penalties as well when the tax adviser provides advice on a substantive tax issue.

Reliance on the advice of a tax adviser is limited to issues generally considered technical or complicated. The taxpayer's responsibility to file, pay, or deposit taxes cannot be excused by reliance on the advice of a tax adviser.[16]

III. Underestimate Penalty

A. In the case of an individual underestimate penalty, there is a special waiver provision. No underestimate penalty will be imposed if the taxpayer can show special circumstances such as casualty or disaster and the imposition of the penalty would be against "equity and good conscience."[17]

B. There is also a reasonable cause exception in the case of an underestimate penalty, but the taxpayer must have retired (after turning sixty-two) or become disabled in the year the penalty was imposed.[18]

IV. Abatement Procedures

A. Reasonable cause penalties are appealed first by filing an abatement request with the governing IRS service center or a taxpayer advocate office. If denied, then the file is transferred to the local Appeals Office for a settlement conference.[19] The taxpayer may also file suit in court.

B. IRS Collection personnel can also consider penalty abatement requests.[20] One would want to file an abatement request with a local representative if he or she is dealing with a person in the local office assigned to the particular case.

C. IRS employees who deny a penalty waiver request based on reasonable cause are required to give the taxpayer a written explanation of his or her appeal rights.[21]

V. Specific Examples Discussing Reasonable Cause

A. *10 Percent Rule*
If the balance of tax due (after an automatic extension has been obtained) is less than 10 percent of the total liability, then reasonable cause is presumed and the late filing penalty will not be imposed.[22]

B. *Reasonable Business Judgment*
The I.R.C. does not define reasonable cause. But, under the regulations, reasonable cause for nonpayment will exist where a taxpayer has exercised reasonable business judgment (ordinary business care) in providing for payment of his or her tax liability.[23] The regulations do not elaborate on what constitute ordinary business care and prudence.

C. *Isolated Errors*

An isolated computational or transcription error can be evidence of reasonable cause and good faith.[24]

D. *Overworked Staff*

An overworked accounting staff will generally not constitute reasonable cause.[25]

E. *Reliance on Employee*

Where an employer has established a successful, longtime pattern of trusting a longtime employee, he or she cannot be penalized because of an inadvertent omission of that employee.[26]

F. *Ignorance of the Law*

The ordinary business care and prudence standard requires that taxpayers make reasonable efforts to determine their tax obligation. However, if there are recent changes in the tax forms or law that a taxpayer could not reasonably be expected to know, this may constitute reasonable cause. An honest misunderstanding of facts or law (given the experience and education of the taxpayer), or reliance on professional advice, constitutes reasonable cause.[27] The IRM takes a slightly different view and requires that taxpayers make a reasonable effort to determine their tax obligations. However, factors such as the taxpayer's education and whether there have been recent changes in the tax law may be taken into consideration.[28]

G. *Death, Serious Illness, or Unavoidable Absence*

Illness, especially involving hospitalization, will usually suffice to establish reasonable cause for late filing of a return.[29] For individuals, the death, serious illness, or unavoidable absence must involve the taxpayer or his or her immediate family (spouse, sibling, parents, grandparents, or children). For corporations the absence must involve someone who has sole authority for executing a return, making a deposit, or paying a tax.[30]

H. *Belief of No Liability*

Simply believing that you owe no tax is no excuse for not filing. Courts have ruled in favor of the IRS in virtually all of these cases.

I. *CPA Negligence*

In one case a taxpayer gave his records to his CPA one month before his return was due. The CPA put the records in the trunk of his car, then loaned his car to his grandson, who disappeared for two months. The court held this to be reasonable cause.[31]

J. *Erroneous Written Advice*
The IRS must abate any penalty attributable to erroneous written advice furnished to a taxpayer by an IRS employee.[32] The IRM also discusses IRS "advice" as a basis for penalty relief.

VI. First-Time Abatement (FTA) Rules

A. The IRM provides penalty relief for § 6651 and § 6656 penalties if the taxpayer:
- Was not previously required to file a return or has no prior penalties.
- Has filed a return (or extension) for all currently required returns and paid any tax due. In other words, the taxpayer must have a clean compliance record.

The FTA waiver can only apply to a single tax period.[33]

VII. Notes

1. IRM 20.1.1.2.2.
2. I.R.C. § 6651(a)(1),(2).
3. I.R.C. § 6664(c).
4. I.R.C. § 6656(a).
5. I.R.C. § 6652(a).
6. I.R.C. § 6724(a).
7. I.R.C. § 6664(d).
8. *See generally* I.R.C. § 7491.
9. I.R.C. § 7491(c).
10. I.R.C. § 6703(a).
11. Terri Gutierrez, *Will a Phobia of Tax Forms Exempt a Taxpayer from the Failure-to-File Penalty?*, 72 TAXES—TAX MAG. 570 (Sept. 1994).
12. Treas. Reg. § 6664-4(b)(1).
13. United States v. Boyle, 85-1 USTC ¶ 3,602 (S. Ct. 1985).
14. *Id.*
15. Steven M. Harris & Richard E. Warner, *Boyle and Beyond: Recent Trends for Excusing the Late Filing Penalty*, 67 TAXES—TAX MAG. 301 (May 1989).
16. IRM 20.1.1.3.3.4.3; *see* Neonatology Assoc. v. Comm'r, 115 T.C. at 98–99 for a three-prong test for reasonable reliance on a tax adviser to avoid the penalty.
17. I.R.C. § 6654(e)(3)(A).
18. I.R.C. § 6654(e)(3)(B).
19. IRM 20.1.1.3.
20. IRM 20.1.1.3.1.
21. IRM 20.1.1.1.3.
22. Treas. Reg. § 301.6651-1(c)(3).
23. Treas. Reg. § 3091.6651-1(c).
24. Treas. Reg. § 1.6664-4(b)(1).
25. United States v. Craddock, 98-1 USTC ¶ 50,392 (10th Cir. 1998).
26. Willis v. Comm'r, 84-2 USTC ¶ 9555 (4th Cir. 1984).

27. Zurcher v. Comm'r 73 T.C.M. (CCH) 2697 (1997); *see also* Holowinski v. Comm'r, 73 T.C.M. (CCH) 2532 (1997); Allied Marine Sys., Inc. v. Comm'r, 73 T.C.M. (CCH) 2124 (1997).
28. IRM 20.1.1.3.2.2.6.
29. Freeman v. Comm'r, 40 T.C.M. (CCH) 1219 (1980); *see also* United States v. Isaac, 91-2 USTC ¶ 50,314 (E.D. Ky. 1991).
30. IRM 2.1.1.3.2.2.1.
31. Gravett v. Comm'r, 67 T.C.M. (CCH) 2651 (1994).
32. I.R.C. § 6404(f).
33. IRM 20.1.1.3.6.1.

Interest on Underpayments and Overpayments

I. Underpayments

A. General Rule

Regardless of the type of tax imposed by Title 26 of the U.S. Code (U.S.C.), if it is not paid when it is due, the IRS charges a statutory interest on the unpaid balance. The period of interest accrual starts on the due date for the payment and ends on the date of actual payment.[1]

B. When Payable

Interest is payable on notice and demand, just as the underlying tax liability is so payable.[2]

C. Effect of Filing Extensions and Installment Agreements

Statutory interest starts accruing on the return due date ("last date prescribed for payment") regardless of any filing extensions[3] obtained or installment agreements[4] that may have been entered into.[5]

D. Jeopardy and Termination Assessments

If there is a jeopardy assessment on early termination of a tax year,[6] no interest will be charged prior to the normal due date of the tax return in question.[7]

E. Accumulated Earnings Tax

Interest accrues on the accumulated earnings tax[8] in exactly the same way that it does on income tax, with the accrual starting date being the return due date.[9]

F. Interest Treated as Tax

Interest is assessed, collected, and paid in the exact same manner as the underlying tax liability, whether the tax relates to a liability reflected on a return or one generated during the examination process as a deficiency.[10]

G. *Satisfaction by Credit*

If a tax liability is satisfied by means of an overpayment credit, for interest accrual purposes it is treated as if it were a direct payment.[11]

H. *Statute of Limitations*

The same statute of limitations (for assessment and collection) applies to interest as that which applies to the underlying tax.[12]

I. *Deferred Estate Tax*

If payment of estate tax has been deferred under I.R.C. § 6166, the interest rate charged depends on the size of the estate. The first million dollars of a taxable estate carry an interest rate of 2 percent on the balance of tax due. The portion that exceeds the tax on more than $1 million carries a rate of 45 percent of the normal underpayment rate specified in I.R.C. § 6621.[13]

J. *Erroneous Refunds*

If the IRS makes a refund in error and later recovers the amount erroneously refunded, that amount bears interest at the § 6621 underpayment rate, running from the date of the erroneous refund.[14]

K. *Payment Extensions*

The granting of an extension of time for the payment of tax[15] does not relieve the taxpayer from liability for the payment of interest thereon during the period of the extension.[16]

II. Overpayments

A. *General Rule*

If a taxpayer overpays his or her tax, the IRS must pay interest on the overpaid balance.[17] The period of accrual runs from the date of the overpayment to a date preceding the date of the refund check by not more than thirty days. Acceptance of the refund check does not prejudice a taxpayer's right to claim any additional overpayment and interest thereon.[18]

B. *Carryback Adjustments*

If there is a tax reduction in a carryback year as a result of a (1) net operating loss (NOL), (2) capital loss, or (3) credit, there is no effect on interest accrual for any period[19] prior to a year giving rise to the unused loss or credit.[20] In the case of a net operating loss, capital loss, or credit carryback, for interest calculation purposes the overpayment is deemed not to have been made prior to the filing date for the return for the year giving rise to the loss or credit.[21] This is the so-called restricted interest rule.

If an NOL carryback to a prior taxable year eliminates or reduces a tax deficiency in such prior period, the full amount of the deficiency will bear interest until the filing date of the year of the NOL. The amount of deficiency not eliminated by the carryback will continue to bear interest beyond such filing date.[22]

C. *Late-Filed Returns (Overpaid)*

If a taxpayer files a return late (i.e., after its due date, whether normal or extended), then there will be no accrual of interest on the overpaid return for any period prior to the actual filing date.[23] This prevents taxpayers from filing late and using the IRS like a savings bank.

D. *"Forty-Five-Day" Rules*

No interest will be paid on an overpaid tax return within forty-five days after it is filed. This is the IRS's "grace" period.[24] The same rule is followed whether the overpayment is on an original return or a subsequent amended return (claim).[25] For purposes of late-filed returns or the forty-five-day rule, returns will be treated as *filed* only if they are in "processable" form. That is, they must contain information sufficient to identify the taxpayer and verify his or her tax liability.[26] Moreover, if the IRS makes an audit adjustment resulting in a refund, forty-five days is subtracted from the normal accrual period.[27]

E. *Prepayment Rule (for Overpayments)*

For purposes of establishing the overpayment date, wage withholding, estimated tax payments, and similar prepayments attributable to a particular year are deemed to be paid on the due date of the return for that year. That is, payments made or credits available on or before the due date of a return are credited at the normal due date.[28]

F. *Overpaid Tax—Next Year's Estimate*

When a taxpayer elects to apply an overpayment to a succeeding year's estimated tax, the overpayment will be credited to the unpaid installments of estimated tax due on or after the overpayment arose, in the order in which they are required to be paid.[29]

III. Rates

A. *Pre-1983 Rates*

Prior to 1983, there was no daily compounding of interest rates. Instead, the rates were annual, simple rates, as follows:

After	And Before	Rate per Annum (%)
—	7-1-75	6
6-30-75	2-1-76	9
1-31-76	2-1-78	7
1-31-78	2-1-80	6
1-31-80	2-1-82	12
1-31-82	1-1-83	20

For amounts outstanding after 12/31/82, the adjusted rates established by the IRS under § 6621(b) were in effect.[30]

B. *Post-1982 Rates*

Interest rates are prescribed in revenue rulings generally issued before the beginning of the relevant quarter. The quarterly changes are summarized in the Wolters Kluwer Standard Federal Tax Reports at ¶ 39,455.02. Factors published in Rev. Proc. 95-17 enable taxpayers to calculate the exact interest, depending on the number of days during the quarter that the interest is owed. For periods between 1-1-83 and 1-1-95, the applicable interest tables are contained in Rev. Proc. 83-7. As a practical matter, most practitioners use commercially issued software packages to make these calculations.

C. *Interest Rates—Generally*

The underpayment rate and the overpayment rate of interest have now been brought into parity for individuals. Both rates are calculated as the federal short-term rate plus 3 percentage points. However, in the case of corporations, the overpayment rate is 1 percentage point less than it is for individuals and other entities.[31]

D. *Federal Short-Term Rates*

The federal short-term rates change each quarter, and the rate changes are effective on the first day of the first month of each calendar quarter.

The determination of the rate occurs in the quarter prior to the quarter for which it is effective. These quarterly rate changes also impact the underestimate penalties of I.R.C. §§ 6654–6655. See I.R.C. § 1274 for the rules regarding "applicable federal rates."[32]

E. *Large Corporate Underpayments*

In the case of a corporation that owes an audit deficiency of greater than $100,000, the interest rate charged is the federal short-term rate plus 5 percentage points (in lieu of the normal 3 points). This rate substitution occurs on the later of the date of the "thirty-day letter" or the date of the deficiency notice.[33]

F. *Daily Compounding*

In calculating interest on overpayments and underpayments, such interest is compounded daily.[34] However, this daily compounding is not used for purposes of the underestimate penalty.[35]

G. *Tax-Motivated Transactions*

Purely as a point of historical reference, between the years 1985 and 1989, and largely as a response to abusive tax shelters, the IRS charged a special interest rate where a deficiency was attributable to a "tax-motivated transaction." In selected cases where the IRS determined a particular loss or transaction was "tax motivated," the interest rate was increased to 120 percent of the normal rate. This law has now been repealed.[36]

IV. Interest on Penalties

A. *Interest and Penalties Distinguished*

Statutory interest is to be distinguished from a time-sensitive penalty, although it is similar in many respects. For example, the underestimate penalty[37] accrues, but is not compounded, daily. The late payment penalty[38] accrues, but is not compounded, monthly. Penalties are never deductible,[39] whereas interest payable to the IRS may be deductible depending on what the interest relates to.[40] But the question inevitably arises as to whether one must pay statutory interest on a penalty in addition to the underlying tax. The answer is "Yes," subject to the rules discussed below.

B. *Filing Delinquency and Other Penalties*

Interest accrues on the filing delinquency penalty[41] starting with the due date[42] of the return in question. For all other types of penalties, interest accrues thereon only if the tax is not paid within twenty-one days after demand by the IRS for payment of the penalty. This period is shortened to ten business days if the penalty amount is $100,000 or greater.[43]

C. *Estimated Tax Penalty Exception*

Interest does not accrue on the unpaid portion of the estimated tax penalty of §§ 6654–6655.[44]

D. *Failure to Deposit FUTA Tax Exception*

No interest accrues with respect to unpaid quarterly Federal Unemployment Tax Act (FUTA) deposits.[45]

V. Interest on Tax Deficiencies

A. *Interest on Agreed Deficiencies*

If there is an audit deficiency and the taxpayer has agreed to it (usually by executing a waiver of assessment restrictions via a Form 870), then the statutory interest accrual is suspended from thirty days after the waiver is signed until the IRS issues a "notice and demand" for payment.[46] This applies to income, estate, gift, and certain excise taxes, but not to employment taxes.

B. *Overpaid Years*

When a taxpayer elects to apply an overpayment to the succeeding year's estimated taxes, the overpayment is applied to unpaid installments of estimated tax due on or after the date(s) the overpayment arose, in the order in which they are required to be paid to avoid an underestimate penalty. The IRS will assess interest on a subsequently determined deficiency, for the overpayment year, from the date(s) that the overpayment is applied to the succeeding year's estimated taxes.[47]

C. *Deductibility of Interest on Deficiencies*

In reversing a North Dakota district court, the Eighth Circuit has upheld the regulation denying a deduction for interest attributable to a deficiency even though the deficiency related to the activities of a business.[48] Assuming such interest were deductible, if the underlying tax was contested, there would certainly be no deduction until there was some overt manifestation of agreement to the tax deficiency. Typically this agreement is accomplished by execution of Form 870 or 870-AD.[49]

VI. Litigation Issues

A. *U.S. Tax Court*

Prepayment of a proposed deficiency to minimize the interest accrual can have unintended consequences. For example, if a deficiency is paid in full following the issuance of a deficiency notice, solely for the purpose of stopping the accrual of statutory interest, the tax court will be deprived of jurisdiction because there is no "deficiency."[50]

After a tax court decision, a taxpayer has one year within which to file a motion with the court solely for the purpose of determining whether the taxpayer has overpaid or underpaid interest on any deficiency assessed after the tax court decision is rendered.[51]

B. *U.S. District Court*

To recover tax, penalty, *or* interest in a refund suit, the full amount of the interest accrual must be paid before instituting suit. Otherwise, the court will not acquire subject matter jurisdiction.[52]

VII. Interest Abatement and Suspension

A. *Abatement*

Since interest is statutory, it normally cannot be abated through a negotiation process. Nor does the tax court normally have jurisdiction to abate or reduce interest on deficiencies.[53] But see limited jurisdiction, discussed below, regarding I.R.C. § 6404 abatements.

The interest assessment is viewed as a mathematical calculation based on an established liability; therefore, the only way to reduce the interest is to reduce the underlying tax liability. However, where there is an audit deficiency and there has been an unreasonable error or delay by an IRS employee acting in his or her official capacity in performing ministerial or managerial acts, the IRS may abate all or part of such interest.[54] Requests for abatement should be made by using a Form 843.[55] This is a process completely separate from the controversy involving the underlying tax liability. If the interest has already been paid, the 843 claim constitutes a claim for refund instead of a claim for abatement.

For example, if the IRS cannot explain the reasons for an inordinate delay in processing a deficiency case, it will be considered an abuse of discretion not to make a partial abatement of interest.[56]

The U.S. Tax Court has exclusive jurisdiction to review, on an abuse of discretion basis, a decision of the IRS not to abate interest under I.R.C. § 6404.[57]

Practice Tip

In the event that the IRS, during an audit, requests an extension of the assessment statute of limitations, one might execute such a consent to extend, conditioned on abatement of interest during such extended period.

B.   *Suspension—Lack of Notice*
     If the IRS does not provide a notice to the taxpayer specifically stating the taxpayer's liability and the basis for the liability within one year (eighteen months for years 2003 and prior) of the return filing date, then the IRS is required to suspend the imposition of any interest.[58] The reason for this law is to encourage the IRS to act promptly in reviewing the return instead of letting the statute of limitations continue to run and allowing a taxpayer's interest to grow.

VIII. Miscellaneous Topics

A.   *Notice Requirement*
     On all "balance due" notices mailed out by the IRS, a computation of how the interest due was arrived at must be included with the notice. This applies to all notices issued after December 31, 2000.[59]

B.   *Global Interest Netting*
     For periods beginning after July 22, 1998, an interest rate of zero applies to overpayments and underpayments for any period of mutual indebtedness between a taxpayer and the IRS. No interest will be imposed

to the extent that the underpayment and overpayment run simultaneously on equal amounts[60]

C. *Bankruptcy—Nondischargeable Tax*

If, in a bankruptcy case, the underlying tax (e.g., trust fund liability tax) is not dischargeable, then the postpetition interest accrual is likewise not dischargeable.[61]

IX. Conclusion

It should never be assumed that statutory interest has been correctly calculated by the IRS, even if done by its computers. Many such calculations are, in fact, done manually. As a general rule, it is always wise for a practitioner to do his or her own calculations, using established principles, and then compare them with the IRS' calculation.

X. Notes

1. I.R.C. § 6601(a).
2. I.R.C. § 6155(a).
3. *See* I.R.C. § 6081.
4. *See* I.R.C. § 6159.
5. I.R.C. § 6601(b)(1).
6. *See* I.R.C. §§ 6851–6873.
7. I.R.C. § 6601(b)(3).
8. *See* I.R.C. §§ 531 *et seq.*
9. I.R.C. § 6601(b)(4).
10. I.R.C. § 6601(e)(1).
11. I.R.C. § 6601(f).
12. I.R.C. § 6601(g).
13. I.R.C. § 6601(j).
14. I.R.C. § 6602.
15. *See* I.R.C. § 6161.
16. Treas. Reg. § 301.6601-1(c)(1).
17. I.R.C. § 6611(a).
18. I.R.C. § 6611(b)(2).
19. That is, on any underpayment for the same accrual period.
20. I.R.C. § 6601(d).
21. I.R.C. § 6611(f).
22. Treas. Reg. § 301.6601-1(e).
23. I.R.C. § 6611(b)(3).
24. I.R.C. § 6611(e)(1).
25. I.R.C. § 6611(e)(2).
26. I.R.C. § 6611(g).
27. I.R.C. § 6611(e)(3).
28. I.R.C. § 6611(d).
29. May Dep't Stores Co. v. United States, 96-2 USTC ¶ 50,596 (Fed. Cl. 1996).
30. Treas. Reg. § 301.6621-1(a).
31. I.R.C. § 6621(a).

32. I.R.C. § 6621(b).
33. I.R.C. § 6621(c).
34. I.R.C. § 6622a).
35. I.R.C. § 6622b).
36. *See* former I.R.C. § 6621(d).
37. I.R.C. §§ 6654–6655.
38. I.R.C. § 6651(a)(2).
39. I.R.C. § 162(f).
40. *See generally* I.R.C. § 163.
41. I.R.C. § 6651(a)(1).
42. Including extensions. I.R.C. § 6601(e)(2)(B).
43. I.R.C. § 6601(e)(2)(A).
44. I.R.C. § 6601(h).
45. I.R.C. § 6601(i).
46. I.R.C. § 6601(c).
47. Rev. Rul. 99-40, 1999-40 I.R.B. 441
48. Temp. Reg. § 1.163-9T(b)(2)(A)(I); Miller v. United States, 95-2 USTC ¶ 50,485 (8th Cir. 1995); Redlark v. Comm'r, 98-1 USTC ¶ 50,322 (9th Cir. 1998). This rule has been also followed in the Fourth, Sixth, and Seventh Circuits.
49. Phillips Petrol. Co. v. Comm'r, 61 T.C.M. (CCH) 2836 (1991).
50. Huene v. United States, 81-1 USTC ¶ 9133 (E.D. Cal. 1980); but see the alternative procedures available under Rev. Proc. 84-58, 1984-2 CB 501, including designation of prepayments as a "cash bond."
51. I.R.C. § 7481(c).
52. Horkey v. United States, 89-2 USTC ¶ 9399 (D.C. Minn. 1989).
53. Costanza v. Comm'r, 50 T.C.M. (CCH) 280 (1985).
54. I.R.C. § 6404(e).
55. Rev. Proc. 87-42, 1987-2 CB 589.
56. Jacobs v. Comm'r, 79 T.C.M. (CCH) at 1840 (2000).
57. I.R.C. § 6404(h); Hinck v. Comm'r (Fed. Cl. 2005).
58. I.R.C. § 6404(g).
59. I.R.C. § 6631.
60. I.R.C. § 6621(d), as added by the IRS Restructuring and Reform Act of 1998.
61. Bruning v. United States, 13 AFTR2d 962 (S. Ct. 1964).

Underestimate Penalties

I. General Rules

A. General Rule
All individuals must make estimated tax payments if they have income that is not subject to withholding. This is part of Congress's theory of a pay-as-you-go system of tax collection.

B. Rate
The underestimate penalty is calculated at the same rate as the one used to calculate interest on underpayments.[1]

C. Daily Compounding
The underestimate penalty is not compounded daily, as is the interest on tax underpayments.[2]

D. Required Installments
Each "required" installment amount must be at least 25 percent of 90 percent of the ultimate tax liability for the current year.[3]

E. De Minimis Rule
No penalty is imposed if the net tax due on a return is less than $1,000.[4]

F. Waiver
The underestimate penalty can be waived if any underestimate can be attributed to a casualty, a disaster, or other unusual circumstances.[5]

G. Assumption Regarding Wage Withholding
Tax withheld from wages is deemed to be paid equally on each of the four due dates unless the taxpayer can prove that the actual withholding amounts are not equal.[6]

> **Practice Tip**
>
> If a taxpayer has salary income subject to withholding as well as self-employment or other income not subject to withholding, a year-end extraordinary withholding on the last paycheck of the year may suffice to avoid the underestimate penalty altogether.

H. *Annualization*

The annualization method (to avoid the penalty) is suitable for taxpayers whose income is received or accrued more heavily toward the end of the year.[7]

I. *"Catch-Up" Payments*

Paying more later during the year does not offset a shortfall from a prior installment.

II. "Underpayment" Rules

A. *Underpayment Amount*

The underpayment amount is the excess of the following:
1. The required installment amount, over
2. The amount of the installment paid on or before the due date.[8]

B. *Underpayment Period*

The "underpayment period" runs from the installment due date to the earlier of the following:
1. April 15 after the close of the taxable year, or
2. The date of payment.[9]

C. *Prior Year Overpayment*

In the case of a prior year overpayment having been designated to apply to a current year estimated tax, a question arises as to what is considered to be the date of payment. The IRS has ruled that it is the date a taxpayer elects to have the overpayment applied (instead of refunded) that controls. Generally, this will be the date the prior year return was filed, not the date the overpayment actually occurs.[10]

III. Due Dates

The four required installment due dates[11] are as follows:

1st	April 15
2nd	June 15
3rd	September 15
4th	January 15 (of the following year)[12]

IV. "Exception #1"

A. *General Rule*

No underestimate penalty is imposed if there was no tax liability in the preceding tax year. But this rule applies only if the preceding year covered a full twelve months and the individual was a U.S. citizen or resident.[13]

B. *Deferral*

The so-called exception #1 (100 percent of prior year liability) is a safe harbor that eliminates the underestimate penalty. But this allowed individuals to defer tax payments on significantly increased income by as much as 15.5 months![14] Note, however, that if the adjusted gross income (AGI) of the return for the preceding year exceeds $150,000, then the 100 percent of the prior year's liability becomes 110 percent.[15]

V. Estates and Trusts

A. *General Rule*

Prior to 1987 estates and trusts did not have to make estimated tax payments, but pursuant to Public Law No. 99-514, they are now subject to the same underestimate penalty rules as are individuals and corporations.[16]

B. *Exception*

Estates with years ending before two years after the decedent's death do not have to make estimated tax payments.[17]

VI. Required Forms

A. *General Rule*

Form 2210 is used to figure the underestimate penalty, but is not generally attached to the Form 1040.[18] There is a helpful flow chart at the top of Form 2210 for taxpayers to determine whether to file the Form 2210.

However, you *do* attach the Form 2210 to the 1040 if one of the following applies:
1. You claim a waiver;
2. You use the annualizing method; or
3. You have unequal wage withholding.

B. *1040 Reporting*

If there is a 2210 penalty, it is added to the tax due and included in the total on line 64.[19]

VII. Corporate Rules

A. *Due Dates*

For corporations on a calendar year, the estimated tax due dates are exactly the same as those for individuals except that the fourth payment is due on December 15 instead of the following January. For fiscal year corporations, simply convert to months 4, 6, 9, and 12 of the corporate fiscal year.[20]

B. *Payment Forms*

There is no prescribed form for corporations. Corporations must now use electronic funds transfer to make all federal tax deposits, including estimated tax payments.

C. *Additional Differences*

Unlike individuals, corporations do not have a de minimis rule and cannot avoid the penalty by showing zero tax in the preceding year.[21]

D. *Exception*

Exception #1 (100 percent of the prior year's liability) can also be used for corporations.[22] There is an important exception to this exception for large corporations: those with taxable incomes in excess of $1 million.[23]

E. *Current Year Rule*

Unlike individuals, who must pay in 90 percent of the current year's liability, corporations must pay in 100 percent of the current year's liability if they cannot meet exception #1.[24]

F. *Original Return Rules*

A corporation may not avoid the estimated tax penalty by filing an amended return. The penalty is based on tax shown on the original return.[25] Nor may a taxpayer use an original return filed *after* a deficiency notice has been issued to avoid the "required annual payment."[26] Thus, a 6654/6655 penalty is based on the information contained in the earlier occurrence of the (1) issuance of a deficiency notice or (2) filing of an original return.

VIII. Miscellaneous Rules

A. *Early Filing*

If an individual's return is filed by January 31, no penalty is imposed with respect to the fourth required installment.[27]

B. *Rule for Farmers*

If the taxpayer is a farmer, only one estimated tax payment is required to be made—on January 15 of the following year.[28]

C. *Tax Court Jurisdiction*

In cases involving disputes over imposition of the underestimate penalty, the U.S. Tax Court has jurisdiction to hear these cases.[29]

D. *Self-Employment Tax*

For individual taxpayers, estimated tax includes self-employment tax as well as income tax.[30]

E. *Other Penalties*

The delinquency and underpayment penalties do not apply to estimated tax payments.[31]

F. *Bankruptcy*

No corporate or individual estimated tax penalty can be imposed for a period during which the taxpayer has a bankruptcy case pending.[32]

IX. Notes

1. I.R.C. §§ 6654(a)(1), 6621(a)(2).
2. I.R.C. § 6622(b).
3. I.R.C. § 6654(d)(1)(B)(i).
4. I.R.C. § 6654(e)(1).
5. I.R.C. § 6654(e)(3).
6. I.R.C. § 6654(g)(1).
7. I.R.C. § 6654(d).
8. I.R.C. § 6654(b)(1).
9. I.R.C. § 6654(b)(2).
10. Rev. Rul. 83-111, 1983-2 CB 245.
11. Assuming a calendar-year individual.
12. I.R.C. § 6654(c).
13. I.R.C. § 6654(e)(2).
14. I.R.C. § 6654(d)(1)(B)(2).
15. I.R.C. § 6654(d)(1)(C).
16. I.R.C. § 6654(1)(1).
17. I.R.C. § 6654(l)(2).
18. Form 1040 instructions.
19. *Id.*
20. I.R.C. § 6655(c).
21. I.R.C. § 6655(d).
22. I.R.C. § 6655(d)(1)(B)(ii).
23. I.R.C. § 6655(d)(2)(A), 6655(g)(2)(A).
24. I.R.C. § 6655(d)(1)(B)(i).

25. Evans-Cooperage, Inc. v. United States, 82-2 USTC ¶ 9665 (E.D. La. 1982), *aff'd*, 5th Cir. 1983.
26. Mendes v. Comm'r, 121 T.C. 308 (2003).
27. I.R.C. § 6654(h).
28. I.R.C. § 6654(i).
29. Conovitz v. Comm'r, 39 T.C.M. (CCH) 929 (1980).
30. I.R.C. § 6654(a).
31. I.R.C. § 6651(e).
32. I.R.C. § 6658(a).

Handling Trust Fund Liability Cases

I. Background

A. General Rule

When an employer withholds FICA and income tax (WHT) from an employee's paycheck, he or she is required by law to do the following:
1. Collect;
2. Account for; and
3. Pay over the collected amount to the IRS.[1]

B. Penalty Rate

Section 6672 is technically not a penalty at all. Instead, it is merely an IRS collection device used whenever there is no other way for the IRS to recover tax that has been withheld from employees' paychecks. Thus the "penalty" is equal to 100 percent of the withheld portions of the payroll tax, but does not include the employer's share of FICA.[2] At a rate of 100 percent, this penalty is the highest rate in the I.R.C. This is the reason the § 6672 penalty is sometimes referred to as the "100 percent penalty."

C. Reasons for Enactment of Section 6672

I.R.C. § 6672 was enacted to deter partnerships and corporations from willfully failing to collect, account for, and pay over any tax. The purpose of § 6672 is quite simple: to discourage decision makers in failing businesses from appropriating employee withholding and FICA taxes for the benefit of other creditors.[3] The reason that corporations and partnerships are focused on in this subchapter is that individual proprietorship employers are already personally liable for any payroll tax. Therefore, there is no need for a derivative statute to impose liability for proprietors.

D. Motivations of Employers

Unsophisticated and unsuspecting owners of financially troubled small to medium-sized businesses view payroll tax funds as a convenient and inexpensive source of working capital when cash flow diminishes. Businesses unable to obtain outside financing or having insufficient funds to pay all of their obligations may attempt to continue in business by failing to pay employment taxes. In many of these cases, however, the business fails anyway, and the IRS attempts to collect the full amount of the taxes from the person responsible for not remitting them.

Decision makers of delinquent corporate employers often believe, incorrectly, that the corporate entity will shield them from personal liability for unpaid payroll taxes. Section 6672 of the I.R.C., however, ensures that personal liability does, in fact, exist.

E. *Manner of Assessment*
The trust fund liability (penalty) falls into the category of penalties that may be assessed and collected in the same manner as tax.

F. *Joint and Several Nature of Liability*
1.   In a trust fund liability case, it is customary for the IRS to assess the same tax against all potentially responsible parties and let the court decide which one is ultimately responsible. Therefore, the liability is considered to be "joint and several."[4] In other words, when confronted with conflicting claims of responsibility, the IRS generally assesses everyone and forces the parties to litigate the matter.
2.   However, trust fund taxes are collected only once, either from the entity or from one or more responsible persons.
3.   Prior to July 30, 1996, if there were multiple responsible parties in a corporation, and one party paid the tax, he or she had no legal right to recover from any of the others for their "share." The law now alleviates this inequity and provides that if any party pays all or part of the penalty, then he or she can recover from other responsible persons an amount equal to the excess of the amount paid by such person over such person's proportionate share of the penalty.[5]

Query: Is the amount paid pursuant to I.R.C. § 6672 tax deductible under either § 162 or § 165? The answer is clearly "no" under current case law.[6] The reason for nondeductibility is that a payment under § 6672 constitutes the payment of a penalty, which is nondeductible for public policy reasons.[7]

II.   Trust Fund

A. *General Rules*
Under the provisions of I.R.C. § 7501(a), the amount of any internal revenue tax collected or withheld from other persons constitutes a special fund in trust for the United States. Each time a corporation meets its

payroll, it is presumed to have withheld the taxes required by law to be withheld. The payment of wages to employees charges responsible persons with having in their hands the withholding and Social Security taxes, which are held as a "trust fund." Unless the government can collect the withheld taxes from the employer or those charged with the responsibility for the payment, then the withheld taxes are forever lost to the government.[8]

B. *Standard of Responsibility*
The trust fund liability penalty is so stringent because Congress recognized that people who collect money from employees to pay tax liabilities are creating a trust fund and must be held to a higher standard of responsibility.

C. *Parties to the Trust Arrangement*
A trust is typically a three-party arrangement. The employer acts as the trustee, the employees are the grantors, and the beneficiary is the government; the trust res is the withheld taxes.[9]

D. *Exclusion from the Trust Fund*
The § 6672 penalty does not include the employer's matching share of the FICA tax. Thus, the liability for the penalty is limited to the amount of the trust fund, which is composed of only the withheld taxes. Employer FICA is a corporate obligation that does not pass to the individual as a personal liability. It is a good idea for a practitioner to verify that the IRS's calculation of the trust fund portion is correct.

E. *Employee Credit*
If the taxes are not paid, the ultimate loss falls on the government, as the employee's account is credited as if the taxes were paid.[10] This is one of the reasons that the IRS views these cases as very serious matters.

III. Willfulness

A. The first of two elements necessary for asserting trust fund liability is "willfulness" (i.e., that the individual willfully failed to pay over collected taxes).

B. To be subjected to the penalty, a person "required" to collect, and so on, must have failed to do so in a manner that was "willful." Willful does not equate to "fraudulent." Generally, the employer is not trying to defraud the government; it is merely preferring other creditors and hoping that business will turn around so that the taxes may be eventually remitted to the IRS.[11]

C. The courts have given the term "willfulness" a very liberal interpretation. The definitions include deliberate choice, voluntarily, consciously, and intentionally. No bad motives need be present. Willfulness may be found in merely preferring to pay other creditors before paying the IRS.

D. Knowledge of the unpaid tax plus an "ability" to pay it satisfy the willfulness test.[12] Note, however, that lack of knowledge of liability can be used as a successful defense against an allegation of willfulness.[13]

E. Willful conduct includes failure to investigate or to correct mismanagement after having notice that withholding tax has not been remitted to the IRS.[14]

F. Advice and counsel received from a taxpayer's accountant or lawyer will not absolve him or her for responsibility for withheld taxes.[15]

G. In one case, a corporate employee was forced by his superiors to pay creditors other than the IRS for fear of losing his job. Thus, even a choice not freely made but consciously undertaken results in a liability.[16] This is an example of the "My boss made me do it" defense. This is also sometimes referred to as the "Nuremberg" defense. It will rarely ever work.[17]

H. Note that where there are no funds, nonpayment of taxes is not willful, and the trust fund liability penalty may not be assessed.[18]

I. Normally, willfulness is a fact question for the jury to determine.[19] However, there have been cases where the government's motion for summary judgment on the question of willfulness has been granted on the theory that the issue of willfulness is not a material question of fact in every case.[20]

J. Willfulness has been interpreted differently, depending on which circuit is considering the case. Some circuits impose a fairly strict liability standard, while others are more liberal, deferring instead to the jury determination, based on the factual circumstances of each case, as to whether a responsible person willfully failed to pay over withheld payroll taxes.[21]

IV. Responsible Person

A. The second element required for asserting the trust fund recovery penalty is the "responsible person" test. Succinctly stated, liability attaches to those with power and responsibility within the corporate structure for seeing that withheld taxes are remitted to the IRS.

B. *Definition of Person*
The term "person," as defined in § 6671(b), includes an officer or employee of a corporation who is under a duty to perform the act in respect of which the violation occurs. Any person may be subject to the penalty. The term "person" includes (but is presumably not limited to) the following:

1. A corporate officer,
2. A corporate employee,
3. A member of a partnership, and
4. An employee of a partnership.[22]

Section 6671(b) has been construed to include all those so connected with a corporation as to be responsible for the performance of the prohibited act.[23] The responsible person test for persons so connected with a business as to be in a position to exercise full authority over financial affairs has been widely accepted.[24]

Thus, the duty is generally found in high corporate officers who are charged with general control of corporate affairs and who participate in decisions concerning payment of creditors and disbursement of funds, although it can be asserted against other persons as well. On the other hand, if an officer holds a title as a mere figurehead and lacks true authority, he or she can usually avoid the penalty. This is true of many officers who are truly nothing more than passive investors.[25]

More than one person can be a responsible officer of a corporation.[26] The responsible person status is determined for each quarterly period, so an individual may be responsible for some quarters but not others.

C. *Check-Signing Authority*
   1. In determining liability, the IRS focuses on the outward indicators of responsibility such as check-signing authority. Such an approach does not necessarily automatically subject a check signer to liability since the individual signing the checks may do so only at another's direction. Thus, a mere titular officer without any real authority can become a target of an IRS investigation. The great weight given to objective signs of authority must be overcome by testimonial evidence on behalf of the client.
   2. In a 1979 Fifth Circuit case, a general manager in charge of a corporation's day-to-day operations and possessing check-signing authority was held to be a responsible person.[27]
   3. A check signer can be held liable, despite the fact that the check signer would have lost his or her job had he or she paid the payroll taxes in violation of the orders of a superior.[28]
   4. It has been held, however, that mere check-signing authority, without more, is insufficient to clothe a check signer with "responsibility."

D. *Outside Entities*
   1. Responsible persons do not necessarily have to be persons within the entity that incurred the liability; they can easily involve outside entities or even lenders.

2. Section 6672 is broad enough to reach any entity (including an outside lender) that assumes the function of determining whether or not the employer will pay over taxes withheld from its employees.[29]

3. A parent company can also be assessed the trust fund penalty where a subsidiary company is delinquent even though the parent was never involved in the day-to-day operations of the subsidiary.[30]

E. *Other Persons*

Usually the IRS seeks to assess the penalty on corporate directors and officers. However, creditors, bookkeepers, and purchasers are not beyond the scope of the statute. The IRS has issued a policy statement that says that nonowner-employees who act solely under the dominion and control of others and who are not in a position to make independent decisions for the business generally are not subject to the trust fund recovery penalty.[31]

It has even been held that a decedent's personal representative can be held personally liable for failure to properly supervise a business owned by the decedent prior to his or her death. This gives new meaning to the old rule that "you can't even die and get rid of the penalty."[32]

V. Preassessment Procedures

A. *Collection Division Investigative Jurisdiction*

Trust fund liability cases are handled and investigated by the Collection function of the IRS, *not* the Examination function. Therefore, in the field, you are dealing with revenue *officers*, not revenue *agents*. Revenue agents possess little or no knowledge of this type of case.

B. *Revenue Officer Investigative Duties*

During the investigation, the revenue officer reviews a variety of relevant records, including cancelled checks, bank signature cards, bank resolutions, payroll tax returns, corporate bylaws, minutes of meetings of directors and shareholders, and other corporate documents that tend to establish the identity of those persons who exercise corporate fiscal control. Quite often, the revenue officer will issue an administrative summons to the bank used by the corporation and obtain thereby copies of relevant records in their possession.

If the revenue officer is unable to make a conclusive determination of responsibility, then, in general, the president, secretary, and treasurer are considered responsible. Revenue officers follow nationwide guidelines in determining responsible persons. In instances where insufficient records or testimony is available, the officers of record are usually determined to be liable.

Revenue officers generally propose the liability against all persons involved with any apparent authority. This forces each such person to mount a defense and give valuable information to the revenue officer in seeking absolution.

The best defense from the corporate officer's perspective may be to identify the true responsible person. The practitioner's goal when defending a client from the penalty is to remove the onus from the client and place it on some other person, or, in the alternative, to limit the amount of liability. That is, you should shift the blame to someone else. Typically, this results in a great deal of "finger pointing" among potentially responsible persons. Asserting that other persons are liable is the most common tendency for most individuals.

In summary, one of the best ways to protect your client is to use the "He did it" defense. Blame someone else. This defense should be asserted at the initial IRS interview. Be prepared to present documentation to support allegations regarding the person with ultimate responsibility for payment of taxes. The best evidence may be affidavits from third parties and the client's assertions as to who was truly responsible. Always point out the client's dire financial situation when appropriate. The IRS may pass on the client based on uncollectibility.

C. *Interview Forms*

For each prospective responsible person, the revenue officer will usually conduct a personal interview and fill out a Form 4180, a multipage form requiring the taxpayer's signature. However, it should be noted that the revenue officer cannot *force* a taxpayer to sign. In any event, this form serves as the revenue officer's script during the initial contact when the penalty is being considered. Also, certain employees and officers may be asked to complete Form 4180, "Questionnaire Relating to Federal Trust Fund Tax Matters of Employer." When appropriate, the revenue officer completes Form 4183k, "Recommendation re 100-Percent Penalty Assessment." This form requires the approval signature of both the examiner's group manager and the chief of the collections field office.

Practice Tip

If the revenue officer fills out Form 4180 during the interview process, it is not a good idea for the interviewee to sign the form, even though there is a place for his or her signature on the last page. The reason is that the words written on the form are those of the interviewer, not the interviewee, and they typically contain "government spin" instead of exactly what the interviewee says. Occasionally, you will be able to convince the revenue officer to let the corporate officer or his or her representative fill out the form and mail it in. This is preferable, but not always possible.

D. *Opportunity to Agree*

At the conclusion of the revenue officer's investigation, he or she will usually ask the target of the investigation if he or she would like to agree to being named as a responsible person. If so, the taxpayer may sign a Form 2751. If not computer generated, this form will be in multiple parts. It will reflect only the trust fund portion of the tax, broken down by calendar quarter. It may also indicate an assessment date.

If a target person is clearly a "responsible" person and there are no available defenses, there is no reason not to sign the Form 2751 and allow the assessment to go forward. On the other hand, if there is a possibility, however slight, of shifting all or part of the blame to someone else, then under no circumstances should this form be signed. Instead, the target person should plan on preparing a protest.

E. *Periods Covered*

A trust fund liability assessment against an individual may cover more than one quarterly period. This causes a great deal of confusion among practitioners because the period indicated on a trust fund assessment will be the *last* (but not necessarily the *only*) quarter covered by the assessment. The revenue officer or other IRS employee will, however, be able to give you all the quarters covered by the trust fund penalty (often abbreviated "CIV PEN") assessment.

F. *Statute of Limitations*

1. *General Rule*

   The normal three-year assessment statute of limitations[33] applies to trust fund liability cases just like it does to income tax cases. For statute of limitations purposes, however, a 941 form is deemed to be filed on April 15 of the year following the year of liability accrual. Therefore, the three-year assessment period begins well after most practitioners might assume that it would.[34]

2. *Extensions of the Statute*

   If the "assessment" statute of limitations period is about to run on a trust fund liability assessment, the revenue officer may ask a potentially responsible party to sign a waiver of the statute. This is accomplished by him or her signing a Form 2750. This form extends the statute to a date certain. That is, it is not "open ended" like the Form 872-A for income tax. Note that, effective October 1990, the six-year collection statute is ten years.

   Note also that if a protest is filed in response to a sixty-day letter (see below), the assessment statute is suspended until thirty days after the IRS Appeals Office makes a final administrative determination with respect to the protest.[35]

G. *Sixty-Day Letter*

After a revenue officer determines that one or more persons are potentially "responsible," he or she will issue to each one a letter proposing liability. This is accomplished by mailing out a Form 1153(DO) letter. This letter is generally accompanied by the Form 2751 agreement form and an explanation of appeal rights. It is also sometimes referred to as a "sixty-day letter." Failure to respond within sixty days will result in automatic assessment. There are no instructions for IRS consideration of a request for extension of time to file a protest. However, there have been circumstances where, depending on need, extensions have been granted.

This 1153 letter satisfies the "notice" requirement of I.R.C. § 6672(b). In the event that the IRS does not mail such notice to a potentially responsible person, any subsequent assessment is invalid. Occasionally, and usually just before the assessment statute of limitations is about to expire, the IRS will not mail out the sixty-day letter; instead, they forward the case to the service center for assessment. If this should happen, the proposed responsible party should obviously contest the validity of the assessment on the grounds that the Section 6672(b) notice requirement has not been met.

H. *Preparation of a Protest*

After receipt of a sixty-day letter, the taxpayer or his or her representative has sixty days within which to prepare a protest and thereafter present his or her case before the IRS Appeals Office. The contents of a protest are specified in the procedural regulations promulgated by the U.S. Treasury. The format of the protest is also set forth on the back or the IRS's letter.

Even if a client is clearly a responsible person who willfully failed to pay the taxes, he or she may still protest the computation of the liability. It is not unusual for the IRS to miscalculate the penalty.

A protest should be sent by certified mail, with return receipt requested. The IRS has shown a remarkable propensity to lose protests and erroneously assess the penalty. If the deadline for a protest is imminent, hand-deliver the protest and secure an acknowledgment of receipt from the IRS.

Contemporaneous with the submission of the protest, request a copy of the IRS file including the computation sheet, Forms 4180 and 4183, a transcript of the account, and documentary evidence. Most IRS offices will voluntarily provide such information upon request. If you are denied access to these documents, you may make a request for the data pursuant to the Freedom of Information Act (FOIA). Privacy Act requests are submitted to the district disclosure office and must contain an offer to pay copying costs.

I. *Appeals Officer's Function*

If a protest is filed, the sixty-day-letter noticee is entitled to a conference with an officer of the IRS Appeals Office. The appeals officer (or settlement officer) reviews the evidence adduced by the IRS as well as the taxpayer and makes an independent determination of culpability. The taxpayer may be represented by a CPA or lawyer and present evidence and witnesses. Unlike collection personnel, the appeals officer may consider hazards of litigation and can recommend settlement of the case on a basis far more favorable than that likely to be recommended by the revenue officer.

Appeals officers are much more flexible during negotiations than are revenue officers. Many appeals officers solicit settlements and are open for suggestions that benefit all parties. However, they will not recommend settlement based on a hardship of the responsible person.

J. *Appeals Officer's Determination*

If the appeals officer is convinced that the taxpayer is not a responsible person, nonassertion of the penalty is recommended by him or her. An appeals officer's recommendations are subject to approval by his or her appeals team leader, who has complete veto power over the appeals officer's determination. If an approved determination, following an appeals conference, is in favor of the taxpayer, no assessment is made; the potentially responsible person is "off the hook." If, however, the appeals officer finds that the person is responsible, he or she forwards the file to the IRS service center for assessment. Unlike income tax cases, no issuance of a deficiency notice is required prior to assessment.

There is a stark contrast to the approach an appeals officer takes on a § 6672 case compared with a normal estate, employment, or income tax case. This is because there is a higher standard to which taxpayers are held in a § 6672 case. The other problem deals with the possibility of the government being "whipsawed" where there are multiple parties involved. For these reasons, appeals officers more often than not take a very hard-line approach on these cases and are reluctant to make any concessions. Another reason the Appeals Office is reluctant to concede is that, in the event of litigation, the Justice Department often brings in a party as a third-party defendant, despite the Appeals Office's prior determination of a lack of responsibility. Consequently, a much lower percentage of these types of cases are settled at the appeals level compared with other types of cases. In fact, many practitioners prefer to bypass appeals altogether and initiate litigation in either the claims court or federal district court.

VI. Postassessment Procedure and Litigation

A. *General Rules*

After assessment of a trust fund penalty, the taxpayer can prevent collection enforcement by doing three things:

1. Paying the withholding tax for one employee for one quarter;
2. Filing a claim for refund (using a Form 843); and
3. Furnishing a surety bond equal to 1.5 times the amount of the penalty assessment.

These three things must be done within thirty days after notice and demand for the assessed penalty.[36] Thus, the allegedly responsible person may obtain judicial review without paying the full tax as is generally required in income tax cases.

B. *Initiation of Litigation*

The trust fund recovery penalty is divisible[37] (i.e., any assessment consists of separate tax liability for each transaction or period). Thus, a taxpayer may pay the tax for only one employee for one quarter and have standing to file a refund suit. The better practice is actually to pay for one employee for *each quarter* of liability. The taxpayer should expect the IRS to counterclaim for the entire balance of the recovery penalty under § 6672(b)(1) so all periods can be resolved at the same hearing.

The taxpayer can either request immediate rejection of his or her claim or wait for six months for the rejection. If either the six months expires or the claim is denied (which is usually the case), then the taxpayer must commence a proceeding in either the federal district court or the U.S. Court of Federal Claims. Once a suit is filed, the matter is handled by the Department of Justice, Tax Litigation (civil) Division.

C. *Appropriate Court Jurisdiction*

1. Once a § 6672 penalty has been assessed, and notice and demand for payment have been made, the taxpayer must pay an amount of at least one employee's portion to challenge the assessment in court. Since a § 6672 penalty is an "assessable penalty," a notice of deficiency does not have to be issued. Thus, a taxpayer is precluded from challenging the assessment in U.S. Tax Court since its jurisdiction does not extend to employment tax cases. The better practice is to make such a payment for each quarter of liability.
2. Since the U.S. Tax Court has no jurisdiction to hear trust fund liability cases, they must necessarily be tried in either the U.S. District Court or the U.S. Court of Federal Claims.[38]
3. The U.S. Tax Court is one of national jurisdiction and, therefore, its decisions are reasonably consistent. But since trust fund cases

are heard by district courts and the claims court, their decisions are far more divergent.

4.   If a potentially responsible person also happens to be in bankruptcy, either before or after assessment, he or she can litigate the § 6672 issues as a separate proceeding within the bankruptcy case and have a judicial determination just as he or she would have in district court or claims court. This is actually a very good plan, as the IRS often finds that the bankruptcy court is an unfriendly forum. In bankruptcy court, the IRS is represented by a lawyer from chief counsel's office, as opposed to the Department of Justice. The proper procedure is to file a separate complaint within the bankruptcy case for a determination of tax liability pursuant to 11 U.S.C. § 505. This complaint will be assigned a separate adversary number, and the case will then be set for trial by the bankruptcy judge.

D. *Stay of Collection*
A taxpayer may bring a trust fund penalty assessment before a court by paying a divisible portion of the tax, but the IRS is not prohibited from action to collect the balance of the assessment by administrative means unless a bond is filed equal to 1.5 times the amount of the penalty asserted.[39]

E. *Counterclaim by the IRS*
After suit is filed, the IRS will counterclaim for the balance of all the payroll tax. Additionally, the Department of Justice will join in the suit parties who have been eliminated as responsible persons by the IRS in either the district or appeals proceedings.

F. *Recovery of Lawyer Fees*
Successful litigants in trust fund liability cases can recover their lawyer fees if the government's position is not substantially justified.[40] A detailed analysis of recovery of litigation costs can be found in chapter 3.

G. *Postassessment Settlement*
In multiparty situations, sometimes the IRS will settle with one of the joint obligors but not the others. The question that arises is whether the settlement with one party automatically releases the co-obligors. The law is now well settled that in the compromise of tax liability cases, the IRS can specifically reserve the right to proceed against co-obligors.[41]

The IRS now follows a policy of not securing a settlement with an assessee for less than the proportionate share of his or her liability when the settlement is not part of an overall agreement with all co-obligors. Part of the reason for this is that sometimes local law controls. In Texas, for example, the rule is that settlement should not be secured with one co-obligor for less than his or her proportionate share unless it is part of a settlement of the entire liability.

VII. Payment Designation

A. *General Rules*

In a postassessment period, a taxpayer's right to designate how payments are to be applied is a very valuable one for the reason that the IRS is loath to compromise § 6672 penalties.

One of a taxpayer's options is, of course, to pay the tax. If he or she does so, the IRS must apply such voluntary payments of assessed tax, penalties, and interest in trust fund liability cases in a manner designated by the taxpayer. In the event of a failure to designate, the IRS policy is to apply the payment first to the non—trust fund portion, including penalty and interest.[42] Obviously, the IRS will act in a manner that best serves its interest.[43]

It is important to note that for a taxpayer to take advantage of the payment designation rule, any payment must be *voluntary*. If it is not a voluntary payment, then the IRS can apply the payment any way it wants, even if to the detriment of the taxpayer.[44] If payment is made pursuant to a levy, the IRS takes the position that the payment is not voluntary. Therefore, they will not comply with a request for designation to trust fund taxes.[45]

Usually, if the corporation is viable and there is an installment agreement in effect, the IRS will not let the taxpayer designate a payment to the trust fund portion.[46]

B. *Authority to Make Payment*

Only a taxpayer, not a third party, has the right to designate how a payment is to be applied. Thus, a former corporate officer could not tell the IRS to apply proceeds of a forced sale to the trust fund portion of the liability. (Note: The obvious plan here is to give the instruction to the IRS before the officer resigns.)

C. *Planning Opportunity*

A clearly responsible person, who sees that his or her corporation is becoming delinquent in paying its trust fund taxes, should remit payments and designate that such payments are to be applied to the trust fund portion first. One should be careful, however, not to merely make the designation via notations on a check. Instead, such payments should be sent directly to the IRS with a cover letter (preferably certified) requesting the designation.[47]

VIII. Bankruptcy Issues

A. *Bankruptcy Code versus the Internal Revenue Code*
When the Bankruptcy Code (U.S.C. Title 11) and the Internal Revenue Code § 6672 intersect, issues are generally resolved in the government's favor.

B. *Dischargeability*
In either the employer's or the responsible person's bankruptcy, if funds are not available to pay the trust fund obligation, then such obligation is not dischargeable, regardless of when assessed.[48] The U.S. Supreme Court has also ruled that an adjudication of bankruptcy will not discharge a debtor's liability to pay over withheld taxes.[49] Congress's specific intent in this situation overrides the overall policy of the Bankruptcy Act of giving a debtor a "fresh start."

C. *Payment Application in Bankruptcy Context*
Whether payments made in a bankruptcy context are "voluntary" is an issue that has been resolved by the U.S. Supreme Court.[50] The holding in that case was that a bankruptcy court has the authority to order the IRS to treat tax payments made by a Chapter 11 debtor as "trust fund" payments where the court has determined that this designation is necessary for the success of a reorganization plan.

D. *Priority Status*
In the Bankruptcy Code, all payroll taxes are given payment priority regardless of whether they fall into the trust fund category.[51]

E. *Proof of Claim*
The IRS's failure to file a timely proof of claim in a bankruptcy proceeding has been held not to preclude it from collecting against a responsible corporate officer.[52]

IX. Miscellaneous Rules

A. *Change of Business Ownership*
A taxpayer, although "responsible," does not violate § 6672 because of the use of funds acquired after assuming control of a business after the liability accrued to pay other creditors, if there were no funds available to pay the IRS at the time of assuming control.[53]

With the exception of this "Slodov" rule, a new owner of a business, individual or corporation, can be held liable for failing to pay withholding taxes collected for the IRS prior to the acquisition. In one case a corporation acquired a 49 percent interest in another corporation. As part of the agreement, the acquiring corporation was given check-signing authority. The court held that the new 49 percent shareholder was liable for the penalty even for the period *prior* to the time the acquisition was made.[54]

B. *Death*
The trust fund liability penalty survives the death of the responsible person.[55]

C. *Transferee Liability*
Transferee provisions do not apply to trust fund liability assessments in the absence of corporate liquidation. Therefore, if you can get personal assets transferred through death or divorce prior to assessment, an injunction will lie if a levy is attempted.[56]

D. *Obligation to Pursue Employer*
The IRS has no obligation to pursue the employer first before going after a responsible person.[57]

E. *Criminal Penalty*
There is also a criminal penalty for failing to comply with the collection and paying over of payroll taxes. If such failure was willful, the penalty is $10,000 plus jail time of five years.[58]

F. *Negligence Penalty*
The penalties under § 6672 and § 6662(c) are mutually exclusive. That is, the negligence penalty cannot be imposed in addition to the trust fund liability penalty.[59]

G. *Contract Laborers*
A corporation cannot avoid the consequences of § 6672 by classifying all workers as contract laborers.[60] However, in the event of an employment tax issue raised in an audit, if the audit is conducted pursuant to the I.R.C. § 3509 procedures, the IRS cannot thereafter pursue any individuals under § 6672.[61]

H. *Backup Withholding*
Note that trust fund liability can be imposed in reference to backup withholding assessed under I.R.C. § 3406, but only in rare cases.[62]

I. *Partnerships and Limited Liability Companies (LLCs)*
Trust fund liability penalties can be asserted in a partnership context. Moreover, because of the joint and several liability, the penalty is not confined to the trust fund, but includes the entire liability! In the case of a single-member LLC that does not elect to be taxed as a corporation, the member has direct (not derivative) liability just as he

or she would if he or she were a sole proprietor.[63] Therefore, the IRS need not rely on the trust fund provisions to collect the tax from such member.

J. *Planning Opportunities*
   1. The possible trust fund liability exposure should be the subject of a shareholder agreement. Areas to be addressed are responsibility issues and contribution and indemnification issues.
   2. With proper planning and cooperation, all prospective responsible persons can minimize their individual risks and enhance the prospects of complete avoidance of liability. One possible approach is for the prospective responsible persons to identify, prior to assessment, the least culpable party against whom the assessment is proposed. Once identified, this person pays the trust fund portion of the tax in full. After the assessment statute of limitations expires on any other potentially liable person, he or she then files a claim, and, following disallowance thereof, litigates his or her case.
   3. Advise financially troubled businesses to pay the IRS first before paying other creditors, even though this may not be the best way to keep the business going.
   4. Make sure employment tax audits are conducted under § 3509.
   5. If you can delay the assessment as long as possible (and possibly shut down the corporation), then you may be able to let the three-year assessment statute of limitations go by on a § 6672 assessment on the corporate officers.
   6. If only a portion of the payroll tax liability can be paid, make sure that payments are designated to the trust fund portion as outlined in VII.C., *supra*.
   7. If marital difficulties seem imminent, a potentially liable person can transfer his or her assets to a spouse in an agreed divorce settlement, wait for the trust fund assessment, then file an offer in compromise based on doubt as to ability to pay. The IRS cannot thereafter proceed against the spouse under the transferee provisions of the I.R.C.

X. Notes

1. I.R.C. § 6672.
2. I.R.C. § 7501.
3. Charles E. Falk & Maureen Dougherty, *Designating Payments to Avoid or Mitigate the Section 6672 Penalty*, 66 TAXES—TAX MAG. 529 (July 1988).
4. *See* Rev. Proc. 69-26, 1969-2 CB 308.
5. I.R.C. § 6672(d).
6. Medeiros, Jr. v. Comm'r, 77 T.C. 1255 (1981).
7. *See* I.R.C. § 162(f); Duncan v. Comm'r, 66 T.C.M. (CCH) 420 (1993).
8. Carter v. United States, 71-2 USTC ¶ 9661 (D. S.C. 1971).

9. Kenneth C. Weil, *Impact of Pending Bankruptcy on Trust Fund Liability*, 72 J. TAXATION (Jan. 1990).

10. Sorenson v. United States, 75-2 USTC ¶ 9694 (9th Cir. 1975).

11. *See* Dillard v. Patterson, 13 AFTR2d 301 (5th Cir. 1963); White v. United States, 372 F.2d 513 (Cl. Ct. 1967).

12. Messina v. Scanlon, 15 AFTR2d 944 (E.D.N.Y. 1965); *In re* Fontenot, 93-1 USTC ¶ 50,186 (Bankr. W.D. La. 1993).

13. Macagnone v. United States, 2000-1 USTC ¶ 50,207 (M.D. Fla. 2000).

14. Kalb v. United States, 34 AFTR2d, 74-6104 (2d Cir. 1974).

15. Newsome, Jr. v. United States, 26 AFTR2d 5078 (5th Cir. 1970); Alioto v. United States, 84-2 USTC ¶ 9736 (N.D. Cal. 1984).

16. Freeman v. United States, 85-1 USTC ¶ 9255 (D. Ariz. 1985).

17. *See, e.g.*, Howard v. United States, 83-2 USTC ¶ 9620 (5th Cir. 1983); Jay v. United States, 89-1 USTC ¶ 9154 (10th Cir. 1989); Roth v. United States, 86-1 USTC ¶ 9172 (11th Cir. 1986).

18. Campbell v. United States, 207 F. Supp. 826 (D. Mich. 1962).

19. Turpin v. United States, 92-2 USTC ¶ 50,383 (4th Cir. 1992).

20. Skouras v. United States, 94-1 USTC ¶ 50,274 (2d Cir. 1994).

21. *See, e.g.*, the discussion in Finley v. United States, 97-2 USTC ¶ 50,613 (10th Cir. 1997).

22. I.R.C. § 6671(b).

23. United States v. Graham, 10 AFTR2d 5808 (9th Cir. 1962).

24. Frazier v. United States, 304 F.2d 528 (5th Cir. 1962).

25. O'Connor v. United States, 92-1 USTC ¶ 50,074 (4th Cir. 1992).

26. Monday v. United States, 25 AFTR2d 70-548 (7th Cir. 1970).

27. Mazo v. United States, 79-1 USTC ¶ 9284 (5th Cir. 1979).

28. Howard v. United States, 83-2 USTC ¶ 9528 (5th Cir. 1983).

29. Adams v. United States, 34 AFTR2d ¶ 74-5280 (7th Cir. 1974).

30. Farris v. United States, 84-1 USTC ¶ 9263 (Cl. Ct. 1984).

31. I.R.S. Policy Statement P-5-60, Feb. 2, 1993.

32. Keller v. United States, 95-1 USTC ¶ 50,088 (8th Cir. 1995).

33. *See* I.R.C. § 6501.

34. Morales v. United States, 92-2 USTC ¶ 50,597 (D.P.R. 1992).

35. I.R.C. § 6672(b)(3).

36. I.R.C. § 6672(c)(1).

37. IRM 5.7.7.4.2.

38. Gordon v. Comm'r, 39 T.C.M. (CCH) 769 (1979).

39. I.R.C. § 6672(c)(3).

40. United States v. Payne, 82-1 USTC ¶ 9416 (D. Colo. 1982).

41. United States v. Wainer, 50 AFTR 595 (7th Cir. 1957), dealing with distilled spirits.

42. Rev. Rul. 79-284, 1979-2 CB 83.

43. For payment designation in a bankruptcy context, *see United States v. Energy Res. Co, Inc.* 90-1 USTC ¶ 50,281 (S. Ct. 1990). In that case it was held that a bankruptcy court has the authority to order the IRS to treat payments made by a Chapter 11 debtor corporation as trust fund payments where the court determines that this designation is necessary for the success of the reorganization plan. Subsequent decisions have held this rule not to apply, however, in a Chapter 7 context. *See, e.g.*, United States v. Pepperman, 92-2 USTC ¶ 50,465 (3d

Cir. 1992). The Sixth and the Ninth Circuits have also concurred with the Third Circuit on this issue.

44. *See, e.g.,* Sotir v. United States, 978 F.2d 29, 92-2 USTC ¶ 50,548 (1st Cir. 1992).
45. *See* Stevens v. United States, 95-1 USTC ¶ 50,123 (7th Cir. 1995).
46. IRM 5.14.7.5.
47. For a discussion of the payment designation issue in a "willfulness" context, *see Wood v. United States*, 87-1 USTC ¶ 9165 (5th Cir. 1987), and *Oakey v. United States*, 93-1 USTC ¶ 50112 (W.D. Va. 1992).
48. 11 U.S.C. § 507(a)(8)(C).
49. United States v. Sotelo, 78-1 USTC ¶ 9446 (S. Ct. 1978).
50. United States v. Energy Res. Co. , 90-1 USTC ¶ 50,281 (S. Ct. 1990).
51. 11 U.S.C. § 507(a)(8)(C).
52. Roth v. United States, 83-2 USTC ¶ 9650 (S.D. Cal. 1983).
53. Slodov v. United States, 78-1 USTC ¶ 9447, 436 U.S. 238 (S. Ct. 1978).
54. Purdy Co. of Ill. v. United States, 87-1 USTC ¶ 9227 (7th Cir. 1987).
55. Larson v. United States, 29 AFTR2d 72-1111 (E.D. Wis. 1972).
56. Lawrence v. United States, 19 AFTR2d 624 (N.D. Tex. 1967).
57. Turchon v. United States, 87-2 USTC ¶ 9541 (E.D.N.Y. 1987).
58. I.R.C. § 7202.
59. I.R.C. § 6672(a).
60. IRM 5.7.3.4.
61. *Id.*
62. IRM 4.90.4.6.
63. Littriello v. United States, 2005-1 USTC ¶ 50,385 (W.D. Ky. 2005).

CHAPTER 6

Collection Enforcement

Dealing with the IRS Collection Function

I. Introduction and Background

A. Prior to the 1998 IRS Restructuring Act, the IRS consisted of numerous functional "divisions," the most important of which, from a tax practitioner's viewpoint, are as follows:
   1. Appeals,
   2. Collection,
   3. Criminal Investigation (CI), and
   4. Examination (formerly Audit).
   Presently the Collection function of the IRS is under the Small Business/Self-Employed Operating Division. Collection groups and examination groups are combined under "territory managers."

B. In many cases a tax practitioner gets a tax case after the tax liability has already been determined. In most cases an assessment will have been made. Once an assessment has been made, the case is in the hands of the Collection function. At that point the practitioner is not concerned about either the Examination function or the Appeals function. Even if the assessment is the result of an audit, the Examination personnel will no longer have the files, and contact with them is pointless. At this juncture, then, the practitioner needs to know and understand the Collection operations, such as the Automated Collection System (ACS) and the Special Procedures Function (SPF). A working knowledge of the Taxpayer Advocate Service (TAS) is also important.

C. The primary functions of the Collection personnel are as follows:
   1. To collect unpaid federal taxes that have been assessed;
   2. To solicit unfiled tax returns that are due; and
   3. To investigate and make recommendations in "trust fund liability" (formerly known as "100 percent penalty")[1] cases.

II. TDAs versus TDIs

A. Revenue officers (ROs), the primary collection field employees, generally handle two types of cases:
   1. Taxpayer delinquent accounts (TDAs)
   2. Taxpayer delinquency investigations (TDIs)
      TDAs are cases where a taxpayer has filed a return, but has not paid the tax; TDIs are cases where a taxpayer simply has not filed a required return.

B. In a TDI case, where a taxpayer refuses to file a return (either income tax or employment tax), ROs are empowered to file a return for him or her. This authority is contained in I.R.C. § 6020(b). Note that if the IRS executes a return under § 6020(b), the statute of limitations (for assessment purposes) does not start to run.[2]

Practice Tip

If an RO requests that a delinquent return be filed, send it to the IRS service center and give a copy to the RO. This prevents mishandling by the RO.

C. It is important to remember that ROs know little, if anything, of substantive tax law. They are trained in neither tax law nor accounting. Consequently, they cannot generally read or interpret the substantive aspects of a tax return. Therefore, in TDI cases, it does not really matter much how accurate the return is; it only matters that the return gets filed.

III. Revenue Officers

A. *Titles*
   Field collection employees are known as ROs. Do not confuse them with revenue "agents." Agents are IRS Examination employees. ROs, on the other hand, are generally not trained in accounting, and do not necessarily have a college degree.

B. *Powers*
   ROs have a difficult and unpleasant job, dealing with delinquent and often recalcitrant taxpayers. But Congress has given them broad, sweeping powers to do their job effectively, including the power to file liens and to levy on wages and other property.

C. *RO Perspectives*
   Revenue agents (RAs) have a totally different perspective than ROs. As a practical matter, RAs could not care less whether the tax ever gets paid; they are concerned only with the accuracy of the returns. On the

other hand, ROs could not care less about the accuracy of the return; they care only about the tax being paid.

D. *Challenging RO Aggression*

If an RO appears to be taking an overly aggressive position, the taxpayer should consider requesting a review of these actions by his or her group manager. There is a certain risk in making this request, however, since the group manager usually sides with the RO, and the request for review may not be welcomed by the RO. In challenging an RO's actions, one should keep in mind the official chain of command. The chain of command within each district, from bottom to top, is (1) revenue officer, (2) group manager, (3) territory manager, and (4) area director.

E. *Oral Statements Made by ROs*

Verbal representations made by ROs (or any IRS employee, for that matter) may not be relied on by taxpayers or representatives.[3] Such statements are useless.

Practice Tip

On critical matters, always try to get revenue officers to commit to promises or agreements in writing where possible.

F. Due to the broad, sweeping powers of ROs to seize property, it is important to treat IRS Collection cases with a great deal of delicacy.

IV. Automated Collection System (ACS)

A. Smaller and more routine IRS Collection matters are often assigned to the ACS.

B. ACS employees do not make field visits. Instead, they operate exclusively by making telephone contacts with delinquent taxpayers. Each ACS employee has a computer terminal and can access any taxpayer's account simply by entering a Social Security number. ACS has access to levy source information and has the power to issue liens and levies in appropriate cases.

C. In smaller cases, ACS has the power to take financial information over the telephone and work out installment agreements.

V. Financial Statements

A. Revenue officers will in virtually all cases request that a taxpayer fill out and sign a Form 433-A. This is a very detailed form requiring disclosure of all assets and liabilities as well as a listing of monthly income and living expenses. If the taxpayer has a business (corporation, partnership, or LLC), the IRS will also request that he or she fill out a Form 433-B.

B.   The purpose of the monthly income and living expense analysis is to indicate a taxpayer's ability to pay a monthly amount to the IRS. For this purpose, ROs will not allow certain expenses. For example, they will not allow the cost of vacations, entertainment, gifts, private school tuition, boat payments, eating out, and so on.

C.   The danger of submitting a financial statement is that this document provides a road map of levy sources that the IRS can immediately attach if they want to. The only problem with not providing a financial statement is that the IRS will not enter into a part-payment agreement without it. Note that if there is little or no exposure to levy action, there may be no advantage to be gained in submitting a Form 433.

VI. Special Procedures Function

A.   The Special Procedures (as it was formerly known) Staff is now a part of the Technical Compliance Function, and deals with the following specialized matters:
   1.   Applications for certificates of discharge, subordination, or nonattachment;
   2.   Recommendations for suit by the United States;
   3.   Suits against the United States;
   4.   Trust fund liability (the 100 percent penalty; I.R.C. § 6672) assessments;
   5.   Summons enforcement; and
   6.   Bankruptcy cases.

VII. Miscellaneous

A.   *Payment Extension*
The IRS also has statutory authority to extend the time for payment of income tax for a period of up to six months. This will only be done in cases of "undue hardship."[4] An application for an extension is made on Form 1127 and must be accompanied by evidence of hardship and a detailed statement.[5]

B.   *Zip Code Designation*
RO groups in IRS local offices are generally assigned cases based solely on postal zip codes. They go by the zip code as reflected on the tax return filed by the taxpayer.

C.   *Internal Revenue Manual*
The collection part (Part 5) of the Internal Revenue Manual (IRM) consists of the following:

Description	Chapter
Field Collecting Procedures	5.1
Reports	5.2
Entity Case Management Systems	5.3
Case Processing	5.4
Decedent Estates and Estate Taxes	5.5
Collateral Agreements	5.6
Trust Fund Compliance	5.7
Offer in Compromise	5.8
Bankruptcy and Other Insolvencies	5.9
Seizure and Sale	5.10
Notice of Levy	5.11
Federal Tax Liens	5.12
Collection Quality Measurement	5.13
Installment Agreements	5.14
Financial Analysis	5.15
Currently Not Collectible	5.16
Legal Reference Guide for Revenue Officers	5.17
Liability Determinations	5.18
Liability Collection	5.19
Abusive Tax Avoidance Transactions (ATAT)	5.20
International and Insular Issues	5.21
Central Withholding Agreement (CWA) Program	5.24

D. *Officer of the Day (OD)*

In each RO group, there is designated each day what is called an "officer of the day." The OD is present to handle walk-in taxpayers. That is, any taxpayer with a collection problem can walk into any IRS office and demand to see the OD, and he or she will be granted an interview.

E. *Bankruptcy Options*

When the administrative avenues for resolution have been exhausted, the taxpayer should begin to consider filing a bankruptcy petition. Bankruptcy is the taxpayer's "ace in the hole." The effects of bankruptcy on the collection of tax are well-known to the RO and, in some circumstances, may provide some additional leverage in the negotiation of an administrative resolution.

F. *Form 53*

When the RO becomes convinced that the taxpayer has no collectible assets and no future source of collection, the RO closes the case by completing Form 53, Report of Currently Not Collectible Taxes. This action (commonly called to "53 the account") removes the case from the RO's inventory. Thereafter, the case remains closed as long as the taxpayer's income stays below certain limits.[6]

G. *Transcript of Account*

If there is any question about the proper amount of an assessment or the proper application of any payments or credits, then one should order a transcript of account. A taxpayer is entitled to this document as a matter of law.[7] The IRS must furnish it to a taxpayer free of charge. To order it, one can telephone or send a fax request to the IRS's Practitioner Priority Service:

Telephone: 866-860-4259
Fax: 901-546-4400

H. *Fair Tax Collection Practices*[8]

In its collection of federal taxes, the IRS may not use certain unfair tactics. IRS restrictions are similar to federal and most state statutes involving fair debt collection practices. The IRS must observe the following rules:

1. The IRS may not contact a taxpayer at an unusual or inconvenient time or place.
2. The IRS may not contact a taxpayer (in person or by telephone) who has an authorized representative.
3. The IRS may not contact a taxpayer at his or her place of work.
4. The IRS may not contact a taxpayer before 8:00 A.M. or after 9:00 P.M.
5. The IRS may not use threats, abusive language, or repeated calls with an intent to annoy the taxpayer.

VIII. Notes

1. I.R.C. § 6672.
2. I.R.C. § 6501(b)(3).
3. Treas. Reg. § 601.201(k)(2); United States v. Guy, 92-2 USTC ¶ 50,581 (6th Cir. 1992); First Ala. Bank NA v. United States, 93-1 USTC ¶ 50,138 (11th Cir. 1993).
4. I.R.C. § 6161.
5. Treas. Reg. § 20.6161-1.
6. *See generally* IRM 5.16.
7. I.R.C. § 6203.
8. *See generally* I.R.C. § 6304.

Federal Tax Liens

I. Background and General Rules

A. Introduction

The federal tax lien (FTL) is the backbone of the federal tax collection process. The filing of a notice of federal tax lien (NFTL) can have a devastating effect on a taxpayer. Since it is a matter of public record, it is quickly picked up by title companies and credit-reporting services. Accordingly, a taxpayer's credit status is adversely affected, and he or she will usually be unable to obtain loans until the lien is somehow released. Furthermore, the taxpayer will be unable to obtain a mortgage on real estate purchases. In addition, a taxpayer with a tax lien against him or her also will be unable to sell real estate in the county in which a lien is recorded. The reason is that a title company will refuse to issue a title policy until the lien (as a "cloud on the title") is removed or otherwise satisfied.

B. Definitions

Webster's definition of a lien is as follows: "a charge upon real or personal property for the satisfaction of some debt or duty ordinarily arising by operation of law; the security interest created by a mortgage." The word "lien" is a generic term and, standing alone, includes liens acquired by contract or by operation of law.

C. General Rule

If any taxpayer refuses to pay tax owed to the IRS (assuming demand for payment has been made), the amount of the unpaid tax (together with statutory interest and any assessable penalties) constitutes a lien in favor of the IRS upon all property or rights to property belonging to the taxpayer.[1]

D. Period of Lien Existence

A federal tax lien arises at the time an assessment is made and continues in force until the tax liability is satisfied (i.e., paid) or becomes unenforceable by reason of lapse of time.[2] If there has been no assessment, there obviously can be no lien. The lifetime of a lien is the period of time that the IRS is allowed to collect the tax by levy. This period is ten years pursuant to I.R.C. § 6502(a)(1).

E. *Notice*
   1. *General Notice Rule*
      Until the notice of federal tax lien has been properly filed, the lien is not perfected against bona fide purchasers and certain classes of creditors.
   2. *"First-in-Time-First-in-Right" Rule*
      This is also known as the "race to the courthouse" rule. Although the general rule is that the first secured lien in time has priority, there are exceptions regarding FTLs. For example, if a third-party creditor gets a judgment against a taxpayer but does not record ("abstract") it before the NFTL is filed, then the IRS lien will prevail. Conversely, if the IRS does not perfect its lien prior to a perfected third-party lien, it will not prevail in a contest regarding conflicting liens.[3]

      If a delinquent taxpayer's property is transferred prior to the filing of the NFTL, then the FTL will not attach to the property even if the transfer is fraudulent and even if the ultimate purchaser of the property has knowledge of the lien.[4]
   3. *"Super Priority" Liens*
      There are ten exceptions to this rule that are contained in the statute.[5] These are referred to as super priority interests, which have priority over an FTL regardless of when the FTL was created or perfected. The IRS even recognizes an eleventh category to include purchase money security interests.[6] Also, purchasers of automobiles are protected against prior FTLs of the seller if they had no notice thereof.[7]
   4. *Notice and Demand*
      Unless a "notice and demand" for unpaid tax is mailed to the taxpayer or left at his or her home, a subsequent FTL is rendered invalid.[8]
   5. An NFTL can cover more than one tax period. It will specify each period and the amount of tax owed for each period.[9]

F. The seven principal aspects of the FTL are as follows:
   1. Creation;
   2. Attachment;
   3. Perfection;
   4. Priority;
   5. Relief from lien;
   6. Duration; and
   7. Enforcement.

G. *Judgment*

There is no requirement that the IRS obtain a judgment against the taxpayer prior to getting a lien; yet, the FTL gives the IRS more power than that given to a judgment lien creditor.

II. Lien Litigation

A. *Necessary Parties*

If suit is filed by the IRS to enforce an FTL, all persons having liens or claiming an interest in the property must be made parties to the suit.[10]

B. *Order of Sale*

If suit is brought under § 7403, the federal district court determines the merits of all claims and may order a sale of the property and distribution of the proceeds.[11]

C. *Intervention in Third-Party Suits*

If the IRS is not a party to a civil action by a third party, it may nevertheless intervene in such suit to assert its lien.[12]

D. *Judicial and Other Sales*

If there is a judicial sale of property in a civil lawsuit and the IRS has a lien on such property, any such sale is subject to the FTL as long as notice of the IRS lien was filed prior to the date the lawsuit was commenced.[13] The Fifth Circuit has ruled that a levy by the IRS on property sold at a sheriff's sale was valid even though the IRS held a junior lien on the property. All other liens on the property were discharged by the sheriff's sale; however, because the IRS had not been given proper notice of the sale as required under I.R.C. § 7425(b), the tax lien followed the property into the hands of the third-party purchaser. The third party's reliance on the county records was held not to be proper.[14]

Nonjudicial sales of property are governed by I.R.C. § 7425(b)–(d). In general, these provisions are sufficient to defeat an IRS lien that is in a junior position as long as proper notice of sale is given by the taxpayer.

E. *Injunction Suits*

Suit may be brought against the IRS to remove an FTL as a cloud on the title to realty, but only if such suit is not brought to enjoin the collection of a tax (see I.R.C. § 7421).[15]

III. Attachment Rules

A. *General Rules*

An FTL is considered to arise and "attach" to the taxpayer's property as of the date of the tax assessment. The date of assessment can be determined by inspecting one of three documents:

1. The taxpayer's transcript of account;
2. The certificate of assessment; or
3. The notice of federal tax lien, Form 668(Y).
   An FTL attachment cannot be effective, however, until three things have happened:
1. The tax has been assessed;
2. The IRS has demanded payment (which demand must occur within sixty days of assessment); and
3. The taxpayer has failed to make payment after such demand.

B. *Nonattachment*

If the IRS determines that, because of confusion of names or otherwise, any person (other than the taxpayer) may be injured by the appearance that a notice of lien refers to such person, the IRS may issue a certificate of nonattachment.[16] An application for a certificate of nonattachment can be submitted to the local IRS Collection office.[17]

C. *After-Acquired Property*

Anything acquired by the taxpayer after the lien arises is immediately attached by the lien. On the other hand, property transferred prior to assessment of the tax and attachment of the lien (e.g., property divided pursuant to a divorce decree) is not subject to the lien.

D. *The "Secret" Lien*

When the federal tax lien first attaches, it is sometimes referred to as the "secret lien" because the lien is not yet of public record. The lien is said to "attach" because it acts as an encumbrance on the taxpayer's property. The secret lien takes priority over any interest of the taxpayer in the property and over the interests of certain other persons even though they may be completely unaware of the existence of the lien.

IV. Enforcement

A. *General Rule*

The FTL is an encumbrance on property. The lien itself, however, does not result in the direct collection of any amount. Rather, the following devices are provided to enforce the FTL:
1. Administrative levies and
2. Judicial remedies.

B. *Levies and Litigation*

The way an FTL is normally enforced is by means of a levy.[18] Although levies are beyond the scope of this subchapter, generally they mean seizure and distraint of a taxpayer's property. However, there is an alternate enforcement mechanism. The IRS can ask the Justice Department to file a civil action in a U.S. district court to enforce a lien and subject any of the taxpayer's property to the payment of delinquent tax.[19]

C. *Injunctions*

A U.S. federal district court has jurisdiction to grant, in appropriate cases, an injunction against the IRS from enforcing an FTL if, for example, a deficiency notice is determined to be invalid.[20]

V. Estate or Gift Tax Liens

A. *Deferred Estate Tax Payments*

In the case of an estate consisting largely of an interest in a closely held business, the executor can elect to pay out the estate tax in deferred installments over an extended period of time.[21] If this occurs, a special lien arises in favor of the IRS with respect to the "§ 6166 property."[22]

B. *Estate Considerations*

Unless estate tax is paid (or becomes unenforceable), it is a lien upon the gross estate for ten years following death.[23] Where estate property has been specially valued under I.R.C. § 2032A, the tax difference resulting from such special valuation constitutes a tax lien for the ten years after death specified in I.R.C. § 2032A(c).[24]

VI. Definition of Property and Property Rights

A. *General Rules, and Applicability of State Law*

I.R.C. § 6321 refers to "property" or "rights to property." Unfortunately, the term "property" is nowhere defined in the Internal Revenue Code. Thus the term "property" draws its content from state law; however, even though the definition of property is left to state law, the consequences that attach to those interests are a matter of federal law. For example, the IRS can enforce its lien and foreclose on a Texas community homestead even though one of the spouses is clearly not liable for the tax.[25]

B. *Intangibles*

The FTL clearly attaches to general intangibles such as accounts receivable, licenses, and franchises. (Note that the Uniform Commercial Code recognizes the value of intangibles as "property rights.")

C. *Pension Plan Benefits*

Pension plan benefits payable to the taxpayer (including individual retirement accounts [IRAs]) are subject to attachment by the FTL even if such payments are exempt from attachment by judgment creditors under state law.

D. *Trusts*

The interest of a taxpayer in a trust is subject to the force of a tax lien.[26]

E. *Inherited Property*

If a taxpayer inherits property at a time when he or she has an outstanding federal tax liability, whether a lien immediately attaches depends entirely on state law. For example, if a taxpayer in Arizona exercises his or her state statutory right to renounce or disclaim the inheritance in favor of third parties, the IRS cannot thereafter attach his or her interest in the estate.[27] But in an Arkansas case, the U.S. Supreme Court has held that a federal tax lien attached to a delinquent taxpayer's interest in an estate, despite his disclaimer. The reason was that, under Arkansas law, the interest had pecuniary value and was immediately transferable at the time the estate was created.[28]

VII. Release and Relief Measures

A. *Release*

Within thirty days after the tax (including interest) has been paid, or the liability has become legally unenforceable, the IRS is required to issue a certificate of lien release.[29] The NFTL (Form 668(Y)) has printed language that operates as an automatic lien release as of the "last date for refiling." That is, pursuant to the language on this form, the FTL is "self-releasing." If credit-reporting agencies, lenders, or title companies refuse to accept this language as a certificate of release, it may be necessary to secure from the IRS a Form 668(Z) release certificate. This issue normally arises when the liability becomes unenforceable due to the expiration of the ten-year collection statute of limitations. Lien releases are currently handled out of a central location in Cincinnati, Ohio.

B. *Subordination*

1. *General Statutory Rule*

The IRS may issue a lien subordination certificate if one of three circumstances exists:

a. The amount of the lien is fully paid;

b. The taxpayer is able to convince the IRS that the amount realizable from the property to which the certificate relates will ultimately be increased by issuing the certificate, thus facilitating the ultimate collection of the tax; or

c. The IRS believes that the government will be adequately secured after the subordination.[30]

2. *Mortgage Example*

If an NFTL is filed and a delinquent taxpayer secures a mortgage loan on property subject to the lien and pays over the proceeds of the loan to the IRS, a certificate of subordination can be issued to put the mortgagee's security interest ahead of the IRS.[31] Other examples are in the regulations as well.

3. *Procedure*

Complete instructions for filing an application for a certificate of subordination are contained in the two-page Publication 784.

There is no specific form for submitting the application. All you have to do is make sure that all the required information is submitted.[32] In the author's experience, it is very difficult to convince a revenue officer to issue a certificate of subordination, even in the face of compelling reasons.

4. *Form of Certificate*

If the application is approved, the IRS will issue the certificate as Form 669-D.

C. *Judicial Relief*

If the IRS knowingly or by reason of negligence fails to release a lien under § 6325, a taxpayer may bring a civil suit for damages against the IRS.

D. *Appeal*

Any person may appeal to the IRS local office for a release of a lien if there has been an error in the filing of an NFTL. This appeal is made to the Special Procedures Section of the IRS.[33]

E. *Lien Withdrawals*

The IRS has the authority to withdraw NFTLs under certain circumstances.[34] The NFTL may be withdrawn if the IRS determines that

1. the filing of the NFTL was premature or not in accordance with IRS administrative procedures;
2. the taxpayer entered into an installment agreement under I.R.C. § 6159 to satisfy the tax liability for which the lien was imposed, unless such agreement provides otherwise;
3. the withdrawal will facilitate the collection of the tax liability; or
4. with the consent of the taxpayer or the National Taxpayer Advocate (NTA), the withdrawal would be in the best interests of the taxpayer and the government, as determined by the NTA.[35]

There is an important distinction between "releasing" a federal tax lien and "withdrawing" a filed notice of that lien. A lien release not only extinguishes the lien itself but also automatically extinguishes the underlying tax liability. A withdrawal, on the other hand, only withdraws public notice of the lien.

All requests for withdrawal of the NFTL must be in writing and must contain the following:

1. The taxpayer's name;
2. Current address;
3. The taxpayer's identification number;
4. A copy of the NFTL affecting the property, if available; and
5. A statement or basis for the withdrawal request.

A request for withdrawal may be sent to the revenue officer assigned to the account, the IRS Technical Support Group, or the NTA, whichever applies.

If the taxpayer is fortunate enough to convince the IRS to withdraw its lien, upon the request of the taxpayer, the IRS is required to make reasonable efforts to notify the credit-reporting agencies and creditors specified in the request.[36]

Practice Tip

As a practical matter, it is unlikely that the IRS will withdraw its notice of lien absent extraordinary circumstances.

F. *Collection Due Process (CDP) Hearing*
When an NFTL has been filed under § 6323, the IRS must hand-deliver or send by certified mail to the taxpayer a notification of such filing. This notice must be delivered within five days of the filing date. Included with the notice must be an explanation of the taxpayer's right to have an impartial hearing with the IRS's Appeals Office.[37] If there are irregularities or mistakes in the filing of the lien, it is an excellent idea to ask for a CDP hearing.[38] Details of the CDP process are contained in chapter 2.

VIII. Miscellaneous

A. *Notice*
The lien imposed by I.R.C. § 6321 is not effective as against any other security interest holder until "notice"[39] has been duly filed by the IRS.[40]

B. *Bona Fide Purchasers*
Even though the IRS may have filed a lien notice, it may not be effective as against a good faith, bona fide purchaser of certain property.[41]

C. *Place of Filing*
In the case of real property, notice of a tax lien is required to be filed in the county courthouse in the county in which such realty is located.[42] State law may not require the IRS to "acknowledge" an FTL. The only function of state law is to designate a place for filing the lien notice.[43]

D. *Refiling*
The running of the ten-year collection period may, in some circumstances, be suspended. For example, if the taxpayer is out of the country[44] or has agreed in writing to extend the collection period, the ten-year statutory period may be considerably longer. In such cases, it is necessary for the IRS to refile its NFTL to maintain the continuity of its lien priority

as against third-party creditors. The government has eleven years plus thirty days after assessment within which to refile its NFTL.[45]

E. *Marital Issues*

Funds owned by a wife prior to marriage and maintained separately are not subject to a lien attributable to the husband and his former spouse's tax liability.[46] Similarly, in a non–community property state (Wisconsin), a tax lien against a husband for a liability arising prior to marriage cannot be enforced against separate property owned by the wife.[47] For purposes of these rules, the sex of the spouse is irrelevant.

F. *Bankruptcy Issues*

IRS Collection Division employees are cautioned to make prompt lien-filing determinations, particularly where a taxpayer is perceived to be in financial distress. However, if a bankruptcy petition has been filed, a notice of tax lien cannot be filed without the consent of chief counsel.[48]

Liens can attach to property exempt from inclusion in the bankruptcy estate, including the homestead exemption. To acquire this status, a lien must be secured by the proper filing of an NFTL prior to the commencement of the bankruptcy. The amount of a secured tax lien in bankruptcy is limited to the unencumbered property's equity, with the balance of the obligation reduced to unsecured status.

A discharge in bankruptcy prevents the IRS from taking any action to collect tax as a personal liability of the debtor. However, property possessed at the time of the filing of the petition remains subject to the tax lien. Thus, while in personam liability may be discharged, in rem liability remains enforceable for purposes of I.R.C. § 6325.

In negotiating a lien buyout in the postdischarge period, look carefully at the copies of the recorded liens. If they are for real estate only, then they will not attach to nonrealty assets such as pension funds.

G. *Statute of Limitations*

The filing of the NFTL has no effect on the expiration of the ten-year collection statute of limitations as provided in I.R.C. § 6502.

H. *The following forms are pertinent to FTLs:*
    1. Notice of Federal Tax Lien (Form 668(Y))
    2. Certificate of Release of Federal Tax Lien (Form 668(Z))
    3. Certificate of Discharge of Property from FTL under I.R.C. § 6325(b)(1) (Form 669-A)
    4. Certificate of Discharge of Property from FTL under I.R.C. § 6325 (b) (2) (A) (Form 669-B)
    5. Certificate of Discharge of Property from FTL (Form 669-C)
    6. Certificate of Subordination (Form 669-D, E, or F)

I.   Nominee Liens

Unfortunately, some delinquent taxpayers have attempted to place their property beyond the reach of government collections by putting it in the name of someone else, typically a relative or "alter ego" entity such as a trust or controlled corporation. Whenever this occurs, the IRS will generally place what is known as a "nominee lien" against the property in question. Nominee liens are judicial in origin, as they are mentioned nowhere in the I.R.C. These nominee liens have been held to be valid in a variety of different circumstances.[49]

IX. Notes

1. I.R.C. § 6321.
2. I.R.C. § 6322.
3. United States v. Romani Estate, 98-1 USTC ¶ 50,368 (S. Ct. 1998); United States v. Crisp, 2000-1 USTC ¶ 50,130 (E.D. Cal. 1999).
4. TKB Int'l, Inc., 93-1 USTC ¶ 50,346 (9th Cir. 1993).
5. I.R.C. § 6323(b).
6. Rev. Rul. 68-57, 1968-1 CB 553.
7. I.R.C. § 6323(b)(2).
8. Bauer v. Foley, 23 AFTR2d 69-307 (2d Cir. 1968); *see* I.R.C. § 6303 (re notice and demand).
9. Treas. Reg. § 301.6320-1(a)(2), Q-A A3.
10. I.R.C. § 7403(b).
11. I.R.C. § 7403(c).
12. I.R.C. § 7424.
13. I.R.C. § 7425(a).
14. Myers v. United States, 647 F.2d 591, 81-2 USTC ¶ 9490 (5th Cir. 1981).
15. Campagna v. United States, 35 AFTR2d ¶ 75-400 (D.N.J. 1974).
16. I.R.C. § 6325(e).
17. Treas. Reg. § 301.6325-1(e).
18. *See* I.R.C. §§ 6331 *et seq.*
19. I.R.C. § 7403(a).
20. Austin v. United States, 80-2 USTC ¶ 9581 (E.D. Mo. 1980).
21. I.R.C. § 6166.
22. I.R.C. § 6324A(a).
23. I.R.C. § 6324(a).
24. I.R.C. § 6324B.
25. United States v. Rodgers, 461 U.S. 677, 83-1 USTC ¶ 9374 (S. Ct. 1983).
26. Magavern v. United States, 451 F. Supp. 217 (W.D.N.Y. 1976).
27. In *Mapes v. United States*, 15 F.3d 138 (9th Cir. 1994), the IRS lost the case in an attempt to attach an Arizona taxpayer's interest in his mother's estate following the taxpayer's renunciation in favor of his children; see also a similar result in a Texas case, *Leggett v. United States*, 97-2 USTC ¶ 50,635 (5th Cir. 1997).
28. Drye v. United States, 99-2 USTC ¶ 51,006 (S. Ct. 1999), *aff'g* 98-2 USTC ¶ 50,651 (8th Cir. 1998).
29. I.R.C. § 6325(a). I.R.S. Form 668(Z) is used for this purpose.
30. I.R.C. § 6325(d); also discussed in IRM 5.12.10.7 and I.R.S. Publ'n 784.
31. Treas. Reg. § 301.6325-1(d)(1).

32. IRM 5.12.10.7.
33. Reg. § 301.6326-1T(b).
34. I.R.C. § 6323(j).
35. I.R.C. § 6323(j)(1).
36. I.R.C.§ 6323(j)(2). The three major credit-reporting agencies are TransUnion, Experian, and Equifax.
37. I.R.C. § 6320(a).
38. *See* Forms 9423, 12153. *See also* I.R.S. Publ'n 1660.
39. *See* I.R.C. § 6323(f).
40. I.R.C. § 6323(a).
41. I.R.C. § 6323(b).
42. I.R.C. § 6323(f)
43. Rev. Rul. 71-466, 1971-2 CB 409.
44. *See* I.R.C. § 6503(c).
45. I.R.C. § 6323(g)(3); Griswold v. United States, 95-2 USTC ¶ 50,419 n.17 (11th Cir. 1995).
46. Bice v. Campbell, 13 AFTR2d 1612 (N.D. Tex. 1964), arguably overruled by Broday v. United States, 29 AFTR2d 72-663 (5th Cir. 1972).
47. United States v. Garsky, 86-2 USTC ¶ 9501 (D. Wis. 1986).
48. *See* discussion in CCA 200215052.
49. See the discussion in *Andrews v. United States*, 99-1 USTC ¶ 50,359 (N.D. Ohio 1999) (citing G.M. Leasing Corp. v. United States, 97 S. Ct. 619, 77-1 USTC ¶ 9140 (S. Ct. 1977)).

Federal Tax Levies

I. Background and General Rules

A. *Background*

Congress has given the IRS all the weapons necessary to collect revenue for the U.S. Treasury, including levies and seizures that, while never pleasant, are frequently necessary. These procedures are generally referred to as "enforced collection."

The IRS is the largest collection agency in the world and has been compared to the Gestapo in its exercise of unchecked power and its propensity to harass defenseless taxpayers. The IRS's favorite "levy" targets are wages and bank accounts. And frequently these techniques are used by the IRS as a "wake-up call" to get the taxpayer to consider an installment agreement or an offer in compromise.

Seizures and levies can be initiated from one of three sources:

a. The various service centers around the country (also known as "campuses");

b. The Automated Collection System (ACS); or

c. A revenue officer (RO).

B. *General Rules and Notice Requirements*

If any taxpayer refuses or neglects to pay any federal income tax within ten days after notice and demand, the IRS can collect such tax by levy upon all the taxpayer's property.[1] Note that subsection (d) requiring a thirty-day written notice effectively overrides this ten-day rule.[2] A "notice and demand" is nothing more than a computer-generated notice that tax is owed, sent by regular mail. On the other hand, a "notice of intent to levy" is typically a Notice # CP504, sent by certified mail, and this is what triggers the thirty-day period. Additionally, the IRS must send out a notice of a right to a collection due process (CDP) hearing before levy can be made. This type of notice must also be sent via certified mail. In other words, a taxpayer is given at least three statutory notices before his or her property is at risk of being seized.

C. *Definitions*

The term "levy" includes the power of distraint and seizure of property by any means. There is no practical or legal distinction between the word "levy" and the word "seizure." The right to seize also encompasses the right to sell the seized property.

II. Types of Property Subject to Seizure

A. *General Rule*

The IRS has the right to seize and sell all types of property owned by a taxpayer, including, but not limited to, real, personal, tangible, or intangible property.[3] Except for the continuing levy on salary or wages, a levy extends only to property possessed or obligations existing *at the time of the levy*. Should property come into the possession of the taxpayer or a third party later, another levy must be made to seize the property, regardless of the fact that the federal tax lien attaches automatically to after-acquired property. Where a right to money is contingent upon the performance of future services, a levy is ineffective as to future payments owed to the taxpayer.[4] On the other hand, the IRS takes the position that where a taxpayer has an unqualified fixed right, under a trust or a contract, or through a "chose in action," to receive periodic payments or distributions of property, a levy is effective to reach subsequent payment coming due.[5] A chose in action is defined as a personal right not reduced into possession, but recoverable by a suit at law.

B. *Pension Plan Benefits*

The IRS has the unqualified right to levy on pension plan benefits.[6] However, a distribution from a qualified pension plan and the like, including an IRA, pursuant to an IRS levy, does not subject the participant to a 10 percent penalty.[7] The IRS is required to use "discretion" before levying on pension or retirement benefits.[8] Levies on pension or retirement accounts also require managerial approval.[9] While the IRS may levy on a pension benefit, collection must wait until the participant has an immediate right to receive benefits from the plan.[10] Stated another way, if the plan participant can't reach the assets inside the pension trust, neither can the IRS.

C. *Life Insurance Contracts*

The cash value of life insurance contracts must be paid over to the IRS as long as the taxpayer-insured (who is presumably the policy owner) could have had the amount advanced to him or her.[11]

III. Bank Accounts

A. Obviously the IRS has a right to levy on a taxpayer's bank account, credit union account, and the like. However, the bank that is served with such a levy must wait twenty-one days before surrendering any of the taxpayer's funds on deposit to the IRS.[12] Bank accounts are some of the easiest IRS enforcement targets. There are several ways the IRS can discover the location of a taxpayer's bank account. If the taxpayer issues a check to the IRS on a particular account, the IRS logs the account information into its computer system. The account thereafter becomes a levy source. The account can also be disclosed voluntarily on a Form 433-A. If the bank is also a lender to the depositor, the bank may also have a UCC-1 on file, and this is a public record, discoverable by anyone, including the IRS. (A UCC-1 is a financing statement form, filed pursuant to the Uniform Commercial Code.)

B.   *Subsequent Bank Deposits*
What happens to money a taxpayer puts into the account after the levy is served? A levy on a bank account does not attach to subsequent bank deposits. That is, unlike a wage levy, it is not a "continuing" levy. The levy only attaches to the right, title, and interest held by the taxpayer at the time of the service.

C.   *Bank's Right to Offset against a Defaulted Loan*
The IRS has a right to issue a levy on a taxpayer's bank account even though the bank may have a loan to the taxpayer that is in default, with the right of offset with respect to any of the borrower's accounts.[13]

D.   *Partnership Bank Accounts*
Since a partnership checking account is an asset and property of the partnership and not an asset or property of the individual partner, a partnership checking account in a bank is not subject to levy to satisfy a tax assessed against an individual partner.[14]

E.   *Planning Suggestions*
Obviously if there is no bank account or the balance is extremely low, there is not much the IRS can do. Additionally, there is no law against a taxpayer paying his or her bills with cash or money orders.

F.   *Erroneous Bank Levies*
If the IRS levies on a bank account in error, the taxpayer may be entitled to file a claim for reimbursement of any bank charges incurred. For this purpose, a Form 8546 is used. Reimbursement is limited, however, to $1,000.[15]

IV. Wages

A.   *General Rule, and Comparison with Texas Law*
The IRS also has a right to levy on a delinquent taxpayer's salary or wages. But note that this is in stark contrast to the rule in the State of

Texas with regard to normal judgment creditors. The Texas Constitution and state statute provide that current wages for personal service are not subject to garnishment. But it is important to remember that these state laws simply do not apply to the IRS![16] One should note also that other states may not offer the same state judgment protections that are available in the author's home state of Texas.

B. *Portion of Wages Exempt from Federal Tax Levy*
A portion of a taxpayer's wages is exempt from levy. Determined on a weekly basis, the sum of the standard deduction plus personal exemptions divided by fifty-two is exempt from levy. If a taxpayer is paid on a basis other than weekly, the IRS prescribes "equivalency" formulas so that the exemption amount is comparable.[17] Virtually all payroll deductions are allowable in determining "net pay" against which the employer computes the amount exempt from levy.[18]

C. *Effect on Wages of Nonliable Texas[19] Spouse*
Where Texas taxpayers are married, the separate tax liability of one spouse can subject the nonliable spouse's earnings to levy, but only to the extent of 50 percent of the nonliable spouse's earnings.[20] But 100 percent of the liable spouse's wages can be levied since, under Texas law, it is subject to his or her "sole management and control." Note, however, that where there is a premarital agreement, the IRS's levy attempt on the innocent spouse's income will fail.[21]

D. The IRS knows that the typical wage levy will not leave the taxpayer with enough money to live on. Therefore, it usually uses this remedy as a means to "get the taxpayer's attention" so that the taxpayer will come forward and give enough financial information to allow them to arrive at a mutually acceptable payout agreement.[22] Once this happens, the wage levy can be released.

E. *Determination of Uncollectibility*
If the IRS determines that the tax is not collectible, it must release a wage levy as soon as is practicable.[23]

F. *Definition of "Wages"*
Frequently there are controversies regarding what constitute "wages." The IRS typically takes an expansive view of what the definition is.[24]

V. Other Exemptions

A. Wearing apparel and schoolbooks are exempt from levy.[25]
B. Personal effects (furniture, etc.) are exempt from levy, but only to the extent of $6,250 in value.[26]
C. Business books and tools are also exempt, but only up to $3,125 in value.[27]

D. Also exempt are the following:
   1. Unemployment benefits,
   2. Undelivered mail,
   3. Railroad retirement benefits,
   4. Workers' compensation benefits,[28]
   5. Amount of income necessary for child support payments, and
   6. Military disability benefits.[29]

E. But note that Social Security benefits are *not* exempt from levy.[30]

VI. Marital Issues

A. *General Rule Regarding Premarital Liability*
   A spouse's property is subject to a tax levy of the other spouse for taxes arising prior to marriage.[31]

B. *The Broday Case*
   In the *Broday* case, a wife owed a prior federal income tax liability attributable to a year in which she was married to her first husband. At the time of her marriage to her second husband, Mr. Broday, this tax was still unpaid. The IRS then levied on Mr. Broday's bank account, which held funds received as a dividend from Mr. Broday's separate property. In reversing the finding of the district court, the Fifth Circuit held that under Texas community property law, the community property bank account, of which the husband had sole right to manage and control, is subject to levy for federal income tax of the wife incurred prior to marriage.

C. *Texas Homesteads*
   According to the U.S. Supreme Court, a federal district court may, at its discretion, order the sale (under I.R.C. § 7403) of a Texas homestead in which a delinquent taxpayer had an interest at the time the tax debt was incurred. A nondelinquent spouse's separate homestead right (under state law) will not bar a judicial sale, but the nondelinquent spouse is entitled to a portion of the sales proceeds that represents complete compensation for his or her loss of the homestead estate.[32]

D. *Spouse's Bank Account*
   Whether a delinquent taxpayer has an interest in a joint bank account subject to a federal tax lien turns on whether the delinquent taxpayer has a unilateral right under state law to withdraw funds from the account. The obvious planning technique here is for the delinquent spouse *not* to have any signature authority or withdrawal rights on the nondelinquent spouse's account.[33]

E. *Qualified Domestic Relations Orders (QDROs)*
   In the case of a divorce, a wife's (or husband's) awarded interest in the spouse's pension fund may trump the IRS's prior lien interest. If the divorce occurs before the IRS files its notice of federal tax lien on

the pension fund, the spouse's lien interest (acquired pursuant to a QDRO) is superior to that of the IRS even though the QDRO may have been finalized subsequently.[34]

F. *Tenancy by the Entirety*

A tenancy by the entirety is a common law form of ownership and is created whenever property is conveyed to husband and wife. The unique feature of this type of estate is that the survivor automatically takes the entire estate following the death of his or her spouse. Unlike a joint tenancy, a tenancy by the entirety may be terminated only by joint action of the spouses during their lives. It is now clear that the IRS can levy on property held in this manner even though only one of the spouses owes the tax.[35]

VII. Nominee Levies

A. An area of increased concern in the past few years is the use by the IRS of "nominee levies." This is an extraordinary remedy being used by IRS Collection personnel.

B. A nominee levy may occur when the IRS determines that a person is holding property as a "nominee" of the delinquent taxpayer. The IRS then seizes the property to satisfy the delinquent tax liability. Or, in some cases, a court will order the enforcement of the IRS nominee lien.[36]

C. The nominee generally does not owe any tax. The IRS initiates these collection actions generally without any judicial determination that the person holding the property is an alter ego or nominee of the taxpayer or that the property has been conveyed to the holder in a fraudulent conveyance or without consideration.

D. Before the IRS can initiate a nominee levy, the revenue officer must secure written approval of area counsel.[37]

Unfortunately, nominee liens and levies do not enjoy the same "due process" protections that non-nominees have.

VIII. Internal Revenue Manual Provisions

A. The IRS's Internal Revenue Manual (IRM) is the internal document that directs the policy, nationwide, that all revenue service personnel are obliged to follow in determining whether to issue a levy.

B. The IRM provides that the RO is to personally contact the taxpayer and advise him or her that seizure is the next action planned and give the taxpayer the opportunity to resolve the tax liability voluntarily.[38] In practice, however, this is often not done. Taxpayers are generally entitled to a CDP hearing before a levy actually takes place.[39] Details of the CDP hearing process are discussed in chapter 2.

C. Generally, revenue officers are not permitted to force their way into a private residence to seize property or conduct an interview with the taxpayer if they are denied entrance.[40]

D. Although it is not a statutory requirement, it is the IRS's policy to file a notice of federal tax lien before issuing a levy.

E. Seizures of tangible property are always done in teams of two revenue officers so that more than one individual can testify as to the regularity of the proceeding.

IX. Miscellaneous Provisions

A. *Notice before Levy*

There is a notice requirement before a levy can be made. This written notice of intent to levy must be sent to the taxpayer at least thirty days before levy can be attempted. There are only three ways this notice may be given:

1. By hand delivery in person;
2. By leaving it at a taxpayer's residence or place of business; or
3. By mailing it to the taxpayer by certified or registered mail.[41]

If any of the periods covered by the levy have not been properly "noticed" under I.R.C. § 6331(d), then the levy is defective and must be released. It may be necessary to file a Form 911, Application for Taxpayer Assistance Order, to get this accomplished.

The IRS must also have given "notice and demand" for payment under I.R.C. § 6303 before an administrative levy is attempted. This is a statutory sixty-day notice by regular mail or home delivery. If the IRS does not give this notice, then all it can do is initiate a lawsuit to collect the tax.[42]

B. *Bankruptcy*

The filing of a bankruptcy petition acts as an automatic stay against the IRS and prevents it from taking enforcement action, including levies.[43] If a bankruptcy filing occurs after a seizure of property by the IRS, but before the sale thereof, the IRS must release the property back to the bankruptcy trustee.[44]

C. *Third Parties*

If a third party is in possession of property belonging to the taxpayer, and subject to the levy, such party must surrender the property to the IRS.[45] Failure to surrender the property subjects the third party to personal liability in an amount equal to the value of the property in question. Such failure can also subject the third party to a penalty equal to 50 percent of the value of the property.[46]

D. *Books and Records*

If a levy has been or is about to be made, any person (usually a bank) is required, after demand by the IRS, to exhibit any relevant documents to the IRS.[47]

E. *Principal Residence*

A principal residence of the taxpayer is exempt from levy if the amount of the total tax liability is less than $5,000. If the amount owed exceeds $5,000, the IRS may levy on a principal residence only if a federal district court judge or magistrate approves in writing such a seizure.[48] As a practical matter, residence seizures are infrequent.

F. *Notice of Sale*

After seizure of property, the IRS is required to give the owner of the property written notice thereof.[49] Notice of an IRS sale is also published in a local newspaper.[50] Obviously, if privacy is an important consideration to the taxpayer, it would not be a good idea for the situation to reach this critical point.

G. *Ownership of Less Than 100 Percent Interest in Property*

If the taxpayer owns less than a full interest in the property sought to be levied on, the IRS can sell the whole property and then take the amount that the taxpayer would have been entitled to.[51]

H. *Time of Sale*

The time of the sale cannot be less than ten days or more than forty days from the time of giving public notice.[52] In the case of real estate, the sale cannot be upon less than twenty days' notice.[53]

I. *Auction Procedures*

The IRS usually sells seized property at a public auction. Before the sale of any property, the IRS sets a minimum bid price.[54] The IRS is authorized to hire professional auctioneers to conduct the sale of seized property.[55]

J. *Redemption*

Any taxpayer whose property has been levied on has the right to redeem it by paying the tax due at any time prior to the actual sale.[56] In the case of real estate, taxpayers have an additional 180 days after the sale to redeem the property.[57]

K. *Certificate of Sale*

After the sale, the IRS gives the purchaser either a certificate of sale or a deed.[58]

L. *Expense of the Sale*

The proceeds of a sale are first used to pay the expenses of the proceedings.[59]

M. *Effect on Underpayment Penalty*
Ten days after a levy notice is mailed under I.R.C. § 6331(d), the IRS can increase the underpayment penalty from 0.5 percent per month to 1 percent per month.[60]

N. *Uneconomical Levies*
1. Uneconomical levies are not allowed. If the estimated amount of expenses that would be incurred with respect to the levy and sale of such property exceeds the fair market value of the property, then no levy can be made on the property.[61]
2. If it is determined, after seizure of property, that the taxpayer's equity in the property is insufficient to yield net proceeds from sale to apply to the unpaid tax, the revenue officer must immediately release the seized property back to the taxpayer.[62]

X. Release and Other Relief Provisions

A. *Releases*
1. *General Rule*
After the levy has been served, it can only be released if the tax has been paid or the liability becomes unenforceable (e.g., if the statute of limitations has run). Remember that the collection statute of limitations is ten years from the date of assessment. Additionally, the IRS will release a levy if it can be shown that notice was not given pursuant to I.R.C. § 6331(d).[63]
2. *Installment Agreement*
A levy can also be released if an installment agreement (i.e., a payout agreement) is entered into or the IRS determines that the levy is creating an economic hardship.[64] Moreover, no levy may be made if the taxpayer has made a *request* for an installment agreement under I.R.C. § 6159 (including an appeal period, if necessary).[65]

Practice Tip

A good planning technique is always to request an installment agreement if there is a danger of an imminent levy.

---

3. *Offers in Compromise (OIC)*
The IRS may not levy on a taxpayer's property during the period of time that an OIC is pending with the IRS.[66]

B. *Lawsuits against the IRS*
1. A taxpayer may now sue the IRS for civil damages in federal district court if any officer or employee of the IRS recklessly or

intentionally disregards any statutory or regulatory provision in connection with the collection of any federal tax. For example, a taxpayer can sue a revenue officer for civil damages resulting from the IRS serving a levy on a bank account after an installment agreement has been entered into.[67]

2. A third party who claims an interest in property wrongfully levied on may also sue the IRS for damages. However, an employee of the IRS may not be sued personally under this provision.[68]

C. *Taxpayer Assistance Orders (TAO)*

1. A taxpayer, or his or her representative, can file with the IRS's Taxpayer Advocate Service an application for a TAO if he or she is suffering or is about to suffer a significant hardship as a result of the manner in which the IRS laws are being administered. This is done by filing a Form 911.[69]

2. 911 forms are submitted to the Taxpayer Advocate Office for consideration. Sending by fax is recommended for faster handling. The IRS may, depending on the circumstances, route the 911 back to the revenue officer in charge of the case or to his or her group manager. This tends to delay the case. Therefore, pressure must be kept up on the Collection function to get the levy released. And you may have to submit documentary evidence to satisfy the revenue officer that your numbers on the 433-A form are correct. Be sure to review bank statements ahead of time to ferret out any "snakes."

XI. Notes

1. I.R.C. § 6331(a).
2. I.R.C. § 6331(d)
3. I.R.C. § 6331(b).
4. United States v. Long Island Drug Co., 25 AFTR 1108 (2d Cir. 1940), *rev'g* 23 AFTR 738 (E.D. N.Y. 1939).
5. Rev. Rul. 55-210, 1955-1 CB 544.
6. Treas. Reg. § 1.401(a)-13(b)(2).
7. I.R.C. § 72(t)(2)(A)(vii).
8. IRM 5.11.6.1.
9. CCA 200935026, involving a postdeath levy.
10. F.S.A. 199930039.
11. I.R.C. § 6332(b).
12. I.R.C. § 6332(c).
13. Citizens & S. Nat'l Bank v. United States, 76-2 USTC ¶ 9665 (5th Cir. 1976).
14. Rev. Rul. 73-24, 1973-1 CB 602.
15. 31 U.S.C. § 3723.
16. I.R.C. § 6331(d)(1); Tex. Civ. Pracs. & Rem. Code § 63.004; Tex. Const. art. 16, § 28.
17. I.R.C. § 6334(d).

18. I.R.S. Priv. Ltr. Rul. 8149061; note that, as a private letter ruling, this authority is of questionable use to the tax practitioner should the IRS decline to follow it.
19. Including other community property states as well.
20. Medaris v. United States, 89-2 USTC ¶ 9565 (5th Cir. 1989).
21. *See, e.g.,* Calmes v. United States, 96-2 USTC ¶ 50,336 (N.D. Tex. 1996), a Texas case in which the IRS had claimed that the premarital agreement was fraudulent. *See also* United States v. Elam, 97-1 USTC ¶ 50,339 (9th Cir. 1997), a California case involving a premarital agreement in the context of an overpayment allocation, for a similar result. Even a verbal postmarriage partition agreement has been held to convert community earnings of a nonliable spouse to separate earnings, thereby avoiding an IRS levy. Venie v. United States, 88-1 USTC ¶ 9106 (E.D. Wash. 1987).
22. *See* I.R.C. § 6159.
23. I.R.C. § 6343(e).
24. *See* United States v. Jefferson-Pilot Life Ins. Co., 95-1 USTC ¶ 50,263 (4th Cir. 1995) regarding amounts paid to independent contractor insurance salespeople.
25. I.R.C. § 6334(a)(1).
26. I.R.C. § 6334(a)(2), indexed for inflation beginning after 1999; I.R.C. § 6334(g).
27. I.R.C. § 6334(a)(3), indexed for inflation beginning after 1999; I.R.C. § 6334(g).
28. However, once a workers' compensation payment is deposited into a bank account, it loses its exempt status.
29. I.R.C. § 6334(a)(4) through (10).
30. § 207 of the Social Security Act (42 U.S.C. 407), which generally exempts social security benefits from levy and garnishment, is superseded by I.R.C. § 6334(c), which does not provide that such benefits are exempt from IRS levy. United States v. Cleveland, 94-2 USTC ¶ 50,421 (N.D. Ill.1994). *See also* Leining v. United States, 97-1 USTC ¶ 50,254 (D. Conn. 1996).
31. Broday v. United States, 29 AFTR2d 72-663 (5th Cir. 1972).
32. United States v. Rodgers, 83-1 USTC ¶ 9374 (S. Ct. 1983).
33. *See* United States v. Nat'l Bank of Commerce, 472 U.S. 713, 85-2 USTC ¶ 9482 (S. Ct. 1985); *see also* Internal Revenue Serv. v. Gaster, 94-2 USTC ¶ 50,622 (3d Cir. 1994).
34. Cooper Indus., Inc. v. Compagnoni, 2001-2 USTC ¶ 50,626 (S.D. Tex. 2001).
35. Hatchett v. United States, 2003-1 USTC ¶ 50,504 (6th Cir. 2003).
36. *See, e.g.,* United States v. Turner, 2000-2 USTC ¶ 50,815 at 85,993 (D. Haw. 2000).
37. IRM 5.11.1.3.6.
38. IRM 5.10.1.7.2.
39. For pre-levy procedures, *see generally* IRM 5.11.1.
40. IRM 5.10.2.14.
41. I.R.C. § 6331(d).
42. United States v. McCallum, 92-2 USTC ¶ 50,448 (5th Cir. 1992); *see also* Bauer v. Foley, 23 AFTR2d 69-307 (2d Cir. 1968).
43. IRM 5.9.3.6.
44. United States v. Whiting Pools, Inc., 83-1 USTC ¶ 9393 (S. Ct. 1983).
45. I.R.C. § 6332(a).
46. I.R.C. § 6332(d).
47. I.R.C. § 6333.
48. I.R.C. § 6334(a)(13), 6334(e)(1)(A).

49. I.R.C. § 6335(a).
50. I.R.C. § 6335(b)
51. I.R.C. § 6335(c).
52. I.R.C. § 6335(d).
53. I.R.C. § 7506(b).
54. I.R.C. § 6335(e).
55. IRM 5.10.5.9.
56. I.R.C. § 6337(a).
57. I.R.C. § 6337(b)(1).
58. I.R.C. § 6338.
59. I.R.C. § 6342(a)(1).
60. I.R.C. § 6651(d)(2)(A).
61. I.R.C. § 6331(f).
62. IRM 5.10.1.
63. I.R.C. § 6343(a)(1)(A); United States v. Arford, 95-1 USTC ¶ 50,046 (9th Cir. 1994).
64. I.R.C. § 6343(a)(1)(C), (D).
65. I.R.C. § 6331(k)(2).
66. I.R.C. § 6331(k)(1).
67. Rorex v. Traynor, 85-2 USTC ¶ 9636 (8th Cir. 1985).
68. I.R.C. § 7426.
69. I.R.C. § 7811.

Seizure of Tangible Personalty by the IRS

I. Background and Definitions

A. Decisions by the IRS to seize a taxpayer's property are the most sensitive that revenue officers are called upon to make.[1]

B. The IRS considers "enforcement," including seizure of property, to be a necessary component of a *voluntary* assessment system.[2] That statement is an obvious oxymoron. How can the surrender of property under threat of force be considered "voluntary"?

C. IRS revenue officers are more inclined to take seizure action when there has been a history of a taxpayer's delinquency or failure to show good faith.[3]

D. *Definitions*
   1. The term "levy" is determined statutorily as "distraint and seizure" by any means.
   2. The term "distrain" means to force or compel to satisfy an obligation by means of a distress.
   3. To "seize" means to take possession of or confiscate.[4]

II. Statutory Authority

A. If a taxpayer refuses to pay a properly assessed tax when it is due, the IRS has the statutory authority to levy on all property and rights to property belonging to the delinquent taxpayer.[5]

B. A levy is proper only after ten days have elapsed following "notice and demand" (assuming there is no "jeopardy").[6] If the IRS fails to give proper notice, a cause of action is available to the taxpayer to set aside the levy as invalid.[7]

C. A recalcitrant taxpayer is also required to pay the expenses incurred by the IRS in collecting by means of a levy.[8]

D. A levy is made by serving a "notice of levy" on any person in possession of property belonging to the taxpayer.[9]

III. Internal Revenue Manual Seizure Procedures

A. The overwhelming majority of rules regarding forcible seizure of a taxpayer's property are contained in the Internal Revenue Manual (IRM). Unfortunately, case law has universally held that IRM procedures are not "law," and failure by the IRS to follow them does not render a particular action by the IRS ineffective.[10]

B. However, there have been cases holding that the IRS may not gain unfair advantage where revenue officers have not followed the mandates of the IRM that they are obligated to follow.[11]

C. *Team Approach to Seizure*
Anytime there is a seizure of property, at least two revenue officers will participate. This rule is designed to ensure that at least one person is available to testify regarding the regularity of the proceeding.[12]

D. *Armed Escort*
If revenue officers attempting a seizure are concerned about their personal safety, they may request an armed escort, usually two special agents of Criminal Investigation, especially if firearms are to be seized.[13]

E. *Equity Determination*
All seizures require the approval and concurrence of the revenue officer's group manager. The group manager will also review the equity determination (Form 2434-B), which is required to be filled out prior to seizure recommendation. Equity determination is required in all seizures regardless of whether a writ of entry or other judicial approval is required.[14] There is no legal requirement to conclusively prove the existence of equity to obtain a writ of entry[15]

F. *Use of Private Vendors*
Revenue officers can arrange to purchase services from private vendors for towing, storage, guard, and locksmith services.[16]

IV. Consent to Enter Private Premises

A. The IRM provides that before assets located in private premises can be seized, consent to enter will be sought from the taxpayer. For this purpose, the IRS uses a Form 2421, Consent to Enter Private Premises.

B. Only after consent has been denied will the revenue officer request a writ of entry. Exceptions to this provision are as follows:
   1. It is believed that advance notice will jeopardize the safety of the revenue officers;

2. Attempts to contact the taxpayer have failed; or
3. Other unforeseen reasons.[17]

C. In situations where consent is not being sought prior to requesting a writ of entry, concurrence by the level of management *above the group manager* is required. This authority is to be used advisedly. Mere loss of the element of surprise will generally not be sufficient cause to warrant an exception.[18]

D. Consent to enter private premises cannot be obtained verbally; it must be in writing. Pattern Letter P-576 or Form 2421 may be used for this purpose.[19]

E. The seizure should be made not more than seven working days from the date of the consent.[20]

F. Consents to enter are voluntary and may be revoked at any time by the person giving consent.[21]

G. If consent to entry is denied by the taxpayer, the revenue officer will explain that a writ of entry to seize the assets is the probable next step.[22]

H. If consent is denied, the revenue officer will, within two working days of the denial, prepare a data sheet and an affidavit to secure a writ of entry.[23]

V. Writs of Entry

A. A writ of entry is not a search warrant or its equivalent. A search warrant cannot be issued to a revenue officer authorizing entry upon private premises to search for property to be seized for distraint purposes.[24]

B. When a writ of entry is required, the revenue officer will prepare an affidavit (Pattern P-577) and a data sheet (Pattern P-584).[25]

C. The data sheet should include all pertinent information necessary to provide a complete background on the case, as the sheet may be used to answer questions that the judge or magistrate might have regarding the request for a writ of entry.[26]

D. As soon as the writ of entry is received, the revenue officer will proceed with the seizure. A copy of the writ will be given to the taxpayer at the time of the seizure or as soon after as possible if the taxpayer is not present at the seizure.[27]

E. All writs are requested through IRS Counsel.[28]

F. Federal district courts and magistrates have jurisdiction to hear and adjudicate applications for writs of entry.

G. The standard for probable cause for an IRS writ of entry is not the same as for a criminal warrant. In an application for such a writ, the IRS must establish the following by affidavit:
1. There is a proper assessment, notice, demand for payment, and nonpayment by the taxpayer; and
2. There is probable cause to believe that there are assets that may be seized on the premises to be entered.

H. I.R.C. § 6331 has withstood numerous constitutional challenges predicated on lack of preseizure judicial hearings.[29] Thus, due process of law does not require a prior hearing before the magistrate issues the writ of entry.[30]

I. Applications for writ of entry may be done on an ex parte basis.[31]

J. An affidavit supporting an application for writ of entry may be based on hearsay information.[32]

VI. Miscellaneous Provisions

A. *Levy Exemptions*

Personal household belongings are exempt from levy to the extent of $6,250 in value, adjusted for inflation.[33]

A revenue officer who seizes tangible personalty is required to appraise and set aside to the owner the property declared to be exempt under I.R.C. § 6334. If the taxpayer objects at the time of the seizure to the valuation fixed by the officer making the seizure, the IRS is required to summon three disinterested individuals who are to make the valuation.[34]

B. *Wrongful Levy*

A levy is wrongful if any of the following conditions apply:
1. It is placed on property exempt under § 6334;
2. It is placed on property in which the delinquent taxpayer has no interest;
3. It is invalid under § 6323 or § 6324; or
4. The plaintiff's interest in the property is senior to the federal tax lien and will be destroyed by the levy.[35]

If property has been wrongfully levied on, the IRS's choices are as follows:
1. Return the specific property levied on;
2. Return the amount of money equal to the value of property levied on; or
3. Return the amount of money equal to the sales proceeds of the property.[36]

Typically, wrongful levy suits under I.R.C. § 7426 are brought by third parties (not the taxpayer) who claim an interest in the property wrongfully levied on.[37] Such suits must be brought within nine months from the date of the levy.[38]

The appropriate procedural remedy for the taxpayer is to file a quiet title suit against the United States questioning the procedural validity of the assessment under § 6203 or the validity of the levy under § 6331. Section 2410 of 28 U.S.C. is a waiver of sovereign immunity in quiet title actions against the government.[39]

A transfer of tangible personalty to an investment partnership will not avoid a seizure by the IRS if the IRS can prove an alter ego theory.[40]

C. *Notice of Intent to Levy*
Revenue officers must always ensure that the taxpayer has received a notice of intent to levy (see I.R.C. § 6331(d)) within the last 180 days prior to any seizure action.[41] Failure to send a notice of intent to levy under § 6331(d) will render the sale null and void, requiring the IRS to schedule a new sale after proper notice.[42]

D. *Bankruptcy and Receivership Cases*
Note that taxes cannot be collected by levy if the assets sought by the IRS are in the custody of a court, whether or not such custody is incident to a bankruptcy or receivership proceeding.[43]

E. *Successive Seizures*
The IRS may continue to levy with successive seizures as often as may be necessary to collect the delinquent tax.[44]

F. *Uneconomical Levies*
Uneconomical levies (i.e., where the anticipated expenses with respect to the levy and sale will exceed the value of the property) are strictly forbidden.[45]

G. *Surrender of Property*
Any person in possession of property subject to levy must surrender such property to the IRS assuming there has been proper notice of levy and demand for surrender.[46]

H. *Notice of Federal Tax Lien*
It is the IRS's policy to file a notice of federal tax lien (NFTL) before taking seizure action, although it is not required to do so by statute.[47]

I. *Warrantless Seizures*
Warrantless automobile seizures that occur on a public street, parking lot, or other open areas involve no invasion of privacy and are not, therefore, an unconstitutional invasion of privacy in violation of the Fourth Amendment of the U.S. Constitution.[48] However, a warrantless entry into private premises, either a home or an office, violates the Fourth Amendment of the U.S. Constitution, as it constitutes a search of private property without proper consent, unless it has been authorized by a valid search warrant (a writ of entry in the case of the IRS).[49]

J. *Use of Force*
Revenue officers are not authorized to use force in the seizure of property.[50] Similarly, it is not a good idea for taxpayers or their friends to

use force in resisting a revenue officer's attempt to seize property, as a criminal conviction can be the result.[51]

K. *Notice of Seizure*
A taxpayer is entitled to notice of seizure at the earliest possible time after seizure.[52]

L. *Inventory*
Items of property seized should be described and identified with reasonable certainty on an inventory, Form 2433, which is sent to the Special Procedures function within five working days after seizure is made.[53]

M. *Redemption*
Both real and personal property may be redeemed before sale by the person whose property is seized.[54]

N. *Sale Following Seizure*
The IRS is required to advertise the sale of the property with a "notice of sale" within ten days of the seizure.[55] Property not sold within the statutory period must be released to the owner.[56]

O. *Failure to Sell Property*
Where the IRS attempts to sell seized property but is unable to do so, the property must be released back to the taxpayers, but is still subject to the IRS's lien. When the IRS fails to do so, the taxpayers may file suit for damages under I.R.C. § 7433. However, the taxpayers have only two years within which to file such an action. Their cause of action accrues on the date of failure to release the property.[57]

P. *Managerial Approval*
As of 1997, all proposed seizures must be approved by someone in IRS Collection upper management. Prior to this date, collection group managers could approve most seizures.[58]

VII. Conclusions

Practitioners representing clients before the Collection Division of the IRS must be constantly aware of the inherent threat of seizure of tangible property by a revenue officer. Because of the cumbersome procedures and constitutional safeguards regarding seizure, the IRS will typically use other enforcement means[59] before resorting to seizure of tangible personalty. If a taxpayer is in possession of property that does not belong to him or her, then he or she should be prepared to prove the nonownership at the time of the seizure. Otherwise it is much more difficult to obtain a release of the property by the true owner.

VIII. Notes

1. IRM 5.10.1.1.
2. *Id.*
3. *Id.*
4. *See* I.R.C. § 6331(b).
5. I.R.C. § 6331(a).
6. I.R.C. § 6342(a)(1).
7. Gonsalves v. United States, 92-1 USTC ¶ 50,067 (D. Me. 1992); Simpson v. United States, 93-1 USTC ¶ 150,248 (N.D. Fla. 1992).
8. *Id.*
9. Treas. Reg. § 301.6331-1(a)(1).
10. Wiley v. United States, 96-1 USTC ¶ 50,089 (S.D. Ohio 1995).
11. *See, e.g.*, Romagnolo v. United States, 96-1 USTC ¶ 50,301 (Bankr. M.D. Fla. 1996).
12. IRM 5.10.3.2.
13. IRM 5.10.2.8.
14. I.R.C. § 6331(f).
15. IRM 5.10.2.
16. IRM 5.10.2.22.
17. IRM 5.10.2.
18. *Id.*
19. *Id.*
20. *Id.*
21. *Id.*
22. *Id.*
23. *Id.*
24. *Id.*
25. *Id.*
26. *Id.*
27. *Id.*
28. *Id.*
29. Baddour, Inc. v. United States, 802 F.2d 801, 86-2 USTC ¶ 9748 (5th Cir. 1986).
30. *Id.* at note 28.
31. United States v. Coppola, 96-1 USTC ¶ 60,233 (2d Cir. 1995).
32. *Id.*
33. I.R.C. § 6334(a)(2).
34. I.R.C. § 6334(b).
35. N. Am. Royalties, Inc. v. United States, 96-2 USTC ¶ 50,677 (E.D. Tenn. 1996).
36. I.R.C. § 6343(b).
37. *Coppola*, 96-1 USTC ¶ 60,233. A spouse may also bring a third-party wrongful levy suit under § 7426. *See* Progressive Bank & Trust Co. v. Moore, 91-1 USTC ¶ 50,192 (E.D. La. 1991).
38. I.R.0 § 6532(c).
39. *But see* Olson v. United States, 90-2 USC ¶ 50,457 (W.D. Pa. 1990).
40. Grant Invs. Fund v. United States, 91-2 USTC ¶ 50,406 (9th Cir. 1993).
41. IRM 5.11.1.3.3.8.
42. Typically this will result following a quiet title action filed by the taxpayer, as in *Kulawy v. United States*, 917 F.2d 729, 90-2 USTC ¶ 50,565 (2d Cir. 1990).
43. Treas. Reg. § 301.6331-1(a)(3).

44. Treas. Reg. § 301.6331-1(b)(2).
45. I.R.C. § 6331(f); Treas. Reg. § 301.6331-2(b)(1).
46. I.R.C. § 6332(a).
47. IRM 5.10.1.3.3.
48. G.M. Leasing Corp. v. United States, 77-1 USTC ¶ 9140 (S. Ct. 1977).
49. *Id.*
50. IRM 5.10.3.6.
51. I.R.C. § 7212; United States v. Afflerbach, 85-2 USTC ¶ 19625 (10th Cir. 1985).
52. IRM 5.10.3.10.
53. *Id.*
54. I.R.C. § 6337.
55. I.R.C. § 6335(b).
56. IRM 5.10.5.10.1.
57. Dziura v. United States, 99-1 USTC ¶ 50,296 (D. Mass. 1998).
58. I.R.S. News Release 97-46.
59. For example, levies on wages and bank accounts, as these procedures are much simpler to accomplish.

Transferee and Fiduciary Liability

I. Background and General Rules

  A. *Types of Transfer*
  A transfer giving rise to transferee liability can be direct or indirect, actual or constructive.

  B. *Applicability of State Law*
  Section 6901, the primary governing statute in this area, affords the IRS a procedural remedy, but the existence and extent of a transferee's liability are governed by state law.[1]

  C. *Remedies Available to the IRS*
  There are two methods by which the IRS may proceed where property has been transferred to avoid payment of tax:
  1. Have the transfer set aside and the property subjected to the collection of the transferor's tax liability; or
  2. Collect the unpaid tax from the transferee's property. This may be done by either bringing suit in federal district court or issuing a deficiency notice, which may lead to a hearing in U.S. Tax Court.[2]

  D. *Transfers for Full Consideration*
  The mere fact that a transferor owes tax does not preclude him or her from conveying property for valuable consideration.

  E. *Liability at Law or in Equity*
  1. Transferee liability may be imposed either at law or in equity. This means that if a judge has no legal grounds to impose a liability, he or she may do so on "equitable" considerations.[3]
  2. Liability in equity exists when the transfer of assets is without adequate consideration and leaves the taxpayer unable to meet his or her liabilities.[4]

F. *Primary versus Secondary Liability: Ordering Rules*
    1. Transferee liability is secondary rather than primary; therefore, all reasonable possible remedies against the taxpayer-transferor must first be exhausted to hold the transferee liable.[5]
    2. The statute does not require, however, that an assessment be made against the transferor before proceeding against the transferee.[6]
    3. Upon termination of a trust and distribution of the trust property, the IRS may proceed against the distributee-beneficiary without first proceeding against the trustee.[7]

G. *Method of Assessment*
    Transferee liability is assessed, paid, and collected in the same manner as direct taxpayer liability.[8]

H. *Types of Tax Covered by Transferee Liability*
    In addition to income tax, transferee liability can be imposed in respect of estate tax (in the case of a transfer by a decedent) or gift tax (in the case of a transfer by a donor).[9]

II. Definitions

A. *Transferee*
    The definition of "transferee" includes the following: heir, legatee, devisee, the distributee of an estate of a deceased person, the shareholder of a dissolved corporation, the successor of a corporation, or a party to a reorganization.[10]

B. *Fiduciaries*
    A fiduciary is defined to include a guardian, a trustee, an executor, an administrator, a receiver, a conservator, or any person acting in a fiduciary capacity.[11] For purposes of I.R.C. § 6905, the term "executor" also includes "administrator."[12]

III. Statute of Limitations Rules Applicable to Transferees

A. *General Rule: One Year Extra*
    There is a special statute of limitations (S/L) rule with respect to a transferee. Regarding the initial transferee, the IRS has an extra year after the assessment S/L has expired against the transferor within which to make an assessment against the transferee.[13]

B. *Second Transfers*
    In the case of a second transfer (i.e., a transfer by the initial transferee), the IRS gets another year after the S/L period expires against the initial

transferee, but not more than three years after the S/L period expires against the initial transferor.[14]

C. *Effect of Court Proceedings*
If a court proceeding has begun against the initial transferor or last preceding transferee, then the assessment S/L is suspended until one year after the conclusion of the court proceeding.[15]

D. *S/L Rules Applicable to Fiduciaries*
A special assessment S/L rule exists in the case of a fiduciary. The S/L against fiduciary liability expires ten years after the liability arises.[16]

E. *Extension of the S/L for Transferees*
S/L periods for assessments may be voluntarily extended by agreements in writing executed at the option of the fiduciary or transferee. Of course, if such an agreement is executed, it extends the S/L period for refunds and credits as well.[17]

F. *S/L Rules for Deceased Persons and Dissolved Corporations*
If the transferor is a deceased person or a dissolved corporation, the S/L rules apply as if death or dissolution had not occurred.[18]

G. *Effect of a Deficiency Notice on the S/L*
The mailing of a deficiency notice to a transferee tolls (i.e., suspends) the assessment S/L and gives the transferee an opportunity to file a petition and litigate his or her case in the U.S. Tax Court.[19]

IV. Fiduciary Liability

A. *General Rule for Fiduciaries*
In the case of an estate, fiduciaries may also be held liable for any tax liability due from the estate.[20]

B. *"Notice" Rules*
1. Fiduciaries are required to give notice, at the time they qualify as a fiduciary, to the IRS that they are acting for another person.[21]
2. To give proper notice of a fiduciary relationship, an executor ordinarily prepares a Form 56 and files it with the IRS service center, where the person for whom he or she is acting is required to file his or her returns.
3. If a fiduciary fails to give the required notice to the IRS, a deficiency notice is sufficient if it is mailed to the last known address of the person alleged to owe the tax, even if that person is deceased.[22]

C. *Applicability of Other Statutes*

For purposes of I.R.C. § 6901(a)(1)(B) (regarding fiduciary liability), one must look to Title 31 of the U.S. Code to determine the circumstances to which this provision applies. Title 31 provides that the executor or administrator of an estate who pays any debt of or claim against an estate is liable for any unpaid claims of the government.[23]

V. Discharge or Release of Fiduciary from Liability

A. *Application for Discharge*

If the decedent owed income, estate, or gift tax, the executor can make application for discharge after the return in question has been filed.[24]

B. *Date of Discharge*

After application for release, the executor is forever discharged from personal liability on the earlier of the following two dates:
1. Upon written notification of discharge sent to him or her by the IRS or
2. Nine months after the IRS's receipt of the application.[25]

C. *Form Required*

To request a discharge from personal liability, an executor or other fiduciary must file a Form 5495.

VI. Litigation of Transferee Liability in Tax Court

A. *General Rule*

A transferee may litigate a transferee liability by filing a petition with the U.S. Tax Court. This follows from the rule that a transferee has rights identical to the transferor (person with respect to which the liability was incurred).[26] When the IRS has chosen to use the deficiency procedures to impose personal liability upon those in possession of the taxpayer's transferred assets, the tax court has jurisdiction to review the commissioner's determination as set forth in the notice of transferee liability. The grant of jurisdiction for these so-called transferee liability cases is implicit from the cross-reference in I.R.C. § 6901 to the "provisions and limitations . . . [governing the] taxes with respect to which the liabilities were incurred."

B. *Right to Examination of Records*

In litigating transferee liability in the tax court, the petitioner has the right (through the court's subpoena power if necessary) to examine books and records of the transferor-taxpayer as well as records in the possession of the IRS.[27]

C. *Burden of Proof Issues*
  1. In tax court, the IRS has the burden of proof that the transferee is liable for the tax of the transferor, but not that the transferor was liable for the tax.[28]
  2. To sustain its burden of proof in court, the IRS must establish five things:
     a. That the transferor did not receive fair consideration;
     b. That the transferor was insolvent at the time of the transfer or was rendered insolvent by it;
     c. That the transfer was made after the tax liability of the tax-payer accrued;
     d. That the IRS has exhausted its remedies against the transferor; and
     e. The value of the assets transferred.[29]

D. *Valuation Problems for the IRS*
  If the IRS fails to prove insolvency by showing the value of all of the transferor's assets, then the petitioner-transferee will prevail in tax court.[30]

VII. Estate and Gift Tax Liability Issues

A. *Estate Tax Rule*
  If estate tax is not paid when due, then the transferee of any property includible in the estate is personally liable for any such unpaid estate tax.[31]

B. *Gift Tax Rule*
  Similarly, if a gift tax is not paid, a tax lien continues for ten years, and the donee becomes personally liable for the unpaid gift tax.[32]

VIII. Interest Issues

A. *General Rule Regarding Interest*
  Transferee liability also includes assessed interest that otherwise would have been due from the transferor.[33]

B. *Estate Tax*
  The tax court has held that a life insurance beneficiary's personal liability for the decedent's estate tax:
  1. Is not limited to the amount of the life insurance proceeds he or she got and
  2. Includes statutory interest, in addition to the tax.[34]

C. *Gift Tax*
  In the gift tax context, the Third Circuit[35] has held that the donee's transferee liability is limited to the value of the gift, even if what

pushes the liability over the value of the gift is statutory interest. This case appears to be in direct conflict with the *Baptiste* case.

IX. Miscellaneous Provisions

A. *Original Return Liability versus Deficiency*
Transferee liability can be in respect to either a tax liability shown on a tax return or a tax deficiency determined by the IRS.[36]

B. *Life Insurance Beneficiaries*
If a life insurance policy names the insured's estate as the beneficiary, the ultimate distributee of the insurance proceeds is liable as transferee for unpaid income taxes of the insured if the distribution renders the estate insolvent.

C. *Applicability of Injunctions*
Transferees are prohibited from filing injunction suits against the IRS, just as primary taxpayers are.[37]

D. *Employment and Excise Taxes*
The IRS cannot do a transferee assessment of taxes such as employment tax or excise tax unless there has been a corporate or partnership liquidation, or unless there has been a § 368 reorganization.[38]

E. *"Trust Fund" Liability (I.R.C. § 6672) Cases*
Transferee provisions do not apply to I.R.C. § 6672 trust fund assessments in the absence of a corporate liquidation.

Practice Tip

The *Lawrence* case presents an obvious planning opportunity. For example, if a culpable spouse can arrange to get a divorce prior to assessment of this kind of liability, then his or her former spouse can enjoin an attempted levy on his or her property by the IRS. *See* Lawrence v. United States, 19 AFTR2d 624 (N.D. Tex. 1967).

F. *Corporate Officer Excessive Salary*
It is difficult for the IRS to show that a corporate officer's allegedly excessive salary constitutes a transfer within the meaning of I.R.C. § 6901.[39]

G. *When Does Tax "Accrue" for Transferee Purposes?*
Transferee liability cannot be asserted prior to the time that tax has *accrued* against the primary taxpayer. Thus, in the case of estimated tax payments, the date of accrual is the date the estimated payments

are due. And any transfers after said accrual can subject the transferee to § 6901 liability.[40]

X. Notes

1. Villani v. Comm'r, 52 T.C.M. (CCH) 8 (1986).
2. IRM 5.17.14.
3. *See* I.R.C. § 6901(a)(1)(A).
4. IRM 5.17.14.2.3.
5. *Id.*
6. IRM 5.17.14.1.
7. IRM 5.17.14.2.2.
8. I.R.C. § 6901(a).
9. I.R.C. § 6901(a)(1)(A).
10. Reg. § 301.6901-1(b).
11. Reg. § 6901-1(c)(4); I.R.C. § 7701(a)(6).
12. I.R.C. § 6905(b).
13. I.R.C. § 6901(c)(1).
14. I.R.C. § 6901(c)(2).
15. I.R.C. § 6901(c).
16. I.R.C. § 6901(c)(3); *see* I.R.C. § 6502(a)(1).
17. I.R.C. § 6501(d)(1).
18. I.R.C. § 6901(e).
19. I.R.C. § 6901(f).
20. I.R.C. § 6901(a)(1)(B).
21. I.R.C. § 6903.
22. I.R.C. § 6901(g).
23. 31 U.S.C. § 3713(b).
24. I.R.C. § 6905(a); I.R.C. § 2204(a).
25. I.R.C. § 6905(a).
26. I.R.C. § 6901(a).
27. I.R.C. § 6902(b); T.C. Rule 73.
28. I.R.C. § 6902(a); T.C. Rule 142(d).
29. Rose v. Comm'r, 17 T.C.M. (CCH) 732 (1958).
30. Brown v. Comm'r, 24 T.C. 256 (1955).
31. I.R.C. § 6324(a)(2).
32. I.R.C. § 6324(b).
33. Treas. Reg. § 301.6901-1(a)(3)(i).
34. Baptiste v. Comm'r, 100 T.C. 252 (1993).
35. Poinier v. Comm'r, 88-2 USTC ¶ 13,783 (3d Cir. 1988).
36. I.R.C. § 6901(b).
37. I.R.C. § 7421(b)(1).
38. I.R.C. § 6901(a)(2).
39. Rose v. Comm'r, 17 T.C.M. (CCH) 732 (1958).
40. Villani v. Comm'r, 52 T.C.M. (CCH) 8 (1986).

CHAPTER 7

Collection: Defenses and Remedies

Applications for Taxpayer Assistance Orders

I. General Information and Background

A. *Statutory Authority*

Taxpayers are authorized to file with the Taxpayer Advocate Service (TAS) an application for a taxpayer assistance order (ATAO). The TAS office was, prior to July 30, 1996, known as the Office of Ombudsman.[1] The term "taxpayer advocate" (TA) also includes any designee of the TA (typically, the TA caseworker in each major city).[2]

II. "Hardship" Issues

A. *General Rule*

For an application for an ATAO to succeed, the taxpayer must be "suffering" or "about to suffer" a significant hardship as a result of the manner in which the internal revenue laws are being administered by the IRS.[3] This determination of hardship is required to be made by the TA prior to the issuance of a TAO.[4]

B. *Definition of Hardship*

1. The term "significant hardship" means a serious privation; it does not include mere economic or personal inconvenience to the taxpayer.[5]
2. Significant hardship is a subjective determination and is to be made on a case-by-case basis. IRS employees have been advised to use good judgment and not to let personal values or opinions bias their determinations. The following factors are to be considered:
   a. The imminence of the hardship;
   b. The taxpayer's ability to retain housing, utilities, or employment;

     c. The taxpayer's ability to obtain food, clothing, or medical treatment;

     d. The chance of irreparable damage to the taxpayer's credit rating;

     e. The likelihood of serious financial hardship, such as inability to meet payroll or an imminent bankruptcy;

     f. Loss of education to the taxpayer or his or her family; and

     g. The taxpayer's physical or mental state as a result of his or her tax situation, as demonstrated by depression, despair, or threat of personal harm.

All doubts concerning the existence and extent of the hardship are to be resolved in favor of the taxpayer.[6]

3. TA case workers can decide that hardship exists, but only the TA can decide that hardship does *not* exist.[7]

4. If a taxpayer is simply getting tax due notices, this is not considered a threat of hardship sufficient to require the filing of an ATAO.[8]

5. Moreover, enforcement action (levies, etc.), in and of itself, is not a significant hardship without additional factors being present.[9]

III. Relief

A. The TAO (following the filing of an ATAO), if issued, may require the IRS to do one of the following things:
- Release any property levied on or[10]
- Cease taking any other collection action.[11]

B. A finding of significant hardship by the TA will not always result in the granting of the relief requested. The TA will also look at the behavior of the taxpayer and action or inaction of the IRS that is causing the hardship.[12]

C. *Timing of Response by the TA's Office*
The TA's office is required to notify the taxpayer and complete certain action within prescribed time limits.[13] The TA's office should complete its review of the ATAO and come to a decision within two work-days of receipt of the ATAO.[14]

IV. Form 911 Procedures

A. The application for a TAO should be made on a Form 911 or in a written statement containing the following information:
1. Name and Social Security number of the taxpayer;
2. The kind of tax involved;
3. A description of IRS action causing the hardship;
4. A description of the specific hardship; and
5. The signature of the taxpayer or his or her representative.[15]

B. *Place of Filing*

ATAOs (911s) should be filed with the Taxpayer Advocate Office of the IRS where the taxpayer resides.[16] If other field or office employees of the IRS receive the ATAO, they are to be immediately forwarded to the TA's office for handling.[17]

C. *Timing of Filing*

An ATAO should be submitted within a reasonable time after the taxpayer becomes aware of the significant hardship or the potential significant hardship.[18]

D. *Alternative Ways to File*

Although the Form 911 is the preferred way to file an ATAO, one can always file by means of a letter or a telephone call. Actually, the fastest way to file is to fill out the 911 form and then fax it to the local TAS office.

V. Statute of Limitations Issues

A. *General Rule*

The collection statute of limitations[19] is suspended during the following period:

Start date: date of application for TAO

End date: date of TA's decision on the application

The collection statutory period is also suspended for any period specified by the TA in the issued TAO.[20]

B. *Unilateral Action by the TA*

The statute of limitations is *not* suspended if the TA acts on his or her own without an application being filed by the taxpayer.[21]

C. *"Decision" Date*

For statute of limitations purposes, the decision date is the date on which the TA makes a decision with respect to the application.

D. *Written Explanation Required*

If the statute of limitations is extended, the taxpayer must be given a written response from the TA explaining which statute was extended, why it was extended, and for how long.[22]

VI. Other Miscellaneous Rules

A. *Rescission*

Once issued, a TAO can only be rescinded by the TA or by the IRS commissioner (or his or her deputy).[23]

B. *Unilateral Action by the TA*
The TA is also authorized to take any action on his or her own without the necessity of a taxpayer filing an application for a TAO.[24]

C. *IRS Divisions Affected by a TAO*
A TAO may affect the actions of the Collection, Examination, and Appeals Divisions of the IRS, but not the Criminal Investigation (CI) Division or chief counsel.[25]

D. *Limited Scope of a TAO*
An ATAO (Application for Taxpayer Assistance Order) does not deal with the technical aspects of a tax account. For example, an ATAO cannot be used to change the determination of an audit deficiency.[26]

E. *Stay of Enforcement Action*
Under most circumstances while an ATAO is being reviewed, all enforcement action will be suspended.[27]

F. *Adverse Decision*
A final adverse decision on the ATAO must be provided to the taxpayer or his or her representative in writing.[28]

G. *Taxpayer's Burden of Proof*
It is the obligation of the taxpayer to provide the IRS with sufficient facts to make a determination of hardship. Mere vague allegations of hardship, without specificity, will not satisfy the statute.[29]

H. *Suit for Damages*
Section 7811 does not authorize a suit for damages against the IRS.[30]

VII. Conclusion

The Taxpayer Bills of Rights (versions 1 and 2) create a significant defensive weapon available to taxpayers who feel helpless to deal with overly zealous collection personnel. A Form 911 should always be considered whenever the IRS serves a levy. For example, wage levies invariably create hardships. Your defensive strategy should be formulated well in advance of the levy, however. Ideally, by the time the notice of intent to levy is issued, your client should be postured to deal with the IRS with one of the following: (1) an installment agreement, (2) bankruptcy, (3) an offer in compromise, or (4) a Form 911.

VIII. Notes

1. I.R.C. § 7811(a).
2. I.R.C. § 7811(f).
3. I.R.C. § 7811(a).
4. Treas. Reg. § 301.7811-1(a)(4).
5. Treas. Reg. § 301.7811-1(a)(4)(ii).
6. IRM 13.1.1.2.
7. IRM 13.1.
8. *Id.*
9. *Id.*
10. Treas. Reg. § 301.7811-1(c).
11. I.R.C. § 7811(b).
12. Treas. Reg. § 301.7811-1(a)(5).
13. IRM 13.1.18.2.
14. *Id.*
15. Treas. Reg. § 301.7811-1(b)(1). Note also that if a representative is filing the 911, a copy of his or her power of attorney, Form 2848, should also be attached.
16. Treas. Reg. § 301.7811-1(b)(2).
17. IRM 13.1.17.2.
18. Treas. Reg. § 301.7811.
19. *See* I.R.C. § 6502.
20. I.R.C. § 7811(d). *See also* Gore v. United States, 76 AFTR2d 95-5673 (Bankr. N.D. Ala. 1995).
21. Treas. Reg. § 301.7811-1(e)(4).
22. IRM 13.1.14.
23. I.R.C. § 7811(c).
24. I.R.C. § 7811(e).
25. Treas. Reg. § 301.7811-1(d).
26. IRM 13.1.
27. IRM 13.1.14.1.
28. IRM 13.1.21.1.2.
29. Nuttle v. Comm'r, 96-1 USTC ¶ 50,081 (10th Cir. 1995).
30. Inman v. Comm'r, 75 AFTR2d 727 (E.D. Cal. 1995).

Installment Agreements (IAs)

I. Background and History

A. When Should an Installment Agreement Be Used?

Approximately 17 percent of all taxpayers pay their taxes partially, late, or not at all. In the majority of cases where a taxpayer cannot pay his or her federal income tax in full, a monthly installment agreement is the remedy of choice. This is usually the case where the taxpayer is unable to qualify for or unwilling to undertake one of the following procedures:

1. Obtain a loan (from a bank or a relative) and pay the tax in full;
2. File for bankruptcy protection;
3. File an offer in compromise;[1] or
4. Convince the IRS to place his or her account in "collection suspense."[2]

B. History: The 1988 Act

Prior to the passage of the first taxpayer Bill of Rights Act in 1988, the use and availability of IAs were not uniform. The 1988 Act gave the IRS statutory authority to enter into written installment payment agreements with taxpayers and required the IRS to include in its notice of intent to levy a clear description of this potential solution.[3]

C. Authority for Agreements

The IRS has statutory authority to enter into an agreement with a taxpayer for the payment of his or her tax liability in installments. This authority is generally discretionary with the government and will only be invoked under circumstances where such an agreement will facilitate collection of the tax.[4] Note that, unless the liability is relatively small, there is no statutory or judicial mechanism to *force* the IRS to enter into an IA.

II. Termination and Modification

A. Duration (Term) of Agreement

Unless one of the exceptions occurs, an IA must remain in effect throughout its term.[5] It is effective from the day the IRS signs it to the day the agreement ends by its own terms.[6] Obviously the agreement also ends on the earlier of either the date the liability is paid in full or the collection statute of limitations expiration date.

B. *Grounds for Termination*

The IRS can abort a previously executed IA if such agreement was premised on inaccurate or incomplete information furnished by the taxpayer. Termination can also occur if the IRS has reason to believe that collection of the tax may be in "jeopardy."[7] The IRS may also alter, modify, or terminate an IA if it determines that a taxpayer's financial condition has significantly improved.[8]

C. *Events of Default*

The IRS has the authority to alter, modify, or terminate an existing agreement if any one of the following occurs:
1. Failure to pay an installment payment on its due date;
2. Failure to pay any *other* liability that the taxpayer may owe; or
3. Failure to furnish financial condition updates as may be requested by the IRS.[9]

Practitioners with clients who have an IA in effect, who have made all required payments, who are current on all subsequent taxes, and who have responded fully to all requests for information should respond vigorously to the IRS's threat to void the agreement. Note that the IRS may not terminate an IA on the grounds that the taxpayer's liability will not be paid in full before the statute of limitations on collections expires.[10]

D. *Notice Requirement for Termination*

Even though the IRS can terminate an agreement upon an event of default, it may not do so without prior notice. The IRS must first give the defaulting taxpayer thirty days' prior notice. That notice must include an explanation of the reasons for the IRS's termination or alteration of the agreement. Notice is not required, however, if the IRS believes that collection of the tax is in jeopardy.[11] Upon receiving this notice, the taxpayer may provide information showing that the reason for the modification is incorrect.[12]

E. *Administrative Review*

The IRS has established procedures for an independent review of IA terminations where the taxpayer requests such a review.[13] If the taxpayer disagrees with the IRS's decision to terminate an IA, an administrative review is initiated by calling the telephone number listed in the notice within thirty days of the date of the termination notice. If, after speaking with a manager, the dispute is still not resolved, the taxpayer may request an independent review in the IRS Appeals Office.[14]

This review procedure is similar to the appeal procedure available for rejected offers in compromise.[15] The Internal Revenue Manual (IRM) goes even further and provides that the taxpayer has a right to appeal a *rejection* of an IA as well as a termination thereof.[16]

F. *Taxpayer Requests for Modification*
A taxpayer may request that the terms of an IA be modified, and the IRS has discretion to do so if it determines that a taxpayer's financial condition has significantly changed.[17]

G. *Enforcement after Termination*
If the IRS terminates an IA and assuming all appeals are exhausted, it may thereafter pursue collection of the unpaid balance through all available legal means, including levy.

III. Forms Used

A. *Types of Agreements*
There are two major categories of IAs:
1. Agreements entered into by the Automated Collection System (ACS) or the Service Center Collection Branch (SCCB); and
2. Written agreements on Form 433-D (Installment Agreement) and Form 2159 (Payroll Deduction Agreement).
Agreements falling into category #1, above, are neither negotiated face-to-face nor based on an in-depth examination of the taxpayer's financial condition. These agreements are confirmed in a letter from the IRS, signed only by the IRS. Agreements falling into category #2, above, are negotiated with an IRS employee who has done an extensive investigation of the taxpayer's financial circumstances.

B. *Installment Agreement Requests (Form 9465)*
The IRS has published Form 9465 for taxpayers to use in requesting an IA. It cannot be used if the taxpayer is already making installment payments for some other year or liability. If the Form 9465 request is prepared prior to filing the tax return in question, it should be attached to the front of the return. If the return is already filed or is being filed electronically, or the taxpayer is responding to a "balance due" notice, the Form 9465 is filed as a stand-alone form with the local IRS service center office.[18] Note that there is no statutory requirement that a request for an IA be in writing, although it is a good idea to put it in writing.[19]

C. *Negotiated Installment Agreements*
If the taxpayer is already dealing with a revenue officer, after the IRS's due diligence is complete, a Form 433-D is prepared as the written agreement for monthly installment payments. This form

sets forth the terms and duration of the agreement, as well as conditions that must be met by the taxpayer for the agreement not to be deemed "in default."

D. *Collection Information Statements*
Generally, unless the amount owed is small, the IRS will require the submission of a signed financial statement before it will enter into an IA. For this purpose the IRS will ask for the submission of a Form 433-A (personal financial statement), Form 433-B (business financial statement), or Form 433-F (wage earners). 433-B forms are necessary for proprietorships, corporations, partnerships, and the like. On these forms are listed assets, liabilities, and monthly income and expenses. All 433 forms are signed under penalties of perjury.

IV. Liens, Levies, Interest, and Penalties

A. *Actions by the IRS during the Period of the Agreement*
Entering into an IA will normally not preclude the IRS from taking certain actions, including issuing summonses.[20] Similarly, the agreement, even if approved, will not prevent any of the following actions:
1. The filing of a lien notice at the local courthouse;
2. Accrual of statutory interest on the unpaid balance; or
3. Accrual of the "underpayment" penalty.[21]

However, the IRS may not levy on a taxpayer's property or wages during the period of time that a request for a § 6159 installment agreement is pending. Nor may a levy be attempted during the thirty days following a rejection by the IRS, plus the period during which any appeal is pending.[22] When the IRS receives a request for an IA, it must input a levy "freeze" code within twenty-four hours of receipt of the request. All that is required to have an effective request is (1) the identification number of the taxpayer, (2) the identification of the tax liability, and (3) a proposal of a monthly amount.[23] This is a *very* important benefit of requesting an IA as a defensive ploy.

B. *Withdrawal of Lien Notice*
Within the IRS's discretion, it may withdraw a notice of federal tax lien (NFTL) if it determines that the taxpayer has entered into an IA under § 6159, unless the agreement provides otherwise.[24] As a practical matter the IRS rarely does this, as it is not generally in the best interest of the government to do so.

C. *Levy Release*
It is mandatory, however, that the IRS release a levy if the taxpayer has entered into an IA under § 6159, unless the agreement provides otherwise.[25] The IRS is not required to release the levy if such release would jeopardize its secured status.[26]

D. *Trust Fund Penalty and Designation Rule*

The standard government form recites in the agreement that payments will be applied in the "best interest of the United States." Accordingly, taxpayers are not permitted to designate IA payments to the "trust fund" portion of payroll taxes.[27] This is one of the disadvantages of having an IA in place.

V. User Fees

A. The IRS has authority to impose a user fee on the taxpayer for entering into an IA. The amount of the fee ranges from $43 to $105, depending on the taxpayer's circumstances.[28] This provision is not in the Internal Revenue Code (I.R.C.), but is contained in the regulations under Title 31.[29] This fee is deducted from the first payment made under the agreement; it is not submitted with a Form 9465.[30]

B. The fee charged by the IRS for restructuring or reinstating an IA is only $24. This fee is payable by the taxpayer who requests a reinstatement.[31]

VI. Miscellaneous Provisions

A. *Mandatory Agreements*

If the amount of tax owed (*not* including interest and penalties) does not exceed $10,000, the IRS *must* agree to enter into an IA. However, this mandatory rule does not apply in the case of any one of the following within the prior five years:

1. Any prior failures to file a return;
2. Any prior failures to pay any tax when due;
3. Any prior IAs; or
4. Where the IRS determines that the taxpayer has the ability to pay in full.

A mandatory agreement will not be entered into if it stretches out the payments beyond three years. Additionally, the taxpayer must agree to comply with all provisions of the I.R.C. during the period of the agreement.[32]

Mandatory IAs are available only for income tax liability. Thus, estate, gift, employment, or excise tax liabilities are not eligible for this relief.[33]

B. *Conditional Agreements*

The IRS may require, as a condition of entering into an IA, that the taxpayer first extend the collection statute of limitations. The IRS may also require that the taxpayer authorize direct debit bank transfers as the method for making payment.[34]

C. *Execution of Agreement*

An IA is always in writing and is normally signed by both the taxpayer and a representative of the IRS.[35]

D. *Extension of Time for Paying Tax*

To be distinguished from the IA rules are the "payment extension" rules. In its discretion the IRS may extend the time for payment of any tax on a return for up to six months (twelve months in the case of estate tax). Likewise, the IRS may extend the time for paying a deficiency for up to eighteen months. No deficiency extension will be granted, however, if any part of the deficiency is due to fraud or negligence.[36]

E. *Deferral and Installment Payment of Estate Tax*

If the value of an interest in a closely held business exceeds 35 percent of the adjusted gross estate, the amount of the estate tax attributed to such interest may be paid out in installments. The first installment does not have to be paid until five years from the due date of the Form 706, and the period of the installment payments can be up to ten years.[37]

F. *Fast-Track Approval*

The IRS has streamlined its approval process for IAs and will also grant installments to taxpayers who agree to pay a balance due of $25,000 or less within a five-year period. Under the streamlined process, agreements do not require the collection manager's approval or the filing of liens. Taxpayers may ask for an installment plan when they file their return. Form 9465 (Installment Agreement Request) should be attached to the front of the tax return.[38]

G. *Interactive Calculator*

An interactive calculator is available through the IRS website[39] to help taxpayers figure their monthly payment amount. Taxpayers who qualify for the streamlined process can find out how long their payments would last. Other taxpayers can compare their monthly expenses to the amounts allowed under the IRS's Collection Financial Standards to determine their appropriate tax payment amount.[40]

H. *Form of Payment*

Each month the taxpayer's payment to the IRS can be made by a payroll deduction (Form 2159), by direct debit from the taxpayer's bank account, or by the taxpayer mailing a check.

I. *Reminder Notices*

If an IA is negotiated, the IRS inputs the agreement into its computer system and thereafter mails out reminder notices until the liability is fully satisfied. Reminder notices are also mailed out if a Form 9465 request has been approved.[41]

J. *Date of Monthly Payment*

The IRS will normally let you select the particular day of the month you would like to make each monthly payment.

K. *Annual Statement*

The IRS is required to provide any taxpayer who has an IA in effect with an annual statement setting forth the taxpayer's beginning of the year balance, all payments made during the year, and the remaining balance at year's end. The IRS must begin providing the IA statements no later than July 1, 2000.[42]

L. *Payment Application—Ordering Rule*

If a written IA is entered into, there is a provision that states that "all payments will be applied in the best interest of the United States." Thus, even if a taxpayer specifically designates that payments are to be applied in a particular manner or to particular years, the IRS has the right to, and will, apply the payments to the oldest year(s) open under the collection statute of limitations.[43]

M. *Statute of Limitations Suspension*

Curiously, neither § 6161 nor § 6159 provides for the suspension of either the assessment or collection limitations as a precondition of or during the course of either extended payment period. Note, however, that regulations have been promulgated effective December 18, 2002, that do provide for suspension of the collection statute of limitations during the period that a proposed IA is pending.[44] This is also in accordance with a careful reading of the statute. But keep in mind that once the agreement has been entered into, the collection statute continues to run.

Practice Tip

The planning opportunity for IAs is clear, subject to the regulatory caveat: If there is a short period left in the collection period, then obviously an installment agreement is preferable to one of the other defensive plans.

N. *Underpayment Penalty*

Note that the failure to pay penalty is reduced by one-half during the period of time that an IA is in place.[45]

O. *Partial Payment Installment Agreements (PPIAs)*

If full payment cannot be achieved before the Collection Statute Expiration Date (CSED), and taxpayers have some ability to pay, the Service can enter into a Partial Payment Installment Agreement (PPIA). This means that if the taxpayer complies in full with the IA, the entire unpaid liability will not be fully paid within the I.R.C. § 6502 period. The American Jobs Creation Act of 2004 amended I.R.C. § 6159 to provide this authority.

CSEDs may *not* be extended during regular IAs. CSEDs may be extended (via Form 900) during PPIAs only in special circumstances such as defaults.[46]

VII. Notes

1. I.R.C. § 7122.
2. Also known as CNC (currently not collectible).
3. Bill of Rights Act § 6234(a), adding I.R.C. § 6159.
4. I.R.C. § 6159; IRM 5.14.
5. I.R.C. § 6159(b)(1).
6. Treas. Reg. § 301.6159-1(c)(3).
7. I.R.C. § 6159(b)(2); *see generally* I.R.C. § 6861 (for "jeopardy" definitions and procedures).
8. Treas. Reg. § 301.6159-1(e)(2).
9. I.R.C. § 6159(b)(4).
10. CCA 200040007.
11. I.R.C. § 6159(b)(5).
12. Treas. Reg. § 301.6159-1(e)(4).
13. I.R.C. § 6159(e).
14. Treas. Reg. § 301.6159-1(e)(5).
15. I.R.C. § 7122(e).
16. IRM 5.1.9.1.
17. Treas. Reg. § 301.6159-1(e)(3).
18. Per Form 9465 instructions.
19. Seagrave v. United States, 2007-01 USTC ¶ 50,479 (7th Cir. 2007).
20. Treas. Reg. § 301.6159-1(d).
21. Form 9465 instructions.
22. I.R.C. § 6331(k)(2).
23. IRM 5.14.1.3.
24. I.R.C. § 6323(j)(1)(B).
25. I.R.C. § 6343(a)(1)(C); IRM 5.10.2.6.
26. I.R.C. § 6343(a)(1).
27. IRM 5.14.7.5.
28. *See* Form 9465 instructions.
29. 31 U.S.C. § 9701; 31 C.F.R. § 300.0, 300.1, 300.2.
30. Form 9465 instructions.
31. 31 C.F.R. § 300.2.
32. I.R.C. § 6159(c).
33. *Id.*
34. Treas. Reg. § 301.6159-1(b)(1).
35. Treas. Reg. § 301.6159-1(b)(2).
36. I.R.C. § 6161.
37. *See* I.R.C. § 6166 and the regulations thereunder.
38. I.R.S. News Release IR-1999-36, Apr. 7, 1999.
39. Visit http://www.irs.gov, then search for "installment agreement" and follow the links.
40. IR-1999-69.
41. Form 9465 instructions.

42. Act § 3506, IRS Restructuring and Reform Act of 1998 (Pub. L. No. 105-206).
43. Bierhaalder v. Comm'r, 70 T.C.M. (CCH) 43 (1995).
44. Treas. Reg. § 301.6331-4(c).
45. I.R.C. § 6651(h).
46. IRM 5.12.2.2.

Offers in Compromise

I. Introduction

A. Background Information

What does a taxpayer do when he or she simply cannot pay an IRS debt? There are a number of options available to settle or compromise a tax liability when funds are not available. Sometimes even an installment agreement will not suffice to effectively reduce the liability. And, of course, the IRS has little to gain by forcing a taxpayer into insolvency or bankruptcy.

The IRS, like any other business, will encounter situations where an account receivable cannot be collected in full or there is a dispute as to what is owed. It is an accepted business practice to resolve these collection and liability issues through a compromise. Additionally, the compromise process is available to provide delinquent taxpayers with a fresh start toward future compliance with tax laws.[1]

The position of the IRS is that it will accept an offer in compromise (OIC) when it is unlikely that the tax liability can be collected in full and the amount offered reasonably reflects collection potential. An OIC is a legitimate alternative to declaring a case as currently not collectible or entering into a protracted installment agreement. The goal is to achieve collection of what is potentially collectible at the earliest possible time and at the least cost to the government.[2]

As part of its Compliance 2000 initiative, the IRS issued Policy Statement P-5-100 in early 1992 to announce a new policy aimed at OICs. At the time, IRS officials professed that the government was adopting a more businesslike approach to collecting accounts that were considered not collectible or had extended installment agreement payments that did not even cover accruals. This effort was directed at bringing more taxpayers back into the taxpaying system by the year 2000.

B. Statutory Authority

The statutory authority for compromising a federal tax liability is in I.R.C. § 7122, which states, in part, "The Secretary [IRS] may compromise any civil or criminal case arising under the internal revenue

325

laws."[3] The treasury secretary's authority to compromise tax liability has been delegated to revenue officers of the IRS's Collection function as well as other specifically designated OIC examiners in campuses located in New York and Tennessee.[4]

C. *Offer Forms*

An OIC can be submitted only on a form prescribed by the IRS.[5] This Form 656 must be submitted on original IRS forms; a photocopy of a form will not suffice. For this purpose, the most recent version of Form 656 is used.[6] In doubt as to collectibility cases, a signed Form 433-A(OIC) must also be attached (see discussion later in section IV). All required supporting documentation should be included with your package as instructed by the 433 form. None of the standard forms may be stricken or altered, and the forms must be signed under penalty of perjury.

The offer form should indicate all the liabilities to be covered by the compromise, the legal grounds for compromise, the amount the taxpayer proposes to pay, and the payment terms.

An OIC Form 656 may be signed by a representative, but only if he or she holds a valid power of attorney specifically authorizing the execution of an OIC. Otherwise, the taxpayer must sign.[7]

D. *Closing Agreement Distinguished*

The difference between a compromise agreement (§ 7122) and a closing agreement (§ 7121) is that the latter is the appropriate settlement vehicle where the underlying proposed deficiency is being contested either administratively or in litigation. An OIC, on the other hand, is used exclusively on a postassessment basis.

E. *Processability*

After initial submission of an OIC, the IRS will make a determination as to whether it is processable. The initial submission of an OIC will be summarily rejected if the proponent is not in compliance with current filing and paying requirements. Noncompliance by a controlled corporation, however, will not prevent the processing of a shareholder's OIC.[8] To ensure processability, all required attachments to the Form 656 should be included.

Offers that are not processable are returned by the IRS to the proponent with no appeal rights.

II. Conclusive Nature

A. *General Rules*

All questions as to the entire liability of the taxpayer are conclusively settled when an OIC is accepted.[9] That is, once a compromise is reached, the parties are bound by its terms. If the taxpayer fails to fulfill his or her obligations, however, the compromise is no longer binding on the IRS, which may then proceed to collect the full original liability.

B. *Reopening of an Offer*

After an OIC has been accepted, the case may not be reopened except upon a showing of one of the following:
1. Falsification or concealment of assets by the taxpayer or
2. Mutual mistake of a material fact sufficient to cause a contract to be reformed or set aside.[10]

C. *Litigation Subsequent to an OIC*

In the absence of fraud or mutual mistake of fact, an OIC is valid and binding. It, therefore, prevents the proponent from thereafter filing a refund suit for the years covered by the OIC.[11] Moreover, a taxpayer may not litigate a trust fund liability (§ 6672) after entering into an OIC and collateral agreement.[12]

D. *Refunds*

As a condition of the offer, proponents are required to forfeit any tax refunds that may be due (including interest) on any return for any period extending through the calendar year in which the IRS accepts the offer. However, this condition does not apply if the offer is based on doubt as to liability.[13]

III. Legal Opinions and Public Records

A. If a liability is compromised, an opinion of general counsel is required to be placed on file with the IRS. This opinion must contain information regarding the following:
1. The amount of tax originally and subsequently assessed;
2. The amount of interest and penalties assessed;
3. The amount paid in accordance with the terms of the compromise; and
4. The reasons for recommending acceptance of the offer.[14]

IRS Counsel has been delegated the responsibility to provide legal opinions as to OICs. A revenue officer or appeals officer must always get IRS Counsel to approve an agreement before an official acceptance letter is sent out.[15] An opinion of chief counsel is *not* required, however, if the amount of the unpaid tax, etc., is less than $50,000.[16]

Copies of the abstract and statement and the attached narrative report for each accepted OIC are available for inspection and copying in the local IRS office where the taxpayer resides.[17]

IV. Grounds for Submission of an Offer

A. *General Rules*

An OIC may be based only upon one of the following three grounds:
1. Doubt as to liability (DATL);
2. Doubt as to collectibility (DATC); or[18]
3. Effective tax administration (ETA).[19]

Effective in 1999, temporary regulations were issued allowing OICs to be submitted based on economic hardship, even though the taxpayer may have equity in assets that could be seized and sold to satisfy the tax.[20] This is known as the "effective tax administration" or "ETA" provision.

B. *Doubt as to Liability (DATL)*

DATC means, "I owe the tax but I can't pay all of it." DATL means, "I don't think I owe the tax." If the OIC is being filed based on DATL, this is normally an examination function.[21] If a deficiency has been settled administratively, or resolved in litigation, a compromise on the basis of DATL will normally be rejected. OICs based on DATL are rare because there are so many other procedures to challenge an assessment or proposed assessment.

C. *Doubt as to Collectibility (DATC)*

1. *General Policy for Acceptance*

An OIC based on DATC generally will be considered acceptable if it is unlikely that the tax can be collected in full and the offer reasonably reflects the amount the IRS could collect through enforcement means.[22]

2. *Forms to Be Attached*

If an OIC is based on DATC, a Form 433-A(OIC) or Form 433-B(OIC) must be signed and submitted with the Form 656. The Form 656 also contains instructions and a worksheet for taxpayers to use in calculating asset and income numbers they would put on the 433 forms. A revenue officer or offer examiner will be assigned to investigate the OIC and may require additional financial information during the investigation.[23]

3. During the investigation of a DATC offer, the IRS will consider the following factors in evaluating the OIC:

   a. The past, present, and future income of the taxpayer; and

   b. The taxpayer's age, health, and educational background.

4. *Asset Valuation*

In DATC offers, the starting point in an analysis of the OIC is the value of the assets minus the encumbrances that have priority over the federal tax lien. Ordinarily, the "quick sale" value (QSV) of the property is used.[24] The QSV is essentially the amount that could be realized when financial pressures cause the taxpayer to sell in a short period of time. Generally, the QSV is an intermediate value between a forced sale and fair market value (FMV). In practice, this value is approximately 80 to 85 percent of FMV. For OIC purposes, the IRS can accept realty values somewhere between QSV and minimum bid prices. QSV is defined as something more than "forced sale value" but not less than 75 percent of FMV.[25]

5. Net realizable equity (NRE) is a minimum compromise amount. To arrive at the NRE of an asset, any encumbrances superior to the IRS liens must be subtracted from the QSV. Therefore, a practitioner's objective should be to ascertain the minimum acceptable offer (generally based on the assets' NRE) and seek its acceptance.

6. In addition to the amount offered being in excess of the equity in a taxpayer's assets, giving due regard to present and future earnings, the proponent of the OIC must be in compliance with all paying and filing requirements for periods not included in the OIC, including estimated tax payments, federal income tax deposits, and so on.

7. Taxpayers are considered to have certain resources. For example, even if a spouse is not liable to pay the tax, the spouse's assets are considered, as well as the ability to borrow from friends or relatives.

8. In determining assets to support the amount of the offer, there are no exempt assets except those exempt from levy as enumerated in the I.R.C.[26]

9. In the case of partnership employment tax liability, the IRS will consider assets of the partnership *plus* the assets of each *general* partner.[27]

10. With regard to a taxpayer's income, the IRS will consider income in excess of necessary expenses over a specified period. For this purpose, the monthly income analysis on Form 433-A(OIC) is used. The formula is simple: the excess monthly income is multiplied by the number of months. The resulting answer is then added to the equity in nonexempt assets to arrive at the amount offered. For a one-time cash payment offer, the number of months is discounted to a present value computation depending on the current underpayment interest rate being charged by the IRS. The IRM contains tables for determining this discount factor.[28]

11. *Future Income*
    The IRS also takes into account the amount that can be collected from future income. In evaluating the future income prospects, the following taxpayer attributes will be considered: age, health, education, experience, profession or trade, and past and present income.[29] There have even been cases in which the IRS will attempt to arbitrarily determine an earning capacity even if the taxpayer is

unemployed. If the taxpayer is employed, the investigating officer will simply take the income information directly from the taxpayer's most recent pay stub.

In the case of self-employed taxpayers with fluctuating income, the IRS generally uses an average of the last three years of income. For cash offers (payable within five months), the monthly disposable income is projected over twelve months. For short-term deferred offers (payable within six to twenty-four months), such income is projected over twenty-four months. The deferred payment option which allows payment over the life of the statute is no longer available. With implementation of the twelve- and twenty-four-month multipliers, the maximum number of months for a periodic payment offer cannot exceed twenty-four months.[30]

A taxpayer's ability to pay may change during the period the OIC is being considered because expenses or debts may increase or decrease. Therefore, the monthly amount may have to be adjusted as of a future date.[31]

Practice Tip

Refinance vehicles using renewable loans with no fixed monthly payments.

---

12. *Necessary Expenses*

   In determining necessary expenses in the excess cash flow component of an OIC, the IRS now for the most part uses national and local guidelines.[32] In addition to items covered by local and national guidelines, the IRS will allow other "necessary" expenses as well. These include dependent care, taxes, health care, court-ordered payments, involuntary deductions, secured debt payments, union dues, and tax professional fees.[33]

13. *Documents and Evidence*

   In evaluating and investigating DATC offers, the revenue officer will typically ask for the submission of a number of documents. These documents include, but are not limited to, the following:
   a. Copies of the last three income tax returns
   b. Copies of the last several months' bank statements
   c. List and current value of all securities
   d. Statement from any life insurance companies indicating cash values of policies, if any
   e. Deeds and land contracts for any realty owned
   f. Copies of titles of all vehicles and similar personalty
   g. On loans with pledged collateral, copies from lending institutions of any mortgage or loan balances

h. Inventory of contents of safe deposit boxes
i. List of business assets, including inventory
j. List of accounts receivable, with aging analysis
k. Full consumer credit report (Note: The IRS will obtain this directly from the credit-reporting agencies.)

D. *Effective Tax Administration*
The IRS may compromise a liability to promote effective tax administration where it determines that, although collection in full could be achieved, collection of the full liability would cause the taxpayer economic hardship. Economic hardship is defined as the inability to pay reasonable basic living expenses.[34]

V. Acceptance, Rejection, and Withdrawal

A. *Rejection*
When a Form 656 is first received by the IRS, it is first subjected to an initial scrutiny to determine whether the OIC is "processable." If it is not processable (if, for example, there is no Form 433 attached), the 656 will be summarily rejected and returned to the proponent. If the 656 is processable, the proponent-taxpayer is notified and an investigation process begins. Depending on the workload of the IRS, this process may be delayed by several months.

If the proponent-taxpayer has assets subject to seizure (levy) by the IRS that approximately equal or exceed the federal income tax liability, the OIC almost certainly will be rejected. Rejection does not occur until the IRS formally rejects the offer. Mere abandonment of consideration of the OIC does not constitute rejection. In the event that an OIC is rejected by the IRS, the taxpayer is required to be promptly notified in writing. Frivolous offers or offers submitted for the purpose of delaying payment of tax are immediately rejected.[35]

If a taxpayer does not offer enough money, rejection is not automatic. He or she will be contacted by the investigating revenue officer, who will give him or her an opportunity to adjust the amount offered. In determining the amount of money to offer, it is suggested that the OIC worksheet in the instructions be completed to serve as the basis for the offer amount. This is referred to as the reasonable collection potential (RCP).

If the proponent-taxpayer and the investigating officer cannot come to terms on what should be an acceptable offer, the IRS will issue a nonacceptance letter offering the taxpayer a right to appeal. Assuming the revenue officer has done an investigation, current IRS policy is not to reject the OIC with no appeal rights. Offers returned for lack of documentation are also subject to independent review.[36] The appeal process requires the preparation of a protest that must be submitted to the OIC examiner within thirty days from the date of the nonacceptance letter. The examiner will then forward the case file to the nearest Appeals Office, where it will be assigned to a settlement officer who will schedule an appeals conference.

B. *Acceptance*

If the IRS determines that a taxpayer's resources and future available income are less than the amount being offered, an OIC is likely to be accepted. Acceptance of an OIC will require the taxpayer to fully comply with all filing and paying requirements of the law for five years. If the taxpayer does not comply with this provision, the offer will be considered in default.[37]

An OIC is considered to be accepted only when the proponent thereof is notified in writing.[38] After the revenue officer or appeals officer has indicated that he or she will accept the offer, it still takes another thirty to forty days to achieve managerial and district counsel approval. If an OIC is accepted, this information is public record and may be disclosed to members of the general public.[39]

Federal tax liens will remain in place until final payment is made under the accepted offer.

Interest does not accrue from the date of acceptance of the OIC to the date of final payment.[40]

C. *Withdrawal*

An OIC may be withdrawn by the proponent thereof at any time prior to its acceptance.[41] If an offer is withdrawn or rejected, the amount tendered with the OIC, including all installments paid, is refunded *without* interest, unless the taxpayer has agreed that the amount tendered is to be applied to the liability with respect to which the offer was submitted.[42]

VI. Collateral Agreements

As a condition to acceptance of an OIC, a taxpayer may be required to enter into a collateral agreement. (Note: A collateral agreement is generally used to establish basis for depreciable property. Collateral agreements are used when considered useful to express the understanding of the parties. They do not achieve statutory finality.) A taxpayer may also be required to post security to protect the government's interests.[43]

Collateral agreements are typically used when a significant increase in income is expected, but are not used for windfalls such as winning the lottery.[44]

The IRS may demand a collateral agreement in the form of a Form 2261, Future Income Agreement. Future income agreements are usually for five years, but can be shorter or longer.

VII. Statute of Limitations Issues

A. *General Waiver Rule*
No OIC can be accepted unless the taxpayer waives the running of the statutory period of limitations (S/L) on both or either assessment or collection of the tax liability involved for the period during which the offer is pending, or the period during which any installment remains unpaid, and for one year thereafter.[45] This includes the period of time the offer is being considered by IRS Appeals.[46]

B. *IRS Authority*
The S/L period is not suspended until an authorized IRS employee signs and dates the Form 656.[47] This means that if the OIC is rejected as not being processable, the S/L is not tolled. The IRS has the burden of proving a waiver of the S/L.[48]

C. *Contract Rules*
A waiver of the S/L in OIC cases is a unilateral waiver and is not governed by contract rules.[49]

D. *Effect of Withdrawal*
A withdrawal of an OIC restarts the S/L clock.[50] The effective date of a withdrawal is not when the taxpayer notifies the IRS of the withdrawal; instead, it is effective when the IRS issues a withdrawal acknowledgment.[51]

E. *Planning Consideration*
If the ten-year collection S/L is about to expire, then a preferable alternative may be not to file the OIC but, instead, to simply wait out the time.

VIII. Criminal Issues

A. *Justice Department Jurisdiction*
If a case has been referred to the attorney general (U.S. Justice Department) for prosecution or defense, the authority for compromising a tax liability shifts from the IRS to the Department of Justice (DOJ).[52] At the moment of referral to the DOJ, the IRS's Collection function loses jurisdiction to make a compromise.

B. *Compromise of Criminal Liability*
A criminal liability can be compromised only if it involves a violation of a regulatory provision of the I.R.C. and then only if the violation was not deliberately committed with intent to defraud.[53]

C. *Criminal Immunity*
An agreement with the government for immunity from criminal prosecution will not compromise a civil tax liability.[54]

D. *False Form 656*

The penalty for falsifying information, or concealing a taxpayer's property, on Form 656 is as much as $100,000 ($500,000 for a corporation) or three years of imprisonment.[55]

E. *Civil Fraud*

A prior finding of civil fraud in reference to the underlying tax liability most likely will not preclude the filing and acceptance of an OIC.

IX. Miscellaneous Provisions

A. *Bankruptcy Alternatives*

An OIC may be preferable to bankruptcy for the following reasons:
1. The taxpayer may not be eligible for bankruptcy discharge of the taxes for a variety of reasons.
2. The taxpayer may not want a bankruptcy to adversely affect his or her retail credit rating. Note that a bankruptcy filing stays on your credit report for ten years. An OIC, on the other hand, does not affect your credit rating. Note also that, while an OIC acceptance is technically public record, as a practical matter hardly anyone ever accesses these records.
3. Therefore, when the IRS is the largest (or only) creditor, the filing of an OIC may be preferable to a bankruptcy.

If a tax deficiency has been determined and an OIC is filed before the date of assessment, it has no effect on the running of the 240-day period of 11 U.S.C. § 507(a).[56]

The threat of bankruptcy can be a very effective negotiating tool where it is obvious that the IRS would get less in a bankruptcy proceeding than what is being offered with the OIC.[57] Where part, but not all, of the tax is dischargeable, a possible option is to base an OIC solely on the nondischargeable portion of the tax.

Note that the IRS position is that an OIC may not be submitted while a taxpayer is in bankruptcy.[58] This policy is, however, at variance with a considerable amount of case law. Bankruptcy courts have uniformly ordered the IRS to receive and consider offers in compromise submitted by debtors in bankruptcy cases.[59]

B. *Remittance with an Offer and during Consideration Thereof*
1. Effective in 2006, lump sum offers must be accompanied by a cash payment equal to 20 percent of the amount offered. A lump sum offer is defined to mean any offer payable in five or fewer payments.[60]

> **Practice Tip**
>
> There is no reason one cannot designate the 20 percent lump sum payment as he or she wishes (I.R.C. § 7122(c)(2)(A)). Thus, it would be advantageous to designate that it be applied to the most recent year of liability in the event that the offer is ultimately rejected.

    2.   For periodic payment offers, the offer itself must be accompanied by the first monthly installment. Additionally, during the pendency of the offer, each monthly installment must be made. Failure to make such payments will result in the IRS treating the offer as having been withdrawn.[61]

    3.   The IRS is also permitted to waive any of the above payments for offers submitted by low-income taxpayers.[62]

    4.   Installment payments during OIC consideration and the 20 percent lump sum prepayment are nonrefundable. No $150 user fee or 20 percent prepayment is necessary if it is a DATL OIC.[63]

    5.   The source of funding of a cash offer should always be indicated as a part of the Form 656. For example, bank loans, liquidation of assets, credit cards, and loans from friends or relatives are typical sources. If it is not so indicated, an investigating officer may request verification of the source.[64] A taxpayer should *not* indicate "to be determined" as a source.

  C. *User Fee*

      Effective November 1, 2003, the IRS has imposed a $150 user fee whenever an OIC is submitted. A check payable to "United States Treasury" must accompany the Form 656. Lower income taxpayers are exempt from the fee as are taxpayers submitting offers based solely on DATL. Other taxpayers may be eligible to have the fee applied to the amount of their offer. The rationale behind such a fee is to discourage the filing of frivolous offers. If a taxpayer withdraws his or her OIC, the fee will not be refunded. The IRS will also keep the fee if the offer is rejected or is returned as nonprocessable. No fee will be charged for resubmitted offers.[65]

  D. *Substitute or Informal Compromises*

    1. *General Rules*

        Informal attempts at reaching a compromise will always fail; the technical requirements of § 7122 and the regulations thereunder must be followed to the letter. That is to say, § 7122 is the exclusive method of compromising a tax liability.[66]

2. *Check Endorsements*

The negotiation of a check will not create an agreement binding on the IRS.[67] Closing agreements and compromises are the exclusive vehicles for settling claims with the IRS. Anything else will fail. Therefore, putting a notation on the back of a check to the IRS, to the effect that negotiating the check will constitute full payment, is ineffective despite the fact that this technique may constitute "accord and satisfaction" under the Uniform Commercial Code.[68]

E. *Effect of Judgment against a Taxpayer*

If the IRS has obtained a judgment against a taxpayer[69] the remedy of an OIC is unavailable.[70]

F. *Penalties*

Note that specific penalties can be compromised separately from the underlying tax and interest.[71]

G. *Stay of Collection*

There is a very important procedural safeguard provided by OICs. By statute, no levy may be made by the IRS during the period that an OIC is "pending." This period includes not only the investigation period but also, in the event of an adverse determination, the period for appeal as well. The word "pending" means a period beginning on the date the IRS accepts the OIC as processable.[72] This statutory provision does not, however, mandate the release of levies preexisting on the date of the offer.[73]

H. *Amount and Timing of Offer*

There is no statutory authority for compromising an unassessed liability; therefore, a taxpayer must wait until after the tax is assessed before filing his or her OIC.[74]

I. *Periodic Payment Offer*

A periodic payment offer is payable in six or more installments. It must be accompanied by the payment of the amount of the first proposed installment and additional installments must be paid while the offer is being evaluated by the IRS. The total installments may not exceed twenty-four months.[75]

J. *Marital Issues*

If a joint tax return was filed, either of the spouses may submit an OIC to compromise just his or her portion of a joint liability. However, in this case the proponent will be asked to execute a "co-obligor" agreement before the offer will be accepted.

If one of the spouses is an innocent spouse, the IRS will nevertheless look at the economic capacity of the innocent spouse in arriving at an acceptable OIC. In community property states, both spouses' income and assets must be considered unless there is a valid prenuptial agreement.

If part of the liability (e.g., 941 tax) is not joint, then a husband and wife may not submit a joint offer. In that case a separate Form 656 must be submitted for the nonjoint liability.[76]

K. *Verbal Offers Forbidden*
Section 7122 is facially ambiguous. It does not specify that compromise agreements must be in writing, nor does it explicitly sanction oral settlements. Nevertheless, the IRS regulation requiring written OICs is generally upheld.[77]

L. *"Horse Trading"*
The proponent's initial offer is not usually accepted. There is usually negotiation of the terms of the offer when an inability to pay is demonstrated.

M. *Inconsistency among Different Districts*
In past years the reception accorded an OIC differed depending on the district office in which it was submitted. To expedite processing and ensure consistency, OICs are now submitted to one of two processing centers, one in Memphis, Tennessee, and one in Brookhaven, New York.

N. *Subsequent Refunds*
Any refund subsequently due for any year covered by an OIC automatically goes toward payment of the compromised liability and may not be refunded to the taxpayer.

O. *Subsequent Default*
An accepted OIC constitutes an enforceable contract. One of the written provisions of that contract is that, for a period of five years, the proponent agrees to file all required tax returns and pay all taxes that come due. In the event of a default, the IRS has the right to reinstate the full amount originally compromised.

P. *Deemed Acceptance Rule*
By statute, if the IRS does not make a determination within two years of the submission of an OIC, the OIC is deemed accepted.[78]

X. Conclusion

In recent years the IRS has become somewhat more liberal in its acceptance of offers. On the offers that were accepted, the dollars accepted represented an average of 15 percent of the original liability. Nevertheless, there is still wide diversity across the country from district to district in acceptance rates. Additionally, the number of OICs has declined substantially as a result of the "20 percent down" rule. See earlier under section IX.B. for a discussion of this rule.

Whenever a client comes to you and is financially distressed because he or she cannot pay his or her tax liability even under the best of circumstances, then an OIC should always be considered as one of the alternatives, along with bankruptcy.

A practitioner must be careful, however, in not using the OIC provisions solely to delay collection action by the IRS.

XI. Notes

1. IRM 5.8.1.1.3.
2. *Id.*
3. I.R.C. § 7122(a).
4. *See* Delegation Order No. 11 (Rev. 18), effective May 10, 1988.
5. Treas. Reg. § 301.7122-1(d).
6. A proponent should obtain the most recent version from the IRS website, http://www.irs.gov. Doubt as to liability offers are submitted on Form 656-L.
7. IRM 5.8.1.5.6.
8. CCA 200040006.
9. Treas. Reg. § 301.7122-1(e).
10. *Id.*
11. Waller v. United States, 91-1 USTC ¶ 50,288 (E.D. Cal. 1991).
12. Sprowles v. United States, 89-2 USTC ¶ 9467 (W.D. Ky. 1989).
13. IRM 5.8.6.4; Barkley v. Comm'r, 81 T.C.M. (CCH) 1552 (2001); Form 656, Item 8(g).
14. I.R.C. § 7122(b).
15. *See* IRM 5.8.8.12.
16. I.R.C. § 7122(b).
17. Treas. Reg. § 601.702(d)(8).
18. Treas. Reg. § 301.7122-1(b).
19. IRM 5.8.11.
20. IRM 5.8.1.1.2.
21. IRM 5.8.1.3.4.
22. Policy Statement P-5-100; Rev. Proc. 2003-71, 2003-36 I.R.B. 517.
23. IRM 5.8.5.3.1.
24. IRM 5.8.5.4.1.
25. *Id.*
26. *See* I.R.C. § 6334.
27. IRM 5.8.4.22.2.
28. *See* IRM 5.8.5.
29. IRM 5.8.5.20.
30. IRM 5.8.5.25.
31. IRM 5.8.5.20.
32. See Publication 1854 for an explanation of these guidelines and for more explanations. The current guidelines can also be downloaded from the Internet at http://www.irs.gov.
33. IRM 5.8.5.2.

34. *Id.*
35. Treas. Reg. § 301.7122-1(f)
36. IRM 5.8.7.7.3.
37. IRM 5.8.9.3.
38. Treas. Reg. § 301.7122-1(e).
39. I.R.C. § 6103(k)(1).
40. *See* IRM 5.8.1.11.
41. Treas. Reg. § 301.7122-1(d)(3).
42. IRM 5.8.7.4.1.
43. Treas. Reg. § 301.7122-1(e).
44. Treas. Reg. § 7122-1(e)(2).
45. Treas. Reg. § 301.7122-1(i).
46. IRM 5.8.10.7.
47. IRM 5.8.10.8.
48. United States v. McGee, 93-2 USTC ¶ 50,406 (9th Cir. 1993).
49. United States v. McGoughey, 93-1 USTC ¶ 50,010 (7th Cir. 1992).
50. *Id.*
51. United States v. Donovan, 04-1 USTC ¶ 50,189 (N.D. Ohio 2004).
52. I.R.C. § 7122(a).
53. *See* IRM 5.8.1.3.1.
54. Finch v. Comm'r, 66 T.C.M. (CCH) 1030 (1993).
55. I.R.C. § 7206(5).
56. Aberl v. United States, 96-1 USTC ¶ 50,151 (6th Cir. 1996).
57. See the discussion in IRM 5.8.10.2.
58. IRM 5.8.10.2.1.
59. *See, e.g., In re* Holmes, 2003-02 USTC ¶ 50,685 (Bankr. M.D. Ga. 2003).
60. I.R.C. § 7122(c)(1)(A); *see also* I.R.S. News Release 2006-106.
61. I.R.C. § 7122(c)(1)(B).
62. I.R.C. § 7122(c)(2)(C).
63. I.R.S. News Release 2006-106.
64. IRM 5.8.4.12.
65. I.R.S. News Release 2003-99.
66. Overseas Inns S.A. P.A. v. United States, 90-2 USTC ¶ 50,506 (5th Cir. 1990).
67. Brown v. Comm'r, 67 T.C.M. (CCH) 2162 (1994); Whitaker v. Comm'r, 67 T.C.M. (CCH) 2408 (1994).
68. Bear v. Comm'r, 64 T.C.M. (CCH) 1430 (1992).
69. Treas. Reg. § 301.6502-1(a)(1).
70. IRM 5.8.1.3.1.
71. Treas. Reg. § 301.7122-1(c).
72. I.R.C. § 6331(k)(1).
73. United States v. Ryals, 99 AFTR2d 2007-1419 (11th Cir. 2007).
74. IRM 5.8.1.5.1.
75. IRM 5.8.1.9.4.
76. *See* Form 656 instructions.
77. Boulez v. Comm'r, 87-1 USTC ¶ 9177 (Fed. Cir. 1987).
78. I.R.C. § 7122(f).

Tax Issues in Bankruptcy

I. Background and Introduction

A. Goals and Rationale of Bankruptcy

In seeking relief under the Bankruptcy Code (U.S. Code, Title 11), an individual has one of two main goals: (1) the reorganization of his or her financial affairs, or (2) the orderly liquidation of his or her nonexempt assets for distribution to creditors.

In either instance, the debtor is seeking to obtain a fresh start from his or her dischargeable debts. While debts are not guaranteed a discharge, one of the primary purposes of bankruptcy is to free the individual from the burden of debts so that he or she can face the world afresh or reduce debts to a level that will give the individual or his or her business an opportunity to prosper.[1]

Bankruptcy courts are courts of equity, and they have the power to adjust claims to avoid injustice or unfairness.[2]

B. Operative Chapters

There are three primary operative chapters in the Federal Bankruptcy Code. They are Chapter 7 (straight liquidation followed by discharge),[3] Chapter 11 (business reorganization rehabilitation),[4] and Chapter 13 (individual "wage earner" reorganization).[5]

C. Voluntary versus Involuntary

Bankruptcy cases are commenced either voluntarily by the debtor or involuntarily by three or more creditors. A voluntary case is commenced with the filing of a petition in bankruptcy court involving Chapter 7, 11, or 13.[6]

D. Legislative History

The rules enacted in the Bankruptcy Reform Act of 1978 regarding the determination of tax liability in bankruptcy proceedings were reconciled with the provisions of the I.R.C. regarding assessment and collection procedures by the Bankruptcy Tax Act of 1980.[7]

E. *Requirement to Have a Trustee*

A trustee is required in Chapter 7 and 13 proceedings but not in Chapter 11.

II. Creation of Separate Entity

A. *General Rules*

Under bankruptcy law, the commencement of a liquidation or reorganization case involving an individual debtor creates an "estate" that consists of property formerly belonging to the debtor. The bankruptcy estate generally is administered by a trustee for the benefit of creditors, and it may derive its own income and incur its own expenditures. Meanwhile, the individual debtor is given a fresh start since wages earned by the individual after the commencement of the case and after-acquired property do not become part of the bankruptcy estate but belong to the individual, and certain property may be set aside as exempt.[8]

B. *Separate Taxable Entity*

The property held by a trustee in bankruptcy for an *individual* is treated as a separate taxable entity under Chapter 7 (liquidation) or Chapter 11 (reorganization) of Title 11 of the U.S. Code (U.S.C.).[9]

C. *Chapter 13 Cases*

A separate taxable entity is *not* created, however, if the case is brought under Chapter 13 of Title 11 of the U.S.C., which involves adjustment of debts of an individual with regular income.[10]

D. *Corporations or Partnerships*

No separate taxable entity is created in a bankruptcy where the debtor is a corporation or a partnership.[11]

E. *Bifurcation Issues*

A debtor can elect to split his or her year of petition filing into two separate taxable years.[12] By making this election, the tax liability attributable to the first short taxable year becomes an allowable claim against the bankruptcy estate. If the election is not made, the debtor's tax liability for the year in which the bankruptcy case commences is not allowable as a claim against the estate.[13]

III. Return Filing Requirements

A. *Fiduciary Reporting*

The trustee of an *individual* debtor (in Chapter 7 and 11 cases only) is required to file a fiduciary income tax return by preparing a Form

1041. However, a return need not be filed and no tax would be due if gross income for the year is less than $2,700. The tax year for which the fiduciary files a return begins on the date of the filing of the petition in bankruptcy. The return may be for a calendar year or a fiscal year.[14]

B. *Individuals*
A trustee in bankruptcy has no authority to file a return on Form 1040 for a bankrupt individual. The individual must file his or her own return.

C. *Partnerships*
The estates of bankrupt partnerships must file their returns on the U.S. Partnership Return of Income, Form 1065.

D. *Corporations*
A receiver, trustee in dissolution, trustee in bankruptcy, or assignee who, by order of a court, has possession of or holds title to all or substantially all the property or business of a corporation must file the income tax return for such corporation on Form 1120. A receiver, etc., must file the return on behalf of the corporation whether or not he or she is operating the property or business of the corporation. A receiver in charge of a corporation, such as a receiver in a mortgage foreclosure proceeding involving merely a small portion of its property, need not make the return.[15]

IV. Section 108 Exclusion Rule

A. *General Rules*
In defining gross income, the I.R.C. includes "income from discharge of indebtedness." However, some relief from this provision is allowed in the I.R.C. Gross income does not include any amount that (but for § 108) would be includible in gross income by reason of the discharge of debt of the taxpayer if the discharge occurs in a Title 11 case.[16]

B. *Tax Attributes*
The amount excluded from gross income in a Title 11 case reduces certain tax attributes of the taxpayer (such as net operating losses) (I.R.C. § 108(b)(1)).

C. *Order of Tax Attributes*
Tax attributes are reduced in the following order:
1. Net operating losses and carryovers;
2. Investment tax credit carryovers;
3. Capital loss carryovers;
4. Basis of assets; and
5. Foreign tax credit carryovers.[17]

D. *Special Rule for Corporations*

Insolvent companies now may pay debts with stock in certain cases without incurring debt-forgiveness income and without having to reduce "tax attributes," including loss carry-forwards.

V. Statute of Limitations Rules

A. *Assessment*

The running of the three-year "assessment" statute of limitations in bankruptcy cases is suspended for the period during which the IRS is prohibited (by reason of the bankruptcy) from assessing the tax and for sixty days thereafter.[18]

B. *Collection*

Similarly, the running of the ten-year "collection" statute of limitations[19] in bankruptcy cases is suspended until six months after the collection prohibition period.[20]

C. *Assets in Control or Custody of a Court*

The ten-year collection statute is likewise suspended as long as a taxpayer's assets are in the control or custody of any state or federal court, and for six months thereafter.[21]

D. *Effect of Notice Requirement*

Every bankruptcy receiver or trustee must give notice of his or her qualification as such to the IRS.[22] Unless prior notice has been given under the Bankruptcy Act, this notice must be given within ten days of appointment or authorization.[23] If the notice under I.R.C. § 6036 is not received by the IRS, the statute of limitations (for assessment) is suspended until the sooner of the following:

1. Thirty days after the notice is received; or
2. Two years after it otherwise would expire.[24]

VI. Taxes Dischargeable in Bankruptcy

A. *Overview*

Often the debtor believes that bankruptcy discharges him or her from all debts, including federal taxes. On the other hand, debtors' lawyers and accountants frequently advise that some debts and especially federal taxes are never discharged. Like most things, the truth lies somewhere between these two extremes.

Section 523(a) of the Bankruptcy Code enumerates the kinds of debts, including certain taxes, that are nondischargeable.

B. *General Three-Year Rule*

Income taxes incurred within three years of filing a bankruptcy petition are not dischargeable. In determining whether the three-year period has expired, one counts backward from the petition date.[25] For example, if a bankruptcy petition were to be filed on April 16, 2014, and all prior tax returns had been filed in a timely manner, all liabilities for 2010 and prior are dischargeable under the general rule.[26] Note that an approved filing extension[27] may place the last due date of the tax return within the three-year prepetition period, thereby rendering the tax liability non-dischargeable.[28] In the case of a conversion from a Chapter 11 or Chapter 13 case to a Chapter 7 case, the three-year period is determined from the earlier petition date and not the later conversion date.[29] It is not necessary for the IRS to file a proof of claim in bankruptcy cases where the tax is on returns filed within three years of the filing of the bankruptcy petition.[30]

C. *Two-Year Rule*
For tax returns that are not filed in a timely manner,[31] the Bankruptcy Code provides that tax liabilities reflected on returns that were filed late are not discharged if the return was filed within two years of the bankruptcy petition date.[32]

D. *240-Day Rule*
Obviously the IRS has the right to audit a tax return and propose additional tax deficiencies, interest, penalties, and so on. In such cases the examination, appeal, or court proceeding can extend beyond the three-year period. In those cases, the IRS is allowed 240 days following the "assessment"[33] date to file (perfect) its lien.[34] If IRS does not file its lien within the 240-day period, then its claim for unpaid taxes is treated as unsecured and subordinate to those of other secured creditors.[35] If an OIC[36] is submitted within such 240-day period, the running of the 240-day period is tolled.[37] The three-year rule and the 240-day rule are not mutually exclusive or alternative avenues to dischargeability. Both of these statutory tests must be satisfied before an income tax liability will become dischargeable.[38]

It is the debtor's responsibility to calculate properly the time period of the 240-day rule to make sure more than 240 days have passed from the assessment date. The 240-day period will also be tolled for any period during which an OIC is pending with the IRS and for thirty days thereafter.[39]

E. *Nonfiled and Fraudulent Returns*
For obvious policy reasons, there is no tax discharge where a return has not been filed[40] or if the return is false[41] or fraudulent.[42] If an individual debtor fails to file a required tax return, willfully tries to avoid paying taxes, or files a fraudulent return, the tax liability owing for that particular tax year or period is not discharged.

Moreover, if the IRS prepares a substitute for return (SFR) for the taxpayer, that is not considered a return filing for bankruptcy discharge purposes.[43] There is a dispute regarding whether the civil or criminal fraud standard should apply to the determination of fraud for bankruptcy purposes.

F. *Payroll Taxes and Trust Fund Liability[44] Cases*

An adjudication of bankruptcy will not discharge a debtor's liability to pay over taxes withheld from employees of a corporation or similar entity, regardless of the length of time such taxes remain unpaid. Congress's specific intent in this situation overrides the overall policy of the Bankruptcy Code of giving the debtor a fresh start.[45] See the "trust fund" liability provisions of I.R.C. § 6672.[46] The only exception to this rule is in a Chapter 13 proceeding.[47]

G. *Other Penalties*

If the tax to which the penalty relates is dischargeable, the penalty is dischargeable. If, however, the penalty does not relate to an underlying tax, discharge will not occur unless the transaction or event giving rise to the penalty occurred more than three years prior to the filing of the bankruptcy petition.[48]

H. *Interest[49]*

The filing of a bankruptcy petition stops the accrual of interest on unsecured tax claims. Prepetition interest is considered in the same category as the taxes to which the interest relates and, therefore, is not dischargeable if the underlying tax liabilities are not discharged.[50] Postpetition interest is not recoverable from the bankruptcy estate after the petition date unless a tax lien has been perfected.[51]

I. *Secured Tax Claims*

If a notice of federal tax lien (NFTL) was recorded prior to the petition date, the IRS will be a secured creditor and the priority rules of Bankruptcy Code § 507(a)(7) will be inapplicable to that secured claim.[52] If, however, an NFTL is not recorded before the petition date, the IRS's claims will be unsecured. Thus the "secret lien" against a debtor will be discharged if the underlying tax liability is a nonpriority dischargeable tax liability.

Although the underlying tax liability may be discharged, the tax lien itself will not be discharged if the IRS has recorded an NFTL against the debtor. Thus, the lien will survive a Chapter 7 discharge or Chapter 11 or 13 plan to the extent of the value of the collateral. Stated another way, the debtor's personal liability for the tax may be discharged, but the in rem claim against his or her assets is not discharged until paid in full to the extent of their FMV.

VII. Tax Court Proceedings

A. *Deficiency Notice*[53]

Most tax court proceedings must necessarily be preceded by the issuance of a notice of deficiency (ninety-day letter). The automatic stay following a bankruptcy petition does not preclude the IRS from issuing such a deficiency notice.[54] Similarly, a deficiency notice proposing additional tax liability is not precluded, following confirmation of a Chapter 11 plan involving the same year, under a res judicata theory.[55]

B. *Tax Court Petition*

To prevent assessment and collection of a proposed tax deficiency, a taxpayer must file a petition with the U.S. Tax Court within ninety days of the date of the statutory deficiency notice. However, in a Title 11 case, this ninety-day period is suspended for the period during which the debtor is prohibited by the Bankruptcy Code from filing the petition and for sixty days thereafter.[56] In the case of a receivership proceeding, however, no petition may be filed with the tax court after the appointment of a receiver.[57]

C. *Pending Tax Court Cases*

The IRS may present tax claims to a court before which a receivership (or a Title 11 bankruptcy) action is pending, despite the pendency of the debtor's proceedings in the U.S. Tax Court.[58]

VIII. Litigation and Choice of Forum

A. *General Rule*

The tax liability of bankrupts is often, if not usually, settled by a different tribunal than in the case of other taxpayers. Current bankruptcy law gives the bankruptcy court broad jurisdiction to determine tax questions unless the tax issue was previously adjudicated by a court of competent jurisdiction before the bankruptcy case commenced.[59]

B. *Res Judicata*

If IRS proposes a tax deficiency, such a deficiency (plus statutory additions or accruals) may be assessed on one of the following:
1. A debtor's "estate" in a Title 11 case or
2. On the debtor him- or herself, but only if the tax liability has become res judicata pursuant to a determination of the bankruptcy court.[60]

After a tax claim has been decided in the bankruptcy court, the liability may not be relitigated in either the tax court or the federal district court.

C. *Mutually Binding*

A bankruptcy court's decision regarding liability for a nondischargeable tax binds both the individual debtor as well as the IRS.

IX. Miscellaneous Provisions

A. *Immediate Assessment of Deficiency*
   Prior to the Bankruptcy Tax Act of 1980, the IRS could immediately assess prepetition tax deficiencies upon the institution of bankruptcy proceedings. Under the present statute, the IRS may do so only in the event that a receiver is appointed in receivership proceedings.[61] Moreover, bankruptcy judges do not have the power to appoint a receiver in a Title 11 case. They are limited to appointment of a trustee when needed.[62]

B. *Payment Required after Receivership*
   After the termination of a receivership proceeding (non–Title 11), any unpaid tax that is "allowed" by the court must be paid immediately upon notice and demand from the IRS.[63]

C. *Extension of Time to Pay Taxes*
   The IRS may grant an extension of time for payment of a tax claim allowed by a bankruptcy court.[64]

D. *Proceedings in Equity*
   Claims for taxes, interest, and so on, may be collectible in equity or under other provisions of law although no claim was allowed in the bankruptcy proceedings because, for example, such items were not included in a proof of claim filed in the proceedings, or no proof of claim was filed.[65]

E. *Waiver of Certain Penalties*
   No underpayment[66] or underestimate[67] penalties will be imposed on a taxpayer involved in a bankruptcy proceeding where the tax was incurred by the bankrupt estate and the failure occurred pursuant to an order of the court finding probable insufficiency of funds to pay administrative expenses.[68]

F. *Effect of Nonfiling of Tax Lien*
   Until a tax lien is filed of record (i.e., perfected) it is considered to be inchoate, and is subject to being subordinated to other secured claims, to wit, security interest, judgment liens, and so on.[69] Where no lien has been filed, the IRS's claim is either "unsecured" or "unsecured priority" depending on the date of assessment. If a lien has been filed, the IRS is either a "secured" or an "unsecured" creditor depending on whether the debtor has sufficient property to secure the claim.

G. *Net Operating Loss Carryback Claims*
   If the year of bankruptcy filing results in a net operating loss[70] for that year, any tax refund resulting from a carryback claim properly belongs

to the bankruptcy trustee on behalf of the bankrupt estate and not to the individual debtor.[71]

H. *Offers in Compromise*
The IRS position is that a taxpayer may not submit an OIC while he or she is in bankruptcy. Their reasoning is that the Bankruptcy Code provides procedures for resolving the IRS's claim. Any such submitted offer will be rejected and returned to the taxpayer.[72] Case law is, however, to the contrary. It has been held that the IRS's policy as reflected in its manual is impermissibly discriminatory. Moreover, the IRS's investigation of an OIC does not violate the Bankruptcy Code's automatic stay provision.[73]

X. Conclusions and Recommendations

A. *Interaction*
The conflicting objectives of tax law and bankruptcy law do not lend themselves to easy reconciliation. Nevertheless, the interaction between the Bankruptcy Code and the I.R.C. provides great flexibility in obtaining a binding determination of tax liability.

B. *Planning*
If a taxpayer is being audited, and if bankruptcy is the course of action to be followed, a taxpayer should push for a conclusion of the audit and assessment of the taxes, and hope that it will take more than 240 days for the IRS to start collecting the tax or filing its liens.

C. *Disclosure in Title 11 Cases*
In a Title 11 case, or in a receivership proceeding, the trustee or receiver is entitled, upon written request, to inspect prior years' tax returns of the debtor. That is, the receiver or trustee may obtain copies thereof directly from the IRS, but only if he or she has a "material interest" in the information contained therein.[74]

XI. Notes

1. Local Loan Co. v. Hunt, 292 U.S. 234 (1934).
2. Morgan v. United States, 99-2 USTC ¶ 50,712 (11th Cir. 1999).
3. 11 U.S.C. §§ 700 *et seq.*
4. 11 U.S.C. §§ 1100 *et seq.*
5. 11 U.S.C. §§ 1300 *et seq.*
6. 11 U.S.C. §§ 301, 303.
7. Sen. Report No. 96-1035, Pub. L. No. 96-589.
8. I.R.C. § 1398.
9. I.R.C. § 1398(c)(1).
10. I.R.C. § 1398(a).
11. I.R.C. § 1399.

12. I.R.C. § 1398(d)(2).
13. *In re* Turboff, 93 B.R. 523 (Bankr. S.D. Tex. 1998).
14. I.R.C. § 6012(a)(8); Treas. Reg. § 1.6012-3(b)(5).
15. Treas. Reg. § 1.6012-3(b)(4).
16. I.R.C. § 61(2); I.R.C. § 108(a)(1)(A).
17. I.R.C. § 108(b)(2).
18. I.R.C. § 6503(h)(1).
19. *See* I.R.C. § 6502.
20. I.R.C. § 6503(h)(2).
21. I.R.C. § 6503(b).
22. I.R.C. § 6036.
23. Treas. Reg. § 301.6036-1.
24. I.R.C. § 6872.
25. 11 U.S.C. § 507(a)(8)(A)(i).
26. *Id.*
27. I.R.C. § 6081(a).
28. *See, e.g., In re* Gidley, 138 B.R. 298 (Bankr. M.D. Fla. 1992).
29. *In re* Rassi, 140 B.R. 490 (Bankr. C.D. Ill. 1992); *In re* Cross, 119 B.R. 652 (Bankr. W.D. Wis. 1990). *But see* Young v. United States, 2002-1 USTC ¶ 50,257 (S. Ct. 2002), where equitable tolling kept a claim for income tax alive when a Chapter 7 petition was filed, effectively dismissing an earlier Chapter 13 filing.
30. 11 U.S.C. § 523(a)(1)(A).
31. *See* I.R.C. § 6072.
32. 11 U.S.C. § 523(a)(1)(B)(ii).
33. *See* I.R.C. §§ 6201 *et seq.*
34. *See* I.R.C. §§ 6321 *et seq.*
35. 11 U.S.C. § 507(a)(8)(A)(ii); United States v. Aberl, 96-1 USTC ¶ 50,151 (6th Cir. 1996).
36. *See* I.R.C. § 7122.
37. 11 U.S.C. § 507(a)(8)(A)(ii).
38. *In re* Torres, 117 B.R. 379 (Bankr. N.D. Ill. 1990).
39. 11 U.S.C. § 507(a)(8)(A)(ii).
40. *See* I.R.C. § 7203.
41. *See* I.R.C. § 7201.
42. 11 U.S.C. § 523(a)(1)(C).
43. I.R.C. § 6020(b); Swanson v. Comm'r, 121 T.C. 111 (2003).
44. Formerly known as the "100 percent penalty" provisions of the I.R.C.
45. 11 U.S.C. § 507(a)(8)(C).
46. 11 U.S.C. § 1328.
47. United States v. Sotelo, 78-1 USTC ¶ 9446 (S. Ct. 1978).
48. 11 U.S.C. § 523(a)(1),(7).
49. *See* I.R.C. § 6621.
50. 11 U.S.C. § 502(b)(2).
51. City of New York v. Saper, 336 U.S. 329 (1949).
52. *See In re* Reichert, 138 B.R. 522 (Bankr. W.D. Mich. 1992).
53. *See* I.R.C. §§ 6212 *et seq.*
54. 11 U.S.C. § 362(a)(9)(B).
55. Hambrick v. Comm'r, 118 T.C. 348 (2002).
56. I.R.C. § 6213(f)(1).

57. I.R.C. § 6871(c)(2).
58. I.R.C. § 6871(c)(1).
59. 11 U.S.C. § 505(a).
60. I.R.C. § 6871(b).
61. I.R.C. § 6871(a).
62. 11 U.S.C. § 105(b).
63. I.R.C. § 6873.
64. I.R.C. § 6161(c).
65. Treas. Reg. § 301.6873-1(b).
66. I.R.C. § 6651.
67. I.R.C. § 6654, 6655.
68. I.R.C. § 6658.
69. I.R.C. § 6323(c).
70. I.R.C. § 172.
71. Segal v. Rochelle, 17 AFTR2d 163, 382 U.S. 375 (S. Ct. 1966).
72. IRM 5.8.10.2.1.
73. *In re* Mills, 2000-1 USTC ¶ 50,103 (Bankr. S.D. W. Va. 1999).
74. I.R.C. § 6103(e)(4).

Innocent Spouse Defenses

I. General Background Information

A. One of the most important defenses available to counsel for a spouse who is either separated from or divorced from his or her spouse is the so-called innocent spouse defense. These cases typically arise in a postassessment period when the IRS is attempting to collect tax arising from a joint return filed during marriage.

B. A prevalent misconception exists regarding a divorce-related agreement between spouses as to the allocation of income tax liability between the parties. A spouse cannot depend on a court-approved divorce decree to avoid joint and several liability on a joint income tax return. The IRS has every legal right to ignore such decrees. All the divorce decree does is to create a contractual right on the part of the "nonliable" spouse to sue his or her spouse for indemnification if he or she has to pay any tax to the IRS. In the meantime the "nonliable" spouse, under the agreement, can be relentlessly pursued by the IRS in its collection enforcement efforts.

C. In 1998 substantial changes were made to the innocent spouse provisions related to joint and several liability. I.R.C. § 6015 replaced the former § 6013(e), which was enacted in 1971 in response to judicial pleas for statutory language enabling relief from liability in situations where the result of joint and several liability was particularly harsh and inequitable. The critical elements necessary to obtain relief under current law are similar in many respects to those contained in the original rule. For that reason, pre-1998 case law cannot be disregarded in attempting to interpret the present § 6015.

D. The 1998 Act makes innocent spouse status easier to obtain than under prior law. The new law eliminates all of the understatement thresholds and requires only that the understatement of tax be attributable to an erroneous (not "grossly erroneous") item of the "other" spouse.[1]

E. The IRS Restructuring and Reform Act of 1998 gave § 6015 retroactive effect in that it was made applicable to any liability for tax arising after July 22, 1998, and to any liability for tax arising before such date that remained unpaid as of July 22, 1998.[2]

II. Section 6015 Rules

A. Exception to "Joint and Several" Rule

But for § 6015, tax liability on a joint income tax return would always be joint and several due to I.R.C. § 6013(d)(3). This rule results in full exposure to both spouses for 100 percent of the total tax liability.[3] In some circumstances a spouse may choose to limit his or her liability instead of seeking total relief from a deficiency assessment.[4]

B. Election for Relief: Five Conditions

Either spouse may elect innocent spouse relief, but only if the conditions of § 6015(b) are met. The conditions of subsection (b) are conjunctive; therefore, all of the conditions must be met for relief to be granted.[5]

Relief for joint tax liability (including related interest, penalties, and other amounts) resulting from a tax deficiency (understatement) is dependent on a claimant's satisfaction of *all* of the conditions of subsection (b). If a single one of these conditions is not met, relief will not be granted:

1. The first condition is that a joint return[6] be filed for the tax year in question.
2. The second condition is that there must be an understatement of tax attributable to erroneous items of the other spouse. The word "understatement" suggests a "deficiency." That is, under subsection (b), tax reported on an original return by the taxpayers will not be forgiven under this subsection.
3. The third condition is that the "innocent" spouse has the burden of proving that he or she did not know, or have reason to know, that there was an understatement.
4. The fourth condition is that, taking all the facts and circumstances into consideration, it is "inequitable" to hold the innocent spouse liable.
5. The fifth and last condition for relief involves a matter of timing. The innocent spouse must elect the benefits of § 6015 not later than two years after the date on which the IRS begins "collection activities" against the innocent spouse.[7] It has been held that something as simple as the IRS offsetting a liability with another year's overpayments constitutes "collection activity" and starts the running of the two-year period.[8]

C. Knowledge Apportionment

If a spouse knew, or should have known, about some but not all of an understatement, then the I.R.C. provides for a measure of limited relief. In such a case, innocent spouse relief is apportioned to the part of the understatement that such spouse did not know about.[9]

D. *Knowledge Issues*
   Among the facts and circumstances that the IRS will consider in evaluating "reasons to know" are the following:
   1. The spouse's educational background and business experience;
   2. The extent of the spouse's participation in the activity that resulted in the erroneous item(s);
   3. Whether the requesting spouse failed to inquire (at the time of signing the return) about matters that a reasonable person would question; and
   4. Whether the erroneous item represented a departure from a recurring pattern reflected in prior year returns.[10]

E. *Definition of "Understatement"*
   An understatement for innocent spouse purposes is calculated by subtracting the tax liability reflected on the return from the correct tax liability. This is also the definition of a "deficiency."[11] For all practical purposes, the two terms can be considered to be synonymous.

F. *Election to Allocate the Deficiency*
   The innocent spouse may elect to obtain relief by separation of liabilities. To qualify, an individual must have filed a joint return and either
   1. Be no longer married to, or be legally separated from, the spouse with whom the joint return was filed; or
   2. Must *not* have been a member of the same household with the spouse for a twelve-month period ending on the date of the filing of Form 8857.

   The burden of proof on income and deductions is on the taxpayer who elects relief under separation of liability.[12]

G. *Allocation of Deficiency—Procedures*
   Items are generally allocated between spouses in the same manner as they would have been allocated had the spouses filed separate returns. For this purpose, community property laws are ignored.[13]

H. *Allocation of Deficiency—Actual Knowledge*
   If the IRS demonstrates that the requesting spouse had *actual* knowledge of an erroneous item (at the time the return was filed) allocable to the nonrequesting spouse, the election to allocate the deficiency to that item is invalid.[14]

I. *Spousal Notification*
   The joint return spouse who does not make an innocent spouse election must, by law, be given notice and opportunity to participate in any tax court proceeding.[15] After a § 6015 request is filed with the

Cincinnati IRS office, the IRS will automatically mail out a letter to the estranged or former spouse, requesting corroboration of the facts alleged by the requesting spouse. This is the reason that Form 8857 asks for the address of the nonrequesting spouse.

Even where a nonrequesting spouse was not given the required notice, he or she will be allowed to intervene in a tax court proceeding and assert a claim that his or her former spouse is not entitled to innocent spouse relief.[16]

J. *Tax Court Review—Petition*
In the event of an adverse determination by the IRS regarding innocent spouse status, the aggrieved spouse can seek a judicial ruling. The I.R.C. gives the U.S. Tax Court jurisdiction to determine the appropriate relief available. To appeal to the tax court a spouse must file a petition at any time *after* the *earlier* of (1) the IRS's mailing (by certified mail) of a final determination, or (2) six months after the Form 8857 (innocent spouse election) is filed. However, in no event can the petition be filed after ninety days following the receipt of the IRS's final determination.[17]

K. *Tax Court Review: Restrictions on Collections*
The IRS is prohibited from taking collection action (levy) against the innocent spouse if he or she has filed a petition with the tax court or if the ninety-day period following the IRS's "determination" has not expired. Despite the normal anti-injunction rule,[18] the tax court has been granted equitable jurisdiction to enjoin the IRS from taking premature collection action.[19]

L. *Tax Court Review—§ 6015(f) Relief without a Deficiency*
The tax court has jurisdiction to review a denial of § 6015(f) relief in a stand-alone petition where the taxpayer is seeking relief from liability of tax shown on the return, without a deficiency having been asserted.[20]

M. *Other Miscellaneous § 6015 Rules*
1. *Equitable Relief*
One of the most important changes brought about by the 1998 Act was the "equitable" relief provisions. Under that new law the IRS is permitted to examine the facts and circumstances of each case for the purpose of determining whether it would be "inequitable" to hold an individual liable. This provision allows an innocent spouse to be relieved of tax shown on the original return in addition to being relieved of any "deficiency." Prior to 1998 this kind of relief would have been impossible.[21] Moreover, if a liability was unpaid prior to the enactment of the 1998 statute, § 6015 relief is available anyway.[22]

2. *Preassessment Consideration*
   There is no requirement that a deficiency be assessed before an innocent spouse claim can be made. Congress intended the proper time to raise and have the IRS consider a claim to be at the same point where a deficiency is being considered and asserted by the IRS. This permits every issue, including the innocent spouse issue, to be resolved in a single administrative and judicial process.[23]

3. *Fraudulent Transfer of Assets*
   If the IRS demonstrates that assets were transferred between the spouses in a fraudulent scheme joined in by both spouses, neither spouse is eligible to make the election (and consequently, joint and several liability attaches to both spouses).[24]

4. *Offer in Compromise and Closing Agreement*
   Innocent spouse relief is unavailable where a spouse has entered into a prior closing agreement[25] or an offer in compromise.[26]

5. *Form to Be Used for Innocent Spouse Request*
   To request innocent spouse relief, the IRS has prescribed the use of Form 8857. However, this form need not be used if the requesting spouse submits a statement, signed under penalty of perjury, containing the same information as required by Form 8857. This form is a stand-alone form in that it is not to be attached to any tax return. Instead the form is filed with the IRS representative considering the spouse's case, or the IRS employee named in the deficiency notice. If neither of these two situations applies, then the form is filed with the IRS service center in Cincinnati, Ohio. Generally this form requires the attachment of detailed statements of fact.[27]

III. Section 66 Rules

A. If a joint return is not filed for a given year (or if no return is filed), then a potential innocent spouse claimant may not avail him or herself of relief under I.R.C. § 6015. Indeed, there cannot be joint and several liability unless a joint return has been filed. Instead, and assuming the claimant is a resident of a community property state, he or she would be relegated to the relief provisions of I.R.C. § 66(c). Residents of separate property states do not need the relief of § 66 for the reason that they would never be tagged with the separate income of their spouses under the income-splitting rule. The income-splitting rule is not of statutory origin; its roots are judicial.

B. To obtain relief under I.R.C. § 66(c), a potential innocent spouse must meet all of the following conditions:

   1. He or she must not have filed a joint return for the year in question;
   2. He or she must not have included an item of income attributable to the other spouse (under the rules of I.R.C. § 879(a));

3. He or she establishes that he or she did not know of, and had no reason to know of, such item of community income; and

4. It would be inequitable to include the community income in his or her tax return.[28]

C. In the event the "innocent" spouse meets all four tests of § 66(c), then what otherwise would have been taxed to him or her becomes taxable automatically to the "noninnocent" spouse.[29]

D. I.R.C. § 66 also deals with other situations in which community income laws may be ignored. For example, § 66(a) provides that community income laws may be ignored where all five of the following tests have been met:

1. Two individuals are married at some point during the year;

2. They live apart for the entire year;

3. They do not file a joint return for the year;

4. At least one of the spouses has earned income; and

5. No portion of the earned income has been transferred (directly or indirectly) between such individuals before the close of the year.

E. For purposes of the income transfer test, de minimis amounts or amounts spent on dependent children are not treated as transfers to an abandoned spouse.[30]

F. There is also a provision that protects the IRS in the event that a taxpayer spouse wants to take undue advantage of the community property laws. For example, if a husband

1. acts as if he is solely entitled to an item of income, and

2. fails to notify his spouse of the nature and amount of the income, then the IRS will deny him the income-splitting benefits and tax it all to him.[31]

G. Section 66(b) is directed against a culpable spouse, rather than a relief provision designed to aid an innocent one. Example: Mr. Smith received $1,000 in income during the tax year. He acted as if it were all his and did not notify his wife of the nature and amount of the income. The IRS will tax him on the full $1,000 even though, under local community property laws, only $500 is considered to be his property.

H. Note that § 66 was designed to relieve hardship in the taxation of "earned income" only. All other types of income are determined in accordance with applicable community property laws.[32]

IV. Section 7703(b) Rules

A. There are some circumstances under which, for tax purposes, a married individual can be considered as unmarried, but only if all four of the following tests are met:

1. The taxpayer must be married as of the close of the tax year;

2. He or she must not have filed a joint return with the spouse;

3. He or she must have furnished over half the cost of a home for a dependent child; and

4. During the last six months of the tax year, the taxpayer's spouse was not a member of the household.[33]

B. If a taxpayer qualifies under I.R.C. § 7703(b), three things are affected:

1. A taxpayer can claim personal and dependency exemptions without regard to what the other spouse does;

2. A taxpayer can take his or her own itemized deductions (or decide not to itemize) without regard to what his or her spouse does; and

3. His or her filing status is affected in that under § 7703(b), he or she may use the head of household tax rates.

C. Apparently, qualifying under § 7703(b) does not, however, mean that one can ignore community property laws. A taxpayer is relegated to qualifying under § 66 for this.

V. Other Rules

A. *Self-Employment Tax*

There is automatic statutory relief of self-employment tax where, for example, a husband owns a proprietorship business. Even though the wife may be taxed on half the net income from that business, she pays none of the self-employment tax attributable thereto unless she "exercises substantially all of the management and control of the business."[34]

B. *Separate Deficiency Notices*

If spouses have separated, and the IRS has been put on notice to that effect, then the IRS is required to send separate deficiency notices to each spouse by certified mail to each of their respective addresses.[35]

VI. Notes

1. Comm. Report on Pub. L. No. 105-206 (1998 Act).
2. *See* Restructuring and Reform Act 1998, § 3201(g)(1), 112 Stat. 740.
3. I.R.C. § 6015(a).
4. I.R.C. § 6015(a)(2).
5. I.R.C. § 6015(a)(1).
6. I.R.C. § 6013(a).
7. I.R.C. § 6015(b)(1).
8. Campbell v. Comm'r, 121 T.C. 290 (2003).
9. I.R.C. § 6015(b)(2).
10. Prop. Treas. Reg. § 1.6015-3.
11. I.R.C. § 6015(b)(3); 6662(d)(2)(A); 6211(a).
12. I.R.C. § 6015(c), (d).
13. I.R.C. § 6015(d); Comm. Report, Pub. L. No. 105-206 (1998 Act).
14. Prop. Treas. Reg. § 1.6015-3.
15. I.R.C. § 6015(e)(4).
16. *See, e.g.*, King v. Comm'r, 115 T.C. 118 (2000).

17. I.R.C. § 6015(e)(1)(A).
18. *See* I.R.C. § 7421(a).
19. I.R.C. § 6015(e)(1)(B).
20. Ewing v. Comm'r, 118 T.C. No. 31 (2002).
21. I.R.C. § 6015(f). See Rev. Proc. 2000-15 for factors that will influence the IRS's decision in this regard.
22. Flores v. United States, 88 AFTR2d 2001-7020 (Fed. Cl. 2001).
23. Comm. Report on Pub. L. No. 106-554 (Community Renewal Tax Relief Act of 2000).
24. I.R.C. § 6015(c)(3).
25. I.R.C. § 7121.
26. I.R.C. § 7122; Prop. Treas. Reg. § 1.6015-1(c)(1).
27. Prop. Treas. Reg. § 1.6015-5(a).
28. I.R.C. § 66(c).
29. *Id.*
30. *See* Comm. Reports on Pub. L. No. 96-605.
31. I.R.C. § 66(b).
32. *See* I.R.C. § 879(a).
33. I.R.C. § 7703(b).
34. I.R.C. § 1402(a)(5).
35. I.R.C. § 6212(b)(2).

CHAPTER 8

Fraud

Federal Tax Crimes

I. Introduction

A. Statutory Provisions in Title 26

The Internal Revenue Code (I.R.C.) contains a number of different criminal sanctions, generally found in Chapter 75 of the I.R.C.[1] Additionally, many criminal provisions affecting taxpayers are contained in Title 18 of the U.S. Code (the federal criminal code).[2]

B. Nature of Criminal Penalties

The criminal penalties of the I.R.C. are in addition to the civil penalties for fraud. Unlike civil penalties, criminal penalties are not collected through the assessment procedures, but are only imposed after conviction or a guilty plea in criminal proceedings.

C. Omissions versus Affirmative Acts

Omissions, such as willful failure to file a tax return or willful failure to pay tax, are generally misdemeanors. Tax evasion, on the other hand, must be proved by an affirmative act, such as the filing of a false or fraudulent tax return. Other examples of affirmative acts would include keeping a double set of books, making false entries, and concealing assets.[3]

D. Felony versus Misdemeanor

The structure of the federal criminal tax statute is one broad felony[4] followed by a series of misdemeanors.[5] Congress intended that the felony and the misdemeanors be totally separate offenses. A violation of either a misdemeanor statute or a felony statute does not necessarily entail a violation of the other.[6]

At common law a misdemeanor offense was one that was simply less grave than a felony. Many states have defined misdemeanors statutorily to mean a crime that carries no sanction more severe than a fine or a jail term not to exceed one year.[7] There are misdemeanor criminal sanctions in the I.R.C.[8] but felony prosecution is the rule for most fraud investigations.

II. Misdemeanor Statutes

A. *Failure to File, Pay, or Supply Information*

Any person who is required to pay any tax (including estimated tax), file a return, keep records, or supply information and who fails to do so is guilty of a misdemeanor. The punishment is a fine of up to $25,000 ($100,000 in the case of a corporation) and imprisonment of up to one year. In the case of failure to pay estimated tax, no criminal penalty can apply unless the civil penalty of § 6654 or § 6655 also applies. In the case of failure to file a currency receipt form,[9] this crime becomes a felony, with up to a five-year jail term.[10]

If a return is filed, but required information or schedules are omitted, a taxpayer can be convicted under § 7203. For example, if a partnership return is filed, but the balance sheet information is omitted, this satisfies the "failure to supply information" standard.[11]

The government's burden in "failure to pay" cases under § 7203 is to prove that the taxpayer possessed sufficient funds to meet his or her obligations to the government and that the taxpayer voluntarily and intentionally did not pay the tax due.[12]

For a variety of reasons, very few failure to file cases are prosecuted.

B. *Failure to Furnish W-2 Form*

In case an employer furnishes a false W-2 form (or fails to furnish one at all) and does so, or fails to do so, willfully, he or she is guilty of a misdemeanor and can be fined up to $1,000 and jailed for one year.[13]

If an employee fails to give his or her employer a W-4 form or supplies false information thereon, he or she is guilty of a misdemeanor and can be imprisoned for up to one year and fined up to $1,000.[14] In construing the term "false" under this section, cases hold that a statement is false if it is untrue when made and known to be untrue by the person making it.[15]

C. *Fraudulent Document*

Any person who willfully delivers to the IRS any return or other document known by him or her to be fraudulent or false as to any material matter is guilty of a misdemeanor, and can be fined up to $10,000 ($50,000 in the case of a corporation) or jailed for up to one year.[16] Although a willful misstatement of a material fact on an income tax return that does not affect the stated tax liability may be a punishable offense, such conduct does not amount to willful tax evasion in violation of § 7201.[17]

D. *Failure to Obey Summons*

If any person is served with an administrative summons[18] to appear and testify, or to appear and produce books and records, and such person fails to appear, he or she can be fined up to $1,000 and imprisoned for up to one year.[19] To compel compliance with a summons, the government must bring suit in district court. At this point, and not before, the summoned party may challenge the summons in district court. If the district court compels compliance, only then might noncompliance result in the imposition of sanctions under § 7210.[20]

E. *Antibrowsing Provision*

Starting in 1997 it is a misdemeanor offense for an IRS employee to "browse" through or otherwise inspect a taxpayer's return information. The penalties for violation of this provision are as follows:
1. A $1,000 fine;
2. Imprisonment for up to one year; and
3. Dismissal from office.[21]

F. *Collected Payroll Taxes*

Any person who fails to comply with § 7512(b)[22] (re depositing payroll taxes in a separate bank account) can be fined up to $5,000 or imprisoned up to one year.[23]

G. *Preparer Disclosure*

A person who is engaged in the business of preparing tax returns and who, knowingly or recklessly, discloses any information obtained by him or her in connection with preparing any return can be fined up to $1,000 and imprisoned up to one year.[24] The preparer disclosure rule does not apply, however, if such disclosure is made pursuant to a court order. Nor does it prohibit using federal information to prepare state returns or disclosing information during a quality or peer review.[25]

III. Felonies

A. *Evasion Statute*

Any taxpayer who willfully attempts to evade or defeat any federal tax is guilty of a felony and can be fined up to $100,000 ($500,000 in the case of a corporation), or imprisoned for up to five years.[26]

The elements that the prosecution must prove in a § 7201 case are as follows:
1. An attempt to evade or defeat tax in any manner;
2. The existence of a tax deficiency or tax due;

3.   An affirmative act of fraud; and
4.   Willfulness.[27]

As in all prosecutions in a criminal tax case, the government has the burden of proving every element of the crime charged beyond a reasonable doubt.[28]

B.   *Failure to Collect and Pay Over Tax*

Any person required to collect, account for, and pay over any federal tax, and who willfully fails to do so, is guilty of a felony and can be fined up to $10,000 and imprisoned up to five years.[29] This criminal provision is related to the trust fund recovery penalty imposed by I.R.C. § 6672.

C.   *Fraud and False Statement (False Return)*[30]

A person is guilty of a felony and can be jailed for up to three years and fined up to $100,000 ($500,000 in the case of a corporation) if he or she commits any of the following offenses:
1.   Signs a tax return or other document that contains a written declaration that is made under penalties of perjury and that he or she does not believe to be true and correct as to every material matter;
2.   Willfully aids or assists in the preparation of a return, claim, affidavit, or other matter whether or not such presentation is with the knowledge or consent of the taxpayer; or
3.   Destroys, conceals, or falsifies any document relating to the financial condition of the taxpayer in connection with an offer in compromise or closing agreement.

To sustain a conviction under § 7206(1), it is not necessary that there be a material underpayment of tax. It is sufficient if the falsity has the potential for impeding the IRS's performance of its responsibilities.[31] An example of this kind of violation is incorrectly answering the question regarding a foreign bank account on a tax return.[32]

The source of one's income as stated on his or her tax return, standing alone, is a material matter within the meaning of § 7206(1), and a taxpayer may be prosecuted for a misrepresentation thereof. This is true regardless of whether one's taxable income had been materially understated.[33]

Section 7206(1) is a perjury statute, making any person who knowingly makes and subscribes a false statement on any return criminally liable. Section 7602(2) has a broader sweep, making all forms of willful assistance in preparing a false return an offense. Perjury in connection with the preparation of a federal tax return is chargeable under either section.[34] Because § 7206(1) is a perjury statute, the literal truth is a defense, even if the answer is highly misleading. Using the wrong form (e.g., 1040-EZ) does not violate § 7206(1).[35]

Section 7206(2) is not limited to tax return preparers, but includes all persons who participate in a fraudulent scheme.[36]

In a § 7206 prosecution, venue is appropriate both where the return was made and subscribed and in the district in which the return was filed.[37]

"Materiality" in § 7206 violations is generally a question of law as opposed to a jury question.[38]

D. *Unauthorized Disclosure*[39]

It is unlawful for specified persons to disclose any tax return or tax return information to another person. The punishment for violation of this provision is a fine of up to $5,000 and imprisonment for up to five years. The persons subject to this penalty are as follows:

1. IRS employees;
2. State employees;
3. Corporate shareholders; and
4. Any other person.

A violation of this statute requires bad faith on the part of IRS agents or an improper purpose for the investigation.[40]

E. *Crimes Committed by Revenue Agents and Officers*

IRS revenue agents and revenue officers can be dismissed from office, fined up to $10,000, and imprisoned up to five years if they commit any of the following offenses:

1. Extorting or committing willful oppression under color of law;
2. Knowingly demanding greater sums than are authorized by law;
3. Failing to perform any of the duties of office;
4. Conspiring with anyone to defraud the United States;
5. Knowingly making opportunity for any person to defraud the government;
6. Doing or omitting to do any act with intent to enable any other person to defraud the government;
7. Making or signing any fraudulent document;
8. Knowingly failing to report any violation of any tax law; or
9. Accepting payments, gifts, and so on, in exchange for compromise, settlement, or adjustment of any charge or complaint for violation of any law.

In the discretion of the court, up to one-half of the fine imposed can be paid to the informant who brings a matter to the attention of the authorities.[41]

F. *Executive Branch Influence over Tax Audits*

Effective in 1998 the U.S. president, vice president, and any employees of their respective executive offices may not request the IRS to audit or terminate any audit of any taxpayer. Violations of this provision carry a punishment of up to $5,000 in fines and five years of imprisonment.[42]

G. *Attempts to Interfere with Revenue Laws*

Whoever attempts to interfere (corruptly, by force, or otherwise) with the administration of tax laws can be fined up to $5,000 per count and imprisoned up to three years.

IV. Willfulness

A. *Definition of Willful*

The textbook definition of "willful" is a voluntary, intentional violation of a known legal duty. It requires bad faith or an evil intent. It requires an element of mens rea, which separates the purposeful tax violator from the well-meaning, but easily confused, mass of taxpayers.[43]

B. *Ignorance or Misunderstanding of the Law*

Generally ignorance of the law or a mistake of law is no defense to criminal prosecution. This is based on the common law presumption that the law is knowable and definite and, therefore, every person knows or should know the law. However, the statutory term "willfully," as used in the federal criminal statutes, is an exception to the old common law rule. This special treatment of criminal tax offenses is largely due to the complexity of the tax law. An illustration of this principle is the *Cheek*[44] case, which held that a jury is entitled to an instruction that a taxpayer's good-faith understanding of the tax laws may be taken into consideration in determining whether he or she acted in a *willful* manner.

C. *Legal Doubt*

A tax return is not criminally fraudulent simply because it is erroneous. A taxpayer cannot willfully evade a tax if there exists a reasonable doubt in the law that a tax is due.[45]

D. *Alcoholism Defense*

Evidence of chronic alcoholism will most likely not indicate a lack of requisite criminal intent. A jury can find that a defendant may be capable of conducting his or her business affairs despite having an alcoholic condition.[46]

E. *Reliance on Counsel*

A jury in a criminal tax case is entitled to an instruction that reliance on tax counsel may indicate that the element of willfulness was lacking.[47]

F. *Circumstantial Evidence*

Since bad faith and evil intent involve intangible mental processes, proof of willfulness usually must be accomplished by means of circumstantial evidence.[48] There are many examples of circumstantial evidence indicating willfulness. For example, filing a false W-4 form claiming to be exempt from income tax four days after filing such a form with contradictory information has been held to be such circumstantial evidence.[49] A taxpayer's entire course of conduct must be examined to determine whether the requisite fraudulent intent exists. There are a number of indicia of fraud that courts consider, including, inter alia, a taxpayer's lack of credibility, inconsistent testimony, and evasiveness on the witness stand. No single factor is necessarily sufficient to establish fraud, but the existence of several factors is persuasive circumstantial evidence.[50]

V. Conspiracy and Title 18 Cases

A. *Title 18 Cases*

The following sections of Title 18 of the U.S. Code are frequently used in tax prosecutions: § 2 (aiding and abetting), § 201 (bribery), § 371 (conspiracy), § 1001 (false statements), and § 1621 (perjury).

B. *Conspiracy*

In addition to crimes specified in the I.R.C., a criminal tax case may be cast in the form of a conspiracy prosecution.[51] A conspiracy conviction carries a maximum penalty of five years in prison and/or a $10,000 fine. The elements of the crime of conspiracy are (1) an agreement between two or more persons to commit an offense against or to defraud the United States and (2) an overt act in furtherance of the conspiracy.[52] The classic definition of a conspiracy is "an agreement between two or more persons to commit a crime."[53] One of the reasons why the government selects the conspiracy statute as its prosecution vehicle is that in a conspiracy to defraud case, the government need not prove the existence of a tax deficiency, as would be the case in an evasion prosecution.

It is possible for a jury to convict a defendant for conspiracy[54] as well as for aiding and abetting.[55] Nevertheless, these two crimes are separate and distinct. A conviction under § 7602(2) requires proof that a person willfully aided and assisted another in the filing of materially false returns, whereas a conviction for conspiracy requires proof that two or more people knowingly and voluntarily entered into an agreement to file false returns.[56]

C. *False Statements*

Taxpayers are frequently charged with a violation of this criminal statute,[57] a felony offense if convicted. This statute has been broadly interpreted to cover all false statements made to any branch of the federal government. However, a defendant's mere negative responses to questions propounded by an investigating agent during a meeting not initiated by the defendant cannot be prosecuted under § 1001.[58] "False statements" do not have to be made under penalty of perjury to be a prosecutable offense. Making an untrue statement to a government agency is a violation of this federal criminal statute.

D. *Mail and Wire Fraud*

The mail and wire fraud statutes[59] provide for felony penalties for the use of mail, wire, radio, television, and the like, for the purpose of executing a fraudulent scheme. The mailing of a fraudulent tax return can be held to violate these statutes. A defendant can be convicted of both mail fraud and tax fraud in the same case. This becomes important in that conviction of either crime is a predicate criminal act for purposes of the Racketeer Influenced and Corrupt Organizations Act (RICO).[60]

VI. The Lesser Included Offense Doctrine

A taxpayer may be found guilty of an offense necessarily included in the offense charged.[61] Thus a defendant is normally entitled to a jury instruction that would permit a finding of guilt of the lesser offense. An example of this statutory overlapping is found, for example, in the interplay between § 7201 (evasion felony) and § 7203 (failure to file misdemeanor).[62]

Where one offense is included in another offense, it (the lesser) cannot support a separate conviction and sentence. Thus, where a defendant is improperly convicted of a lesser included offense, the proper remedy is to vacate both the conviction and sentence on the lesser included offense, leaving the conviction and sentence on the greater offense intact.[63]

VII. Methods of Proof

A. *Net Worth Method*

A "net worth" case is generally used by the IRS where the taxpayer's records are inadequate to allow a determination of income tax liability. Under this method the IRS establishes an opening net worth, then proves the increases in net worth for each succeeding year, then calculates the differences between the adjusted net values of the taxpayer's assets at the beginning and end of each of the years involved. The taxpayer's nondeductible expenditures, including living expenses, are added to these increases, and if the resulting figure for any year is substantially greater than the taxable income reported by the taxpayer for that year, the IRS claims that the excess represents unreported taxable income.[64]

B. *Cash Expenditures Method*

The "cash expenditure" method is a variant of the net worth method of establishing unreported taxable income. This method is appropriate for taxpayers who tend to spend all they make and end up no wealthier than before. Under this method the IRS establishes the amount of purchases of goods and services that are not attributable to resources on hand at the beginning of the period analyzed or to nontaxable receipts during the year.[65]

C. *Bank Deposits Method*

Under this method, the IRS must prove that the defendant was engaged in an income-producing business and that regular deposits of funds having the appearance of income were in fact made to bank accounts during the course of business.[66]

VIII. Miscellaneous Topics

A. *Tax Court Jurisdiction*

One will never see a criminal tax prosecution in the U.S. Tax Court. The tax court, while having jurisdiction over civil penalties (including civil fraud), does not have jurisdiction over tax matters involving criminal penalties. All federal tax crimes are tried in federal district courts.

B. *Maximum Fines—Sentencing Guidelines*

Although fines and punishment are provided for by the I.R.C., the U.S. Sentencing Commission Guidelines[67] provide alternative maximum criminal fines that apply to crimes committed on or after November 1, 1987.

For tax crimes, the sentence depends on the tax loss involved and the criminal history of the defendant. The maximum fine under the Criminal Code may be greater than that provided for in the I.R.C.

Note, however, that in 2005[68] the Supreme Court held that the federal sentencing guidelines are now only advisory and that trial courts must do only what is "reasonable."

C. *Entrapment Defense*

Occasionally a criminal tax defendant will raise a defense of entrapment. Entrapment occurs when the criminal design originates with agents of the government, and they implant in the mind of an innocent person the disposition to commit the alleged offense and induce its commission so that they may prosecute. On the other hand, there is no entrapment if the intent was formed in the mind of the defendant.[69]

D. *Constitutional Defenses*

A taxpayer claim that the federal income tax is unconstitutional will always fail. This argument has repeatedly been rejected by the courts as frivolous.

E. Criminal Acts of Corporations

A corporation can be held liable for criminal tax fraud based on the illegal acts of an employee, officer, director, or shareholder. A corporation is held liable for the criminal acts of a responsible person when the acts are committed in an official capacity, are to the benefit of or in furtherance of the corporation, and are authorized (or acquiesced in) by the corporation.

F. Badges of Fraud

The proof of tax evasion can be inferred in many ways. Typically the government likes to prove one or more of the following so-called badges of fraud, also sometimes referred to as indications of fraud:

1. A consistent pattern by the taxpayer of underreporting income or overstating deductions;
2. Omission of an entire source of income on a tax return (e.g., not reporting any dividend income);
3. Claiming completely fictitious deductions;
4. Keeping two sets of books, or no books at all;
5. Making false entries in the books;
6. Providing an accountant with false information concerning the preparation of a tax return;
7. Destroying tax records, especially if just after an IRS audit is started;
8. Filing a false Form W-4 with an employer claiming excess exemptions to reduce the taxes withheld;
9. Backdating tax records;
10. Dealing in large sums of cash without an adequate explanation; and
11. Concealment of bank accounts, brokerage accounts, and other property.

IX. Conclusion

Those who believe that the system of taxation in the United States is one of voluntary assessment are delusional. The fact is that the IRS has a very big cannon aimed at your head in the form of incarceration.

Tax practitioners and their clients must be constantly aware of where "the line" is between legitimate tax planning (to avoid or minimize tax liability) and criminal tax evasion. This line is often not clear or apparent. Because of government prosecutorial zeal, it is the better part of wisdom not to try to go right up to the line. It is always best to stay well clear of it.

X.   Quick Reference Chart

Statutory Grid

I.R.C. Code §	Short Title	Maximum Fine	Maximum Jail Time in Years	Remarks
7201	Evasion	$100,000	5	$500,000 fine in the case of a corporation.
7202	Failure to Pay Over	10,000	5	Failure to remit payroll taxes.
7203	Failure to File	25,000	1	Misdemeanor; $100,000 fine for corporation.
7204	Fraudulent W-2	1,000	1	Also includes failure to furnish W-2.
7205	Fraudulent W-4	1,000	1	Requires willfulness.
7206	False Return, Etc., Fraudulent Aiding and Assisting	100,000	3	$500,000 fine for corporation; includes destruction of documents, aiding and assisting, etc.
7207	Fraudulent Document	10,000	1	$50,000 in case of corporation; no perjury declaration required.
7210	Failure to Obey Summons	1,000	1	Requires prior "show cause" hearing in federal district court.
7212	Corrupt Interference	5,000	3	Bribery of IRS employee, physical threats, etc.
7213	Unauthorized Disclosure	5,000	5	Generally applies to IRS employees.
7213A	Antibrowsing	1,000	1	Misdemeanor; generally applies to IRS employees; added in 1997.
7214	Unlawful Acts by IRS Employees	10,000	5	Extortion; willful oppression under color of law.
7215	Collected Taxes	5,000	1	Violation of § 7512(b).

(continued)

Statutory Grid (*Continued*)

I.R.C. Code §	Short Title	Maximum Fine	Maximum Jail Time in Years	Remarks
7216	Preparer Disclosure	1,000	1	Exceptions: (1) court order and (2) waiver.
7217	Ordering IRS Audits	5,000	5	Applies to employees of executive branch.
18 U.S.C. § 371	Conspiracy to Commit Any Offense against the United States	250,000	5	This is a Title 18 [of the U.S. Code] violation that is often employed in federal tax cases.
18 U.S.C. § 1001	False Statements	10,000	5	Title 18 violation; does not require statement under penalty of perjury.

XI. Notes

1. I.R.C. §§ 7201 *et seq.*
2. 18 U.S.C.
3. See the discussion in *Spies v. United States*, 317 U.S. 492, 30 AFTR 378 (S. Ct. 1943).
4. I.R.C. § 7201.
5. I.R.C. §§ 7202–7203.
6. United States v. Foster, 86-1 USTC ¶ 9327 (7th Cir. 1986).
7. *See, e.g.,* Tex. Penal Code § 12.21.
8. *See, e.g.,* I.R.C. § 7203—willful failure to file a tax return.
9. *See* I.R.C. § 6050I and Form 8300.
10. I.R.C. § 7203.
11. Pappas v. United States, 216 F.2d 515, 46 AFTR 1019 (10th Cir. 1954).
12. United States v. Ausmus, 774 F.2d 722, 85-2 USTC ¶ 9742 (6th Cir. 1985).
13. I.R.C. § 7204; *see also* §§ 6051 and 6674 for civil requirements.
14. I.R.C. § 7205(a).
15. Brister v. United States, 96-1 USTC ¶ 50,246 (Fed. Cl. 1996).
16. I.R.C. § 7207; Treas. Reg. § 301.7207-1.
17. United States v. Garber, 79-2 USTC ¶ 9709 (5th Cir. 1979).
18. *See* I.R.C. §§ 7602 *et seq.*
19. I.R.C. § 7210.
20. Caesar Elecs., Inc. v. United States, 86-2 USTC ¶ 9693 (E.D.N.Y. 1986).
21. I.R.C. § 7213A.
22. Regarding collected payroll taxes.
23. I.R.C. § 7215(a).
24. I.R.C. § 7216(a).
25. I.R.C. § 7216(b).
26. I.R.C. § 7201.
27. United States v. Terrell, 85-1 USTC ¶ 9249 (5th Cir. 1985).

28. United States v. House, 75-2 USTC ¶ 9782 (3d Cir. 1975).
29. I.R.C. § 7202.
30. I.R.C. § 7206.
31. United States v. Greenberg, 735 F.2d 29, 84-1 USTC ¶ 9509 (2d Cir. 1984).
32. *See* Form 1040, Schedule B.
33. United States v. DiVarco, 343 F. Supp. 101 (N.D. Ill. 1972); *aff'd*, 484 F.2d 670 (7th Cir. 1973).
34. United States v. Shortt Acct. Corp., 785 F.2d 1448, 86-1 USTC ¶ 9317 (9th Cir. 1986).
35. United States v. Reynolds, 919 F.2d 435, 91-1 USTC ¶ 50,267 (7th Cir. 1990).
36. United States v. Crum, 529 F.2d 1380, 76-1 USTC ¶ 9214 (9th Cir. 1976).
37. United States v. Griffin, 87-1 USTC ¶ 9299 (1st Cir. 1987).
38. *Greenberg*, 735 F.2d 29.
39. I.R.C. § 7213.
40. United States. v. Tex. Heart Inst., 755 F.2d 755, 85-1 USTC ¶ 9283 (5th Cir. 1985).
41. I.R.C. § 7214(a).
42. I.R.C. § 7217.
43. United States v. Bishop, 412 U.S. 346 (S. Ct. 1973); *see also* United States v. Pomponio, 429 U.S. 10 (S. Ct. 1976).
44. 91-1 USTC ¶ 50,012 (S. Ct. 1991), rev'g 882 F.2d 1263 (7th Cir. 1989).
45. United States v. Garber, 607 F.2d 92, 79-2 USTC ¶ 9709 (5th Cir. 1979); *but see* United States v. Curtis, 782 F.2d 593, 86-1 USTC ¶ 9195 (6th Cir. 1986).
46. United States v. Jalbert, 504 F.2d 892, 74-2 USTC ¶ 9788 (1st Cir. 1974).
47. Bursten v. United States, 395 F.2d 976, 21 AFTR 2d 1403 (5th Cir. 1968).
48. United States v. Collorafi, 90-1 USTC ¶ 50,188 (2d Cir. 1990); United States v. Brown, 591 F.2d 307 (5th Cir).
49. States v. Shivers, 86-1 USTC ¶ 9404 (5th Cir. 1986).
50. Hammett v. Comm'r, 53 T.C.M. (CCH) 636 (1987).
51. 18 U.S.C. § 371.
52. *See* United States v. Montalvo, 87-2 USTC ¶ 9546 (5th Cir. 1987).
53. United States v. Rabinowich, 238 U.S. 78 (1915).
54. 18 U.S.C. § 371.
55. 26 U.S.C. § 7206(2).
56. United States v. Rubin, 844 F.2d 979 (2d Cir. 1988).
57. 18 U.S.C. § 1001.
58. United States v. Hajecate, 83-1 USTC ¶ 9192 (5th Cir. 1982).
59. 18 U.S.C. §§ 1341, 1343.
60. Racketeer Influenced and Corrupt Organizations Act, 18 U.S.C. § 1961.
61. *See* Fed. R. Crim. P. 31.
62. See the discussion in *Sansone v. United States*, 380 U.S. 343, 15 AFTR2d 611 (S. Ct. 1965).
63. United States v. Buckley, 79-1 USTC ¶ 9290 (5th Cir. 1978); *see also* United States v. Newman, 468 F.2d 791 (5th Cir. 1972).
64. *See* Holland v. United States, 348 U.S. 121, 46 AFTR 943 (S. Ct. 1954).
65. Taglianetti v. United States, 398 F.2d 558 (1st Cir. 1968).
66. United States v. Esser, 520 F.2d 213 (7th Cir. 1975).
67. Sentencing Reform Act of 1984, Pub. L. No. 98-473 (codified at 18 U.S.C. §§ 1335–3742 and 28 U.S.C. §§ 991–998).
68. United States v. Booker, 543 U.S. 221 (S. Ct. 2005), a non-tax case decided under the 6th Amendment.
69. *Buckley*, 79-1 USTC ¶ 9290.

Civil Fraud

I. Background Information

The civil fraud penalty is combined with the "accuracy-related" penalty to compose Part II of Subchapter A (nonassessable penalties) of Chapter 68 (additions to tax and assessable penalties) of the Internal Revenue Code (I.R.C.). Prior to 1990, the civil fraud penalty was contained in I.R.C. § 6653(b). It was recodified as § 6663(a) as a part of Public Law No. 101-239.

II. General Statutory Rule

The I.R.C. provides for a 75 percent civil fraud penalty, but only on the portion of a tax "underpayment" (see discussion in III, *infra*) that is attributable to fraud.[1]

III. Definition of "Underpayment"

A. No civil fraud penalty can be imposed unless there is an underpayment of tax (usually involving a deficiency).
B. For purposes of civil fraud, the term "underpayment" is defined by the following formula:
   - Correct amount of tax liability
   - Less: tax shown on the tax return
   - Less: previous assessments
   - Plus: previous abatements, credits, and refunds
   - Equals: underpayment[2]
C. If *any portion* of an underpayment is proved to be attributable to fraud, then the *entire* underpayment is presumed to be attributable to fraud unless the *taxpayer* can prove (by a preponderance of evidence) that the remaining portion is not fraudulent.[3]

IV. Definition of Fraud

A. Fraud requires a specific intent; mere negligence or ignorance of the law does not constitute fraud.

    B.   Fraud is defined as an intentional wrongdoing designed to evade tax believed to be owing.[4]

    C.   Even a sincere belief that federal income tax laws are unconstitutional is not a defense to a finding of fraud.[5]

    D.   Fraud may not be found under circumstances that create at most only a suspicion.[6]

V. Burden of Proof Issues

    A. *General Rule*

        The burden of proving (by clear and convincing evidence) that civil fraud exists is on the IRS.[7]

    B. *"Clear and Convincing" Standard*

       1. In establishing civil fraud, the IRS must meet its burden of proof by clear and convincing evidence.[8] Such fraud is never presumed.

       2. The clear and convincing standard of proof is easier for the government to meet than the criminal burden of proof "beyond a reasonable doubt," but harder than the standard of proof for nonfraud civil penalties.[9]

    C. *Civil versus Criminal*

        The criminal standard is more restrictive and requires a showing by the IRS of an affirmative act by the taxpayer calculated to defraud the government. The civil standard, on the other hand, requires a showing only that the taxpayer voluntarily, consciously, or intentionally attempted to evade taxes.[10]

    D. *Government Must Show Intent*

        To meet its burden, the IRS must show that a taxpayer intended to evade taxes known to be owing by conduct intended to conceal, mislead, or otherwise prevent the collection of taxes.[11]

    E. *Precision Not Required*

        The IRS need not prove the precise amount of underpayment resulting from fraud, but only that some part of the underpayment of tax each year in issue is attributable to fraud.[12]

    F. *Burden Shifting*

        Once the IRS has met its burden of showing that some portion of the underpayment is attributable to fraud, the burden shifts to the taxpayer to establish which, if any, items are *not* attributable to fraud, and these items are exempt from the 75 percent penalty. The taxpayer's burden of proving nonfraudulent items is, however, one of preponderance of the evidence.

G. *Circumstantial Evidence*

Since direct proof of a taxpayer's fraudulent intent is rarely available, fraud may be proved by circumstantial evidence and reasonable inferences drawn therefrom.

VI. Statute of Limitations

A. *General Civil Rule*

There is no statute of limitations on assessment or collection if the IRS has proved that a false or fraudulent return has been filed. That is, tax may be assessed at any time, in effect resulting in *no statute of limitations!*[13]

B. *Criminal Rule Distinguished*

Unlike the civil rule, the criminal prosecution statute provides for a six-year statute of limitations for cases involving fraud. Therefore, an indictment must be brought within six years of the commission of the offense (e.g., the signing of a false tax return).[14]

VII. Nonfiling

A. The civil fraud penalty *cannot* be imposed where
   1. No tax return was ever filed or
   2. The IRS has prepared a return under I.R.C. § 6020(b).[15]
B. Of course, one cannot avoid the penalty by simply not filing; a corresponding 75 percent delinquency penalty applies where there has been a fraudulent failure to file.[16]

VIII. Miscellaneous Issues

A. *Spousal Issues*

In the case of a married taxpayer who files a joint return, no fraud penalty can attach to the spouse unless "some part" of the underpayment is due to fraud of the spouse.[17]

B. *Prior Criminal Case*

A taxpayer's acquittal of criminal charges does not prevent a tax court in a subsequent civil proceeding from finding him or her liable for the civil fraud penalty.[18]

The courts are split on whether a criminal conviction estops a taxpayer from challenging a civil fraud assertion. However, the Fifth Circuit takes the position that collateral estoppel does apply.[19]

C. *Penalty Stacking*

Stacking penalties is prohibited. Thus, the 20 percent accuracy-related penalty of I.R.C. § 6662 does not apply to any portion of the underpayment on which the fraud penalty is imposed.[20]

D. *Voluntary Disclosure*

Voluntary disclosure does not necessarily mitigate the civil fraud penalty. For example, the filing of an amended return by a taxpayer who has previously filed a fraudulent return and payment of the tax shown to be due on the amended return do not bar assessment of fraud penalties.[21]

IX. Notes

1. I.R.C. § 6663(a).
2. I.R.C. § 6664(a).
3. I.R.C. § 6663(b).
4. Miller v. Comm'r, 94 T.C. 316, 332 (1990).
5. Niedringhaus v. Comm'r, 99 T.C. 202 (1992).
6. Toussaint v. Comm'r, 743 F.2d 309, 312 (5th Cir. 1984).
7. I.R.C. § 7454; T.C. Rule 142(b). This is unlike normal civil tax litigation, where the burden of proof is clearly on the taxpayer.
8. Carroll v. Comm'r, 69 T.C.M. (CCH) 1711 (1995).
9. Mattingly v. United States, 91-1 USTC ¶ 50,068 (8th Cir. 1991).
10. *In re* Irvine, 63 B.R. 983 (Bankr. E.D. Pa. 1994).
11. Webb v. Comm'r, 394 F.2d 366, 68-1 USTC ¶ 9341 (5th Cir. 1968).
12. Lee v. United States, 466 F.2d 11 (5th Cir. 1972).
13. I.R.C. § 6501(c)(1).
14. I.R.C. § 6531.
15. I.R.C. § 6664(b).
16. I.R.C. § 6651(f).
17. I.R.C. § 6663(c).
18. Oliver v. Comm'r, 66 T.C.M. (CCH) 1192 (1993).
19. Tomlinson v. Lefkowitz, 14 AFTR2d 5169 (5th Cir. 1964).
20. I.R.C. § 6662(b).
21. Badaracco v. Comm'r, 104 S. Ct. 756, 84-1 USTC ¶ 9150 (S. Ct. 1984).

Failure to File Tax Returns

I. Introduction

A. A surprising number of U.S. citizens and residents, although required to do so, fail to file annual income tax returns. Literally millions of U.S. taxpayers are delinquent in their filings, resulting in a loss of billions of dollars of tax revenue to the U.S. Treasury. Why do people fail to file? The overwhelming majority of cases involve a lack of money with which to pay the tax. If everyone was due a refund, there would be a minimal nonfiler problem.

B. And while many persons are able to "escape the system" and go largely undetected, the vast majority are ultimately detected by the IRS and are asked to comply with the filing requirements. The IRS has an active nonfiler program and some very sophisticated techniques for determining who has not filed. Nevertheless, the IRS will typically require the filing of tax returns for only the last six years.

C. Most of those who go undetected are part of the "underground" economy where all business transactions are done in currency. In such cases there is a lack of an audit trail. Furthermore, there is no information reporting to alert the IRS to a possible failure to file situation.

D. If the IRS becomes aware of a potential failure to file situation, the IRS service center usually issues an inquiry, hoping thereby to generate a voluntary filing. Sometimes these inquiries result in a taxpayer delinquency investigation (TDI) and possible personal contact by a member of the IRS Collection function. Once the TDI begins, a series of computer-generated notices are sent to the taxpayer. Typically, three notices are sent over a period of sixteen weeks. If the IRS receives no response, the case may be assigned to the Automated Collection System (ACS), which maintains a computerized inventory of taxpayers who have delinquent taxes and returns. If the ACS cannot secure the delinquent return, the case is usually referred to a revenue officer group for personal contact.

E. Failure to file an income tax return is an "omission" as opposed to an "act," and whether such an omission is fraudulent is in every case a question of fact.

II. General Filing Requirements

A. I.R.C. § 6012 sets out the general filing requirements for individuals, estates, trusts, corporations, political organizations, homeowners' associations, and bankruptcy estates.

B. *Filing Deadlines*

Form Type	Authority	Deadline
709 Gift Tax	I.R.C. § 6075(b)	April 15 after year of gift date
706 Estate Tax	I.R.C. § 6075(a)	Nine months after date of death
990 Exempt Organization	I.R.C. § 6072(e)	Fifteenth of fifth month after year end
1040 Individual	I.R.C. § 6072(a)	April 15 after calendar year end
1041 Fiduciary	I.R.C. § 6072(a)	April 15 after calendar year end
1120 C Corporation	I.R.C. § 6072(b)	Fifteenth of third month after year end
1120-S S Corporation	I.R.C. § 6072(b)	Fifteenth of third month after year end
5500 Pension	IRS Instructions	End of seventh month after plan year

C. *"Dummy" Returns*

If a taxpayer fails to make a return, the IRS can prepare one for him or her under statutory authority. If it does so, such return as prepared by the IRS is prima facie good and sufficient for all legal purposes.[1] For internal administration purposes, the IRS refers to these returns as "substitutes for returns," or SFRs. Note that this procedure will *not* start the running of the three-year assessment statute.[2]

It is definitely *not* in the taxpayer's best interest to have the IRS prepare returns for him or her. Typically, the IRS will report all known sources of income and calculate the tax according to the method that maximizes the liability. Unless they are aware of deductions, dependents, and a favorable filing status (and they usually are not), the IRS will not allow any of these benefits.

Thus, there are two ways for the IRS to handle a nonfiling situation when they encounter it: (1) solicit a voluntary return from the taxpayer; or, failing which, (2) go through the SFR procedures.[3]

> **Practice Tip**
>
> Whenever a nonfiling situation occurs, have the taxpayer sign and file (preferably by hand delivery) an original return, reporting the correct liability. The IRS is then forced to deal with this original return in one way or another; it cannot just ignore it. If the return is accepted as filed, without audit, the SFR assessment will be partially abated along with any interest and penalties associated with the excess tax.

III. Criminal Sanctions

    A. Statutory Sanction

Typically nonfiling situations are uncovered by the Collection function. If a revenue officer discovers such a delinquency, he or she may solicit the delinquent return from the taxpayer, or he or she may turn it over to the Examination function, assuming he or she does not believe there is any fraud involved.[4] If there is a pattern of noncompliance, he or she may, however, get Criminal Investigation involved.

Most taxpayers are not aware that it is a misdemeanor not to file a tax return on time. The willful failure to file a tax return, pay a tax, or supply required information is a misdemeanor punishable by a $25,000 fine ($100,000 for corporations) plus up to one year in jail.[5] In nonfiler cases, willfulness means the deliberate and intentional failure to file a return when the taxpayer knows that one ought to be filed and that he or she is disobeying the law by failing to file.[6] Prosecutions are numerous under § 7203; many of them in recent years have involved so-called tax protestors.[7]

    B. *Separate Offenses*

Each year of filing delinquency constitutes a separate offense. Therefore, for example, if one fails to file a return for five successive years, he or she could face a maximum incarceration of five years.

    C. *Scope of § 7203*

       1. The term "any person" as used in I.R.C. § 7203 includes not only an individual but also an officer of a corporation or a member or employee of a partnership.

       2. Criminal versus Civil

Fraud that incurs a civil penalty is not necessarily "willful" to incur a criminal penalty. On the other hand, fraud that is "willful" to incur criminal penalties necessarily requires "intent" and invokes also the civil penalties.[8]

3. The elements of § 7203 are (1) willfulness and (2) the omission of at least one of the acts enumerated in the statute at the lawfully prescribed time.

4. Misdemeanor versus Felony

   The U.S. Supreme Court has ruled that a mere failure to file a tax return cannot, without more, be elevated to the status of a felony. Failure to file involves an "omission," not a "commission," and, therefore, a felony tax evasion charge may not be instigated, except where an overt act of evasion has occurred.[9]

D. *Effect of Failure to Assess*

   Failure by the IRS to assess the tax does not preclude indictment for willfully failing to file a return or pay the tax.[10]

E. *Venue*

   Venue for prosecution for failure to file lies in the internal revenue district where the taxpayer lives and conducts business.[11]

F. *Interplay between § 7201 and § 7203*

   Sansone is the leading case explaining the interplay between § 7201 (the felony evasion statute) and § 7203 (the misdemeanor failure to file statute). There, the Supreme Court held that *Sansone* was not entitled to the lesser included offense instruction. The § 7203 misdemeanor is "completely encompassed" by the greater § 7201 offense when the elements of the latter are made out, and the IRS is entitled to the felony conviction.[12]

G. *Referrals from Compliance*

   If IRS employees in the Compliance functions become aware of a fraudulent nonfiling situation, they are required to make a referral to Criminal Investigation (CI) by preparing a referral Form 2797.[13]

IV. Defenses

A. *Ignorance*

   In one case a judge was justified in not accepting the explanation of a lawyer that he did not know that the law required the filing of returns if he did not have the money to pay the tax.[14]

B. *Fifth Amendment*

   The privilege in the Fifth Amendment against self-incrimination is not a defense to an indictment charging failure to file.[15]

C. *Reliance on Professionals*

   Generally, reliance on the advice of accountants is not a defense in failure to file cases. However, it has been held that such reliance is an issue for jury consideration.[16]

D. *Statute of Limitations Defense*

Charges for tax crimes generally must be brought within six years. When a taxpayer willfully fails to file a tax return, the limitations period generally expires six years after the due date of the return plus the period of any extension to file the return. This is most likely the reason that normally only six years of delinquent returns are pursued by IRS examiners and revenue officers.[17] Note that the unlimited statutory period of I.R.C. § 6501(c)(3) (for nonfilers) relates solely to *assessment, not prosecution.*

V. Delinquency (Late-Filing) Penalty[18]

A. *General Statutory Rule*

The IRS can assess 5 percent per month (or a fraction thereof) up to 25 percent in the aggregate when an income tax return is filed late. The penalty can be avoided if "reasonable cause" is shown. The penalty is applicable only to the net amount of tax due. If the return is filed within an approved extension period, the penalty cannot be assessed. Note that if a taxpayer miscalculates his or her estimated tax with an automatic extension request, the delinquency penalty can be retroactively imposed.

If the failure to file is *fraudulent*, the penalty percentages increase dramatically. In such a case, the IRS can assess 15 percent per month (or a fraction thereof) up to 75 percent in the aggregate.[19]

B. *Retroactive Effect*

The delinquency penalty will be applied where the tax is paid within the filing extension period (but after the original due date), and the actual filing date is after the extension period has expired. That is, the full 25 percent penalty will apply retroactively to the original due date.[20]

C. *Reliance on Counsel*

The Supreme Court has ruled that reliance on the advice of counsel will not avoid the delinquency penalty.[21]

VI. Information Returns

A. *Interest and Dividends*

For 1099-INTs and 1099-DIVs, the delinquency penalty is $1.00 per return.[22]

B. *Exempt Organization Returns*

A failure to file a Form 990 can result in a penalty of $20 per day up to a maximum of the lesser of $10,000 or 5 percent of the annual gross receipts of the organization. However, the 990 delinquency penalty can be avoided upon a showing of "reasonable cause."[23]

C. *Pension Plans*

The penalty for failure to file an information return for deferred compensation (pension) plans (i.e., 5500 forms) is $25 per day, up to a $15,000 maximum, unless reasonable cause is shown.[24]

D. *Wage and Tax Statements*

A willful failure to furnish a W-2 form can result in a $1,000 fine plus one year in jail.[25]

E. *Treasury Currency Reports and 8300 Forms*

In the case of any willful failure to file information returns in the case where a business receives more than $10,000 in currency, the criminal sanction applies by substituting five years for one year.[26]

F. *Information Returns*

Effective in 1987, the failure to file an information return can result in a penalty of $100 per failure up to $1,500,000 per year.[27]

VII. Partnerships

A. *General Filing Requirements*

The I.R.C. contains a requirement that partnerships must file a return. Essentially, a partnership return is an "information" return in that it does not incur any tax liability. These return forms (Form 1065) must be filed annually.[28]

B. *Sanctions for Failure to File Partnership Returns*

Failure to file a partnership return (or late filing) can result in the imposition of a penalty. The failure to file penalty continues for only five months. The penalty is calculated at $195 times the number of partners times the number of months of delinquency (up to 12 months maximum). This penalty can only be assessed against the partnership. Presumably, this means that the IRS could not go against a limited partner personally to collect the penalty.[29] The same rule applies to S Corporations.[30]

VIII. Miscellaneous Provisions

A. *Statute of Limitations*

If no return is filed, the three-year assessment statute of limitations does not begin to run.[31] Note also that if a filing delinquency exceeds three years and there is an overpayment on the return, no refund check will be issued by the IRS.[32] Moreover, if *no* return is filed, any refund claim must be filed within two years of the tax payment.[33]

B. *Applicable Forum*
The U.S. Tax Court generally has jurisdiction over civil failure to file penalties, while the U.S. District Court has jurisdiction over criminal penalties for failure to file.

C. *Validity of Deficiency Notice*
Failure to file a return will not preclude the IRS's subsequent issuance of a valid statutory notice of deficiency.[34]

D. *Incomplete Returns*
Tax returns that contain the defendant's name and address but no data as to his or her income or expenses are not a return for purposes of a criminal failure to file violation.[35]

E. *Bankruptcy Dischargeability*
If a court holds that a failure to file a tax return was willful, then the tax liability of the debtor is nondischargeable in a Title 11 proceeding.[36] Before filing for bankruptcy, then, a debtor would be well advised to ensure that all required tax returns have been filed prior to his or her petition date.

F. *Voluntary Disclosure*[37]
Voluntary disclosure is a procedure invoked by taxpayers to avoid criminal prosecution for past tax crimes. A voluntary disclosure occurs where a taxpayer, prior to the initiation of an investigation, advises the IRS that he or she has failed to file returns or has filed false returns.[38] Generally the IRS will consider a voluntary disclosure as a reason for refraining from prosecution of a delinquent taxpayer for past tax crimes, including the nonfiling of tax returns. The theory is that voluntary disclosure negates the willfulness element that must be proved at trial.

It must be emphasized that there are no guarantees of nonprosecution following a voluntary disclosure.[39] The IRS's position is that voluntary disclosure does not bar criminal prosecution, but rather, is a factor to be considered when deciding to recommend prosecution.[40]

IX. Conclusions

If a tax practitioner discovers that a client has failed to file a federal tax return, his advice to that client should depend on whether the IRS has commenced an investigation of the delinquency. If an investigation has not commenced, there is no absolute assurance that there will be no prosecution. However, in the author's forty-eight years of experience, no prosecution has ever resulted where there has been a voluntary filing of a delinquent return prior to a CI inquiry. This is also the informal policy of the IRS.[41]

A taxpayer should never delay the filing of a tax return simply because of a shortage of funds. There are all sorts of available procedures for dealing with money owed to the IRS. These include installment agreements, offers in compromise, bankruptcy, and even determinations of uncollectibility. Just remember, it is generally not a crime to owe money to the IRS, but failure to file is definitely a crime.

There is another reason why many people fail to file: unavailability of records from which to prepare an accurate return. But this should never be a rationalization for failure to file. Where exact figures cannot, because of missing or incomplete records, be used in completing a return, the use of reasonable estimates can be used. The recommended procedure is to attach a full-disclosure disclaimer to the return putting the IRS on notice that the return has been prepared using estimated numbers. Remember that it is far better to file a return based on good-faith estimates than not to file at all. Additionally, one should keep in mind that the IRS employees charged with the responsibility of soliciting delinquent returns are not auditors; they do not work for the *Examination* function. Therefore, they are not really concerned with the *accuracy* of the return.

X. Notes

1. I.R.C.§ 6020(b).
2. I.R.C. § 6501(b)(3).
3. IRM 4.12.1.1.
4. IRM 5.1.11.2.2.
5. *See* I.R.C. § 7203; IRM 9.1.3.3.4.1.
6. United States v. Aitken, 755 F.2d 188, 85-1 USTC ¶ 9209 (1st Cir. 1985).
7. *See* IRM 9.1.3.3.4.1 re the elements of the offense of failure to file.
8. *See* I.R.C. § 6663 for civil fraud penalties.
9. Spies v. United States, 317 U.S. 492, 30 AFTR 364 (S. Ct. 1943); IRM 25.1.7.1.
10. United States v. Commerford, 12 AFTR 364 (2d Cir. 1933).
11. United States v. Gorman, 21 AFTR2d 1177 (7th Cir. 1968).
12. Sansone v. United States, 380 U.S. at 351, 15 AFTR2d 611 (S. Ct. 1965).
13. IRM 25.1.7.5.
14. Ripperger v. United States, 52 AFTR 944 (4th Cir. 1957).
15. Sullivan v. United States, 274 U.S. 259, 6 AFTR 809 (S. Ct. 1926).
16. United States v. Platt, 26 AFTR2d 70-5829 (2d Cir. 1970).
17. IRM 4.20.2.5.
18. *See* IRM 20.1.2.1.1 for a discussion and summary of I.R.C. §§ 6651 and 6698.
19. I.R.C. § 6651(f).
20. I.R.C. § 6651(a)(1).
21. United States v. Boyle, 469 U.S. 241, 85-1 USTC ¶ 13,602 (S. Ct. 1985).

22. I.R.C. § 6652(a).
23. I.R.C. § 6652(c).
24. *See* I.R.C. §§ 6058, 6652(e).
25. I.R.C. § 7204.
26. I.R.C. §§ 6050I, 7203.
27. I.R.C. § 6721(a)(1).
28. I.R.C. § 6031; *see* § 6231(f) for foreign partnership filing requirements.
29. I.R.C. § 6698. *But see* Simons v. United States, 89-1 USTC ¶ 9238 (S.D. Fla.1989), which held that general partners in a partnership that owned an apartment building were individually liable for the § 6698 penalty.
30. I.R.C. § 6699.
31. I.R.C. § 6501(c)(3).
32. I.R.C. § 6511(b)(2)(A); Rev. Rul. 76-511, 1976-2 CB 428.
33. I.R.C. § 6511(a).
34. *See* Treas. Reg. § 301.6211-1(a); Hartman v. Comm'r, 65 T.C. 542 (1975).
35. United States v. Pryor, 78-1 USTC ¶ 9391 (8th Cir. 1978).
36. 11 U.S.C. § 523(a)(1)(B)(i); Toti v. United States, 94-1 USTC ¶ 50,235 (6th Cir. 1994).
37. For an excellent discussion of this topic, see Webb, *High Income Nonfilers Can Preclude Criminal Prosecution through Voluntary Disclosure*, 70(2) TAXES—Tax MAG. 100 (Feb. 1992).
38. Chad Muller & Farley Katz, *IRS Makes Important Changes to Its Voluntary Disclosure Policy*, 98 J. TAXATION 79 (Feb. 2003); *see also* Charles P. Rettig & Steven R. Toscher, *IRS Revised Voluntary Disclosure Policy: Feel Lucky?*, 5 J. Tax PRAC. & PROCEDURE 15 (June–July 2003).
39. United States v. Hebel, 668 F.2d 995, 82-1 USTC ¶ 9162 (8th Cir. 1982). This court pointed out that the IRS's policy of nonprosecution of voluntary disclosures was formally abandoned in 1952. Thus, the defendant could not argue that there was a violation of due process.
40. Crystal v. United States, 99-1 USTC ¶ 50464 (9th Cir. 1999).
41. *See* I.R.S. News Release No. IR 432 (1961).

Criminal Tax Investigation and Prosecution

I. Introduction

A. Nothing strikes fear in the heart of the average taxpayer so much as the thought of being taken to jail for cheating on income taxes. The purpose of this subchapter is to introduce the reader to the inner workings of the criminal section of the IRS. A criminal tax case usually develops from an investigation by the Criminal Investigation (CI) section of the IRS.

B. *Publicity*
Obviously the IRS does not have the resources and manpower to prosecute every tax cheat in the United States. Therefore, to obtain the most "bang for the buck," the CI picks its cases very carefully. The IRS's CI will typically investigate and recommend for prosecution only high-profile taxpayers to create the maximum possible impact on the compliance attitudes of taxpayers.[1] Additionally, the IRS is fond of contacting the media for exposure to would-be tax cheats, giving the idea that the IRS vigorously prosecutes fraudulent taxpayers. A good example of such media coverage is the famous case of hotelier Leona Helmsley (now deceased).[2] Thus, the deterrent effect of criminal tax prosecutions is the most important consideration to the government.

II. Referral Sources

A. *General Sources*
Criminal tax cases develop from a number of different sources, including the following:
1. Referrals from IRS Examination personnel (revenue agents and tax auditors);
2. Referrals from IRS Collection personnel (revenue officers);
3. Referrals from other law enforcement agencies such as the Drug Enforcement Administration (DEA);
4. Currency transactions reports (CTRs); and, most importantly,
5. Informants.[3]

B. *The Internet*

In addition to the traditional third-party sources of information (informants, public records, etc.), the IRS uses Internet search engines to collect news reports about taxpayers. Moreover, a taxpayer's own website is a continuing source of information.

> **Practice Tip**
>
> Practitioners should advise their clients *never* to put data or information on their website that they would not like the IRS to read. This rule applies equally to social media such as Facebook and Twitter.

C. *Informant Profile*

People seeking revenge or a reward are an important source of information leading to criminal investigations. Ex-spouses, ex-girlfriends, ex-boyfriends, neighbors, and ex-employees with detailed knowledge of the taxpayer's history are a great source for CI leads.

III. Investigation by Special Agents

A. *In General*

Investigation of a criminal tax case is usually assigned to a single agent known as a "special" agent. These agents have as their sole duty the development of the case in a manner sufficient to support a successful prosecution of the targeted taxpayer. They may also recommend that the case be referred to the civil agents (known as revenue agents) for development as a noncriminal (i.e., civil) case. If the case is accepted for prosecution, the special agent develops all the facts and sees the case all the way through trial in federal district court.[4] Special agents of CI investigate both Title 26 crimes as well as Title 18 crimes. Tax crimes that come to light from other agencies such as the DEA do not go forward for prosecution until CI has investigated them. CI investigates tax crimes involving illegal- as well as legal-sourced income. Once a case is screened by CI and criminal potential is determined, the case is "numbered" and assigned to a special agent. The person being investigated may be issued what is known as a "target" letter. This type of letter comes well before an indictment is issued.

Criminal tax investigations take a long time to complete. The average length of time from onset to completion of the special agent's report can range from eighteen to thirty months.

B. *Authority*

Any agent charged with the duty of enforcing the criminal tax statutes[5] has the authority to

1. Carry firearms;
2. Execute search warrants;[6]
3. Execute arrest warrants;
4. Serve subpoenas and summonses;
5. Make arrests without a warrant for offenses committed in his or her presence; and
6. Seize property subject to forfeiture.[7]

There are only two provisions in the I.R.C. that empower IRS agents to make arrests, execute searches, or seize evidence. In both instances the authorization is limited to a specific class of IRS agent. 26 U.S.C. § 7608(a) grants to agents who are charged with enforcing the provisions of Subtitle E (alcohol, tobacco, and certain excise taxes) the power to make arrests, execute and serve search warrants, and carry firearms. Similar powers are granted to an IRS agent who is a criminal investigator with CI or of the Treasury Inspector General Office of the IRS. Essentially, this means that there are three types of agents who have these powers:

1. Special agents of CI;
2. Inspection (internal security) agents; and
3. ATF (alcohol, tobacco, and firearms) agents.

C. *Team Approach*

Although a single special agent is in charge of a particular case, whenever it is necessary to interview a taxpayer or third-party witness a second agent usually accompanies the agent in charge. It is desirable from the government's standpoint to have a corroborating witness in case of difficulty. The special agent in charge will often call in a civil revenue agent to assist with the technical aspects of the case. Chief counsel lawyers may also be consulted on legal aspects of the case during the investigation phase.

One of the agents will generally take copious notes, and then return to his or her office later to prepare a contemporaneous memorandum of interview.

D. *Element of Surprise*

Special agents love to catch taxpayer-targets when they least expect a visit. Often they show up at a taxpayer's residence early in the morning or at dinnertime, when it is inconvenient for the taxpayer to call his or her accountant or lawyer. In an effort to be "cooperative," most taxpayers will talk willingly. That is a big mistake. By catching taxpayers by surprise and off-guard, agents can get information (and often untrue statements). Much work will already have been done by the agents before they ever show up, so it will be easier for them to catch the taxpayer in a lie.[8]

Often a different set of agents will show up simultaneously at the taxpayer's accountant's office so that there is no opportunity for the taxpayer and his or her accountant to get their stories straight.

Practice Tip

A lawyer-practitioner is well advised to hire an independent *Kovel* accountant to assist him or her in the case (other than the taxpayer's regular accountant) so that the attorney-client privilege can be protected. *United States v. Kovel*, 9 AFTR2d 366 (2d Cir. 1961), established the rule cloaking an accountant with attorney-client privilege if hired directly by the attorney in a criminal tax case.

E. *Identification*

All investigative agents of the IRS are required to carry identification known as a "pocket commission." The distinctive character of a special agent's commission is the gold badge on the exterior. They also carry business cards with distinctive gold badges on them.

F. *Classification of Interviewees*

In any tax-related investigation, the Department of Justice or the IRS CI must make contact with and interview numerous individuals. Practitioners representing persons so contacted must be sensitive to how the government views the person they are interviewing. Generally, the IRS classifies interviewees in one of three categories:
1. Target;
2. Subject; or
3. Witness.

If the person contacted is a "target," that means that the government considers him or her to be a defendant and likely to be indicted. By identifying individuals as "subjects," investigators indicate that they believe these individuals engaged in suspicious behavior and fall within the scope of the investigation, but fall short of being a target. All others contacted by investigation fall into the category of "witnesses," who generally have no criminal culpability. An example of persons the government considered to be subjects were employees of KPMG as a part of the widely publicized tax shelter probe.[9]

G. *Tape-Recorded Conversations*

Neither the U.S. Constitution nor any act of Congress requires that official approval be secured before conversations are overheard or recorded by government agents with the consent of one of the conversants. Indeed, even if such a recording were made in violation of a regulation or IRM provision, evidence obtained thereby would not be excludable at trial.[10]

Practice Tip

Any practitioner who speaks with a criminal investigator of the IRS should always assume that the conversation is being audio-recorded surreptitiously. It is not without precedent that the lawyer or other practitioner finds him or herself the target of an investigation, and these sorts of conversations become evidentiary in that proceeding.

H. *Search Warrants*

CI agents are permitted to search a taxpayer's business or personal premises but only if they apply to a U.S. magistrate for a search warrant that must be supported by probable cause. Moreover, the Fourth Amendment requires that a search warrant describe the things to be seized with sufficient particularity to prevent a "general, exploratory rummaging in a person's belongings."[11]

I. *Use of Administrative Summons*

Special agents of CI are authorized to issue administrative summonses[12] in the course of their investigations. A typical CI investigation will make extensive use of this power.[13]

A *blanket* objection to the issuance of an IRS summons based on the Fifth Amendment privilege against self-incrimination is not a viable defense. The recipient of the summons must appear before the issuing agent and claim the privilege on a question-by-question and document-by-document basis.[14] That the evidence obtained through the summons may later be used against the taxpayer in a criminal prosecution is no barrier to the summons enforcement.[15] A witness may properly invoke the privilege when he or she reasonably apprehends a risk of self-incrimination even though no criminal charges are pending against him or her and even if the risk of prosecution is remote.[16]

J. *Grand Jury Investigations*

Investigations of particular cases or projects may be conducted by means of the administrative process, or by seeking a grand jury investigation. A grand jury investigation is considered to be necessary and appropriate in the following circumstances:

1. It is apparent that the administrative process cannot develop the relevant facts within a reasonable period of time, or

2. Coordination of the tax investigation with an ongoing or proposed grand jury investigation would be more efficient; and

3. The case has significant deterrent potential.[17]

In grand jury investigations, the special agent in charge of the case works closely with the Assistant U.S. Attorney (AUSA) and may serve subpoenas to fact witnesses during the investigation. Note that administrative summonses are not used in grand jury investigations.

K. *CI Withdrawal from Prosecution*

If CI determines that a case should not be forwarded for consideration of prosecution, it sends a withdrawal letter to the "target" taxpayer and a copy thereof to his or her lawyer.

IV. Role of Civil Revenue Agents

A. *Civil Examiner's Duty*

Every audit conducted by the IRS has potential for criminal investigation and prosecution. The IRM contains instructions on what an agent must do if he or she suspects fraud. If, during a routine civil audit, a revenue agent suspects fraud, he or she is required to suspend the civil inquiry and refer the case to CI without telling the taxpayer the reason for the suspension.[18] If this does not occur, the revenue agent runs the risk of being accused of actually gathering evidence for a criminal investigation. Evidence obtained by revenue agents after fraud is suspected can be excluded at trial, but only if it can be proved that the revenue agent acted in bad faith. This is a difficult burden of proof for defense counsel. Note that revenue agents do not give partial Miranda warnings; only special agents of the CI do this.[19]

In recent years the line between civil and criminal cases has become somewhat blurred. In fact there are now fraud specialists within the civil Examination function to advise agents about what to look for in civil cases when fraud is suspected.

Practice Tip

If a revenue agent starts asking "why" questions, then a practitioner should be on the alert that the agent may be suspecting fraud. "Why" questions tend to establish things like intent and motivation.

B. *Agent Referral*

After a revenue agent suspects fraud and suspends his or her audit, he or she prepares a Form 2797 ("Referral Report for Potential Fraud Cases") and forwards it to the group manager for review. If the group manager concurs in the recommendation, the case is forwarded to the CI for prosecution evaluation.

C. *Agent Latitude in Making Referrals*

Revenue agents and their managers enjoy some latitude in making referral decisions, and usually a reviewing court will not disturb their decision since a referral decision is inescapably a discretionary one. A mere suspicion, or a "first" indication of fraud, does not rise to the level of a "firm" indication of fraud.[20]

D. *Revenue Agent Deception*

A revenue agent cannot deceive a taxpayer or his or her representative into believing that an audit is being conducted as a purely civil matter when, in fact, it has criminal overtones. If this happens, the evidence obtained through deception will be suppressed at trial.[21]

V. Miranda Warning

A. *Applicability to Tax Investigations*

Tax investigations are not immune from the *Miranda*[22] requirements for warnings to be given to a potential defendant. As long as there is the likelihood that an investigation will end up in a criminal prosecution, a modified Miranda warning must be given.[23]

Practice Tip

Practitioners should always advise clients to discontinue communicating with IRS special agents after being read their rights and immediately secure experienced criminal tax counsel.[24]

B. *Right to Counsel*

Special agents are always careful, during a Miranda warning, to advise a taxpayer of his or her right to speak with a lawyer. Nevertheless it is noteworthy that the agents often appear unannounced at a taxpayer's residence in the early morning or during evening hours, when most lawyers are not typically in their office. Thus the taxpayer cannot make a quick call to his or her lawyer. At the risk of cynicism, this timing of the interview is not coincidental.

C. *Custody*

When CI special agents interview a taxpayer at his or her home or office, the taxpayer is not in "custody." Therefore, only a partial Miranda warning is given. A full Miranda warning would include advising a taxpayer that he or she has a right to free legal representation. And that would be appropriate if the taxpayer were in custody or otherwise deprived of his or her freedom.[25]

D. *Statement Admissibility*

When CI special agents fail to give the partial Miranda warning, any statements they receive are still admissible in court. This is because, according to case law, the IRS need not follow its own procedural requirements (IRM) when such requirements are not mandated by statute or the U.S. Constitution.[26]

VI. Other Constitutional Issues

A. *Right of Silence*

The Fifth Amendment to the U.S. Constitution states that no person "shall be compelled *in any criminal case* [emphasis supplied] to be a witness against himself." Thus a potential defendant in a criminal tax case has the right at all times to remain totally silent. As a practical matter, however, this is often difficult. As mentioned above, special agents of CI have an annoying habit of appearing at a taxpayer's home at odd hours to question a taxpayer. If the taxpayer is a "target" of the investigation, the CI agents are required to give the Miranda warning, which includes a reminder of the right to remain silent. Despite this, however, a typical taxpayer's impulses are to want to "explain" away any misunderstandings the agents have, and this inevitably leads to statements made by a taxpayer that are harmful. The best advice, of course, is for the taxpayer to say nothing and immediately call his or her lawyer.

Assuming the criminal nature of an inquiry, if the answer to any question would furnish the prosecution with a link in the chain of evidence against the witness, the witness may refuse to testify. Defense counsel must be vigilant in making an early determination as to whether the client should assert the privilege. The privilege may be asserted in response to questions posed by the following:

1.   A CI special agent;
2.   A civil revenue agent;
3.   A collection revenue officer; and
4.   An "inspection" agent.[27]

The witness is under no obligation to explain to any IRS employee the specific reason why the privilege is being asserted. In other words, the Fifth Amendment privilege is self-actuating.

Note that in cases involving prosecution for failure to file a tax return, the privilege against self-incrimination is not a defense.[28]

B. *Wrongful Search and Seizure*

A court may not exclude evidence under the Fourth Amendment unless it finds that an unlawful search or seizure violated the defendant's own constitutional rights. And the defendant's rights are violated only when the challenged conduct invaded *his or her* legitimate expectation of privacy rather than that of a *third party*.[29]

C. *Rights of Witnesses*

A witness, when interviewed or questioned by CI agents, is entitled to have his or her own counsel present to represent and advise him or her. This is true whether or not the witness is the "target" of the investigation. Generally the witness is also entitled to have a copy of any affidavit or "Q&A" transcript furnished to him or her promptly.[30]

VII. Post-investigation and Trial

A. *Damage Control*

A lawyer may not be retained until after the criminal investigation has commenced or been concluded. Regardless, having been informed of CI's involvement in a client's tax affairs, a lawyer's first task is to determine what information has already been turned over to the IRS and what verbal statements have been made by the client. Once the potential damage has been assessed, the lawyer should ensure that no further damage is done. In this connection, there should be absolutely no further cooperation with the CI investigators.

B. *Preindictment Conference*

Prior to a taxpayer's indictment, he or she will be given an opportunity to meet with the IRS's special agent in charge (SAC). At this conference the taxpayer (or his or her representative) will present reasons why he or she feels that prosecution is not appropriate. The government will not be willing to provide the defense with "free discovery" at this conference. The taxpayer is not given a copy of the special agent's report. The SAC will rarely provide any information beyond what is in his or her letter offering a conference. The SAC, if he or she believes that prosecution is warranted, will forward the case file to the Department of Justice. The Tax Division of the Department of Justice will usually provide an opportunity for the taxpayer to come to Washington, D.C., for an additional conference.

Practice Tip

Practitioners should always take advantage of an opportunity to meet with a special agent, as it offers a reasonably good chance to convince the government that its case is weak. Requests for these conferences should be made by letter as early as possible in the investigation.

C. *Decision to Prosecute—Factors Considered*
In deciding whether to prosecute a tax crime, CI and the Department of Justice will typically consider the following factors:
1. Whether the taxpayer has made a preinvestigation voluntary disclosure;
2. Whether there is a substantial amount of tax involved;
3. Whether the taxpayer has any health problems; and
4. Whether there is any evidence of willfulness.

D. *Multiple Prosecutions*[31]
It is the current policy of the Department of Justice that several offenses arising out of a single transaction should be alleged and tried together and should not be made the basis of multiple prosecutions. This is a policy directed by considerations both of fairness to the defendant and of orderly and efficient law enforcement. Thus, tax indictments are typically of the multiple-count variety.

E. *Burden of Proof*
As in all criminal matters, the burden of proof remains on the government in criminal tax investigations and the subsequent trial, although the burden of going forward with the evidence may shift from one side to the other. It is the government's burden to prove beyond a reasonable doubt that the defendant intended to commit a crime and intended willfully to defraud the government.[32]

F. *Use of Summary Witnesses and Charts at Trial*
In criminal tax trials, unlike some other criminal trials, either party is entitled to present a summary expert witness to explain the numbers for the judge or jury. This summary witness may also present charts and other visual aids for this purpose. Summary charts may not be admitted into evidence unless a proper foundation is established connecting the numbers on the chart with the underlying evidence. For this reason the designated summary witnesses are permitted to sit through and observe the entire trial.[33]

VIII. Statute of Limitations Issues

A. *General Rules*
Tax crimes specified in the Internal Revenue Code have their own special limitations period. Generally the indictment (formal charge issued by a grand jury) must be brought within six years of the commission of the offense. This statute accrues (begins to run) on the date of signing the tax return in question. In the case of failure to file a return, the key date is the due date of the return.[34]

B.   *Amended, Nonfraudulent Returns*

In the case of a false or fraudulent return, the tax may be assessed at any time.[35] That is, the assessment statute (normally three or six years, depending on whether there was a 25 percent income omission) never even starts to run. Where a fraudulent return is followed by a subsequent nonfraudulent amended return, the three-year statute is not triggered. As stated by the Supreme Court, "[N]othing is present in the statute that can be construed to suspend its operation as a consequence of a fraudulent filer's subsequent repentant conduct."[36]

IX. Immunity from Prosecution

A.   *Immunized Testimony*

If a witness asserts his or her Fifth Amendment privilege to refuse to incriminate him or herself, or the government believes that he or she will do so, the Department of Justice may obtain immunity from prosecution for the witness under federal statutory authority. The government has no inherent power to grant immunity; it must resort to obtaining immunity under 18 U.S.C. § 6002. Testimony procured under this statute may not be used against the witness in any criminal case, even if information obtained is only indirectly derived from the immunized testimony.

B.   *Types of Immunity*

There are two types of immunity: "use" immunity and "transactional" immunity. Transactional immunity means that a witness may not be prosecuted for offenses to which the compelled testimony relates. Use immunity—the type granted under 18 U.S.C. § 6002—is much more restrictive, and the witness is only protected from the "use and derivative use" of compelled testimony and evidence derived therefrom. The transactional immunity affords a witness considerably broader protection than does the Fifth Amendment privilege.[37]

X. Miscellaneous Issues

A.   *Government Success Rate*

Because of the resources required for a successful prosecution and the government's desire for maximum publicity, it only takes cases to trial where there is a reasonable probability of conviction. In the recent past, the government's success rate in criminal tax cases exceeded 90 percent.

Practice Tip

If you can convince a prosecutor that he or she has less than, say, a 70 percent chance of success at trial, chances are that you can successfully kill the case.

B. *Voluntary Disclosure*

If a taxpayer is aware of errors on a tax return and has not been contacted by an investigator, a typical strategy is to come forward and file an amended return—a so-called voluntary disclosure. And while there have been relatively few prosecutions of true voluntary disclosures, the IRS has consistently reserved the right to do so. Thus disclosure will not, ipso facto, necessarily insulate a taxpayer from prosecution under any administrative policy or recognized practice.[38]

C. *Grand Jury Proceedings*

Absent a waiver, the government may prosecute a federal tax defendant only after an indictment returned by a grand jury, composed of twenty-three individuals. This takes place after the termination of the investigation and after various review procedures are concluded. A grand jury may also instigate an investigation. If it does so, the defense has a much more difficult job. Witnesses must testify before the grand jury without the presence of their lawyer and consult with counsel only by leaving the room for this purpose.

Grand jury proceedings are generally considered to be secret, and transcripts thereof are not subject to disclosure except in judicial proceedings. The Supreme Court has held that an IRS audit, including administrative appeals, is not a judicial proceeding, and the government may not obtain disclosure of grand jury transcripts for purposes of a civil tax audit.[39]

D. *Venue*

Venue for federal criminal prosecution lies in the district in which the offense was committed. In failure to file cases, venue is proper in the district in which the return should have been filed. In evasion cases, venue is proper in the district in which any affirmative act of fraud was committed.[40]

E. *Vicarious Admissions*

Since 1986 the vicarious admissions rule (for statements made by lawyers attending conferences before the Criminal Section of the Tax Division of the Department of Justice) is no longer used by the Tax Division, except where the lawyer authenticates a written instrument.[41]

F. *Spousal Communications*

Communications between a husband and wife, privately made, are generally assumed to have been intended to be of a confidential nature and are, therefore, held to be privileged. Communications made in the presence of a third party, however, are not privileged. Note that the marital communications privilege belongs to, and therefore may be invoked by, the defendant spouse.[42] There also exists an independent privilege of one spouse to refuse to testify adversely against another. In a civil tax controversy, the spousal privilege does not apply.

G. *Pattern of Behavior*

The government prefers cases that cover a number of years rather than a single-year case. The reason for this is that showing a pattern of behavior may convince a jury of a criminal intent rather than relying on an isolated event.

H. *Sentencing Guidelines*

Although the I.R.C. provides sentencing maximums for various types of tax crimes, courts are generally guided by what are known as sentencing guidelines. There has been some litigation recently as to whether courts are bound by the guidelines, but generally they are followed. In tax cases, the number of months to be served is based on the loss of revenue to the government, according to a sliding scale. Health of the taxpayer or of his or her spouse can sometimes be a mitigating factor in sentencing considerations.

Practice Tip

Practitioners should try to minimize the tax deficiency numbers as much as possible in the early stages of a CI investigation.

XI. Notes

1. IRM 9.1.1.4.
2. *See* United States v. Helmsley, 91-2 USTC ¶ 50,455 (2d Cir. 1991).
3. *See* I.R.C. § 7623 regarding payment by the IRS of discretionary rewards to informants; *see also* IRM 9.4.2.5.
4. IRM 9.6.
5. This does not include "revenue" agents, only "special" agents.
6. United States v. Rosnow, 92-2 USTC ¶ 50,506 (1992); IRM 9.4.9.1.
7. I.R.C.§ 7608.
8. And thus be a basis for a 18 U.S.C. § 1001 violation. Note that false statements do not have to be in writing or under oath to be the basis of this violation.
9. Cassell Bryan-Low, *KPMG, Tax-Shelter Probe Grows; U.S. Classifies 30 as "Subjects,"* WALL ST. J., Mar. 5, 2004.
10. United States v. Caceres, 440 U.S. 741 (S. Ct. 1979).
11. Voss v. Bergsgaard, 774 F.2d 402 (10th Cir. 1985).
12. *See* I.R.C. § 7602.
13. *See* IRM 9.1.2.2.
14. United States v. Allee, 89-2 USTC ¶ 9615 (1st Cir. 1989).
15. United States v. Stewart, 77 AFTR2d 96-510 (5th Cir. 1996).
16. United States v. Argomaniz, 91-1 USTC ¶ 50,135 (11th Cir. 1991).

17. IRM 9.5.2.2.
18. *See generally* IRM 25.1.
19. See the result in *United States v. Toussaint*, 78-2 USTC ¶ 9793 (S.D. Tex. 1978), where all evidence and statements obtained by a revenue agent after finding firm indications of fraud were excludable at trial.
20. Groder v. United States, 87-1 USTC ¶ 9259 (4th Cir. 1987).
21. United States v. Tweel, 77-1 USTC ¶ 9330 (5th Cir. 1977); However, a civil audit is not criminal in nature merely because the referral source was CI. United States v. Caldwell, 87-2 USTC ¶ 9423 (5th Cir. 1987).
22. Miranda v. Arizona, 384 U.S. 436 (1966).
23. United States v. Sturgis, 91 AFTR2d 2003-1557 (D. Del. 2003).
24. *See id.*
25. *Id.*
26. United States v. Irvine, 83-1 USTC ¶ 9166 (1st Cir. 1983), regarding failure to use the word "criminal" in connection with an agent's reading of the *Miranda* warning.
27. I.e., Treasury Inspector General for Tax Administration (TIGTA) agents.
28. Garner v. United States, 424 U.S. 648, 76-1 USTC ¶ 9301 (S. Ct. 1976).
29. United States v. Payner, 447 U.S. 727 (S. Ct. 1980).
30. Treas. Reg. § 601.107(b)(1); *see* IRM 9.4.5.7.3.
31. *See* United States v. Rigas, 605 F.3d 194 (3d Cir. 2010).
32. I.R.C. § 7454.
33. United States v. Citron, 783 F.2d 307 (2d Cir. 1986).
34. *See generally* I.R.C. § 6531.
35. I.R.C. § 6501(c).
36. Badaracco v. Comm'r, 104 S. Ct. 756, 84-1 USTC ¶ 9150 (S. Ct. 1984).
37. See the discussion in *Kastigar v. United States*, 406 U.S. 441 (S. Ct. 1972).
38. United States v. Hebel, 668 F.2d 995 (8th Cir. 1982); SAH 342.14.
39. United States v. Baggot, 463 U.S. 476 (S. Ct. 1983).
40. Fed. R. Crim. P. 18.
41. Tax Div. Directive 86-58, May 30, 1986.
42. *Id.*

Use of Informants by the IRS

I. Introduction and Background

A. The IRS receives, and must evaluate, many informant communications each year. Typically such informants fall into one of the following categories:
   1. Profiteer (i.e., one seeking a reward for the information);
   2. Jealous neighbor;
   3. Scorned lover;
   4. Estranged spouse;
   5. An underpaid (or recently fired) bookkeeper;
   6. A beaten competitor; or
   7. A co-conspirator recently come to religion.

   While one might suppose that an informant may be motivated by a desire to do his or her civic or patriotic duty, such is rarely the case. In virtually all cases, informants are motivated by one of three things: (1) revenge, (2) greed, or (3) government coercion.

B. *Who Is an Informant?*
   An informant is an individual who furnishes information to the IRS. Such information may be furnished on the informant's own initiative or as a result of being directed to furnish information by a special agent or other IRS employee.[1]

C. In some cases (the exact number is unknown), IRS audits, either civil or criminal, are commenced as a direct result of an informant's communication. That communication can take the form of a letter, telephone call, or personal visit.[2]

D. *Statutory Authority for Payment of Rewards*
   Many, if not most, of the persons who furnish information about another person's tax liability do so because they want to be paid for the information. Congress has recognized that without some sort of a reward system, much of the information from informants would not

be forthcoming. Accordingly, the IRS has the statutory authority to pay such sums as are deemed necessary for either of the following:

1. Detecting underpayments of tax or
2. Detecting and bringing to trial any person found guilty of violating the tax laws.

Payments made under this statute are payable directly from the proceeds of the collected tax. Note that proceeds are payable from tax, fines, and penalties only. Statutory interest is not included.[3]

II. Delegation for Approval of Payment of Rewards

Approval for payment of informants' awards has been delegated to the IRS Whistleblower office in Washington, DC[4] or a designated regional service center.[5]

III. Eligibility for Reward

A. *General Rule*
The person who submits information related to the tax law violation is eligible to file the claim for reward under I.R.C. § 7623.[6]

B. *Federal Employees*
Department of Treasury employees are ineligible to receive § 7623 rewards if they were federal employees at the time they came into possession of the relevant portions of the divulged information. Any other current or former federal employee is eligible to file a claim for reward if the information provided came to the individual's knowledge other than in the course of the individual's official duties.[7]

C. *Deceased Informants*
In an informant dies before submitting a claim for reward, it may nevertheless be submitted on his or her behalf by his or her legal representative, such as an executor. To make such a claim, the representative must attach to the claim evidence of his or her authority, such as letters testamentary.[8]

IV. Determination of Payment and Amount of Reward

A. *Regulations*
All relevant factors, including the value of the information furnished in relation to the facts developed by the investigation of the violation, will be taken into account in determining whether a reward will be paid and, if so, the amount of the reward. The amount of the reward will represent "adequate compensation" for the value of the reward, between 15 and 30 percent[9] of the amounts (other than interest) collected due to the information provided. Payment of the reward will be

deferred until after the government collects the tax in question. The informant may, however, waive any claim for taxes not yet collected, and, if so, his or her claim may be immediately processed. Partial reward payments may be made without waiver in cases where a criminal fine has been collected prior to completion of the civil aspects of a case and also where there are multiple tax years involved and the deficiency for one or more of the years has been paid. No person has the authority to contractually bind a district or service center director with respect to the payment of any reward or the amount of the reward.[10]

B. *Limits on Amount of Reward*
   The amount of the award will be determined as follows:
   1. For specific and responsible information that caused the investigation and resulted in recovery, the reward shall be between 15 and 30 percent of the amounts recovered.[11]
   2. For information that caused the investigation and was of value in the determination of tax liabilities (but was from public sources), the reward is limited to 10 percent of the amount recovered.[12]
   3. For information that caused the investigation, but had no direct relationship to the determination of tax liabilities, the reward is limited to 1 percent of the amount recovered, with the total reward not exceeding $2 million.
   4. No reward of less than $100 will be paid.
   5. An informant who has received a direct payment for information provided to the IRS is not precluded from filing a claim for reward for the same information. However, to prevent duplicate payments, the amount of the reward payment will be reduced by the amount of the direct payment.
   6. Due to federal antidisclosure laws, the IRS will not provide information to the informant (or anyone else) about specific actions taken on the information provided.
   7. If an investigation is initiated as a result of the information provided, it can take two or more years before there is a final disposition of the investigation.[13]

V. Procedures for Submission of Claims for Reward

A. *Submission of Information*
   Claims for reward may be submitted in writing to the following:
   Assistant Commissioner (CI)
   1111 Constitution Ave. NW
   Washington, D.C. 20224
   They may also be submitted in writing to the local CI representative.[14] The CI chief in whose jurisdiction a criminal investigation is being contemplated or taking place has the responsibility to evaluate

the use of informants. In deciding whether to use an informant's tip, the CI chief takes into account such factors as the informant's criminal background, his or her previous reliability, and his or her source of information.

B. *Form to Be Used*
Filing a claim for reward under § 7623 is accomplished by preparing Form 211, Application for Reward for Original Information. This form must contain the informant's true name and signature.[15]

C. *Informant Claims Examiner*
Each IRS service center has a person whose duty is to pass on all filed claims for reward. They are known as informant claims examiners.[16]

D. *Informant Letters*
If an informant submits information via a letter, the letter is acknowledged in writing. This acknowledgment letter states that the matter will be given immediate attention.[17]

E. *Verbal Information*
An informant may give his or her information over the telephone to a representative of customer service located at an IRS service center. The toll-free number is 800-829-0433.[18] This is known as the "informants' hotline."[19]

F. *Minimum Recommended Information*
The IRS recommends that an informant's communication contain as much of the following information as possible:
1. Tax years of violations;
2. Aliases, if any;
3. Addresses;
4. Social Security numbers and/or employer ID numbers;
5. Financial data (bank accounts, assets, etc.) and their location;
6. Documents to substantiate the allegation (e.g., books and records); and
7. Dates of birth.[20]

VI. Disclosure of an Informant's Identity

A. *General Rules*
IRS informants fall into one or more of several categories:
1. Anonymous;
2. Confidential;
3. Nonconfidential; and
4. Controlled.

Anonymous informants are either those who refuse to identify themselves or those who use fictitious names and whose true identities are unknown to the IRS. Confidential informants are those who request that their names be held in strict confidence, while nonconfidential informants make no such requests. Controlled informants are those informants who are paid for the information they voluntarily provide or who provide such information involuntarily under some kind of threat by the government.

The IRS is strictly forbidden to disclose the identity of any informant, whether or not a claim for reward has been filed, except on a need-to-know basis.[21]

B. *The Informant Privilege*
Traditionally the IRS has protected informants from possible harassment or retaliation by keeping their identities secret. Generally the IRS will not reveal the identity of a confidential informant without his or her consent.[22] This privilege affords protection to the informant, who has been assured by the government that his or her communications are confidential. However, the informant privilege is qualified in that the government must show that the interest of effective law enforcement outweighs a litigant's need for the information.

C. *Disclosure to State and Local Law Enforcement*
Generally the IRS may disclose tax return information to a state or local government employee for purposes of administering state or local tax law. However, such information cannot be disclosed if the IRS determines that such disclosure would identify a confidential informant.[23]

D. *IRS Liability to Third Parties*
If the IRS improperly discloses the identity of an informant and the informant is subsequently sued by a third party as a result, the informant cannot generally recover damages from the government.[24]

VII. Informants' Tax Liability

A. *General Rule*
Rewards received by informants are fully taxable as ordinary income under I.R.C. § 61. Presumably, however, they are not subject to self-employment tax unless a claimant is in the "business" of turning taxpayers in. To ensure that the informant reports the reward, he or she is required to reflect his or her Social Security number and a date of birth on the claim Form 211.[25]

B. *Compromising an Informant's Tax Liability*
The Taxpayer Bill of Rights (TBOR 2) provides for a prohibition on compromising an informant's tax liability. This reflects the IRS's

long-standing prohibition against special agents compromising the tax liability of an informant in exchange for information about another taxpayer.[26]

VIII. Litigation Issues

A. *Credibility of Informant during Trial*
The IRS must carefully assess an informant's reliability. Otherwise, an entire case may be damaged if a jury or judge questions his or her credibility.[27] If an informant testifies at the taxpayer's trial, he or she will undoubtedly be asked on cross-examination whether he or she was offered or will claim a reward for supplying information to the IRS. If so, such a question is not objectionable. If the answer is yes, the jury is entitled to conclude that the financial stake the informant has in the outcome adversely affects the witness's credibility.[28]

B. *Constitutional Issues*
A constitutional objection to the government's use of an informant will most likely fail. The rationale is that a defendant's conversations with an informant are generally voluntary.[29] In a tax trial, the testimony of a paid informant—even from one expecting a huge reward under I.R.C. § 7623—will not violate the taxpayer's constitutional right to due process. However, the jury may take that fact into consideration, upon proper instruction, in assessing a witness's credibility.[30]

C. *Informant Disclosure at Trial*
At the trial of a taxpayer, a court will generally not order that the identity of an informant be revealed.[31]

IX. Miscellaneous Issues

A. *Expenses Incurred by IRS Employees*
IRS agents who incur expenses to "develop" informants may be reimbursed for such expenses by the government.[32]

B. *IRS's Duty to Pursue*
Once information is turned over by an informant to the IRS, there is no requirement that the IRS must pursue the taxpayer to the extent that the informant may deem appropriate. If the IRS could have, but did not, collect back taxes, the informant's reward claim can be commensurately reduced or denied.[33] Similarly, the IRS has no duty to maximize the taxes collected and, commensurately, the reward.[34]

C. *Related Taxpayers*
Where the information provided relates to related taxpayers (such as investors in a single tax shelter), the reward maximum will apply just once, and not separately to each taxpayer.[35]

D. *Multiple Informants*

If more than one informant jointly provide essentially the same information to the IRS, the appropriate reward will usually be divided among them at the discretion of the IRS.

X. Notes

1. *See generally* IRM 9.4.2.5.
2. *Id.*
3. I.R.C. § 7623(a).
4. Note that as a result of the IRS Restructuring Act of 1998, the position of district director has been eliminated. This will undoubtedly require the redrafting of thousands of sections of statute and regulations.
5. Treas. Reg. § 301.7623-1(a).
6. Treas. Reg. § 301.7623-1(b)(1).
7. Treas. Reg. § 301.7623-1(b)(2).
8. Treas. Reg. § 301.7623-1(b)(3).
9. Ten percent prior to 1997.
10. Treas. Reg. § 301.7623-1(c).
11. I.R.C. § 7623(b)(1).
12. I.R.C. § 7623(b)(2)(A).
13. *See* I.R.S. Publ'n 733.
14. Treas. Reg. § 301.7623-1(d); Form 211 also contains an address where the claim form may be mailed.
15. Treas. Reg. § 301.7623-1(f).
16. *See generally* IRM 9.4.2.5.
17. *See* Ltr. 639 SC.
18. *See* I.R.S. Publ'n 733.
19. *Id.*
20. *Id.*
21. Treas. Reg. § 301.7623-1(e).
22. IRM 25.2.1.2.
23. I.R.C. § 6103(d)(1).
24. Jarvis v. United States, 99-1 USTC ¶ 50,559 (Fed. Cl. 1999).
25. Form 211 instructions.
26. Ann. 96-5, 1996-4 I.R.B. 99.
27. *See* Jackson v. Comm'r, 73 T.C. 394 (1979).
28. Wheeler v. United States, 16 AFTR2d 5845, 351 F.2d 949 (1st Cir. 1965).
29. *See* Hoffa v. United States, 385 U.S. 293 (S. Ct. 1966).
30. United States v. Wilson, 90-2 USTC ¶ 50,368 (11th Cir. 1990).
31. Escobar v. United States, 388 F.2d 661, 21 AFTR2d 427 (5th Cir. 1967).
32. I.R.S. Priv. Ltr. Rul. 8125006.
33. Lagermeier v. United States, 77-1 USTC ¶ 9447 (Cl. Ct. 1977).
34. *Id.*
35. Merrick v. United States, 89-2 USTC ¶ 9645 (Cl. Ct. 1989).

CHAPTER 9

Ethical Considerations

Practice before the IRS

I. Background Material

A. Governing Regulations

Title 31 of the U.S. Code authorizes the Secretary of the Treasury to regulate lawyers, certified public accountants, enrolled agents, enrolled actuaries, and others who practice before the IRS.[1] Regulations under 31 U.S.C. § 330 are promulgated in 31 C.F.R. part 10 and are reprinted as Treasury Department Circular 230.[2]

B. Director of the Office of Professional Responsibility (OPR)

The OPR director is appointed by the Commissioner. It is the director's responsibility to act upon all applications for enrollment to practice before the IRS. He or she also presides over all matters involving disciplinary proceedings.[3]

C. Definition of Practice

"Practice" includes all matters connected with a presentation to the IRS or any of its employees relating to a client's rights, privileges, or liabilities under any law or regulation administered by the IRS.[4]

D. Parallel Authorities

In addition to Circular 230, practitioners who are lawyers or CPAs must also observe the rules of their respective professional organizations. These rules are contained in the American Bar Association (ABA) Model Rules and the American Institute of Certified Public Accountants (AICPA) Code of Professional Conduct. These professional association rules overlap with, but are not identical to, the rules contained in Circular 230.

II. Persons Entitled to Practice

A. *Persons Covered by Circular 230*
The rules contained in Circular 230 govern the recognition of lawyers, certified public accountants, enrolled agents, and other persons representing clients before the Internal Revenue Service.

B. *Authority to Practice*
Lawyers and CPAs who are not under suspension or disbarment may practice before the IRS. Enrolled agents and enrolled actuaries may also practice. Practice by enrolled actuaries is limited to matters involving qualified and nonqualified employee plans. Government employees may not practice before the IRS.[5]

C. *Enrolled Agents (EAs)*
Any person who successfully passes a written examination administered by the IRS, demonstrating special competence in tax matters, may be granted enrollment status. Former IRS employees may also be granted enrollment status if they meet certain conditions. For example, they must apply for enrollment within three years of leaving the IRS's employ, and they must have been employed there for five continuous years in a position that required interpreting the Internal Revenue Code (I.R.C.) and regulations.[6] Applicants who have been approved will receive from the director of practice an enrollment card, sometimes called a "treasury card." These cards must be renewed every three years.[7] This three-year period is referred to as the "enrollment cycle."

D. *Continuing Education for EAs*
To qualify for renewal enrollment, EAs must complete a minimum of sixteen hours of continuing education in each year of an enrollment cycle. Continuing education courses must be conducted by a qualifying sponsor.[8]

E. *Nonlicensed Representation*
A person who is not a lawyer, CPA, or EA may represent a taxpayer before the IRS if he or she fits within one of the following situations:
1. Individuals may appear on their own behalf before the IRS.
2. An individual may represent a member of his or her immediate family.
3. A regular full-time employee of an individual employer may represent the employer.
4. A general partner or a regular full-time employee may represent a partnership employer.
5. An officer or employee of a corporation may represent the corporation (or similar organization).

6. A fiduciary may represent a trust, estate, and the like.
7. Any individual may prepare a tax return, appear as a witness for the taxpayer before the IRS, or furnish information at the request of the IRS.[9]

III. Client Issues

A. *Fees*

A tax practitioner cannot charge an "unconscionable" fee for representing a client before the IRS. Moreover, practitioners may not (with certain exceptions) charge contingency fees for services rendered in connection with any matter before the IRS. "Matter before the IRS" includes tax planning or advice rendered in connection with preparation of claims for refund. One of the exceptions to this general rule is where such a claim is filed within 120 days of a taxpayer's receipt of notice of examination of the original return.[10]

Tax practitioners may disseminate the following information to the general public:
1. Fixed fees for specific routine services;
2. Hourly rates;
3. A range of fees for particular services;
4. Fees charged for an initial consultation; and
5. Responsibility for costs incurred.

B. *Advertising and Solicitation*

In any kind of advertising or other public communication, a tax practitioner may not use statements that are false, deceptive, or misleading in any way. Enrolled agents may not use the word "certified." However, they may use the terms "enrolled" or "admitted to practice," or the designation "EA." Tax practitioners may not make uninvited verbal solicitations of business regarding IRS matters, including in-person contacts and telephone communications, if such solicitation would violate state or federal law. All permitted solicitations must clearly identify the source of the information used in choosing the recipient.[11]

It is a violation for a practitioner to persist in attempting to contact a prospective client if such client has made it known that he or she does not wish to be solicited. In the case of a radio or television ad, the practitioner is required to retain a copy of the actual audio or video transmission. In the case of direct mailing, the practitioner must retain a copy of each mailing along with a list of recipients. All such copies must be retained for three years.[12]

C. *Conflicts of Interest*

A tax practitioner is expressly forbidden to represent conflicting interests in his or her practice before the IRS. The only exception to this prohibition is where full disclosure has been made and express consent of all directly interested parties has been obtained.[13] A classic trap into which CPAs often fall is the representation of both husband and wife where there is a separation or pending divorce. A wise course of action is to withdraw from representing one or the other. The safest course of action is to withdraw completely from representing either spouse.

D. *Return of Client's Records*
In general, a practitioner must, at the request of a client, promptly return any and all records of the client that are necessary for the client to comply with his or her federal tax obligations. The records returned may be first copied and retained by the practitioner. A fee dispute will not relieve a practitioner of his or her duties under this provision. If applicable state law permits a practitioner to retain original documents, then the practitioner must allow his or her client to copy such records.[14]

IV. Miscellaneous Provisions of Circular 230

A. *Failure to Furnish Information*
No lawyer, CPA, or EA can refuse to submit promptly any records or information requested by the IRS, nor interfere with any attempt by the IRS to obtain such information. However, a representative may refuse to furnish information believed in good faith to be privileged. Refusal may also be justified if the request is of doubtful legality. Under certain limited conditions a practitioner must provide information to the IRS regarding the identity of persons who may have possession or control of requested documents[15]

B. *Knowledge of Client's Omission*
Any qualified representative who learns that his or her client has not complied with tax laws or has made an error or omission on any document must advise his or her client promptly of such error or omission and the consequences thereof. Note, however, that this rule does not require the representative to notify the IRS of the error.[16] This rule is identical to the AICPA's Statements on Standards for Tax Services (SSTS) No. 6.[17]

C. *Diligence as to Accuracy*
Each tax practitioner is required to exercise due diligence in the preparing or filing of tax returns or other documents with the IRS. Similar diligence is required when making oral or written representations to IRS employees and to his or her own clients.[18] An example of lack of due diligence would be the deduction of commuting expenses when the practitioner has no authority for such a deduction.

D. *Delay*

No tax practitioner can be the cause of any unreasonable delay in the prompt disposition of any matter before the IRS.[19]

E. *Negotiation of Refund Checks*

No tax practitioner (who is also a return preparer) may negotiate or endorse a tax refund check issued to his or her client.[20]

F. *Best Practices for Tax Advisers*

Circular 230 contains suggestions regarding providing client advice and preparation of submissions to IRS. Also discussed are (1) clear communications, (2) establishing the facts, (3) avoidance of penalties, (4) acting fairly and with integrity, and (4) establishing firm procedures.[21]

G. *Positions on Tax Returns*

A practitioner may not sign a return (or advise with regard to a return) if a position taken in such return lacks a reasonable basis. Whether a return may or may not be audited may not be considered in assessing a likelihood of an issue being sustained.[22] Thus, practitioners may no longer consider the "audit lottery" when considering the reasonableness of tax return positions.[23]

H. *Reliance on Client Information*

A practitioner may rely in good faith without verification on information furnished by his or her client. However, the practitioner must probe further if he or she has reason to believe that such information may be incorrect or incomplete.[24]

V. Enforcement Provisions

A. *Authority to Disbar or Suspend*

The treasury secretary has authority to suspend or disbar any tax practitioner from practice before the Internal Revenue Service, but only after due process has been granted.[25]

B. *Examples of Disreputable Conduct*
1. Being convicted of a federal criminal offense, or any criminal offense involving dishonesty or breach of trust;
2. Giving false or misleading information to an IRS employee;
3. Using misleading solicitations of employment;
4. Counseling a client to evade assessment or payment of tax;
5. Failing to file a tax return or attempting to evade taxes;
6. Misappropriating tax payments;
7. Being disbarred or suspended of license by any state;
8. Attempting to influence the official actions of an IRS employee;

9. Assisting a suspended practitioner;
10. Using abusive language to or making false accusations about an IRS employee;
11. Failing to sign a tax return (when required); or
12. Knowingly misrepresenting facts to the IRS.[26]

C. *Referral to the Director of OPR*

An IRS employee who has reason to believe that there is a violation of Circular 230 by a practitioner is required to make a report to the director OPR.[27] After the practitioner has been notified of a possible violation, the director of practice may institute proceedings for reprimand, disbarment, or suspension.[28]

D. *Complaint and Answer*

Disciplinary proceedings are instituted by the director of practice (or his or her delegate) by filing a complaint, setting out the allegations, which is sent by certified mail to the practitioner. The respondent practitioner is then required to submit a written answer.[29]

E. *Administrative Law Judge*

If the initial appeals conference is unsuccessful in resolving the matter, a disciplinary hearing is held before an administrative law judge. This hearing is stenographically recorded.

VI. Powers of Attorney

A. *General Rule*

The regulations have always allowed a taxpayer to be represented in tax controversy matters. The authority of a representative must be evidenced by a power of attorney (POA) and declaration of representative filed with the appropriate IRS office.[30]

The written POA must contain certain specific information, including information about the representative who is authorized to act. The POA must contain an attachment that constitutes a "declaration" by the representative that states the following:

1. That he or she is not currently under suspension or disbarment from practice before the IRS;
2. That he or she is aware of the regulations contained in U.S. Treasury Department Circular 230;
3. That he or she is authorized to represent the taxpayer(s) identified in the POA; and
4. That he or she is an individual described in Treas. Reg. § 601.502(a).[31]

Note that there is no provision for corporations, partnerships, or any entity other than an individual to hold a valid POA. Law firms and accounting firms must designate specific qualified individuals to be the designated representatives on a POA. However, an individual may represent any kind of taxpayer, including a partnership.

B. *Minimum Required Information for a POA*
A POA must contain the following information:
1. The name and address of the taxpayer;
2. The taxpayer(s) federal identification number(s);
3. Employee plan number, if applicable;
4. The name and address of the representative(s);
5. A description of the subject matter of the representation, including
   a. type of tax,
   b. federal tax form number,
   c. specific years or periods involved, and
   d. in estate matters, date of death; and
6. A clear expression of the taxpayer's intention regarding the scope of authority granted.[32]

C. *Form of POA*
The government has provided a preprinted form that, if properly completed, will satisfy all the requirements of the procedural regulations. This is Form 2848. The use of this form is not, however, mandatory. A mere letter, as long as it contains all the required information, will suffice.[33]

D. *Future Years*
Powers of attorney may cover years extending into the future, but the periods must end no later than three years after the date the POA is received by the IRS.[34]

E. *Multiple Matters/Spouses*
A POA may (and often does) cover more than one matter (e.g., a 1040 and 941).[35] If a 941 or 940 (employment tax) matter is reflected, the applicable employer identification number must also be placed in the box provided therefor. A representative who represents both a husband and a wife must prepare separate POAs for each.

F. *CAF System*
The IRS maintains a central authorization file (CAF) for each authorized representative, who is assigned a unique CAF alphanumeric, ten-character number.[36] Information from powers of attorney is recorded onto the CAF system for ease of retrieval by computer. The CAF system automatically directs copies of notices and correspondence to the authorized individuals.[37] However, it is noteworthy that a POA will *not* be rejected on the basis that it does not contain a CAF number.[38]

If a representative desires to receive copies of all notices relating to his or her client, it is advisable to fax a copy of the POA to the POA unit in a service center designated for that purpose in addition to furnishing a copy to the local field personnel.

G. *IRS Communication with Taxpayers*

IRS employees are forbidden to communicate directly (either in person or by telephone) with a taxpayer if they are aware that there is an authorized representative who holds a valid POA.[39] Even if the IRS is not aware of the existence of a POA but could, through database access or otherwise, readily ascertain the representative's name and address, it may not communicate directly with a taxpayer. Of course, the IRS may contact the taxpayer directly where the representative is unresponsive or dilatory or where the representative consents to such contact.[40]

H. *Bypass of a Taxpayer's Representative*

If a representative has unreasonably delayed or hindered an examination by failing to furnish, after repeated requests, nonprivileged information, the examiner may report the situation, through channels, to his or her division chief and request permission to contact the taxpayer directly for such information. If permission is granted, the investigator must document his or her files with the reasons sufficient to justify the bypass. Written notice of the bypass will be given to the taxpayer and his or her representative.[41]

The bypass procedures contained in the Internal Revenue Manual (IRM) and the procedural regulations do not violate procedural due process. Bypass procedures do not require notice and hearing in that they do not deprive a practitioner of the ability to practice law.[42]

I. *Taxpayer Interviews*

Any authorized representative who holds a valid POA may attend any interview conducted by an IRS employee and represent his or her client therein. In the absence of an administrative summons, an IRS employee may not require the taxpayer to accompany the representative to such an interview.[43]

J. *Delegation of Authority*

Any authorized representative, acting under a valid POA, may delegate his or her original authority to any other recognized person. The IRS must thereafter recognize both the delegator and delegatee as having requisite authority.[44] This right is available only if the representative checks the appropriate box on a Form 2848 or otherwise indicates the desire to have the ability to delegate.

K. *Representation—Mere Furnishing of Information*

Merely furnishing information to the IRS does not constitute "representation" and does not require the submission of a POA.[45]

L. *Joint Returns*

In the case of a joint return, both husband and wife may, but are not required to, appoint the same representative but must do so with separate POAs.[46] Conversely, the IRS may not object if the husband and wife have different representatives, or if one of the spouses elects to have *no* representation.

M. *Signing of Tax Returns*

The filing of a POA does not authorize the recognized representative to sign a tax return for a taxpayer unless such act is permitted by the I.R.C. and regulations[47] and is specifically authorized in a POA.[48] If such authority is desired, the practitioner must add the specific language to the preprinted Form 2848 and ensure that the requirements in the regulation are met. Otherwise the client must personally sign his own tax return.

N. *Submission of Copies*

Often IRS employees insist on receiving the original copy of the POA. However, the rules say that the IRS must accept either an original or a photocopy of the POA. POAs will also be accepted by facsimile (fax) transmission.[49] There is a legal reason for this rule. The POA is a legal document, either a contract or an agency agreement, between two parties, the taxpayer and his or her representative. The IRS is not a party to this agreement and should not, therefore, be entitled to the original document. Of course, the POA could always be executed in multiple originals.

O. *Revocation and Withdrawal*

All revocations and withdrawals must be in writing.[50] A copy of the existing POA should accompany a revocation or withdrawal with the notation "REVOKE" or "WITHDRAW" clearly indicated in the top margin of the form.

There are two ways a taxpayer can revoke a previously executed POA:

1. File a written statement of revocation with the IRS or
2. Execute a new POA authorizing a different representative.

If a new representative is appointed, the existing POA is automatically revoked unless an exception is noted in the new POA.[51]

Any representative may withdraw his or her POA at any time for any reason. The withdrawal statement must be filed with the IRS office handling the controversy matter and must be signed by the representative.[52] This withdrawal must identify the taxpayer and the matter(s) covered.

The recommended method for quickly and efficiently accomplishing a revocation of a POA is to write at the top of the form the word "REVOKE" and to sign and date it. This form should then be mailed or faxed to the CAF unit so that the IRS can update its records accordingly.

P. *Tax Court Cases*
In cases docketed before the U.S. Tax Court, a POA is not required to be submitted by a lawyer of record in a particular case. Any other person is required to submit such a POA, however.[53]

Q. *Copies of Communications to Taxpayers*
Copies of all IRS written communications must be furnished to the authorized representative holding a valid POA. A taxpayer may designate up to two representatives to receive such copies. If the taxpayer does not designate which representative is to receive copies, the IRS will send copies only to the first representative listed in the POA. Failure to furnish a copy to the representative will not affect the validity of any notice or written communication delivered to a taxpayer.[54]

When a POA requests that "all" (not just copies thereof) communications be sent to the representative, the representative's address will be considered to be the last known address of the taxpayer.[55]

R. *Closing Agreement*
A representative may not execute a closing agreement for a taxpayer unless his or her POA specifically authorizes him or her to do so.[56]

S. *Date of Receipt by the IRS*
The IRS must receive the POA within sixty days of the date of the taxpayer's signature whenever a representative is seeking disclosure of tax returns or return information from the IRS.[57]

T. *Tax Preparers*
Effective with the 2001 filing season, a taxpayer can check a box on his or her 1040 to allow an IRS customer service representative to speak directly with a preparer.[58]

U. *Signing of Form 656 or Form 433-A*
A representative, acting under authority of a POA, may legally sign a Form 656 (Offer in Compromise) or a Form 433-A (Collection Information Statement) on behalf of his or her taxpayer-client.[59] In the author's opinion, however, the better practice is to have the taxpayer sign such documents.

VII. Tax Practitioner Privileged Communications

A. *General Rules*

It is important to note that the ethical obligation of confidentiality is not the same as the attorney-client privilege. In some cases, the attorney-client privilege may survive a court order to testify, whereas the ethical obligation of confidentiality ends whenever a practitioner encounters a legal obligation to make disclosure.

With respect to tax advice, the same common law protections of confidentiality that apply to a communication between a taxpayer and a lawyer also apply to any federally authorized tax practitioner.[60] The term "federally authorized tax practitioner" means, generally, those practitioners authorized to practice under Circular 230.[61] The term "tax advice" means advice given by an individual in the scope of his or her authorized federal tax practice.[62]

B. *Limitation to Civil Tax Matters*

The nonlawyer privilege clearly may not be asserted in any criminal investigation or prosecution under the jurisdiction of the IRS or any federal tribunal where the IRS is a party to the proceeding.[63]

Practice Tip

The time-tested *Kovel* procedure should be used in any criminal tax matter. Under this procedure, an accountant hired by a criminal defense lawyer to assist the lawyer will be covered by the lawyer's "privilege umbrella." (United States v. Kovel, 296 F.2d 918, 9 AFTR2d 366 (2d Cir. 1961).)

C. *Corporate Tax Shelters*

The nonlawyer privilege does not extend to communications between a practitioner and a representative of a corporation with respect to that corporation's participation in any "tax shelter" as defined in I.R.C. § 6662(d)(2)(c)(iii).[64]

D. *Other Rules*

Privileged information furnished to a client-taxpayer also includes communication with *a potential* client-taxpayer.[65]

I.R.C. § 7525 does not expand privilege beyond what a lawyer would otherwise have. For example, information furnished to a lawyer for the purpose of preparing a tax return is not presently privileged. Therefore, such information would not be privileged under I.R.C. § 7525 to a nonlawyer.[66]

VIII. Practitioner Traps

A. *General Observation*

In the opinion of this author, there is a disturbing trend among federal prosecutors and investigative zealots within the IRS. Too often, whenever an aggressive practitioner's client cannot be successfully prosecuted, government employees turn instead to his or her representative as a target. Because of this, practitioners are well advised to be ever alert to government tactics in this regard.

B. *Recording of Telephone Calls*

A practitioner should always assume that his or her telephone conversations with personnel of the IRS are being monitored and/or recorded. Therefore, one should never say anything in such conversations that he or she would not like to hear played back in a court of law.

C. *Written Communications*

The general rule is that one should never create a document (either electronically or in hard copy) that you would not like to see introduced into evidence in a court of law. Even notes and memoranda contained in a file are subject to subpoena unless the attorney-client privilege applies. The government is famous for conducting raids on practitioners' offices in their zeal to obtain evidence against taxpayers. Even deleted e-mails are capable of being retrieved with today's technology.

D. *Section 7212*

One of the government's favorite weapons used against practitioners is I.R.C. § 7212.[67] This section was used effectively in the *Popkin* case[68] against a lawyer who advised his client to form a corporation for the purpose of disguising the true nature of illegal income and repatriating it to the United States. It would not take a great deal of imagination to foresee the government's stretching this tactic to cover any aggressive, but legitimate, tax planning by a practitioner.

E. *Tax Court Representation*

A practitioner must be extremely careful when representing a client in tax court. If a lawyer or other authorized practitioner "appears" to have multiplied the proceedings "unreasonably and vexatiously," the court has the authority to assess counsel personally for excessive costs incurred.[69]

F. *Monetary Fines*

The Jobs Act of 2004[70] added censure and monetary penalties on a representative (or his or her firm) where there has been a finding of proscribed conduct.[71]

IX. Notes

1. 31 U.S.C. § 330(a).
2. 31 C.F.R.§§ 10.0–10.93.
3. 31 C.F.R. § 10.1.
4. 31 C.F.R. § 10.2; *see also* Treas. Reg. § 601.501(b)(10).
5. 31 C.F.R. § 10.3.
6. 31 C.F.R. § 10.4.
7. 31 C.F.R. § 10.6.
8. 31 C.F.R. § 10.6.
9. 31 C.F.R. § 10.7.
10. 31 C.F.R. § 10.27.
11. 31 C.F.R. § 10.30(a)(1).
12. 31 C.F.R. § 10.30(c).
13. 31 C.F.R. § 10.29.
14. 31 C.F.R. § 10.28(a).
15. 31 C.F.R. § 10.20.
16. 31 C.F.R. § 10.21.
17. For a complete text of the SSTSs, see http://www.aicpa.org/members/div/tax/index.htm.
18. 31 C.F.R. § 10.22.
19. 31 C.F.R. § 10.23.
20. 31 C.F.R. § 10.31; *see also* I.R.C. § 6695(f) for civil penalties imposed for such negotiation of refund checks.
21. 31 C.F.R. § 10.33.
22. 31 C.F.R. § 10.34.
23. Estate of Trompeter v. Comm'r, 111 T.C. 57, 69 (1998) (concurring opinion).
24. 31 C.F.R. § 10.34.
25. 31 C.F.R. § 10.50.
26. 31 C.F.R. § 10.51.
27. 31 C.F.R. § 10.53.
28. 31 C.F.R. § 10.60.
29. 31 C.F.R. §§ 10.63, 10.64.
30. Treas. Reg. § 601.501(a).
31. Treas. Reg. § 601.502(c).
32. Treas. Reg. § 601.503(a).
33. Treas. Reg. § 601.503(b).
34. Treas. Reg. § 601.506(d)(3)(ii).
35. Treas. Reg. § 601.504(a).
36. Treas. Reg. § 601.501(b).
37. IRM 5.1.23.
38. Treas. Reg. § 601.506(d)(2).
39. I.R.C. § 6304(a)(2).
40. Treas. Reg. § 601.506(b).
41. *See generally* I.R.C. § 7521(c); IRM 5.1.23.5.
42. Wegge v. Egger, 84-2 USTC ¶ 9753 (9th Cir. 1985); *see also* Treas. Reg. § 601.506(b). *See* I.R.C. § 7521(c) for statutory authority to bypass.
43. I.R.C. § 7521(c); Treas. Reg. § 601.506(b).
44. Treas. Reg. § 601.501(b)(5), 601.505(b)(2).

45. Treas. Reg. § 601.501(b)(13).
46. Form 2848 instructions.
47. *See* Treas. Reg. § 1.6012-1(a)(5).
48. Treas. Reg. § 601.504(a)(6).
49. Treas. Reg. § 601.504(c)(4).
50. IRM 5.1.23.4.4.
51. Treas. Reg. § 601.505(a).
52. Treas. Reg. § 601.505(b).
53. Treas. Reg. § 601.509.
54. Form 2848 instructions.
55. Rev. Proc. 61-18, 1961-2 CB 550.
56. Treas. Reg. § 601.504(a)(4).
57. Treas. Reg. § 301.6103(c)-1(b)(2).
58. Notice IR 2000-23.
59. I.R.S. Priv. Ltr. Rul. 200115031.
60. I.R.C. § 7525(a)(1).
61. I.R.C. § 7525(a)(3)(A).
62. I.R.C. § 7525(a)(3)(B).
63. I.R.C. § 7525(a)(2).
64. I.R.C. § 7525(b).
65. Comm. Reports on Pub. L. No. 105-206.
66. *Id.*
67. I.R.C. § 7212(a) reads, in part, "Whoever . . . obstructs or impedes, or endeavors to obstruct or impede, the due administration of this title, shall, upon conviction thereof, be fined not more than $5,000, or imprisoned not more than 3 years."
68. United States v. Popkin, 91-2 USTC ¶ 50,496 (11th Cir. 1991).
69. I.R.C. § 6673(a)(2); Johnson v. Comm'r, 116 T.C. 111 (2001), *aff'd*, 2001 USTC ¶ 50,402 (7th Cir. 2002).
70. Pub. L. No. 108-357.
71. I.R.S. Notice 2007-39, 2007-20 I.R.B. 1243.

Civil Preparer Penalties

I. History and Statutory Scheme

A. History

I.R.C. § 6694, Understatement of Taxpayer's Liability by Income Tax Return Preparer, was enacted as a part of the Tax Reform Act (TRA) of 1976, Pub. L. No. 94-455, 90 Stat. 1520. This statute was substantially amended as a result of the 2007 Tax Act.

Several provisions of the 1976 TRA were designed to regulate the conduct of paid income tax preparers. These provisions reflected congressional concern over various abuses by preparers in the reporting of their clients' income tax liabilities. Congress wanted the IRS to be able to more closely monitor the activities of the tax return preparation industry. Their goal was to promote a higher standard of care in the preparation of returns for compensation and to deal with the problem of the fraudulent, unscrupulous, or incompetent preparer.[1]

B. Basic Statutory Scheme

Section 6694 is a penalty provision with a civil sanction. A penalty equal to the greater of (1) $1,000 or (2) 50 percent of the income derived by the preparer with respect to the return or claim is imposed on a "tax return preparer," but only if *both* of the following conditions exist:

1. There is an understatement of liability with respect to a tax return or a claim for refund, if the understatement is attributable to a reasonable belief that more likely than not the position taken would not be sustained on its merits;[2] and
2. Such position was not disclosed, or there was no reasonable basis for the position.[3]

C. Penalty Cumulative

Preparer penalties can be imposed *in addition to* any other penalties provided by law.[4]

D. *Comparison with Prior Law*

I.R.C. § 6694(a) is to be interpreted in a manner similar to the former I.R.C. § 6653(a), relating to negligence on the part of a taxpayer. Thus, negligence has been defined as the lack of due care. For example, if due care would have resulted in the discovery of an alternative minimum tax (AMT) liability, then failure to report AMT will result in § 6694 liability.[5]

II. Definitions

A. *Who Is a "Preparer"?*

1. *General Rule*

The term "income tax preparer" means any person who prepares an income tax return for compensation[6] or employs a person or persons to prepare such a return. The preparation of a substantial portion of a return or claim is the equivalent of preparing the entire return.[7]

2. *Exclusions*

An "income tax return preparer" does *not* include someone who

a. merely furnishes typing or copying services;

b. prepares a return for an employer;

c. acts as a fiduciary in the preparation of a return; or

d. prepares a refund claim in response to a deficiency notice.[8]

3. *Multiple Preparers*

No more than one individual associated with a firm (for example, as a partner or employee) is treated as a preparer with respect to the same return or claim for refund. If a signing preparer is associated with a firm, that individual, and no other individual associated with the firm, is a preparer with respect to the return for the purposes of § 6694.[9] Note that this is in apparent conflict with a private letter ruling that avers, "The Code and regulations contemplate that more than one person can be a preparer with respect to a given return."[10] At this writing no judicial authorities have addressed this issue. The return signer may not have actually prepared the return, but designating the signing preparer as the responsible party is an administratively workable rule.

4. *Employer or Partner Rule*

An employer or partner of a preparer can also be held liable for a § 6694 penalty if any one of three conditions exist:

a. If a member of management of a firm *knew* of the proscribed conduct;

b. If the firm failed to provide adequate review procedures; or

c. If review procedures were disregarded.

This rule applies regardless of whether a subsection (a) or a subsection (b) penalty is being asserted.[11]

5. *Furnishing Substantial Information*

A person who furnishes to a taxpayer or other preparer sufficient information and advice so that completion of the return or claim for refund is largely a mechanical or clerical matter is considered an income tax preparer, even though that person does not actually place or review placement of information on the return.[12]

6. *Exposure of Legal Adviser*

A person who only gives advice on specific issues of law is not a preparer unless the advice affects a substantial portion of the return and the following two tests are satisfied:

a. The advice is given with respect to events that have occurred when the advice is rendered and is not given with respect to the consequences of contemplated actions, and

b. The advice is directly relevant to the determination of the existence, characterization, or amount of an entry on a return or claim.

B. *Partnership Issues*

A general partner is not a "preparer" of his or her partnership's return. Nor would the general partner be considered to be the preparer of another general partner's return or the return of an employee of the partnership.[13]

However, a general partner *may* be the preparer of a limited partner's return. Because the general partner rendered advice directly relevant to determining the existence, characterization, and amounts of entries that constitute a substantial portion of a limited partner's return, and if the general partner is compensated for preparing the partnership return and Schedule K-1 from which those entries were derived, the general partner is a preparer with respect to the limited partner's return.[14]

Several court cases have held that a preparer of a partnership return can be held liable under § 6694 even though he or she never spoke with the limited partners who claimed overstated K-1 losses.[15]

C. *Definition of Understatement of Liability*

The term "understatement of liability" means an understatement of net income tax payable or overstatement of tax refundable.[16] Note that a preparer penalty can only be imposed relative to Subtitle A income taxes. It cannot be imposed with respect to estate, gift, or excise taxes.[17]

D. *Definition of Frivolous Position*

A "frivolous position" (for purposes of I.R.C. § 6694(a)(3)) with respect to an item is one that is patently improper.[18]

III. Section 6694(b) Issues

A. *Willfulness*

If any part of the understatement of tax is due to willfulness or recklessness of the preparer, the penalty amount is increased to the greater of $5,000 or 50 percent of income derived.[19] Section 6694(b) requires either a willful understatement or a willful assistance before liability can be imposed. Congress intended that the preparer be directly involved in aiding or abetting before liability is imposed. This requirement mandates an "actual knowledge" jury instruction.[20]

On the issue of willfulness, the doctrine of collateral estoppel may apply. For example, in the *Richey* case, the return preparer was convicted of assisting in the preparation of a false tax return. He was also assessed a preparer penalty for willful understatement of his client's tax liability.

The Ninth Circuit held that the issues in the criminal and civil cases were substantially identical, and therefore the doctrine of collateral estoppel prevented the preparer from claiming a lack of willfulness.[21]

B. *Mutual Exclusivity*

The penalties of subsections (a) and (b) are mutually exclusive, not cumulative. That is, they cannot be "stacked"; the government must choose which penalty amount to assert.[22]

C. *Definition of Reckless*

A preparer is "reckless" in not knowing of a rule or regulation if the preparer makes little or no effort to determine whether a rule or regulation exists, under circumstances that demonstrate a substantial deviation from the standard of conduct that a reasonable preparer would observe in the situation.[23]

D. *Burden of Proof on the IRS*

The IRS bears the burden of proof only on the question of willfulness. The preparer bears the burden on all other elements required to be proved.[24]

IV. Administrative Appeal

A. *Underlying Examination*

Typically, preparer penalties result from audits of the tax returns of the preparer's clients. The return preparer penalty will not be proposed until the income tax audit is completed at the group level.[25] If the agent or auditor concludes that a preparer penalty should be imposed, he or she will secure manager approval and modify the exam report accordingly.[26]

B. *Protest of Agent's or Auditor's Determination*

After the investigation of the preparer is complete, the IRS will send a report of the examination to the preparer before the assessment of either a subsection (a) or subsection (b) penalty. Along with this report will be sent a notification offering the preparer the opportunity to seek further administrative review. Since these penalties are both less than

$2,500, no written protest is required. The only requirement is that the preparer must submit (within thirty days) a written request for an IRS Appeals conference.[27]

C. *Assessment Procedures*

The IRS will not actually assess the penalty until after an adverse determination by the Appeals Division or in the event that the preparer chooses not to request an IRS Appeals conference. After assessment, the IRS will send a "notice and demand" to the preparer.[28]

D. *Further Appeal Following Assessment*

After the notice and demand for payment are received, the I.R.C. provides a way for the preparer to appeal the assertion of the penalty by paying only a portion thereof. To appeal, the preparer must pay an amount of at least 15 percent of the assessed penalty and then file a claim for refund of the amount paid. The preparer can then file a refund lawsuit against the government following the expiration of the earlier of the following:
1. A denial of the claim, or
2. Thirty days after the expiration of six months after the filing of the claim.[29]

E. *Refund after Final Determination*

If there is a final administrative or judicial determination that there has been no understatement resulting in a preparer penalty, any payment must be refunded, and any assessment must be abated.[30]

V. Litigation

A. *Initial Claim*

Filing a claim for refund is a jurisdictional prerequisite for litigation of a preparer penalty issue. And in filing this claim, the preparer must clearly set forth each ground for his or her position that the penalty does not apply.[31]

B. *Choice of Forum*

The normal deficiency procedures[32] do not apply with respect to preparer penalties.[33] Therefore, one cannot litigate them in the U.S. Tax Court. The preparer must litigate in the U.S. District Court or not at all. It is important that a preparer not let the time limits of § 6694(c) (1) expire for fear of being deprived of a forum in which to be heard.[34]

C. *Counterclaim*

Typically, the government will file a counterclaim for the balance (i.e., the 85 percent unpaid part) of the penalty. However, one court has ruled that in § 6694 suits, the IRS need not file a counterclaim for the other

85 percent of the penalty because any court decision with regard to the refund of the 15 percent will apply equally to the remaining 85 percent.[35]

D. *Stay of Collection Enforcement*
If a suit is filed following denial (or nonaction) of the refund claim, the IRS is precluded from collecting the penalty by levy and may be enjoined from doing so, § 7421 notwithstanding, until there is a final resolution of the refund litigation.[36]

VI. Statute of Limitations Rules

A. *General Assessment Rule*
Section 6694(a) and § 6695 penalties must be assessed within three years after the return to which the penalty relates was filed.[37] That is, the government has no more time to assess a preparer penalty than it has to assess the underlying income tax deficiency.[38]

B. *Claim-Filing Deadline*
A claim for refund of an overpayment of a § 6694 or § 6695 penalty must be filed within three years from the date the penalty was paid.[39]

C. *Exception for Intentional Penalties*
Note, however, that there is no statute of limitations on assessments of penalties under § 6694(b), § 6700, or § 6701. Similarly, there is no statute of limitations to enjoin preparers or promoters under § 7407 or § 7408.

D. *Tolling of Collection Statute*
As one would expect, the collection[40] statute of limitations is tolled during the pendency of a § 6694(c)(1) proceeding.[41]

E. *Extensions of the Statute*
The statute of limitations on preparer penalties arising under § 6694(a) or § 6695 can be extended by using Form 872-D.

VII. Disclosure and Realistic Possibility

A. *Realistic Possibility*
  1. *50 Percent Standard*
    A position is considered to have a "reasonable basis"[42] for being sustained on its merits if a reasonable and well-informed analysis by a person knowledgeable in the tax law would lead such a person to conclude that it has a 50 percent or greater, likelihood of being sustained on its merits. In making this determination, the possibility that the position will not be challenged by the IRS (e.g., because the taxpayer's return may not be audited) is not to be taken into account.[43]

2. *Relationship to Accuracy-Related Penalty*
In determining the "reasonable basis" standard under Treas. Reg. § 1.6694-2(b), the authorities and the weight given them are the same under § 6694 as they are under the "accuracy-related" penalty of § 6662.[44]

3. *Determinative Date*
The appropriate date for determining if the reasonable basis standard is satisfied is the date the preparer signed the return. If a non-signing preparer is the subject of the penalty, the relevant date is the date the advice was given. Thus, preparers should be aware of changes in the law occurring between the end of the tax year and the date the return is signed or the advice is given.

B. *Disclosure*
1. *Form 8275 Required*
If the realistic possibility standard is not met, then the § 6694 penalty can be avoided if there is "adequate disclosure" of the position. However, disclosure is adequate only if a Form 8275 is attached to the tax return.[45]

2. *Comparison with § 6662*
The standard for whether disclosure of a position on a return is adequate to reduce an "understatement" is virtually the same for the accuracy-related penalty of § 6662 as it is for the preparer penalty of § 6694.[46]

3. *Adequacy Defined*
For purposes of adequate disclosure, a taxpayer must furnish all required information in accordance with the applicable forms and instructions, and the money amounts on these forms must be verifiable.[47]

VIII. Defenses

A. *Reasonable Cause and Good Faith*
The "unrealistic position" assertion by the IRS can be avoided if a preparer demonstrates that there is reasonable cause for the understatement and that he or she acted in good faith.[48] Therefore, this should be a practitioner's first line of defense.

B. *Five Factors to Be Considered*
Under the "reasonable cause" and "good faith" exceptions of § 6694, the following five factors are generally considered:[49]
1. The nature of the error causing the understatement
2. The frequency of the errors
3. The materiality of the errors
4. The preparer's normal office practice
5. Reliance on the advice of another preparer

C. *Reliance on Client Information*

A preparer generally may in good faith, without verification, rely upon information furnished by his or her client. Thus, he or she is not required to audit, examine, or review books and records, business operations, or documents to verify independently the taxpayer's information. However, the preparer may not ignore the implications or information furnished to the preparer or actually known to the preparer. The preparer must make reasonable inquiries if the information as furnished appears to be incorrect or incomplete. In the event that the I.R.C. requires specific documentation (such as entertainment expenses under § 274), then a preparer inquiry is required before a deduction can be claimed.[50] A return preparer who does not ask for assurances that § 274(d) substantiation requirements have been met is subject to a § 6694 penalty.[51]

D. *Isolated Errors*

If the error is isolated and nonrecurring, this fact can be an important defense. An isolated mathematical or clerical error will not cause imposition of the preparer penalty.[52] But although the reasonable cause and good-faith exception generally applies to an isolated error, it does not apply if the isolated error is so obvious, flagrant, or material that it should have been discovered during a review of the return or claim.[53]

E. *Normal Office Practice*

If the preparer can demonstrate that the understatement would not normally have occurred given the preparer's normal office procedures for such things as checklists and review procedures, a successful defense may be launched under that theory. "Normal office practice" must be a system for promoting accuracy and consistency in the preparation of returns or claims and generally would include checklists, methods for obtaining necessary information from the client, a review of the prior year's return, and manager review procedures.[54]

For example, a failure to report alternative minimum tax will not result in a preparer penalty where a practitioner can demonstrate that, because of his or her office's normal review policies, such an error would rarely occur.[55]

F. *Working Paper Adequacy*

The only way for a practitioner to meet his or her burden of proof is to ensure that his or her files adequately reflect the circumstances leading up to the adoption of the position being challenged by the IRS. This should include at least (1) research notes, (2) factual questions asked of the client, and (3) reasons for relying on another professional's advice, where applicable. Documentation is king when defending yourself.

IX. Miscellaneous Topics

A. *Other Preparer Penalties*

1. *Miscellaneous Summary*

An income tax preparer can also be penalized for

a. failing to furnish his or her own identifying number[56] on a tax return;[57]

b. failing to retain a copy of a tax return[58] (see below);

c. failing to comply with I.R.C. § 6060 (information returns of income tax preparers);[59] or

d. endorsing or negotiating a client's refund check.[60]

2. *Failure to Furnish a Copy of a Tax Return*

An income tax return preparer is required to furnish a completed copy of a return or refund claim to his or her taxpayer-client not later than such time as the return is presented to his or her client for signature.[61] Failure to comply with this provision of the law subjects a preparer to a $50 penalty for each such failure. The maximum penalty during any calendar year cannot exceed $25,000. This penalty can be avoided if a preparer can demonstrate reasonable cause and lack of willful neglect.[62]

3. *Failure to Sign a Return*

Failure by a preparer to sign a return requiring a preparer signature can subject the preparer to a $50 penalty per occurrence.[63]

4. *Preparer ID Number and Address*

Although the regulations require that a preparer show his or her tax ID number and address on a return or a claim, there appears to be no penalty provision for failure to do so.[64]

B. *Rules and Regulations*

When there is any doubt about an issue, a preparer should research it to ensure that the position is not contrary to a regulation.

The term "rules or regulations" includes provisions of the Internal Revenue Code, temporary or final Treasury Regulations, and revenue rulings or notices issued by the IRS and published in the *Internal Revenue Bulletin*. Note that this does *not* include private letter rulings.[65]

When a preparer follows instructions of a client regarding the exclusion of an item of income, without consulting the regulations, the preparer penalty will be imposed.[66]

A position contrary to regulations must be disclosed with a Form 8275-R (Regulation Disclosure Statement) even when the preparer, in good faith, believes that his or her position meets the "more likely than not" standard.

C. *NOL Carrybacks, and Unclaimed Items*

Preparer penalties will not be abated where a taxpayer's liability is eliminated or not assessed because of a net operating loss (NOL) carryback. However, such a penalty will be abated because of an unclaimed item arising in the same year.[67]

In a case involving a § 6701 (aiding and abetting) penalty, a district court in Arizona established a rule that would seem to apply equally to § 6694. Both § 6701 and § 6694 require an "understatement" of tax liability. Where a preparer files a 1040-X reflecting no change to his or her client's liability *for that year*, the penalty is appropriate anyway for the reason that the 1040-X may affect carry-back and carry-forward losses.[68]

D. *Corporation and Shareholder Issues*
If a preparer prepares a corporate tax return and the return of its majority shareholder, he or she must be sure to take consistent positions. If the corporation deducts interest on a loan to the shareholder, the shareholder must report the interest income. If not, the preparer can be assessed a § 6694 penalty.[69]

E. *Pattern of Error*
Where there is a pattern of errors on a return, the preparer penalty will apply. For example, where not all 1099 income was reported, itemized deductions were overstated, and the wrong tax table was used, the penalty will apply.[70]

F. *Inadvertent Errors*
Inadvertent errors in entering numbers on tax software computer sheets will not result in a preparer penalty.[71]

G. *Year-to-Year Discrepancy*
Claiming deductions in one year while being aware that similar deductions were disallowed in a previous year will subject a preparer to a penalty.[72]

H. *Family Trusts*
The IRS has attempted unsuccessfully to argue that the preparation of family trust tax returns is per se unreasonable and automatically subjects a preparer to a § 6694 penalty. But the Ninth Circuit has taken a contrary view.[73]

I. *Standard of Knowledge and Ability*
Under IRS guidelines, a tax return preparer is held to a higher standard of tax knowledge and ability than a normal taxpayer. That a preparer has charged a fee to prepare a complex tax return implies a reasonable ability to do it correctly. However, a penalty should not be imposed on a preparer who does not find an obscure provision or who misapplies a difficult one.[74]

Nevertheless, licensed CPAs are *not* held to a higher standard than the one imposed on unlicensed preparers.[75]

X. Conclusions

Preparer penalties must be avoided at all costs. This does not mean, however, that a tax practitioner must always take the most conservative approach on an issue. If a position is well justified, even though it may be challenged later by the IRS, the risks must be explained (preferably in writing) to the client.

If a preparer penalty is imposed on a practitioner by the IRS, it must be vigorously defended, no matter what the cost. The reason is that imposition of preparer penalties may lead to fines, injunctions, license revocations, or referrals to the Office of Professional Responsibility (OPR). While imposition of § 6694 penalties will not automatically subject a practitioner to discipline under Circular 230, it is likely that if the penalty is sustained, there will be a referral to the OPR and an ensuing investigation by that office.

Note also that the § 6662 and § 6694 penalties and the defenses available under each section can have the effect of pushing the tax practitioner and his or her client into a conflict. And this can lead to undesirable civil litigation.

XI. Notes

1. *See* IRM 4.10.6.8.2.
2. I.R.C. § 6694(a)(2)(B).
3. I.R.C. § 6694(a)(2)(C).
4. I.R.C. § 6696(a).
5. *See* I.R.S. Priv. Ltr. Rul. 8001007, 8001008, and 8001015.
6. Presumably this means that a practitioner who prepares returns for friends and relatives for free will not be subject to a preparer penalty. Additionally, in the opinion of this author, no penalty is appropriate where a preparer does a tax return under a pro bono engagement.
7. I.R.C. § 6694(f); I.R.C. § 7701(a)(36)(A).
8. I.R.C. § 7701(a)(36)(B).
9. Treas. Reg. § 1.6694-1(b)(1).
10. I.R.S. Priv. Ltr. Rul. 8731004.
11. Treas. Reg. § 1.6694-2(a)(2), 1.6694-3(a)(2).
12. Treas. Reg. § 301.7701-15(c).
13. Treas. Reg. § 301.7701-15(f).
14. Rev. Rul. 81-270, 1981-2 CB 250.
15. Goulding v. United States, 92-1 USTC ¶ 50,174 (7th Cir. 1992), followed by Adler & Drobny, Ltd. v. United States, 93-2 USTC ¶ 50,602 (7th Cir. 1993).
16. I.R.C. § 6694(e).
17. *Id.*, including estate, gift, and excise taxes, effective May 25, 2007.
18. Treas. Reg. § 1.6694-2(c)(2).
19. I.R.C. § 6694(b).

20. Mattingly v. United States, 91-1 USTC ¶ 50,068 (8th Cir. 1991).
21. Richey v. United States, 93-2 USTC ¶ 50,647 (9th Cir. 1993).
22. I.R.C. § 6694(b).
23. Treas. Reg. § 1.6694-3(c)(1).
24. Treas. Reg. § 1.6694-3(h). *See also* I.R.C. § 7427.
25. IRM 4.10.6.8.2 and 20.1.6.2.
26. IRM 20.1.6.1.1.2.
27. Treas. Reg. § 1.6694-4(a)(1).
28. Treas. Reg. § 1.6694-4(a)(2).
29. I.R.C. § 6694(c)(1).
30. I.R.C. § 6694(d).
31. *See* Treas. Reg. § 301.6402-2(b).
32. I.R.C. §§ 6211 *et seq.*
33. I.R.C. § 6696(b).
34. I.R.C. § 6694(c)(2).
35. Nielson v. United States, 92-2 USTC ¶ 50,618 (5th Cir. 1992).
36. I.R.C. § 6694(c)(1).
37. I.R.C. § 6696(d)(1).
38. *See* I.R.C. § 6501.
39. I.R.C. § 6696(d)(2).
40. I.R.C. § 6502.
41. I.R.C. § 6694(c)(3).
42. *See* I.R.C. § 6694(a)(1).
43. Treas. Reg. § 1.6694-2(b)(1).
44. See regulations promulgated under § 6662.
45. Treas. Reg. § 1.6694-2(d)(3).
46. *See, e.g.,* Rev. Proc. 97-56, 1997-52 I.R.B. 18.
47. *Id.*
48. I.R.C. § 6694(a)(3).
49. Treas. Reg. § 1.6694-2(e).
50. Treas. Reg. § 1.6694-1(e).
51. Rev. Rul. 80-266, 1980-2 CB 378.
52. Rev. Rul. 80-262, 1980-2 CB 375.
53. Treas. Reg. § 1.6694-2(e)(2).
54. Treas. Reg. § 1.6694-2(e)(4).
55. *See, e.g.,* Rev. Rul. 80-264, 1980-2 CB 377.
56. I.R.C. § 6109(a)(4).
57. I.R.C. § 6695(c).
58. I.R.C. § 6695(d).
59. I.R.C. § 6695(e).
60. I.R.C. § 6695(f).
61. I.R.C. § 6107(a).
62. I.R.C. § 6695(a).
63. I.R.C. § 6695(b).
64. Treas. Reg. § 1.6109-2.
65. Treas. Reg. § 1.6694-3(e).
66. Rev. Rul. 78-344, 1978-2 CB 334.
67. Rev. Rul. 82-25, 1982-1 CB 214.
68. Bailey v. United States, 96-1 USTC ¶ 50,270 (D. Ariz. 1996).

69. Rev. Rul. 80-265, 1980-2 CB 377.
70. Rev. Rul. 80-263, 1980-2 CB 376.
71. I.R.S. Priv. Ltr. Rul. 8218005.
72. I.R.S. Priv. Ltr. Rul. 8022027.
73. Swayze v. United States, 86-1 USTC ¶ 9291 (9th Cir. 1986).
74. *See generally* IRM 20.1.6.
75. Wilfong v. United States, 93-1 USTC ¶ 50,232 (7th Cir. 1993).

Preparer Disclosure

I. Background of Statutory Provision

A. The I.R.C. contains many provisions that are nothing more than traps into which tax practitioners can unwittingly stumble. For example, tax practitioners can, and often do, run afoul of the following statutory provisions:
   1. Aiding and abetting in the preparation of a false document;[1]
   2. Acts resulting in injunctions;[2]
   3. Understatement of tax liability;[3]
   4. Various administrative failures;[4] and
   5. Failure to furnish copies to clients.[5]

B. One of the least understood and appreciated statutory provisions affecting return preparers is contained in Chapter 75 of the I.R.C., which is titled Crimes, Other Offenses, and Forfeitures. The final section of Subchapter A (Crimes), in Part I, is I.R.C. § 7216, Disclosure or Use of Information by Preparers of Tax Returns. I.R.C. § 7216 was newly enacted in 1971 as a part of the Revenue Act of 1971.[6] Its effective date is January 1, 1972.[7]

C. *Basic Statutory Scheme*
   Any person who discloses any information obtained during a tax return preparation engagement can be fined $1,000 and be jailed for one year.[8]

II. Who Is a "Preparer"?

A. While "tax practitioner" is a more all-inclusive term, the I.R.C. typically targets practitioners who are "return preparers." A tax return preparer is defined as one who prepares tax returns for compensation or remuneration.[9]

B. Any person who is in the business of preparing, or providing services in connection with the preparation of, federal tax returns and who discloses "any information" for or in connection with the preparation of a tax return is subject to the criminal sanction.[10] Thus, someone who furnishes advice, or consults with a return preparer, concerning a reporting position on a tax return would easily come within the purview of § 7216.

C. A preparer can include a financial institution, a preparer's secretary, and a computer service bureau.[11]

D. If you "hold yourself out" to the public as being a preparer, you are subject to the statute even if you do not charge a fee for your service.[12]

III. Criminal Sanctions

A. Make no mistake about it. I.R.C. § 7216 is a criminal statute, violation of which can lead to time in the federal penitentiary.

B. Violation of § 7216 can have very serious consequences. Just because a violation constitutes a misdemeanor[13] does not mean that the punishment is a mere slap on the wrist. Upon conviction under this statute, a preparer can face up to one year in prison and a $1,000 fine for each violation. The consequences of such a conviction are such that no practitioner would want to face them. One of the results of a conviction would be the inevitable censure by the state licensing board, which has the power to remove or suspend a practitioner's license to practice.

IV. Other General Rules

A. For § 7216 to be invoked, the prohibited disclosure must be done "knowingly OR [emphasis supplied] recklessly." The author does not know, nor does anyone, quite what "recklessly" means. That notwithstanding, however, it does not tax the imagination to envision almost any disclosure coming within the definition of "knowingly." At the risk of being rhetorical, how can one do something without knowing that he or she did it? Of course, one could easily imagine a situation in which a clerical person in the preparer's employ inadvertently puts a wrong address on an envelope and thereby mails a tax return to the wrong person. Clearly, this would not be "knowingly" on the part of the preparer.

B. What a preparer may not disclose is "information."[14] Information obviously can be either verbal or written and would include all the client's documents in the preparer's possession. Such term would also include correspondence, notes, and memoranda that may be in a preparer's files. In short, whatever a preparer has learned about his or her client's tax affairs, and whatever may be in his or her client's tax or working paper files, may not be disclosed to a third party. Tax return information includes a taxpayer's name, address, and identifying number.[15]

C. Moreover, a preparer may not "use" any such client information for purposes other than preparing his or her client's return. Though it seems far-fetched, a practitioner would thus be precluded from using such information for practice management or marketing purposes.[16] If so, it is likely that every CPA firm in the United States is guilty of violating this provision. Fortunately, the statute does provide an exception for disclosure of tax information during quality or peer reviews.[17]

D. It has been judicially held that the act of authenticating a tax return during courtroom testimony is an example of a prohibited disclosure where the tax return relates to a taxpayer who is not a party to the litigation. In such cases, the taxpayer to whom the return relates is the only one who can authenticate the return.[18] The preparer cannot.

V. Exceptions to the General Rules

A. There are exceptions for disclosures pursuant to other parts of the I.R.C. For example, obviously a preparer can make disclosures to his or her own client and to the IRS. Similarly, a preparer can make disclosures in connection with the preparation of state or local tax returns.[19]

B. Further, an exception to the statute exists for any one of the following:
  1. The order of any federal, state, or local court;
  2. Any state or federal grand jury subpoena; or
  3. A subpoena issued by a state or federal agency, including a state licensing agency.[20]

C. The regulations provide yet another exception to the disclosure statute. A preparer may legally disclose tax return information to third parties if his or her client signs a separate, written consent for each disclosure. This consent must contain the following:
  1. The name of the preparer;
  2. The name of the taxpayer;
  3. The purpose for which the consent is being furnished;
  4. The date the consent is signed;
  5. A statement that the tax return information may not be disclosed or used by the preparer for any purpose not stated in the consent; and
  6. A statement that the taxpayer consents to the disclosure for the stated purpose.[21]

D. An accountant may disclose tax return information pursuant to an order of a state board of accountancy.[22]

E. Disclosure by an accountant pursuant to a summons issued by the IRS will not violate § 7216.[23]

F. An issue involving § 7216 frequently arises in civil litigation where a client of the tax practitioner is one of the litigants. It is not uncommon, for example, for an accountant to receive a subpoena to appear and testify at a trial or a deposition. If it is a subpoena duces tecum, the witness is required to bring and produce documents or papers. If the testimony or the documents of the accountant involve tax return information, a question inevitably arises as to whether he or she is permitted to disclose such information in light of the § 7216 statutory prohibition.

G. In the author's opinion, the only logical exception to the nondisclosure rule would occur where the subpoena could legally be construed as tantamount to a "court order" as specified in I.R.C. § 7216(b)(1)(B).

H. A subpoena is nothing more than a process by which a litigant, through his or her lawyer, can compel a witness to appear and give testimony. Subpoenas are not typically issued by a court in civil litigation but are, instead, issued by one of the parties to the case. A judge's signature appears nowhere on the subpoena.

I. A court order, on the other hand, is a command or direction authoritatively given by a court or a judge. The conclusion of the author is, therefore, that subpoenas and court orders are not the same and that they are mutually exclusive.

J. Refusal to disclose information pursuant to a subpoena issued by a private party to civil litigation is not the same as the assertion of a "privilege." A privilege suggests some advantage or benefit enjoyed by a particular class of persons that is unavailable to other persons. For example, communications between a lawyer and his or her client are said to be "privileged" and may not be disclosed in the absence of a waiver or consent.

K. An accountant's refusal to respond to a subpoena by invoking § 7216 is not client protective in nature; instead, it is purely witness protective.

L. So what is a subpoenaed tax practitioner expected to do? Is he or she required to hire a lawyer and file a motion to quash the subpoena? Or is he or she required to appear, refuse to testify, and thereby force the opposing lawyer to file a motion to compel? As a practical matter, this would only be problematic in a deposition setting where a judge is not present to give a verbal order. In a trial or hearing, it is inconceivable that a judge would not issue an appropriate order compelling the witness to testify and produce his or her client's tax records.

VI. Miscellaneous Private Letter Rulings

A. Section 7216 does not prevent a computer service bureau from furnishing to a preparer comparative client data.[24]

B. A tax return preparer (who is also a life insurance agent) cannot disclose return information for advertising purposes unless the client executes an explicit written consent.[25]

C. An insurance agency that offers tax preparation services may disclose "sanitized returns" to a third party as a part of a quality control review.[26]

D. Return information disclosed to a state agency regulating the practice of accounting is not subject to § 7216 sanctions.[27]

E. If a return preparer operates through a franchise, his or her disclosure of "quality review" copies of tax returns to the franchisor does not constitute improper disclosure.[28]

F. Section 7216 does not apply to a farm lender that gathers tax information to be used on Schedule Fs.[29]

G. A cooperative association of farmers will be considered a "preparer" if it gives members specific advice on their Schedule Fs.[30]

VII. Conclusion

Any tax return preparer must be at least generally familiar with the provisions of I.R.C. § 7216 for fear of criminal sanctions. He or she must also be cautioned not to be intimidated into producing a client's tax information merely because he or she receives a subpoena. The preparer must always wait for either a verbal or written order of a court, or written client permission, before producing such information.

VIII. Notes

1. I.R.C. § 7206(2).
2. I.R.C. § 7407(a).
3. I.R.C. § 6694.
4. I.R.C. § 6695.
5. I.R.C. § 6107.
6. *See* Comm. Reports on Pub. L. No. 92-178, *reported at* 1972-1 CB 648.
7. Treas. Reg. § 301.7216-1(b)(2).
8. I.R.C. § 7216(a).
9. I.R.C. § 7701(a)(36); Treas. Reg. § 301.7216-1(b)(2)(C).
10. I.R.C. § 7216(a).
11. Treas. Reg. § 301.7216-1(b)(2)(i).
12. Treas. Reg. § 301.7216-1(b)(2)(ii).
13. Treas. Reg. § 301.7216-1(a).
14. I.R.C. § 7216(a)(1).
15. Treas. Reg. § 301.7216-1(b)(3).
16. *See* Rev. Rul. 79-114, 1979-1 CB 441, for a prohibition against using return information for the purpose of compiling statistical data or for marketing purposes.
17. I.R.C. § 7216(b)(3); *see* Comm. Reports on Pub. L. No. 101-239 (Omnibus Budget Reconciliation Act of 1989).
18. Loftus v. Comm'r, 63 T.C.M. (CCH) 2944 (1992).
19. I.R.C. § 7216(b)(2).
20. Treas. Reg. § 301.7216-2(c).
21. Treas. Reg. § 301.7216-3.
22. Rev. Rul. 85-5, 1985-1 CB 385; I.R.S. Priv. Ltr. Rul. 8316050 (1-14-83).
23. Buckner v. United States, 95-1 USTC ¶ 50,228 (W.D. Wash. 1995).
24. I.R.S. Priv. Ltr. Rul. 9253030.

25. I.R.S. Priv. Ltr. Rul. 8717008.
26. I.R.S. Priv. Ltr. Rul. 8429052.
27. I.R.S. Priv. Ltr. Rul. 8316050.
28. I.R.S. Priv. Ltr. Rul. 8242034.
29. I.R.S. Priv. Ltr. Rul. 8227082.
30. I.R.S. Priv. Ltr. Rul. 8035069; I.R.S. Priv. Ltr. Rul. 8034159.

Government Disclosure and Other Misconduct

I. Introduction

The I.R.C. contains significant restrictions on the government's ability to disclose information about a taxpaying citizen's financial affairs. I.R.C. § 6103 was drafted by Congress to balance two important but competing interests. First, it was recognized that our system of taxation depends on a taxpayer's reasonable expectation of confidentiality of his or her tax return information. I cannot imagine a much worse effect on a person's reputation than to have his or her friends, neighbors, and business associates learn that he or she is being "investigated" by the Internal Revenue Service. Nevertheless, Congress also realized that the government has a legitimate concern for using tax return information for effective tax administration and enforcement purposes. Thus, § 6103 was crafted to satisfy those competing interests.

Additionally there are many provisions of Title 26 under which an IRS employee can be sued, sanctioned, or prosecuted criminally. Most of those provisions are discussed in this subchapter.

II. Definitions re Disclosure

A. *Definition of Return*
The term "return" includes any of the following items filed with the IRS:
1. Tax return or claim;
2. Amendments to tax returns; or
3. All supplementary information that forms part of a return.[1]

B. *Definition of Return Information*
The I.R.C.'s all-inclusive definition of "return information" encompasses virtually anything and everything related to a taxpayer. Most importantly the definition includes whether a taxpayer or his or her return is being or will be audited or investigated. Additionally, the IRS is precluded from disclosing information contained in a "written determination"[2] or in a closing[3] agreement.[4] The phrase "return

information" has been broadly construed by the courts. Thus, special agents who contact third parties, suggesting various taxpayer improprieties, violate the provisions of § 6103.[5]

C. *Definition of Disclosure*

The term "disclosure" means the making known to any person *in any manner whatever* a return or return information.[6]

III. Components of Section 6103

A. *General Nondisclosure Rule*

Tax returns and tax return information are considered to be confidential. Therefore, no IRS employee can legally disclose any such information obtained by him or her in any manner in connection with his or her official duties. This rule also applies to all former IRS employees.[7]

B. *Disclosure to Designee of the Taxpayer*

1. Any taxpayer may voluntarily allow the IRS to disclose information to his or her designee, typically the holder of a power of attorney.[8] The IRS has published a convenient form to use for representation and disclosure.[9]
2. If the taxpayer signs an authorization form (typically a Form 8821 or a Form 2848), such forms are strictly limited, regarding both the information to be disclosed and the named appointee. If the IRS strays beyond the limits of the consent, a violation of § 6103 occurs.[10]
3. The IRS may disclose tax return information to a third party such as a lender only under prescribed circumstances. An authorization by a taxpayer or loan applicant must be signed and must contain very specific information.[11]

C. *Disclosure for Tax Administration*

The IRS may disclose return information to any of its employees whose duties require inspection or disclosure of such information. This rule of administrative necessity permits employees to have discussions with each other about tax enforcement matters.[12]

The phrase "tax administration" has been broadly construed by the courts. For example, disclosure of a former IRS employee's tax return information during a related civil rights (wrongful termination for tax return improprieties) action is not actionable under § 7431.[13]

In a federal or a state judicial or administrative proceeding regarding a taxpayer's tax liability, return information can be disclosed, but only if the taxpayer is a party to the proceeding. Disclosure can also be made of a transaction between a party and a taxpayer that affects the resolution of an issue in the proceeding.[14] Note that for this purpose, an IRS audit is not the same thing as an "administrative proceeding."[15]

The IRS may disclose return information to certain other agencies in matters not involving tax administration.[16]

D. *Disclosure to State and Local Officials*
The IRS may generally disclose return information to any state or local government agency that is charged with tax administration.[17]

Disclosure to a state agency must be pursuant to a written request by the agency. Verbal permission or request by a taxpayer will not suffice. Moreover, IRS personnel are expected to know this rule, and violation of the rule cannot be defended on the basis of "good faith."[18]

E. *Disclosure Regarding Joint and Several Liability*
1. *Joint Return Collection Activities*
   If a deficiency has been assessed on a joint return and the spouses are divorced or no longer living together, the IRS must (if requested in writing) disclose to the requesting spouse the following information:
   a. Whether collection from the other spouse has been attempted;
   b. The nature of the collection activities; and
   c. The amount collected.[19]

   Note that this provision does *not* apply to collection of tax reported, but not paid, on a filed tax return.
2. *Disclosure Regarding Trust Fund Liability*
   If the IRS determines that a person is liable for a penalty under I.R.C. § 6672, such person may request the following information regarding any other such person:
   a. The name of the co-obligor determined to be liable and
   b. The nature of the collection activities against the other person or persons.[20]

F. *Disclosure to Persons Having a Material Interest*
The IRS *must* disclose return information to the following (upon written request):
1. An individual taxpayer (as to his or her own information);
2. The spouse of a taxpayer (but only if a joint return was filed);
3. A member of a partnership (as to partnership information);
4. A 1 percent shareholder of a corporation;
5. The legal representative of an estate;
6. The fiduciary of a trust; or
7. A trustee or receiver in a bankruptcy case.[21]

G. *Notices of Federal Tax Liens*
Obviously, if the IRS files a notice of a federal tax lien (NFTL) pursuant to I.R.C. § 6323(f), this information becomes part of the public domain and is easily accessible by credit-reporting agencies, title companies, and anyone else who is interested. The filing of an NFTL should be

avoided at all costs due to its chilling effect on the taxpayer who wants to sell property or obtain credit.[22]

H. *Copies of Tax Returns*

If a person is entitled to have disclosure of his or her own tax return or tax return information, he or she may request that the IRS furnish him or her with a copy for a reasonable fee.[23] Form 4506 is used for this purpose. The cost is $23 per return copy. A requester should allow three to four weeks for delivery.

IV. Civil Investigations

A. *Disclosure for Investigation Purposes*

An IRS employee may, in connection with his or her official duties, disclose tax return information. However, this disclosure may be made only under circumstances where it is necessary to obtain information that is not "otherwise reasonably available."[24]

B. *"Verification of Correctness" Rule*

Per the IRS regulations, a revenue agent is authorized to make a disclosure of return information to "verify the correctness" of a return.[25] (Note: The author views this regulation as an invalid interpretation of the statute, as it makes no provision for circumstances under which the substantiation may be otherwise available.)

C. *"Otherwise Reasonably Available"*

The phrase "not otherwise reasonably available" used in § 6103(k)(6) invites unique factual scrutiny. Litigation over this phrase illustrates that a fact question is raised that must be resolved by the trier of the facts. For example, disclosure by a revenue agent in sending letters to a doctor's patients regarding cash payments raises a fact issue regarding whether such information could have been obtained from other sources.[26]

V. Criminal Investigations and Prosecutions

A. *Disclosures during Criminal Investigation and Prosecution*

In a criminal tax case it frequently happens that the special agents have contact with other agencies, including state agencies. They will also frequently talk with prosecutors. Disclosures made during these contacts will generally not violate § 6103 or result in a § 7431 civil damages award.[27]

B. *Restrictions on Special Agents of Criminal Investigation*

Special agents may not show a taxpayer's tax return to a third party. They may sometimes make investigative disclosures under the guidelines of § 6103(k)(6); however, the fact that information may already be on public record should not normally be considered by a special agent in making an investigative disclosure.[28]

C. *Mailing of "Circular" Letters*
The mailing of "circular" letters by a special agent to business associates of the taxpayer is not a per se violation of § 6103. If the § 6103(k)(6) standards are met, the disclosures of name, Social Security number, and address are not wrongful. In litigation over this issue a taxpayer would be well advised, therefore, to argue and prove that the information sought was readily available elsewhere.[29]

D. *Disclosure by a U.S. Attorney*
A U.S. attorney's gratuitous and cavalier attachment of tax returns as an exhibit to a memorandum of law filed with a court is clearly proscribed conduct and may result in sanctions against the government.[30]

VI. Disclosures during Collection Activities

A. *Disclosures during Asset Seizures*
In the process of a revenue officer's levying or seizing business assets, it is sometimes necessary for him or her to make disclosures. For example, disclosure to employees on the premises or local law enforcement personnel can be an inevitable consequence of seizure of business assets and will not result in liability under § 7431.[31]

B. *Wrongful Levies*
There is currently a split among the circuits as to disclosures made in the process of serving levies that turn out to be wrongful. The Eighth Circuit takes the position that a disclosure in pursuance of an unlawful levy violates § 6103. The Fifth Circuit, on the other hand, takes the contrary position that the validity of the underlying levy is irrelevant to the question of disclosure.[32]

C. *Location of Assets*
One of the functions of revenue officers is to locate taxpayer assets for the purpose of levy, if necessary, to collect the tax owed. Generally, the IRS may disclose return information if necessary in the location of assets in which the taxpayer may have an interest.[33]

VII. Criminal Sanctions

A. *General Statutory Rule*
The provision in the I.R.C. most feared by IRS employees is one that provides for a felony in the event of an unauthorized disclosure. If any IRS employee *willfully* discloses tax return information (as described in

§ 6103(b)), he or she may be subject to being prosecuted. If convicted, he or she can be subjected to a fine of up to $5,000 and five years of imprisonment. This punishment is in addition to being dismissed from office.[34]

B.   Revenue Agent Disclosure

A former revenue agent's disclosure to the media about auditing a tax return while employed at the IRS can result in indictment. Obviously, communicating with the media satisfies the willfulness aspect of the proscribed conduct.[35]

VIII. Lawsuits for Civil Damages

A.   General Rule

If an IRS employee knowingly, or by reason of negligence, inspects or discloses any return or return information with respect to a taxpayer, that taxpayer may sue the government in federal district court for civil damages.[36] Taxpayers may also bring such a suit if disclosure is made by a third party who is not a government employee.[37]

B.   Defenses

No liability arises under § 7431 if a disclosure results from a good faith, but erroneous, interpretation of § 6103.[38] In the author's opinion this provision effectively emasculates the right to sue the government for civil damages.

If a court finds disclosure authority under § 6103(k)(6), it will decline to rule on a "good faith" defense.[39]

C.   Damage Limits

If a taxpayer is found to be entitled to a recovery, the government's liability is limited to the greater of the following:
1. $1,000; or
2.   the sum of
     a.   actual damages sustained,
     b.   punitive damages (if willfulness is shown),
     c.   costs of the action, plus
     d.   lawyer fees, under the guidelines of § 7430.[40]

A recent case illustrates the circumstances warranting punitive damages. During 1991 and 1992, special agents of the IRS conducted a criminal investigation of a lawyer in Houston, Texas. During the course of that investigation, the agents contacted a number of the lawyer's clients and advised them that their lawyer was under criminal investigation by the IRS. The lead agent on the case, on several occasions, asked third parties whether the lawyer was a drug dealer. Because of this egregious conduct of the agent, the court awarded both actual and punitive damages.[41]

D. *Statute of Limitations*

Suits must be brought under § 7431 within two years after the date of discovery by the plaintiff of the unauthorized inspection or disclosure.[42] Suits brought after two years will be time-barred and will not confer jurisdiction on a federal district court.[43]

E. *Suits against IRS Employees Personally*

Litigants may only recover damages under § 7431 against the United States, and not against the IRS employees in their individual capacities.[44]

F. *Proof of Intent*

In claiming § 7431 damages, it is not necessary that a taxpayer prove that the IRS acted with intent or willfulness. Thus, the IRS's mistake in recording an incorrect Social Security number, resulting in an unlawful levy, can lead to a recovery by the aggrieved taxpayer.[45]

IX. Other Misconduct by IRS Employees

A. *Criminal Acts*

IRS employees commit a criminal act if they engage in any of the following activities. Such activities will result in dismissal from office and, upon conviction, can result in a $10,000 fine and a five-year prison term. These consequences result if the IRS employee is guilty of any of the following:

- Extortion or willful oppression under color of law;
- Demanding greater sums than are authorized by law, or receiving compensation or reward, except as prescribed by law, for the performance of any duty;
- Failing to perform any of his or her duties, with intent to defeat the application of tax law;
- Conspiring with another person to defraud the United States;
- Knowingly making an opportunity for any person to defraud the government;
- Omitting to do an act to enable another person to defraud the United States;
- Making a fraudulent entry in any book;
- Failing to report a violation of any tax law; or
- Taking a bribe for the compromise, adjustment, or settlement of any charge or complaint regarding any violation of law.[46]

B. *Private Cause of Action*

The statute provides also for a damages remedy (judgment) against an offending IRS employee.[47] However, this private cause of action, statutorily implied, can be enjoyed only after prosecution and conviction of the offending IRS employee.[48]

X. Treasury Inspector General for Tax Administration (TIGTA)

A. *Background Information*

TIGTA is the IRS's internal policing organization, set up to ensure that its employees adhere to rules designed to establish minimum ethical standards. Additionally, TIGTA is charged with the responsibility of monitoring the IRS's compliance with various provisions of the IRS Restructuring and Reform Act of 1998.[49]

Much of TIGTA's authority is derived from Title 5 as opposed to Title 26.[50]

B. *IRS Disclosure*

1. Under the antidisclosure rules, no disclosure of return information can be disclosed to the IRS Oversight Board.[51]
2. Employees of TIGTA, in connection with official duties, may disclose tax return information to the extent necessary to obtain information relating to such duties.[52]
3. For disclosure purposes, the term "Treasury Department" includes TIGTA.[53]

C. *Semiannual Reports*

TIGTA is required to issue a semiannual report on the IRS's compliance with various restrictions.[54] TIGTA is also required to report semiannually on the number of taxpayer complaints about IRS employee misconduct and a summary of the disposition of such complaints.[55]

D. *Toll-Free Complaint Number*

TIGTA is required by law to establish and maintain a toll-free telephone number so that taxpayers can register complaints of misconduct of IRS employees.[56]

E. *Executive Branch Restrictions*

The I.R.C. contains a restriction on the U.S. president and vice president requesting an audit or termination of an audit on any taxpayer. A violation of this provision is to be reported to TIGTA.[57]

F. *TIGTA Discretion*

TIGTA's decision to initiate an investigation or refer a matter for criminal prosecution is completely discretionary. Indeed, its authority to make such investigations and reports relating to the programs of the IRS encompasses those that are necessary or desirable. Accordingly, a taxpayer may not obtain a mandamus writ ordering TIGTA to investigate an IRS service center for failing to allow deductions.[58]

G. *Freedom of Information Act (FOIA)*
Results of TIGTA investigations may generally not be obtained through the filing of FOIA[59] requests because of exemption 7(c).[60]

H. *Regulation of Practitioner Conduct*
TIGTA also, to a certain extent, investigates unethical behavior of tax practitioners. To a degree its jurisdiction in that regard is co-extensive with that of the Office of Professional Responsibility. TIGTA is responsible to protecting IRS employees against external attempts to corrupt or threaten them.[61] If a tax practitioner is involved in unethical behavior along with an IRS employee, referral to TIGTA is required by the IRS Manual.[62] Similarly, threats to an IRS employee or tax evasion by a practitioner should be referred to TIGTA.[63]

XI. Miscellaneous Provisions

A. *Currency Transaction Disclosure*
The IRS may disclose "currency" information contained in a Form 8300 authorized by I.R.C. § 6050I to any federal agency or any local government agency that files a written request therefor.[64]

B. *"Antibrowsing" Rule*
In 1997 Congress enacted the so-called antibrowsing rule. This law prohibits IRS employees from willfully inspecting returns or return information. Violations of this provision can result in prosecution and dismissal from office.[65] These cases are investigated by the Treasury Inspector General's office and local agents.

C. *Disclosures to Card Issuers*
IRS employees may disclose information to credit and debit card issuers as may be necessary in connection with tax payments made via such cards.[66]

D. *Accidental Disclosure*
Accidental or inadvertent inspection that may occur (such as, for example, by making an error in typing a Social Security number) would not be subject to damages under § 7431. Such disclosure would not meet the standard for negligence eligible for discovery.[67]

E. *Tax Shelter Cases*
During an audit of a tax shelter, the IRS may obtain names of investors and potential investors. If the IRS thereafter sends out letters to these investors, warning them not to claim deductions purportedly allowed by the shelter, this could be construed as an unauthorized disclosure.[68]

F. *Public Disclosures and Press Releases*
As noted herein, disclosures otherwise proscribed, if made in a judicial forum, are perfectly permissible. Nevertheless, subsequent disclosure is

wrongful if the immediate source of the information is a tax return.[69] On the other hand, a press release detailing charges contained in a federal criminal indictment will not constitute an unauthorized disclosure.[70]

The government can be held liable if it knowingly or negligently discloses a taxpayer's return information to the media. Thus, an IRS employee's disclosure on a live radio talk show resulted in liability even though prior approval had been obtained from the IRS's Disclosure Office. The Disclosure Office's information regarding a taxpayer's prior consent was incorrect.[71]

G. *Tax Return Preparers*

Only taxpayers, not their return preparers, are entitled to file a § 7431 lawsuit. Thus a district court will lack jurisdiction to hear a preparer's civil damages action following the IRS's issuance of letters to the preparer's clients.[72]

H. *State Statutes*

State statutes that require the filing of copies of federal tax returns in conjunction with the filing of local returns do not violate § 6103 of the I.R.C.[73]

I. *Offers in Compromise*

The IRS must disclose (upon request) information about a taxpayer's accepted offer in compromise filed pursuant to I.R.C. § 7122.[74]

J. *Prior Court Disclosure*

A revenue agent's testimony in court will not remove the cloak of confidentiality from tax return information. Thus, a subsequent suggestion to a taxpayer's business associate that the taxpayer was "stealing oil" is a willful violation of § 6103, justifying an award of punitive damages.[75]

K. *Acts Requiring Termination*

Misconduct by IRS employees can result in their dismissal from office. In fact, the IRS must terminate an employee upon a final administrative or judicial determination that, in the course of his or her official duties, the employee committed one of the following "ten deadly sins":

1. Failing to obtain proper authorization before seizing a taxpayer's assets;
2. Providing a false statement under oath regarding a taxpayer or his or her representative;
3. Violating a taxpayer's constitutional or civil rights;
4. Falsifying or destroying documents to conceal mistakes involving a taxpayer;
5. Assaulting or battering a taxpayer or his or her representative;
6. Violating policies or regulations for the purpose of retaliating against or harassing a taxpayer or other employee of the IRS;

7.   Willfully violating I.R.C. § 6103 (disclosure rules);
8.   Failing to file any tax returns;
9.   Understating his or her own tax liability; or
10. Threatening to audit a taxpayer for the purpose of extracting personal gain.[76]

L. *Fair Debt Collection Practices*[77]

The IRS collection function has a great deal more power than normal creditors. Nevertheless, there are some constraints on certain behavior. In connection with any collection of unpaid tax, the IRS is subject to the following rules: (1) IRS may not communicate with taxpayers at unusual times (before 8 A.M. or after 9 P.M.) or places, (2) IRS must not communicate with taxpayers directly when they are represented by counsel, and (3) IRS must not call the taxpayer's place of employment. IRS may also not engage in harassing or abusive behavior. Taxpayers who have been subjected to this kind of behavior may sue the government under I.R.C. § 7433.

XII. Notes

1.   I.R.C. § 6103(b)(1).
2.   *See* I.R.C. § 6110(c).
3.   *See* I.R.C. § 7121.
4.   I.R.C. § 6103(b)(2).
5.   United States v. Bischoff, 95-1 USTC ¶ 50,308 (5th Cir. 1995).
6.   I.R.C. § 6103(b)(8).
7.   I.R.C. § 6103(a).
8.   I.R.C. § 6103(c).
9.   *See* Form 2848.
10. Baskin v. United States, 96-2 USTC ¶ 50,424 (S.D. Tex. 1996).
11. Treas. Reg. § 301.6103(c)-1(a).
12. I.R.C. § 6103(h)(1).
13. Hobbs v. United States, 2000-1 USTC ¶ 50,403 (5th Cir. 2000).
14. I.R.C. § 6103(h)(4).
15. Mallas v. United States, 93-1 USTC ¶ 50,302 (4th Cir. 1993).
16. I.R.C. § 6103(j).
17. I.R.C. § 6103(d).
18. Huckaby v. United States, 86-2 USTC ¶ 9565 (5th Cir. 1986).
19. I.R.C. § 6103(e)(8).
20. I.R.C. § 6103(e)(9).
21. I.R.C. § 6103(e)(1).
22. I.R.C. §§ 6103(k)(2), 6323(f).
23. I.R.C. § 6103(p)(2)(A).
24. I.R.C. § 6103(k)(6); Treas. Reg. § 301(k)(6)-1(a).
25. Treas. Reg. § 301.6103(k)(6)-1(b)(1).
26. Barrett v. United States, 86-2 USTC ¶ 9571 (5th Cir. 1986). Note that the Barrett case went up to the Fifth Circuit on four separate occasions, each one dealing with a different aspect of alleged government agent misconduct.

27. McQueen v. United States, 98-1 USTC ¶ 50,388 (S.D. Tex. 1998).
28. IRM 9.3.1.3.1; *see also* Gandy v. United States, 9802 USTC ¶ 50,838 (E.D. Tex. 1998).
29. Nordbrock v. United States, 2000-1 USTC ¶ 50,247, 96 F. Supp. 2d 944 (D. Ariz. 2000).
30. United States v. Sapp, 33 AFTR2d 74-479 (S.D. Fla. 1974).
31. Morales v. United States, 90-1 USTC ¶ 50,275 (W.D. Tex. 1990).
32. Rorex v. Traynor, 85-2 USTC ¶ 9636, 771 F.2d 383 (8th Cir. 1985); Wilkerson v. United States, 95-2 USTC ¶ 50,569 (5th Cir. 1995). *See generally* Robert P. Butts, *IRS Liability for Wrongful Disclosures Made in the Process of Tax Collection: Should the Validity of the Underlying Collection Be Considered?*, 102(1) Dickinson L. Rev. 67–92 (1998).
33. Treas. Reg. § 301.6103(k)(6)-1(b)(a).
34. I.R.C. § 7213(a)(1).
35. *See* United States v. Richey, 91-1 USTC ¶ 50,055 (9th Cir. 1991).
36. I.R.C. § 7431(a)(1).
37. I.R.C. § 7431(a)(2).
38. I.R.C. § 7431(b).
39. Wilkerson v. United States, 95-2 USTC ¶ 50,569 (5th Cir. 1995).
40. I.R.C. § 7431(c).
41. Payne v. United States, 2000-1 USTC ¶ 50,217 (S.D. Tex. 2000).
42. I.R.C. § 7431(d).
43. Gandy v. United States, 98-2 USTC ¶ 50,838 (E.D. Tex. 1998). *See also* Amcor Capital Corp. v. United States, 95-2 USTC ¶ 50,395 (C.D. Cal. 1995).
44. Hassell v. United States, 99-2 USTC ¶ 50671 (N.D. Tex. 1999).
45. Chandler v. United States, 88-2 USTC ¶ 9541 (D. Utah 1988).
46. I.R.C. § 7214(a).
47. *Id.*
48. Cody v. United States, 82 AFTR2d 98-7277 (W.D. La. 1998).
49. I.R.C. § 7803(d). For example, TIGTA must ensure compliance with restrictions on the use of enforcement statistics to evaluate IRS employees and restrictions on contacting the taxpayer directly when there is a power of attorney.
50. 5 U.S.C. § 552; United States v. Lovern, 89 AFTR2d 2002-2957 (4th Cir. 2002).
51. I.R.C. § 7802(a); I.R.C. § 6103(h)(6)(A).
52. Temp. Treas. Reg. § 301.6103(k)(6)-1(a)(1).
53. Treas. Reg. § 301.6103(n)-1(f)(1).
54. I.R.C. § 7803(d)(1)(A)(i).
55. I.R.C. § 7803(d)(2).
56. I.R.C. § 7803(d)(3)(B).
57. I.R.C. § 7217(b).
58. Craig v. Gardner, 93 AFTR2d 2004-987 (Va. 2003).
59. 5 U.S.C. § 552.
60. Lewis v. United States, 92 AFTR2d 2003-5963 (C.D. Cal. 2003).
61. 5 U.S.C. § app. 3, § 8D(d)(1)(C).
62. IRM 8.10.2.1.2.1.
63. *Id.*
64. I.R.C. § 6103(1)(15).
65. I.R.C. § 7213A.
66. Treas. Reg. § 301.6103(k)(9)-1.
67. Comm. Report on Pub. L. No. 105-35 (Taxpayer Browsing Protection Act of 1997).

68. Mid-South Music Corp. v. United States, 756 F.2d 23, 85-1 USTC ¶ 9262 (6th Cir. 1984).
69. Johnson v. Sawyer, 97-2 USTC ¶ 50,616 (5th Cir. 1997).
70. *Id*.
71. Ward v. United States, 97-2 USTC ¶ 50,504 (D. Colo. 1997).
72. Hernandez v. United States, 99-2 USTC ¶ 50,887 (5th Cir. 1999).
73. Rev. Rul. 70-454, 1970-2 CB 296.
74. I.R.C. § 6103(k)(1).
75. Rodgers v. Hyatt, 83-1 USTC ¶ 9139 (10th Cir. 1983).
76. IRS Restructuring and Reform Act of 1998, Act § 1203.
77. I.R.C. § 6304.

APPENDIX A

Abbreviations and Acronyms Used in Federal Tax Procedure Matters

ACS	Automated Collection System
AFTR	American Federal Tax Reports
AO	Appeals Officer (IRS)
AOD	Action on Decision
ASED	Assessment Statute Expiration Date
ATAO	Application for Taxpayer Assistance Order
ATAT	Abusive Tax Avoidance Transaction
ATE	Appeals Technical Employee
AUR	Automated Underreporter Report
BLS	Bureau of Labor Statistics
BMF	Business Master File
BR	Bankruptcy
BSA	Bank Secrecy Act
BUW	Backup Withholding (IRC 3406)
CAF	Central Authorization File
CAP	Collection Appeal Program
CAWR	Combined Annual Wage Report
CB	Cumulative Bulletin
CCA	Chief Counsel Advice
CDP	Collection Due Process
CFR	Code of Federal Regulations
CI	Criminal Investigation
Cir.	Circuit

(continued)

Cir. 230	Circular 230 (see 31 CFR)
CIS	Collection Information Statement (Form 433)
CNC	Currently Not Collectible
CSED	Collection Statute Expiration Date
CSP	Classification Settlement Program (re worker classification)
CTR	Currency transaction report
DATC	Doubt as to Collectibility (for offers in compromise)
DATL	Doubt as to Liability (for offers in compromise)
DDIA	Direct Debit Installment Agreement
DIF	Discriminant Function Formula (for NRP)
DISC	Domestic International Sales Corporation
DN	Deficiency Notice (see ND)
DO	Delegation Order
DOJ	Department of Justice
ECC	Enterprise Computing Center (Detroit)
EIN	Employer Identification Number
EO	Exempt Organizations
EP	Employee Plan
ERSED	Erroneous Refund Statute Expiration Date
ETA	Effective Tax Administration (for offers in compromise)
ETE	Employment Tax Examination
Exam.	Examination, Audit
FBAR	Foreign Bank Account Report
Fed. Cl.	Court of Federal Claims
FICA	Federal Insurance Contribution Act
FIT	Federal Income Tax
FOIA	Freedom of Information Act
FPAA	Final Partnership Administrative Adjustment
FSA	Field Service Advice
FTD	Federal Tax Deposit
FTL	Federal Tax Lien
FTS	Fast-Track Settlement
FUTA	Federal Unemployment Tax Act
GCM	General Counsel Memorandum
IA	Installment Agreement
IAT	Integrated Automation Technology
IDR	Information Document Request
IDRS	Integrated Data Retrieval System

IE	International Examiner
IMF	Individual Master File
IRB	Internal Revenue Bulletin, a/k/a Cumulative Bulletin
IRC	Internal Revenue Code (title 26 U.S.C.)
IRM	Internal Revenue Manual
IRP	Information Return Program (see wage & income transcripts)
IRS	Internal Revenue Service
LB&I	Large Business and International (formerly LMSB)
LRG	Legal Reference Guide
MCAR	Mutual Collection Assistant Requests (international situations)
ND	Notice of Deficiency (statutory)
NFTL	Notice of Federal Tax Lien
NOPA	Notice of Proposed Adjustment
NRA	Nonresident Alien
NRP	National Research Program (formerly TCMP)
OD	Officer of the Day (collection function)
OIC	Offer in Compromise
OPR	Office of Professional Responsibility
PAM	Post Appeal Mediation
PCS	Partnership Control System
PLE	Personal Living Expenses
PLR	Private Letter Ruling
PMTA	Program Manager Technical Advice (issued by Chief Counsel)
POA	Power of Attorney
PPIA	Partial Payment Installment Agreement
PPS	Practitioner Priority Service
RA	Revenue Agent
RAR	Revenue Agent Report
RCP	Reasonable Collection Potential
Reg.	U.S. Treasury Regulation
Rev. Proc. or RP	Revenue Procedure
Rev. Rul. or RR	Revenue Ruling
RH	Refund Hold
RO	Revenue Officer
SA	Special Agent (see CI)
SAC	Special Agent in Charge
SB/SE	Small Business / Self-Employed
SCA	Service Center Advice

(continued)

S. Ct.	Supreme Court (US)
SE	Self-Employment, Self-Employed
SEP	Special Enforcement Program (resulting from strike force)
SFR	Substitute for Return
SH	Shareholder, Stockholder
S/L	Statute of Limitations
SO	Settlement Officer (IRS Office of Appeals)
SSN	Social Security Number
TAM	Tax Advice Memorandum
TAO	Taxpayer Assistance Order
TAS	Taxpayer Advocate Service
TC	U.S. Tax Court
TCO	Tax Compliance Officer (office auditor)
TDI	Taxpayer delinquency investigation (nonfilers)
TDS	Transcript Delivery System
TFRP	Trust Fund Recovery Penalty
TIGTA	Treasury Inspector General for Tax Administration
TIN	Taxpayer Identifying Number
TMP	Tax Matters Partner
TP	Taxpayer
USC	United States Code
USCA	United States Code Annotated
USTC	United States Tax Cases (CCH publication)
UTP	Uncertain Tax Positions
VCSP	Voluntary Classification Settlement Program (re worker classification)
WBO	Whistleblower Office
W&I	Wage & Investment (see also IRP)
WPs	Working Papers or Workpapers

APPENDIX B

IRS Forms[1] and Notices Used in Federal Tax Procedure Matters

Form No.	Form Name	I.R.C. §	Explanation
23C	Assessment certificate	6201	Now replaced by computer-generated RACS 006
53	Currently not collectible (CNC)	6301	Internal IRS use only by revenue officers
56	Notice of fiduciary relationship	6903, 6036	For use by trustees, executors, etc.
105C	Claim disallowance	6511(a)	Notice of claim disallowance, usually because it's untimely
211	Informant reward application	7623	For use by whistleblowers; see also publ. 733 and Form 3949A
231	General power of attorney to negotiate check drawn on U.S. treasury	6695(f)	Where TP is unable to do so
369C	Response to request for penalty abatement	6651	Usually denies the request
393	FOIA exemptions	6103	
433-A	Collection information statement (CIS)	7122(d)	Use 433-B for entities; use 433-A (OIC) for OIC cases
433-A (OIC)	Collection information statement	7122(d)	Used by wage earners & self-employed persons in OIC cases
433-B	Collection information statement	7122(d)	Don't use for sole proprietorships

(continued)

---

[1] Access http://www.irs.gov to download and print government forms. However, government internal-use only forms are not available on this website.

Form No.	Form Name	I.R.C. §	Explanation
433-D	Installment agreement payout agreement	6159	May be signed by a representative under POA
433-F	Collection information statement	6159	Simpler version, used mostly by wage earners
433-G	Direct debit IA	6159	Automatic bank draft for installment payments
433C	Collection acknowledgment of information	6301	Notification of resolution of collection matter
531, or 531-T	Deficiency notice	6212(a)	Statutory notice of deficiency; contains last date to file petition with Tax Court
538 (SWR)	Examiner activity record [case history]	7602	Daily record of activity on each particular case; filled out by RA
544C	Collection acknowledgment	6301	Notification of resolution of collection matter
656	OIC, doubt as to collectibility	7122	$150 filing fee; 20% down payment required if lump sum offer
656-A	OIC, additional basis	7122	Attach to 656; for use in economic hardship cases
656-B	OIC booklet	7122	Offer in compromise booklet
656-L	OIC, doubt as to liability	7122	For doubt as to liability offers; no $150 user fee required
656-PPV	OIC, partial payments	7122	Voucher can designate where payments are to be applied
667	Currency & banking data base	7602	National base of bank account info, sorted by SSN & EIN, available to RAs
668-A	Notice of levy	6331	Issued to banks; shows type of tax & periods; bank holds funds for 21 days before releasing to IRS
668-B	Notice of levy	6331	Sent by IRS to banks, etc.
668-D	Notice of release of levy	6343	Levy release; ACS (not TAS) can issue these
668-F	Lien refiling notice	6325(a)	This form, used to refile a lien, is not self-releasing; IRS must manually release it
668-W	Notice of wage levy	6331(e), 6334(d)	Served on employer; continuing in nature
668(Y)	Notice of federal tax lien	6321	Notice of federal tax lien filed with county clerk; shows periods of liability

Form No.	Form Name	I.R.C. §	Explanation
668(Z)	Certificate of lien release	6325(a)	RO can prepare this upon pay-off if TP wants to record the release himself
669-A	Lien discharge	6325(b)(1)	Property double the amount of the liability
669-B	Lien discharge	6325(b)(2)(A)	Issued when equivalent value paid to IRS
669-C	Lien discharge	6325(b)(2)(B)	Where interest in part to be discharged has no value
669-D	Certificate of lien subordination	6325(d)	Certificate of subordination of federal tax lien
784	TFRP notice	6672	Information only; explains personal liability
843	Claim for refund or abatement	6511, 6404, 6672	Use for other than FIT refund claims; also used for abatement; do not use for employment tax; use 941-X instead; for TFRP cases, send separate 843 for each period
866	Closing agreement	7121	Final determination
866-A	Explanation of items	7602	Used by revenue agents to explain adjustments
870	Waiver of restrictions on assessment	6213(d), 6601(c)	Agreement form used following more complicated audits
870-AD	Agreement form, appeals case	1313(a)(4)	Used in appeals to close cases; not a closing agreement
870-IS	Innocent spouse waiver of restrictions	6015	Waiver of collection restrictions in innocent spouse case
870-LT	TEFRA agreement on partnership items, etc.	6231(b)(1)(C), 6229(f)	Agreement for partnership items & affected items, penalties, etc.
870-P	TEFRA partnership settlement agreement	6224	Sent along with FPAA notice
872	Extension of assessment S/L	6501(c)(4)	Extends statute of limitations to a date certain; it cannot be terminated; there is no reason for this form to be signed except in unusual circumstances
872-A	Extension of assessment S/L	6501(c)(4)	Unlimited in duration unless terminated by 872-T
872-D	Preparer penalty, consent to extend assessment	6694(a), 6695	Extends to date certain
872-N	Termination of partnership S/L extension	6229(b)	Re partnership items

(continued)

Form No.	Form Name	I.R.C. §	Explanation
872-P	Partnership extension of S/L	6229(b)	Must be signed by TMP unless another partner is authorized
872-T	Termination of 872-A S/L extension	6501(c)(4)	See notice 88-79
875	Partnership audit agreement	6224	Acceptance of examiner's findings (re flow-thru entity)
886-A	Examination explanation of items	7602	Explains reason for audit adjustment; generally prepared by RA in unagreed cases
886-X	S corp exam changes, by shareholder	1366, 7602	Shareholder's share of income, deductions, credits
890	Waiver of restrictions on assessment of estate tax	6601	For estate tax (890-AD if in appeals)
895	S/L control sheet	6501	(gov't use only) Used to track S/L expiration on returns where < 180 days left in statute period
900	Tax collection waiver	6502(a)(2)	Extends to date certain; used only in limited circumstances
906	Closing agreement	7121	As to specific matters; IRM 8.13.1.2
907	Extension form (refund suit)	6532(a)	Agreement to extend time to bring refund suit
911	Application for taxpayer assistance order	7811	To stop imminent IRS action; use in case of hardship
941c	Correction of payroll tax return	6413(a)(1)	To correct 941
941-X	Claim for refund of employment tax	6511, 3101	Use in lieu of form 843 to obtain jurisdiction of federal district court
945-X	Correction of withholding tax return	3406	To correct an erroneous 945
1003	Bond for postponement of tax payment	6165	Must be signed by principal and surety
1010	Informant award denial	7623	Notifies informant that information furnished did not result in tax collection
1040-X	Amended individual income tax return	6511	Use for filing claims for refund or abatement; reg. 301.6402-3(a)(2)
1045	Application for tentative refund	6411	Used for NOL carrybacks
1058	Notice of intent to levy & right to CDP hearing	6330	Triggers a 30-day appeal window

Form No.	Form Name	I.R.C. §	Explanation
1098	How to stop interest	6601	Information on how to stop interest on your account
1120-X	Amended corporate return	6511	Use in lieu of Form 843
1139	Application for corporate tentative refund	6411	Used for corporate NOL carrybacks
1153	Notice of proposed TFRP assessment	6672	Sent to proposed responsible officer, who has 60 days from mailing date to file protest
1157	Witness fee voucher	7610	For witness to be reimbursed
1219B	Third-party contact notice	7602(c)	Notice of potential third-party contact
1331-B	Notice of adjustment	7602	
1341	Foreign bank account warning	1471	Contains terms of "last chance offer" to limit penalties re FBAR
1356	How to submit a FOIA request	6103	Instructions on how to submit a freedom of information act request
1862	Failure to file notice	6651(a)	Contains attachment with proposed deficiency
1902-B	Examination change report	7602	For individuals; often used in TCO audits
1902-E	Report of audit changes	7602	Report of audit (examination) changes (adjustments)
2014	Wage levy exemptions	6331(e)	See publication 1494; tables for figuring amount exempt from levy on salary
2039-A	Summons, administrative	7602–7610, 7402	Can be issued by RA, RO, TCO, SA; must be personally served if on TP
2045	Statement of transferee status	6901	Issued by appeals
2159	Payroll deduction agreement	2159	For automatic withholding from paycheck for agreed IA amount
2212SWR	Cash transaction account	7602(e)	Also known as "cash T"; used for indirectly determining income
2261	Collateral agreement, future income	7121	Used when significant increase in income is expected
2261-C	Collateral agreement	7121	Waiver of NOL, capital loss, & unused investment credit carryovers

(continued)

Form No.	Form Name	I.R.C. §	Explanation
2270	Notice to Exhibit (books/records)	6333	Delivered by IRS to person in possession of taxpayer books or records
2297	Waiver of statutory notice of claim disallowance	6511, 7422, 6532	Begins 2-year period for filing suit
2358C	Return filing (no need)	6012	Advises TP that he doesn't need to file a return
2421	Consent to enter private premises	7606, 7342	If this form isn't signed, the RO will secure a writ
2433	Notice of seizure	6331(b)	Prepared by revenue officer; IRM 5.10.3.10
2434-B	Equity determination for asset seizure	6331(j)	Filled in & approved by group manager prior to seizure of assets by RO
2504	Employment tax deficiency agreement	3101	Agreement to assessment of additional tax; used at conclusion of audit
2504-WC	Agreement to assessment of employment taxes	3101	Used in worker classification cases
2511	Request for missing information	6411	Re form 1045
2645C	Correspondence acknowledgment	6301	Says will respond in 90 days
2725	Document receipt	6001	IRS must sign to acknowledge receipt of documents from TP
2747	RO investigation history	6301	Used by revenue officers re actions, by date
2750	TFRP S/L extension	6672(b)(3)	Extends assessment statute in TFRP cases
2751	Consent to TFRP assessment	6672	Has all periods of liability listed; has place for TP signature; TP should not sign this unless he is prepared to pay the TFRP in full
2788C	Address change inquiry	6212(b)	Requests that 8822-B be filled out for change of business address
2797	Criminal referral form	7201	Used by compliance (e.g., in nonfiler situations)
2848	Power of attorney	6304(a)(2), 7521(c), 6103(c)	POA & declaration of representative
3050	Certificate of lack of records	6001	

Form No.	Form Name	I.R.C. §	Explanation
3174-A	Notice of unpaid tax	6303	Can accompany a summons for appearance before a RO
3219(SC)	Deficiency notice	6212	Sent from service center, after correspondence audit
3363	Acceptance of proposed disallowance of claim	6511	Acceptance of proposed disallowance of claim for refund
3531	Request for missing information	7602	Accompanies tax return that has been returned to the taxpayer
3610	Audit statement	7123	Used to reflect agreed tax and penalty in settled appeals case
3623	Statement of account	7453	Tax Court settlement statement; reflects correct agreed tax & penalty
3870	Request for adjustment	6402	Request for adjustment between spouses, e.g.
3877	Deficiency notice, mail-out	6212	List of all deficiency notices mailed; see *Barrash* case
3911	Statement regarding refund	6402	Used to determine status of lost refund check
3949 A	Report of suspected fraud	7623	Information referral from whistleblower
4089	Deficiency notice waiver	6213(d)	Waives restrictions on assessment; similar to F870; waives right to go to Tax Court
4180	TFRP interview sheet	6672	8-page form. The representative should fill this out and submit it to the revenue officer (RO); if the RO prepares it, he will put a "government spin" on it; client is not required to sign a 4180, and I do not recommend that he do so
4183	RO recommendation for TFRP liability	6672	Prepared by RO and submitted to group manager for approval
4188	Adjustment to account	6511	Issued 60 days after amended return filed
4235	Collection advisory group (re liens)	6321	Contains telephone numbers & addresses for releases, etc.
4340	Assessment and payment certificate	6203	To establish that notice and demand was sent within 60 days; see *Lundsford* case
4422	Application for lien discharge re estate tax	6325(b)	Application for certificate discharging property subject to estate tax lien

(continued)

Form No.	Form Name	I.R.C. §	Explanation
4463	Request for technical advice	6110	See reg. 601.105(b)(5)(iii)(k)
4466	Application for estimated corporate tax refund	6525	For quick refund of current year tax; not signed by preparer
4485	Employer ID No., IRS assignment	6109	Partnership can retain EIN if it merely changes its name
4506-T	Request for transcript of account	6203	Request for account, W&I transcripts
4506T-EZ	Transcript request, short form	6203	Short form request for individual tax return transcript
4549	Exam (audit) changes to income	7602	For simple or correspondence audits; signed by TP when agreement secured as to audit adjustments
4549-A	Audit (exam) report	7602	Contains income tax discrepancy adjustments
4564	Information document request (IDR)	7602	Used by RAs & TCOs to request documents during a tax return audit; in LB&I audits, these IDRs are strictly controlled
4571	Explanation for penalties	6651	Explanation for filing return or paying tax late
4602	Estimated tax correction statement	6654	
4605, 4605-A	TEFRA examination changes	6221	Report of exam changes for partnerships
4665	RA transmittal report	7602	Prepared by RA at conclusion of unagreed case; good idea to obtain through FOIA
4666	Employment tax examination summary	3101, 7636	Summary of results of employment tax audit
4667	FUTA examination changes	3301	Report of examination changes to form 940
4668	Schedule of adjustments to employment tax	3101	Follows a 941 audit
4668-B	Examination report of withheld income tax	7602	Report of examination of withheld federal income tax
4669	Statement of payments received	3402(d)	Relief for employer where employee already paid the tax
4670	Request for withholding relief	3402(d)	Filed by employer to prove that worker reported income & paid SE tax

Form No.	Form Name	I.R.C. §	Explanation
4764	Examination plan	7602	16-page document to be discussed with RA at beginning of LB&I audit
4789	Currency transaction report (CTR)	6050I	Used by banks to report currency transactions > $10K; see Bank Secrecy Act; also see Form 8300
4790	Transportation of currency	6867	U.S. customs form used for transportation of currency, etc. > $10K out of the U.S.
4810	Request for prompt assessment	6501(d)	For estate taxes
4822	Personal & family living expenses	7602(e)	Don't EVER fill this out during an audit
4852	Substitute for W-2	6051	Use when unable to obtain W-2 or it's incorrect; attach to 1040
4903 (ASC)	Filing delinquency notice	7203	Computer generated; warns of criminal penalties for nonfiling
4945-B	Examination changes	7602	Lists adjustment, by issue; can be used by flow-thru entities
4986C	Notification of favorable determination for innocent spouse	6015	Letter granting innocent spouse relief
5204	Record of account	6203	Submitted in response to request for transcript of account
5278	Statement of income tax changes	6212, 7602	Summarizes adjustments to income; accompanies DN; has penalties
5344	Examination closing record	7602	Prepared by RAs; contains, in summary form, what happened to the case
5402	Appeals transmittal of case back to exam	7602	Used by AOs to send underdeveloped cases back to agent or auditor
5438	Excise tax examination report	7602	
5495	Fiduciary discharge request	6905	For use by fiduciary to apply for relief from liability for decedent's income and gift tax
5564	Deficiency notice waiver	6212, 6601(c)	Sent w/ deficiency notice in case TP wants to agree; interest cut-off after 30 days

(continued)

Form No.	Form Name	I.R.C. §	Explanation
5601	Deficiency notice	6212(a)	Statutory notice of deficiency; 90-day response time
5701	Notice of proposed audit adjustment [NOPA]	7602	Issued by RAs in LB&I cases; can request fast-track after 5701 issued
5713	International boycott report	999	Report by TP required if business is done in country on "list"
5777	Proposed changes to income tax	7602	Gives options if you don't agree
5816	Report of preparer penalty	6694	Prepared by revenue agent to propose preparer penalty
6014	Authorization for third-party records	7602(c)	Authorization for IRS to access third-party records
6118	Claim of preparer to recover penalty	6684, 6695, 6701, 6700	Claim for refund of return preparer and promoter penalties
6209	Transaction codes (used on transcripts)		Access through http://www.irs.gov
6338(C)	Proof of claim in bankruptcy case	1398	Proof of claim in bankruptcy proceeding
6401	Request for missing information	6011	Sent by IRS to taxpayers who omit information from return
6637	summons	7603	Issued by RO to get CIS (433) information
6641	Statement of changes to account	7602	Shows increase in tax, penalty, and interest
6863	Expense reimbursement for compliance with summons	7610	Invoice & authorization for payment
6884	Consent to search	7201	Voluntary consent to a search of person, premises or conveyance; used by special agents; see IRM 9.4.9.2
8009	Missing information on amended return	6511	Sent back with 1040-X if information is missing
8082	TEFRA inconsistent treatment notice	6222(b)	For use by partners
8125	Notice of tax due	6303	Calculates interest & penalty; precedes "notice of intent to levy"
8126	Final notice before levy	6331(d)	Gives 30 days to appeal
8176	Request for delinquent tax return	3406	Computer generated; may contain IRP

Form No.	Form Name	I.R.C. §	Explanation
8275	Disclosure of position	6662(d)(2)(B)	To disclose positions in order to avoid penalty; notice 90-2
8275-R	Disclosure of position	6662(d)(2)(B)	To disclose position contrary to regulation
8278	TFRP balance due notice	6672	TFRP balance due notice
8300	Report of currency payments	6050I, 6103(l)(15), 7203, 6721(e)(2)(B)	Also includes cash "equivalents"
8355	Backup withholding information	3406	Gives 30 days to respond; if no response, 31% BUW may result
8362	Currency transactions	6050I	Used by casinos
8379	Injured spouse claim and allocation	6402(c)	For wife to claim part of refund on joint return, past-due obligation of spouse
8453	Electronic filing declaration	6061	Contains signature information re the return filer; ERO must send in
8484	Report of practitioner misconduct	6694	Submitted by IRS to OPR; see IRM 5.1.1.7.6.2
8488	Statement of change to account	6213	Calculates interest & penalty; precedes notice of intent to levy
8489	Partnership late-filing penalty notice	6698	$195 per month × no. of partners (same for S Corp)
8519	Notice of levy	6331	Comes from ACS; served on bank (see 668-W for wage levies)
8546	Claim for expenses resulting from bad levy	6343, 6503, 7426	Reimbursement of bank charges due to erroneous levy
8626	Agreement to rescind deficiency notice	6212(d)	See RP 88-17, 88-1 CB 692
8821	Tax information authorization	7521(c)	Use 2848 instead
8822	Address change	6212(b)	Change of address notification for individuals
8822-B	Address change	6212(b)	Change of address notification for businesses
8633	Electronic filer application	6011	
8655	Reporting agent authorization	3101	Where someone other than the TP reports employment tax information to the IRS

(continued)

Form No.	Form Name	I.R.C. §	Explanation
8802	Application for U.S. residency certification	6013(g), 6039E, 7701(b)	$35 user fee
8833	Treaty-based return disclosure	6114	
8849	Claim for refund of excise tax	6511	Where 720, 730, or 2290 form filed
8857	Request for innocent spouse relief	6015	Must file within 2 years of IRS collection action; for relief from joint & several liability
8879	Electronic filing signature authorization	6011(f)	Don't send to IRS; for TP records; must be signed by TP
8879F	E-file signature authorization for 1041	6011(f)	Kept in TP records, not sent to IRS
8888	Split refunds	6511	New as of 2006; to allow TPs to split refunds into multiple accounts
8919	Uncollected SS/Medicare	3401, 3121	Filed by employee if employer didn't withhold; NA to independent contractor
8948	Explanation for not filing electronically	6011	Submitted by preparer
8952	Application for voluntary classification settlement	3509, 3401	Re worker classification settlement program; see Ann. 2011-64
9264	Penalty abatement	6651(a)	Delinquency & failure to pay
9297	Document request	7603	Issued by RO; summary of contact; contains deadline
9423	Collection appeal request	6301, 6331(d)(4)(C)	See Publ. 1660; request must be in writing; must discuss with group manager first; can file these after receiving CP504
9440	Levy sources	6331	TP levy source & contact info (used by RAs at end of unpaid audit)
9465	Request for IA	6159	For individuals only; no 433F if tax < $25K
9456-FS	Request for IA	6159	For amounts owed > $25K; submit 433-F
9984	Examining officer's activity report [case history]	7602	Record of all contacts & activities of revenue agent (very useful info)

Form No.	Form Name	I.R.C. §	Explanation
11369	Reward claim evaluation report	7623	Confidential evaluation report on claim for reward; used by WBO
12153	Request for CDP hearing	6320, 6330	Request for collection due process hearing or equivalent hearing; 30 days to file
12203	Request for appeals	7602	Request for appeals review (sent following TCO audit) (note that this form is *not* required by the regulations)
12233	Request for IA review	6159	Request for independent review prior to rejection
12256	Withdrawal of request for CDP hearing	6320, 6330	Withdrawal of request for collection due process hearing
12277	Application for withdrawal of form 668(Y)	6323(j)	5 possible reasons listed
12507	Innocent spouse statement	6015(e)(4)	Submitted by nonclaimant spouse
12508	Innocent spouse questionnaire	6015(a)(4)	Filled out by nonrequesting spouse
12510	Innocent spouse questionnaire	6015	Filled out by requesting spouse
13586	Settlement initiative declaration	7602	See Ann. 2004-46
13683	Protest (short form)	7602	Used where change is $25K or less for each period audited
13711	Request for OIC appeal	7122(e)(2)	Request for appeal of offer in compromise rejection; attach documents, if applicable
13873-B	Transcript rejection	6203	Rejection notice in response to 4506-T
14039	Identity theft affidavit	6109	For us by TP who has been a victim of identity theft
14135	Application for lien discharge	6325(b)	Application for discharge of property from FTL
14157	Preparer complaint	6694	Return preparer complaint form
14157-A	Preparer fraud	6694	Tax return preparer fraud or misconduct affidavit
CP11	Notice of tax due on 1040NR	6072	Notice of tax due resulting from change to 1040NR
CP14	Tax due notice	6303	Contains billing summary with penalty & interest calculated; precedes CP504

(continued)

Form No.	Form Name	I.R.C. §	Explanation
CP15B	TFRP balance due notice	6672	Shows period & balance due; shows EIN of employer entity
CP21A	Notice of tax due	6303	Adjustment to liability; shows reduction in tax due to requested changes
CP21B	Notice of refund	6511	Notice of refund due; shows account balance before changes and adjustments
CP21C	TFRP changes to liability	6672	Reflects changes to prior trust fund recovery penalty assessment
CP21E	Notice of refund due	6511, 7602	As a result of a 1040 audit
CP22A	Tax due notice	6303	Tax due resulting from income mismatch, also for TFRP liability
CP22E	Notice of changes to 1040	6303	Shows balance of tax due, including interest and penalty
CP23	Notice of tax due	6303	Notice of tax due on a 1040 after changes made to payments & credits
CP24	Notification of refund	6511	Notification of adjusted refund due to payment, etc.
CP39	Notification of overpayment application	6402	To offset balance due on another year (form 1040)
CP42	Notification of overpayment application	6402	To offset balance due on another year
CP44	Refund offset against potential liability	6402	Delays refund by 6–8 weeks, depending on whether another tax owed
CP45	Estimated tax application	6402(b), 6654	Failure to apply overpayment to next year because of problem with current year
CP49	Notification of overpayment application	6402(a)	Tax applied to another period or another type of tax
CP 59	Delinquent tax return notice	6012	Request for unfiled income tax return
CP60	Statement of adjustment to account	6204	To adjust for erroneous credits, misapplied payments, etc.
CP63	Refund hold	6402	Due to nonfiling of prior year return(s)
CP71A	Reminder of tax due (annual)	7524	Reminder of overdue taxes; shows year & type of tax, but no calculation of P&I

Form No.	Form Name	I.R.C. §	Explanation
CP71C	Annual reminder of tax due	7524	Reminder of past-due tax (1040 or CIV PEN)
CP71D	Annual reminder of tax due	7524	Notice of tax due (can be for 1040 or CIV PEN)
CP79	Information needed to claim EIC	32	See also form 8862
CP89	Annual IA statement	6159	Annual installment agreement statement; shows payments made during year
CP90	Notice of intent to levy & right to hearing	6330	Notice of intent to levy & notice of right to CDP hearing; requires a response in order to prevent levy
CP91	Final notice of intent to levy on social security benefits	6331(h)(1)	Re 15% levy on SS benefits
CP128	Notification of overpayment application	6402	Re application of 941 or 1120 overpayment to another period
CP132	Change to tax return	7602	Reflects changes to corporate tax return; shows balance due (incl. P&I)
CP 134	FTD discrepancy notice	6302(g)	Re 941 liability; shows refund amount
CP134B	FTD payment discrepancy notice	6302(g)	FTD/employment tax payment discrepancy notice (re payroll tax deposits)
CP134R	FTD discrepancy notice re refund	6302(g)	Re 941 liability; shows refund amount
CP136	941 tax deposit requirements	6302(g)	Explains payroll tax deposit requirement for current year based on look-back period
CP141	Request for payment	6155	
CP161	Request for payment	6155, 6303	Shows tax, penalty, & interest due; can be used for 941 taxes unpaid
CP162	S Corp late-filing penalty	6699(a)(1)	Notification of penalty charge for late filing of 1120S
CP171	Reminder of tax due	6303	Reminder of tax due; form 941 or 945; calculates P&I
CP210	Statement of overpayment	6404	Shows tax & penalty reduction, but does not indicate a reason

(continued)

Form No.	Form Name	I.R.C. §	Explanation
CP220	Notice of changes to 1120	6303	Shows tax increase due to changes; shows penalty & interest as well; usually follows an IRS examination
CP240	Employment tax discrepancy	3121	Notifies employer of discrepancy between 941 and W-2 amounts
CP259	Request for tax return	6012, 7203	Notice of nonfiling of tax return (941 or 1120)
CP260	Credit adjustment (balance due)	6402	Shows form # and period; removes previous credit incorrectly applied
CP297A	Final notice of intent to levy & right to CDP hearing	6330	Triggers a 30-day appeal period
CP501	Reminder of tax due	6303	Precedes CP503 by 30 days
CP503	Notice of unpaid tax	6303	Individual tax due, one of the early (2nd reminder) notices; precedes CP504
CP504	Final notice of intent to levy	6331(d), 6303(a)	"notice & demand"; Can't do 12153 after receiving one of these; use CAP instead
CP504B	Notice of intent to seize property	6331	Shows period & 941 balance due (including P&I)
CP515	Request for tax return	6012, 7203	Has IRP information; requests filing of return or explanation of why return not due
CP518	Notice of delinquent tax return	6012, 7203	Notice of overdue tax return; has response page
CP521	Monthly IA statement	6159	Reminder of monthly payment due on installment agreement
CP523	Intent to terminate IA	6159(b)(3)	Where installment agreement was defaulted
CP539	Backup withholding	3406	Due to nonreporting of passive income
CP2000	Cross-match proposal	7602	Results from 1099 discrepancies; has tax & interest calculated; requires response
CP2005	Cross-match; closing	7602	Indication that cross-match notice discrepancies have been cleared up
CP2100	TIN mismatch notice	3406, 6109	For document filers who file more than 50 documents

Form No.	Form Name	I.R.C. §	Explanation
CP2100A	Notice of future backup withholding	3406	Notice of required future backup withholding for small filers
CP2501	Cross-match inquiry	7602	Does not calculate tax; requires a response; precedes CP2000
CP3219A	Deficiency notice	6212(a)	Notice of deficiency sent after CP2000 unresolved
FinCen 114	Report of foreign bank account (FBAR)	1471	Formerly TD F 90-22.1 (which is now obsolete); must be filed electronically by 6/30 of each year (no extension available)
LT11	Notice of intent to seize (levy) property	6331(d)	Shows amount due; right to CDP hearing shown in small print on 2nd page; usually follows CP504
LT16	Tax due notice	6303	Threatens "enforcement" action
SS-4	Application for employer ID number	6109	Can do this online at http://www.irs.gov
SS-8	Employee status inquiry	3121(d)	Use by IRS to determine whether worker is employee for withholding purposes
SS-10	Consent to extend employment tax S/L	6501(c)(4)	Extends to a date certain for FUTA, FICA, & WHT, but not I.R.C. § 6672 (TFRP)

APPENDIX C

IRS Form Letters Sent to Taxpayers[1]

Letter No.	Subject of Letter	I.R.C. §	Explanation
86C	Transfer of collection file	6301	Acknowledges TP correspondence; transfers matter to another IRS office
99C	CAWR	7602	Notifies TP that W-2 totals don't match 941 amounts for year in question
105C	Claim disallowance	6511(a)	Notice of claim disallowance re an individual taxpayer
168C	Penalty removal notification	6651(a)(1)	Notification of late-filing penalty removal based on explanation
238 (AOIC)	OIC rejection	7122	Signed by territory manager; asset and income tables are enclosed; also encloses Form 13711 for appeal within 30 days
288C	Account adjustment	6204	Adjustment (favorable) resulting from taxpayer inquiry
402	Commitment to lien discharge	6325(b)	Conditional commitment to discharge property from federal tax lien
484C	CNC status	6330	Notifies taxpayer of CNC status due to financial situation
504	Levy intent	6330	Can't do 12153 after receiving one of these, but you can do a CAP
510C	Refund in error	7405	See IRM 21.4.5.6
525	Audit notification	7602	From correspondence audit unit; specifies a year and asks for response

(continued)

---

[1] There are many other form letters utilized by the IRS, but these are the ones most frequently encountered by tax practitioners.

Letter No.	Subject of Letter	I.R.C. §	Explanation
528	Transfer of case	7602	Transfer of exam case; see regs re requirement to transfer
531	Deficiency notice	6212(a)	90-day letter; also see form letter 5601; must contain petition due date
531-T	Deficiency notice	6212(a)	Contains last date to file petition with U.S. Tax Court
569	Claim disallowance	6511	For full or partial disallowance of a claim; accompanies Form 4549-A
639 SC	Informant claim	7623	Acknowledges receipt of information from informant
672C	Overpayment application	6402	Re 941, notification of application of overpayment per taxpayer request
692	Examination report transmittal	7602	Used by TCOs; acknowledges information provided; accompanies audit report; if not signed, a deficiency notice will be issued
725	Collection appointment	6301	scheduling
728	Tax due	6303	Signed by a revenue officer; has periods & amounts owed; this letter is not a valid "notice and demand"; see *Conway v. Comm'r*, 137 T.C. 209 (2011)
728A	Tax due	6303	Shows form, tax period, prior balance, and total amount due, including penalties
854C	Penalty abatement denial	6051, 6674, 7204	Notice of failure to establish reasonable cause for late filing of W-2 forms
890	Office audit (TCO)	7602	Appointment letter
906	Claim disallowance	6532(a)	Starts the 2-year period running for filing a refund suit
907	Statute of limitations (S/L)	6501(c)(4)	Extension request; explains TP right to refuse to extend the S/L
915	Exam report	7602	Accompanies TCO exam report; this is the 30-day letter
937	Power of attorney (POA)	7521(c)	Transmits other documents to representative holding a POA
950	30-day letter	7602	Issued at end of audit; gives 30 days to respond to exam report; describes protest procedure
950-D	Exam (employment) report	7602	30-day letter giving TP right to appeal examiner's findings

Letter No.	Subject of Letter	I.R.C. §	Explanation
967	S/L extension	6501(c)(4)	Accompanies form 872; explains why an extension of the statute is needed (note: the author's practice is not to extend the statute unless there is a really good reason)
1020	Acknowledgement letter	7602	Used by TCOs; acknowledges receipt of information or asks for additional information; has response due date
1025	Return of protest	7602	Accompanies returned protest for additional information
1058	Notice of intent to levy	6330	Gives TP 30 days to file form 12153 to request CDP hearing; TPs should always file the 12153 to forestall a levy (note: these letters should always be responded to with a request for hearing under I.R.C. § 6330)
1058A	Notice of intent to levy	6330	Same as 1058
1058-D	Notice of intent to levy	6330	Same as 1058
1153(DO)	Proposed TFRP assessment	6672(b)	This letter satisfies the preliminary notice (before assessment) requirement; it gives the individual 60 days to prepare a protest. Unless the individual is clearly liable, these letters should always be followed with a protest.
1154	Re non-TFRP liability	6672	Advises TP that he does not owe trust fund recovery penalty
1155	TFRP agreement, transmittal	6672	Transmits agreement Form 2751 re an agreed liability (note: one should never sign a Form 2751 unless you are clearly liable and ready for an immediate assessment)
1285	Final determination letter	7803	Issued by taxpayer advocate service (TAS)
1722	Transcript of account	6203	Shows assessments, payments, credits (by year)
1829	Partnership adjustments	6224	60-day letter; explains procedures if there is no agreement
1844	Promoter penalty investigation	6700	Letter to promoter or participant in tax avoidance scheme
1912	TCO exam report transmittal	7602	Accompanies TCO audit report

(continued)

Letter No.	Subject of Letter	I.R.C. §	Explanation
2050	Reminder of tax due	6303	"Please call us about overdue taxes or returns".
2203	Office audit appointment	7602	Sets 10 days to respond and set appointment; has boxes (items to audit) checked
2205-A	Exam audit notification	7602	Advises TP that his tax return has been selected for examination; signed by revenue agent
2206	Appointment confirmation	7602	Used by revenue agents and IRS auditors to set appointment for examination
2272C	Rejection of request for IA	6159	Lists periods of liability
2273C	Acceptance of IA request	6159	Sets forth terms and agreements re accepted installment agreement
2290	Interest abatement	6404(e)	Notifies taxpayer of decision on abatement claim due to unreasonable delay
2566	Proposed assessment	6041	Can be sent out when return has been filed but which contains a possible cross-match problem
2644C	Additional time needed	6151	Notifies TP of additional time needed to do research
2645C	Acknowledgment of correspondence	6301	Correspondence acknowledgment; says that IRS will respond in 90 days
2675C	POA revocation	6103(c)	Sent to a taxpayer whose representative has withdrawn his POA
2737	Audit reconsideration notification	7602	Indicates the result of an audit reconsideration
2797	Taxpayer address inquiry	6212(b)	Used by IRS to update records re address, etc. for TP
2908	Lien release	6325(a)	Notification of upcoming lien release, after full payment of an accepted OIC
3030C	Tax due letter	6502	Sent to a TP when the collection S/L is due to expire soon
3164-A	TFRP notice of third-party contacts	7602	Sent by revenue officer to notify taxpayer that 3rd party contacts may be made
3164B	Tax due notice	6303	This letter is not a valid notice & demand; see *Conway v. Comm'r*, 137 T.C. 209, 218 (2011)
3172	Lien notice, CDP right	6320	Notice of federal tax lien filing and right to CDP hearing; 30-day deadline to file 12153 in response; this is an after-the-fact notice; lien has already been filed

Letter No.	Subject of Letter	I.R.C. §	Explanation
3174	Tax due notice	6303	Advises TP of unpaid tax; can be signed by RO; lists periods & amounts due
3193	Notice of determination	6320, 6330	Notice of determination concerning collection action; follows CDP hearing; a Tax Court petition can be filed following receipt of this letter
3254	Examination appointment letter	7602	Schedules a time and place for commencement of SBSE audit
3262	Notice of lien appeal rights	6321	Form letter accompanying a notice of federal tax lien (668(Y))
3284	Innocent spouse	6015(e)(4)	Letter to other spouse notifying him of right to participate in proceeding
3391	Exam report	7602	Accompanies examination report; gives taxpayer 30 days to request an appeals conference if no agreement
3401-S	Exam no-change	7602	Issued by revenue agent when corporate audit is finished w/ no change to liability
3500	Acknowledgment of correspondence	7602	Issued by correspondence exam function
3501	Response to inquiry	7602	From correspondence exam technician; Acknowledgment of receipt of inquiry; postpones response date
3505C	Penalty, abatement request inquiry	6651	Requests evidence of hardship
3523	Notice of determination	3121, 7436	Notice of determination of worker classification (and opportunity to go to Tax Court)
3572	Appointment letter	7602	Exam (TCO) appointment letter; shows items to be audited
3573	Appointment letter	7602	Sets appointment for TCO examination (audit)
3586	Request for meeting	6301	Request for meeting with (collection) revenue officer (RO)
3783	Claim disallowance	7422(a)	Sent via certified mail. Starts period running to file refund suit
3884C	Rejection letter	6330	Re CDP hearing "you aren't entitled to a hearing" (citing reasons)
3990	Foreign bank account	1471	See notice 1341, offer to limit penalties where no FBAR was filed
3996	Related tax return	7602	Sent by LB&I agent to corporate officer; says "not an audit" (IRM 4.46.3.6.7)
4016-A	POA bypass letter	7521(c)	Initial bypass letter; See IRM 5.1.1.7.7.1

(continued)

Letter No.	Subject of Letter	I.R.C. §	Explanation
4016-B	POA bypass letter	7521(c)	Final bypass letter; IRM 5.1.1.7.7.1
4052	IA rejection letter	6159	Rejection of request for installment agreement (IA); gives 30 days to respond to rejection
4121-E	Employment tax exam report	7602	Letter transmitting report of employment tax examination (audit)
4141	Appeals case receipt	6330	Signed by appeals team manager; indicates the SO who is assigned to the case
4383	CDP hearing request, withdrawal of	6330	States effective date of withdrawal; signed by SO
4462	Appeals acknowledgment	7122	Acknowledges receipt of OIC rejection in appeals office
4476	Correspondence acknowledgment	7602	Sent from exam to the taxpayer
4624	CNC status	6330	Notification of determination that taxpayer can't pay; classifies TP as currently not collectible
4735	Computational adjustment	6230(a)	Notice of computational adjustment as a result of a TEFRA audit
4836	Appeals acknowledgment of CDP hearing request	6320, 6330	Arranges a conference date and time; asks for documents to be sent in advance of the hearing
4837	CDP hearing	6330	Acknowledgment letter setting telephonic hearing date and time
5077	IDR, delinquency notice	7602	Used by LB&I where the TP does not provide a complete response to an IDR
5264	Examination report transmittal	7602	Threatens a deficiency notice if requested information is not received
5441	Examination report transmittal	7602	Accompanies a revised revenue agent report (RAR)
9774	Tax due notice	7524	For non-master file only
LT40	Appeals information	7123	Information about appeals office
SSA-L-93-SM	CAWR (Combined Annual Wage Report)	3121	Sent by Social Security Administration to employer whenever 941 information does not match W-2/W-3 totals

APPENDIX D

IRS Publications on Procedural Topics

Publ. No.	Publ. Name	I.R.C. §	Explanation
1	Taxpayer rights	7521(b), 7602(c)	"Your rights as a taxpayer"; contains notice regarding I.R.C. § 7602(c)third-party contacts, examination, appeal, collection, and refunds
5	Appeal rights	7123	Explains appeal rights available at the conclusion of an audit that is not agreed to; explains how to prepare a protest
556	Examination, appeals, claims	7602	Explains all procedures for examination of returns, appeal rights, and claims for refund
594	IRS collection process	6301	General description of the IRS collection process against delinquent taxpayers
733	Informant rewards	7623	See Form 211 (reward claim form); who may file a claim; amount & payment of reward
783	Lien discharge	6325(b)	Instructions on applying for certificate of discharge from federal tax lien (FTL); removes the U.S.'s lien from the property named in the certificate
784	Lien subordination	6325(d)	Procedures for applying for certificate of lien subordination; to move junior creditor position ahead of the U.S.' position
947	Practice before the IRS and power of attorney	7521	See Circular 230; discusses who can represent a taxpayer before the IRS
971	Innocent spouse relief	6015	Information regarding community property laws, relief from joint and several liability, etc.; see also Pub. 504 (divorced or separated individuals) and Pub. 555 (community property) and Pub. 3512

(continued)

Publ. No.	Publ. Name	I.R.C. §	Explanation
1035	Statute of limitations	6501(c)(4)	Explains the (optional) process for extending the assessment statute of limitations
1153	Lien subordination, estate tax	6325(d)(3)	Explains how to apply for a certificate of subordination of federal estate tax lien
1450	Lien releases	6325(a)	Explains how to secure a release of a federal tax lien
1494	Wage levy exemptions	6331(e)	Contains table for figuring the amount exempt from levy on wages, salary, etc.
1544	Reporting of cash payments	6050I	Explains the reporting of (> $10,000) currency transactions on Form 8300
1546	Taxpayer advocate service (TAS)	7803(c)	For resolving tax problems that can't be resolved through normal channels
1635	Employer identification number (EIN)	6109	Understanding the EIN; what it is; how to apply; use of form SS-4
1660	Collection appeal rights	6330	Explains CDP and CAP procedures; rights to a hearing in Appeals
1872	Tip reporting	3402(k)	Guide to tip reporting for employers in food/beverage industry
1976	Section 530 (safe harbor) employment tax relief	530 (Act §)	See Act Sec. 530, 1978 Revenue Act; re worker classification issues; how to avoid liability
3498	The Examination process	7602	Contains the formal requirements for preparing a protest following an unagreed examination
3512	Innocent spouse	6015	Explains how to request innocent spouse relief by filing form 8857; see also publication 971
3598	Audit reconsideration	6404	Explains the audit reconsideration process; see IRM 4.13
3605	Fast-track mediation	7123	Explains process for prompt resolution of tax issues; no protest required
4235	Collection advisory offices	6325	Re questions regarding liens and release thereof
4524	Identity Theft and security awareness	6109	Describes prevention and assistance if someone uses a TP's SSN or name without consent to file a tax return
4539	Fast-Track Settlement (FTS)	7123	Explains the process for prompt resolution of LB&I issues
11734	Transaction codes pocket guide		Abbreviated version of Document 6209

INDEX